LONDON

About the author

Andrew Gumbel is a journalist as well as a travel writer, currently living in Los Angeles. His London guide first appeared in 1995.

Acknowledgements

Andrew would like to thank Mary-Ann and Claudia, and everyone at the Cadogan office, for their hard work and dedication.

About the contributor

Mary-Ann Gallagher is a travel writer and editor who has written and contributed to several titles in the Cadogan series. She has lived all over the world, but has spent much of the last decade within spitting distance of the Thames. Her idea of perfect happiness is a deckchair in St James's Park on a sunny day.

Acknowledgements

Mary-Ann would like to thank Mark Ludmon and Claire White, who helped out enormously with research, and Alex Haworth for the maps. Big thanks to Kate and co., Andrew, Emma, Matt, Laurine and Ramizan for top tips. Most of all thanks go to my endlessly patient, hard-working editor Claudia Martin.

Cadogan Guides
Network House, 1 Ariel Way, London W12 7SL
cadoganguides@morrispub.co.uk
www.cadoganguides.com

The Globe Pequot Press
246 Goose Lane, PO Box 480, Guilford, Connecticut
06437–0480

Copyright © Andrew Gumbel 2002

Series design: Andrew Barker
Series cover design: Sheridan Wall
Art direction: Jodi Louw
Designer: Tracey Ridgewell
Cover photo: © Dennis Gilbert/VIEW
Photography: © Olivia Rutherford 2002
Maps © Cadogan Guides, created by Oxford Cartographers
Additional map work: Angie Watts

Editorial Director: Vicki Ingle
Series Editor: Claudia Martin
Editorial: Catherine Charles, Georgina Palffy, Tori Perrot, Philippa Reynolds, Nick Rider and Christine Stroyan – and thanks to all the rest of the Cadogan team
Proofreading: Linda McQueen
Indexing: Hilary Bird
Production: Book Production Services
Printed in Italy by Legoprint
A catalogue record for this book is available from the British Library
ISBN 1-86011-850-X

Contents

Introduction

London, like all great cities, has a habit of going through drastic mood swings: grey, worthy and dull one minute, hip and ultra-modern the next. And so, just when it was being written off as the crumbling capital of a dead empire, the city has come roaring back to life. These days, London has the breezy confidence of a city on top of the world. Although it has neither the weather nor the sheer architectural beauty of a Paris, Venice or Barcelona, London has long since been proclaimed the cultural capital of Europe, a locus of teeming creative energy and irresistible hipness. Gone are the dowdy days when London comported itself like a fussy old duchess; now the capital is being redefined by a new, highly creative generation of artists and designers iconoclastic enough to break apart the once fusty capital and rebuild it in their own image. Everyone is talking about London's architects, its clothes designers, its film-makers, its musicians, its artists – even, in this most culinarily challenged of capitals, its chefs.

But be warned: London is still beset by many of its old pitfalls – pollution, gridlocked traffic, creaky public transport and more besides. Like an eccentric aristocrat who forgets to wash, London is certainly not a city that shouts its beauties from the rooftops. There is an art to exploring London: you have to engage on a personal level, ferreting out neighbourhoods you feel at home in, finding little backstreets, discovering the museums and theatres and pubs that give you a sense of personal satisfaction. You could tramp around Hampstead Heath or pick your way through the former docks beside the Thames; gaze at the stunning glass courtyard at the British Museum or take a peek at the brand-new British Galleries in the Victoria and Albert Museum; spend the evening star-spotting at The Ivy restaurant, or watching world-class ballet, opera and theatre in the West End; try out the new bars, clubs and galleries around trendy Hoxton Square or get a great cheap Indian meal on Brick Lane.

Once you have got over the sheer vastness and inconvenience, once you have traced out your own route through the labyrinth, the sense of diversity and discovery can be immensely liberating. Nobody can know all of London – not poets, not politicians, not even guidebook writers. Make up your own version of the city. Pop out of an Underground station at random and you may well find yourself in the sort of anonymous urban wasteland the city's millions of commuters pass through every morning and night, or you might just find a charming unknown corner of the metropolis you can call your very own.

The Neighbourhoods

In this guide the city has been
divided into 12 neighbourhoods,
outlined on the map below,
each with its own sightseeing
chapter. This map also shows our
suggestions for the Top Ten activities
and places to visit in London. The
following colour pages introduce the
neighbourhoods in more detail,
explaining the distinctive character
and highlights of each.

**Marylebone and
Regent's Park**

Soho
Chinat

St James's,
Mayfair and
Regent Street

**South Kensington
and Knightsbridge**

Buckingham
Palace and th
Royal Parks

9 The National
Gallery, p.103

2 Big Ben, p.90

3 Westminster
Abbey, p.86

5 The London Eye,
p.202

10 Pub-crawling in Soho, p.343

6 The British Museum, p.166

1 St Paul's Cathedral, p.216

Bloomsbury and Fitzrovia

The Strand, Holborn and Fleet Street

The City

Covent Garden and Around

Trafalgar Square and Around

The South Bank

Westminster

8 The Tower of London, p.229

4 Tate Modern, p.205

7 Bargain-hunting in one of London's many markets, p.209

Westminster

Two of the city's most august institutions preside over Westminster: the mother of all parliaments, and the mother of all London churches, Westminster Abbey. Politics and pageantry are the keynotes here: government policy is hammered out in Whitehall as Big Ben chimes the hour, and kings and queens are crowned, married and buried in the Abbey with solemn splendour. Beyond Westminster is Victoria, a chaotic, transient neighbourhood clustered around the city's busiest train station, and beyond that is Pimlico, home to Tate Britain, which contains a spectacular selection of British art spanning eight centuries.

Clockwise from top: Horse Guards Parade, Tate Britain, Houses of Parliament, Big Ben.

Westminster

Westminster chapter p.83
Hotels p.296 Restaurants p.314 Bars p.341
Royal London walk p.276

Anticlockwise from top: Piccadilly Circus, Eros, National Gallery Sainsbury Wing, Trafalgar Sq. fountain, Piccadilly street sign.

Trafalgar Square and Around

Trafalgar Square was conceived in the early 19th century, but politicking and financial problems stunted it from the beginning. Surrounded by whizzing traffic and clogged with exhaust fumes, the square has even lost its famous beleaguered pigeons. Very much still here, though, is the National Gallery, with a stunning collection of West European painting, and tucked behind it is the unique National Portrait Gallery. To the west lies Piccadilly Circus, tacky, neon-lit and yet as much a symbol of London as double-decker buses; to the north is Leicester Square, packed night and day with cinema-goers, tourists, buskers and touts.

St James's, Mayfair and Regent Street

St James's is one of London's quietest and most exclusive corners, a rarefied enclave of palaces and gentlemen's clubs where the British upper class while away the hours in elegant smoking rooms and libraries. The shopping is equally exclusive, from the traditional tailoring establishments and barbers of Jermyn Street, to the lavish displays at Fortnum and Mason's food emporium. Beyond St James's are the splendid Georgian squares of Mayfair, which have long been home to London's high society, stacked with sumptuous mansion blocks, designer boutiques, and prestigious art galleries and auctioneers. The elegant curve of Regent Street is more proletarian, always bustling with shoppers and commuters.

Buckingham Palace and the Royal Parks

Buckingham Palace has been the royal family's residence in London since Queen Victoria's day. It's surprisingly low-key – visitors have been known to walk past it in search of something grander – but at least the plumbing works nowadays. The main approach to the palace is the Mall, which slices through two of the royal parks: St James's, one of London's loveliest, with a lake full of ducks and pelicans; and quieter Green Park. Flanking the Mall is Nash's handsome Carlton House Terrace, now home to the Institute of Contemporary Arts (ICA), with exhibitions devoted to the latest antics of the Brit Pack artists.

Clockwise from top left: Queen Victoria Memorial outside Buckingham Palace, postcards, St James's Park deckchairs.

Soho and Chinatown

Chaotic, colourful and bustling, Soho and Chinatown are the most beguiling of central London's neighbourhoods. Soho is a curious mixture of the seedy and the flashy: strip joints and trendy bars are squeezed up cheek-by-jowl, media moguls and transvestites strut the streets, and limos and rickshaws (yes, rickshaws) impatiently negotiate the crowds. Much of the city's nightlife is centred here, with hundreds of clubs and restaurants, and an endless stream of people looking for a good time. Chinatown is tiny, but through the vermilion gates on Gerrard Street lies another world, crammed with restaurants, Chinese supermarkets and subterranean gambling dens.

Anticlockwise from top: Madame Jojo's, roasted ducks in Chinatown, Old Compton Street café, shop window.

Soho and Chinatown
Soho and Chinatown chapter p.129
Hotels p.299 Restaurants p.317 Bars p.343

Covent Garden and Around

Covent Garden is the heart of London's theatreland – not just the traditional kind that takes place in the Royal Opera House or the Theatre Royal, but the street theatre which entertains the crowds around the central piazza. Mime artists, puppeteers, buskers and acrobats entertain the tourists browsing among the craft shops and boutiques of the former Flower Market, which is also home to a couple of engaging attractions, the Theatre Museum and the London Transport Museum. There's good shopping to be had along trendy Neal Street, and book-lovers shouldn't miss the secondhand bookshops which line Charing Cross Road.

Covent Garden and Around
Covent Garden and Around chapter p.137
Hotels p.299 Restaurants p.321 Bars p.344

Clockwise from top left: Covent Garden Market, the Tube, Royal Courts of Justice.

The Strand, Holborn and Fleet Street

Holborn is peppered with the medieval buildings, quadrangles and hidden gardens which make up the four Inns of Court, the cradle of the English legal system. This was also Dr Johnson's stomping ground, and a whiff of 18th-century clubbishness still lingers in the creaking old inns. But the great printing presses and journalists' pubs of Fleet Street have almost disappeared, victims of new technology which pushed the newspapers out to Docklands. The Strand is home to the Savoy, London's first luxury hotel, and Somerset House, where you can linger among the Impressionists at the Courtauld Gallery, or the opulent tsarist treasures in the Hermitage Rooms.

The Strand, Holborn and Fleet Street
The Strand, Holborn and Fleet Street chapter p.147
Hotels p.299 Restaurants p.323 Bars p.344

Bloomsbury and Fitzrovia

Bloomsbury, a once-fashionable district of Georgian townhouses and leafy squares, is still dominated by the great British Museum and the University of London. Its reputation as the intellectual heart of London was cemented during the inter-war years, when writers and artists moved in and established the Bloomsbury Group. It has retained its air of shabby gentility and, while the British Museum is undoubtedly its biggest attraction, the cafés, bookshops and a smattering of smaller museums are also worth a look. Nearby Fitzrovia is soaking up the media spillover from Soho, with fashionable new bars and restaurants opening almost daily.

From top: British Museum Great Court, Telecom Tower, restaurant.

Marylebone and Regent's Park

Marylebone, with its teashops, delis, smart boutiques and old-fashioned bookshops, is one of London's most tranquil villages. It's also astonishingly central, just a step away from the hordes battling their way down Oxford Street. Among its charms are the delightful Wallace Collection, housed in a beautiful 18th-century mansion, and the amusing museum devoted to Conan Doyle's fictional detective Sherlock Holmes, on Baker Street. The inexplicably popular attractions of Madame Tussaud's and the Planetarium are just to the north, and beyond them lies the manicured expanse of Regent's Park, also home to London Zoo.

> ### Marylebone and Regent's Park

Clockwise from top: Harrods van, Wellington Arch, cake shop.

South Kensington and Knightsbridge

After the phenomenal success of the Great Exhibition in 1851, three splendid museums dedicated to the arts and sciences, and a grandiose concert hall, were established in South Kensington under the patronage of Prince Albert. The Victoria and Albert Museum contains a mind-boggling collection of art and design; the Science Museum is consistently voted London's best, particularly now that its new interactive wing has opened; and the Natural History Museum is crammed with dinosaur bones and stuffed mammoths. The adjoining chi-chi enclave of Knightsbridge oozes wealth; this is the stamping ground of ladies-who-lunch, and home to Harrods, London's poshest department store.

> ### South Kensington and Knightsbridge

The South Bank

The South Bank Centre was built as a new home for the National Theatre and the National Film Theatre in the 1950s, and for decades provided the only reason to come south of the river. The millennium celebrations changed all that, and the last few years have seen the inauguration of the panoramic London Eye, the Elizabethan-style Globe Theatre, and the vast Tate Modern museum, now linked with the north bank by a pedestrian bridge. The Thames itself, long ignored, has finally come into its own, with a fleet of river taxis and boat cruises doing a brisk trade.

Clockwise from top right: Royal Festival Hall, London Eye, Tate Modern, Millennium Bridge.

The City

At first glance, it's hard to believe that this modern, glassy district is where London began. But beneath the skyscrapers and office blocks, the streets still follow the medieval plan; the airy spires of Wren's churches and the vast dome of St Paul's Cathedral still mark the horizon; and hospital buildings, law courts and markets recall a time when the City *was* London. Its business is still trade, as it has always been, even if it is trade of a most abstract and arcane sort, and the City still clings to the curious traditions and colourful ceremonies of the past.

Clockwise from top right: Tower of London, St Paul's Cathedral, Tower Bridge, market.

The City
The City chapter p.213
Hotels p.304 Restaurants p.327 Bars p.346

Outside the Centre: North London

North London's villages each retain a distinct atmosphere. Leafy, residential St John's Wood is a mecca for cricket-lovers and Beatles fans. Beyond it lie the upmarket streets of Hampstead, which also boasts a surprisingly wild heath. On the other side of the heath is genteel Highgate, with a smattering of teashops and a magnificent Victorian cemetery. Close to the City is newly fashionable Clerkenwell, filling up with loft-apartments and restaurants. Buzzy Islington is home to London's chattering classes, and neighbouring, arty Camden is famous for its market and nightlife.

Outside the Centre: West London

The suburbs of West London, peppered with palaces and parks, are London's most affluent and conservative. There's still a little multicultural spice in trendy Notting Hill, particularly around Carnival time in August, but once-bohemian Chelsea has settled down to become the spiritual home of the Sloane Ranger (well-bred and well-groomed). Beyond the next crook in the Thames lies Richmond, where the city's biggest park stretches out languidly beside the river, flanked by the spectacular gardens at Kew. The aristocrats built their palaces around here; many of them are open to the public, but the finest of all is the Tudor palace of Hampton Court.

From top: Notting Hill Carnival, feet at Notting Hill Carnival, Trellick Tower.

Outside the Centre: South London

South London has recently undergone a dramatic renaissance after years of poverty and deprivation. Yuppies have colonized the former wharves and warehouses of Lambeth and Bermondsey, bringing restaurants, bars and galleries in their wake. This is also where you'll find some of London's quirkiest museums, from the Imperial War Museum to the gruesome 18th-century Operating Theatre and the brand-new Fashion Museum. Downriver is affluent Greenwich, with a royal palace, a famous observatory, and a long and illustrious maritime tradition. Tranquil Dulwich is home to a charming, light-filled Picture Gallery, and Wimbledon is world famous thanks to the prestigious tennis tournament.

From top: Thames Barrier, Peckham Pearly King, Canary Wharf.

Outside the Centre: East London

East London may conjure up images of cockney gangsters and Jack the Ripper, but the reality is very different. Now buzzy, vibrant and multicultural, it's home both to a large Bangladeshi community and a high percentage of trendy Brit artists. The city's hippest nightspots are clustered around Hoxton and Shoreditch, and there are some great markets, particularly the lovely flower market on Columbia Road, to while away a Sunday. Big business shifted east from the City in the 1980s, moving into the dramatically restored former Docklands, now overlooked by a triumvirate of skyscrapers.

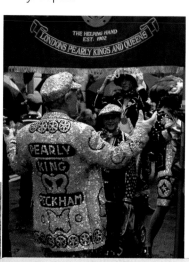

Days Out in London

Londoner's City p.16

Literary City p.18

Contemporary Architecture p.20

Riverside City p.22

Outdoor City p.24

Indoor City p.26

LONDONER'S CITY

Some of the clichés about London are true: cab drivers know everything, everyone talks about the weather, and they really do say 'Mind the gap' on the Tube. There are all kinds of Londoners, from the rosy-cheeked duffers in Clubland (St James's) to the loft-dwellers of Shoreditch, but they share the same affections: black cabs, old double-decker buses, and picnics in the park at the first glimpse of sunshine. In general, it's London's smaller, less glitzy charms that have won the hearts of Londoners – the markets at Borough and Spitalfields, small museums like the Geffrye, and urban parks like Hampstead Heath.

One

Start: Tube Tottenham Court Rd or Holborn.

Breakfast: For maximum artery-clogging, a full English breakfast at **La Brasserie Townhouse**.

Morning: Meet some cockney barrow boys at one of London's markets: at sweet-smelling **Columbia Road Flower Market** (Sun morning only); buzzing **Brick Lane** (Sun morning only); **Portobello Road** (Mon–Sat for fruit and veg, Sat for antiques); or **Spitalfields** (not Sat).

Lunch: Some of the best fish and chips in town at **Sea Shell** on Lisson Grove.

Afternoon: Take a black cab (talk to the driver about the weather – if you can get a word in edgeways) to the **Geffrye Museum**, recently voted a favourite by Londoners, with its reconstructions of British living (lounge) rooms. Head back into town and hire a deckchair in **St James's Park** and feed the ducks. Follow up by checking out the latest Brit Art at the nearby **ICA**.

Evening: A performance at the **Royal Albert Hall** – in particular, the last night of the Proms is a quintessential London experience.

Dinner: A late-night curry (the UK's national dish) at the **Red Fort** in buzzy Soho.

Night: In typical Londoner style, a pub crawl around the trendy **bars of Soho**.

Two

Start: Tube Highgate.

Breakfast: Head for village-like Highgate and try **Café Mozart**, a wood-panelled Viennese café, for mouthwatering pastries.

Morning: Take a tour of eerie **Highgate Cemetery** to see the last resting place of London's great and good.

Lunch: Head back into town and have a bite at the **Old Bank of England** on Fleet Street, a noisy, lively place in a former bank.

Afternoon: Wander around the nearby **Sir John Soane's Museum**, a fascinating place in the former home of one of London's most endearing characters.

Dinner: **Neat Brasserie** in the Oxo Tower, for great views of the Thames and St Paul's.

Evening: 'Go to the dogs' at the **greyhound racing** in Walthamstow – it's much more fun than Ascot.

Night: Clubbing at **Fabric**, one of London's best nights.

LITERARY CITY

Everyone who is anyone in Britain's literary canon seems to have passed through London at some time or another: Shakespeare tussled with his actors at the Globe, Dr Johnson compiled his dictionary, Keats caught consumption, and Dylan Thomas got kicked out of more pubs than he could remember. The city exerts a deep fascination for scribblers of every kind and has featured in everything from Chaucer's *Canterbury Tales* and Dickens' stories of the Victorian slums, to Martin Amis's *London Fields* and Hanif Kureishi's *The Buddha of Suburbia*. In 2000, London even got its own biography thanks to Peter Ackroyd.

Three

Start: Tube Leicester Square.

Breakfast: Spot some up-and-coming talent at the cosy **Pâtisserie Valerie** in Soho.

Morning: Visit **Dickens' House**, the only one of Dickens' homes to survive, then stroll around **Bloomsbury** in the footsteps of E.M. Forster and Virginia Woolf.

Lunch: The **Fitzroy Tavern**, where Orwell and Dylan Thomas used to drink.

Afternoon: Make a pilgrimage to 84 Charing Cross Road (it doesn't really exist but there are plenty of excellent **bookshops** around), made famous by Helene Hanff's novel. If you'd like to visit another entirely fictional address, try the **Sherlock Holmes Museum** at '221B' Baker Street.

Dinner: **Rules**, which has been going since the first edition of Dr Johnson's dictionary was published (well, almost).

Evening: **Ye Olde Cock Tavern** on Fleet Street, where Samuel Pepys used to drink himself into a stupor.

Four

Start: Tube Waterloo.

Breakfast: Pastries at **Konditor and Cooke** in the Young Vic Theatre.

Morning: Stroll around the streets in **Southwark** made famous by Dickens, perhaps following our **Taverns, Stews and Players walk**. Before lunch, tour the **Globe Theatre** (*photo above*), a reconstruction of the original Elizabethan theatre where Shakespeare's plays were first performed in the round.

Lunch: At the **George Inn**, the only surviving Elizabethan coaching inn, on Borough High Street. Chaucer's pilgrims set off for Canterbury from a (long-demolished) inn in this neighbourhood.

Afternoon: Walk off lunch with a stroll around **Hampstead Village**, long renowned as the home of many of London's literati. Visit **Keats' House**, the consumptive poet's home for two years.

Dinner: **Ye Olde Cheshire Cheese** on Fleet Street, where Dr Johnson used to drink.

Evening: See a performance at the **Royal National Theatre**, where Harold Pinter recently directed his own play, *No Man's Land*, to great acclaim.

CONTEMPORARY ARCHITECTURE

London's skyline changed dramatically in the run-up to the millennium. The most obvious additions were the London Eye and the Dome, but things were changing underground, too – some of the best new architecture in London is to be found in the stations along the extension to the Jubilee Line. Out in Docklands, skyscrapers were sprouting until the events of 11 September reopened the debate about tall buildings, with Prince Charles on one side, and London's outspoken mayor on the other. He and his council are about to move into a 41-storey 'erotic gherkin' right by Tower Bridge, designed by the ubiquitous Norman Foster.

Five

Start: Tube Covent Garden.

Breakfast: At **Paul** in the newly extended Covent Garden piazza.

Morning: Take a tour of the **Royal Opera House**, which has been spectacularly expanded and includes the dazzling Vilar Floral Hall. Head up to Bloomsbury for a look at London's other high-profile extension, the Great Court at the **British Museum** (*photo below*).

Lunch: At **Abeno**, for lovely Japanese food right by the museum.

Afternoon: Stroll across the river, from Charing Cross to the South Bank, on the Hungerford Bridge, a railway bridge with an extra new pedestrian walkway added in April 2002. Next, take a twirl on the **London Eye**, the most famous addition to the London skyline, which gives views out as far as the controversial Millennium Dome.

Dinner and evening: At the Damien Hirst-designed **Pharmacy Bar and Restaurant** in Notting Hill.

Six

Start: Tube Charing Cross, Embankment or Holborn.

Breakfast: **Indigo**, the very stylish breakfast bar belonging to the glossy One Aldwych Hotel.

Morning: Take the Tube to Southwark, one of the best of the futuristic stations on the new **Jubilee Line**. Pop up again at **Canary Wharf**, a stunning Tube station famous for its endless escalator. Gaze up at London's tallest building, the 812ft Canary Wharf Tower. It no longer stands alone: two banks, HSBC and Citibank, built the enormous towers which flank it like a pair of bodyguards.

Lunch: **Baradero**, with views over the Docklands developments.

Afternoon: Have a look around **Tate Modern** (*photo bottom right*), a former power station. Then stroll across the nearby **Millennium Bridge**, Foster's famous 'Blade of Light'.

Dinner: **Le Pont de la Tour**, one of Terence Conran's restaurants, with great views of the river and City.

Evening: Wander along the Millennium Walkway to the **Oxo Tower** and have a drink in one of its bars.

Food and Drinks

Sights and Activities

Nightlife

RIVERSIDE CITY

The Thames is Britain's largest and most powerful river, the source of the city's fortune for centuries. Long ignored – largely because it was polluted and stank – the river is now finally back where it should be in any view of London: right in the middle. The slew of millennial projects were all stacked up along the riverbank: the London Eye, the Millennium Bridge, Tate Modern, and even the much maligned Dome. Thanks to a massive clean-up, the fish and birds are back, and river-taxis and cruise boats ply the waters all the way from Hampton Court Palace to the Thames Barrier.

Seven

Start: Tube Southwark.

Breakfast: At the Globe Café (at the **Globe Theatre**) on the South Bank.

Morning: Take the train from Waterloo for **Syon Park**, a stately home set in landscaped gardens by the riverside in the sprawling western suburbs.

Lunch: **Chez Lindsay**, a pretty Breton-style restaurant on the banks of the Thames in Richmond.

Afternoon: Stroll off lunch along the delightful stretch of river just south of **Richmond Bridge**. Or learn about London's history as a port at the **Museum in Docklands** and follow it up with a stroll around the striking **Canary Wharf** developments.

Dinner: Out on the terrace at **Admiralty**, set in Somerset House right on the riverside.

Evening: If the weather's nice, do a crawl of some of the riverside pubs in Hammersmith, such as **The Dove**.

Eight

Start: Tube Waterloo.

Breakfast: At the Film Café (at the **National Film Theatre**) in the South Bank Centre.

Morning: Wander along the Thames Path (which follows the river for 184 miles), from Waterloo Bridge to **London Bridge**. Cross London Bridge and climb the **Monument** for beautiful views.

Lunch: At the Southwark Refectory, part of the ancient **Southwark Cathedral** that sits right on the riverbank.

Afternoon: The **Tower Bridge Experience**, for an insight into how the famous bridge is raised and lowered. Take a boat cruise down-river, past **Greenwich**, and on to the **Thames Barrier** (*photo far left*).

Dinner and evening: At the **Prospect of Whitby**, an old riverside pub with a great beer garden.

OUTDOOR CITY

London is one of the greenest capital cities in the world, with a string of fabulous parks right in the centre – you can walk from Whitehall to Kensington (a good 3 miles) and barely touch concrete. To the west and north lies a clutch of stately homes surrounded by beautiful parklands; there are venerable botanical gardens at Kew, a tiny charming Physic Garden in Chelsea, and outdoor swimming pools (lidos) in suburban parks. Even the urban squares take on a life of their own when the sun shines and a sea of picnickers pours out from the office blocks.

Nine

Start: Tube Marble Arch.

Breakfast: At the **No.6 Brasserie**.

Morning: Go **horse-riding in Hyde Park**, or mess about in a rowing boat on the **Serpentine**, then follow our **walking tour around Royal London**.

Lunch: On the elegant terrace at the **Orangery** at Kensington Palace.

Afternoon: Take an **open-top bus tour** of the city, then enjoy a pint or two at the old **Anchor**, which has an outdoor terrace overlooking the Thames. See a performance of one of Shakespeare's plays in the round at the outdoor **Globe Theatre**.

Dinner: Modern European food at the **Zinc Bar and Grill**, which has tables outside in summer.

Evening: When, and if, the weather's good, pubs spill out into the streets in London, particularly around **Covent Garden** piazza or in the trendy streets of **Soho**.

Ten

Start: Tube Marylebone.

Breakfast: Pick up some croissants at one of London's nicest pâtisseries – **Pâtisserie Valerie** or **Maison Blanc** on Marylebone High Street – and head for Regent's Park for a picnic breakfast.

Morning: Visit the magnificent Queen Mary's Rose Gardens in **Regent's Park**, then potter around **London Zoo** – watch the penguins being fed and pet a camel.

Lunch: At an outdoor table at **Giraffe** in Hampstead.

Afternoon: Window-shop among the smart designer boutiques along **Hampstead High Street**, then fly a kite on nearby **Parliament Hill** or go for a swim in one of the ponds on **Hampstead Heath**.

Dinner and evening: If it's the summer, pack a picnic hamper (with plenty of champagne) and watch an **outdoor concert at Kenwood House**.

INDOOR CITY

Pack an umbrella because it will rain while you're in London. Discussing the erratic weather will win you new friends at bus stops, but the city has long accepted its climate and adapted accordingly. There are plenty of cosy pubs to retreat to in the depths of winter, and a host of exceptional museums built on such a mammoth scale (the British Museum, the Science Museum or the Victoria and Albert, for example) that you could happily lose yourself for a day or two. And London has got all the big-city trappings in spades: great restaurants and bars, and a dizzying array of entertainment from opera to contemporary dance.

Eleven

Start: Tube Tottenham Court Rd or Holborn.

Breakfast: Tuck into a big breakfast at **La Brasserie Townhouse**.

Morning: Spend some time with the mummies at the **British Museum**, and admire the vast new Great Court. On emerging, buy a sturdy English umbrella at **James Smith and Sons**.

Lunch: Linger over an excellent pub lunch at the **Duke of York** in Bloomsbury. Or hear a lunchtime classical concert at **St John's Smith Square**.

Afternoon: Take the Tube and stay dry: the Piccadilly Line from Russell Square to South Kensington. Visit the amazing new British Galleries at the **Victoria and Albert Museum**. Kids will particularly enjoy seeing a 3D film at the IMAX theatre in the nearby **Science Museum**.

Dinner: Dine on oysters and champagne at the fabulous Art Nouveau restaurant **Bibendum**.

Evening: Go to the opera at the **Royal Opera House** or **London Coliseum**, or if you prefer dance, see a ballet at **Sadler's Wells**.

Roots of the City

*When it's three o'clock in New York,
it's still 1938 in London.*

Bette Midler

London is a city in love with the past. Not the unpleasant parts of it, mind you, not the grime, poverty and violence all too present in its long and turbulent history. No, the past that London cares about is glorious, colourful and just a little eccentric; strong on tradition, high on pomp and well larded with nostalgia. Its fondly preserved relics are in evidence everywhere: Beefeaters at the Tower, Horse Guards on parade, Savile Row suits, liveried assistants at Fortnum & Mason and red double-decker buses. History, at least according to folklore, has been very good to London: no foreign invasions since 1066, no major political upheavals since the Civil War, no grand-scale calamities since the Plague and Great Fire of 1665–6. Even when adversity has threatened, as it did during the summer of 1940, London has been strong enough to overcome it. Continuity has been the name of the game, or so London would like to believe.

Of course, London is kidding itself. Life in this most streetwise of capitals has been considerably more precarious than its folklore is prepared to admit. The pursuit of wealth, London's chief *raison d'être*, has always favoured the few at the expense of the many. Crime, disease and destitution have been constant blights, and popular revolt has all too often beckoned. The picture may be rosier in today's modern city, but insecurities about housing crises, transport failures and unemployment are never far from people's minds.

Much of London is dedicated to the deluded proposition that the old world is still with us. They're still changing the guard at Buckingham Palace; the Queen is still on her throne. Barristers and judges still wear wigs, and the Lord Mayor still arrives for his year in office in a gilded 18th-century coach. Of course these are just vestiges of the past, many of them absurdly if charmingly anachronistic, and in some cases actually bogus (*see* 'Keeping the Anachronism Alive', p.116–17, on the fake traditions of the monarchy). The daily Ceremony of the Keys at the Tower, for example, has long since ceased to have a security purpose, if it ever had one. Likewise, the royal guards who stand to attention in their furry busbies and smart red uniforms are largely there for decoration. The more unpleasant aspects of the past have been either forgotten, or sanitized and co-opted into London's 'glorious tradition'. The great criminals of the past have been immortalized as ghoulish anti-heroes at Madame Tussaud's.

So London's history comes with a health warning: don't believe everything you are told. The gulf between the legend and the more complex, often more sordid reality helps explain many of London's insecurities about its place in the world. At times it is a city that yearns to modernize, to be hip and cutting-edge. At others, it likes to look back to a rose-tinted bygone age and sigh for the innocent youth it never had.

Prehistory–AD 410: Rhinos, Romans and Revolt

London's habit of aggrandizing its own past began in the 12th century when Geoffrey of Monmouth, the man who elaborated the legends of King Arthur, spun tales about London's being founded by a Trojan prince called Brutus and populated by heroic giants descended from the Celtic warrior King Lud. In fact, London in the pre-Christian era was an unpleasant swamp inhabited only by wild beasts. Excavations at Heathrow Airport have unearthed evidence of elephants, mammoths, rhinoceroses and hippopotami. At the time of the first **Roman invasion** in 55 BC, there was no city on the Thames, and the main tribe in Britain, the Catuvellauni, had their capital further northeast at Colchester. It was the Emperor Claudius who built the first **London Bridge** to take his army over the Thames towards Colchester in AD 43, and Londinium grew up as a natural consequence on the north bank of the river. The settlement became an important transport hub as new roads radiated outwards towards Chester, Lincoln, Colchester, Dover, Lewes, Brighton and Silchester. Colchester remained the capital for a while, but Londinium's position on the Thames made it an ideal trading centre. By AD 60, according to Tacitus, it was 'famed for commerce and crowded with merchants'.

Such prosperity was short-lived, for revolt was brewing among the Iceni of East Anglia. They had been double-crossed over the inheritance of their king, Prasutagus, who had left half his assets to the invaders in exchange for peace. In AD 61 a group of Romans, in the absence of the governor Suetonius Paulinus, decided to seize the other half as well. Prasutagus's **Queen Boudicca** (often spelt Boadicea) was given a public flogging and her daughters raped. Boudicca rallied an army and overran Colchester and St Albans before marching on Londinium, which she burnt to the ground, hanging or crucifying any Romans in her way. It was the most serious revolt the Romans ever faced in Britain, and made Boudicca into a folk hero. Suetonius struggled long to win back the upper hand, but when he did he was merciless, slaughtering the Iceni indiscriminately and ravaging their territories. Boudicca herself took poison rather than face torture and execution at his hands.

Londinium was rebuilt, only to be beset by fires. The worst of them, in AD 130, did nearly as much damage as Boudicca's army. But the strategic position of the town served it well. Its position on the edge of the Roman Empire kept it out of the internecine rivalries rocking the rest of Europe, and allowed it to concentrate on selling cloth, hides, fur, gold, tin, lead and corn. In exchange it bought up pottery, glass, bronze, silverware, wine jugs and olive oil. The Romans fortified it and built a cluster of public buildings, including a governor's palace, an amphitheatre, a Mithraic temple and a civic centre or basilica containing law

> ### Prehistory–AD 410
> **Museum of London**, with exhibits on the history of London from its beginning to the present day, p.223
> **Natural History Museum**, for dinosaur skeletons and all sorts, p.192

courts, offices and administrative council rooms. The **Roman walls**, fragments of which survive at Tower Hill and the Barbican, were completed by about AD 200.

But by the end of the 4th century the empire was in terminal decline, and even Britain could not avoid feeling the effects. When a British-based career soldier called Magnus Maximus declared himself Roman Emperor in 388, he took most of the colonial army off with him to Gaul and left Londinium at the mercy of the **Picts**, **Saxons** and **Scots**. He was just the first in a succession of pretenders to strip Britain of its garrison. In 410, as Romanized Britons appealed for help against the marauders, a hard-pressed Emperor Honorius could do nothing but tell them to organize their own defences. Nearly 400 years of Roman rule were over.

410–1066: Saxons, Danes and Normans

At this point, London drops out of the history books for 200 years. Nobody knows for sure what became of the city in the 5th and 6th centuries. It seems that it may have been destroyed, because, by the time records resumed, London's street plan had changed and most of its citizens had moved out of the city walls to new settlements along the river. **Christianity** had arrived through the influence of St Gregory and St Augustine, and in 604 the ruler of the time, Ethelbert of Kent, undertook the building of the first St Paul's. The first Westminster Abbey followed later in the 7th century. This spiritual revival did nothing, however, to dampen London's trading instincts. By the 8th century, Bede noted London was 'a market place for many peoples, who come by land and by sea'. The wool trade, which was to form the basis of Britain's wealth for several centuries, began in earnest, and London grew fat as the chief entry point for consignments to and from the continent.

This peace and prosperity was disturbed in the middle of the 9th century by new raiders, this time the **Vikings**, who swooped in from Denmark with horses in the holds of their ships and a terrifying array of battle-axes. Saxon Britain was quite unprepared to beat back their sophisticated army, and found itself overwhelmed. Only **Alfred, King of Wessex**, was able to stand up to them. He drove the Vikings out of his own territories in 871 and out of London 15 years later. On his orders, Londoners moved back inside the city walls as a defensive measure; the move paid off, since in 896 the townsfolk successfully repulsed a new Danish attack.

The situation remained tense but generally quiet for another century until **King Ethelred** (978–1016), nicknamed The Unready, decided he would prefer to pay the Vikings off than fight them. It was a disastrous decision. A band of marauding Danes kidnapped the Archbishop of Canterbury, Alfege, in 1011 and pelted him to death a year later. In 1013 the Danes took London after a brief siege and sent Ethelred fleeing for his life. Only after Ethelred's Norwegian ally Olaf pulled down London Bridge with ropes attached to his ships, thus isolating the invaders, did the Danes call a truce and allow Ethelred back on the throne.

Ethelred was little more than a puppet, however, and his successor in 1016 turned out to be **Canute** (sometimes spelt Cnut), King of the Danes. The Danish occupation brought new, unfamiliar customs to the city; one contemporary document records how Londoners resented having to wash as often as once a week, and complained about having to comb their hair to please Danish women – both activities considered unmanly in the extreme. This tyranny of gallant manners did not last long, however. Canute died in 1035 and his last son, Harthacnut, followed him to the grave seven years later.

The new king was Ethelred's son **Edward**, who had spent the previous quarter-century in exile in Normandy.

Edward hoped that an alliance with the Normans would make Britain stable and keep the Danes out once and for all. He established his court and a new **abbey at Westminster**, earning himself the nickname The Confessor, and fostered strong ties with his former land of exile. Not everybody approved of his policies, and his chief rival, Godwin, seized control of the city in protest. When Edward died in January 1066, eight days after the consecration of his abbey, the scene was set for another showdown. Godwin's son **Harold** took the throne, and in retaliation Edward's Norman protégé **William** launched an invasion. As every schoolchild in the country knows, the two sides met at Hastings on the south coast, Harold was killed, and William (soon to be called the Conqueror) marched on victoriously to London.

1066–1485: Medieval London

William immediately showed he meant business by building a **fortified tower** at the eastern end of the City, so squashing any thoughts the citizens of London may have had about revolt. With the City merchants, William proved rather more malleable (they were, after all, the guarantors of the kingdom's wealth) and promised that their old trading rules would continue unhindered. Tensions between the City and the court at Westminster nevertheless persisted. One of the Tower's first constables, Geoffrey of Mandeville, tried to use his position to extort money from the merchants; he was so reviled that when he died he was left unburied for 20 years. The City made clear that it was not to be messed with, and slowly built itself into a powerful ideological counterweight to the king.

Over the next two centuries, the merchants organized themselves into a series of craft associations, or **guilds**, dotted around the City: saddlers in Fosters Lane, goldsmiths at the eastern end of Cheapside, plumbers in Clement's Lane, candlemakers in Cannon St and shoemakers around St Mary-le-Bow. As their economic power grew, so too did their political confidence. They gave only limited support to **Richard the Lionheart** in his efforts to raise money for the Crusades, preferring to support his brother **John**, who was scheming to take over from him. At one point Richard commented in sheer frustration: 'If I could have found a buyer I would have sold London itself.' John became king on Richard's death in 1199, but immediately lost what credibility he had with the London merchants by demanding further taxes to fight a new war in Normandy. Eventually John's barons forced him to sign away a chunk of his powers in the **Magna Carta** declaration of 1215, obtaining amongst other things the right to elect a **mayor for London** annually without interference from the Crown. Important though the document was for the development of the constitution, it would be a mistake to see the Magna Carta in itself as a great leap towards democracy. The barons were engaged in a power struggle and wanted primarily to look out for their own interests; the appointment of a London mayor gave them an important political platform. The mayor was appointed by the 24 aldermen of the City. His main job was to look after the interests of business; the people – ill-housed, ill-paid and without access to clean water or proper hygiene – did not come under any serious consideration.

Among the worst treated were the **Jews**, who had come over with William the Conqueror and settled north of Cheapside in the area still known as Old Jewry. From the start they had no legal rights. Barred from farming or manufacturing, they were virtually forced into money-lending. They were

also obliged to bury their dead outside the city walls, paying a toll fee for the privilege. For a while they enjoyed some protection from the king, but then the Crusades made anti-Semitism fashionable and they really began to suffer. The Crown frequently fined Jews on the pretext that they had committed some offence; if the king had no particular culprit in mind, he would simply fine the whole community. John's successor **Henry III** squeezed £160,000 out of the Jewish population this way, allowing him to pay for a good part of the rebuilding of Westminster Abbey. What the king couldn't steal from the Jews, he borrowed. There wasn't much difference: most Jews, after granting a loan to the monarch, never saw their money again.

The City merchants, meanwhile, went from strength to strength. As Henry III went deeper into debt, they bailed him out with loans and charged him extortionate interest rates. Henry railed and called them 'nauseatingly rich', but stopped short of imposing direct rule on London because he needed the merchants to plug his finances. The final showdown between Henry and the City came in 1263, when **Simon de Montfort** led a baronial rebellion to overthrow the king. Montfort won the support of Londoners of all classes with his promise of democratic reforms, but could not raise an army large or competent enough to topple the government. He perished at the battle of Evesham in 1265. Henry's revenge on London for its treachery was terrible. He fined the merchants £17,000 and wrote a new crime into the legal records: 'Offence, a Londoner'.

The City soon recovered, and refused all cooperation with the monarchy. Henry's successor **Edward I** had to turn to foreigners for money, inviting **Lombard bankers** to take up residence near Cornhill. **Edward II** meanwhile tried to curb the independence of London by force, with disastrous results. A furious mob chased the king through the streets, and when they failed to catch him they turned on his treasurer, the Bishop of Exeter, whom they tailed from Newgate to Cheapside before hacking off his head with a breadknife. This incident contributed to Edward's deposition by Parliament, and the disgraced king died a gruesome death, run through from behind with a red-hot poker at Berkeley Castle in Gloucestershire.

Riots and street fighting were a constant feature of medieval London and usually underpinned political tensions. In 1222 a wrestling match between Westminster and the City turned into a running battle. A century later, Italian traders fell victim to a mob accusing them of sleeping with English women and siding with the French in the Hundred Years' War. Sometimes the fighting was the result of rivalry between two guilds, as in 1340 when the Skinners and Fishmongers pounced on each other. At other times anger was directed at the Crown, for example after **Edward III** licensed the export of wool exclusively to Westminster, rather than the City, in the 1340s. It was a dirty, precarious time to live, full of **disease, dirt, crime and perverse punishment**. Bad cooks were boiled alive, and crooked vintners were forced to drink their own foul wine in public. The Fleet river, running down from Smithfield Market to the Thames, was an open sewer overflowing with animal blood and offal. A baker called Richard drowned in human faeces when the floorboards he was standing on gave way and landed him in a cesspit.

Perhaps it was no surprise, given the teeming filth of the city, that the **Black Death** of 1348–9 hit London particularly hard. The population fell from 60,000 to less than 30,000 as the bubonic plague, carried by rats from Asia via continental Europe, ravaged house after house and street after street. Once the plague had done its worst, Edward III realized the importance of hygiene for public health and decreed that cattle should be slaughtered outside the city limits; largely as a result of his foresight, the population regained its former strength within 50 years.

Trouble soon came again, in the shape of the **Peasants' Revolt**. In 1381 a mob of peasants from around the country penetrated the capital demanding the repeal of the new poll tax, a levy that penalized all citizens equally, regardless of their ability to pay. The mob leader, Wat Tyler, demanded an audience with the 14-year-old **King Richard II**; while he waited, his men opened debtors' prisons, slaughtered lawyers, destroyed the residence of the corrupt regent John of Gaunt, and burst into the Tower, where they beheaded the Archbishop of Canterbury and his treasurer. The peasant leader eventually gained the royal ear, first at Mile End and then at Smithfield, where the king made vast concessions including the abolition of all feudal services. Many of Richard's courtiers could not believe their ears; William Walworth, the Mayor of London, drew his dagger and stabbed Tyler in fury at his presumption. The crowd erupted, and might yet have turned on Richard had the young king not stood up and offered himself as leader in Tyler's place. It was an extraordinary moment in English history: the mystical power of the monarch was so great that the crowd took him at his word and dispersed peacefully. It was a bad call on their part. Richard immediately rescinded his promises (although, to deter further uprisings, he did abolish the poll tax) and hunted down and killed as many revolt leaders as his men could find. Tyler himself was dragged into Bart's Hospital after his stabbing and then tortured and decapitated. Walworth, meanwhile, stayed in his post; his dagger was later incorporated into the arms of the City of London. With so great a scare so early in life, Richard made sure henceforth that London and its citizens were well looked after. He established a Great Wardrobe to fit his court with lavish furniture and clothes, most of them ordered from City merchants like the celebrated mercer Dick Whittington (*see* 'Turn Again, Whittington', pp.238–9).

The **Wars of the Roses**, a struggle for the crown between the Houses of Lancaster and York that dragged on throughout the mid-15th century, brought considerable disturbance to this calm. The City initially supported **Edward IV** and the House of York, but was happy to change its mind when political expediency demanded, not least because its champion was sleeping with the wives of a number of City merchants. Edward died in 1483 and his two young sons were subsequently murdered in the Tower of London. The hunchback **Richard III**, widely suspected of killing the young princes, took the throne for two years before going down in battle at the hands of the Earl of Richmond. Richmond, a Lancastrian, was crowned **Henry VII** and shrewdly ended the war by marrying a Yorkist.

1485–1660: Tudors and Stuarts

Political turmoil returned with a vengeance in the 1530s after **Henry VIII**'s divorce from his first wife, Catherine of Aragon, in defiance of the Pope, and his consequent break with the Roman Catholic Church. Over the next 15 years a stream of churchmen, politicians and courtiers were executed, most of them at the Tower of London, as Henry closed the monasteries and cracked down on anyone who challenged him. One of the first victims was the humanist thinker Sir Thomas More, who refused to recognize the monarch as head of the Church in England. The political violence continued well after Henry's death in 1547 as the Crown seesawed between Protestants and the Catholic **Queen Mary**. A modicum of order returned with the accession of Mary's Protestant sister **Elizabeth** in 1558, although she too had to resort to violence to fend off threats from her jealous relatives, particularly her Catholic

1485–1660
  Banqueting House, symbol of Stuart kingship, p.94
  Golden Hinde, a reconstruction of Sir Francis Drake's galley, p.209
  Hampton Court, Henry VIII's love nest, p.255
  Museum in Docklands, for the story of London's port, p.274
  Shakespeare's Globe, to find out more about Elizabethan theatre, p.206

cousin Mary Queen of Scots and her brother-in-law, Philip of Spain, who sent an unsuccessful invasion fleet, the **Armada**, to English shores in 1588.

Remarkably, the City kept its cool through this turbulence. For London, the Tudor period was one of unprecedented affluence. **New industries**, such as silk-weaving and glass manufacture, prospered. Commerce was so intense that the Thames turned into a multi-lane highway where boats constantly had to raise their oars to allow traffic to pass. The richer merchants made a killing from the dissolution of the monasteries; they bought up the land on the cheap and then, thanks to the increasing speculative value of property in London, sold or rented it at enormous profit. Without doubt the key commercial event of the 16th century was the opening of the **Royal Exchange** in 1552: for the first time traders of all kinds could meet and fix bulk prices for their wares. It says much about the power of the merchants that, in order to build the exchange, its founder Sir Thomas Gresham simply razed 80 houses along four streets without a thought for their inhabitants.

It was altogether a time of great social gulfs between the rich and the poor. As the population increased (from 75,000 in 1500 to 220,000 a century later), the greatest problem became access to clean and plentiful **water**. One Venetian ambassador to London in the early 16th century complained that he could detect the stink of the city cisterns even in his clean linen. In the early 17th century, a City merchant called Sir Hugh

Myddleton had a trench dug all the way down from the underground springs of Hertfordshire. His New River provided a virtually unlimited water supply and heralded the enormous growth of London in the following centuries. Landed aristocrats moved into town, building palaces where monasteries had been, particularly on the land between Westminster and the City which we now know as the **West End**. This new district was not only near the royal court, it also enjoyed the benefit of the prevailing west wind which kept the stink of the City out of the aristocrats' nostrils.

England's peculiar Reformation, which after all had been motivated by Henry VIII's private interests rather than any theological rift with Rome, proved fragile at first. Soon, however, it was bolstered by the development of a radical anti-Catholic lobby inspired by Calvinist Puritanism. The **Puritans** may have come in for a lot of bad press for their austere ways and their attacks on the Elizabethan theatre, but politically they played a crucial role in questioning the powers of the monarch and the inequalities of English society. When the Stuart family – with its Catholic heritage and High Church sensibilities – came down from Scotland to take over the English crown in 1603, the Puritan agenda shot to the forefront of national debate. The first Stuart king, **James I**, was so careful not to offend the Protestants that a group of disaffected Catholics decided to blow him up along with his Parliament just two years after he came to power. The **Gunpowder Plot** was foiled at the last minute by a vigilant Parliamentary watchman, thereby handing the Puritans a crucial propaganda victory and giving them virtually free rein to rant on about the evils of Roman Catholicism.

James's successor, **Charles I**, fatally underestimated the political importance of the Puritans. He failed to understand how his old-fashioned style of monarchy, based on privilege, favour and the divine right of kings, would anger them and push the country into civil war. The Puritans gained control of

Parliament and tried to force Charles towards reform. The king ignored their calls until 1641, when he was presented with a bill demanding the execution of his chief minister, the Earl of Strafford. He retaliated by dissolving Parliament, only to find himself chased out of London a few months later. London had every reason to support the Puritan Parliament: the merchants had always seen the Crown as an obstacle to their aims, while many ordinary Londoners bitterly resented Charles's lavish spending and lack of interest in the common citizen. Once the fighting started, there was a purge of leading Royalists in the City, including the Lord Mayor. Charles tried to lead his army against the capital in 1642, but could not overcome a tight ring of fortifications and turned back at Turnham Green near Hammersmith. Thereafter, the king did not set foot in London again until he was brought by force to be tried in Westminster Hall and executed outside his beloved Banqueting House in 1649.

The architect of the Parliamentarians' military victory was **Oliver Cromwell**, a descendant of Henry VIII's minister of the same name, who soon became de facto ruler of Britain. Cromwell turned out, however, to be despotic and undependable. All talk of 'levelling' and democratic reform went out of the window when he closed down Parliament in 1653 and accepted the title – and quasi-royal powers – of Lord Protector. By the time he died in 1658 he was almost universally reviled. Many influential London merchants had reconverted to the Royalist cause, and secret negotiations were soon under way to bring the future **Charles II** back from exile. Charles ascended the throne in 1660; Cromwell, on the other hand, was disinterred, hanged and decapitated, and his head displayed on the roof of Westminster Hall, the scene of Charles I's trial 11 years earlier. Despite this reversal of fortunes, the restored monarchy was a chastened institution: never again would a king assert his divine rights, or dare to disdain the will of Parliament.

1660–88:
Plague and Fire

London in the 1660s was a prosperous city of a quarter of a million. The incipient **trade in sea-coal** was making it tremendously rich (and tremendously smog-ridden, too). It was an unsentimental place, but at least it felt it could take any calamity in its stride. Fires would burn down a few buildings now and again, plagues would come along every few years and wipe out a few thousand people, but that was just the way life went. The overall mood, particularly among the governing classes, was one of relentless optimism. Until, that is, the twin calamities of 1665 and 1666 – an appalling plague followed by the worst fire in London's history.

The first **bubonic plague** victims were reported around Christmas 1664. The epidemic was checked by an exceptionally cold winter, but raged with a vengeance from the first warm days of April right through until November. The first sign of the disease was drowsiness, followed by headache, vomiting and delirious fever. Then the buboes would appear: at first no more than a rash, then full-blown black swellings under the arms and in the groin. The rash was called a 'token' which signalled almost certain death. These symptoms inspired the nursery rhyme:

Ring-a-ring of roses
A pocketful of posies
A-tishoo! A-tishoo!
We all fall down.

The 'roses' were skin rashes; the posies were herbs which the healthy carried in the hope of warding off disease. Sneezing was a common sign of impending death.

What made the Great Plague particularly tragic was the complete abdication of responsibility by Parliament, the City fathers and the king. Rich families moved out into the country from April onwards; Charles II prorogued Parliament until September and followed them out, with a swathe of politicians, municipal officials, doctors and

clergymen. The economy started to collapse; shopkeepers went out of business and small companies were forced to close for lack of staff. Only quack doctors, selling amulets and concoctions of pepper and urine, managed to make anything resembling a living. Servants who had been abandoned by their masters either took work driving 'dead-carts' through the streets or else joined marauding gangs of looters and house-breakers. Gravediggers worked day and night. The corpses piled up in the streets and sometimes lay there for days at a time.

By midsummer, one Justice of the Peace decided to have the entire city population of cats and dogs exterminated, in the mistaken belief that it was they who carried the plague. Exterminators were paid two shillings for every animal corpse they could produce – the equivalent of two days' wages for a working man. Most of the cats and dogs were fed poisoned meat, or else clubbed to death. It was a crazy decision. The removal of all the cats gave free rein to the real villains, the plague-carrying rats, who now scurried around and multiplied with impunity. Fear and paranoia were rife. Londoners taking refuge in the country would not open a letter from the city without first washing it or heating it in front of a fire. Plague victims seeking a rural retreat were pelted with stones and manure to keep them away from healthy households. In London itself, any house with a victim was locked and guarded for 40 days, with all the inhabitants – sick or healthy – trapped inside.

As summer wore on, plague victims were seen foaming at the mouth and running naked through the streets. Some hurled themselves out of sheer despair into plague

Samuel Pepys and the Art of Keeping a Diary

Nowadays we know Samuel Pepys (1633–1703) as the greatest diarist in English literature, a painstaking recorder of London in the 1660s. And yet he nearly missed the most dramatic event of his lifetime, the Great Fire. Pepys actually woke up on the night that the fire started, but decided it didn't look like much and went back to bed. Unlike the incompetent Lord Mayor Thomas Bloodworth, who made the same mistake, though, Pepys quickly made up for lost time and proceeded to describe the fire in minute detail, first from the vantage point of his home in the City, and then, as the blaze spread, from Bethnal Green and Woolwich. It is to him and his fellow diarist, John Evelyn, that we owe nearly all our knowledge of the traumatic events of September 1666. In many ways, Pepys and Evelyn also gave London its taste for literature and literary gossip.

Pepys was a top-flight civil servant who sealed the success of his career when he helped bring Charles II back from exile in 1660. Appointed Clerk of the Acts to the Navy Board, he began writing his diary as a chronicle of political events at the outset of the Restoration. It was never meant for public consumption, and indeed was written in a personal shorthand telescoping words and phrases and peppered with a handful of foreign languages. As the diary goes on, Pepys's personal life intrudes more and more: what he has eaten, what he has seen at the theatre, his troubles with servants, his relationship with his wife Elizabeth, his worries about his eyesight and, ultimately, his affair with his wife's companion, Deborah Willett, which caused him to break off his diary in 1669. Because the journal is essentially private (it was not published until 1825), it is not given to great literary flourishes; it is unspectacularly written, but dense and highly detailed nonetheless. Pepys enjoyed access to Charles II, and provides much royal gossip; it is through him that the legend of Charles hiding in an oak tree at the Battle of Worcester in 1651 has been handed down.

pits for the dead. The streets were filled with wailing and delirious moans. Only in late autumn did the death toll begin to wane; as late as Christmas there was still a stench of human putrefaction in the streets. Only when Charles II returned to the capital in February 1666 did London return to something like its normal state. The official death toll from the plague was 69,000. It seems likely, however, that the figure was deliberately underplayed and that the real toll was nearer 100,000.

Catastrophe number two followed a few months later. In the early hours of 2 September, a **fire** broke out at Farynor's bakery in Pudding Lane. Mr Farynor had almost certainly forgotten to damp down his oven, although he denied this in the subsequent investigation, and sparks carried by a strong wind set fire first to the nearby Star Inn and then to the entire neighbourhood. The Farynor family scurried to safety, abandoning their maid, who was left sleeping and burnt to death. At first nobody thought much of the blaze. The Lord Mayor, Sir Thomas Bloodworth, was called out, but returned to bed declaring, 'Pish, a woman might piss it out!'

By morning, more than 300 houses and half of London Bridge were on fire. Soon the coal and tallow stores on Thames St by the river were ablaze; then the London Bridge water wheel, which could have saved the day, was engulfed too. Attacking the inferno with water-filled leather buckets and primitive hoses did not do much good. The diarist **Samuel Pepys** was taken aback by the sheer heat: 'With one's face in the wind you were almost burned with a shower of fire drops,' he wrote. The glow was visible 50 miles away in Oxford. Believing the whole city to be lost, Pepys packed up his valuables and transported most of them by coach and boat to the countryside. His wine and parmesan cheese he buried in his garden.

The fire raged for four days, destroying 13,200 houses, 44 livery halls and 87 churches, including the medieval St Paul's Cathedral. 'London was, but is no more,' wrote the diarist John Evelyn. The damage might have been worse still but for King Charles, who ordered the navy to break the fire by blowing up houses. By the time the flames came under control, the death toll was remarkably low – just eight victims. But the psychological damage was immense, as the fire gave rise to a sinister sort of instant fascism. Rumours spread that the fire had been started deliberately by foreign plotters or Catholics, and angry mobs began attacking French and Dutch families at random in the street. Some had to be locked up for their own protection. One Frenchman, Robert Hubert, was coerced into confessing responsibility for the fire at Farynor's bakery and hanged. King Charles, worried by the growing lynch-mob mentality, made a point of visiting homeless families camped around the city and disabused them of the foreign-plot theory. But superstition persisted. Preachers noted that the blaze had started at Pudding Lane and ended at Pye Corner, near Newgate prison, and concluded that God was punishing the city for its gluttony.

In physical terms, London recovered with remarkable speed. The king rejected radical schemes put forward by Evelyn, Christopher Wren and others, giving free rein instead to building speculators on condition that they used fire-proof brick rather than wood. What this approach lacked in aesthetic finesse, it certainly made up for in practicality: by 1672 nearly everyone who had lost their home was rehoused. Public buildings were replaced with revenue from tax on sea-coal; in this way the King's Surveyor of Works, **Christopher Wren**, refurbished scores of City churches and paid for his masterwork, the modern St Paul's Cathedral. Sadly, the atmosphere of intolerance and religious bigotry did not dissipate as easily as the physical scars. As late as 1681, a plaque in Pudding Lane blamed the fire on 'the malicious hearts of barbarous Papists'.

The death of Charles II in 1685 caused a constitutional crisis: he had no legitimate son, which left only his brother James, an ardent Catholic, to inherit the throne. **James II** suppressed an uprising by Charles's illegitimate but popular son, the Duke of Monmouth, but could not consolidate his military victory with political backing. After three years, James was forced to flee, and Parliament invited his son-in-law, the Dutch prince **William of Orange**, to take over. 1688 is known as the year of the '**Glorious Revolution**', so called because Parliament fixed its legislative role and decreed that no Catholic would be allowed to take the English crown again. The inglorious corollary of this revolution, however, was the institutionalized persecution of Catholics, particularly in Ireland. The merchants of London did not let this bother them unduly, and returned to the important business of making money. They established trading links with the Orient through the **East India Company** and, as the industrial age beckoned, laid the foundations of the modern capitalist system.

1688–1837: London's Golden Age

The 18th century was London's golden age. Every great city has one, a defining moment in its history when all its best characteristics (and usually all its defects) are most in evidence. One thinks of Paris in the 19th century, or New York in the first half of the 20th. Hanoverian London was simply and effortlessly ahead of the rest of the world. For one thing, it was much larger than any other city: its population of 650,000 at the beginning of the century grew to nearly a million by the end, making it twice as big as its nearest rival, Paris. One in 10 of the population of England and Wales lived in London, compared with one in 40 Frenchmen in their capital. The empty spaces between Westminster and the City filled with Palladian mansions, new residential squares, shops, offices and churches. Building stretched south of the river, west towards Kensington and north around Hampstead and Highgate. This **urban sprawl**, which bewildered every commentator of the age, was the direct result of London's economic wealth, boosted by advances in science and commerce and reinforced by the creation of the British Empire.

Along with this physical and economic growth came a **flowering of the arts**: a new-found appreciation of architecture on the Palladian model; the emergence of British painting through Hogarth, Reynolds and Gainsborough; the rise of the theatre under the influence of the actor-manager David Garrick; and above all a thriving literary scene populated by satirists (Swift and Pope), novelists (Smollett and Fielding) and the towering personality of the journalist, lexicographer, literary critic and general man-about-town, Dr Samuel Johnson.

It would be a mistake, however, to take this prosperity and cultural richness as a sign of contentment and well-being. The truth was quite the opposite. If the 18th century saw London at its most typical, that was because it also saw it at its **dirtiest, most crime-ridden and most divided** by class, wealth and ambition. The Hanoverian monarchs were corrupt and lazy, and Parliament acted as their stooges. There was little pretence at democracy: the country was run by rich aristocrats who fed off the misery of the majority. Most ordinary citizens spent their time in a gin-befuddled haze. 'Human life is everywhere a state in which much is to be endured and little to be enjoyed,' said Dr Johnson. But he also noted that by seeing London, 'I have seen as much of life as the world can show.' London contained every form of existence, from the fopperies of powdered aristocrats stuffing themselves with rich food and gambling away their fortunes, to the desperation of ordinary people dying of hunger on the streets. The streets were for the most part unlit, unpaved and unnumbered; filth and refuse was stacked shoulder-high on street corners; the sky was often thick with fog. For the first half

of the century the River Fleet (modern Farringdon St) was an open sewer, and the Thames stank of rotting carcasses and industrial effluent.

Many of the century's most notable figures were rogues or crooks. Conditions were so terrible that anyone who stood up to authority, even by breaking the law, was hailed a folk hero. Gossip on the street was not about politicians or aristocrats, but about such figures as Jonathan Wild, thief-taker (*see* p.144), or Jack Sheppard, master jail-breaker (*see* p.220). Londoners lived at the mercy of a **cruel and arbitrary legal system** that proposed absurd punishments for trivial offences. Imitating a Chelsea pensioner was a crime punishable by death, as was planting a tree anywhere near the Prime Minister's office in Downing St. The government used the law as a way of waging war on the lower classes, deterring them from revolt through fear. While the authorities might hang a child for stealing a single spoon, they were quite happy to let marauding bands of rich young men roam the streets and terrorize the city population. The most notorious of these gangs were the Mohocks, who took pleasure in torturing nightwatchmen, throwing housemaids out of windows or forcing prostitutes to stand on their heads in barrels. Few were ever brought to book.

London needed a radical figure to counter this atmosphere of fear and corruption: it found one in the unlikely form of **John Wilkes**. The cross-eyed son of a Clerkenwell distiller, Wilkes was a notorious libertine, drunk and member of the Hell-Fire Club which organized Satanic banquets. He burst onto the political scene in 1762 with the publication of the pamphlet *North Briton*, which hurled insults at the leading figures of the age. At first Wilkes was treated as a bit of a joke and appreciated mainly for his wit. Once the Earl of Sandwich told him in Parliament: 'Egad, Sir, I do not know whether you will die on the gallows or of the pox.' Wilkes replied: 'That will depend, my Lord, on whether I embrace your principles or your mistress.' Wilkes pushed his luck too far in

1688–1837

1763 and was arrested and imprisoned in the Tower of London before being sent into exile. To his astonishment, however, he attracted a large following of ordinary people who demanded his freedom with the slogan 'Wilkes and Liberty'. When the City hangman tried to burn copies of *North Briton* outside the Royal Exchange, a crowd gathered to pelt him with dirt and recover pamphlets from the flames. In 1768 Wilkes returned to London and tried to get re-elected to Parliament as member for Middlesex. Three times he stood and won, but each time the authorities cancelled the poll. Eventually, however, the establishment realized what damage it was doing to itself and allowed Wilkes to enter the political arena via the City of London. This might seem an odd place for a radical to thrive, but the City merchants had shown in the past that they were not averse to firebrands as long as they could use them as weapons against the power of Parliament and the Crown. Wilkes became Lord Mayor in 1774, and although his agenda for universal suffrage, freedom of the press and reform of the legal system did not come about overnight, he put them irrevocably on the political agenda.

By this stage, popular anger was so great that it could have boiled over at any time.

The explosion eventually came with a revolt led by one of the most trenchant anti-Catholics in Parliament. **Lord George Gordon** was bitterly opposed to a Relief Bill allowing Catholics to inherit land and establish schools, and set up a Protestant Association to give vent to his opinions. In June 1780 the Association brought a vast crowd to St George's Fields in Lambeth for a demonstration; soon London had a full-scale riot on its hands. The protesters were not all anti-Catholic fanatics; rather they used Lord Gordon's demagogy to launch a general protest against the establishment. The mob burnt down five prisons and released the inmates into the streets; they attacked the Prime Minister's office at Downing St and tried unsuccessfully to burst into the Bank of England. They also meant to roast the Archbishop of Canterbury alive, along with other luminaries, but had to content themselves with plundering the Lord Chief Justice's house and tossing his book collection onto a bonfire. The fighting, looting and burning lasted for five days and only abated when government troops opened fire, killing at least 285 people.

The violence of the Gordon Riots scuppered any chances of achieving any concrete political aims. Official reports made much of the fact that a brewery in Holborn had been looted, and dismissed the rioters as drunken hooligans. Politically, the *ancien régime* barely paid any attention to the uprising. Lord Gordon, as an aristocrat, was acquitted of treason and spared his life, while 21 members of the riot mob were picked out more or less at random and hanged. Once again, the Hanoverians showed there was one law for the rich, another for the poor.

The tide was slowly turning, however. Resentment of the Hanoverian order was growing, not only among working people but also within the establishment itself. The ageing, doddery and finally insane **George III** came to look as much of an anachronism as his less fortunate contemporary Louis XVI in France. Luckily for him, it was Louis who fell first, losing his head as well as his crown in

Dickens Reshapes a City

'Dickens,' wrote his contemporary Walter Bagehot, 'describes London like a special correspondent for posterity.' It is the peculiar achievement of Charles Dickens (1812–70) to have succeeded in his vast body of fiction in outstripping the achievements of a whole century's worth of historians, journalists and social researchers. His imaginative vision has managed to convey more of the flavour and density of life in Victorian London to more people than any profusion of facts or faithfully recorded observations.

Dickens was the first and arguably the only English novelist to embrace the whole metropolis in his fictional world without flinching or growing incoherent. His labyrinthine plots and vast social backdrops create an illusion of the complexity of the city itself. To read Dickens is to take on the metropolis and come away feeling as though you have conquered it. And yet the London of his novels is very much an artificial one: his characters have names, like Veneering or Pecksniff or Gamp, that are far too absurd to be plausible; likewise their personalities exaggerate identifiable reality to the point where they become grotesque. With Dickens you are always wavering between realism and caricature, between the city you know and the free flight of your imagination.

The defining experience of the metropolis in Dickens is surface. His London is so big that it is hard to penetrate anyone beyond the outward signposts to their character: clothes, physical features, manner of speech and so on. Surface, not substance, is paramount in determining social status. A book like *Our Mutual Friend* is all about the fragility of identity in the big city and the ease with which one social mask can be exchanged for another, particularly through the power of money. Appearances are everything, for the middle-class snob Mr Podsnap, for the parvenu Veneerings, even for the modest Mr and Mrs Boffin. When the Boffins come into an unexpected fortune, they understand that their characters must change along with their status. 'Our old selves wouldn't do,' Mr Boffin tells his wife. Characters grow rich, grow poor, get lost and are found again with terrifying arbitrariness in this profusion of surfaces that is Dickensian London. The fog is a recurring metaphor; characters pop out of the gloom at crucial moments and then sink back again into anonymity and isolation. The modern city is a lonely place. Dickens wrote in one of his journalistic pieces: 'It is strange with how

the fervour of the **French Revolution**; the shock of events across the channel proved something of a respite for George since the establishment rallied together to prevent similarly radical ideas taking root at home. From 1792 to 1815 Britain was at war with France, rather than with itself, and the Hanoverians clung on a while longer.

1837–1901: Victorian London

The Victorians thought of themselves as the champions of progress in London. To a large extent they were right. Thanks to them, the capital acquired street lighting, sewers, railways, buses, the Underground, a regular police force, fine hotels, clubs, new theatres and, ultimately, a democratic government: all the trappings of a modern city. The trouble was that in the process they savaged London's soul.

Their reaction to the Hanoverian era was a vicious backlash: having established that they did not like it, the more zealous among them set about destroying its every last vestige. They did not just turn away from neoclassical architecture, they destroyed whole chunks of it. They did not merely disapprove of the moral laxities of the Georgian era, they established a code of behaviour so repressive it was just as reprehensible as the one it replaced. It was a time of desperate hypocrisy, not least because many leading Victorians were by temperament as ill-disposed towards democracy and

little notice, good, bad, or indifferent, a man may live or die in London.' It is a sentiment that infuses much of his fiction.

One of the most appealing facets of Dickens is his compassion, a quality which not only brings his characters to life but also makes him seem like something of a social crusader. His moving descriptions of the poorhouse, or the slums of St Giles (called Tom-all-Alone's in *Bleak House*), or the stink of Smithfield Market, or the barbarity of Newgate jail and its gallows, have all been interpreted as appeals for greater social equality; at the same time, his satirical indictments of bureaucracy, whether in the legal system or in Parliament, suggest grave disillusionment with the way Britain was governed.

And yet Dickens turns out to be more slippery about politics than he appears on first sight. In 1869 he made a remarkably equivocal statement when addressing the Birmingham and Midland Institute. He said: 'My faith in the people governing is, on the whole, infinitesimal; my faith in the People governed is, on the whole, illimitable.' Quite a few people in his audience who did not have the advantage of seeing the capital P in print thought he was advocating authoritarianism, although Dickens later insisted on the opposite. The ambiguity is significant and

crops up elsewhere in his work. Dickens decries drunkenness as the consequence of poverty one minute, then speaks out against the degeneracy of drinkers the next. His description of Tom-All-Alone's may be humane and touching, but he also talks about its 'corrupted blood' which 'propagates infection and contagion' as though poverty itself were a sort of disease.

What this indicates is that Dickens was infused with the contradictions of his age, and in particular the contradictions of the big city. Fortunately, he was a good enough writer not to allow preachiness to take precedence over his powers of observation; maybe he was too unsure of his own prejudices to know how to let them intrude. As a result, he could be read and appreciated by just about anyone. The 'bran-new' Veneerings are depicted with such verve and humour that even social climbers of the same ilk could read about them without taking offence. George Orwell wrote that Dickens 'seems to have succeeded in attacking everybody and antagonizing nobody'. Dickens encapsulated a vision of the city so coherent and apparently complete that to take exception to his novels would have been to admit a deficient appreciation of life itself.

social justice as their forebears. Their doctrine was one of 'non-interference', which meant maintaining the status quo under a veil of liberal rhetoric. In their concern for industrial progress and economic prosperity, they very nearly lost control of London altogether. The city population jumped from one million to four million between 1800 and 1880, creating **slums and desperate poverty** on a scale never seen before. Because of London's instinctive abhorrence of central planning, the city lost all shape and purpose. London came to be seen as a place to be feared, not enjoyed. The overriding preoccupation of the country's leaders was to avoid the kind of political violence rocking other European capitals. Reform – for example, the 1832 Act extending voting rights, which

followed closely on the heels of the 1830 uprising in Paris – was almost always a reaction to the threat of revolt rather than a stroke of political enlightenment.

London in the 19th century above all lacked imagination. Heroes of the Georgian era were criminals and radical politicians; now they were worthy bureaucrats like Edwin Chadwick and Joseph Bazalgette. The most exciting event of the century, the **Great Exhibition** of 1851, injected an air of cosmopolitanism into the city, but it was never properly followed up, leaving London lagging far behind other European capitals, such as Paris, in terms of urban planning and life.

The lack of imagination showed itself all too clearly in 1848. The **Chartist movement**,

Sherlock Holmes and the Art of Detection

London in the late 19th century took on a more sinister and bewildering aspect than ever before. Never had the city been so large or so anonymous. The suburbs were sprouting, the population was mushrooming, and all the old codes of city life – the surfaces that Dickens revelled in – were flattening out and disappearing. The slums of the East End were filled with more human misery than anyone dared contemplate; meanwhile the new railway stations were packed with thousands of identical commuters in uniform-like grey suits. Pickpockets and petty thieves could operate with virtual impunity because they had become as faceless as the rest of the urban population. The city seemed incomprehensible and dangerous. Who could make sense of such a place?

Enter Sherlock Holmes, detective extraordinaire, who from his first appearance in *A Study in Scarlet* in 1887 stunned and delighted thousands of avid fans with his powers of observation and deduction. Sir Arthur Conan Doyle's creation, with his trademark deerstalker hat and meerschaum pipe, was a detective whose time had come. A generation after Dickens, the city had become too confusing, too diffuse, too anonymous for a single imagination to grasp. Holmes, exceptionally, knew how to decode the bewildering surfaces and restore a sense of order. What's more, the dramatic context of the stories – mystery tinged with melodrama – gave back to the city its lost sense of variety and excitement. Crime became a thrill, not a threat.

'It has long been an axiom of mine that the little things are infinitely the most important,' says Holmes in the story 'A Case of Identity', as he proceeds to reel off an astonishingly detailed list of facts about a woman he has never met before. Attention to small signs and clues has now become an axiom of city life, the key to becoming fashion-conscious and streetwise. But it was a mildly disturbing idea in late Victorian London, where a sense of propriety and moral uprightness was maintained precisely by not observing too much or asking too many questions.

Holmes is a disconcerting figure who can see into the hearts not only of criminals but of all men. His pronouncements come with a peculiar note of moral authority and he uses them to draw out the innermost secrets and thoughts of both his suspects and his associates; Holmes acts as a kind of secular Father Confessor for the sins of the modern city.

Despite his knack for unearthing hidden desires, Holmes is also a supremely rational detective. One of his greatest attractions to the late Victorians was that he proved, or appeared to prove, that deductive logic could provide the answer to any problem, no matter how great. At a time when London's growth seemed to have veered out of control, here was a man who could make sense of it all. It must have been every civil servant's fantasy to see through the muddle of London with Holmes-like clarity and bring the whole heaving monster under control. Elementary? If only.

which campaigned for universal suffrage, organized a demonstration in Trafalgar Square on 6 March, which turned violent after the police panicked and started attacking participants. Instead of following this up, however, the Chartists withdrew into internal debate for a whole month. By the time they actually marched on Parliament from St George's Fields on 10 April, the 79-year-old Duke of Wellington was waiting for them with 170,000 special constables as well as the full array of the Metropolitan Police force. Then it started raining, and the Chartists dispersed before they had even crossed the river. 'My poor friends,' said Hector Berlioz, the French composer, who was in London at the time, 'you know as much about starting a riot as the Italians about writing a symphony.'

When new movements like the **trade unions** and the **socialists** sprang up later in the century, the government was happy to accommodate part of their demands if it meant averting a showdown. Only once did a demonstration turn nasty. On 13 November 1887, subsequently called **Bloody Sunday**, grenadiers with fixed bayonets fired into a crowd of socialists in Hyde Park, killing two people and injuring scores more. This did much to mobilize the working class into a political force and so create the modern Labour Party.

The Victorians followed the same principle with social problems as they did with political discontent: containment. The government did little to alleviate the plight of the poor until the effects of poverty, such as crime and disease, started affecting the rest of society. 'Let those who are anxious to improve the health of the poor... prove to people of property that the making of these reforms will pay,' wrote the influential political thinker Herbert Spencer. Starting in the early 1830s, London was hit by a series of **cholera epidemics**. Edwin Chadwick, in his landmark *Inquiry into the Sanitary Condition of the Labouring Population of Great Britain* (1842), made a clear link between disease and poverty and deplored the sanitary conditions in London, particularly the water supply, which was at the root of the epidemics. At first Chadwick's report was ignored, but when cholera started hitting the middle classes in the late 1840s and 1850s, the authorities began to sit up and take notice. Disraeli, the Tory leader and future Prime Minister, described the Thames to the House of Commons as 'a Stygian pool, reeking with

ineffable and intolerable horrors'. A Metropolitan Board of Works was established in 1855, and under its chief engineer Sir Joseph Bazalgette built an embankment for the Thames and established the city's first network of underground **sewers**. The Great Stink subsided and the quality of water, which the reformer Sydney Smith had once described as containing 'a million insects in every drop', improved dramatically.

The problems of poverty, however, were not so much overcome as displaced. Slums in central London were pulled down and replaced with broad avenues. The inhabitants were forced to move out to equally miserable lodgings further afield. The **East End**, grimy home to thousands of workers in the London docks and scene of the Jack the Ripper murders in the 1880s, became the most notorious slum of all, which the Board of Works did little or nothing to improve.

1901–45: Our Finest Hour

The late Victorian and Edwardian eras saw the **growth of the suburbs** and the gradual waning of the inner-city population; the City itself turned into a glorified office development, described by one member of Parliament as 'a strange animal pickled in the spirits of time', and the Lord Mayor was just a figurehead for its business interests. By the time the London County Council, the capital's first overall governing authority, came into being in 1889, there was little it could do to influence the urban sprawl. The LCC's proudest achievement, the **Clean Air Act** which finally rid London of its thick fogs, did not make the statute books until 1956.

London in the late 19th and early 20th century had lost much of its glamour. The city was turning into little more than an entry and exit point for goods coming through its docks, a metropolis of contented tradesmen and petty bureaucrats. It took two World Wars and the collapse of the Empire to shake London out of its torpor. The first scare came with a series of German

zeppelin raids in 1915. The LCC silenced Big Ben and drained the pond in St James's Park so that its reflection would not guide the German pilots to Whitehall and Buckingham Palace. The raids proved shortlived, however, and provided only a taste of what was to come in the appalling winter of 1940–41.

The sustained German air raids on London known as **the Blitz** began on 7 September 1940 and lasted for 76 consecutive nights bar one, 2 November, when the weather was too stormy for the Germans to fly. Around 20,000 people died, thousands more were injured, and more than 1.5 million properties were damaged or destroyed. Buckingham Palace was hit on 13 September but suffered relatively minor damage. St Paul's Cathedral survived the bombing virtually unscathed despite being at the centre of some of the heaviest raids of all. But whole blocks in the City and surrounding areas such as Holborn, Shoreditch and Southwark were wiped off the map.

Despite the suffering, Londoners look back on the Blitz with a strange fondness. It is remembered as 'our finest hour', when the threat of German invasion was thwarted through a blend of skill and stiff-upper-lip bravery on the part of an outnumbered and unprepared Royal Air Force. Londoners remember the tremendous community spirit that accompanied the air raids and see the Blitz as a time of great social levelling, when everyone, regardless of background, simply mucked in.

All of these memories have a certain degree of truth in them, of course, and certainly the community worked together with far greater cohesion than it had during earlier disasters in London like the Great Plague and Great Fire. But in truth the Blitz, like so many memories of the Second World War, was not quite as glamorous as the folk-lore version of it would have us believe. The people were chivvied along by the popular press and, in particular, some stirring speeches by the Prime Minister, Winston

> ## 1901–45
> **Cabinet War Rooms**, Winston Churchill's underground HQ during the Second World War, p.93
> **Imperial War Museum**, with exhibitions on the trenches, the Blitz and the Holocaust, p.258

Churchill, who vowed to fight the Germans with 'blood, toil, tears and sweat'.

As for the air war itself, it was not true that the British were outnumbered. Both sides had about 1,000 aircraft at the start of the conflict, and as the battle wore on the British managed to replenish their stock with downed German planes, an advantage their enemy did not share. It was not true, either, that the British were unprepared. They managed to detect the enemy with radio-direction-finding stations (later known as radar) which had been installed in 1936. Indeed, there were so many ground defences that some historians believe shrapnel from anti-aircraft artillery killed more people than the German bombs.

In London itself, social levelling was more limited than was readily admitted. Grand hotels like the Dorchester or the Savoy converted their basements into comfortable dormitories for their guests (the Savoy even had a special section for heavy snorers), and most expensive West End restaurants offered all-night shelter as part of their service. By contrast, poor Londoners, especially those made homeless by the bombing, had little option but to shelter in the Underground stations, which had no sanitary facilities. Rats and lice thrived, and at one stage the government feared an outbreak of typhoid. The Underground was not completely secure either: 100 people were killed at Bank station after a bomb ripped through the water mains. Some people became so addicted to sleeping in the Underground that they stayed long after the bombing was over. Others preferred to stay in their own homes despite the risks.

1945 Onwards: From Multiculturalism to 'New' London

High on the Dunkirk spirit, London recovered quickly after the Second World War. The Labour government of 1945–51, together with the LCC, established the modern social security system, provided free health care for all, began constructing social housing and organized the **1951 Festival of Britain** to kick-start the arts. While the collapse of the British Empire might have been bad for the country's standing internationally, it did wonders for London. Not only did the city reassert itself as a centre of British culture, it absorbed much of the culture of the former colonies. Mass **immigration** began in the early 1950s and continued more or less unabated for 15 years. The main waves were from the Caribbean, India, Pakistan and Hong Kong. Drab pre-war neighbourhoods began to echo to the sound of steel bands; markets filled with exotic vegetables and spices; and unusual new languages took root in the inner city. As a new **youth culture** grew up in the late 1950s and 1960s, the immigrant wave was a strong influence. Students ate cheap Indian or Chinese food, and danced at clubs playing salsa and conga. London latched on to the jazz craze in the 1950s and, after the advent of rock'n'roll, discovered an extraordinary musical talent of its own. The Rolling Stones, the Yardbirds, the Who and Eric Clapton all came from the London area and attracted vast followings. Young people grew their hair and wore eccentric clothes that shocked the sober older generation. London, so the saying went, was swinging.

Well, up to a point. The young of London were pretty conservative compared to their Parisian counterparts, and they didn't put up much of a show in 1968 when students in the rest of Europe and the United States were out in the street demanding social revolution and an end to the Vietnam War. Some youth movements like the Teddy Boys were overtly racist and vented their hostility on the new immigrant population. Much of London society was as inward-looking and xenophobic as it had been when the Jews and Lombards arrived in the Middle Ages. In 1968, the Conservative politician Enoch Powell gave legitimacy to the new anti-immigrant mood with a speech in which he forecast doom if any more foreigners were to be allowed into the country. 'Like the Roman,' he said, 'I seem to see the Tiber flowing with much blood.' This so-called 'Rivers of Blood' speech inspired the growth of the neo-fascist **National Front** in the 1970s and found legislative expression in a raft of tough laws introduced by the Conservatives after **Margaret Thatcher** brought them to power in 1979. The black community in particular became stigmatized, leading to an explosion of anger in 1981, when **riots** broke out in Brixton, a major centre of London's Caribbean community, and again in Tottenham in 1985, when a police constable was hacked to death with machetes on the Broadwater Farm estate.

Under Thatcher, the fabric of London changed almost beyond recognition. Her aggressive free-market policies deprived many public services, particularly the transport system, of badly needed funds. She waged war against the left-wing councils running many of London's boroughs by imposing a ceiling on the rates they were allowed to charge their local residents. Finally she abolished rates altogether in favour of the flat-rate **poll tax** – a short-lived experiment, as it turned out, which led to riots in Trafalgar Square in April 1990 and eventually to her downfall as Prime Minister.

Most seriously of all, Thatcher lost patience with the **Greater London Council**, the LCC's successor which had been created in 1965. Despite the fact that the GLC was a democratically elected – and popular – assembly, Thatcher decided she could no longer tolerate its radical Labour leader, **Ken Livingstone**, and simply abolished it in 1986. London was left with no single political body to oversee its affairs: the work was divided between five government departments, 33 borough councils and around 60 committees and quangos, all of them quite unaccountable to the electorate. The consequences of this erosion of city democracy were grave. Public housing became desperately short, the Underground grew ever creakier, and new developments like the Docklands were left with utterly inadequate amenities or links with the rest of the city.

To many Londoners, the Thatcher years were a nightmare from which they are only now waking up. In her messianic determination to challenge the old certainties of British life and replace them with her vision of self-reliance and wealth-creation, she created deep **ideological divisions** that served only to bring out the worst in London's social structure. The streetwise boys from suburban Essex who were allowed to make their fortunes in an increasingly unfettered City may have adored her, but to many others she was an object of undiluted hatred.

This drastic sense of polarization lingered on under Thatcher's successor, John Major, but vanished almost overnight as **Tony Blair's 'New' Labour Party** swept to a landslide election victory on May Day 1997. London suddenly felt rejuvenated and optimistic again; even people who had not voted for Blair (and there were some) sensed the excitement of change. The Conservative legacy was no longer a cause for grudges, but an opportunity to be seized in both hands. Instead of moaning about the erosion of public funding for the arts, the new government triggered a slew of **public works** projects for the Millennium using the proceeds from a Tory-era innovation, the National Lottery. Instead of exacting revenge in kind for the Conservative onslaught on Labour borough councils, plans were made to re-introduce a London-wide government with a directly elected mayor. The new governing body, the **Greater London Authority**, was duly formed in 2000, and its elected head was none other than Margaret Thatcher's *bête noir* 'Red Ken' Livingstone.

1945 Onwards

Canary Wharf, symbol of London as a global financial centre, p.274

Carnaby St, p.135, **Neal St**, p.144, and **Hoxton Square**, p.271, homes of London's youth culture, past and present

Design Museum, for up-to-the-minute mass-produced objects, p.260

National Portrait Gallery, for a glimpse of whoever's famous today, p.107

Portobello Rd, p.244, **Chinatown**, p.135, and **Brick Lane**, p.269, for multicultural London

Science Museum, with fascinating displays on scientific advances, p.193

South Bank Centre, a post-war and still evolving cultural complex, p.203

Tate Modern, for cutting-edge art, p.205

There has now long been a consensus that the Blair honeymoon is over and the time for the government to take decisive action has come. For now, London clothing fashions, London chefs, London music and London avant-garde art are all the rage, and London is still holding on to its position as capital of Europe's financial markets. But the city's biggest problem remains its struggle for durable modernity: how to square its obsession with new fads and fashions with an old and draughty (and ever more impossibly expensive) housing stock, a down-at-heel public transport network (at the time of writing, plans were going ahead to part-privatize the Tube, largely against public opinion and entirely against the wishes of London's mayor) and a bureaucratic structure that is stuck somewhere in the latter days of empire. The point is not for London to turn its back on the past or, worse still, to pickle it in briny nostalgia – an abiding feature of the Queen's **2002 Golden Jubilee Celebrations**, for which the reception was mixed – but to take a cool unflinching look at its history, sort out the good from the bad, and use it as a springboard into the future.

Growth of the City: Architecture

It is the disaster of London, as to the beauty of its figure, that it is thus stretched out in buildings, just at the pleasure of every builder, or undertaker of buildings, and as the convenience of the people directs, whether for trade or otherwise; and this has spread the face of it in a most straggling confus'd manner, out of all shape, incompact and unequal... whither will this monstrous city then extend? and where must a circumvallation or communication line of it be placed?

Daniel Defoe, *A Tour Through the Whole Island of Great Britain* (1724–7)

One can understand why Defoe, writing in the 1720s, was so bewildered by the rate of London's growth. In his lifetime it was the biggest city in the world; urban sprawl did not exist as a concept until London invented it. But one wonders how it was that this monstrous growth continued into the 19th and 20th centuries, unabated, unchecked and seemingly beyond control. There seems to be something endemic to the place; London is like an obese child that keeps on growing to the despair of its parents. The urban equivalent of crash diets, such as the Great Fire or the Blitz, have had only a temporary effect in countering the spread of great rolls of suburban adipose tissue. Even when the overall population of London has fallen, as it has since the Second World War, the buildings and office blocks and housing estates have still continued to sprout. Where will the city bulge out to next? What can we do to stop it? The questions posed by Defoe have never really gone away.

Yet the reasons behind the phenomenon are not as mysterious or as unfathomable as some of the more florid writers in the London literary canon like to make out. Public policy towards the architecture and development of the capital has been remarkably consistent down the centuries. London has always been a merchant city, and the ethos of the marketplace has infused nearly all its monumental buildings and housing projects. London, alone among the great European capitals, is a private enterprise city.

The landlord, not the prince, has been its inspiration and its master builder. Nobody has ever succeeded in imposing a single, overarching vision, and for that reason London is a city of disparate parts, not a unified whole. There have been few attempts to realize civic projects on a truly grand scale in London; these have always been short-lived and usually ended in failure.

London may not be a planned city in the same way as Paris or Chicago, but the development of its land in individual, privately owned parcels was certainly just as prescriptive and undemocratic. Instead of suffering the monopoly of the state, London has suffered the caprices of the private sector. It is merely planning under a different and less efficient guise. One result of this *laissez-faire* attitude to urban development has been a cavalier disregard for London's historical landmarks and monuments. The taste for demolition has waned appreciably in recent years, but that has not necessarily been a sign of a new aesthetic sense. It is merely a switch of priorities. Nowadays the authorities do not knock down old buildings: they pickle them in nostalgia, dress them up as tourist attractions and market them as part of a London heritage package.

The prevailing tendency in London towards speculation and jerry-building has, generally speaking, left little room for manoeuvre for imaginative architects. Embellishing London with fine buildings has for centuries been something of a hit-and-miss operation. It was easier in the Middle Ages, when the Crown, the religious orders and the City merchants all wielded sufficient power to commission such landmark buildings as Westminster Abbey, Bermondsey Abbey or the first Royal Exchange. After the Great Fire and the beginning of the housing boom, monumental architecture came to depend on Parliamentary whim and the vagaries of fortune, such as the frequent fires that afflicted the city. There might be a chance to build a few churches here, a government building there, but no steady stream of work for any but the most favoured of artists such as Wren or Nash. The talents of less fortunate but equally gifted architects such as Hawksmoor or Soane were largely squandered.

And yet it would be wrong to think of London as a place of little stylistic imagination. Style wars between architects, city planners and landowners have been going on since the early 17th century. London's architectural history has been one long struggle between traditionalists and progressives, from the slow acceptance of Palladian ideals in the 17th and 18th centuries, to the Victorian clash between classical and Gothic styles, right up to the present-day disputes over modernism and its successor movements.

The Age Before Style

The Danish architect and critic Steen Eiler Rasmussen famously described London as a 'scattered city', in contrast to the more familiar 'concentrated' cities of the continent. The reason for London's straggly nature, he argued, was that the original citadel built by the **Romans** was simply too small. When the **Saxons** began settling in the late 4th century, they preferred to set up river communities along the Thames rather than move into the City, which had fallen into decline in the dying days of the Roman empire. An abbey was established on Thorney Island (what we now know as Westminster) in the 7th century, and the royal family set up its residence in Aldwych. It was not until 886 that the Saxons, under Alfred the Great, moved back inside the city walls – largely, it seems, as a defensive measure against the invading Danes. Westminster retained its growing importance, however, and was confirmed as London's second centre when **Edward the Confessor** decided to take up residence in a revamped Westminster Abbey. London's lingering sense of structural unity was gone forever, and the City never got another chance to expand. Indeed, the modern Square Mile is scarcely any bigger than at the time of the Norman invasion in 1066.

The earliest complete building to survive into the modern era is the **Norman** keep of the Tower of London, better known as the White Tower. The chapel of St John inside the tower features one of the few examples extant in London of round Norman arches. Later, in the 12th century, builders began experimenting with pointed Gothic arches alongside the traditional rounded ones in a style known as **Transitional**. You get a good idea of the techniques used in the Temple Church, where points are formed by the intersection of rounded arches.

England developed its own **Gothic** tradition, but it was not until Henry III decided to rebuild Westminster Abbey that London enjoyed its first major monument in the same decorated, or '**flamboyant**', style as the great cathedrals of northern France. Henry knocked down Edward the Confessor's abbey with the somewhat spurious excuse that it was dilapidated and started work on the version we know today, erecting much of the east end and the magnificent Chapter House. Financial problems and the distraction of the Hundred Years' War delayed work on the nave for 100 years, and it was only

The Age Before Style

Roman: Temple of Mithras, p.226; 3rd-century Roman walls, p.223 and p.232

Saxon: arch in All Hallows-by-the-Tower, p.232

Norman: crypt of St Mary-le-Bow, p.218; St Bartholomew-the-Great (Norman arches), p.221; the Tower of London's White Tower, p.230

Transitional: St Marie Overie, incorporated into Southwark Cathedral, p.209; Temple Church, p.155

Gothic: crypt of the Guildhall, p.226; crypt of St John's, Clerkenwell, p.235; Lady Chapel of St Bartholomew-the-Great, p.221; retro-choir of Southwark Cathedral, p.209; St Etheldreda's, p.159; St Helen's Bishopsgate, p.227; Westminster Abbey, p.86; Westminster Hall, p.90

Tudor: Hampton Court Palace, p.255; Lady Chapel of Westminster Abbey, p.86; Middle Temple Hall, p.154; Prince Henry's Room, p.160; Staple Inn, p.158

under Richard II that construction went into full swing. From 1375 the man in charge of the work was Henry Yevele, the first named architect in London's history, who scrupulously respected the ground plan as originally conceived while adding some decorative touches in the **Perpendicular** style, a late Gothic idiom peculiar to England. The Henry VII Chapel, completed in 1517, is at once the high point of the Abbey and, with its astonishing fan-vaulted ceilings, the apotheosis of English Gothic. But finding other remnants of medieval London is no easy task, since so much of it was destroyed during the dissolution of the monasteries in the late 1530s or else burnt down in the Great Fire. Brick was not used to build houses until the Tudor era and did not become popular until the reign of James I in the early 17th century.

For the most striking building of the Tudor age, you have to head all the way out to Henry VIII's palace at Hampton Court, the pinnacle of what is now known as **English Renaissance**. The term is something of a misnomer, since England largely ignored the artistic revolution going on in Italy and other parts of the continent in the 15th and 16th centuries. For its real Renaissance, London had to wait another 100 years and the advent of Inigo Jones.

Jones versus Wren: The Style Wars Begin

Inigo Jones (1573–1652) was London's first modern architect and a man with an uncompromising mission: he sought to impose the tenets of Palladian Renaissance architecture in England. The son of a Smithfield cloth-worker, Jones spent much of the early part of his career as a stage designer and worked closely with Ben Jonson in the production of theatrical masques. Then in 1613 he was invited by Lord Arundel to spend 18 months in Italy. The experience was tantamount to a religious conversion. Jones became an assiduous student of Andrea Palladio's *I Quattro Libri dell'Architettura* and, like his Italian

> ## Jones versus Wren
>
> **Inigo Jones**: Banqueting House, p.94; Queen's Chapel, p.122; Queen's House, p.263; St Paul's Church, p.140
>
> **Christopher Wren**: Fountain Court at Hampton Court, p.255; King's Bench Walk in Inner Temple, p.155; Marlborough House, p.122; Monument, p.229; Octagon Room in the Old Royal Observatory, p.262; Royal Hospital, p.247; Old Royal Naval College, p.265; St Bride's, p.162; St Clement Danes, p.151; St James Piccadilly, p.125; St Magnus the Martyr, p.229; St Mary-le-Bow, p.218; St Paul's, p.216; St Stephen Walbrook, p.225

mentor, became fascinated with the theories of Vitruvius and other architects of classical antiquity. Like many converts, Jones ended up more zealous than the man who inspired him, more **Palladian** than Palladio himself. He became a mathematical purist, one might say a fundamentalist, who believed in an architecture that was 'solid, proportionable according to the rules, masculine and unaffected'.

Such ideas were little short of revolutionary in an England still stuck in a 200-year-old Gothic time warp, and the shock was soon felt when Jones was appointed Surveyor-General to James I on his return from Italy in 1615. His first, and arguably most impressive, completed building was the Banqueting House (1622) at Whitehall, which he intended to be the centrepiece of a massive new royal palace – until a row over his style caught up with him.

Jones's fate as an architect became inextricably linked with the political fortunes of his most influential patron, James's son Charles I, who got him to complete the Queen's House at Greenwich and encouraged Francis Russell, the fourth Earl of Bedford, to execute Jones's plans for an arcaded piazza at Covent Garden. When it was first built in the 1630s, Covent Garden offered a vision of urban planning that could have set a precedent for the whole of London: a genuinely public space where the populace could meet and go about their commerce surrounded by fine aristocratic buildings. At first the scheme appeared to be a success, and Jones began work on a similar development in Lincoln's Inn Fields. But then the Civil War broke out, and his notions of urban planning, deemed anti-Puritan, were ditched along with the monarchy itself. Covent Garden began its slow decline and Jones, an ardent monarchist, had to flee London for his life. He was bundled out of Basing House in the City in a blanket in 1647 after the place was set on fire.

Hostility to Jones's aesthetics did not wane following the return of the monarchy in 1660. Jones's plans to restore the medieval cathedral of St Paul's were ditched and a new architect, the young **Christopher Wren** (1632–1723), was appointed to take over the task. A comparison between Jones and Wren helps explain much about London's aesthetic sensibilities. Both were visionary, multi-talented men (Jones worked in the theatre; Wren was a professor of astronomy at Oxford as well as a first-rate mathematician), with boundless energy and technical expertise. And yet the former was reviled while the latter became the most revered architect Britain has ever known. What did Jones do wrong? As we have seen, the political climate in the years leading up to the Civil War was against him. He did not live long enough to seize the rebuilding opportunities that fell into Wren's lap after the Great Fire of 1666. Most of all, though, he was simply ahead of his time in a country unbending in its cultural conservatism. Palladio may have died 35 years before Jones even discovered him, but London simply was not ready to receive such pure classicism at the beginning of the 17th century.

Wren, on the other hand, was a pragmatist who somehow managed to hit the right note with his patrons. He successfully blended the lessons of Renaissance classicism with those of **Baroque** to produce a style that was majestic but at the same time not over-assertive. It was just this lack of ostentation that the London authorities were looking for – new, but not too new – and soon the commissions were pouring in. Not only did Wren design the new St Paul's, he oversaw the rebuilding of more than 50 City churches and worked extensively in Greenwich and elsewhere. Not that he didn't have his failures. He had to tone down his plan for St Paul's and only managed to sneak the dome – deemed too Baroque and hence too Roman Catholic – past the authorities by a sly piece of political subterfuge. He also failed to realize his ambition to rebuild the City on a rational grid plan after the Great Fire. Wren wanted to dispense with the medieval layout and create a series of radiating roads spreading out from two focal points, St Paul's and the Royal Exchange, but the notion was deemed too disruptive and revolutionary.

Both Jones and Wren tried to act as ambassadors for the new styles being developed on the continent, and the English critics acted as a peculiar breed of customs officer, approving the more acceptable tenets of classicism and Baroque while turning down the more rigorous, flashy or Papist notions contained within them. In doing so, they probably sentenced London for ever to a watered-down, generally unadventurous architectural heritage. In Wren (and arguably in Wren alone), at least London had a genius who could make the most of the limiting conditions. Wren used the tall steeples of his churches to create a graceful skyline for London even though many of his façades were perforce hidden behind other buildings. He also made revolutionary changes to church interiors, opening them up to make them airier and focusing attention on the pulpit and lectern as well as the altar. In Wren, the Church of England found its perfect architectural voice: his churches removed much of the mystery of Catholic ritual and for the first time made the priest visible, and audible, to the whole congregation.

The Rise of Landlords

The rejection of Jones's aesthetics was more than a question of style: it affected for ever the way Londoners were destined to live. At the time of the Great Fire, there were only two residential **squares** in the rapidly growing chunk of London between Westminster and the City: Covent Garden and the brand-new development of aristocratic houses at St James's Square. They represented two very different models of urban living. Covent Garden was a public space in the manner of an Italian piazza or the Place des Vosges in Paris; St James's a hallowed and very private domain, the home of aristocratic tenants. Jones's defeat in the style wars meant it was St James's that proved the model for virtually all subsequent development in London. Future squares were not necessarily so exclusive, but they were all obsessively private. Indeed, most squares built in the 18th and 19th centuries were little more than an extension of the upper-middle class drawing room: often the entrance would be guarded by a caretaker, while the garden in the middle would be fenced off with railings and locked.

If the squares of London's West End are not all as upmarket as St James's, it is largely because the Great Fire transformed the housing market in the capital, creating an urgent need to provide the largest possible number of houses in the shortest possible time. One man soon hit upon the winning formula: **Thomas Wriothesley**, the fourth Earl of Southampton. After the Great Fire, the Earl devised a system of development which has persisted to this day: the **leasehold**. At Bloomsbury Square, which he had begun developing in the early 1660s, he divided the land into plots and leased them out individually at a low rent for 42 years, on condition that the properties all be built to a prescribed style. It was a system that worked with great efficiency. Building speculators leapt at the chance to develop land cheaply, erecting their houses as tall and as thin as they could to extract maximum profit from the ground space.

So successful was the Earl of Southampton that, over the next 150 years or so, other aristocrats followed his example and developed their agricultural estates. Only the royal parks, the Crown's former hunting grounds,

The Rise of Landlords

escaped the encroachment of bricks and mortar. The names of the speculators who moved in on these estates are commemorated in the street names of the West End: Panton, Clarges, Storey, Bond and Frith. The squares around which the buildings were arranged were intended primarily to increase the value of the property: they offered space and light and a place where coaches could comfortably draw up. One speculator, **Thomas Neale**, tried to dispense with the square to squeeze more money out of his land at Seven Dials north of Covent Garden. The result of his star-shaped development was catastrophe: nobody wanted to live on dark, narrow streets and the area quickly deteriorated into slumland.

The consequences of the leasehold were manifold. On the plus side, it provided decent and plentiful housing to make up for the losses of the Great Fire and to accommodate the fast-growing population. In some quarters, the uniform series of estates inspired admiration: John Evelyn described Bloomsbury Square as the 'epitome of town planning'. As time went on, however, abuses in the system led to poor building standards and the entire subordination of aesthetics to the profit motive. The Lighting and Paving Acts of 1761 and the Building Act of 1774 curbed the worst excesses of the jerry-builders but only accentuated the conformity of design through their various prescriptions. The estate-building went on largely unabated well into the 19th century and beyond.

The most lasting effect of the leasehold system was one of lifestyle: it made the house, rather than the flat, the norm for residential living. Speculators could cut down on their ground rent by building narrow, tall houses destined for one family each, rather than gambling on grander developments subdivided into apartments. The architecture of the houses reflects this. In 1709 the sash window began to replace the more mundane casement to provide more light for the family living room; in the absence of public squares, sunken gardens at the front or rear became popular. While the fronts of houses looked out onto the squares, the backs gave onto narrow alleys known as mews where horses were tethered.

Palladio Returns

Ceremonial building did not stop in the Georgian era, but Sir Christopher Wren was a hard act to follow and it took some time for London's architects to regain their confidence and find their niche. In his long lifetime, Wren eclipsed even the most talented of his students, such as **Nicholas Hawksmoor** and **John Vanbrugh**, who only came fully into their own towards the end of their master's life. Their chance came in 1711, when the newly elected Tory Parliament passed an act for the building of 50 new churches. The act was over-pompous in its ambitions, and only a dozen or so of the churches were ever completed, but these included Hawksmoor's Christ Church Spitalfields and **James Gibbs**'s St Martin-in-the-Fields. The dour grandeur of Hawksmoor's work expressed the full if somewhat belated flowering of **English Baroque**, while Gibbs, in his experiments with models from antiquity, signalled a surprising comeback for classicism in general and Palladianism in particular.

Clearly, those critical customs officers who had previously rejected Palladio decided that he could now safely be taken out of quarantine. Why this change of heart? As Sir Reginald Blomfield has pointed out, maybe he was just too useful to be ignored. 'With the touch of pedantry that suited the times and invested his writings with a fallacious air of scholarship,' Blomfield wrote in his *Studies in Architecture*, '[Palladio] was the very man to summarize and classify, and to save future generations of architects the labour of think-

ing for themselves.' But, in two architectural forms at least, **neo-Palladianism** came fully into its own in Georgian England: the smart townhouse and the stately country home.

In London, **Lord Burlington** set the ball rolling with Burlington House (1720), now home to the Royal Academy in Piccadilly, and continued with lovely country houses such as Chiswick House. The two greatest exponents of the Palladian tradition in London were probably the much underrated **William Kent**, who worked largely on interiors, and **Robert Adam**. Adam, along with his brothers William, John and James, perfected the art of creating lively but regular exteriors and matching them with graceful, finely detailed interiors. There are examples dotted all over London but, sadly, much of the Adams' work was wrecked by the Victorians, who found it offensive to their High Church sensibilities.

In 1766, **John Gwynn**'s landmark book *London and Westminster Improved* brought home just how straggly and ill-formed London had become. Gwynn described the new London and its leasehold estates as 'inconvenient, inelegant, and without the least pretension to magnificence or grandeur'. He encouraged a number of changes, including the introduction of stucco to liven up the drab façades of the brick buildings, and welcomed the invention of Coade stone, a cheap but very hardy imitation of ornamental terracotta. With these

---

Palladio Returns

Nicholas Hawksmoor: Christ Church Spitalfields, p.268; St Alfege, p.264; St Anne Limehouse, p.273; St George's Bloomsbury, p.171; St Mary Woolnoth, p.226

James Gibbs: Octagon Room in Orleans House, p.254; Royal Academy of Arts, p.126; St Bartholomew's Hospital, p.221; St Martin-in-the-Fields, p.108; St Mary-le-Strand, p.151

William Kent: Chiswick House, p.249; Horse Guards Barracks, p.95; State Apartments of Kensington Palace, p.195

Robert Adam: Kenwood House, p.241; Osterley Park House, p.250; Spencer House, p.123; Syon Park House, p.250

materials, London's houses could at least be livened up, like a middle-aged face dusted with rouge and powder. Under Gwynn's influence, architects were encouraged to exercise their imaginations once more, and slowly they started dreaming of grand projects to give London some of the monumental glory that it lacked. England's victory in the Napoleonic Wars, and the rise to power of the Prince Regent (later to become George IV) provided the political and financial opportunities for such dreams to be realized. Everyone started drawing up plans to change the face of London.

Nash versus Soane: The Clash of Ideals

The two most prominent architects of the moment were John Nash and John Soane. Of the two, there is little doubt that **Sir John Soane** (1753–1837) was the more talented. He had studied classical models more profoundly, his structures were more interesting and innovative, and his buildings, those that made it into bricks and mortar, were more solidly built than Nash's. And yet Soane missed out on nearly every major commission going under the benevolent regency of the Prince of Wales. If you visit the John Soane Museum in Lincoln's Inn Fields, you will gain some insight why: Soane's grandiose schemes for royal palaces and neoclassical Parliament buildings were hopelessly idealistic and paid scant attention to the strictures of space or budget. As a result, only a few major London projects of his made it to completion. Sadly, none of these have survived in their original form; all that is left of Soane's Bank of England is a mutilated version of his exterior curtain wall and a few bowdlerized rooms inside.

John Nash (1752–1835) was an idealist too, and a spendthrift to boot, but for reasons that have never been entirely explained he won the Prince Regent's near-exclusive favour and ended up doing more than any architect since Christopher Wren to change the face of London. His early career was

hardly auspicious: he was declared bankrupt after dabbling in a doomed property scheme in Bloomsbury Square and retreated to Wales, where he concentrated on designing fanciful country houses. The turning point came in 1798 when, at the age of 46, he married the 25-year-old Mary Ann Bradley. The story goes that Bradley was a mistress of the Prince Regent's, and that Nash nobly pitched in with an offer of marriage to save George's embarrassment at the first of five pregnancies. True or not, there has yet to be a more convincing explanation for Nash's meteoric rise from provincial obscurity to national stardom.

Nash thought big and managed to persuade the Prince Regent, a fellow spendthrift, to sponsor his projects for Regent St and Regent's Park. The original plan, drawn up in 1813, was intended to bring revolutionary changes to the way London was organized. Nash's idea was to make Regent St the main north–south artery linking the prince's residence at Carlton House on The Mall to the newly landscaped expanse of Regent's Park; as such it would have been the centrepiece of a carefully planned ensemble of squares, palaces and public thoroughfares. The prince was effusive about the scheme and predicted it would 'quite eclipse Napoleon'. Parliament, however, was not so sure and fretted about how much the whole thing would cost. The main problem was the lack of precedent for urban planning in London; one by one suspicious noblemen whose land lay on the proposed route for Regent St raised objections to selling out to the Crown. By the time Nash had haggled his scheme to completion, Regent St was no longer the straight line of his plans, but a series of curious wiggles that had to be bent and twisted into something resembling an elegant shape.

Nash converted one such wiggle, at Piccadilly Circus, into a graceful quarter-turn and christened it The Quadrant, endowing it with arcades and balustrades that provided the perfect walkway for strollers in central London. The idea caught on, and Regent St became the centre of fashionable London society, with shops that attracted customers from around the world. But the splendour of The Quadrant was not to last. Victorian shopkeepers complained that the arcaded pavements were too dark and attracted too many louche characters, particularly in the evenings. As a result, the authorities decided in 1848 to pull down the colonnade, thus wrecking the harmony of Nash's design. At the beginning of the 20th century, the buildings themselves came under attack, again because of the complaints of shopkeepers who said their floorspace was too restricted. Demolition began in 1916 and the present desperately unimaginative buildings were in place by the mid-1920s. The reconstruction represented a triumph of commerce and petty-mindedness over imagination, a problem that has beset London more than once in its long history.

Nash also laid the foundations of Trafalgar Square and started work on Buckingham Palace. At his best, Nash was capable of buildings of great charm and elegance (for example, the admirable sweep of Park Crescent at the entrance to Regent's Park). But at other times he could be sloppy, with a tendency to kitsch (his indiscriminate use of stucco at Chester Terrace was once described as 'spray-on architecture'), and his contemporaries found his primacy in the architectural community ever harder to take. Foreign observers tended to be more indulgent about his weaknesses. The German landscape architect Prince Pückler-Muskau wrote: 'The country is, in my opinion, much indebted to him for conceiving and executing such gigantic designs for the improvement of the metropolis... Now for the first time, [London] has the appearance of a seat of government, and not an immeasurable metropolis of shopkeepers.'

Nash's fortunes, like those of Inigo Jones, depended in the end on the popularity of the monarch of the day: when George IV died in 1830, Nash's career was over. He was immediately dismissed from work on both Buckingham Palace and Trafalgar Square and

> ### Nash versus Soane
> **John Soane**: Dulwich Picture Gallery, p.266; Sir John Soane's Museum, p.157
> **John Nash**: Institute of Contemporary Arts, p.117; Regent's Park and surrounding terraces, p.182; Royal Opera Arcade, p.123

allowed to sink back into the obscurity from which George IV had plucked him. With hindsight we can begin to understand why his sensibilities were deemed so out of place in the London of the 1830s. The social make-up of the city had altered radically as the population shot up from just under one million in 1801 to nearly two million in 1837. A banking crisis in 1825 had severely squeezed state funds. Industrialization was developing apace and poverty was spreading rapidly. This was not the right atmosphere for the refinements of classical architecture; London was seemingly sinking into anarchy and Parliament desperately sought some sort of moral as well as practical guidance. It found its answer in a peculiar mixture of architecture and fundamentalist religion.

Victoriana: The Bigots Have It

The demise of Nash did not entirely banish classical style from London. The tail-end of the classical movement, known as the **Greek Revival**, lasted through to the 1840s, and classical architecture made periodic comebacks throughout the Victorian era. What did die with Nash, however, was his idealistic dream of a new rational city. Ideas kept pouring in, but Parliament rejected every one of them. Austerity and practicality were in; grand dreams and lavish spending were deemed mere frivolity.

In 1836 **Augustus Welby Pugin** (1812–52), a fanatic and a genius, published his pamphlet 'Contrasts'. In one fell swoop Pugin dealt the deathblow to English classicism and heralded a return to Gothic forms. The classical movement was for him an irreligious aberration: 'What madness, while neglecting our own religious and national types of architecture and art, to worship at the revived shrines of ancient corruption, and profane the temple of a crucified Redeemer by the architecture and emblems of heathen Gods.' Pugin rejected Protestantism as the root of all moral decay and called for a 'revival of Catholic art and dignity'. He soon got his chance: the Palace of Westminster burnt down in 1834, and he was nominated to work with **Charles Barry** to rebuild it. The detail of Pugin's work on the new Parliament, notably in the interiors, testified to his prodigious talent, but that did not alter the fact that his mind was a touch possessed – he died in the madhouse at Bedlam at the age of 40.

But to a new generation of architects, Pugin was a rousing inspiration. **Gothic Revival** meant a profusion of brick turrets and highly embellished terracotta, a rejection of the bland white of classicism for a profusion of reds and greys and purples. Nowadays we tend to think of such overblown Victoriana as the Albert Memorial in Hyde Park (by **George Gilbert Scott**, one of the chief architects of the Revival) as rather ugly. But whatever our instinctive revulsion to these monuments, they remain fascinating as indications of the deep contradictions in Victorian thought. On the one hand, this was supposed to be the age of Progress; on the other, here were the age's leading artists peering far back into the medieval past for inspiration. The 19th century saw the rise of capitalism in all its shining ghastliness; and yet the Victorians liked to think of themselves as devotees of God, not Mammon.

The Victorians' greatest contribution to the age was, of course, material not spiritual: the development of the docks, which had begun in 1800; the building of countless bridges, river tunnels and railway stations; and, eventually, the development of the world's first underground railway. It was also the Victorians who finally installed a proper sewerage system and built the Thames Embankment (although only after the health of the middle classes came under serious threat from cholera). 'Railway termini and hotels are to the 19th century what

monasteries and cathedrals were to the 13th century,' wrote *Building News* in 1875. But London could not then keep up with a city like Paris, with its new boulevards, department stores and monumental architecture. The public displays of grandeur and style that made Paris what it was were considered distasteful in conservative London, and the typical materials of 19th-century Paris, iron and glass, were scarcely exploited in the British capital at all. One exception was **Joseph Paxton**'s wondrous Crystal Palace, built for the 1851 Great Exhibition, which went thoroughly unappreciated by the architectural critics of the day and was soon put out to grass at Sydenham in southeast London, where it eventually burnt down in 1936. The very idea of a Great Exhibition had been rather continental in the first place, encouraged by the cosmopolitan Prince Albert, who wanted to landscape part of South Kensington along Parisian lines into a municipal park dotted with great museums and centres of learning. The scheme was only partly realized at the time of Albert's death in 1861 and severely truncated thereafter.

If the Victorians were shy about construction, they showed no such compunction

Victoriana

Greek Revival: Athenaeum Club, p.123; British Museum, p.166; Screen at Hyde Park Corner, p.197; University College, p.172

Gothic Revival: Albert Memorial, p.195; All Saints Margaret Street, p.174; Houses of Parliament, p.89; Natural History Museum, p.192; Royal Courts of Justice, p.152; St Pancras Station, p.174; Strawberry Hill, p.254; Tower Bridge, p.232

Neo-Roman: Royal Albert Hall, p.194

Neo-Byzantine: Westminster Cathedral, p.98

Baroque Revival: Brompton Oratory, p.192; Port of London Authority, p.232

Exotica: Leighton House, p.246

Tudor Revival: Public Records Office, p.157

Arts and Crafts: Horniman Museum, p.266; Morris Room, Victoria and Albert Museum, p.188; William Morris Gallery, p.274

about tearing down parts of the city and rearranging them to meet their own requirements. Armies of church restorers went about 'improving' Wren's interiors, tinkering with the geometry and the furnishings and wrecking his lighting effects by putting stained glass in the windows. The anti-classical backlash also produced a veritable orgy of destruction of Georgian masterpieces that continued well into the 20th century. Among the victims were the first Westminster Bridge, the old criminal law courts designed by Sir John Soane, and large chunks of Georgian Whitehall. The Victorians could not very well destroy the Georgian townhouse that had spread so far over the city, but they did turn it upside down. Servants were now put below stairs, not at the top of the house. The Victorian household was like a microcosm of the Empire: rulers on top, underlings below. New housing spread through the London hinterland with the rage of a forest fire: first in Belgravia and Pimlico, thanks to the entrepreneurial zeal of the speculator **Thomas Cubitt**, then throughout Kensington, Chelsea, Bayswater and Notting Hill, and finally out towards such established villages as Wimbledon, Richmond, Ealing, Hampstead and Highgate.

With the population mushrooming, Victorian London also saw a growing anonymity in the city. The ties that bind small communities loosened under the sheer weight of people; street life disappeared and even the clothes became greyer and less distinctive. Commuting, that most alienating of urban rituals, started in earnest in the 1860s. Privacy and, by extension, **home-owning** became something of a cult: it was the Victorian age that popularized the expression 'an Englishman's home is his castle'. Living in a house rather than a flat was still a point of great pride for middle-class Londoners, despite the growing shortage of space in the city. The apartment was considered a foreign vulgarity allowing little privacy because the neighbours could register every entrance and exit. It was also thought profoundly immoral because of the proximity of the living rooms to the bedrooms. Worst of all, flat courts encouraged the mingling of different classes on the stairs. 'As for the ladies,' commented *The Architect*, 'it is difficult to assign a limit to the distress and shame that would be occasioned by an habitual encounter on mutual steps between one caste and another.' **Blocks of flats** did, nevertheless, make their first hesitant appearance in the 1850s, usually provided with plenty of entranceways to keep those unpleasant cross-cultural encounters down to a minimum, and often described not as 'flats' but as 'mansions' to give them a more refined social cachet.

Here Come the Suburbs

In 1856 the *Saturday Review* described London as 'the least beautiful city in the world'. Clearly, it was time for the middle classes to get out, and they deserted in their thousands to the suburbs. The immediate effect of this **suburbanization** was simply to spread the metropolitan jumble out into the Home Counties. 'The deadening uniformity that we noted in the terrace-houses of the City reaches its peak in the suburbs,' wrote the architectural critic Hermann Muthesius. 'There are no bends, no variety, no squares, no grouping to relieve the unease that anyone who strays into these parts must feel.' The lower middle-classes had effectively been conned. True, they had escaped the inner-city slums, but at the price of overwhelming dullness. Even interior décor became heavy and oppressive, relieved only by the flights of fancy in wallpaper and furniture pioneered by William Morris's **Arts and Crafts** movement.

What about wealthy families? Clearly, they were not going to stand by and watch this distressing trend grow if they could help it. Some stayed in town, picking exclusive riverside locations like Cheyne Walk to build new houses, or else indulging in a new fad for **exotica**. Leighton House in Holland Park, for example, was kitted up for the painter Lord Leighton as an oriental palace with fountains, mosaics and patterned tiles from Cairo and Damascus. Escapism duly became the architectural watchword well into the Edwardian era. Like cooks trying to liven up a bland dish with hot spices, designers called forth every style they could think of to breathe a little new life into the city. There was a **Tudor Revival** and even a Baroque revival of sorts, dubbed the **Wrenaissance**.

Meanwhile, there was a concerted effort at **urban improvement**. The authorities cleared the slums around St Giles to create Shaftesbury Av and Tottenham Court Rd. Theatres, dance halls and smart hotels took the place of miserable working-class dwellings. Slum clearance also attracted the attention of such philanthropists as the American businessman **George Peabody**, who left half a million pounds on his death in 1869 for the construction of decent low-rent dwellings. The forbidding, prison-like Peabody Estates designed by H.A. Darbishire are still with us today. They did nothing to make London more beautiful, and had only a limited impact on the city's housing problems.

Towards the end of the Victorian era, a new generation of architects grew up with the belief that the only enduring solution to London's problems was to abandon the metropolis and start again in the surrounding countryside. The chief theorist of this movement was **Ebenezer Howard** (1850–1928), who pioneered the concept of the garden city. His idea was to create a balanced environment for a community outside the city centre where there was plenty of space and greenery for children to play and respectable adults to go about their daily business. New towns duly sprouted in Hertfordshire, Berkshire and Surrey, and many comfortably off families moved there. Closer to London, architects designed islands of upper middle-class respectability, such as Hampstead Garden Suburb. The problem with Howard's vision was that its liberal veneer concealed a profound hostility to the lower classes. One of his ideal drawings of London shows the inner city divided carefully into secure areas to contain waifs, drunks

20th Century

Edwardian: Admiralty Arch, p.117; County Hall, p.202; Selfridge's, p.178
Inter-war: Battersea Power Station, p.96; Broadcasting House, p.179; Michelin Building, p.247; Odeon Cinema, p.109; Oxo Tower, p.205; Royal Institution of British Architects, p.179; Senate House, p.172
50s and 60s: Barbican Arts Centre, p.223; South Bank Centre, p.203; Telecom Tower, p.174
80s: Lloyd's of London, p.228; Storm Water Pumping Station, p.274; Thames Barrier, p.266
90s: Canary Wharf Tower, p.274; Embankment Place, p.109

and the insane, while respectable folk are placed safely out in suburban communities with pious names like Concord, Morrisville and Gladstone. Howard only succeeded in creating ghettos of pleasantness for a relatively narrow band of society.

The move to the suburbs and the commuter belt beyond had deleterious effects on the inner city. Architecturally, the first 40 years of the 20th century were a disaster in London. The kind of monumental architecture popular on the continent found only a muted echo in Edwardian London; schemes like County Hall, Admiralty Arch and the Victoria Memorial were hardly on the same scale as the Grand Palais and the Gare d'Orsay in Paris.

The interwar years were even more barren for London architecture. Of the few buildings to be commissioned in that time, perhaps only the **Art Nouveau** Michelin Building on the Fulham Road, Sir Giles Gilbert Scott's Battersea Power Station and the occasional purpose-built cinema showed any sign of innovation or liveliness. The rest were an amorphous and unpleasant mass of grey, none more so than the breathtakingly ugly Senate House of London University, which George Orwell used as the model for his Ministry of Truth in *Nineteen Eighty-Four*. Meanwhile, the destruction of the city's Georgian heritage, begun in the Victorian era, continued apace. Regent St was pulled down and rebuilt in drab stone, as was

Soane's Bank of England. It was not until the postwar generation that anybody seemed to notice or care about what was going on. The traditionalist critic James Lees-Milne wrote in his 1947 book *The Age of Adam*, 'In concerts of jubilation bishops, aldermen and captains of commerce urged the tearing down of churches by Wren, bridges by Rennie, terraces and town palaces by Adam...' Even Hitler's bombs could not eclipse that kind of unthinking architectural barbarism.

Carbuncles and Wobbles?

The bombsites left all over London after the Blitz presented a wonderful opportunity for architectural improvement throughout the city, an opportunity that was for the most part entirely squandered. The one beneficial side-effect of the Nazi bombing campaigns was to slow down the growth of the suburbs and encourage the creation of a Green Belt around the outside of the city where building could be strictly controlled. Inside London, the postwar building boom became an architectural disaster as vacant lots fell prey to the worst kind of functionalism. The **modern movement** hit London like a slab of concrete landing on a bird's nest, creating soulless **inner-city housing estates** and residential tower blocks. The new generation of publicly subsidized housing projects, while laudable in intent, was built on the cheap by speculators interested only in short-term profit. The best buildings of the 1950s and 1960s, such as the South Bank Centre, at least made up in practicality what they lacked in aesthetic appeal. But most of the projects of the period were eyesores that should not have passed the planning officer's desk, such as the towering Centre Point building at the eastern end of Oxford St.

It was not all bad. Whatever the new buildings might have been like, it was the old buildings that underwent the greatest transformation. London was becoming a place of great social and racial diversity, and all those stuck-up Victorian townhouses were quickly gutted and filleted and converted into series of two- and three-room flats. Mews properties, considered fit only for horses in the 18th century, became hotly sought after for their seclusion and bijou elegance. While the modern movement was pointing misguidedly to a monolithic brave new world, the old Victorian certainties of bricks and mortar were melting visibly.

Reaction to the modern movement came in several waves. First, in the 1970s, came the remorse, signalled by a decision to call a halt to the building of insipid skyscrapers. Then came nostalgia and a hankering for the lost elegance of the past. The fashion was to prettify and restore old houses rather than destroy them, as previous generations had done. The **redevelopment** of Covent Garden after the fruit and vegetable market moved out in the early 1970s was a turning point.

It was only in the 1980s that new building emerged with any confidence. The two key events were the deregulation of the City in the mid-1980s and Margaret Thatcher's free-for-all invitation to **private speculators** to develop the derelict docks. The profit motive has proved a rather unreliable promoter of civic order, however, and the results have been distinctly uneven. Among the notable failures is the NatWest Tower in Bishopsgate, which has little to recommend it except its height. Among the successes are **Richard Rogers**' hi-tech Lloyd's of London in the heart of the City and **Terry Farrell**'s reworking of Charing Cross railway station as a glasshouse complex called Embankment Place. The redevelopments in the Docklands have come in for vehement criticism because of the social upheavals they have caused and the initial lack of basic services such as transport and shopping. Some of the new buildings there are nevertheless rather successful, at least as pieces of architecture – the new marina at Surrey Quays, for example. Even **Cesar Pelli**'s monstrous 800ft tower at the heart of Canary Wharf is impressive in its way, if only for its sheer audaciousness in an architecturally timid city like London. But you don't have to look far for the horrors, a prime example being the Cascades housing estate on the Isle of Dogs, which has become a seedbed of new far-right nationalism.

Plenty of people began asking themselves whether all this unrestricted construction was really wise, among them **Prince Charles**, who took the architectural community completely by surprise in 1984 by slagging off a slew of new building projects in a speech to the Royal Institute of British Architects. He ridiculed a proposed extension to the National Gallery as 'a carbuncle on the face of a much-loved and elegant friend'. What Charles wanted to see was a return to solid, tasteful architecture that people could enjoy as part of an integrated urban environment. Reaction to the prince's speech was fast and furious. Many architects accused him of turning his back on progress and yearning for a non-existent past: a nostalgic return to 'traditional' building forms, that is to say imitations of Georgian classical design. His main objection to the National Gallery extension was that it did not look like William Wilkins' (less than successful) original. The effect of his speech was astonishing. The National Gallery extension was recommissioned from a more conservative firm of American architects. Traditionalist buildings started popping up everywhere, and many architects lost their jobs. Richard Rogers said: 'Modern architecture is in danger of being obliterated by an indiscriminate wave of nostalgia.'

Not entirely. The arrival of the new millennium was marked by a series of ambitious **public works projects**, most notably the transformation of the old Bankside power station into a new art gallery, the Tate Modern; the reorganization of the British Museum to include a new covered square; the British Airways London Eye observation wheel by the river, affording vertiginous views over the whole city; a slender and innovative Millennium Footbridge across the Thames; and the huge Millennium Dome rising out of the derelict docks of Greenwich.

New Millennium

British Airways London Eye, p.202; British Museum Great Court, p.166; GLA Building, p.259; Jubilee Line extension stations, p.205; Millennium Dome, p.265; Millennium Bridge, p.206; Millennium Village, p.266; Tate Modern conversion, p.205

These various projects have had a mixed success. The Tate Modern, the new-look British Museum and the London Eye have all received a thumbs-up from both architects and punters. The Footbridge was admired – except, that is, by those who tried to walk on it. The 'wobble factor' was too high and the bridge was closed after two days – for two years. It finally reopened in early 2002, after 2,000 volunteers agreed that the 'wobble' had been corrected. Despite bringing much-needed money and attention to a forgotten part of the city, the Millennium Dome has been an unmitigated disaster. It was supposed to celebrate a millennium of human endeavour, but for many it was a monument to human stupidity – whether it be a waste of public money, an architectural disaster (Prince Charles likened it to a blancmange) or the triviality of its contents, which were more Disney than Einstein. Its first incarnation is now over and the government and private business are seeking ways of giving it a new role as a conference centre or entertainment venue. A much more hopeful project on the Greenwich Peninsula is the Millennium Village, an environmentally friendly and 'affordable' housing community.

The future of London's architectural development is unclear. Throughout its history, London has refused to learn the lesson that private enterprise alone cannot build a successful city. That is why so much of London is a mess, and will continue to be unless the government takes some bold and energetic planning decisions. The creation of the GLA, with an avowed mandate to build a city that takes the measure of its inhabitants, gives reason for hope.

Travel

GETTING THERE

By Air

From the USA and Canada

London has five airports, with flights landing frequently from practically every major city in the USA and Canada. Cheap or last-minute deals are often available. Shop around and consider the less obvious airlines as well as major carriers like British Airways. Travel time for direct flights from New York or Montreal is 6 hours, from Los Angeles 9 hours. Flights from New York start at around $250, from LA at $350, from Montreal or Toronto at $350 and from Vancouver at $400.

Flights on the Internet

The best place to start looking for flights is the Internet – just about everyone has a site where you can compare prices (*see* the airlines listed below), and booking online usually confers a 10–20% discount.

In the USA
w *www.air-fare.com*
w *www.airhitch.org*
w *www.expedia.com*
w *www.flights.com*
w *www.orbitz.com*
w *www.priceline.com*
w *www.travellersweb.ws*
w *www.travelocity.com*
w *www.smarterliving.com*

In Canada
w *www.flightcentre.ca*
w *www.lastminuteclub.com*
w *www.newfrontiers.com*

In the UK and Ireland
w *www.airtickets.co.uk*
w *www.cheapflights.com*
w *www.flightcentre.co.uk*
w *www.lastminute.com*
w *www.skydeals.co.uk*
w *www.sky-tours.co.uk*
w *www.trailfinders.com*
w *www.travelocity.com*
w *www.travelselect.com*

Scheduled Flights

The biggest transatlantic carriers are:

Air Canada, t *1888 247 2262, Toronto t (416) 798 2211,* **w** *www.aircanada.ca.*

American Airlines, *USA* **t** *1800 433 7300,* **w** *www.aa.com.*

British Airways, t *1800 247 9297,* **w** *www.britishairways.com.*

Continental Airlines, t *1800 231 0856,* **w** *www.continentalairlines.com.*

Delta Airlines, *USA* **t** *1800 627 241 4141,* **w** *www.delta.com.*

United Airlines, *USA* **t** *1800 241 6522,* **w** *www.ual.com.*

Virgin Atlantic, t *1800 862 8621,* **w** *www.virgin.com.*

Student and Youth Travel

Council Travel, t *(212) 822 2700,* **w** *www.counciltravel.com.* Branches across the USA.

CTS Travel, t *(212) 760 1287,* **f** *(212) 760 0022,* **e** *info@ctstravelusa.com.*

Educational Travel Centre, t *608 256 5551,* **t** *800 747 5551,* **f** *608 256 2042,* **w** *www.edtrav.com.*

STA Travel, t *800 781 4040,* **w** *www.statravel.com.* Branches at most universities.

Travel Cuts, *(Canada)* **t** *(416) 979 2406,* **w** *www.travelcuts.com.* Canada's specialists.

From the UK and Ireland

Several UK-based airlines operate services between the major cities. Prices vary hugely. Return flights between Edinburgh or Glasgow and London, for example, can range from £300 for a fully flexible ticket on British Airways to less than £50 with one of the low-cost airlines such as easyJet, Ryanair or Go. For the best deals, book well in advance: if you're booking at the last minute, 'no-frills' airlines are often no cheaper than the standard airlines.

Scheduled Flights

Aer Lingus, *Ireland* **t** *0818 365000,* *UK* **t** *0845 973 7747.* **w** *www.aerlingus.com.*

bmi British Midland, t *0870 607 0555,* **w** *www.flybmi.com.*

British Airways, t *0845 779 9977,* **w** *www.britishairways.com.*

Low-cost Airlines

easyJet, *t 0870 600 0000, w www
.easyjet.com.*

flybe.com British European, *t (UK) 0870
5676 676, Ireland t 1890 925 532.*

Go, *t 0345 605 4321, w www.go-fly.com.*

Ryanair, *t 0870 333 1231, w www
.ryanair.com.*

Student and Youth Travel

The following agencies have branches in
most UK cities or on university campuses:

Council Travel, *t (020) 7437 7767, w www
.destinations-group.com.*

STA Travel, *t (020) 7361 6161, w www
.statravel.co.uk.*

Trailfinders, *t (020) 7938 3939, w www
.trailfinders.com.*

By Train

If you're travelling to London from the
Continent, Eurostar's Channel Tunnel service
trains take 2hrs 40mins from Brussels (11
trains a day; around £129 return) or 3hrs
from Paris Gare du Nord (about 20 trains a
day; £79–£298 return). Special deals are
frequently on offer.

Otherwise, the main ferry-train links from
the rest of Europe bring you through Dover,
Newhaven or Portsmouth. If you are coming
from Ireland, you can link up with the
InterCity service to Paddington from the
landing dock (Holyhead or Fishguard).

Whatever your itinerary, be prepared to
battle with an underfunded and badly
managed network. A painful privatization
split the system up into separate companies
according to activity – track, stations and

signals under one management, rolling stock
under another – a loopy idea that has
wreaked organizational disaster and raised
prices. Railtrack, the network operating
company, is in receivership at the time of
writing, pending a bail-out by taxpayers.
There are no fewer than 26 individual
companies running trains in different areas –
many overlapping and competing. It is
notoriously difficult to get accurate and
comprehensive information on fares and
timetables across the network. Companies
include First Great Western, Virgin, South
West Trains, Connex, GNER, Anglia, Chiltern,
Thames Trains, First Great Eastern, etc.

Eurostar, *Waterloo Station, t 0870 518
6186, w www.eurostar.com.* If you need
help with baggage or mobility, mention
this when booking.

National Rail Enquiries, *t 08457 48 49 50,
w www.nationalrail.co.uk.* The best central-
ized information and reservations service for
rail travel. The Web site has links to all train
operating companies, and details of which
ones will provide impartial information on
fares and timetables across the network.

Qjump.co.uk, *w www qjump.co.uk.* Online
ticket sales.

The Train Line, *w www.trainline.co.uk.*
UK Railways on the Net, *w www.rail.co.uk.*

By Coach

National Express runs a network of coaches
throughout Britain from Victoria Coach
Station, while its Eurolines service offers
routes to and from the Continent.

National Express: *t 08705 808 080,
w www.gobycoach.com.*

By Car

Before you decide to drive, remember that
traffic in London is slow-moving, and parking
is difficult and expensive (*see p.70*). If you
think you need a car in town or plan to make
day trips by car, make sure you familiarize
yourself with the British Highway Code
(available from newsagents) and take note of
the strict drink-drive laws. You don't need to

carry your driving papers with you, but if you are stopped you can be asked to show them at a police station within five days. You won't need an international licence if you are from any of the main English-speaking countries, although it is best to check with your local British consulate. Get valid insurance before you leave and remember that wearing seat-belts in Britain is compulsory, front and back.

Check out fly-drive deals before you leave home, since they are usually the cheapest. For rental companies in London, see p.70. To hire a car in the UK, you must be over 21 and have at least one year's driving experience.

Remember that in Britain cars drive on the left-hand side of the road. This eccentricity goes back to the time when riders would walk alongside their horses by the road; since it was easier for most people to hold their animal's bridle in their right hand, it made sense for them to walk on the left-hand side of the road so they could be on the pavement. Logical, when you think about it.

TOUR OPERATORS

USA and Canada

Abercrombie and Kent, *152 Kensington Rd, Oak Brook, Il 60523, t 1 800 323 7208, w www.abercrombie.kent.com.* Smart, upmarket tailor-made tours.

Britain Travel International, *PO Box 299, Elkton, VA 22827, t 1 800 327 6097, w www .britishtravel.com.* Made-to-measure pack-ages – flights and accommodation.

Cit Tours, *15 West 44th St, New York, NY 10173, t (212) CIT-TOUR, w www.cit-tours.com, and 9501 West Devon Avenue, Rosemount, IL 60018, t 800 CIT-TOUR, and in Canada, 80 Tiverton Ct, Suite 401, Markham, Ontario L3R 0GA, t 800 387 0711.* London city breaks.

Classic Custom Vacations, *t 800 221 9748, w www.classiccustomvacations.com.* Customized holiday itineraries.

EC Tours, *12500 Riverside Drive, Suite 210, Valley Village, CA 91607-3435, t 800 388 0877, w www.ectours.com.* Tours and city packages.

Euro Vacations, *851 Southwest Sixth, Suite 1010, Portland OR 97204, t 1 888 281 EURO, w www.eurovacations.com.* Package deals to London.

Globus, *t 1 866 265 2651, w www .affordableglobustours.com.* London pack-ages, with as much guiding as you want.

Jet Vacations, *880 Apollo St, Suite 243, El Segundo, CA 90245, t 800 JET 0999, f 310 640 1700, w www.jetvacations.com.* Independent travel packages and customized group pack-ages specializing in Europe.

Kesher Tours, *347 Fifth Av, Suite 706, New York, NY 10016, t (212) 481 3721, t 800 847 0700, f (212) 481 4212, w www.keshertours .com.* Fully escorted kosher tours.

Virgin Vacations, *465 Smith St, Farmingdale, NY 11735, t 1 888 937 8474.* Virgin's package-holiday section.

Worldwide Classroom, *PO Box 1166, Milwaukee, W1 53201, t (414) 351 6311, t 800 276 8712, w www.worldwide.edu.* Database listing worldwide educational organizations.

UK

Crystal Holidays, *Kings Place, 12–42 Wood St, Kingston upon Thames, Surrey KT1 1JY, t 0870 160 9030, f 0870 888 0243, w www.crystalcities.co.uk.* Short-break pack-ages to London.

Eurotours, *St Georges House, 34–6 St George's Rd, Brighton, East Sussex BN2 1ED, t (01273) 883838, f (01273) 383123, w www.eurotours.co.uk.* Hotel packages with rail transfer.

Interhome, *383 Richmond Rd, Twickenham, Middx TW1 2EF, t (020) 8891 1294, f (020) 8891 5331, w www.interhome.co.uk.* Self-catering accommodation.

Radisson Edwardian Hotels, *140 Bath Rd, Hayes, Middx UB3 5AW, t 0800 33 55 88, t (020) 8757 7905, f (020) 8757 7906, w www.radisonedwardian.com.* Luxury hotels, theatre and concert packages and leisure breaks.

Sovereign, *Groundstar House, London Rd, Crawley, West Sussex RH10 2TB, t 08705 768 373, f (01293) 457760, w www.sovereign.com.* City breaks to London.

Superbreak, *Ryedale Building, 60 Piccadilly, York YO1 9WX, t (01904) 628992, f (01906) 652592, w www.superbreak.com.* Organizes short breaks to London.

Theatre Breaks, *PO Box 1, St Albans AL3 5EQ, t (01727) 840244, w www.theatrebreaks.co.uk.* Hotel and theatre packages to top West End shows.

Thomas Cook, *t 0870 0100 437, w www.thomascook.co.uk.*

Turquoise Tours and Travel, *31 Theobald Rd, WC1 85P, t (020) 8288 2835, w www.london hotels-net.com.* Hotel booking service; often has reduced rates.

Ireland

Abbey Travel, *44–5 Middle Abbey St, Dublin 1, t (01) 708 863 198, f (01) 708 860 514, w www.abbeytravel.ie.* City breaks.

Go Holidays, *28 North Great George's St, Dublin 1, t (01) 874 4126, f (01) 872 7958, w www.goholidays.ie.* City breaks.

ENTRY FORMALITIES

Passports and Visas

Britain has opted not to join the eight-strong group of European countries practising an open-border policy (the so-called Schengen Group), so European Union citizens will still have to bring their passports or identity cards. That means a few delays and detours, but basically they can expect to breeze through Customs in a separate queue to avoid hold-ups. Anyone else can expect a fair grilling, particularly at airports. If you are a national of the United States, Canada, Australia, New Zealand, South Africa, Japan, Mexico or Switzerland, you won't need a visa to get into the country if you are just on holiday or on a business trip. Other

nationalities should check with their local British consulate (*see* p.76).

Customs

There are very few customs restrictions if you're coming **from another EU country**: you can bring any amount of wine, spirits, tobacco or perfume that you can reasonably argue is for your own personal consumption. There is no duty free within the EU.

For anyone arriving **from outside the EU**, duty-free restrictions are 220 cigarettes or 100 cigarillos or 50 cigars or 250 grams of tobacco; 2 litres of still table wine; 1 litre of spirits or strong liqueurs over 22% volume, or 2 litres of fortified wine, sparking wine or other liqueurs; 60 ml perfume; 250 ml toilet water; £145 worth of all other goods including gifts and souvenirs. Anything above these limits must be declared.

Non-EU citizens generally face restrictions on how much they can return home with. If they have been away for more than 48 hours, Americans can take 1 litre of alcohol (over-21s), 200 cigarettes and 100 cigars home with them, plus $400 worth of tax-free goods, paying 10% tax on the next $1,000 worth of goods. After that, the tax is worked out on an item by item basis.

US Customs, *P.O. Box 7407, Washington, DC 20044, t (202) 927 6724, w www.customs .ustreas.gov.* For more detailed information, visit the Web site or request the free booklet *Know Before You Go.*

Canadians can take back 200 cigarettes, 50 cigars, 200 tobacco sticks or 220 grams of manufactured tobacco; 1.5 litres of wine, 1.14 litres of spirits or 8.5 litres of beer. There is a $750 tax-free limit for trips of more than 7 days ($200 for 2–6-day trips).

Revenue Canada, *2265 St Laurent Bd, Ottawa K1G 4KE, t 800 461 9999, t (613) 993 0534, w www.ccra-adrc.gc.ca.* Provides a booklet, *I Declare*, with further information.

ARRIVAL

London's Airports

Heathrow

The largest of London's airports, with four passenger terminals, Heathrow is about 15 miles west of the centre. Terminal 1 is mainly short-haul British Airways flights; Terminal 2 the European services of non-British airlines; Terminal 3 non-British long-haul services; and Terminal 4 Concorde and British Airways intercontinental flights. All terminals have bureaux de change, transport and hotel information desks.

Airport information: *t 0870 0000 123, w www.baa.co.uk.*

Getting to and from Heathrow

Central London can be reached by London Underground (Tube), bus, train or taxi.

By Tube: Heathrow is on the Piccadilly Line. There are two stations: one serves Terminals 1–3 and the other serves Terminal 4. Tube trains depart every 5–9 minutes and the average journey time to the city centre is 50 minutes. This can be considerably longer during rush hour. A single fare into the city centre costs £3.60, but check out the various passes before you buy your ticket (*see* p.68).

By bus: The Airbus A2 (*t 0870 575 7747, w www.gobycoach.com*) departs from all terminals every 30 minutes and makes several stops before terminating at King's Cross. Tickets cost £8 single or £12 return. Most hotels near the airport operate a shuttle service (*t 0870 574 7777*). Call for information. A night bus (N97) connects Heathrow with Trafalgar Square. It's a long, dreary ride.

By train: The relatively new Paddington Express is the fastest and most painless option to reach the West End; trains depart every 15 minutes between 5.10am and 11.40pm from Paddington Station. Tickets cost £12 (single) and £22 (return).

By taxi: There are taxi ranks outside all terminals. Fares into the centre of London with a black cab are about £35–£50, depending on traffic.

Gatwick

With two terminals, Gatwick is about 20 miles south of London and handles a lot of charter flights. There are two terminals, North and South, linked by a shuttle service.

Airport information: *t 0870 000 2468, w www.baa.co.uk.*

Getting to and from Gatwick

By bus: Airbus A5 and Jetlink coaches run hourly from outside both terminals to Victoria Coach Station. Tickets cost £8 single or £12 return.

By train: The fastest service is the Gatwick Express (*t 0870 530 1530*), which runs from the South Terminal to Victoria every 15 minutes and takes about 30mins. Tickets cost £10.50 for a single, or £20 return. There are two other train services: one with Connex to Victoria, and one with Thameslink via King's Cross and London Bridge. These are slower, stopping trains, but slightly cheaper.

By taxi: There are taxi ranks outside all terminals. Fares into the centre of London with a black cab are about £40–£60 depending on traffic.

Stansted

Stansted is the furthest from London, about 35 miles to the northeast, but is far and away the most modern and pleasant. It is currently being expanded, and long-haul flights from the US have just begun landing here. It's also the home of low-cost airlines Go and Buzz.

Airport information: *t 0870 000 0303, w www.baa.co.uk.*

Getting to and from Stansted

By bus: Airbus A6 and Jetlink coaches (*t 0870 575 7747, w www.gobycoach.com*) run every 30 minutes from Stansted to London Victoria via Marble Arch and Hyde Park Corner. There are less frequent services all through the night. Tickets cost £8 single or £12 return.

By train: The Stansted Express (**t** *0845 748 4950*, **w** *www.stanstedexpress*) runs every 15 minutes during peak times, and every 30 minutes outside of peak times between 5am and 11pm to and from Liverpool St, in the City. Tickets cost £13 single and £21 return.

By taxi: A black cab from one of the ranks outside the terminal will cost £40–£60.

City

Some 9 miles east of the centre, London City is small, modern and pleasant; it serves mainly business passengers arriving from continental Europe.

Airport information: t *(020) 7646 0000*, **w** *www.londoncityairport.com.*

Getting to and from City

By Tube: Shuttle buses connect the airport with Canning Town Tube Station. The Docklands Light Railway also runs from Canning Town to Canary Wharf and Bank.

By bus: There's a regular Airbus, which shuttles between the airport and Liverpool St every 10mins.

By taxi: A black cab to Trafalgar Square or the city centre costs around £15–£20.

Luton

Luton airport mostly provides charter flights for British tourists heading for the sun. It is also easyJet's base. After a recent facelift, it's no longer quite the nightmare it once was, but it's still a long way out (north of London) and more basic than the rest.

Airport information: t *(01582) 405 100*, **w** *www.london-luton.com.*

Getting to and from Luton

By bus: Greenline coaches (**t** *0870 608 7261*, **w** *www.greenline.co.uk*) run roughly every half-hour between Luton Airport and Victoria Coach Station via the West End. Tickets cost £7 single or £8 return.

By train: Thameslink (**t** *0845 330 6333*, **w** *www.thameslink.co.uk*) run frequent trains into King's Cross Station 8am–10pm. Tickets cost £9.50 for a single and £15 for a return.

By taxi: A black cab will cost you around £40–£60 to central London.

By Train

London has eight main railway stations (Paddington, Euston, St Pancras, King's Cross, Liverpool St, Charing Cross, Waterloo and Victoria), all quite central and with their own corresponding Underground stations and, in some cases, inner London rail links.

The Channel Tunnel terminus is at **Waterloo Station**, in a concourse designed by architect Nicholas Grimshaw. Waterloo station is just south of the Thames and is on the Northern and Bakerloo Underground lines, either of which will take you straight into the West End in about 10 minutes. There is a direct link to the Underground from the international Eurostar terminal, about a five-minute walk inside the station; just follow the signs. If you take a taxi to the centre, it will cost you £5–£10; there's a taxi rank just as you exit the Eurostar gate. If you're taking a taxi to Waterloo from central London, make sure to specify you want the international terminal.

By Bus

London's main coach station is about 10 minutes' walk along Buckingham Palace Rd from Victoria Train Station, where you can find Underground links, buses and taxis.

GETTING AROUND

Maps

If you're planning to leave central London, you may need additional maps to those included in this book. Wandering around clutching a map in London does not automatically mark you out as a visitor; few Londoners venture out of familiar territory without a copy of the *London A–Z* street atlas, a thick map book with an index of street names. This essential London survival tool comes in a variety of formats, from a simple black-and-white paperback to glossy colour editions with leatherette binding, and can be bought at almost any newsagent or petrol station. The Clever Map Company's **London Backstreet Map** suggests routes from one part of central London to another avoiding the major roads – a far more enjoyable and intriguing option than trudging along dusty dual carriageways.

Bus and tube maps are available from most main Underground stations; the large Journey Planner maps show both Tube and British Rail links. For motorists the **AA** (Automobile Association) and **Ordnance Survey** both publish excellent road atlases which are updated annually. Motorists who want to survive London's draconian traffic schemes and parking regulations should consult the **London Parking Map** and the **London Speed Trap Map**, both published by the Clever Map Company.

Cyclists will find the **Central London Cyclists' Map** a helpful guide to the quickest, safest and most pleasant routes through London's traffic mayhem. Published by the London Cycling Campaign, it can be bought from their office (*Unit 228, 30 Great Guildford St, London SE1 0HS, **t** (020) 7928 7220, **w** www.lcc.org.uk*) and from some bookshops and cycle shops.

These and many other maps can be found at London's largest specialist map shop, Stanford's (*12–14 Long Acre, WC2E 9UP, **t** (020) 7836 1231, **w** www.stanfords.co.uk*).

By Underground

London's Underground system (also known as the Tube) is 100 years old, and it shows. Creaky, unpunctual, smelly, unfriendly and nearly always overcrowded, it is everyone's favourite urban nightmare. The Tube is the most expensive city transport system in Europe, a single adult ticket costing £1.60, compared with less than 50 pence in Paris. But for better or worse, it is still the quickest way to cross London, especially during office hours, so you will just have to learn to love its shortcomings. Trains run from around 5.30am (7am on Sundays) until at least 11.30pm and as late as 1am on some lines.

There is no service on Christmas Day, but a reduced service runs on all other public holidays. Allow plenty of time for your journey: don't be surprised if you have to wait 20 minutes for a train to arrive on some lines, although on others they come every two or three minutes. Do anything in your power to avoid the rush hour, when train carriages turn into solid packs of distressed human flesh and your face is ineluctably pressed into the sweaty armpit of a fat middle-aged accountant with bad breath. Don't, by the way, try to talk to anyone – unless you're in genuine need of assistance. There is a mysterious unwritten code of silence on the Tube, and any attempts at conversation will be countered with steely stares. London commuters are a shy lot, at least below ground, and they like to suffer their Tube train misery alone.

The Underground fare system is organized in concentric **zones**. Zone 1 is the centre and Zone 6 the outermost ring (including Heathrow Airport). Pick up a map from any station; the lines are colour-coded to make them easier to follow. Among the worst lines are the Circle, District and Hammersmith and City Lines, particularly on their northernmost stretch from Paddington to Moorgate, and the Northern Line. Among the best are the Victoria and Jubilee Lines, mainly because they were built most recently, and the refurbished Central Line. The East End, Docklands and Greenwich are served by the **Docklands Light Railway**, or DLR, an overground monorail which links up with the Tube at Bank and Tower Hill. DLR trains now run all week, until at least 11.30pm.

The most practical ticket is a **One Day Travelcard**, which you buy to cover as many zones as you need and allows you unlimited Tube travel and is valid on buses and urban train lines as well. Daily Travelcards are available after 9.30am; weekly and monthly passes are available any time, although you'll need a passport photo to get them. A Zone 1 and 2 Travelcard currently costs £4.10. Zone 1 tickets are also sold in useful carnets which cost £11 for 10 tickets (saving you £4).

London Transport: *t (020) 7222 1234,*
w www.londontransport.co.uk. Tube and bus information and maps.

w www.thetube.com. Up-to-date information on Tube timetables, first and last trains and how services are running.

DLR: *24-hour hotline t (020) 7918 4000.*

By Bus

London's buses are slow, slightly cheaper than the Underground, and very often don't stop where they are supposed to because there are too many passengers on board already. On the plus side, you can see trees and sky, as well as the life of the city crawling by. And there are still bright red double-deckers (called Routemasters).

Since the late 1980s, when the bus system was deregulated, any number of vans, minibuses and coaches have been running services. All are integrated into the London Transport network and charge 70p for a single journey in inner London, £1 further afield. Your best bet is to buy a pass (a **One Day Bus Pass** costs just £2). You can now also buy a book of six tickets (which work out at just 65p each) from newsagents. If you plan to use the bus a lot, get a **bus map**, available from major Tube stations, including Euston, King's Cross, Oxford Circus, Piccadilly Circus, Victoria and Heathrow.

By Train

National Rail Enquiries: *t 0845 748 4950,*
w www.nationalrail.co.uk.

Overground trains around London can be useful for crossing large chunks of town, for accessing parts that the Underground neglects, and in particular for reaching suburban areas. Three useful services are Thameslink, which starts at Luton Airport and snakes through West Hampstead, Kentish Town, King's Cross and Blackfriars to the South London suburbs, including Greenwich; the North London Silverlink, which starts in Richmond and goes through Kew Gardens, Hampstead and Highbury on

its way round to the East End; and the quick, efficient Waterloo and City Line between Waterloo and Bank. The rail lines are all marked on the larger Underground maps (called Journey Planners), and you don't have to pay extra if you have a Travelcard.

By Taxi

Taxis are part of the mythology of London, perhaps because their drivers are the only people who can make sense of the great metropolitan labyrinth. Cabbies train for three years to take their qualifying exam, The Knowledge, for which they have to be able to locate every street, every major building and all the main tourist attractions as well as memorizing 468 basic routes. The test goes back to the early days of motorized cabs, which first hit the streets in 1906. For years taxis conformed to a single black design, but recently there have been changes, notably the advent of advertising stickers and different colours. You can recognize them by the distinctive old-fashioned curvy shape and the 'For Hire' signs on the roof which light up in orange when the cab is free.

You can simply hail a taxi off the street, or pick them up at taxi ranks, by stations and randomly scattered around town. Licensed cabs are metered. They are more expensive than in most cities, but you can be confident of getting to your destination by the quickest route and not being unfairly ripped off. If you have a complaint, make a note of the driver's number displayed on his or her left lapel as well as the cab number, and call the Public Carriage Office (*t (020) 7941 7800*).

Lost property: *t (020) 7918 2000.* If you leave something in a cab.

Dial-A-Black-Cab: *t (020) 7253 5000.* To order a taxi.

Black cabs used to be harder to find at night, but more cruise the streets after dark since London Mayor Ken Livingstone allowed them to raise their night-time fares – which are extortionate after 8pm. You may choose to call a minicab instead. These tend to be much cheaper, but can be a little hazardous (they are unregulated, although a licensing system is under discussion). The best way to stay out of trouble is to call a reputable firm, like those listed below or in the Yellow Pages, and negotiate the price before you travel. Don't ever get into one of the minicabs that tout for business off the street.

Atlas Cars, t *(020) 7602 1234.*

Greater London Hire, t *(020) 8340 2450.*

Lady Cabs, t *(020) 7254 3501.* A specialist service run by women for women.

Town and Country Cabs, t *(020) 7622 6222.* Good for South and Central London. Male or female drivers, as requested.

By Car

Traffic in London moves at eight miles an hour during the day – roughly the same speed as in the horse-drawn days of the 19th century. In other words, unless you are carrying your fridge around, you will be much better off forgetting about a car and using some other means of transport.

Parking is also a huge problem. Many spaces are for residents only. Car parks and meters are very expensive and can prove ruinous if you outstay your welcome – around £40 for a parking fine (or £80 if you leave it for longer than two weeks). If you're very unlucky you will have a nasty yellow clamp placed around one of your wheels. If this happens, look at the ticket to find out which Payment Centre you need to go to to liberate your vehicle (the main ones are at Marble Arch, Earl's Court and Camden). You will have to fork out £45 to have the clamp removed plus a parking fine (£40), and then return to your vehicle under your own steam. If you don't wait patiently for the declampers – and they can take up to four hours to arrive – you risk being clamped all over again. One even worse horror in store is having your car towed away altogether. Call **t** *(020) 7747 4747* to find out where your vehicle is and bring at least £165 in cash to the vehicle pound.

A car can nevertheless be useful in the evenings and for trips out of town. Familiarize yourself with the British Highway Code (available from newsagents) and take particular note of the strict drink-drive laws. Technically you are allowed a glass of wine or two, but to be safe it's best either to stay dry or to leave the car behind. The police will be businesslike but unforgiving if they catch you over the limit. You don't need to carry your driving papers with you, but if you are stopped you can be asked to show them at a police station within five days.

Car Hire

To hire a car, you must be over 21 and have at least one year's driving experience. Here are some addresses:

Avis, *lots of branches, central booking office* **t** *0870 590 0500, open 24 hours.*

easyRentacar, w *www.easyrentacar.com.* Online car rental service; prices as low as £7 a day but watch out for hidden charges.

Hertz, *lots of branches, central booking office* **t** *0870 599 6699.*

By Bicycle

In many ways, the bicycle is the perfect mode of transport in London. It is faster than going by car, at least during the day, and 10 times more pleasant than the Tube, especially if you make use of London's extensive parkland. There are drawbacks, however: the city is too big and too hilly to make bikes practical for all journeys (try going from Clapham to Highgate and you'll see the problem); it also rains a distressingly large proportion of the time and can get very cold in winter; and the pollution in the centre isn't pleasant. Contrary to popular wisdom, however, the London streets are not particularly dangerous for cyclists as long as you assert yourself. Cars get out of the way if you shout loud enough, and bus drivers are positively sympathetic as long as you don't commit the cardinal sin of trying to overtake when they are signalling to pull out of a bus stop. For bike hire try:

Dial-a-Bike, *51 Marsham St*, *t (020) 7234 4224*. Full range of bikes available all year.

On Your Bike, *52–4 Tooley St (by London Bridge)*, *t (020) 7378 6669*. Wide selection of bikes at reasonable prices.

You could also telephone the **London Cycling Campaign** (*t (020) 7928 7220, w www.lcc.org.uk*) for advice and maps of safe routes around the city.

By Boat

Over the last few years, London has invested heavily in new piers and encouraged river traffic. A plethora of commercial companies run services from Westminster Pier or Charing Cross Pier, both just south of Trafalgar Square. Services downriver to Greenwich and the Thames Barrier – the most attractive destinations – run every half-hour and take about 45–50 minutes (*t (020) 7930 4097* for up-to-the-minute information). Services upriver to Kew, Richmond and Hampton Court are more erratic and may not run more than four times a day, and then only in summer (*t (020) 7930 4721*). Hampton Court can be up to four hours' journey.

Circular Cruises, *t (020) 7839 2111*. This company runs services between the Tower and Westminster.

City Cruises, *t (020) 7740 0400, w www.citycruises.com*. Offers a 'River Red River' ticket which offers unlimited 'hop-on hop-off' travel between Westminster, Tower and Greenwich piers. Good value at £7.50 for an adult and £3.75 for a child.

There are plenty of other stops and local services (for instance, from Richmond) all along the river, as well as along the canal from Little Venice to Camden and beyond (*see* p.246). The London Tourist Board has a leaflet with full, up-to-date timetables, called *Discover the Thames*, available in tourist information centres, or you can call for more information (*t 09068 663344*; calls are charged at 60p per minute).

Note that holders of Travelcards are entitled to a discount on riverboat services.

Guided Tours

Countless operators offer one- or half-day coach tours of London, and day trips to Stratford-upon-Avon and the Cotswolds, Canterbury and Kent, Oxford, Cambridge, Hampton Court, Windsor and so forth. The London Tourist Board Web site (*w www.londontouristboard.co.uk*) has links to operators, as does London Mayor Ken Livingstone's (*w www.london.gov.uk/greatlondondeals/shortbreaks*). A selection is listed below, or look in the pages of *Time Out*.

Taxi Tours

Black Cab Tours, *w www.blackcabtours.com*. Personalized tours in a London cab.

Black Taxi Tours, *7 Durweston Mews, London W1V 6DF*, *t (020) 7289 4371, w www.blacktaxitours.co.uk*. A similar service in a London taxi.

Walking Tours

Guided London Walks, *t (020) 8881 2933, w www.walklon.ndirect.co.uk*. Specialize in small, friendly groups. Themed walks include Brothels, Bishops and the Bard, the Old Jewish East End, Bohemians and Bluestockings, or Hidden Hampstead.

London Walks, *t (020) 762 3978, w www.londonwalks.co.uk*. Guided walks around London. Haunted London, Ripper Walk, etc.

Mystery Walks, *t (020) 8558 9446*. Jack the Ripper guided walking tours of the East End.

The Original London Walks, *t (020) 7024 3978*. Offers over 40 different walks including ghost, Shakespeare and Dickens walks.

Zig Zag Audio Tours, *t (020) 8458 5310*. Self-guided audio tours in six languages. Tours include Royal and Parliamentary, City of London, and Soho and the West End. All tours include compact audio pack and map and are delivered free to hotels. Adults £7.95 and students £4.75.

Cycle Tours

The London Bicycle Tour Company, *1A Gabriel's Wharf, 56 Upper Ground SE1*, *t (020) 7928 6838, w www.londonbicycle.com*. Bicycle tours of London (bike, tandem and roller-blade rental as well).

Helicopter Tours

Aeromega Helicopters, *Stapleford Aerodrome*, *t (01708) 688 361*, *w www.aeromega.co.uk*. Short flights over London.

Cabair Helicopters, *Elstree Aerodrome*, *t (020) 8953 4411*, *w www.cabair.com*. Half-hour flights over London.

Bus and Coach Tours

There is a vast range of tourist buses. If you don't fancy any of the following, sightseeing buses line up at Trafalgar Square and outside other major tourist sights.

Astral Travels, *72 New Bond St, London W1Y 9DD*, *t 0700 078 1016*, *w www.astraltravels.co.uk*. Offers a tour following the path of London's history from the Romans to the present day in 1920s-style mini coaches. Also a Magical Tour of Glastonbury Abbey and Avebury Stone Circle.

The Big Bus Company, *t (020) 7233 9533*, *w www.bigbus.co.uk*. Daily open-top double-decker bus tours with live commentary, or audio tours in 12 languages.

Harrods Luxury Sightseeing, *t (020) 7225 6596*. Book on the ground floor of Harrods. Complimentary drinks and live commentary.

Hop-on Hop-off, *t (01708) 631 122*. Takes you round all the main tourist sights of the centre and allows you to get on and off as many times as you like. Call for details of the route so you know where to catch it.

Original London Sightseeing Tour, *t (020) 8877 1722*, *w www.theoriginaltour.com*. Daily open-top double-decker bus tours with live commentary.

21st Century Travel (UK) Ltd, *t 0870 745 1046*, *w www.sightseeingtours.co.uk*. Coach tours including London's West End and Westminster Abbey, Rock and Roll Tour, etc.

Coach Tours (Out of Town)

The following companies offer half- or full-day tours to towns like Brighton, Bath, Oxford and Cambridge.

Big Value Tours, *t (020) 7233 7797*.

British Tours, *49 Conduit St, London W1S 2YS*, *t (020) 7734 8734*, *e info@britishtours.com*, *w www.britishtours.com/bt*. Guided tours, special interests, 'meet the owner' country-house tours, helicopter and river trips, including London by night, Greenwich, Oxford, Cambridge, Stratford-upon-Avon and the Cotswolds, Hampton Court and Windsor.

English Tours, *w www.englishtours.com*. Upmarket Charles Dickens tours by car.

Evan Evans Tours, *t (020) 7950 1777*, *w www.evanevans.co.uk*. History, Pageantry and Sights of London, as well as out-of-town tours to Oxford and Cambridge galore.

Frames Rickards, *t (020) 7637 4171*, *w www.grayline.com*. The usual destinations.

Golden Tours, *t (020) 7233 7030*, *w www.goldentours.co.uk*. An assortment of tours.

London Country Tours, *w www.londoncountrytours.co.uk*. Kent and Castles and other trips to the area around London.

Visitors Sightseeing Tours, *t (020) 7636 7175*, *w www.visitorssightseeing.co.uk*.

Riverboat Tours

There are dozens of boat rides to choose from – from cabaret cruises to rides with running Cockney commentary.

Bateaux London, *t (020) 7695 1804*. Cabaret and dancing.

Catamaran Cruisers, *t (020) 7987 1185*, *w www.catamarancruisers.co.uk*. A Thames Circular Cruise between Westminster and Tower piers, and a 50-minute commentated tour along the river. Also trips to Greenwich, and lunch and dinner cruises.

London Showboat, *t (020) 7237 5134*. Music from West End musicals over dinner.

Practical A–Z

Climate

'When two Englishmen meet,' wrote Dr Johnson, 'their first talk is of the weather.' The English are weather-crazy, constantly hoping it will brighten up if it is raining – it usually is – or else complaining about the heat on the rare occasions that the sun actually deigns to come out. English people use the weather as a way of filling in embarrassing gaps in the conversation. Not for them the direct approach at parties ('So who are you then?'); rather they begin with some meteorological platitude.

The strange thing about the English weather is that there is nothing much to talk about. London's climate is so stable it could be on tranquillizers – rarely too hot, rarely too cold and rarely too wet. Heat waves and snow are each so unusual that they tend to trigger a state of national panic. The rain is at its worst in November (2.5 inches or 64mm on average), but keeps up a steady trickle all year. You rarely get drenched, but on the other hand you can't count on it staying dry for more than a few hours at a time, whatever the season.

Spring usually finds London at its best, with the trees in bloom and the air light and balmy. Autumn can also be magical, especially on Hampstead Heath and in the larger parks, while winter is ideal if you want to see lots of museums and plays. Summer is probably the worst time to visit: London can get surprisingly oppressive even in moderate heat, and the tourist buses quickly become a strain on the nerves. Don't think you'll escape the rain in the summer, either. July and August are two of the wettest months of the year.

Average daily temperatures in °C (°F)

Jan	April	July	Oct
7 (45)	13 (55)	22 (72)	15 (59)

Crime and Police

British tabloid newspapers are full of crime stories, often involving attacks on children or old people, car-jackings or, sometimes, shootings between rival drug gangs. Something of a siege mentality has set in, which is curious, as serious crime in London has been pretty stable for years: firearms are still fairly uncommon, even police officers do not carry them as a matter of course, and the murder rate is still one-tenth that of New York City. However, there has been an unpleasant increase in street crime, in bag thefts, pickpocketing and so on. As a visitor, areas where you need to be particularly on your guard include, for bag thefts, Oxford St, and markets like Camden and Portobello. Mobile/cell phones are a special magnet for theft. To limit your chances of being robbed, follow the usual precautions: keep bags closed and close to your body; never leave bags or coats where you can't see them in bars or restaurants, or dangling on the back of a chair; never carry wallets or purses in pockets where you won't notice if they disappear.

If you need to report a crime to the police, visit the nearest police station, or, in the centre, look for a police officer. Unfortunately, it's unlikely that you will get any stolen goods back, but you will need the police report for any insurance claims. In case of emergency, dial either **t** 999 or **t** 112. If for any reason you get picked up by the police, you can insist on calling your embassy or consulate, or a lawyer if you know one. Keep your cool and remain polite – the more cooperative you seem, the more leniently you are likely to be treated.

Disabled Travellers

London is reasonably wheelchair-conscious, certainly by comparison with the rest of Europe, and most of the major sights have proper access and help on hand if necessary. In **museum** entries throughout this book, we use the term 'wheelchair accessible' for those places that are most accessible to disabled travellers. In **hotel and restaurant** entries we have indicated those places that fulfil the strictest wheelchair requirements, but many others are largely or mostly accessible – ring for details.

There are still problems, however, with the **transport** system and many theatres and cinemas. The London Tourist Board has a special leaflet called *Information for Wheelchair Users Visiting London*, which you can find in tourist offices and which covers hotels, tourist sights and transport. London Transport publishes *Access to the Underground*, with information on lift-access to stations, available free from Tube stations or by post from the London Transport Unit for Disabled Passengers, 172 Buckingham Palace Rd, London SW1W 9TN, **t** (020) 7918 3312. *Transport For All* gives information on door-to-door transport services and accessible buses and Underground stations in London, **t** (020) 7482 2325, **w** *www.transportforall.com*.

Artsline, **t** (020) 7388 2227, **w** *www.artsline .org.uk*, provides free information on access to arts venues in London.

Organizations in the UK

Greater London Action on Disability, *336 Brixton Rd, London SW9 7AA*, **t** *(020) 7346 5819*, **w** *www.glad.org.uk*. Provides advice and information on disability issues to Londoners and visitors.

Holiday Care Service, *2nd Floor, Imperial Buildings, Victoria Rd, Horley, Surrey RH6 9HW*, **t** *(01293) 774535*, **f** *771500*, **w** *www .holidaycare.org.uk*. Up-to-date information on destinations, transportation and suitable tour operators.

RADAR (Royal Association for Disability and Rehabilitation), *Unit 12, City Forum, 250 City Rd, London EC1V 8AF*, **t** *(020) 7250 3222*, **f** *7250 0212*, **w** *www.radar.org.uk*. Publishes several books with information for travellers with disabilities.

Royal National Institute for the Blind (RNIB), *224 Great Portland St, London W15 5TB*, **t** *(020) 7388 1266*, **w** *www.rnib.org.uk*. Advises blind or partially sighted people about travelling by plane. Can also advise on accommodation.

Royal National Institute for the Deaf (RNID), *19–23 Featherstone St, London EC1Y 8SL*, infoline **t** *0808 808 0123*, textphone **t** *0808 808 9000*, **f** *(020) 7296 8199*, **e** *informationline@rnid.org.uk*, **w** *www.rnid .org.uk*. Their information line has advice on travelling.

Tripscope, *The Vassall Centre, Gill Av, Bristol BS16 2QQ*, **t** *(020) 8580 7021*, **e** *tripscope@ cableinet.co.uk*, **w** *www.justmobility.co.uk/ tripscope*. Practical advice (by letter, tape or over the telephone) on travel and transport for the elderly and disabled.

Organizations in the USA

American Foundation for the Blind, *15 West 16th St, New York, NY 10011*, **t** *(212) 620 2000*, **t** *800 232 5463*. The best source in the USA for visually impaired travellers.

Mobility International USA, *PO Box 3551, Eugene, OR 97403*, **t** *(541) 343 1284*, **f** *343 6812*, **w** *www.miusa.org*. Offering information, advice and tours; there is a US$35 annual membership fee.

SATH (Society for Accessible Travel and Hospitality), *347 5th Av, Suite 610, New York, NY 10016*, **t** *(212) 447 7284*, **w** *www.sath.org*. Advice on all aspects of travel for the disabled. Their Web site is a good resource.

Other Useful Contacts

Access Ability, **w** *www.access-ability.co.uk*. Information on travel agencies catering specifically to disabled people.

Access Tourism, **w** *www.accesstourism.com*. Pan-European Web site with information on hotels, guesthouses, travel agencies and specialist tour operators, etc.

Australian Council for Rehabilitation of the Disabled (ACROD), *PO Box 60, Curtin, ACT 2605, Australia*, **t**/TTY *(02) 6682 4333*, **w** *www.acrod.org.au*. Information and contact numbers for specialist travel agents.

Disabled Persons Assembly, *PO Box 27-524, Wellington 6035, New Zealand*, **t** *(04) 801 9100*, **w** *www.dpa.org.nz*. All-round source for travel information.

Emerging Horizons, **e** *horizons@emerging horizons.com*, **w** *www.emerginghorizons. com*. International online travel newsletter for people with disabilities.

Irish Wheelchair Association, *Blackheath Drive, Clontarf, Dublin 3*, **t** *(01) 833 8241*, *w www.iwa.ie.* They publish guides with advice for disabled holidaymakers.

Electricity, Weights and Measures

Britain uses three-prong square-pin plugs unlike anything else in Europe or North America. So far, the British government has resisted conforming to the rest of Europe on safety grounds – all British plugs have detachable fuses of three, five or 13 amps. You'll need an adaptor for any electrical device you bring in from abroad (you can get one at the airport). The electricity supply is 240 volts AC.

Britain's slow but never-quite-halted adaptation to membership of the European Union is perhaps best reflected in its constant, confusing mixing of traditional Imperial (feet, miles, pints) and international metric (metres, grams, litres) measurements. Metric will (probably) eventually overcome, but as of now which system you use tends to vary according to what you want. Most ready-bottled products (milk, petrol/gasoline, paint, sugar) are sold and distributed in metric sizes, while more intimate things are still dealt with in Imperial – everyone says their own height in feet and inches, and draught beer is still served up in pints. In shops, markets and supermarkets, packaged goods are nearly all sold in metric, though no one will fail to understand if you ask for loose goods in Imperial. The road system, still measured and signposted entirely in miles, is the one major area where the metric system has not yet made any impact, in part because changing over would be horrifically expensive.

Note that the US and British Imperial liquid measures have never been the same in any case. One US gallon is equivalent to 0.83 of a British gallon, or 3.78 litres.

Embassies and Consulates

In London

Canada: *38 Grosvenor St, W1,* **t** *(020) 7258 6600,* **w** *www.canada.org.uk;* **tube** *Bond St (O10).*

Ireland: *17 Grosvenor Place, SW1,* **t** *(020) 7235 2171;* **tube** *Hyde Park Corner, Victoria (O14).*

USA: *24 Grosvenor Square, W1,* **t** *(020) 7499 9000,* **w** *www.usembassy.org.uk;* **tube** *Bond St (N10).*

Abroad

Canada: *British High Commission, 80 Elgin St, Ottawa, Ontario K1P 5K7,* **t** *(613) 237 1303,* **f** *237 6537,* **w** *www.britainincanada.org.*

Ireland: *29 Merrion Rd, Dublin 4,* **t** *(01) 205 3700,* **f** *205 3890,* **w** *www.britishembassy.ie.*

USA: *3100 Massachusetts Av, Washington DC, 20008,* **t** *(202) 588 6500,* **f** *588 7870,* **w** *www.britainusa.com/consular/embassy.*

Health, Emergencies and Insurance

Police, ambulance, fire brigade: **t** *999 or* **t** *112.*

Citizens of the European Union and some Commonwealth countries enjoy free medical care in Britain under the state National Health Service. The days when you could get free treatment on production of just a passport are probably over, so you'll need to fill out the appropriate paperwork before you leave home (in the EU the form is called an E111). Thus armed, the only things you will have to pay for are prescriptions and visits to the optician or dentist, although these should not cost more than a few pounds. Be warned that the bureaucracy is hellish and seriously consider taking out private travel

Clothing Size Conversion Chart

Women's Shirts/Dresses

UK	10	12	14	16	18
USA	8	10	12	14	16

Women's Shoes

UK	3	4	5	6	7	8
USA	4	5	6	7	8	9

Men's Shoes

UK	5	6	7	8	9	10	11	12
USA	7.5	8	9	10	10.5	11	12	13

insurance. Anyone else, and that includes visitors from the USA and Canada, should take out medical insurance.

If you need urgent medical treatment, head for the casualty department of a major hospital. These include St Thomas's on the South Bank, University College Hospital on Gower St, and the Charing Cross Hospital on Fulham Palace Rd.

There are several telephone helplines dealing with **HIV and AIDS**, including the Body Positive Helpline (*t (020) 7373 9124; open daily 7pm–10pm*), the National AIDS Helpline (*t 0800 567 123; free of charge, 24 hours*) and the Terrence Higgins Trust (*t (020) 7242 1010; open daily noon–10pm*).

The following numbers may also be useful:

Bliss Chemist, *5 Marble Arch; tube Marble Arch (L9). Open daily until midnight.* Details of other late-opening chemists are available from police stations.

Dental Emergency Care Service, *t (020) 7937 3951. Open 24 hours.* Directs you to the nearest clinic for emergency dental care.

Family Planning Association, *t 0845 310 1334.* Will tell you where your nearest family planning clinic is and give you advice on morning-after pills, abortions and so on.

Great Chapel Street Medical Centre, *13 Great Chapel St, t (020) 7437 9360; tube Tottenham Court Rd (R8). Open Mon–Fri 2–4pm.* A general NHS clinic that accepts EU, Commonwealth and Scandinavian visitors for free treatment.

NHS Direct, *t 0845 4647.* The National Health Service helpline, offering medical advice on all topics.

Internet

London has a variety of Internet centres, ranging from cosy cafés to large warehouse-style venues. The big department stores on Oxford St (e.g. Debenhams) often provide Internet access too. Try one of the following:

Cyberia, *39 Whitfield St, t (020) 7681 4200, w www.cyberiacafe.net; tube Goodge St. Open Mon–Fri 9am–9pm, Sat 11am–7pm, Sun 11am–6pm; from 50p per 15 mins.*

easyEverything, *358 Oxford St, t (020) 7436 0459, w www.easyeverything .com; tube Bond St. Open daily 24 hours; from 50p per half-hour.* Large branch of the famous Internet café chain, with 350 PCs. There are five other branches: on Kensington High St, Tottenham Court Rd, the Strand, Wilton Rd and King's Rd.

Global Cafe, *15 Golden Square, t (020) 7287 2242, w gold.globalcafe.co.uk; tube Piccadilly Circus. Open Mon–Fri 10am–11pm, Sat noon–11pm, Sun 2–9pm; from £2 per hour.*

Nethouse Café, *138 Marylebone Rd, t (020) 7224 7008, w www.nethousecafe*

London on the Internet

There are literally thousands of Web sites offering information on London. The following are just a few to get you started:

w funkyuk.com/london Clubbing, drinking, cafés, cinemas and theatres.

w www.groupline.com The place to book for all famous West End shows.

w www.londondudes.co.uk Claim to be hip 'n' trendy: check it out for yourself.

w www.londonnet.co.uk 'Virtually, the best guide to London.'

w www.londontouristboard.com The official London Tourist Board site.

w www.londontransport.co.uk For maps and info (including ticket prices). Mainly for visitors, with help in many languages.

w www.mylondonvacation.com/guides.htm A little more conservative than some sites, but worth a look.

w www.netlondon.com/directory.html Portal for almost any area of London life you can think of: if it's on the Web, you'll find it here... somewhere.

w www.squaremeal.co.uk If food is your thing, this site has all the better-known establishments grouped by categories such as trendiest, best, etc. Also has divisions for various types of cuisine.

w www.surflondon.co.uk One stop for all London info.

w www.welcometolondon.com For the visitor: weather info, what clubs are hot, eating out and plenty more.

.co.uk; *tube* Baker St. *Open daily 24 hours; from £1 per hour.*

Lost Property

To retrieve lost property, try the **London Transport Lost Property Office**, 200 Baker St, **t** (020) 7486 2496 (*open weekday mornings only*); or the **Black Cab Lost Property Office**, 15 Penton St, Islington, **t** (020) 7833 0996 (*open Mon–Fri 9–4*).

Media

Britain once had both the best and the worst **newspapers** in the world. Its quality press was feared and respected for its opinions, its fine writing, its probing analyses and its depth of reporting both at home and abroad; the tabloid press, meanwhile, was feared and detested for its jingoism and prurient muck-raking. Neither stereotype really holds true any more. The upper end of the market has dropped its standards markedly in a bid to reach wider audiences, while the tabloids are getting some stiff competition in the sleaze department from supermarket gossip rags.

At the quality end of the range of **dailies** there is the *Daily Telegraph* (true-blue Tory, with some bright writing), *The Times* (maverick conservative, with a large appetite for showbiz trash), the *Independent* (once the pacemaker among the quality broadsheets, now sliding downmarket in its struggle to keep up), the *Guardian* (bastion of the liberal left), and the *Financial Times* (a bellwether for the business world, printed on pink paper).

Further down the greasy journalistic pole come the mainly right-wing middle-range papers: the *Daily Express* (very anti-Europe) and the *Daily Mail*. The *Evening Standard* comes out in London in the afternoons and enjoys a captive commuter audience. It can be useful for information about the capital. There's a free paper called *Metro* available at Tube stations in the mornings.

At the bottom of the pile are the down-market '**tabloids**' (so called because of their format) with their lurid sex scandals and tone of moral righteousness. The *Sun*, notorious for its page-3 topless pin-ups, is the biggest seller, followed by the similar *Daily Star*. The *Sport* does not even attempt to cover news and devotes itself entirely to sex and phone sex instead. The *Daily Mirror* was once an excellent popular left-wing paper but has abandoned many of its principles for the sake of flashy celebrity scoops.

The British press was once dominated by **Sunday newspapers**; now these tend to be owned by the daily titles and differ only slightly in tone from their sister publications. They are, however, two or three times as fat. The right-wing, establishment-bashing *Sunday Times* is the biggest-selling quality paper, but has some dubious journalistic ethics. The *Observer* is now a struggling offshoot of the *Guardian*. The *Independent on Sunday* has an interesting culture section.

Britain is relatively poor on **weeklies**. Anyone in London should buy *Time Out* (see 'Entertainment', p.355). Otherwise there is the *Economist* (conservative and informative, if a little patronizing), the *Spectator* (occasionally witty but rather reactionary), and the *New Statesman and Society* (centre-left; occasionally stimulating but rather dull). Every two weeks comes the satirical and often very funny *Private Eye*. Finally, you should take a look at the *Big Issue* (£1.20), a magazine sold on the streets by the homeless.

You can get hold of most **foreign titles** quite easily in London. Broadly speaking, the more cosmopolitan the area, the more varied its newspaper range. Some of the best shops are Borders, 203 Oxford St; Moroni's, 68 Old Compton St, Soho; and Gray's Inn News, 50 Theobald's Rd, Bloomsbury. There are also two or three international shops at the top end of Queensway.

Radio is still dominated by the public service BBC, which runs five national networks devoted respectively to pop (Radio 1, 98.8 FM), light entertainment (Radio 2, 89.2 FM), classical music (Radio 3, 91.3 FM), the spoken word in all forms (Radio 4, 198 kHz and 93.5

FM) and rolling news and sport (Radio 5 Live, 693 kHz or 909 kHz). Radio 4 is one of the great institutions of the airwaves, with news and arts programmes, opinion forums, plays and quizzes. Commercial stations include Jazz FM (102.2 FM, devoted to jazz, blues and soul), Classic FM (100.9 FM), the news and phone-in channel London Newstalk (97.3 FM and 1152 kHz), and the popular music station Capital FM (95.8 FM). Less commercial music can be found on Kiss (100FM), which specializes in dance music, and XFM (104.9 FM), home of new and alternative indie and rock music. You'll also stumble across numerous pirate stations charting the latest underground sounds.

On **television**, network broadcasting is shared between the BBC and three independent channels, ITV 1 (Carlton/LWT), Channel 4 and Channel 5. All five have their fair share of trash, but – with the exception of the underwhelming Channel 5 – also produce excellent documentaries, news and arts programmes, comedies and drama serials. BBC1 and BBC2 carry no adverts and are supported by government subsidy and licence-payers. The main news bulletins are at 6pm and 10pm on BBC1, 7pm on Channel 4 and some time between 10pm and 11pm on ITV. BBC2's *Newsnight*, perhaps the best digest of all, starts at 10.30pm.

That leaves **satellite TV**, dominated by Rupert Murdoch's Sky empire, which has most of the world's important sporting events. The BBC also has a 24-hour rolling news channel. The better London hotels will also give you CNN, MTV and Eurosport.

Money and Banks

The currency in Britain is the pound sterling, divided into 100 pence. You'll come across notes worth £5, £10, £20 and £50, and coins worth 1, 2, 5, 10, 20 and 50 pence, and £1 and £2. Britain did not convert to the euro in 2002 along with the rest of Europe, but some major shops in central London do accept euros; apparently one in three Oxford St shops plan to accept the currency. At the

moment it seems to be confined to the major stores such as BhS, Debenhams, Dickens and Jones, Dixon's, Hamley's, Liberty, Marks & Spencer, Selfridge's and Virgin Megastore.

London is also fully up to speed on **credit card** technology, and many shops, restaurants and hotels will accept Visa, MasterCard or AmEx for all but the smallest purchases.

Minimum **bank opening hours** are Mon–Fri 9.30am–3.30pm, although many banks in central London stay open later and, in some cases, on Saturday morning, too. The biggest banks are Barclays, HSBC, NatWest and Lloyds TSB. Most branches have automatic cash dispensers open 24 hours; check the stickers to see if your card and PIN number will be accepted, although if you don't have a British card you can expect your bank to charge a commission fee for any transaction.

You can change **travellers' cheques** at any bank or bureau de change, but remember to bring a passport or similar ID along with you. By and large, the big banks offer a better rate and lower commission fees, but shop around. If you need non-British currency, bureaux de change will be more likely to stock it. Try:

American Express, *6 Haymarket*, **t** *(020) 7484 9600; **tube** Piccadilly Circus (S10)*.

Chequepoint, *548 Oxford St*, **t** *(020) 7723 1005; **tube** Marble Arch (M9)*. Also other branches.

Thomas Cook, *Victoria Station (P15), Marble Arch (L9) and many other branches*, **t** *(020) 7302 8600*.

Opening Hours

Traditionally, **shops and offices** open Mon–Fri 9am to 5.30 or 6pm, with shops opening the same hours on Saturday and many bigger shops opening for shorter hours on Sunday. Later closing hours for shops are becoming more common in London – usually 6.30 or 7pm, and until 9pm on Thursdays. Most areas of London have corner shops that stay open until at least 10pm; quite a few keep going all night.

Public Holidays

With the exception of Christmas and New Year's Day, Britain's national holidays, known as bank holidays, shift slightly every year to ensure they fall on a Monday. This avoids being 'cheated' out of holidays, as happens in continental Europe when they fall on the weekend. Banks and businesses close down on bank holidays, but many shops and tourist attractions stay open. Public transport theoretically runs a Sunday service, but in practice tends to be threadbare.

Bank holidays are:

1 January New Year's Day (plus the following Mon if it falls on a weekend)
March/April Good Friday
March/April Easter Monday
1st Mon in May May Day
Last Mon in May Spring Bank Holiday
Last Mon in Aug Summer Bank Holiday
25 December Christmas Day
26 December Boxing Day (plus 27 Dec if Christmas or Boxing Day falls on a weekend).

Pubs and bars have fairly strict licensing rules and can only serve alcohol 11am–11pm, with shorter hours on Sunday (though there is talk of change).

For post-office opening hours, *see* 'Post Offices', below; for bank opening hours, *see* 'Money and Banks', above.

Post Offices

Post offices are generally open Mon–Fri 9am–5.30pm and Sat 9am–noon. Avoid going at lunchtime as they can get very crowded. They are marked on most London maps (in the *A–Z*, for example, by a black star). Some newsagents also act as sub-post offices (with a Post Office sign outside), while most at least sell books of stamps. Two of the biggest post offices are at 24 King William IV St, next to Trafalgar Square (*open Mon–Sat 8am–8pm*), and at King Edward St, near St Paul's Cathedral. Both have stamp shops and a *poste restante* service, as well as a very useful mail collection on Sunday evenings.

London **postcodes** are fairly confusing, and rely on an intimate knowledge of city geography to be intelligible. Postcodes begin with a direction (W for West, WC for West Central, and so on) and a number from 1 to 28, which can be followed by a further letter. The full postcode then adds a space, a number and two more letters. So a postcode might read EC1R 3ER – gobbledygook to anyone but a post office computer. This book uses postcodes sparingly, preferring to indicate instead the geographical district.

Smoking

There are total bans in theatres, cinemas, museums, buses and Underground stations. Most restaurants have non-smoking areas, and some bars and pubs are introducing a similar partition. If you are invited to someone's home, ask in advance if smoking will be tolerated. It is considered quite normal to send guests wanting a puff into the garden or street.

Students and Pensioners

Students and pensioners are entitled to **discounts** on transport passes, air and rail travel, and entry to many museums and shows. You should have some appropriate ID; in the case of students, an ISIC card is the most practical and is recognized worldwide.

Students with queries should address themselves to the University of London Union (ULU), in Malet St behind the British Museum, **t** (020) 7664 2000 (or go to any branch of STA; *see* p.62).

Telephones

The two biggest companies are British Telecom, the former national monopoly, and Mercury. **Phonecards** are widely available, for example from newsagents. Watch out whose phone you use with a card – they are company-specific. Coins, of course, work fine anywhere (minimum charge 20p). For **prices** and information on cheap times to call, check with any post office (the rates are constantly changing). Obviously, though, evenings and weekends are cheaper, particularly for international calls.

London **phone numbers** differ by area. They begin with the London code, 020, followed by an eight-digit number. For inner London these numbers begin with 7, for outer London with 8 (so a number in the City will be **t** (020) 7xxx xxxx). Within the same area, you need only dial the eight-digit number; from one area to another or outside London you must use 020. Anyone calling from abroad must dial the international prefix 0044, then 20, then the rest of the number.

Directory enquiries are on **t** 192. There is a 20p charge for this service. The telephone directory lists private numbers and businesses in separate volumes. There's also the *Yellow Pages* (**w** *www.yell.com*), ordering businesses by activity.

Operator services: t *100.*
International operator: t *155.*
International directory enquiries: t *153.*

The **international dialling code** is 00, followed by the country code (1 for the United States and Canada, 61 for Australia, 64 for New Zealand).

Time

Britain is one hour behind the rest of Western Europe. During the winter (roughly the end of October to the third week of March) it follows Greenwich Mean Time; in the summer it follows British Summer Time, which is 1 hour ahead of GMT. New York is 5 hours behind GMT and San Francisco 8 hours behind, while Tokyo and Sydney are 10 hours ahead.

Tipping

Britain does not have the United States' established tipping code, but 10–15% is considered polite in restaurants, taxis, hairdressers and the posher hotels. Watch out for restaurant bills which already include a

gratuity but leave space for another – a common occurrence in London.

Toilets

The old-fashioned underground public toilets are disappearing fast – and with good reason, given their dubious hygiene record and reputation for attracting gay men on the prowl for casual sex. In their stead you will find free-standing automatic 'Super-Loos' which are coin-operated (20p) and smell of cheap detergent (there is one, for example, in Leicester Square). Generally speaking, you'll have a more salubrious experience in pubs, bars and restaurants.

Tourist Offices

Abroad

Canada: *British Tourist Authority, 5915 Airport Rd, Suite 120, Mississauga, Ontario, L4V 1T1, t 1 888 847 4885, t 905 405 1720, f 905 405 1835, w www.visitbritain.com/ca.*

Ireland: *Britain Travel Centre, 18–19 College Green, Dublin 2, t (01) 670 8000, f 670 8244, w www.visitbritain.con/ie.*

USA: *British Tourist Authority, 7th Floor, 551 5th Av at 45th St, New York, or 10th Floor, 625 North Michigan Av, Chicago, t 1800 462 2748, w www.travelbritain.org.*

In London

London is one of the tourist brochure capitals of the world: show one faint sign of interest and you will be inundated with glossy paper.

The **London Tourist Board** has a recorded telephone service with up-to-date information (**t** 09068 663344, 60p per minute), and a Web site at **w** *www.londontown.com*, with details of restaurants, shops and current attractions, and 3D maps. Alternatively, you can speak to a person on **t** (020) 7932 2000.

The main tourist offices, which can also help you find accommodation, are:

Britain Visitor Centre, *1 Regent St, Piccadilly Circus, SW1Y 4XT (R10).* **Open** *Mon 9.30am–6.30pm, Tues–Fri 9am–6.30pm, Sat and Sun 10am–4pm (June–Oct Sat 9am–5pm).*

Heathrow Underground Station (Terminals 1, 2 and 3). Open *daily 8am–6pm.*

Liverpool St Underground Station *(DD6–7).* **Open** *Mon–Fri 8am–6pm, Sat 8am–5.30pm, Sun 9am–5.30pm.*

Victoria Station *(P15–16).* **Open** *Mon–Sat 8am–7pm, Sun 8am–6pm.*

Waterloo Station, *Arrivals Hall, International Terminal (W12–13).* **Open** *daily 8.30am–10.30pm.*

Women Travellers

Women have a far more hassle-free time in London than in Rome or Madrid, and it is accepted as normal for a woman to be out on her own. Watch out on the Underground, however, particularly in the evenings and at night; avoid boarding an empty carriage.

Some areas of the city are more dangerous than others late at night: King's Cross is seedy, for example. Take sensible precautions – don't walk alone down quiet, unlit streets, and do carry your bag strapped across you. Be extremely careful about taking cabs alone late at night; you will find drivers approaching you as you leave clubs and other venues, but be warned that there have recently been attacks on women in un-licensed cabs. Either book a cab in advance, take a black cab, or wait for a night bus.

Working and Long Stays

European Union citizens can enter the country with a passport and stay indefinitely. Visitors from the USA, Canada, Australia and New Zealand can stay for up to six months so long as they can prove they have a return ticket and sufficient funds to live on. For longer stays, visitors can apply to the British Embassy or High Commission in their own country for an Entry Clearance Certificate. If you are already in the UK and want to extend your visa, apply in writing to the Immigration and Nationality Department (make sure you

do it several weeks before your visa runs out), Lunar House, Wellesley Rd, Croydon CR9 2BY (**t** 0870 606 7766).

Citizens of most other European countries, with the exception of Albania, Bosnia, Bulgaria, Croatia, Macedonia, Slovakia, Yugoslavia and all the former Soviet Republics (other than the Baltic states) can enter Britain with just a passport and stay for three months.

For more information, contact your consulate. The British Foreign office has a very useful Web site which gives information on visa regulations (**w** *www.fco.gov.uk*), and you can also download the relevant application forms from it. The independent charity Immigration Advisory Service (IAS), County House, 190 Great Dover St, London SE1, **t** (020) 7357 6917, **w** *www.iasuk.org*, offers free, confidential advice to anyone seeking entry to the UK.

Residents of EU countries can legally work in the UK. Citizens from elsewhere will need a **work permit**, which, without the backing of an organization, can be very difficult to obtain. Young people aged between 17 and 27 can apply for a Working Holiday-Maker Entry Certificate, which entitles the holders to stay in the UK for up to two years and take on casual work. These certificates are only available from British Embassies and High Commissions abroad and should be applied for in advance.

Full-time students in North America can apply for temporary UK work permits through Bunac, PO Box 430, Southbury, CT 06488 (**t** 0 800 GO BUNAC, **w** *www.bunac.org*). These are valid for six months and Bunac can help organize accommodation and provide lists of possible employers.

Commonwealth citizens who have a parent or grandparent who was born in the UK are also entitled to work in Britain. Apply for a Certificate of Entitlement to the Right of Abode at the British Embassy or High Commission in your home country.

Westminster

Westminster

Westminster means two things: the mother of all London churches, Westminster Abbey; and the mother of all parliaments, that august institution which has set the benchmark for democratic assemblies all over the world. Actually, there is nothing very motherly, or even feminine, about either place. This part of town has for centuries been the preserve of men of power. Women have not, until very recently, had much of a look-in. Despite the fact that there are now 118 female MPs, Westminster still has the same exclusive, boys-will-be-boys feel as the clubland of St James's across the park.

To the south, Westminster borders on Victoria, a traveller's standby for its rail and bus stations, and the white terraces of Pimlico, with, right by the river, Tate Britain, the national showcase for British art.

Highlights

Londoner's City: Hearing a debate in the House of Commons, p.89

Literary City: Poets' Corner in Westminster Abbey, p.88

Outdoor City: Hearing Big Ben chime the hour, p.90

Indoor City: The excellent collection at Tate Britain, p.96

---

1 Lunch

The Cinnamon Club, *Old Westminster Library, Great Smith St*, **t** *(020) 7222 2555*; **tube** *St James's Park. Open Mon–Fri 7.30–10am, noon–3pm and 6–10.30pm, Sat 6–10.30pm, Sun noon–4pm. Expensive.* The hushed library atmosphere still lingers in this excellent new Indian restaurant.

2 Drinks

Paviours Arms, *Neville House, Page St*, **t** *(020) 7834 2150*; **tube** *Pimlico, St James's Park.* Lovely Art Deco pub with a spectacular sinuous black bar.

PARLIAMENT SQUARE

Westminster started out as a piece of swampy, brambly ground called Thorney Island, a backwater more than a mile upstream from Roman Londinium. Little is known for certain about its development before Edward the Confessor established it as his centre of government in the 11th century. One story has it that St Peter himself pointed out the site of the future abbey to a humble 7th-century fisherman called Edric, who then managed to sell his miraculous story to King Sebert of the East Saxons. An abbey of some sort was almost certainly built at the time, but it did not take on political importance until the reign of Edward the Confessor. After Edward, there was a significant shift in London's balance of power, the City remaining the preserve of the merchants while Westminster became the centre of the royal court. The two poles competed for centuries; a wrestling match between Westminster and the City in 1222 degenerated into a running battle that raged on for several days.

Parliament Square is full of monumental **statues of British statesmen** including Palmerston, Disraeli and Winston Churchill (the stooping Churchill, as fashioned by Ivor Roberts-Jones in 1974, is heated from within to stop the pigeon droppings sticking).

Westminster Abbey T14

*e info@westminster-abbey.org; w www .westminster-abbey.org; **tube** Westminster; wheelchair accessible. **Adm** free for services or prayers. **The nave, Royal Chapels, Statesman's Aisle and Poets' Corner open** Mon–Fri 9.45am–4.30pm, last adm 3.45pm, Sat 9.20am–2.30pm, last adm 1.45pm; **adm** adults £6, children £3, families £12, under-11s free. **Chapter House open** April–Oct daily 10am–5.30pm, Nov–March daily 10am–4pm; **Pyx Chamber and Undercroft Museum open** daily 10.30am–4pm; single **adm** charge of £2.50 gives entry to all three. **Cloisters open** daily 8am–6pm; **adm** free. **Guided tours** conducted by the vergers are available: **t** (020) 7222 7110 to book. Pick up a floor plan at the entrance of the abbey.*

It is impossible to overestimate the symbolic importance of Westminster Abbey in English culture. This is where monarchs are crowned and buried, where the Anglican Church derives its deepest inspiration, and where the nation lionizes its artistic and political heroes. To construct an equivalent in Paris you would have to roll Notre Dame, the Panthéon and the Père Lachaise cemetery all into one, and probably add a bit of the Invalides and Versailles as well. No other country invests so much importance in a single building.

The comparison with France is an apt one, since architecturally the abbey takes its inspiration from the great cathedrals at Rheims and Amiens and the Sainte-Chapelle in Paris. 'A great French thought expressed in excellent English,' one epithet has it. The abbey's origins go back to the Dark Ages; it found a mystical patron in Edward the Confessor, saint and monarch; it was rebuilt from scratch in the finest Gothic traditions from the 13th until the 16th century; and it was completed in 1745 when Nicholas Hawksmoor, one of England's finest architects, added the towers at the western end. The abbey thus spans virtually the whole of English history. To be buried here, or at least to have a plaque erected inside, is still the highest state honour for a British citizen. The tombs of the medieval kings and other royal relics here bestow much of the legitimacy to which the modern monarchy can lay claim. If St Paul's is a monument to the secular wealth of London, Westminster Abbey enshrines the mystical power of the Crown.

History

The story of Edric the fisherman (*see* 'Parliament Square' above), is only one of the founding myths of the abbey church of St Peter at Westminster. Bishop Mellitus, the builder of the first St Paul's, is said to have consecrated an early version in the 7th century; St Dunstan is also believed to have worked on building an abbey here 300 years later. The only thing for certain is that a religious institution was on the site when Edward the Confessor became the Saxon king in 1042. He commissioned a new abbey, which was consecrated just eight days before he died in 1066, and features in a panel of the Bayeux tapestry depicting his funeral ceremony. The importance of Westminster as a royal counterweight to the City was then further reinforced when Edward's protégé William the Conqueror had himself crowned in the new abbey on Christmas Day 1066.

Edward the Confessor was canonized in 1161. His cult served the Crown well, not least in its political struggle with the City merchants, and it is perhaps no surprise that a king with more than his fair share of trouble with the City, Henry III, should have decided to rebuild a bigger, finer abbey in his predecessor's honour, beginning in 1220. The effort almost bankrupted him, and he pawned his own jewels to complete work on the east end; the nave, meanwhile, would not be finished until 1532. This long delay was all to the abbey's benefit, however, for it allowed architectural techniques to catch up with construction; the final result includes such pinnacles of English Gothic as the Chapter House (based closely on the Sainte-Chapelle) and the fan-vaulted Henry VII Chapel, part of the 15th–16th-century late-Gothic extension to the eastern end.

Westminster's association with the Crown saved the abbey during the dissolution of the monasteries in the 1530s, when it escaped with just a few smashed windows and broken ornaments. Its revenues were severely depleted, however, and transferred to the coffers of St Paul's (hence, at least according to folklore, the expression 'robbing Peter to pay Paul'). To this day the abbey remains a 'royal peculiar', which means it is run directly by the Crown rather than by the Church of England. The royal connection made it a target during the Civil War, when Cromwell's army used it as a dormitory and smashed the altar rails. Cromwell himself succumbed to its lure once he was Lord Protector, though, and had himself buried here after his death in 1658. His body was dug up at the Restoration, to be reburied at the foot of the gallows at Tyburn. Civil War over, the abbey was once again given over to burials and coronations. Royals aside, it is stuffed with memorials to politicians (in Statesman's Aisle), poets (in Poets' Corner), actors, scientists and engineers.

The Nave

Measuring 103ft from floor to ceiling, the nave of Westminster Abbey is by far the tallest in England, an indication of the influence of French Gothic architects, for whom height was an important means of expressing their awe before the Almighty. Height, though, was not something the abbey's architects wanted to emphasize too strongly, and its effects are diluted in a number of ways. The nave is very long as well as high, giving an impression of general grandeur ahead of loftiness. The columns, made of Purbeck marble, grow darker towards the ceiling, thus further deadening the effect of height. And the ceiling decoration pushes the eye not upwards, but along the nave towards the altar. Ornamentation is just as important in the overall effect as the manipulation of perspective.

As you enter the nave, you pass a 14th-century gilded **painting of Richard II**. The north aisle is crowded with memorials to politicians, earning it the nickname **Statesman's Aisle**. From the relief memorial to William Pitt the Younger above the west door, to the Earl of Stanhope's monument against the choir screen, you can spot nearly every influential name in British political life of the 18th and 19th centuries. Among the characters who crop up elsewhere in this book are the Prime Ministers Sir Robert Peel (founder of the Metropolitan Police), Palmerston, Gladstone, Disraeli, Neville Chamberlain (as well as his father Joseph), Lloyd George and Clement Attlee. Other walks of life are celebrated in this part of the abbey too, notably scientists and engineers, including Michael Faraday (a fine tablet) and Sir Isaac Newton (a splendid monument by William Kent against the choir screen).

The Choir and St Edward's Chapel

The first attraction beyond the ticket counters, the **choir screen**, is a 19th-century reworking by Edward Blore of the gilded 13th-century original. Note the elegant black and white marble floor, and the heraldic shields commemorating the families who gave money to construct the abbey in the 13th century. Behind the High Altar is **St Edward's Chapel**, the epicentre of the abbey, with its **memorials to medieval kings** set around the Coronation Chair. The finest of all these tombs was the golden memorial encrusted with jewels that Henry III built for Edward the Confessor; however, all that remains of it today is the base. Henry himself lies nearby, in a simple chest built so that the body could be removed at any time and the bones extracted in case the English army wanted to brandish them on their next campaign in Scotland. Richard II and his wife Anne of Bohemia lie together on a single tomb. Their effigies used to hold hands, but their arms have snapped off. Richard's jawbone was also removed, by an enterprising pupil from Westminster School who pulled it out through a hole in the tomb in 1776; the missing bone was only returned to poor old Richard in 1916. Henry V, the man who beat the French at Agincourt, has his own mini-chapel towards the back featuring sculpted scenes of his exploits. Until the 18th century the corpse of his widow, Catherine of Valois, lay embalmed in an open tomb. The diarist Samuel Pepys came to Westminster Abbey on his 36th birthday and gave himself a treat by kissing the leathery ex-queen full on the lips. Perhaps to discourage such behaviour, the abbey authorities bundled her into a tomb in St Nicholas's chapel in 1776.

Henry VII Chapel

The penny-pinching Henry VII managed one great feat of artistic patronage during his reign, this extraordinary fan-vaulted chapel, nominally dedicated to the Virgin Mary but in fact a glorification of the Tudor line of monarchs. It is a supreme example of Perpendicular style – an English offshoot of late Gothic that flowered at a time when most of Europe was already well into the Renaissance. Henrys VII and VIII, Edward VI, Mary and Elizabeth I are all buried here in style, along with a healthy sprinkling of their contemporaries and successors. Elizabeth shares her huge tomb with her embittered half-sister Mary, in a curious after-death gesture of reconciliation. The bodies believed to be the two princes murdered in the Tower of London in 1483 also have a resting place here. The highlight of the chapel, though, is the **decoration**. The wondrous ceiling looks like an intricate mesh of finely spun cobwebs, while the wooden choir stalls are carved with exotic creatures and adorned with brilliantly colourful heraldic flags.

Poets' Corner

The south transept and the adjoining St Faith's Chapel are part of the original 13th-century abbey structure, and boast a series of **wall paintings** and some superbly sculpted figures of angels. **Geoffrey Chaucer** was buried in the south transept in 1400, and ever since then other poets and writers have vied to have a place next to him. When **Edmund Spenser**, author of *The Faerie Queen*, was buried here in 1599, several writers tossed their unpublished manuscripts into the grave with him. His contemporary, the playwright **Ben Jonson**, asked modestly for a grave 'two feet by two feet' and consequently was buried upright. In spite of appearances, few of the writers commemorated in Poets' Corner are actually interred here; among the 'genuine' ones are **Dryden**, **Samuel Johnson**, **Sheridan**, **Browning** and **Tennyson**. Having a memorial in Poets' Corner is deemed the ultimate accolade for a writer, and not conceded easily: **Shakespeare** had to wait 130 years for his, **William Blake** 150, and **Anthony Trollope** 111, while a campaign to have Virginia Woolf honoured is still under way. To free up more space in this increasingly crowded corner, the abbey authorities have recently installed a

stained-glass window with new memorials to such previously passed-over parvenus as Pope, Herrick and Wilde.

Chapter House, Pyx Chamber and Undercroft Museum

A pretty cloister (note the flamboyant tracery of the windows) leads to these three annexes to the abbey. The octagonal **Chapter House**, completed in 1255 and used sporadically as the meeting-place for medieval Parliaments, reproduces in miniature the techniques of weight distribution used in the Sainte-Chapelle in Paris. A single central shaft supports a vaulted roof and eight bays containing tall stained-glass windows. The intricate floor tiles, bearing heraldic symbols, are generally reckoned to be the finest examples of their kind in England.

The **Pyx Chamber**, which dates back to Edward the Confessor's abbey, is named after the box, or *pyx*, which contained the pieces of gold and silver used to set the standard for medieval coins. These coins are still checked and counted in a ritualistic annual ceremony at Goldsmiths' Hall in the City. Finally, the **Undercroft Museum** contains many treasures once displayed inside the church proper, including Henry V's military gear used at Agincourt. The museum also acts as a kind of medieval Madame Tussaud's, with a collection of wax effigies of royalty and other VIPs that were once used in funeral processions.

The Houses of Parliament (Palace of Westminster) T–U14

Tube Westminster; wheelchair accessible.

Most of today's building is the dizzy virtuoso work of Charles Barry and Augustus Pugin, two Victorian architects working at the height of their powers in answer to the commission to replace the old Parliament after it was destroyed by fire in 1834. Their building's neo-Gothic luxuriance is both an expression of Victorian self-confidence and a throwback to the medieval origins of the English Parliamentary system. As you wander

Getting into Parliament

Visiting arrangements for Parliament are hugely complicated, and vary according to your nationality; you may find that telephoning in advance (**t** (020) 7219 3000, or **t** (020) 7219 4272 for information on what is being debated) will avoid wasting time. The usual timetable (open to interruption according to the day's agenda) is: **debates in the House of Commons** (open to all) Mon–Thurs 2.30–10pm, Fri 9.30am–3pm; **Question Time**, the duel between ministers and their detractors, Mon–Wed 2.30–3.30pm, Thurs 11.30am–12.30pm; **Prime Minister's Question Time** Wed 3–3.30pm. To be sure of getting in you need to apply in advance to your MP if you are British, and to your embassy if you are not. If you turn up on spec, you must queue outside St Stephen's entrance (roughly halfway along the complex of buildings); don't expect to get a seat before 5pm. **Debates in the House of Lords** are held Wed from 2.30pm until debates finish, Thurs from 3pm, Fri from 11am, and occasionally Mon. Both houses have long recesses, particularly in the summer. Debates of particular public interest are likely to be very crowded. To see the rest of the Palace of Westminster, including **Westminster Hall**, you need to apply for a permit about two months in advance from your MP or embassy. It's a good idea whatever your arrangements to bring your passport and leave behind any large bags or cameras. You should also dress reasonably formally. The good news amid all this mayhem is that the Houses of Parliament, once you get in, come free of charge.

through its corridors and peer into its grand chambers, you have a sense of several moments in history converging at one point: matters of pressing actuality are debated inside a Victorian secular cathedral, which in turn is modelled on buildings and institutions dating back to the 11th century.

Barry and Pugin's was a near-perfect partnership. Barry sketched out the broad lines of the design, while Pugin attended to the details of ornamentation. Some of Pugin's work was lost due to bombing in the Second World War, but you can still admire the sheer fervour of his imagination in the sculpted wood and stone, stained glass, tiled floors, wallpaper and painted ceilings that abound along every corridor and in every room. Pugin was known for ranting against classicists, but nevertheless was happy to go along with Barry's essentially classical design and then Gothicize it to his heart's content. The Palace of Westminster's blend of architectural restraint (Barry) and decorative frenzy (Pugin) is one of its most appealing aspects.

Big Ben U13

The most celebrated feature of Pugin and Barry's new building was the clock tower at its eastern end, known universally by the name of its giant bell, Big Ben. Nowadays the clock is renowned for its accuracy and its resounding tolling of the hour, but the story of its construction is one of incredible incompetence and bungling. The 320ft-high clock tower was finished in 1854, but thanks to a bitter disagreement between the two clockmakers, Frederick Dent and Edmund Beckett Denison, there was nothing to put inside it for another three years. Finally, a great bell made up according to Denison's instructions was dragged across Westminster Bridge by a cart and 16 horses. Then, as it was being made ready to be hoisted into position, a 4ft crack suddenly appeared, and the bell had to be abandoned. Similar embarrassments ensued over the next two years, until a functioning, but still cracked, bell was at last placed at the top of the tower. It remains defective to this day.

The most common explanation of the bell's title is that it was named after Sir Benjamin Hall, the unpopular Chief Commissioner of Works who had to explain all the cock-ups in his project to an unimpressed House of Commons. Another theory has it that Big Ben was in fact Benjamin Caunt, a corpulent boxer who owned a pub a couple of hundred yards away in St Martin's Lane. The chimes, which are heard around the world through being broadcast by the BBC World Service, are a bastardized version of the aria 'I Know That My Redeemer Liveth' from Handel's *Messiah*. Denison filched the idea from the similar chant emitted by the bells of St Mary's church in Cambridge, where he had been an undergraduate. The words accompanying the bong-bong-bong-BONG are:

All through this hour Lord be my Guide
And by Thy Power no foot shall slide.

Following this inauspicious beginning, the clock has had a remarkably uneventful history, only going seriously wrong during the Second World War, when the belfry stage of the tower was damaged and the clockface shattered by bombing. Once, in 1949, the hands stopped turning under the weight of a flock of starlings. Since then, except for a dry bearing which stopped the clock twice in 1997, Big Ben has proved unfailingly accurate. Its tower has a shadier, less well-known side, though, as an occasional prison. Emmeline Pankhurst, the pioneer suffragette, spent several days in confinement there in 1902.

Westminster Hall

The story of the whole palace begins with Westminster Hall, which has survived the centuries more or less intact. The hall was originally a banqueting chamber built for King William Rufus, the son of William the Conqueror, in 1097. Its true glory dates from the end of the 14th century, when the magnificent oak **hammerbeam roof** was built. The Hall was the meeting-place of the Grand Council, a committee of barons which discussed policy with the monarch, as an early incarnation of Parliament. It also became the nation's main law court, where Anne Boleyn, Sir Thomas More and Charles I were tried and condemned. After the restoration of the monarchy in 1660, Royalists avenged Charles's execution by digging up the body of his Parliamentary foe Oliver Cromwell and sticking his head on the roof of Westminster Hall; there it remained until a strong wind blew it away in 1675. The old hall

Towards Democracy

The role of the modern Parliament was largely defined by the Glorious Revolution of 1688, which overthrew the despotic James II and banned Catholics from occupying the crown. Henceforth legislation was decided by Parliament alone; the monarch had the right only to advise and, in exceptional circumstances, block new laws by refusing the Royal Assent. There was no provision, however, for the very key to a democratic society, universal suffrage. It was not until 1832 that the first Reform Act broadened the base of voters beyond aristocrats and their cronies, and not until 1928 that all adult voters, male and female, had the right to cast their ballot. The swing towards democratic representation was largely the result of fear – fear that the popular revolutions sweeping France in the early 19th century might take hold in Britain if concessions were not made to the will of the people.

was also a rowdy place, with shops and entertainments to distract the lawyers. Henry VIII built a court for real tennis (an early indoor version of the modern game) next door, and as late as the 1940s restorers found balls jammed in the roof. Monarchs were naturally attracted to the hall's splendour, and until 1821 it was used for all their coronation banquets. These were not always an unqualified success. When George III and Queen Charlotte celebrated their investiture in 1761, their dinner was lit by 3,000 candles. The wax dripped onto many a fine dress, and scores of honoured guests were carried out after fainting from the heat.

The House of Commons

From about 1550, the lower house of Parliament, known as the House of Commons, began meeting in St Stephen's Chapel in the main body of the palace. It may seem odd to convene Parliament in a religious setting, but the juxtaposition is curiously appropriate: ever since the Reformation, Parliament has been a symbol of the primacy of Protestantism in English politics. It was only when St Stephen's was destroyed in the Blitz that the House of Commons became an entirely secular chamber, but even today's reconstructed version has an unmistakably religious aura. The benches on which members sit look like choir stalls; the speaker's chair is an altar before which members bow on their way in and out; the division lobby, where votes are counted, resembles a vestry or ante-chapel.

If the atmosphere of the medieval Parliaments has persisted, the same cannot exactly be said for procedure. Parliament's power in the early days was precarious to say the least and depended in large measure on the indulgence of the reigning monarch. The change began with a provocation that even Parliament could not tolerate. In 1621 King James I tore out pages in the *Commons Journal* asserting the right of members to deal 'with all matters of grievance and policy'; Parliament felt so antagonized that it took steps to bar royalty from its proceedings altogether. In 1642 Charles I became the last monarch ever to set foot in the House of Commons, and seven years later Parliament abolished the monarchy outright – albeit temporarily – at the end of the Civil War.

The House of Lords

For much of its history the House of Lords triumphantly performed its role of making the Commons look modern. Until the long-awaited arrival of reform in 1999, a thousand or more peers were entitled to sit in Pugin's finest room as superior Parliamentarians, their job to check and sometimes delay Commons legislation: more than half owed their position only to an accident of birth, having inherited their dukedoms, earldoms and the like from their fathers. There were of course many useful members – elder statesmen, businessmen, even some hereditary peers – who worked assiduously to exploit the Parliamentary system, often obstructing the more objectionable pieces of Commons law-making. Yet the hereditary system ensured that the Lords was always overwhelmingly white, Tory, male and upper class.

Order! Order!

Debates at Westminster are famous for their repartee and banter, which all too often takes precedence over the substance of the topic itself. The daily grilling of ministers known as Question Time, which once a week features the Prime Minister, is an opportunity for the opposition to prove its debating abilities as much as its prowess in unnerving or embarrassing the government. The floor of the House of Commons has produced some wonderful rhetorical moments, not least when one member has set out to insult another. The Victorian statesman Benjamin Disraeli had a particular talent in this department, once saying of his self-satisfied Whig rival William Gladstone, 'He has not a single redeeming defect'; or again of a bumptious member called John Bright, 'He is a self-made man, and worships his creator.' Churchill described Clement Attlee as a 'sheep in sheep's clothing' and 'a modest little man with much to be modest about'. In the 1980s, Labour's Denis Healey said that being attacked by the ineffectual Conservative minister Geoffrey Howe was 'like being savaged by a dead sheep'.

Members of Parliament are also capable of extraordinarily puerile behaviour, even in the quasi-religious atmosphere of the House of Commons. Some of the masculine stuffiness was tempered by the arrival of over a hundred new women MPs in the 1997 intake (there are now 118), but they have been forced to submit a formal complaint about sexist taunts ('Get back in the kitchen!', 'She's got PMT!', etc.) thrown across the chamber. No image of the place is more memorable than that of the Speaker yelling 'Order! Order!' to get unruly members to shut up.

But in Parliament there is bad behaviour and bad behaviour: it might be fine to scream your head off as a member of an opposing party is trying to put a point across, but other lapses are not acceptable. Members must not address each other by name, but rather by the constituency they represent, or at the very least as 'my honourable friend' if it is a party colleague or 'the honourable member' if it is an opponent. The Speaker can call a member to order for instances of what is deemed to be 'unparliamentary language'. Accusing an MP of lying or being drunk is unacceptable; rather they must be demonstrated to have been 'withholding certain facts', or uttering 'terminological inexactitudes', or 'appearing to be tired and emotional'. Terms to which Speakers have taken objection in the past include 'blackguard', 'coward', 'git', 'guttersnipe', 'hooligan', 'rat', 'swine', 'stoolpigeon' and 'traitor'. A member must withdraw such a word if called upon to do so; otherwise he or she faces disciplinary proceedings that can include expulsion from the chamber for a number of days.

Finally, on the anniversary of Guy Fawkes' attempt to blow up Parliament, Tony Blair's reforms sent all but 94 hereditary peers packing. The future of the House is still not certain: currently the chamber is made up of the rump of hereditaries, the 560-odd life peers (who have been ennobled by past governments but cannot pass the title to their children), plus Church of England bishops and senior judges. In the future, the latter may be asked to leave; the whole chamber may be appointed; there has even been talk (good heavens!) of holding elections.

The Jewel Tower T14

Abingdon St, opposite the far tower of the Palace of Westminster, t (020) 7222 2219; tube Westminster. Open April–Sept daily 10am–6pm, Oct daily 10am–5pm, Nov–Mar daily 10am–4pm; closed 24–26 Dec; adm adults £1.50, concessions £1.10, 5–18s 80p.

If you're interested in the origins of the Parliamentary buildings, you should make a detour to the Jewel Tower, which, along with Westminster Hall, is the only surviving relic of the 1834 fire, and is now a museum containing a collection of pre-fire remains. Unfortunately there are no jewels left; instead you can enjoy an excellent exhibition detailing the history of the Houses of Parliament ('Parliament Past and Present'), which includes a new virtual tour of the interior of the entire complex. There is also a small but mind-crushingly dull display on weights and measures, a legacy of the Jewel Tower's 70 years as a public office for this peculiarly uninspiring topic.

St Margaret's Westminster T14

Tube Westminster; wheelchair accessible. *Open Mon–Fri 9.30am–3.45pm, Sat 9.30am–1.45pm, Sun 2–5pm.*

This white stone church alongside Westminster Abbey is best known for its society weddings: its marriage register includes such names as Samuel Pepys, John Milton and Winston Churchill. The building itself, which doesn't usually get much attention what with Big Brother the abbey standing next door, is a patchwork of relics and architectural styles dating back to the late 15th century. Edward VI's evil protector Lord Somerset tried to demolish it to provide stones for Somerset House, but was rebuffed by angry parishioners who chased his men away with clubs and bows. St Margaret's suffered more serious damage in the Second World War, and was extensively rebuilt. Its most prized possession, the **east window**, is a stained-glass depiction of the betrothal of Catherine of Aragon to Prince Arthur, the eldest son of Henry VII. The window, commissioned from Spanish craftsmen, celebrates a fatefully shortlived union, since Arthur died and Catherine married his brother, the future Henry VIII, before it could be installed. The glass was tactfully removed to Waltham Abbey in Essex and only brought back in 1758.

WHITEHALL

In the 17th century the view down Whitehall was rather different. Instead of today's busy traffic funnel lined with self-important Neoclassical offices, the street was a grand thoroughfare flanked on each side by the Renaissance buildings of Whitehall Palace. At the top of the street was the three-storey stone and flint Holbein Gate, thoughtlessly pulled down in 1759 to facilitate the flow of coach traffic. The palace itself was built and established as the main royal residence by Henry VIII in the 1530s. It continued to be embellished until 1689, when William and Mary decided to move to Kensington Palace and the court decamped to St James's. Then in 1698 the whole complex, except only the Banqueting House, burnt to the ground after a Dutch laundry-woman left a stove on overnight. Whitehall has since become a synonym for the British Civil Service, which moved in during the 18th and 19th centuries to take advantage of its proximity to Parliament. Among the bronze plates you'll see on the way down are the Ministry of Defence, the Ministry of Housing and, on the corner of Parliament Square, the Treasury. None of the government buildings is open to the public.

Cabinet War Rooms S–T13

Clive Steps, King Charles St, t (020) 7930 6961, e cwr@iwm.org.uk, w www.iwm.org.uk; tube Westminster; wheelchair accessible. Open April–Sept daily 9.30am–6pm, Oct–March daily 9.30am–5.15pm; closed 24–26 Dec; adm adults £5.40, concessions £3.90, children free.

This is the underground world where British leaders met in secret during the Second World War and the essential work of government was carried out. Winston Churchill had the basements of a number of government buildings converted in preparation for war in 1938, and he, his Cabinet and 500 civil servants worked down here throughout the conflict, protected from the bombing by several layers of thick concrete. The floor below the present exhibition contained a canteen, hospital, shooting range and sleeping quarters. The upper floor, on public display, was where the Cabinet met and communications were maintained with the outside world. Churchill, whose office was a converted broom cupboard, kept a direct line open to President Roosevelt in Washington; all other telephone connections were operated from an unwieldy old-fashioned switchboard, and scrambled, for perverse reasons of security, via Selfridge's department store on Oxford St.

The War Rooms, with their Spartan **period furniture** and **maps** marking the British Empire in red, are a magnificent evocation of the wartime atmosphere. A pity, then, that the curators do not allow the place simply to speak for itself. They have piled on the nostalgia with broadcasts of Churchill's wartime speeches, wailing air-raid sirens in the corridors and any number of trinkets in the gift shop: 'careless talk costs lives' mugs and even a ration-ticket recipe book.

The Cenotaph T13

Tube *Westminster, Charing Cross.*

Just before Downing Street, heading north, in the middle of the road, is the Cenotaph, the nation's chief memorial to the dead of the two World Wars, designed by Edwin Lutyens in 1920. It is the site of an official ceremony attended by the Queen and senior politicians of all parties on every Armistice Day, 11 November.

Downing Street T12

Tube *Westminster, Charing Cross.*

No.10 of this plain-looking street has been home to British Prime Ministers on and off since 1735. Unfortunately, you won't be able to sidle up to the famous Georgian front door without a security pass; the best you can hope for nowadays is a glimpse through the heavy iron gates at the end of the street, installed in 1990 under Mrs Thatcher. Next door at No.11 is the home of the Chancellor of the Exchequer, the British equivalent of treasury secretary or finance minister, and next door to him, at No.12, is the government whips' office, where the party in power keeps tabs on its members in Parliament.

It is rather pleasing to think that this street, the scene of many a heated Cabinet meeting, was once an open venue for cock-fighting. Only in 1675 it was a rather modest building development, later to become the powerhouse of the British establishment, undertaken by one George Downing, a slippery fellow who spied for both Oliver Cromwell and Charles II during the Civil War and came out of it not only alive but stinking rich. It was more accident than design that led to Downing St's lasting fame. When the Prime Minister Robert Walpole succeeded one Mr Chicken as tenant in 1735 he never meant to establish No.10 as an official residence, and many of his successors preferred to conduct the business of government from their more lavish homes elsewhere in London. Only in the early 19th century was 10 Downing Street kitted out with proper facilities, such as John Soane's sumptuous dining room, and not until 1902 did it become the Prime Minister's home as well as office. The shortcomings of the place, though, have never gone away; when Tony Blair became Prime Minister in 1997, he installed his family in the more spacious No.11 next door, swapping places with his then unmarried Chancellor, Gordon Brown. It certainly appeals to the British establishment's keen sense of understatement that 10 Downing Street should be such an ordinary-looking seat of power.

Banqueting House T12

Whitehall, bookings **t** *(020) 7930 4179, general information* **t** *(020) 7839 8919,* **w** *www.hrp .org.uk;* **tube** *Westminster, Charing Cross; wheelchair accessible.* **Open** *Mon–Sat 10am–5pm, last adm 4.30pm; closed for government functions, public hols and 24 Dec–2 Jan;* **adm** *adults £3.90, concessions £3.10, children £2.30.*

The Banqueting House was the first building that Inigo Jones, the Palladio-crazy King's Surveyor of Works, constructed after he returned from his expedition to Italy in 1615. Completed in 1622, it was the first Italianate building in London, a sober design of elegant proportions which enthused foreign visitors but left the home-grown critics stone cold. Jones was not really ahead of his time: the rest of London was just living about 150 years in the past, and it took more than a century before the Banqueting House attracted the admiration it deserved.

It was much more than a place where royalty ate dinner: it became an essential symbol of Stuart kingship, especially after Charles I commissioned the breathtakingly beautiful but supremely arrogant **ceiling frescoes** by Rubens in the main dining hall on the first floor. The theme of these frescoes is the divine right of kings, no less. Of the three main panels, the first is an allegorical celebration of the union of England and Scotland under James I; the second a celebration of James's virtues; and the third, directly above the throne, a depiction of the peace enjoyed in James's reign. For James I you could just as easily read Charles I – this was very much a glorification of the present monarch, rather than a fond tribute to his father. In fact, Charles had less in common with James I than with Richard II, whose own claim to the divine right of kings 250 years earlier is so brilliantly captured in the *Wilton Diptych* (in the National Gallery). Charles should have remembered how Richard II was deposed and murdered for his presumption; a few years later, he wound up on an executioner's block right outside this dining hall.

The Banqueting House inevitably became something of a Royalist shrine after the restoration of the monarchy in 1660, and was chosen as the venue for Charles II's coronation celebrations. James II tried to turn it into a Catholic shrine, and stuck a weather vane on the roof to warn him of any 'Protestant wind' that might blow him off his royal perch. The Protestant wind did indeed come, in the shape of William of Orange, who deposed James and promptly used the Banqueting House for a joint feast with Queen Mary in 1689 to celebrate their accession. Jones's building survived the Whitehall Palace fire of 1698, but its ceremonial role faded fast. For 200 years it was stuffed full of

religious paraphernalia and used as a royal chapel. It was only restored to its original form for its public opening in 1963. It is still occasionally used for a royal ceremony on Maundy Thursday, the day before Good Friday, when the Queen distributes specially minted coins, known as Maundy money, to charitable institutions and the poor.

Horse Guards Parade T12

*Whitehall; **tube** Charing Cross, Westminster, St James's Park. **Changing of the Guard** daily 11am.*

The Horse Guards in question are the Queen's very own knights in shining armour, properly known as the Household Cavalry. Altogether, seven regiments (the 'Household Division') are allocated the task of dressing up in chocolate-soldier costumes and parading in front of Buckingham Palace (although, they occasionally engage in more serious business, too, like peacekeeping in Kosovo). Housed both here and at Wellington Barracks on the south side of St James's Park (*see* p.118) are the Life Guards and the Blues and Royals (the two cavalry regiments, in their helmets and plumes), and the five regiments of 'Foot Guards': the Grenadiers, the Coldstream Guards and the Scots, Irish and Welsh Guards. The best time to see them is on the first weekend in June, when they all take part in a grand parade in front of the Queen known as Trooping the Colour. Otherwise you can make do with the Changing of the Guard, when the detachment on duty outside Buckingham Palace (three officers and 40 men) is relieved in a colourful series of manoeuvres.

This has been parading territory since Henry VIII's day, when Horse Guards Parade was built as an extension to Whitehall Palace. The present-day barracks are Georgian, the work of William Kent; notice the **arch** leading through to the St James's Park side, which is so low that Hogarth once painted a coach coming through it with a headless driver.

PIMLICO

The chunk of residential London that runs from Victoria Station down to the river in Pimlico was the work of one man, 19th-century builder Thomas Cubitt, who lost no opportunity to turn this promising area of residential London into a veritable savannah of blandness. The Victorians already hated it, calling it insipid and tawdry and disparaging it as 'Cubittopolis'. In the 20th century, Pimlico inspired such indifference that it turned briefly into slumland. Now the area is the domain of hotels and foreign embassies, but it is also where you will find the national collection of British art in Tate Britain.

While you're in Pimlico, note the view over the river to the awe-inspiring **Battersea Power Station**, blurring the division between beauty and ugliness, built between 1933 and 1953 by Sir George Gilbert Scott. It's currently used only as a film set, but there are always plans to turn it into something.

Tate Britain T17

Millbank, t (020) 7887 8008, w www.tate .org.uk; tube Pimlico; wheelchair accessible. Open daily 10am–5.50pm; closed Good Fri, May Day and 24–26 Dec; adm free, charges for special exhibitions. Guided tours Mon–Fri at 11.30am (for the Turner collection), 2.30pm and 3.30pm (for Tate Britain highlights); free. 'Painting of the Month' (a short talk discussing a featured work from the collection) Mon at 1.15pm and Sat at 2.30pm. Film programme Wed, Thurs, Sat (feature films and documentaries, check Web site for details). Giftshop, café, restaurant.

This gallery, founded at the end of the 19th century by the sugar baron Sir Henry Tate of Tate & Lyle, was once known simply as 'The Tate' and housed the second great London art collection after the National Gallery. In spring 2000, however, the collection divided into two: 20th-century international art moved across the river to Tate Modern at Bankside (*see* p.205) while, here at Millbank,

Finding Your Way Around Tate Britain

Apart from the huge increase in space, one of the most radical changes made by the 2001 overhaul is that the collection has been regrouped into thematically linked rooms, each exploring particular aspects of British art across history. The galleries have names like 'Landscape and Empire', 'War and Memory', and focus on different groups of artists. Two new rooms are dedicated to confronting the myths about artists and their subjects, 'Painters in Focus' and a gallery of 'Nudes', which explores the relationship between artist and model with works by Lucian Freud, Gwen John and Lord Leighton. Tate Britain's most recent purchases are displayed in one of a suite of rooms entitled 'New Acquisitions in British Art', which features some of the gallery's more controversial, trendsetting works by Damien Hirst, Gillian Wearing and Chris Ofili. The displays change every few months, as the notion of 'Britishness' is explored in different ways, but the underlying display principles remain the same. A broadly consistent chronological approach is similarly maintained, with the earliest art remaining in the western half of the gallery, near the new Manton St entrance, and the more recent work (post 1900) in the eastern half.

Tate Britain reverted to the original purpose of its founder as the national gallery of home-grown art, with a full panorama of works from the Middle Ages until now.

As part of this transformation, the original Tate Britain building was completely overhauled, and now has a new entrance on Manton St, five all-new exhibition galleries and nine renovated galleries. All this new space has allowed works by Gainsborough, Hogarth, Stubbs, Blake, Constable, the Pre-Raphaelites, Spencer, Sickert, Bacon and Moore to be brought out of years of storage. Contemporary painters have also been given a better airing, with more works by Anthony Caro, Richard Hamilton, David Hockney,

Eduardo Paolozzi, Lucian Freud, Howard Hodgkin, Richard Long and Frank Auerbach.

The Highlights

Turner and Landscape Paintings

In 'British Landscape', paintings by **Siberechts**, **Stubbs**, **Gainsborough**, **Nash**, **Lanyon** and Turner show the enormous range of emotional responses to the natural assets of this land. **John Constable** is represented by lyrical depictions of Malvern Hall in Warwickshire and Salisbury Cathedral. **Joseph Mallord William Turner** (1775–1851), the pre-eminent British painter of the 19th century, is particularly well represented. A diehard Romantic, he specialized in seascapes and, in his early work, idealized classical scenes *à la* Claude Lorrain. As his work progressed he grew more audacious in his use of light and colour, prefiguring the experiments of the French Impressionists and often bewildering the artistic establishment in London. Much of his work is a wistful look at the passing of the old rural world and the advent of the industrial revolution, and his classically inspired paintings are often penetrating allegories of the aspirations and cruelties of the British Empire. It is hard to pick out individual pictures, but try to see some of the following: *Rome from the Vatican* (1820), an idealized portrait of the Eternal City reflecting many of Turner's artistic preoccupations; *Snow Storm: Steamboat off a Harbour's Mouth*, a virtuoso whirl of chaos on the waves; *A City on a River at Sunset*, a gorgeous, warm study of sky and water, probably in Rouen; and *Peace: Burial at Sea*, a tribute to Turner's fellow painter David Wilkie in which light, mist and smoke mingle in Turner's typical sea setting.

Blake, Hogarth, Stubbs and Reynolds

Around the galleries, a series of single-room displays are dedicated to some of the most famous British artists. Well worth entering is the terrifying Manichean world of **William Blake** (1757–1827), a man who turned his vivid Biblical and literary nightmares into extraordinarily enigmatic poetry, pen and ink watercolours and prints. We see Adam and Eve in horror as they discover the murdered body of Abel, Nebuchadnezzar crawling in rags like vermin, and Job in all stages of his trials. Blake was a radical anti-materialist, who saw human progress as essentially displeasing to the Almighty. Look at his portrait of Isaac Newton, showing the father of modern physics as a misguided, ape-like figure making drawings in the dirt. Among the most lyrical works in the collection are Blake's illustrations to the *Divine Comedy*, which capture all of Dante's comic perversity as well as the horror of the whirlwinds, the contorted bodies and various tortures, including the gruesome well of fire reserved for Pope Nicholas III.

One display centres on **Hogarth**'s (1697–1764) finest satire, *O the Roast Beef of England*, a depiction of the greed and corruption of France seen through the soldiers, priests and beggars of Calais. Hogarth himself appears, sketchbook in hand, drawing the famous gates of the city while a detachment of soldiers prepares to arrest him. Aside from this picture, however, the Tate catches Hogarth in uncharacteristically sober mood as portrait painter to the great and good, including Thomas Herring, Archbishop of Canterbury. Other galleries give glimpses of **Gainsborough** and **Zoffany**, soft-focus portrait painters in the Watteau mould; **Stubbs** the horse specialist (who used to paint the horses and then fill in the background later); and the founding president of the Royal Academy, **Sir Joshua Reynolds** (1723–92). Reynolds adopted the ideal style and classical themes pioneered in Renaissance Italy, adding to it something of the fragrance of the English countryside. His *Three Ladies Adoring a Term of Hymen*, for example, turns four upper-class English sisters into gossiping Greek nymphs with delicate complexions and dainty clothes.

The Victorians

Highlights among the Victorian paintings in the collection include **John Martin**'s hallucinogenic visions of heaven with bands of angels suspended from dramatic day-glo clouds. Martin serves as a useful counterfoil to the **Pre-Raphaelites**, the group of mid-Victorian painters who strove to reject the ideal style symbolized by Raphael and his followers, in favour of a naturalistic approach more in tune with the real world. The works of Rossetti, Millais, Waterhouse and Burne-Jones cannot really be said to be realistic, however: their strong colours and heart-rending emotions are a heightened reality, like the application of belladonna to a beautiful pair of eyes. Among the works to look out for are Waterhouse's *Lady of Shalott*, Burne-Jones's *King Cophetua and the Beggar Maid* and Millais' *Ophelia*. There are other Victorian curiosities, notably the extraordinary work of **Richard Dadd**, who was shut up in a lunatic asylum after he murdered his father, and **Augustus Egg**'s triptych of a fallen woman called *Past and Present*.

VICTORIA

Victoria is a transitional place: its biggest features are a major train station and a coach station, and its streets are crammed with guesthouses. Everyone ignored that fact that the Catholic cathedral was built in Victoria, and named it after Westminster up the road. It seems poor Victoria's fate is always to be overlooked. If you're not arriving or leaving, head into the streets of Victoria's aristocratic neighbour, swanky Belgravia, to the south-west – a very elegant place for a stroll and shop (head for Elizabeth St; *see* p.370).

Westminster Cathedral Q15

Victoria St, t (020) 7798 9055, w www .westminsterdiocese.org.uk; tube Victoria; wheelchair accessible. Open Mon–Fri and Sun 7am–7pm, Sat 8am–7pm; adm free.

London's main Roman Catholic church, Westminster Cathedral is a striking confection of red brick and Portland stone built according to the Byzantine style of the early Christians, even though the exterior was completed in 1903. Catholicism had a long, hard road to travel to reach acceptability in Britain – a web of legal restrictions on Catholics was not abolished until 1829 – and even after the appointment of the first Cardinal Archbishop of London in 1850 it was not easy to raise the funds needed to build an appropriate central place of worship. In the end, the Church fathers decided to build the outside first, and leave the cost of furnishing the interior to future generations. Hence the curious look of the interior, which is highly ornate in some places and virtually bare in others, an effect accentuated by its vast proportions – 360ft long and 156ft wide (the widest nave in Britain). The sumptuous green marble **pillars** in the nave were cut from the same stone as the 6th-century basilica of Hagia Sophia in Istanbul; it took two years to bring the stone to London because of a local difficulty with the Turkish army in deepest Thessaly. Among other features are a series of bas-reliefs by Eric Gill in the nave of the **Stations of the Cross**, a 15th-century alabaster **Virgin and Child** brought over from France by an anonymous donor, a marble **pulpit**, and a huge **baldacchino** inlaid with mosaics, standing on eight pillars made of yellow Veronese marble. The **organ** is unique because of its dual control system, which allows it to be played at either end of the cathedral.

St John's Smith Square T15

Smith Square, t (020) 7222 1061; tube Westminster. Open Mon–Fri 10am–5pm and for concerts. Café.

This attractive open-plan Georgian church, designed by Thomas Archer and completed in 1728, was grossly under-appreciated in its first 200 years; Queen Anne compared it to an upturned footstool (and indeed the crypt café is called The Footstool). Now the church has been converted into a concert hall staging excellent concerts. There are rehearsals most afternoons which are well worth gate-crashing. The atmosphere is light and airy and the acoustics excellent.

Trafalgar Square and Around

04

1 Lunch

J. Sheekey, *St Martin's Court*, **t** *(020) 7240 2565*; **tube** *Leicester Square*. **Open** *Mon–Sat noon–3 and 5.30–midnight, Sun noon–3.30 and 5.30–midnight*. **Expensive**. A renowned fish restaurant, housed in an elegant suite of wood-panelled rooms.

2 Tea and Cakes

Portrait Café, *National Portrait Gallery, 2 St Martin's Place*, **t** *(020) 732 2465*; **tube** *Leicester Square, Charing Cross*. **Open** *Mon–Wed, Sat and Sun noon–6pm, Thurs and Fri 10am–8.30pm*. The gallery café is tucked away in the basement, but light pours in through the unusual glass roof.

3 Drinks

Chandos, *29 St Martin's Lane, WC2*, **t** *(020) 7836 1401*; **tube** *Leicester Square, Charing Cross*. **Open** *Mon–Sat 11am–11pm, Sun noon–10.30pm*. A busy London pub serving traditional Yorkshire ales from Sam Smith's. Try the spacious first-floor bar.

Trafalgar Square and Around

What should, and could, have been the centrepiece of a grand modern city (this is, after all, the point from which all measurements in London are drawn) is today a noisy, dusty traffic hub of little grace or architectural distinction. If it is the fate of London to be a shapeless jumble with no place to call its heart, then the story of Trafalgar Square goes a long way towards explaining why.

At the beginning of the 19th century the Prince Regent (later crowned George IV) and his chosen architect, John Nash, wanted to create a vast open space glorifying the country's naval power which would also provide a focal point from which other urban projects could spread. It was a fine idea, but one that was destined to be cruelly truncated by the vagaries of history. As economic crisis gripped the nation in the 1820s all George's dreams were brought to a halt by a hostile Parliament. Nash was dismissed as soon as George died in 1830, and from then on Trafalgar Square was left at the mercy of successive Parliamentary committees who argued for the best part of a generation over its final form. The end result has all the allure of a pizza pie concocted by a bevy of squabbling chefs. Its centrepiece, Nelson's Column, has certainly captured public imagination as a symbol of imperial Britain, but it is a monument entirely at odds with its immediate surroundings.

To the north and west lie two more of London's unwieldy squares: Piccadilly Circus, famously lit with neon and overlooked by Eros, and Leicester Square, a broad pedestrianised square full of tourists and street entertainers.

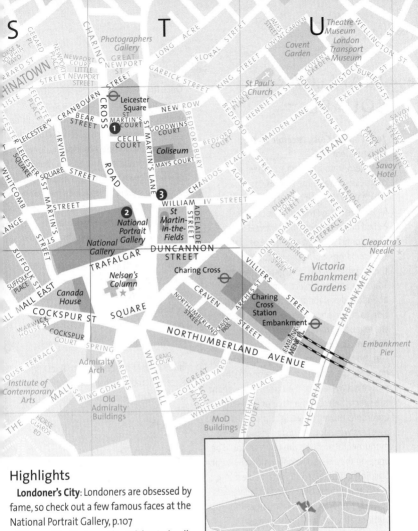

Highlights

Londoner's City: Londoners are obsessed by fame, so check out a few famous faces at the National Portrait Gallery, p.107

Literary City: Seeing a play in 'Theatreland' on St Martin's Lane, p.109

Contemporary Architecture: Terry Farell's Embankment Place at Charing Cross Station, p.109

Outdoor City: Watching the crowds, and your valuables, amid the bustle of these symbolic central squares – Leicester, Trafalgar and Piccadilly Circus, pp.109, 102 and 110

Indoor City: The world-class collection at the National Gallery, p.103

TRAFALGAR SQUARE

Tube *Charing Cross, Leicester Square, Embankment.*

Modern Trafalgar Square evolved partly out of a desire to raise the tone of the area, which until the 19th century was best known as the site of taverns and pillories. Nash pulled down the old King's Mews to make room for his planned ensemble of grand classical buildings, but he never got to build them before his fall from grace. The whole Trafalgar Square project might have been abandoned had it not been for a determination to bestow honours on Horatio Nelson, the legendary naval commander (*see* 'Nelson's Column', below).

In the absence of a coordinating architect, however, the scheme made painfully slow progress. Where Nash had been extravagant, the special select committee of the House of Commons proved downright stingy. The new planners were not interested in producing monumental architecture unless it could be done on the cheap. The only halfway decent building in Trafalgar Square to make it into bricks and mortar, the National Gallery, was severely compromised by Parliamentary stipulations about its design (*see* below).

The other buildings around the square are a late-Victorian–Edwardian assortment. On the eastern side of the square is **South Africa House**. Next door is James Gibbs's church of St Martin-in-the-Fields (*see* below). In the southeastern corner stands a lamp-post known as the **smallest police station** in the world, which contains a telephone linked up to police headquarters at Scotland Yard. On the western side, in a building designed by Robert Smirke, builder of the British Museum, is **Canada House**, home to the Canadian High Commission. **Admiralty Arch**, the grand entrance to the Mall, is to the southwest. Of the statues in the square, that of **George IV** in the northeastern corner was originally commissioned to stand atop the

Symbol of the Nation

Once finished, Trafalgar Square proved a success in one respect only: as a symbol of the nation and its imperial past. Adolf Hitler was so impressed with Nelson's Column that he ordered his bombers to leave it alone, harbouring ambitions instead to haul it off to Berlin once he had invaded and conquered Britain. The square's symbolism has not been lost on generations of political demonstrators who have met here to demand everything from universal suffrage (under the Chartists in 1848) to the abolition of the hated 'poll tax'. It still comes to life on New Year's Eve when thousands of people gather in a drunken crush beneath a vast Christmas tree donated each year by the Norwegian government. The rest of the year it is grey, noisy and unremarkable.

Marble Arch at the entrance to Buckingham Palace. When the arch was moved to Hyde Park, the statue was dumped here, purportedly until a more suitable spot could be found.

Nelson's Column T11

Stiff on a pillar with a phallic air,
Nelson stylites in Trafalgar Square.
                    Lawrence Durrell

Horatio Nelson died at the Battle of Trafalgar in 1805. The victory that the British scored against the French there brought Nelson the kind of adulation one might expect for a martyred saint. Over the years 120 proposals were submitted to honour him, including myriad columns, pyramids and even a colosseum. Nelson's Column did not see the light of day until 1843. Originally, the official committee in charge was against building a column, arguing (correctly) that it would dwarf the new National Gallery and surrounding neighbourhood. But, as so often in London's chequered planning history, nobody had the guts to propose anything more daring, and when a competition was launched in 1838, William Railton's 145ft high hunk of granite won the day.

The Corinthian column, topped by an un-remarkable and scarcely visible likeness of Nelson by E.H. Baily, was erected on a sloping concrete basin prepared by the Neoclassical architect Charles Barry, also responsible for the Houses of Parliament. Railton based his design on a triumphalist precedent from ancient Rome, the Temple of Mars in the Forum of Augustus. The bronze bas-reliefs at the base of the column represent Nelson's greatest victories, at Cape St Vincent, the Nile, Copenhagen and Trafalgar, while the surrounding statuary is of Nelson's admirals. They all face away from the National Gallery, accentuating the lack of cohesion in the square's overall design. The two granite foun-tains at the base arrived in 1845, while the **bronze lions**, the most appealing feature of the ensemble, appeared a quarter of a century later. These were the work of the landscape painter Edwin Landseer, a novice at sculpture called in after a previous commission turned out to be too embar-rassing to put on display.

One of the plinths opposite the National Gallery also suffered from the lack of coher-ence which characterised the planning of Trafalgar Square; it was forgotten about and stood empty for 158 years. Finally, in the run-up to the millennium and afterwards, the plinth was allowed to fulfil its *raison d'être* and became the stage for a series of tempo-rary contemporary sculptures, including one by Rachel Whiteread, *Monument*. Since its dismantling in May 2002, no decisions have been made about what will follow.

The National Gallery S11–T10

Trafalgar Square, information line **t** *(020) 7747 2885,* **e** *information@ng-london.org.uk,* **w** *www.nationalgallery.org.uk;* **tube** *Charing Cross, Leicester Square, Embankment; wheel-chair accessible.* **Open** *Thurs–Tues 10am–6pm, Wed 10am–9pm; closed 1 Jan, Good Friday and 24–26 Dec; adm free.* **Restaurants**.

The National Gallery is an astonishing collection of Western European painting from the 13th to the 19th centuries, including

Finding Your Way Around the National Gallery

The first work of art is a mosaic of Greta Garbo's head by Boris Anrep (1933) on the floor of the main entrance hall. Pick up a floor plan from the information desk and you'll see that the gallery's four wings each concentrate on a different historical period, starting with early medieval Italian painting in the Sainsbury Wing. Rooms devoted to individual painters are clearly marked. At the entrance to each wing, you are given the names of the major paintings to look out for. The gallery is magnificently lit, with intelli-gent explanations displayed alongside each picture. There is a computer database in the Micro Gallery in the Sainsbury Wing, where you can look up and print out information on pictures or artists.

There are also organized lectures on indi-vidual pictures, as well as a constantly changing special exhibition in the Sunley Room to the left of the central hall, where paintings from the collection are grouped to illustrate a specific theme. And if that's not enough for you, there are hundreds of minor paintings stored on lower floors available for public view.

masterpieces from virtually every major school. The great names represented include Leonardo da Vinci, Piero della Francesca, Van Eyck, Raphael, Titian, Veronese, Rubens, Poussin, Rembrandt, Velázquez, Caravaggio, Turner, Constable, Delacroix, Monet, Van Gogh, Cézanne and Picasso. The collection is very much a product of the 19th century: a catalogue of work from the Grand Tradition reflecting the pride and power of the collector nation. It was founded in 1824 when George IV persuaded the government to buy 38 pictures, including a handful of Raphaels, Rembrandts and Van Dycks, from the estate of the recently deceased marine insurance broker and philanthropist John Julius Angerstein. Many of the gallery's master-pieces were bought in the Victorian era, particularly under its first director, Charles Eastlake, who went on annual spending sprees in Italy in the 1850s and 60s. The picture-buying has continued ever since, and, although money has grown tighter, the annual budget remains well over £2 million.

The building was commissioned from William Wilkins soon after the acquisition of Angerstein's collection, but the project, like the rest of Trafalgar Square, fell victim to Parliamentary penny-pinching. By the time it was finished in 1838 it was widely derided and nicknamed the 'national cruet stand' because the cupola reminded critics of a mustard pot and the bell-towers looked like pepper casters. More serious reservations focused on its lack of grace, its awkward symmetries and the apparently needless decision to build a broad 12ft-high staircase up to the main entrance. Wilkins, though, had been given a near-impossible task, since most of the features which earned him derision, including the cupola and the bell-towers, were stipulated in the original commission. Awkwardly, he was also asked to incorporate part of the frontage of the demolished royal palace at Carlton House in his façade – all this for a measly budget of just £100,000. Wilkins kept his cool and did what he was told, even coming in £45 under budget. If the building ended up less than the sum of its parts, it was not entirely his fault.

Architectural controversy was to dog the National Gallery again a century and a half later. In the early 1980s the supermarket chain Sainsbury's sponsored a new extension at the western end of the gallery, and a competition was duly held. The winning entry, by the British firm Ahrends Burton & Koralek, was an audacious Modernist design in glass and steel that set out to be a bit different and lend a provocative new tone to staid old Trafalgar Square. For the first time in years, it looked as though London might be serious about following Paris's example in commissioning ground-breaking new buildings. But then Prince Charles stunned everybody by a speech to the Royal Institute of British Architects in 1984 in which he described the proposed extension as a 'monstrous carbuncle' and called for a return to traditional architectural values.

The competition was hastily scrapped and a new, more sober extension commissioned from the American architects Robert Venturi and Denise Scott Brown, which was completed in 1991. There is nothing much wrong with their version of the Sainsbury Wing, which unlike ABK's goes out of its way to blend in with its surroundings. But its bland conformism is a constant reminder of the design opportunities missed. Charles's remarks proved a severe blow to the morale of young architects promoting bold and innovative design. ABK did not work again for 18 months after the 'carbuncle' speech. Meanwhile, the real carbuncles – the speculator-driven monstrosities in Docklands and elsewhere – sprout with impunity.

The Sainsbury Wing (1260–1510)

The National Gallery's early Renaissance collection concentrates almost exclusively on Italian and Dutch painters. In an annexe off the first room here, Room 51, is **Leonardo da Vinci**'s magnificently expressive *Cartoon*, a full-size chalk sketch for a painting of the *Virgin and Child with St Anne and John the Baptist*, which was commissioned in 1508 for the altar of the church of Santissima Annunziata in Florence. The figure of St Anne, pointing up to heaven, is the main talking point since she looks no older than her daughter Mary. Some critics believe she is in fact St Elizabeth, the mother of John the Baptist, whom she is holding. The *Cartoon* has for years been kept behind thick glass in reduced lighting because of its fragility. In 1987 it was nearly lost forever when a visitor fired a shotgun at it at close range. The attack turned out to be a perverse sort of blessing as the picture underwent the restoration work it had desperately needed for years, the gallery earned plenty of sympathetic publicity, and various curators and restorers won awards for their brave efforts.

We now jump back pre-1400 to the mostly religious paintings of **Duccio** and the **Italian School**. An oddity is the *Wilton Diptych* (Room 53), a piece of propaganda for

Richard II showing the young king protected by John the Baptist, St Edmund and Edward the Confessor as he kneels before the Virgin and a host of angels. Painted by unknown European artists in the late 14th century, it is a striking statement on the divine power of kingship. One begins to appreciate how Richard could end the Peasants' Revolt with little more than a hand gesture. Room 55 contains some of **Uccello**'s set-piece experiments with movement and perspective, notably the *Battle of San Romano* (1450) with its sea of colour and broken lances.

In Room 56 is one of the most influential paintings of the early Renaissance, **Jan van Eyck**'s *Arnolfini Marriage* (1434). The precision and detail in this portrait of an Italian merchant and his new wife in their house in Bruges is astounding. Notice the lapdog, the broom and the pair of clogs – each object swelling the mood of bourgeois contentment. The wife looks about 16 months pregnant; in fact she is merely bunching her thick dress against her stomach to symbolize the couple's hopes for a fecund future. Technically most fascinating is the convex mirror on the back wall, which reflects the whole scene including the painter and his easel like a wide-angled photograph. Generations of later artists have borrowed such gimmicky use of reflection, notably Velázquez (see his *Rokeby Venus* in Room 30).

Bellini is well-represented (see his portrait of *Doge Leonardo Loredan* in Room 61), as are **Antonello** and **Mantegna**. Room 66 has **Piero della Francesca**'s *Baptism of Christ*, a peculiarly Central Italian interpretation of the baptism story. The limpid colours and burnished summer light are unmistakably those of Piero's home town of Borgo Sansepolcro. Christ is baptized not in a broad river, as northern European painters have usually imagined it, but in a trickle of a stream beneath an olive tree.

West Wing (1510–1600)

The smallest display area (just 10 rooms), the West Wing is also the weakest, although it features some fine set pieces such as **Veronese**'s *Family of Darius before Alexander*

(Room 9). More unusual is **Holbein**'s *Christina of Denmark* in Room 2, one of a series of portraits of eligible European women that he undertook for Henry VIII after the king's third wife Jane Seymour died in 1538. Perhaps influenced by Holbein's rather glum depiction, Henry did not ask for Christina's hand but turned to Anne of Cleves instead, whom he then quickly divorced. **Tintoretto**'s *St George and the Dragon* (Room 7) is curious because it makes the damsel in distress the main subject of the painting. The work is bathed in an ethereal light beaming down from the heavens, while the valiant George barely gets a look-in.

North Wing (1600–1700)

Room 15 neatly compares two idealized harbour scenes, **Claude Lorrain**'s *Embarkation of the Queen of Sheba* and **Turner**'s much later Lorrain-influenced *Dido Building Carthage*. There is more Lorrain (whom the National refers to as Claude) in Room 19, including his dreamy *Enchanted Castle*. On the way there are two rare **Vermeers** in Room 16, *Woman Standing at a Virginal* and *Woman Sitting at a Virginal*. Room 20 contains **Poussin**'s *Adoration of the Golden Calf*, a magnificently decadent study of the power of Mammon.

Some of the very best of **Rubens** is in Room 29, including two versions of the *Judgement of Paris*. The later one (1630) is simpler, more pastoral and more satisfying to the modern eye than the earlier one, all rosy-cheeked buttocks and over-voluptuous thighs. In *The Rape of the Sabine Women*, the sensuality of the painting takes on a sinister and frightening quality. *Samson and Delilah* depicts the moment of the Biblical strong man's arrest as he lies draped over Delilah's suggestively exposed midriff. You'd have to be a sucker to believe it was just a haircut that made him so exhausted.

Room 23 is devoted to **Rembrandt**, notably two of his expressive self-portraits. The first, done when he was 34, is self-assured and vigorous, while the second, painted in the last year of his life, is darker and more reflective. Rembrandt beautifully captures the intimacy of the moment in his near-monochrome *Women Bathing in a Stream*, while in *Belshazzar's Feast* he shows his talent for depicting sheer drama. The look of astonishment on Belshazzar's face is at once shocking and almost funny. The words written on the wall in Hebrew read *Mene mene tekel upharsin* ('You have been weighed in the balance and found wanting'). One of Rembrandt's contemporaries, **Gerrit van Honthorst**, painted an equally dramatic (and gruesome) picture of the *Martyrdom of St Sebastian* by arrows, which is in room 24.

Velázquez's *Rokeby Venus* in Room 30 was Spain's first nude, although it bows to contemporary sensibilities by portraying the subject with her back to the viewer. The mirror reflecting her face is a joke on the part of the artist: according to the angle at which it is held, what we should be seeing is her voluminous bust.

In Room 31, we come to a series of state portraits, many of them commissioned by Charles I: a display that highlights much of the Stuarts' pomp and self-satisfaction. The best painting is probably **Van Dyck**'s *Equestrian Portrait of Charles I*, the classic encapsulation of a vainglorious monarch convinced that nothing can touch him. The picture loses some of its power when you remember that in life Charles measured less than 5 feet in his stockinged feet. It was, of course, painted only a few years before the Civil War and Charles's death on the scaffold. Room 32 is most notable for **Caravaggio**'s *Salome Receiving the Head of John the Baptist*, a moody piece contrasting the deep suffering etched on the severed head of John and the near total indifference of a frowning Salome.

East Wing (1700–1900)

Venice dominates Room 38, notably in the vast panoramas of **Canaletto**'s two set-pieces, *The Basin of San Marco on Ascension Day* and *Regatta on the Grand Canal*. Both depict major city festivals, the former the marriage of Venice and the Sea at which the Doge ritually tosses a golden ring into the Adriatic. The room also contains a handful of

Guardis, whose softer-edged versions of the floating city contrast with Canaletto's geometric precision.

Room 34 is devoted to **Turner**, the ultimate English Romantic painter, whose dramatic watercolours of shipwrecks and sunsets experiment boldly with light and colour. The guides all push you towards *The Fighting Téméraire*, a sumptuous tribute to a Nelson-era man-of-war being dragged out to its watery grave by a modern steamer. But the most innovative work here is arguably *Rain, Steam and Speed*, a delicate contrast of the industrial and natural worlds. The Great Western Railway express hurtles straight towards the viewer, the steam from its engine mingling with the colours of the morning mist and the murky River Thames at Maidenhead. Critics who first saw the picture in the 1840s thought it was prepos-terous; in fact it was a good three or four decades ahead of its time, anticipating the light and colour experiments of the Impressionists.

English painting dominates the following rooms, from **Gainsborough**, **Reynolds** and **Hogarth** (don't miss his brilliant satirical series on upper-class life, *Marriage à la Mode*) to the idyllic country scenes of **John Constable**, including *Salisbury Cathedral from the Meadows* and *The Hay Wain*. There is some interesting non-English Romantic painting here too, notably **Paul Delaroche**'s *Execution of Lady Jane Grey* (Room 41) and **Caspar David Friedrich**'s magnificently lit picture of a cripple praying in the snow, *Winter Landscape* (Room 42).

Rooms 43–5 are devoted to the Impressionists and their followers. Many of the pictures are so famous they need no introduction – **Van Gogh**'s *Chair*, **Seurat**'s *Bathers at Asnières*, **Cézanne**'s *Les Grandes Baigneuses* and views of Mont Ste-Victoire, **Monet**'s *Water Lilies* series, **Henri Rousseau**'s *Tropical Storm with Tiger*. More unusual are Monet's *Gare St-Lazare*, a study of Paris at its industrial zenith, and his *Thames from Westminster*, painted in 1871 when the Victoria Embankment with its (then) wooden piers had just opened. No English-born painter has ever captured the moody, foggy atmosphere of industrial London better than Monet. Also don't miss **Degas**'s *Miss La La* for its dramatically angled glimpse of a trapeze artist at the Cirque Fernando, clenching the rope between her teeth.

The turn of the 20th century is just about where the National Gallery leaves off and Tate Modern (at Bankside, across the Thames; see p.205) takes over.

The National Portrait Gallery T10

*St Martin's Place, t (020) 7306 0055, recorded information t (020) 7312 2463, w www.npg .org.uk; **tube** Charing Cross, Leicester Square, Embankment; wheelchair accessible from Orange St entrance. **Open** Mon–Wed, Sat and Sun 10am–6pm, Thurs and Fri 10am–9pm; closed 1 Jan, Good Friday, May Day and 24–26 Dec; **adm** free, charges for some special exhibitions. Basement **café** and a roof **restaurant**.*

This gallery is unique, and a true oddity. Unique, because no other Western country has ever assembled a similar collection of portraits of the glorious names populating its history. Odd, because the kings, generals, ministers, pioneers, inventors and artists on display here have not been chosen according to the quality of the painting – in fact, some of it is downright lousy. They are here because the Victorian aristocrats who originally founded the gallery believed that it would serve as a stern kind of history lesson.

The gallery is a forceful argument for Thomas Carlyle's view that the history of the world is 'but the biography of great men' (and occasionally great women), and that the proper duty of the lower orders is to shut up and be grateful. Of course, this was a highly convenient notion at a time when the aristocratic ruling order was under threat from both the industrial middle classes and the disgruntled urban poor, and spoke volumes about the insecurity of the establishment. Don't be too surprised, then, to find that in here you will see no revolutionaries, few

union leaders, few true dissidents; nobody, in fact, who might be deemed out of place at a society dinner party. Well, almost nobody. In the 20th-century galleries there is a portrait of Arthur Scargill, Marxist miners' leader, erstwhile Thatcher-baiter and, to judge by his blow-dried blond quiff, aspiring dictator of some eccentric Balkan mini-state.

Even with its £12 million millennium extension and development, the gallery has far more pictures than space: only a fraction of the 9,000 portraits are shown in rotation over the six small floors. On the ground floor, the new IT Gallery gives access to the whole collection so you can get a glimpse of what you're missing as well as gaining greater insight into what you're about to see.

The Collection

Chronologically, the collection starts at the top with the new environmentally controlled Tudor Gallery, working its way down towards the present day, with a magnificent 20th-century wing which was designed by Piers Gough in 1995. The best paintings, technically speaking, are probably Holbein's vividly life-like versions of **Henrys VII and VIII** and **Sir Thomas More**. There are also magnificent renditions of the 19th-century Prime Ministers **Disraeli** and **Gladstone** by Millais, self-portraits by **Hogarth** and **Reynolds**, a distinctly ambivalent **Churchill** by Walter Sickert (all yellows and greens) and a Cubist **T.S. Eliot** by Jacob Epstein. Some of the portraits are so reverent as to be absurd. **Lawrence of Arabia** appears in stone effigy like some medieval king imbued with divine powers. Jacques-Emile Blanche's **James Joyce** looks ludicrously respectable in a smart suit in front of an orderly writing desk. You suspect he's dying to light that cigarette dangling between his fingers.

The most entertaining pictures, though, are the modern royals on the first floor, largely because they are pretty awful. Alison Watt's **Queen Mother** looks like a bag lady who has stumbled into the wrong person's living room. **The Queen**, draped in the robes of the Order of the British Empire, is given an air of grandeur and benign severity that she simply does not possess in real life. The artist, Pietro Annigoni, said he did not want to paint her as a film star, but a film star is exactly what she looks like: she could be auditioning for Joan Crawford's role in *Johnny Guitar*. Or maybe she's just trying to look tough for **Margaret Thatcher**, a Prime Minister she never made much secret of disliking, whose portrait lurks on the staircase round the corner. In Rodrigo Moynihan's hands, Thatcher is no longer the bossy, strident nanny of the nation. He casts her in flattering soft-focus; she looks as if she couldn't hurt a fly.

St Martin-in-the-Fields T10

Trafalgar Square, t (020) 7930 0089, w www.stmartin-in-the-fields.org; tube Charing Cross, Leicester Square, Embankment; wheelchair accessible. Open Mon–Sat 10am–8pm, Sun noon–6pm. Lunchtime recitals Mon, Tues and Fri at 1.05pm; free. Crypt café, gallery, shop and brass-rubbing centre, t (020) 7930 9306; open Mon–Sat 10am–6pm, Sun noon–6pm. Market (beside the church) held daily 10am–5.30pm.

The church of St Martin-in-the-Fields is the oldest building on Trafalgar Square, and the only one truly to benefit from the exposure the square affords; its curious combination of Greek temple façade and Baroque steeple quickly catches the eye, even if the mix is a little awkward. James Gibbs's design, built over four years from 1722 to 1726 to replace a decaying 16th-century original, became popular with the royal family, which had several babies christened here. Its **churchyard**, now a daytime souvenir and trinkets market, contains the graves of Charles II's mistress Nell Gwynne and the 18th-century painters Reynolds and Hogarth. In more recent times the church has become known for its concerts and resident orchestra, the Academy of St Martin-in-the-Fields, which celebrated its 40th anniversary at the end of 1999.

The portico's cold stone Corinthian columns lead to a rather bland interior enlivened only by some kitschy plaster cherubs on the ceiling. Look out for the **alabaster font**, a relic of the original medieval church, and the ornate 19th-century oak **pulpit** with its delicately twisted banister rail. The greatest curiosity is the vaulted **brick crypt**, used after the First World War to shelter homeless soldiers returning from the front and again during the Blitz as an air-raid shelter. St Martin's celebrated vicar Dick Sheppard held the first broadcast service in Britain here in 1924.

Charing Cross U11

Tube Charing Cross, Embankment.

This spot entered the history books in 1293 when Edward I built Charing Cross as a memorial to his late queen, Eleanor of Castile. Edward erected 12 crosses, one at each place where her funeral cortège had stopped on its way to Westminster Abbey. Charing Cross was the last stop. The name is probably derived from the Anglo-Saxon word *cerr* meaning a bend in the river. You can see a 19th-century replica of the original Caen **stone cross** in the forecourt of Charing Cross station, just off the Strand. The badly decayed original, which used to stand at the top of what is now Northumberland Av, was pulled down in 1647 and put to practical use, both to fashion knife-handles and to renovate paving stones in Whitehall. A bronze equestrian **statue of Charles I** was commissioned from the French sculptor Hubert Le Sueur to take the place of the cross, but could not immediately be erected because of the outbreak of the Civil War. The statue was finally erected, atop a pedestral carved by Grinling Gibbons, in 1675.

In the 18th century, Charing Cross developed into a popular meeting spot for both the rich in their sedan chairs and the poor who frequented the raucous nearby taverns; Dr Johnson famously remarked that 'the full tide of human existence' appeared to gather there. The main attractions were the public pillories – branding, nose-splitting and ear-lopping – that took place beneath Charles's haughty figure. In the Victorian era, these gave way to a railway station, on top of which a striking giant glasshouse known as **Embankment Place**, designed by Terry Farell, was built in 1991.

St Martin's Lane T10

The black strip at the bottom of the street signs says that this is London's theatreland. The theatres along St Martin's Lane – the Albery and Duke of York's as well as the Coliseum – all date from the start of the 20th century, and so were among the last great playhouses to be built in London. But as early as the 18th century the street was attracting such artistic residents as Joshua Reynolds, first president of the Royal Academy, and Thomas Chippendale, the furniture-maker. Back then this was still a rough neighbourhood: there was a whipping post and a small prison opposite St Martin-in-the-Fields, where the constables regularly got drunk and mistreated their charges. Nowadays it's far more civilized, with numerous rather touristy restaurants and cafés.

The Coliseum T10

St Martin's Lane, **t** *(020) 7632 8300,* **w** *www.eno.org (accepts online bookings);* **tube** *Charing Cross, Leicester Square, Embankment; wheelchair accessible. Box office in foyer (24-hour booking line* **t** *(020) 7632 8300)* **open** *Mon–Sat 10am–8pm.*

Home to the English National Opera and built in 1904, this was the first theatre in England with a revolving stage. The globe on the roof used to revolve too, until it was deemed a hazard by Westminster City Council. The ENO recently had a narrow escape from losing its precious home at the Coliseum and was threatened with having to leap into an uncomfortable house-share with the Royal Opera, but, thanks to some hefty funding, all is well for the foreseeable future.

LEICESTER SQUARE

Tube *Leicester Square, Piccadilly Circus.*

Towards the end of the 19th century, Leicester Square was the place to be seen of an evening, especially for middle-class men looking to let their hair down and flirt with 'unrespectable' women. Attractions included the gaudily decorated Alhambra Music Hall (now replaced by the Art Deco **Odeon Cinema**), Turkish baths, oyster rooms and dance halls. Nowadays the square is a pale shadow of its former self, a characterless jumble of first-run cinemas and hamburger joints. All the fine buildings of the past, including the 17th-century Leicester House which gave its name to the square, are long gone. The Blitz was largely responsible for destroying the buildings and spirit of the place. On 8 March 1941, several high-explosive bombs crashed into the Rialto Cinema and caused the roof of the Café de Paris nightclub to cave in. Thirty-four people were killed, including the trumpeter Ken 'Snake-eyes' Johnson, whose band was playing at the time. To make matters more distasteful, several people, including members of the fire brigade, were caught stealing rings and jewellery from the dead and dying.

Leicester Square has nowadays recovered some of its happy-go-lucky spirit; the square has been pedestrianized and the central garden tidied up. Come here at more or less any time of the day or night and you will find a rough and ready crowd of cinema-goers, student tourists, buskers, street performers, portrait-painters and pickpockets. For the dedicated sightseer, however, the only historical curiosity is a bronze **statue of Charlie Chaplin** with his bowler hat and walking stick, but it is marred by the trite dedication: 'The comic genius who gave pleasure to so many.'

PICCADILLY CIRCUS

Tube Piccadilly Circus, Leicester Square.

The car horns and neon advertising hoardings of Piccadilly Circus have become synonymous with London, along with red double-decker buses and the Queen. Quite why is something of a mystery: the dominant smell of this busy, awkwardly shaped road junction is of traffic fumes and stale chips. For some inexplicable reason, hordes of European teenagers spend afternoons trudging across Piccadilly Circus's crowded traffic islands, from Burger King to the Trocadero Centre to Tower Records, in search of the ultimate cheap thrill. It's a bit like hanging around McDonald's on the Champs-Elysées and saying you've seen Paris.

Eros R10

The best-known feature attraction of Piccadilly Circus is the Eros statue at its centre, a winged aluminium figure fashioned by Sir Alfred Gilbert in memory of the Victorian philanthropist Lord Shaftesbury and unveiled in 1893. Londoners have developed a strange fondness for this statue, an audacious and rather un-British experiment in homoerotic art – strange because it was designed without a shred of enthusiasm, detested by the critics who first saw it and has been plagued ever since by corrosion and overzealous tourists who like to clamber all over it. The figure is not in fact supposed to be Eros, god of love: Gilbert intended it to be an Angel of Christian Charity, in memory of Lord Shaftesbury's work with destitute children. The identity problem (not surprising, given the statue's state of undress and the bow in its right hand) was only one of several sources of anguish for Gilbert. He was reluctant to embark on the project in the first place, describing Piccadilly Circus as 'an impossible site on which to place any outcome of the human brain except possibly an underground lavatory'. Then, having accepted the commission, he tried in vain to have the statue mounted atop a wide basin lapped by gushing fountains. He was overruled by his masters, the Shaftesbury Memorial Committee, which shuddered at the thought of the public getting splashed. So angry was Gilbert at this and other setbacks that he refused to attend the official unveiling by the Duke of Westminster.

The Trocadero R–S10

1 Piccadilly Circus, t (020) 7434 0030, w www.troc.co.uk; tube Piccadilly Circus, Leicester Square; wheelchair accessible. Open daily 10am–midnight; adm free but separate charges for each attraction.

It would be no great loss to miss out on this, arguably the city's brashest, least salubrious attraction. Take a quick look and gasp at the mesmerising atrociousness of it all – the overpriced theme-u-rants (Planet Hollywood and the Thunderdome Café), the screaming kids and intimidating teenagers. Amidst the horrors, there are some thrilling and expensive virtual-reality racing and flight simulators, a dodgem ride (also thrilling and expensive), a ten-pin bowling alley, a seven-screen multiplex and a 3D IMAX cinema. If these are your idea of fun, go ahead. If not, you should be able to see the whole place and be out again in about 20 seconds.

Buckingham Palace and the Royal Parks

Buckingham Palace and the Royal Parks

Buckingham Palace, nestled comfortably in the centre of green parkland, is the heart of Royal London. Creamy mansions, ceremonial avenues and leafy parks provide a grand backdrop to the pomp and circumstance which accompanies any royal event. Oddly, the least flamboyant building of all is Buckingham Palace, which began as a modest little mansion and doesn't seem quite able to shake off its origins, despite countless extra wings and flounces. The French, in particular, with the great palaces of Versailles and Fontainebleau as comparison, come away a touch disappointed, but the Great British Public have taken Buck House to their hearts since Queen Victoria made it the nerve centre of the monarchy over a century ago.

The approach to the Palace is the grand sweep of the Mall, which fringes St James's Park, one of London's dreamiest, filled with the squawking of ducks and pelicans, and the perfect spot to pitch a deckchair.

1 Lunch

ICA Café, *ICA, The Mall,* **t** *(020) 7930 8619;* **tube** *Charing Cross.* **Open** *for food Mon noon–4 and 6–10, Tues–Sat noon–4 and 6–11, Sun noon–4pm.* **Inexpensive**. You have to pay the £1.50 day membership fee to get in, but it's worth it. The food is (almost always) good and attractively presented. It's much quieter at lunchtimes – at night it can overrun with wannabe Brit Packers.

2 Drinks

Tiles Wine Bar, *36 Buckingham Palace Rd,* **t** *(020) 7834 7761;* **tube** *Victoria.* **Open** *pub hours.* A welcoming wine bar (the decorative floor tiles give the place its name) with comfy sofas.

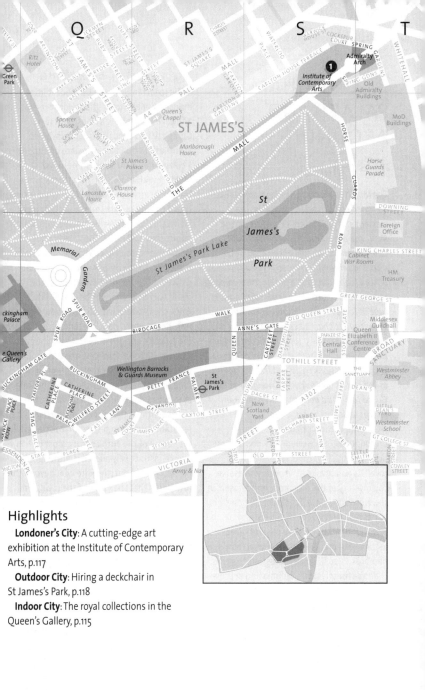

Highlights

Londoner's City: A cutting-edge art exhibition at the Institute of Contemporary Arts, p.117

Outdoor City: Hiring a deckchair in St James's Park, p.118

Indoor City: The royal collections in the Queen's Gallery, p.115

BUCKINGHAM PALACE AND AROUND

The Palace P13

The Mall (the elegant tent-like ticket office, designed by Michael Hopkins, is at the western end of St James's Park just off the Mall, and the entrance is at Ambassadors' Court on the south side of the building), recorded information t (020) 7799 2331, ticket office t (020) 7321 2233, e buckinghampalace@royalcollection.org.uk, w www.royal.gov.uk; tube St James's Park, Victoria, Hyde Park Corner; wheelchair accessible. Open Aug and Sept daily 9.30am–5.30pm, last adm 4.15pm; ticket office open 9am–4pm; adm adults £11.50, concessions £9.50, children £6. Toilets at the end of the tour only. Changing of the Guard May–Aug daily 11.30am, Sept–April alternate days 11.30am.

On 7 August 1993, miracle of miracles, Buckingham Palace opened its doors to the public for the first time. For generations, royalists had invoked the need to preserve the mystery of the monarchy and refused, in the words of Walter Bagehot, to 'let daylight in upon its magic'. But by the early 1990s the British monarchy was in a crisis of quite astonishing proportions. Two royal marriages had broken up in quick succession, Princess Diana's struggles with bulimia and depression had been made glaringly public, Prince Charles had allegedly been taped telling his mistress on the telephone how he fantasized about being her tampon and, to top it all, half of Windsor Castle had burnt down. Little knowing the revelations and tragedies that were still to come, the Queen dubbed 1992, the year of most of these misfortunes, her 'annus horribilis'. To rally public opinion behind the monarchy, she made two unprecedented concessions. The first was to agree to pay income tax for the first time (although, as nobody knows quite how much the Queen earns, it is not clear just how

The Making of 'Buck House'

The royal family bought a modest little mansion called Buckingham House in 1702, and called it the King's House, but it was George IV (1820–30) who commissioned John Nash to build a new palace on the site – a crazy scheme for a vast three-sided building with more than 600 rooms, and a triumphal arch (the Marble Arch which now sits at the top of Park Lane) at its entrance. When the Duke of Wellington became Prime Minister in 1828 he cut the weekly budget from £10,000 to £2,500, and the project was truncated, to be completed by the unimaginative master builder Edward Blore. The result was a total mess. The drains didn't work, the lavatories stank, bells would not ring, doors would not close, and several of the palace's 1,000 windows would not open.

Queen Victoria described it as a 'disgrace to the country', but nevertheless grew quite fond of the place, and by the end of her reign in 1901 had made Buckingham Palace the nerve-centre of the modern monarchy. Its reputation went from strength to strength in the course of the 20th century. Most British people instinctively adored it, although they probably could not say quite why, beyond the firm belief that the home of the royal family must inevitably be tinged with magic.

much she is prepared to plough back into the Exchequer). The second was to unveil some of the mysteries of Buckingham Palace for two months of the year.

So what exactly is all the fuss about? What do you get to see? Certainly not a glimpse of the 'working palace' constantly alluded to by the Queen's public-relations hacks. The tour takes in just 18 of Buckingham Palace's 661 rooms, and even these feel as though they have been stripped down to the bare minimum to ensure they are not sullied by the savage hordes. The usual carpets are rolled away each summer and replaced with industrial-strength red Axminster rugs that clash awkwardly with the fake marble columns, the greens, pinks and blues of the flock wallpapers, and the gold and cream ornamental ceilings. The place feels hollow and spookily empty; in fact it is hard to imagine that anybody lives or works in such soulless surroundings. As for the personal touch, there is not so much as a photograph of the royal family on the whole tour, let alone a flesh-and-blood prince or princess to welcome the guests. As one American tourist commented, 'At least Mickey Mouse is always present in his Disneyland.'

The Tour

The guide that follows only mentions the highlights, and not necessarily in the order in which you will encounter them. There is no free ground plan, but the wardens are excep-tionally helpful and friendly.

The tour route leads you to the inner court-yard and thence to the back part of the palace overlooking the gardens. The **Grand Staircase**, with its elegant wrought-iron banister, leads up to the first of the state rooms, the Green Drawing Room.

The effect sought by Nash was above all a theatrical one. All these rooms are filled with ostentatious chandeliers, somewhat chintzy furniture and ornate gilt and painted plaster ceilings. Much of the decoration has been imported from the fire-damaged rooms of Windsor Castle; there are, however, some impressive pieces giving a hint of the flam-boyant tastes of George IV, who acquired most of the palace's treasures. In the **Green Drawing Room**, for example, there is a deli-cate, beautifully painted Chelsea pot-pourri vase depicting courtly figures in a rustic setting; notice the Regency-era chandelier featuring three weeping women. The **Blue Drawing Room** was originally red and has a handsome 18th-century marble astronomical clock. The **White Drawing Room** contains a vast mirror which swings open to reveal a hidden cabinet. According to the guards, Elton John played the grand piano in the **Music Room**, and Princess Diana practised tap-dancing on the slippery-looking floor.

The lower floor of the tour holds few new surprises, although you can have some fun in the 200ft **Marble Hall** with its yards of sculp-ture – look out for Canova's sensuous *Mars*

and Venus, which George IV commissioned from Napoleon's pet artist after the British victory at Waterloo. The **Throne Room** is an almost laughable exercise in kitsch, with his'n'hers thrones in pink and yellow adorned with the initials EIIR for Elizabeth and P for Philip. On the walls is a plaster frieze, adorned with scenes from the Wars of the Roses, that only adds to the artificial atmosphere. The incidental decoration does not really improve as the tour goes on, although there are some nice French clocks in the **State Dining Room** and some fine if disconcerting Gobelins tapestries depicting famous rapes (Proserpine and Europa) on the **Ministers' Staircase**.

The real highlight is the 155ft-long **Picture Gallery**, which is crammed from floor to ceiling with the cream of the royal collection of some 10,000 paintings. The walls are a bit crowded for comfort, but the gems stand out easily enough: Van Dyck's idealized portraits of Charles I; Rembrandt's *Lady with a Fan*, *Agatha Bas* and *The Shipbuilder and His Wife*; landscapes by Ruysdael, Poussin and Claude Lorrain; portraits by Frans Hals; Rubens' underwhelming *St George and the Dragon*; Albert Cuyp's *Landscape with a Negro Page* – and much more besides. Apart from Charles I, the only royal to receive pictorial justice in Buckingham Palace is Victoria, whose family is cosily captured in Franz Winterhalter's 1846 portrait in the **East Gallery** (the room after the Picture Gallery).

The Queen's Gallery P14

Buckingham Palace, Buckingham Gate, t (020) 7799 2331 (recorded information), e information@royalcollection.org.uk, w www.the-royal-collection.org.uk; tube St James's Park, Victoria, Hyde Park Corner; wheelchair accessible. Open daily 10am–5.30pm, last adm 4.30pm; adm adults £6.50, 5–17s £3, under-5s free. Booking recommended.

At the time of writing, the architectural firm John Simpson and Co. had just completed a £20 million expansion and renovation of the gallery. It now has a

Keeping the Anachronism Alive: The Royal Family

As well as being the year of the Queen's Golden Jubilee, 2002 saw the end of an era for the royal family: the death of the Queen Mother. Following years of scandal, tragedy and disaster for the royals, many people saw the old lady's death as the beginning of the end for the monarchy. Born during the reign of Queen Victoria, she was considered by many to be a true matriarchal figurehead and last representative of old-fashioned family values. With one of the most popular and respected members of the family gone, there is certainly one less barrier to changes in the royal lifestyle.

The death was followed by a period of official national mourning, but the public reaction was in fact muted: how could most young people feel saddened by the passing away in her sleep of a lady of 101? The BBC was criticised for its fairly matter-of-fact treatment of the death, but responded that in light of a changed public mood they had decided to make the coverage less extensive than previously planned.

The truth is, the British monarchy now has to do what it has done ever since the country's unhappy experiment with republicanism in the 17th century: search for ways to adapt and survive even though its discernible usefulness has long since been exhausted. The last few years have seen a profound crisis, no question, but such episodes are by no means unprecedented. One only has to think of Queen Victoria sulking away in Balmoral after the death of her husband Prince Albert; she all but abandoned her constitutional duties and, horror of horrors, the country began to realise that it didn't make much difference.

What saved the monarchy on that occasion was a complete image overhaul. One of Victoria's most astute subjects, the political philosopher Walter Bagehot, wrote a kind of users' manual for royalty called *The English Constitution*. Bagehot decided the royal family's chief role should be not government, but entertainment; the monarchy, he said, should 'commonly be hidden like a mystery, and sometimes paraded like a pageant'. In other words, too much publicity would ruin its magic, while too little would whittle it away. The royal family didn't have much pageantry to speak of at the time, so a great slew of it had to be invented. In 1877 Victoria

striking new entrance, three times more display space, education suites and a multimedia room. To mark the Queen's Golden Jubilee, the inaugural exhibition is called 'Royal Treasures: A Golden Jubilee Celebration' and shows 450 pieces – paintings, furniture, jewellery, books – covering five centuries of collecting. The exhibition will close on 13 January 2003.

Royal Mews P14

Buckingham Palace Rd, ticket office **t** *(020) 7321 2233,* **w** *www.royal.gov.uk;* **tube** *St James's Park, Victoria, Hyde Park Corner; wheelchair accessible.* **Open** *May–Sept 11am–3.30pm, last adm 3.15pm;* **adm** *adults £4.30, concessions £3.30, children £2.10.*

This is the royal equivalent of the Batcave, where the blue-blooded celebs undergo a mysterious transformation before bursting out into the public arena through the grand entrance arch in their ceremonial clothes and outrageous vehicles. You'll find rows of gaudily painted wagons, a fine 18th-century Riding House by William Chambers, and stables for the thoroughbreds. You can take a close look at the Gold State Coach commissioned by George III for coronation ceremonies; Queen Victoria's Irish Coach used for the State Opening of Parliament; the Glass State Coach built in 1910 for royal weddings; and many more.

Back in the 18th century, royal coaches were little different from the carriages owned by a hundred wealthy men around London; it was not until the age of the automobile that they really made the royal family stand out from the crowd. Nowadays they are an essential part of the royal mythology.

was named Empress of India in a lavish but thoroughly meaningless ceremony; in 1887 her Golden Jubilee was marked with street parties and parades, and in 1897 her Diamond Jubilee was celebrated in similar vein. It all worked like a dream.

The illusion held during the Second World War, when George VI and the late Queen Mother boosted national morale during the Blitz with their appearances at bomb sites. The illusion persisted, too, for the first 40-odd years of Queen Elizabeth's reign. Her televised coronation in 1953 was the most lavish – and most phoney – ever, featuring among other things a group of seven 'state' coaches rented from a film production company. She pulled off the public relations coup of the century by persuading the world that Charles loved the fragile, virginal Lady Diana Spencer. And she spun a careful web of mystique around her many state visits around the world. She never travels without her own tea set, or her own toilet seat.

The first bubble to burst was the myth of the Happy Family, and the woman who punctured it was Princess Diana. Recruited to provide fresh blood, Diana succeeded triumphantly in renewing the image of the royals, but for reasons that nobody – not even she – could have imagined on her wedding day. In exchange for the privilege of marrying into the House of Windsor, she was expected to stand dutifully by her husband's side. As time went by and her public opinion ratings went up, she found the modern monarchy ever more unbearable. At last she decided to go into print and onto TV, revealing all those notorious tales of her bulimia and of Charles's long-standing love affair with Camilla Parker Bowles. But maybe Diana showed the House of Windsor the way to move forward. The more she revealed of her personal misery, the more the public loved her. The more she shunned the military establishment and campaigned to abolish anti-personnel landmines, the more she increased her profile worldwide.

Despite the deaths of Princess Margaret and the Queen Mother, at the time of writing plans were going ahead to celebrate the Golden Jubilee, marking it, just like Queen Victoria's Jubilee, with street parties. But as a sign of recognising the public's tastes, there was also to be a national holiday, a pop concert featuring the likes of Elton John, and a 'Notting Hill-style' Carnival.

ST JAMES'S PARK AND THE MALL

The Mall Q13–T11

Admiralty Arch T11
Tube Charing Cross.

A sense of place, and occasion, is immediately invoked by Admiralty Arch, the Mall's grand concave triple-arched entrance from Trafalgar Square. This is the gateway to St James's and the start of the long straight drive along The Mall up to Buckingham Palace. The stone arch, designed by Aston Webb in 1910 as part of an architectural ensemble in memory of Queen Victoria (as stated in the Latin inscription that runs across the top), is one of the few monumental buildings from the Edwardian era in London. Traffic passes through the two side-gates and the larger central gate is opened only for royal processions and state visits.

Institute of Contemporary Arts S11
12 The Mall, box office t (020) 7930 3647, w www.ica.org.uk; tube Charing Cross; wheelchair accessible. Open Mon noon–11pm, Tues–Sat noon–1am, Sun noon–11.30pm; closed all Christmas and public hols; day membership Mon–Fri £1.50 (concessions £1), Sat and Sun £2.50 (concessions £1.50) or £1.50 (concessions £1) when there are no exhibitions. Café (doubles as a very popular bar – a favourite because of its late opening hours) and a small trendy art bookshop.

Perhaps surprisingly given the setting, in John Nash's 1833 Carlton House Terrace (built on the site of George IV's short-lived Carlton House, which he got bored with and had pulled down), the ICA is a mecca for the 'Britpack' school of art, the pre-post-avant-garde and the obscure in all areas of the arts. Come here for lectures on the finer points of Post-structuralism seen through the eyes of a reconstructed Lacanian, or the latest in performance art dancing, or for films with titles like *Life is Cheap but Toilet Paper is Expensive*.

At the top of the bank of steps next to the ICA building, leading to Pall Mall (*see* p.123), is a 126ft **column** commemorating Frederick, the (Grand Old) Duke of York, for whom Lancaster House was built.

St James's Park Q13–S12

Tube St James's Park, Charing Cross, Westminster.

St James's explains much about the spirit of the neighbourhood. It seems perfectly spruce nowadays, even rather romantic in a restrained sort of way, with its tree-lined pond and proliferation of city wildlife; but its elegance is a cunning artifice created to overcome centuries of turbulence and squalor. Back in the early 12th century, Queen Matilda founded a women's leper colony on the site of what is now St James's Palace. The park was then a marshy field where the lepers would feed their hogs. By the mid-15th century leprosy had subsided and the hospital was turned into a special kind of nunnery – special because its young occupants were known for administering to the flesh rather than the spirits of the eminent men who called on them. These so-called *bordels du roi* lasted barely more than 50 years and were closed by Henry VIII, who built St James's Palace in their place and drained the marsh to create a nursery for his deer. The first formal gardens were laid out under James I, who installed, among other things, an aviary (hence the name of the street on the south side, Birdcage Walk) and a menagerie of wild beasts including two crocodiles. The setting was romantic enough for Charles II to use it as a rendezvous with his mistress, Nell Gwynne; unfortunately it also attracted upper-class hooligans in search of both trouble and rumpy-pumpy with the local prostitutes.

It was only under George IV that the park developed its present dignity. George land-scaped the lake as we see it today and added gas lighting to deter the ladies of the night. The sex-crazed aristocrat gave way to an altogether gentler breed, the birdwatcher, as St James's filled with more than 30 ornithological species. Look out for the pelicans, ducks, geese and gulls which have made the lake their home.

Guards Museum, Wellington Barracks Q–R14

Birdcage Walk, t (020) 7414 3428; tube St James's Park; wheelchair accessible. Open daily 10am–4pm; closed 1 Jan, 25 Dec; adm adults £2, concessions £1, childen free.

To underline the fact that the royal Guards regiments are not simply decorative, the exhibits in this museum tell the story of their role in military campaigns from Waterloo onwards. There are a few surprises among the uniforms and weaponry, including a vicious device used to brand deserters, and Field Marshal Monty's picnic basket, used while he was on campaign in Italy.

Nearby, **St James's Park Tube Station** has sculptures by Epstein and reliefs by Eric Gill and Henry Moore.

GREEN PARK

Tube Green Park, Hyde Park Corner.

This pleasant expanse of greenery has much the same history as St James's Park (*see* above). It was originally a burial ground for lepers from a nearby hospital, founded by Queen Matilda (and, in deference to the dead beneath it, has never been planted with flowers). Henry VIII made it a royal park, and Charles II laid out its walkways. Green Park, like its neighbour, was a haunt of trouble-makers and duellists in the 18th century.

St James's, Mayfair and Regent Street

St James's, Mayfair and Regent Street

St James's is a hushed, stately enclave of palaces and private clubs, traditional tailoring establishments, and the odd purveyor of fine food and wine to London's upper crust. It's the preserve of a fast-dying breed, the British upper class. St James's seeps into Mayfair, where the grand Georgian squares are lined with Rollers and Bentleys and money talks a little louder. This is where to shop for big designer labels, pick up a little something from Christie's or Sotheby's at auction, and then retire for cocktails. Regent St, a grand curve, is the most egalitarian of the area's thoroughfares, lined with all kinds of shops and arcades.

Highlights

Londoner's City: An exhibition at the Royal Academy of Arts, p.126

Literary City: Wandering around 'Clubland', immortalised in countless novels, p.124

Indoor City: Shopping in one of the covered arcades, such as the Burlington, p.127

1 Lunch

The Greenhouse, *27A Hay's Mews, t (020) 7499 3331; tube Green Park. Open Mon–Fri noon–2.30 and 5.30–11, Sat 5.30–11pm, Sun 5.30–9pm. Expensive.* For fantastic resurrections of stale old English recipes such as sponge pudding.

2 Tea and Cakes

The Ritz, *Piccadilly, t (020) 7493 8181; tube Green Park. Tea sittings daily at 1.30, 3.30 and 5pm; £27.* The fanciest, most indulgent tea in town. Book well in advance.

3 Drinks

Ye Grapes, *16 Shepherd's Market; tube Green Park. Open Mon–Sat 11am–11pm, Sun noon–10.30pm.* Attractive and popular pub tucked into the corner of the market square.

ST JAMES'S

St James's is the preserve of the establishment, not the vulgar money-making classes of the City but an older, rarefied pedigree that whiles away the hours in the drawing-rooms of fine houses and private clubs. It is a world that has been endlessly depicted on film and on television; incredibly, it still exists. Think of it as a zoo for that endangered species, the upper-class Englishman.

St James's Palace Q–R12

*At the bottom of St James's St, on Cleveland Row; **tube** Green Park. **Closed** to the public.*

For more than 300 years this was the official residence of England's kings and queens; indeed, foreign ambassadors are still formally accredited to the Court of St James even though they are received at Buckingham Palace. Henry VIII built St James's, endowing it with fine buildings (of which only the octagonal towers of the **gatehouse**, at the end of St James's St, survive). The palace became known as a raucous place of ill manners and debauchery, particularly under Queen Anne. Anne was well known for her unseemly appetite for food and drink and for her frequent bodily noises (inspiring Thomas D'Urfey to write his satirical poem 'The Fart', in which courtiers reluctantly accept responsibility for the stink caused by Her Majesty). Not surprisingly, the place soon came to be described as 'crazy, smoky and dirty', and George IV moved out into Carlton House (*see* 'The Institute of Contemporary Arts', p.117). A fire destroyed most of the original buildings in 1809; the rebuilt courtyards now house offices for members of the royal household.

Lancaster House Q12

*The Queen's Walk; **tube** Green Park. **Closed** to the public.*

This was destined to be the residence of Frederick, the bankrupt Grand Old Duke of York of the nursery rhyme (he marched his men up and down a hill). An architectural wrangle delayed the project too long, however, for the duke to live to see it. Robert Smirke, architect of the British Museum, was first hired for the job, then fired in favour of Benjamin Wyatt in 1825. The final result is an elegant three-storey rectangle in Bath stone with a tall Neoclassical portico. After the Duke of York's death it was never used by the royal family, but passed instead through a succession of aristocratic owners. It is now used for high-level conferences and was the scene of the agreement that secured independence for Rhodesia, subsequently known as Zimbabwe, in 1979.

Marlborough House R12

*Marlborough Rd; **tube** Green Park. **Rarely open** to the public.*

Queen Anne leased this part of the grounds of St James's Palace to her closest friend, Sarah, Duchess of Marlborough. The two fell out after the Duchess complained she had once been kept waiting 'like a Scotch lady with a petition'. They never spoke again. In the meantime, the Duchess asked the ageing Christopher Wren and his son to build Marlborough House, instructing them to use the red bricks that her husband had used as ballast in his warships returning from Holland. The house's heyday came under Victoria's heir Prince Edward and his wife Alexandra, who made it the epicentre of London society. Alexandra lived here after her husband died in 1910, and buried her three dogs, Muff, Tiny and Joss, in the garden. Today Marlborough House is the headquarters of the Commonwealth Secretariat.

The Queen's Chapel R12

*Marlborough Rd; **tube** Green Park. **Open** Easter–June for Sunday service, check times in person.*

The chapel was the first Neoclassical church in England, built by Inigo Jones in 1623 to celebrate the prospective marriage of the future Charles I and the Infanta of Spain, although as it turned out Charles married a French princess, Henrietta Maria, instead. It is extraordinarily simple, little more than a box livened up with the odd flourish of stucco; but it is graced with attractive furnishings, including a reredos carved by Grinling Gibbons and a painting of the *Deposition* by Annibale Carracci. Above all, it is uplifted by the light that pours in through the large windows above the altar. This is where both the Princess of Wales' and Queen Mother's coffins were laid in the run-up to their funerals.

Spencer House Q12

27 St James's Place (off St James's St), t (020) 7499 8620, w www.spencerhouse.co.uk; tube Green Park; house wheelchair accessible. Open Sun 10.30am–5.30pm; closed Jan and Aug; adm adults £6, concessions and children £5. Visit by guided tour only; tours begin at regular intervals and last an hour.

This gracious Palladian mansion was born in sorrow: its original backer, Henry Bromley, ran out of money and shot himself moments after reading his will over with his lawyer. The site was then taken over by the Spencer family (ancestors of Princess Diana), who hired a bevy of architects including John Vardy and Robert Adam to produce one of the finest private houses in London. Completed in 1766, Spencer House boasts magnificent parquet floors, ornate plaster ceilings and a welter of gilded statues and furniture. The highlight is Vardy's **Palm Room**, in which the pillars are decorated as gilt palm trees with fronds stretching over the tops of the arched window bays. James Stuart's **Painted Room** features classical murals, graceful chandeliers and a fine, highly polished wooden floor. Unfortunately, only eight rooms are open to the public.

Pall Mall R12–S11

Tube Piccadilly Circus, Green Park.

The street's curious name derives from an ancient Italian ball game called *palla a maglio*, literally ball and mallet, a form of croquet which entailed hitting a ball through metal hoops. The sport, which was known in England first by its French name, *paille maille*, then as pell mell, proved wildly popular on its introduction in the mid-16th century. Charles II liked it so much that he built this pall mall alley close by St James's Palace. In the early 18th century the ball game disappeared, but the street remained fashionable as a row of upper-crust shops and cafés. Café society in turn gave way to the club craze in the 19th century.

Starting at the eastern end, on Waterloo Place, you'll find the Institute of Directors and the Athenaeum. The **Institute of Directors** building is the older of the two, originally designed by Nash in 1827–8 to house the United Service Club. The exterior was given a facelift in the late 1850s to look more like the Athenaeum opposite; both now have Neoclassical friezes just below their roof awnings. The **Athenaeum**, designed by Decimus Burton, is one of the best Greek Revival buildings in London, its frieze inspired by the relief sculptures from the Parthenon housed in the British Museum. The club was known in the 19th century as the haunt of the intellectual elite, which explains the gilt statue of Athena, goddess of wisdom, above the entrance, and the Greek letters of Athena's name in the mosaic above the porch. The **Reform Club**, at Nos.104–5, is where Jules Verne's fictional hero Phineas Fogg made his wager and set out to travel around the world in 80 days.

Royal Opera Arcade S11

Between Pall Mall and King Charles II St; tube Piccadilly Circus.

This was London's earliest covered shopping street (1818), with Regency shop fronts designed by John Nash. The shops here still sell a full range of traditional hunting, shooting and fishing gear. The arcade derives its name from the pre-Covent Garden Royal Opera building, which burnt down in the 1860s and was replaced with the modern

Clubland

The club phenomenon speaks volumes about English class relations; it shows that in London the middle-class gentleman, at least at the height of the British Empire from about 1850 until the Second World War, sought his entertainment privately and in the company of his peers, while the lower orders remained safely in the street and his family stayed forlornly at home. Nowadays the phenomenon is more restricted – largely to former public schoolboys, Conservative Party members and the upper echelons of the armed forces – but still reflects the English predilection for keeping in with one's own.

Despite their exclusivity, clubs became popular because they were relatively cheap. One club aficionado wrote in 1853 that 'a man of moderate habits can dine more comfortably for three or four shillings (including half a pint of wine) than he could have dined for four to five times that amount at the coffee houses and hotels.' To the comfortable but not excessively rich businessman, the club atmosphere gave the feeling of acting and being treated like a lord in his mansion, with a library, smoking room and card room.

As London mushroomed in size in the mid-19th century and increasing numbers of the well-to-do moved out to the suburbs, the club also became a convenient 'home away from home' where a member could drop off his things and stay over for a modest rate. Of course a big attraction was the prospect of spending raucous nights with the boys without fear of intrusion by wife or children. Clubs did not exactly do much for Victorian family values.

The end of the Empire and the emancipation of domestic servants brought about a sharp decline in clubland. With staff no longer prepared to work for a pittance and endure all manner of abuse from members, the establishments could no longer make ends meet. Before the Second World War there were 120 clubs in London; now there are fewer than 40. Standards have risen and so have prices. Many have taken the previously unthinkable step of admitting women; even the arch-conservative Carlton Club broke its strict men-only code to welcome in Margaret Thatcher, which may have been a bad start. The atmosphere at the clubs remains rarefied, although some of the carefree indolence of the past has disappeared.

Her Majesty's Theatre on the corner of Haymarket and King Charles II St.

St James's Square R11

Tube *Piccadilly Circus, Green Park.*

This square was where St James's turned from a mere adjunct to the royal palaces into a fashionable residential district in its own right. Just before the Great Fire of 1666, Charles II granted a lease to Henry Jermyn, Earl of St Albans, charging him to build 'palaces fit for the dwelling of noblemen and persons of quality'. The result was to set the tone for nearly all of London's squares, creating a haven of privacy and seclusion with little resemblance to the more public urban spaces familiar in the rest of Europe. The **equestrian statue** in the middle is of William III; his horse has one hoof atop

the molehill which caused the king's fatal riding accident in 1702.

Nowadays there are no more private residences in the square's spacious, mainly Georgian houses; they have been replaced by a succession of clubs, eminent institutions and company offices. Notice, for example, the **East India, Devonshire, Sports and Public Schools Club** at No.16 (with large bay windows you can peer through for a glimpse of the toffs in the dining room); and in the northwest corner the **London Library**, a superb open-shelved literary and historical book collection founded by Thomas Carlyle in 1841. **No.4**, on the eastern side, served for a time as the headquarters of De Gaulle's Free French during the Second World War, while General Eisenhower directed the First Allied Army and planned the North African and Normandy campaigns from **Norfolk House** at

No.31. No.4 is the new home of the Naval and Military Club, fondly and now almost officially known as the In and Out club. These were the words which greeted you on the pillars either side of its old drive-in entrance on Piccadilly. The current single doorway is far less flamboyant but, true to tradition, the columns either side still bear the words 'In' and 'Out'.

No.5 was, until 1984, home to the Libyan Embassy. In April of that year one of the embassy staff shot and killed a police constable, Yvonne Fletcher, during an anti-Libyan demonstration in the square. There followed a siege, culminating in the severing of all diplomatic ties between London and Tripoli. Fletcher is commemorated by a plaque on the spot where she died.

Jermyn Street Q–R11

Tube Piccadilly Circus, Green Park.

Jermyn Street boasts some of the fanciest shopping in town. Royal and aristocratic patronage has showered down on it over the years, and the names of the establishments hark back to another era: Turnbull and Asser the shirtmakers; George Trumper, barber and perfumer; or Bates the hatter (the spectrum from flat caps to bowlers). The shop assistants more closely resemble manservants from the great aristocratic houses of the past than paid employees of ongoing business concerns. Leading off Jermyn St towards Piccadilly are two arcades lined with more purveyors of quality goods: first **Princes Arcade**, with its brown and white décor, and then, after Duke St, the higher-ceilinged **Piccadilly Arcade**.

PICCADILLY

St James Piccadilly R11

197 Piccadilly, t (020) 7734 4511, w www.st-james-piccadilly.org; tube Piccadilly Circus; wheelchair accessible. Open daily, with lunchtime recitals and evening concerts (call

ahead on t (020) 7381 0441 or email e sjp .concerts@virgin.net for details); craft market Wed–Sat 10am–6pm; antiques market Tues (for markets, call t (020) 7734 4511). Aroma café in the grounds open Mon–Sat 8am–7pm, Sun 10am–7pm.

St James's (1684) is an object lesson in effortless grace and charm. It is the only church that Christopher Wren built from scratch in London (the others were all renovations or rebuildings on medieval sites), and as such most clearly expresses his vision of the church as a place where the relationship between the priest and his congregation should be demystified. It's airy and spacious, with the altar and pulpit in full view and accessible to all. An elegant gilded **wooden gallery** with rounded corners runs around the western end, supported by Corinthian pillars in plaster adorned with intricate decorations. There are some beautiful **carvings** by Grinling Gibbons, notably on the limewood reredos behind the altar (fruit and nature motifs) and on the stone font (depictions of Christ and his apostles).

The exterior is a simple affair in brick and Portland stone. The uncomplicated but effective **spire** is a comparatively recent addition (1968), although it was designed by Wren; for nearly three centuries St James's was topped by a nondescript bellcote put together at a cut-price rate by one of Wren's carpenters.

Fortnum & Mason Q11

181 Piccadilly, t (020) 7734 8040, w www .fortnumandmason.co.uk; tube Piccadilly Circus, Green Park; wheelchair accessible. Open Mon–Sat 10am–6.30pm. There are four restaurants and tearooms, with sumptuous afternoon teas 3–5.45pm (£11.95).

Fortnum & Mason is the kind of luxury food shop that would cause the mouth of even the most suspicious French gourmet to water: wonderful potted meats, homemade breads, smoked fish and caviar, all beautifully packaged and served with fervent attention (at a price). Charles Fortnum was one of George III's footmen, and he and his friend

John Mason opened their first shop in St James's in the 1770s. The rest, as they say, is history. The briskest trade has traditionally been in tea, marmalade and potted Stilton cheese; gift packs of all of these are stored at the front of the shop (on the Piccadilly side).

The building itself is less alluring. Completed in 1925, its centrepiece is a **turquoise mermaid fountain** in rather dubious taste. One more recent addition is quite fun – the **clock** above the entrance (1964). As the hour strikes, articulated figures of Mr Fortnum and Mr Mason emerge from their boxes and bow to each other.

Royal Academy of Arts Q10

Burlington House, Piccadilly, t (020) 7300 8000, w www.royalacademy.org.uk; tube Piccadilly Circus, Green Park; wheelchair accessible. Open Sat–Thurs 10am–6pm, Fri 10am–10pm; closed Good Fri and 24–25 Dec; adm on special exhibitions (prices vary), permanent collection free. Café open Sat–Thurs 10am–5.30pm, Fri 10am–7.30pm; restaurant open daily 10am–5.30pm.

Burlington House, built in 1720 on the lines of Palladio's Palazzo Porta in Vicenza, houses the Royal Academy of Arts, one of London's most important exhibition venues, staging major retrospectives, the famed amateur (and pretty poor) Summer Exhibition, and more cutting-edge and controversial contemporary exhibitions. The RA also has a permanent collection with works from its prestigious members (Reynolds, Gainsborough, Constable and Turner for starters), as well as a marble relief sculpture by Michelangelo of the *Madonna and Child with the Infant St John*.

You won't get much sense of the original Palladian mansion, however, because the building was radically altered by the Victorian architect Sydney Smirke in 1872. Smirke added a second storey, thus upsetting the harmony of the original, rearranged the interiors and stuck **statues of famous artists** onto the outside walls above the windows – look out for Leonardo, Michelangelo, Titian

and Wren. The newest part of the building is the Sackler Wing, designed by Norman Foster. The **bronze statue** in the centre of the courtyard is of Sir Joshua Reynolds, the founder of the RA, shown with palette and paintbrush. It dates from 1931.

The Ritz Q11

Piccadilly, t (020) 7493 8181, w www.the ritzlondon.com; tube Green Park; wheelchair accessible. Open for tea at 3.30 or 5pm, reserve weeks in advance, or try your luck at 1.30pm; the dress code is jacket and tie, with strictly no jeans or trainers; £27.

Tea at the Ritz is a London institution, a challengingly priced but worthwhile indulgence that permits you to spend an hour or two immersed in an Edwardian paradise of gilded statues, interior waterfalls and exotic plants in the Palm Court. This is the sister hotel to the original Paris Ritz, and opened in 1906, eight years after its illustrious relative. The London Ritz has always been quite independent, however: César Ritz may have lent it his name, but he had already retired from public life at the time of its opening and was later to die in a Swiss clinic from a debilitating venereal disease. Some of the hotel's more illustrious guests are celebrated in a mural in the foyer.

MAYFAIR

The area got its name from the annual fair which was once held around the street now known as Shepherd's Market. The goings-on at the fair caused such a scandal that local residents had it banned in the mid-18th century, perhaps mindful of the royal neighbours at St James's Palace. Everyone who could afford it wanted a royal neighbour, and by the time that the disreputable fair was finally banned for good, a swathe of handsome townhouses had grown up around some of London's most elegant squares – Berkeley, Hanover and, grandest of all, Grosvenor. This is where Bertie Wooster would have parked his two-seater, and where the inimitable Jeeves would have got him out of countless scrapes. It's still got an old-fashioned feel in parts – Savile Row is still the place to go for a properly tailored suit, and the stuffy auction houses like Sotheby's and Christie's are tucked away in the exclusive streets. It has always been a neighbourhood where money talks loudest – and, of course, it's still the most expensive stop on the Monopoly board.

Burlington Arcade Q10–11

Tube *Piccadilly Circus, Green Park.*

London never really went in for shopping arcades the way that Paris did at the beginning of the 19th century; arcades nevertheless enjoyed a brief popularity in the final decade of the life of George IV. The Royal Opera Arcade (*see* p.123) was the first; the most famous, however, is Burlington Arcade (1819), no doubt because of its top-hatted beadles who enforce the arcade's quaint rules: no whistling, no singing and no running. The arcade was not, it must be said, commissioned predominantly for aesthetic reasons: Lord Cavendish, the owner of Burlington House next door, was fed up with passers-by throwing oyster shells and other rubbish into his garden and thought the arcade would be a suitable barrier. Nowadays it is elegant enough, its high-ceilinged halls decorated in green and white, but you may not be tempted by its overpriced upmarket clothes shops.

The Albany Q10

Albany Court Yard; **tube** *Piccadilly Circus, Oxford Circus, Green Park.*

Opposite Savile Row, on the other side of Vigo St, is the driveway to the Albany. This elegant Georgian building is one of the most beautiful in London and was once a prestigious address for eminent bachelors including Lord Palmerston, Robert Smirke, William Gladstone, Graham Greene and Terence Stamp.

Bond Street O9–Q11

Tube *Green Park, Piccadilly Circus, Bond St, Oxford Circus.*

Old Bond Street, the lower part of the thoroughfare, concentrates mainly on **jewellery shops** and includes all the well-known international names, including Tiffany's at No.25 (note the fine gold-trimmed clock hanging above the entrance) and Chatila at No.22, with its curious gargoyles above the window displays. On New Bond St you can look into the showrooms of **art dealers** such as Bernard Jacobson and Le Fevre (or, round the corner on Cork St, Waddington and Victoria Miro). **Sotheby's**, the famous auctioneers, are at Nos.34–35 New Bond St; above the front door is the oldest outdoor sculpture in London, an ancient Egyptian figure made of igneous rock dating back to 1600 BC.

Royal Institution/ Faraday Museum P10

21 Albemarle St, **t** *(020) 7409 2992,* **e** *ri@ri.ac.uk,* **w** *www.ri.ac.uk;* **tube** *Green Park; wheelchair accessible.* **Open** *Mon–Fri 10am–5pm; closed 24 Dec–7 Jan;* **adm** *adults £1, concessions 50p.*

This is to science what the Royal Academy is to art. Founded in 1799, the Institution built up a formidable reputation thanks to members such as Humphrey Davy (inventor of the Davy Lamp for detecting methane down mines) and his pupil, Michael Faraday. The small museum (the only part of the building regularly open to the public) is Faraday's old laboratory, where he carried out his pioneering experiments with electricity in the 1830s; his work is explained with the help of his original instruments and lab notes.

Berkeley Square O–P10

Tube *Green Park, Bond St.*

This is a key address for debutantes and aristocratic young bucks, who come for the annual Berkeley Square Charity Ball and vie to join the square's exclusive clubs and gaming houses. The chief interest for the visitor is the elegant row of Georgian houses on the west side. The highlight is **No.44**, described by Nikolaus Pevsner as 'the finest terraced house in London', built in 1742–4 for one of the royal household's maids of honour.

St George's Hanover Square P9

Tube Oxford Circus, Bond St.

A Neoclassical church with a striking Corinthian portico, St George's was built in 1721–4 as part of the Fifty New Churches Act. It is the parish church of Mayfair and has proved enduringly popular as a venue for society weddings, including the match between Shelley and Mary Godwin. The interior, restored at the end of the Victorian era, has some fine 16th-century **Flemish glass** in the east window and a **painting** of the *Last Supper* above the altar attributed to William Kent. Notice also the **cast-iron dogs** in the porch; these once belonged to a shop in Conduit St and were brought here in 1940 after their original premises were bombed.

Handel House Museum P9

25 Brook St, t (020) 7495 1685, e mail@handel house.org, w www.handelhouse.org; tube Bond St; wheelchair accessible. Open Tues, Wed, Fri and Sat 10am–9pm, Thurs 10am–8pm, Sun noon–6pm; adm adults £4.50, concessions £3.50, children £2. Audioguides available. Giftshop.

Handel lived in this house from 1723 until his death in 1759. The interiors have been painstakingly restored using inventories of his belongings after his death, and are a remarkable evocation of a London townhouse in the 1720s. This is where Handel created some of his best-known works – including the *Messiah* and *Music for the Royal Fireworks*. Next door, two centuries later, lived a musical genius of a very different kind – **Jimi Hendrix**.

REGENT STREET

Tube Piccadilly Circus, Oxford Circus.

Regent St was once the finest street in London, thanks to the architect John Nash, who thought big and managed to persuade the Prince Regent, a fellow spendthrift, to sponsor his projects for Regent St and Regent's Park. The original plan, drawn up in 1813, was intended to bring revolutionary changes to the way London was organized. Nash's idea was to make Regent St the main north–south artery, linking the prince's residence at Carlton House on The Mall to the newly landscaped expanse of Regent's Park; as such it would have been the centrepiece of a carefully planned ensemble of squares, palaces and public thoroughfares. But by the time Nash had haggled with the various land-owners, Regent St was no longer the straight line of his plans, but a series of curious wiggles that had to be bent and twisted into something resembling an elegant shape. At the beginning of the 20th century, his fine buildings came under attack again, because of the complaints of shopkeepers who said their floorspace was too restricted. Demolition began in 1916, and the present desperately unimaginative buildings were in place by the mid-1920s.

Now all Regent St boasts is a few fine shops (particularly men's clothes stores), including the famous toy store **Hamley's**. The finest department store is **Liberty**, famous for its silks and fabrics which in the 19th century carried designs by William Morris. It still stocks some attractive furniture from the Arts and Crafts period on the top floor, and excellent kitchenware, women's clothes and jewellery on other floors. There is a bridge leading from the main Liberty building to its fake-Tudor 1925 timbered extension.

Soho and Chinatown

1 Lunch

Golden Harvest, *17 Lisle St*, **t** *(020) 7287 3822;* **tube** *Leicester Square, Piccadilly Circus.* **Open** *Mon–Thurs and Sun noon–12.45am, Fri and Sat noon–1.45am.* **Inexpensive.** Outstandingly good low-priced Chinese food. The owners are Chinatown's fishmongers, so fresh fish is easily guaranteed.

2 Tea and Cakes

Pâtisserie Valerie, *44 Old Compton St;* **tube** *Leicester Square.* **Open** *Mon–Fri 7.30am–8pm, Sat 8am–7pm, Sun 9am–6pm.* Divine French cakes. You may have to wait for a seat (share one of the dark wooden tables).

3 Drinks

Dog & Duck, *18 Bateman St*, **t** *(020) 7494 0697;* **tube** *Tottenham Court Road, Piccadilly Circus.* **Open** *Mon–Fri noon–11pm, Sat 5–11pm, Sun 6–10.30pm.* Soho's smallest pub, on the site of the home of the Duke of Monmouth, who hunted in the area in the 17th century, crying 'So-Ho'.

Soho and Chinatown

'Better a seedy Soho than a tarted-up tourist attraction like Covent Garden,' opines Daniel Farson in his entertaining book *Soho in the Fifties*. Seediness has always proved strangely alluring in this wild and cosmopolitan district, so distinct from the sober calm of the rest of central London. Soho started off as a refuge for French Huguenots, and now counts whole communities of Italians, Cypriots, Greeks, Poles, Chinese, Thais and Bengalis who, along with the new wave of trendies, run the area's zillions of restaurants and bars. Here are the clashing smells of oregano and lemongrass, the competing sounds of jazz and Hong Kong pop, the unlikely mix of bohemian intellectuals, hip zoot-suiters and peepshow pimps.

The establishment has always been suspicious of this area: too many foreigners and loose morals for the liking of respectable ladies and gents. The artistic community has never shown such squeamishness; indeed this is the heart of London's Theatreland, with its haunted nooks and much elaborated legends. Nowadays the sleaze is slowly disappearing, supplanted by the flashy cars and modish whims of the advertising and media darlings. Since the mid-1990s, Soho has also become the fashionable hub of London's gay scene, especially around Old Compton St. Soho is now sleeker and hipper than ever before, but the naked power of money, and particularly the pressure of the property developers, still meets stiff resistance here – and it is the robust, unpretentious old spirit of the place that keeps Soho swinging.

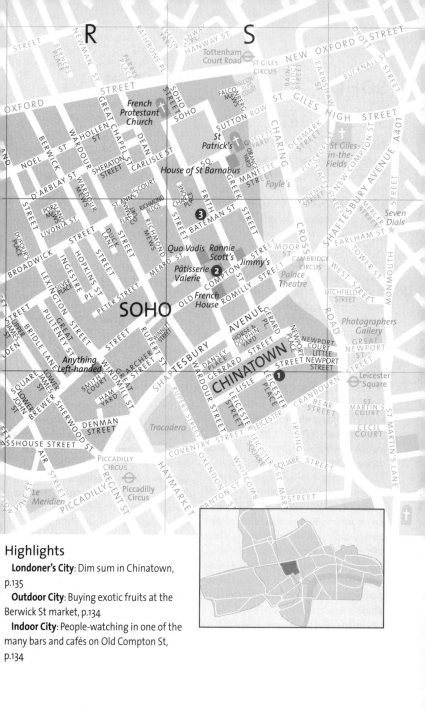

Highlights

Londoner's City: Dim sum in Chinatown, p.135

Outdoor City: Buying exotic fruits at the Berwick St market, p.134

Indoor City: People-watching in one of the many bars and cafés on Old Compton St, p.134

SOHO

Soho Square S8

Tube Tottenham Court Rd.

A contemporary **statue of Charles II** by Caius Gabriel Cibber stands in the square gardens, looking somewhat the worse for wear beside a mock-Tudor toolshed which covers an underground air vent. The square is a popular place to sit in the summer. On the north side is the **French Protestant Church**, originally built for the Huguenots and then reworked by the Victorians in flamboyant neo-Gothic style. To the east is the red-brick tower of **St Patrick's Roman Catholic Church**. Weekly services are held in Spanish and Cantonese, and the priest, Father Sherbrooke, hosts open houses and other events for homeless people and rough sleepers.

House of St Barnabas S8

1 Greek St. **Open** *to the public fortnightly for tours,* **t** *(020) 7434 1846,* **t** *7434 2067.*

On the corner of Greek St, this stern-looking building, according to the plaque by the door, offers 'a temporary home for women who have the necessary recommendations'. Founded in 1846 (although the building dates back exactly a century earlier), the House set out to improve the lot of the poor through Christian teaching, and giving shelter to servants between posts and to people getting ready to emigrate. The House now offers accommodation to 38 homeless women for a limited period of six months at a time.

Its exterior and utilitarian entrance hall, including the disconcertingly thick front door and enormous bolt chain and lock (18th-century London was rife with violent crime and rioting), belie its light and magnificent Rococo interiors, within which are a few architectural rarities. The curve in the banister uprights on the main stairs allowed 18th-century ladies room to swan up and down in their vast dresses; this is one of only three 'crinoline staircases' left in London.

Frith Street S8–9

Tube Tottenham Court Rd, Leicester Square.

Frith St is best known for **Ronnie Scott's** jazz club. Scott, a jazz saxophonist, died in 1996, but his dingy basement club still gets high-profile bookings. There is also a plethora of restaurants, including **Jimmy's**, a basement Greek café serving cheap moussaka and chips and still famous for being where the Rolling Stones ate in the 1960s, even though it has since moved across the street.

Dean Street R8–S9

Tube Tottenham Court Rd, Leicester Square.

At No.28, the restaurant **Quo Vadis** became instantly trendworthy in 1996 after it was bought from its Italian owners by Marco Pierre White, the famous London superchef,

---

Fallen Women

Relief for unfortunate women was something of an obsession for many Victorian figures. Charles Dickens was involved with the philanthropist Angela Burdett-Coutts' home for stray females, and drew up such dictatorial and patronising rules for their behaviour that many fled back to the streets. Prime Minister William Gladstone, that pillar of Victorian politics, would pick up prostitutes (in the nicest possible way) during his extraordinary night-time walks through Soho in the early 1850s. His declared aim was to talk them out of their sinful ways and offer them temporary relief from poverty, but inevitably cynical tongues soon began wagging. 'He manages to combine his missionary meddling with a keen appreciation of a pretty face,' remarked one member of Parliament, Henry Labouchère. As often as not, Gladstone would offer to take the prostitutes home. 'What will your wife say?' his Permanent Secretary asked him in horror while accompanying him on one such trip. 'Why,' Gladstone replied, all innocence and sweet reason, 'it is to my wife that I am bringing her.'

The Making of Soho

The curious name is a medieval hunting call, as in the quaint 15th-century exclamation quoted by the *Oxford English Dictionary*: 'Sohoe, the hare ys founde!' The district was indeed hunting territory up to the 17th century, although it seems Soho took its name not from the cry itself but – not unsuitably given the character of the district – from the name of an inn.

Low life and aristocrats have always dwelt side by side in Soho. In the 18th century it was fashionable with salon hostesses as well as artists and prostitutes. In Victorian times it was full of cowsheds and slaughterhouses, with animal droppings littering the street. For polite society, the area became a byword for depravity and lack of hygiene. The Victorians would have been even more horrified by what was to come: erotic revues, peepshows and the rise of pornography. In 1931 the Lord Chamberlain authorized nudity on stage for the first time for a revue at the Windmill Theatre, although he stipulated that the lighting had to stay low and the showgirls were not allowed to move while they showed off their bodies. The rules remained unchanged during the Second

World War, when showgirls often found themselves standing stock still as everyone around them dashed for shelter from German V-bombs.

It was after the war that Soho really came into its own. In the 1950s it became the centre of the avant garde in jazz, new writing, experimental theatre and cinema. In many ways Soho prefigured the social upheavals of the 1960s, creating a youth subculture based on rebellion, permissiveness, *joie de vivre*, booze and drugs. This was the world of Colin MacInnes's *Absolute Beginners*, of John Osborne and the other Angry Young Men, of Kenneth Tynan and his risqué revue *Oh Calcutta!* Above all, Soho developed its own community of intellectuals and eccentrics, people of all classes mingling, chatting, borrowing money off each other and getting pleasantly tippled in pubs or illicit 'near-beer' bars that stayed open outside the stringent licensing hours.

Walk into the right place and you would meet Nina Hamnett, known as the Queen of the Bohemians, who boasted that Modigliani had credited her with 'the best tits in Europe'; or Ironfoot Jack, an impresario with

and Damien Hirst, Britpack conceptual artist-cum-restaurateur. In 1999, after a major and very public tiff, MPW turfed out all of Hirst's artwork, which had famously lined the walls, knocked up a few parodies, and is doing very nicely on his own, thank you.

In stark contrast, upstairs is where **Karl Marx** lived with his family from 1851 to 1856, in a two-room attic flat in conditions of near-abject penury. Not only did Marx have next to no money, he did little to set about earning any. While he spent his days in the British Library reading room, his wife Jenny struggled to bring up their growing family in a garret without ready access to toilets or running water. Three of their children died of pneumonia. For a while the Marxes shared their digs with an Italian chef, and readily invited all comers to their dwelling to share what little they had. Then Karl started an

affair with the family maid, managing to get both her and his wife pregnant at the same time. In the end, the arrival of inheritances from Jenny Marx's mother and uncle saved the family from the poorhouse and they left for the healthier climes of Primrose Hill.

South of Old Compton St at No.49 is the **French House**, which became the unofficial headquarters of the Free French forces under Charles de Gaulle during the Second World War. Now it's a lively pub-cum-wine bar with a dining room above and its walls covered with photographs of famous Frenchmen.

Two clubs further down the street illustrate the changes in Soho since the 1950s. The **Colony**, at No.41, was once described as 'a place where the villains look like artists and the artists look like villains... burglars and millionaires, tramps and poets, students and countesses are all given an identical

one leg six inches shorter than the other, who went around in colourful silk scarves; or Jeffrey Bernard, a journalist who sat in the Coach and Horses pub in an alcohol-induced stupor writing a column called 'Low Life' for the *Spectator* magazine.

Like all golden ages, 1950s Soho and its low life came to a somewhat sorry end. Nina Hamnett was eventually reduced to an incontinent wreck hobbling around Soho with a permanently damaged thigh bone she broke in a drunken fall; the celebrated local bookseller David Archer died of a drugs overdose; and most of the famous writers moved out to Camden or Notting Hill. The liberalizations of the 1960s and 1970s brought peepshows and strip joints galore that nearly caused the destruction of the neighbourhood. The planning authorities, outraged by prostitutes openly soliciting on every street, threatened to bulldoze the whole district to make way for office blocks. Only Jeffrey Bernard valiantly hung on in there, turning out his column as regularly as his liver would permit (he finally died in 1997, but not before Peter O'Toole had turned him into a legend on the West End stage with the one-man show *Jeffrey Bernard Is Unwell*).

It wasn't until the mid-1980s that new laws regulated the pornography business and Soho regained some of its spirit. The number of peepshows is strictly controlled and prostitutes rarely solicit on the streets. The developers have largely been kept out by the Soho Society, set up in 1972, which succeeded in having the district declared a conservation area. So attractive has Soho become that the trendies have inevitably moved in to join the fun.

The quirky hipness of the 1960s has evolved into a social free-for-all, drawing in movers and shakers in the music, film and advertising worlds, comedians and television personalities, journalists, artists, dealers and agents, hangers-on and drop-outs, and a substantial gay community. Not a week goes by without a new bar, a new restaurant, a new fad. Yesterday it was sushi served by robots; this week these are passé and the new thing is cafés that look like middle-class living rooms. Is the fashion wind blowing towards East Soho or West Soho? Against the odds, the area has become glamorous and limitlessly desirable, the very image of a vibrant new London. The Duke of Monmouth would have loved it.

welcome'. Drunken artists, from Francis Bacon to George Melly, have gathered here since time began. The **Groucho** – a new-model private club for trendy metropolitans and so called because of Groucho Marx's one-liner that he never wanted to join a club that would have him as a member – opened at No.44 in 1985 and has been a hit with the world of television, music, comedy, publishing and film ever since.

Old Compton Street S9

Tube *Leicester Square, Piccadilly Circus.*

In many ways this is the archetypal Soho street, and a popular hangout for London's gay community. Here you'll find cafés like Pâtisserie Valerie at No.44, restaurants, delicatessens, gay clubs and bars, and modest-looking newsagents stocking every

conceivable title. This is the site of the Admiral Duncan, the gay pub that suffered in the nail-bomb attacks of 1999 that also hit Brixton and Brick Lane. There is a memorial in the pub to the dead and wounded.

Berwick Street R8–9

Tube *Leicester Square, Piccadilly Circus, Oxford Circus, Tottenham Court Rd.* **Market held** *Mon–Sat around 9am–4pm.*

This is home to the best **fruit and vegetable market** in central London. You'll hear the barrow-boys hawking their collies and taters as you come round the corner. Berwick St market always has beautifully fresh produce at incredibly low prices for central London. Ever since Jack Smith introduced the pineapple to London here in 1890, the market has also had a reputation for stocking unusual and exotic fruit and veg such as salsify or starfruit. The houses behind the stalls date, like the market itself, back to the 18th century, although there is plenty to distract you from even noticing them. There are a couple of **old pubs** (The Blue Posts is the most salubrious), a scattering of noisy independent **record stores**, and several excellent old-fashioned **fabrics shops** specializing in unusual silks, satins, velvets, Chinese printed silks and printed cottons, sold by the metre: the place to go if you're looking for something exotic for yourself or your sofa.

At the southern end of Berwick St is a poky passage called **Walker's Court**, dominated by peepshows and London's shabby equivalent of the Moulin Rouge, Raymond's Revue Bar.

Brewer Street R9–10

Tube Piccadilly Circus.

This street still offers the ultimate old-Soho mixture of sex joints and eclectic shops. As you wander down it you will notice discreetly signposted **peepshows**, a vintage **magazine and poster shop** at No.39–43, and, at No.67, the shop **Anything Left-Handed**. If, like Michelangelo and John McEnroe, you are what the specialists call sinistro-manual, you might be delighted to find an entire shop full of left-handed scissors, can-openers, cutlery, pens and gardening tools. There are even left-handed mugs. Left-handed mugs? Of course, so all we southpaws can see the illustration on the mug while we are holding it.

Carnaby Street Q9

Tube Piccadilly Circus, Oxford Circus.

Don't be deluded by the name – the caftans, beads and marijuana that characterized this street when it shot to worldwide fame in the 60s have given way to cheap T-shirts, Union Jack underpants, plastic bobby helmets and crass souvenir models of Buckingham Palace and the Tower of London. Carnaby St simply became too famous for its own good, and deteriorated into tourist

trash. More seriously, in the late 1980s it became a hangout for neo-Nazis who openly paraded racist literature on the stalls. Nevertheless, it still has some odd little one-off shops and its own array of even tinier side-alleys. Recently, the area has been on the rise again – funky young designers and ultra-trendy boutiques like the Mac make-up store have popped up in the winding alleys leading off Carnaby St, like **Newburgh St** and **Marshall St**.

The most attractive building is the **Shakespeare's Head** pub on the corner of Foubert's Place. Look up above the doorway and you'll see a painted bust of the playwright smiling down on the crowd. For some reason lost in the mists of time, the figure has one hand missing.

CHINATOWN

Tube Leicester Square, Piccadilly Circus.

London's Chinese population came here mostly from Hong Kong in the 1950s and 60s, victims not so much of the political upheavals in the region as the cruel fluctuations of the Asian rice market. Back then Gerrard St, like the rest of Soho, was cheap and rundown and relatively welcoming to foreigners. It took more than a generation for the new community to be fully accepted, however, and it was not until the 1970s that this street was pedestrianized and kitted out with decorative lamps and telephone boxes styled like pagodas – a spectacular backdrop to the Chinese New Year celebrations which take place here at the end of January or early February. For many people here, English is not their first language, and the area seems a world apart from the rest of the West End. The younger generation has integrated well; those born here are mockingly nicknamed BBCs (British-born children).

London's Chinatown is still very small – just Gerrard St and Lisle St really – but an astonishing number of restaurants, businesses, offices and Chinese-orientated facilities are packed into its mostly 18th-century buildings. The district's trade is overwhelmingly in food and **restaurants**. Bizarrely, one or two of the restaurants are popular because of their famously rude waiters – but others do have extremely friendly staff. There's always been a discreet illegal business in gambling, too – underground dens for *mah-jong*, *pai-kau* and *fan tan*. Triad gangs keep a relatively low profile in London, although in the 80s there were occasional, isolated outbursts of violence.

The eastern end of Gerrard St and Newport Place are crowded with Chinese **supermarkets and craft shops**, which are well worth poking around for a bargain. Cramped but cavernous stores like Sun Luen on Little Newport St, or the giant Loon Fung at 42–44 Gerrard St, are fascinating places to explore, crammed full with Chinese vegetables and spices, unrecognizable frozen fish, dumplings and (if you can think what to do with them) live Asian carp, kept in giant tanks.

Covent Garden and Around

08

Covent Garden and Around

There are those who find modern Covent Garden too ritzy and spoilt with its boutiques, upmarket jewellery stalls and prettified pubs; too much of an easy crowd-pleaser with all those mime artists and hand-clapping bands belting out yet another rendition of 'I'm a Believer' or 'The Boxer'; too much – heaven forbid – of a tourist attraction. Looking into the past, however, one should perhaps be relieved that it's even half as pleasant as it is. When the wholesale fruit and vegetable market moved out to the South London suburbs in the 1970s, the London authorities initially wanted to build office blocks and a major roadway through here. Wouldn't that have been fun? It was the local traders and residents who saved Covent Garden with protests and petitions; it is also the locals who, by and large, have the run of the place today.

Dig a little, and behind the obvious tourist draws are plenty of quieter, more discreet spots. If Covent Garden seems a little derivative, it is because it deliberately and self-consciously echoes its own past – a dash of Inigo Jones's original piazza with its street life and sideshows, several measures of Charles Fowler's covered market, plus plenty of the eating, drinking and general revelry that have always characterized this neighbourhood.

1 Lunch

Calabash, *Africa Centre, 38 King St, t (020) 7836 1976; tube Covent Garden, Leicester Square. Open Mon–Fri 12.30–2.30 and 6–10.30, Sat 6–10.30pm. Inexpensive.* Dishes from all over Africa in a collegey canteen. Nigerian *egusi* (stew of beef, melon and shrimps cooked in palm oil), couscous from the Maghreb, *dioumbre* (okra stew) from the Ivory Coast, with lots of fried plantain.

2 Tea and Cakes

Paul, *29 Bedford St, t (020) 7836 5324; tube Covent Garden, Charing Cross, Leicester Square. Open Mon–Fri 7.30am–9pm, Sat and Sun 9am–9pm.* Part of the plush French chain, this elegant café offers superb cakes and pastries to eat in or take away.

3 Drinks

Lamb and Flag, *33 Rose St, t (020) 7497 9504; tube Covent Garden, Leicester Square. Open Mon–Thurs 11am–11pm, Fri and Sat 11am–10.45pm, Sun 11am–10.30pm.* One of the few wooden-framed buildings left in central London, dating back to the 17th century, with low ceilings and a lively atmosphere. The pub was for a long time nicknamed 'the Bucket of Blood' because it staged bare-knuckle fights. Now you just have to try to knuckle your way past the crowds at the bar.

Highlights

Londoner's City: Shopping in the trendy clothes stores along Neal Street, p.144

Literary City: Learning about the history of the British stage in the Theatre Museum, p.141

Contemporary Architecture: The splendidly revamped Royal Opera House, p.143

Riverside City: Cleopatra's Needle, just slightly out of place on the Embankment, p.146

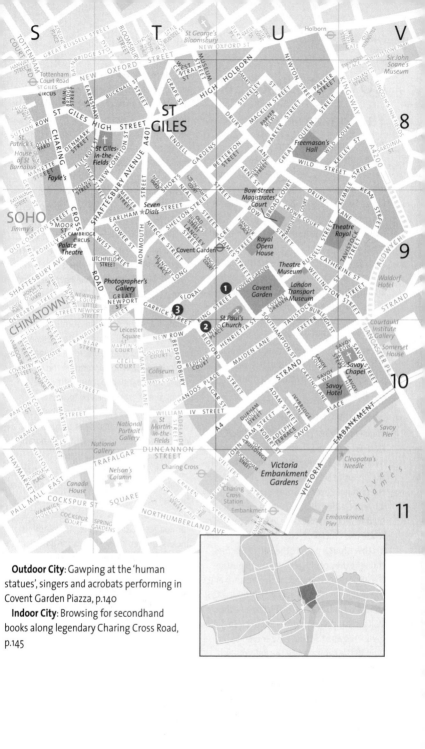

Outdoor City: Gawping at the 'human statues', singers and acrobats performing in Covent Garden Piazza, p.140

Indoor City: Browsing for secondhand books along legendary Charing Cross Road, p.145

COVENT GARDEN

The Piazza U9

Tube *Covent Garden, Charing Cross.*

With the loss of the market (*see* 'Covent Garden's Roots') Covent Garden undoubtedly lost its rough edges. The main hall, once littered with crates and stray vegetables, is now spick and span, while the Flower Market houses museums devoted to transport and the theatre. But the place has not lost its soul. You can still buy roast chestnuts from a street vendor as Dickens did, or watch clowns and jugglers performing in front of St Paul's Church, where Punch and Judy shows first caught the public imagination in the 17th century. And, after you've had your fill of street theatre, wander through South Hall to explore the lower levels of the market with their intriguing little shops and restaurants.

St Paul's Church U9

Inigo Place; wheelchair accessible. **Open** *Tues–Fri 9.30am–4.30pm, Sun service at 11am.*

Although you enter it from Inigo Place, on the opposite side, St Paul's is really part of the original Covent Garden piazza (*see* 'Covent Garden's Roots') which Inigo Jones built in mock-Italian style in the 1630s. Jones made one crucial oversight, however. He and his Low Church patron, the Earl of Bedford, thought they could get away with putting the altar of their church at the western end, so breaking with convention, which insists it should be in the east. The Bishop of London, William Laud, was in no mood to be so indulgent. This was the first new church to be built in the capital since the Reformation, and the arch-conservative Laud was keen not to stir up controversy. He ordered Jones to put the altar where it traditionally belongs, in this case flush against the planned main entrance. Until the 19th century you could still enter by one of the two side doors on the piazza, but in 1871 they were blocked up by the restorer William Butterfield, presumably

to ensure that Godfearing churchgoers would not have to mingle with the drunken riffraff in the market. Now the only way in is on Inigo Place, through the pretty and secluded rose garden churchyard.

The interior is of disarming simplicity: a double square, 100ft by 50ft. Horace Walpole relates how the Earl of Bedford, Francis Russell, was anxious not to spend too much money on the church (he was more or less talked into building it, along with the rest of Covent Garden, by King Charles I). 'In short, I would not have it much better than a barn,' Russell told Inigo Jones. Jones is said to have replied: 'Well then, you shall have the handsomest barn in England.' St Paul's is one of the few pre-Great Fire buildings still left in London, and the only significant part of Inigo Jones's piazza still standing. An overzealous restorer called Thomas Hardwick began reworking the whole interior in the late 1780s, but changed his mind after a devastating fire in 1795 which he took as a providential sign. He ended up rebuilding the whole church as it had been before. A fine new **organ** was added in 1861, incorporating part of the casing of the original.

St Paul's quickly won the affections of the theatre folk of Covent Garden, who preached here as well as attending services. They nicknamed it the Actors' Church. Several luminaries of the stage are buried here, including **Ellen Terry**, the grande dame of the late-Victorian theatre, whose ashes are marked by a plaque in the south wall. There is also a curious floor stone in memory of **Claude Duval**, a highwayman hanged in 1670 who gained his notoriety as much by womanizing as by robbing the rich. He was once seen dancing in the moonlight with an eminent lady he had just held up on a road on Hounslow Heath. The floor stone reads:

Here lies Du Vall: Reader,
if male thou art
Look to thy purse;
if female to thy heart...
Old Tyburn's glory,
England's illustrious thief

Covent Garden's Roots

Covent Garden originally had an extra 'n' – it was pastureland belonging to the Convent of St Peter at Westminster, the original Westminster Abbey. After the dissolution of the monasteries, the Crown gave the land to the Earl of Bedford and his family. Francis Russell, the fourth earl, fancied himself as a building speculator and, with the encouragement of the King, hired Inigo Jones, the King's Surveyor of Works, to construct houses 'fit for the habitations of gentlemen'. Jones, who had won fame for designing the Banqueting House in Whitehall (*see* p.94), duly obliged with an arcaded piazza heavily influenced by his studies of Palladian buildings in Italy. Smart terraced houses on three sides looked onto a large public square where coaches could linger and strollers enjoy the grace of their surroundings. It was a light, elegant piece of work, but failed to make much impression on Jones's contemporaries, who were unused to the concept of the public square and found it simply too un-English. To them, the idea of a square encouraging street life and the mingling of the classes seemed horrifying. When market stalls started appearing in the 1670s, the piazza lost any remaining kudos and fell into rapid decline. Nobody seemed to care much about Jones's fine buildings, which were allowed to disintegrate and disappear. Bedford House, the first and finest house on the piazza, was demolished in 1706 to make room for a row of shops. That tells you something about London's planning priorities.

By the 18th century, Covent Garden was attracting a totally different species of humanity. 'One would imagine that all the prostitutes in the kingdom had picked upon the rendez-vous,' spluttered Sir John Fielding, blind half-brother of the novelist Henry, who

Du Vall, the ladies' joy,
Du Vall the ladies' grief.

It's an elegant little verse, but in fact it is doubtful whether Duval was ever buried here since there are no records of him in the parish register. This could just be the Actors' Church doing a bit of acting of its own.

London Transport Museum U9

*The Piazza, **t** (020) 7379 6344, **e** contact@ ltmuseum.co.uk, **w** www.ltmuseum.co.uk; wheelchair accessible. **Open** Sat–Thurs 10am–6pm, Fri 11am–6pm, last adm 5pm; closed 24–26 Dec; **adm** adults £5.95, concessions £3.95, children free. The **shop**, selling all sorts of London Underground paraphernalia from 'Mind the Gap' boxer shorts to pillows made out of Tube seat covers, is accessible even if you don't pay to go into the museum.*

Londoners like to grumble about London Transport, but in their heart of hearts they are really rather fascinated by it. This cheerful museum celebrates everything that is excellent about the system, from the red London Routemaster bus to the London Underground map, designed in 1931 by Harry Beck and, though much emulated, never surpassed.

In the main gallery, a glass walkway takes you past a series of historic buses, trams and steam locomotives, including the oldest surviving **double-decker horse tram** (dating from 1882, when 1,000 tonnes of horse dung were deposited on the streets of London every day). Unfortunately the superb collection of Art Deco period posters is now accessible by appointment only. Bringing it all to life, there's a simulated Tube train driving seat, actors dressed in period costume, and an interactive trail of 'Kidzones' throughout the museum.

Theatre Museum U9

*Russell St, **t** (020) 7943 4700, **w** www.theatre museum.org; **tube** Covent Garden; wheelchair accessible. **Open** Tues–Sun 10am–6pm; closed all bank hols; **adm** free. **Guided tours** Tues– Sun at 11am, 2pm and 4pm. **Workshops** for aspiring thesps and free **make-up displays** (call for times).*

This museum is mostly subterranean and can therefore seem dark and confusing at

was magistrate for the district in the 1750s. Covent Garden became a byword for vice, a den of iniquity and immorality where criminal gangs ran extortion rackets, gambling houses and brothels. Vice has a funny way of attracting supposedly respectable 'artistic' folk, however, and Covent Garden became a favourite drinking haunt of literary types, including Henry Fielding, Pope, Sheridan and Goldsmith.

Meanwhile, the market grew in importance, especially after the closure of Stocks Market in the City in 1737. But importance was not always a guarantee of quality, and rotting or adulterated food became increasingly common. Bric-a-brac traders gradually joined the fruit and veg sellers, causing such congestion and chaos that by the early 19th century Parliament was forced to reorganize the market's licensing system and authorize the building of a proper market hall. The result was Charles Fowler's grand structure of Tuscan columns and pretty arcades, completed in 1830, which largely survives as the centrepiece of the piazza today. Over the next 80 years, further market halls followed – Floral Hall (1860), the Flower Market (1871) and the Jubilee Market (1904).

Covent Garden became a bustling, popular focal point for central London where people of all classes could mingle. It is no accident that in *Pygmalion*, Bernard Shaw's play unravelling the savage eccentricities of the British class system, his characters Henry Higgins and Eliza Doolittle first meet outside the classical portico of St Paul's Church. In time, however, the market grew too big for the space available and, after decades of overcrowding, the fruit and veg stalls moved out in 1974 to roomier, more modern premises at Nine Elms south of the river.

first; by far the best way to see it, unless you're an expert on theatre, is to join one of the very informative guided tours led by actors. (If you miss the tours, pick up a leaflet at the entrance which lists some of the highlights.) A vast number of exhibits cover the history of the English stage from the Elizabethan public playhouses to the rise of the Royal National Theatre, illustrated by period costumes and plenty of model theatres. **'Theatre Rites'**, on the top floor, is a highly interactive, wacky, touchy-feely exhibit of theatrical paraphernalia with all sorts of pulleys, switches, handles and loops to pull, push and poke.

Theatre Royal U–V9

Drury Lane, **t** *(020) 7494 5000;* ***tube*** *Covent Garden; wheelchair accessible.*

The Theatre Royal was one of the first theatrical establishments to open after the 1660 Restoration, holding a performance of *The Humorous Lieutenant* by Beaumont and Fletcher for its inauguration in 1663. Nell Gwynne made her debut here, as did David Garrick and Edmund Kean in subsequent centuries. Once famous for its classical repertoire, it turned to spectacular dramas in the latter part of the 19th century when its manager Augustus Harris, a theatrical Cecil B. De Mille, staged horse races, snowstorms, earthquakes and avalanches.

The theatre's constant curse, however, has been fire. In 1809 the playwright and politician Richard Sheridan, who was then manager, was alerted to the flames spewing out of his theatre while he was embroiled in an important debate in Parliament. Stoically, he refused to go to the site until his business at Westminster was done. He was later seen nursing a stiff drink at the scene of the fire and commenting with characteristic wry humour: 'Surely a man may take a glass of wine by his own fireside?' Benjamin Wyatt was responsible for the rebuilding, completed in 1812. In 1840 the theatre acquired a different kind of curse, when a man was found in one of the walls with a knife poking through his ribs; a ghost has appeared in the circle from time to time ever since, particularly at matinées.

Royal Opera House U9

*Bow St, **t** (020) 7304 4000, **w** www.royalopera house.org; **tube** Covent Garden; wheelchair accessible. All front of house areas (the Vilar Floral Hall, cafés and restaurants) are **open** daily 10am–3pm. **Box office open** Mon–Sat 10am–8pm, or book on **t** (020) 7212 9460, **w** www.royaloperahouse.org. **Guided back-stage tours** Mon–Sat 10.30am, 12.30pm and 2.30pm; adults £7, concessions £6. You can watch the **Royal Ballet in class** in the Clore Studio about once every three months, call for dates; **adm** adults £10, concessions £5. Ten **bars** and **restaurants**.*

The Covent Garden theatre was advertised as the most luxurious in London when it opened in 1732, but quickly became known for its calamities as much as its perform-ances. An angry mob ripped up the boxes and orchestra pit in 1763 after management broke with the custom of granting free entry for the third act. There was further violence in 1792 when the theatre tried to raise gallery prices to pay for costly restoration work. Then in 1808 a fire razed the theatre to the ground. A new building designed by Robert Smirke was opened just over a year later. By this time Covent Garden was so unfashionable, not to say vice-ridden, that the main entrance of the theatre was moved to Bow St in an effort to create some distance from the lower elements of society. But when the management next had the temerity to raise prices, again the result was fighting in the streets. The Old Price Riots lasted more than two months until the theatre finally gave in to the demands of its rowdy audience.

The second Covent Garden fire broke out during a ball in 1856, just a few years after the theatre had become established as an opera house. The orchestra desperately played 'God Save the Queen' to persuade everyone to leave the building. In the end nobody was seriously hurt, but nothing remained of the theatre apart from the portico frieze *Tragedy and Comedy*. Beating even Robert Smirke's record for speed, the new architect, Edward Barry, incorporated it

into his design and it is still the centrepiece of Bow St's Neoclassical façade.

By the end of the 20th century, some of the House's most thrilling drama focused around a massive redevelopment and extension programme, which involved over 25 years of controversial debate, countless delays, three years of construction and a bill of £214 million. Now that Covent Garden had become so trendy again it was important to reintegrate the Opera House with the piazza, allowing the public direct access from the square as well as from Bow St (hardly known for cutting-edge glamour). Architects Jeremy Dixon and Edward Jones devised a plan for replacing the Georgian houses in the northern corner of the piazza with white vaulted shopping arcades containing cafés, restaurants and the box office, all in a style they call 'stripped classical' and designed to complement Inigo Jones's original Covent Garden. The extension also includes a new 400-seat Linbury Studio for studio opera and experimental dance, new accommodation and rehearsal studios for the Royal Ballet, state-of-the-art backstage facilities and an entirely renovated auditorium with improved sight-lines and 100 new lower-price seats. One of the most spectacular changes to the Opera House is the proper incorporation of the Vilar Floral Hall, built in 1859 as an elegant adjunct to the House; subsequently used as a market hall, it was badly damaged by yet another fire in 1956. It is now a glorious amphitheatre bar, all white cast-iron and glass.

Although most of the prices for actual tickets are still wildly prohibitive, the Opera House feels as though it is truly open to the public for the first time in its history.

Bow Street Magistrates' Court U9

*Bow St (opposite the Royal Opera House); **tube** Covent Garden.*

This was where the Fieldings, Henry and John, held court in the 18th century. Henry, who was a trained barrister as well as the author of *Tom Jones*, used his tenure here to set up the Bow Street Runners, an informal plain-clothes police force that worked to crack down on underworld gangs and challenge the infamous official marshals, or 'thief-takers', who were usually in cahoots with the thieves themselves (*see* 'The Eventual Downfall of Jonathan Wild'). The Runners proved remarkably effective and soon became famous throughout the land. Until Robert Peel's uniformed bobbies appeared in the 1830s, they were the closest thing to a police force that London had. When ill health forced Henry to retire in 1754, his blind half-brother took over and introduced foot patrols to keep an eye on known felons. Legend has it that the 'Blind Beak' could recognize 3,000 thieves by their voices alone. The present court building dates from 1881.

Freemason's Hall U8

Great Queen St, t (020) 7831 9811, w www.grand-lodge.org; tube Covent Garden, Holborn; wheelchair accessible. Open Mon–Fri 10am–5pm, Sat 1pm, for compulsory guided tour; adm free.

The tours offered here are an intriguing PR exercise stressing Freemasonry's principles of truth and brotherly love (the Freemasons are an all-male secret society founded in London in 1717). There's lots of regalia but no elucidation of those handshakes. 'It is not a secret society,' explains a leaflet. Right.

Neal Street T8–9

Tube Covent Garden, Leicester Square.

While Carnaby St, the in place in the 1960s, has faltered and just about died, Neal St, a development from the late 1970s, has survived and is now packed with hip fashion shops as well as a few stalwart hangers-on from the hippy years. Turn down Shorts Gardens and you come to distinctly New Age **Neal's Yard**, a tranquil triangular oasis planted with trees and climbing plants, and an excellent place to sit down, away from the traffic fumes and confusion. Don't miss the

The Eventual Downfall of Jonathan Wild

Most infamous of all the 18th-century thief-takers (official marshals who were often on the wrong side of the law), and the eponymous subject of one of Fielding's own books (a masterpiece of satire against the contemporary popular idolization of criminals as expressed in works such as John Gay's *The Beggar's Opera*), was Jonathan Wild, who built up an entire criminal empire by repossessing property he had more often than not stolen and sold on in the first place. His success depended on playing an elaborate game of deception and counter-deception with his own men; during his career he turned in several dozen of his accomplices to keep his nose clean.

As long as Wild did not hold on to any of the goods he stole, it was hard for the magistrates to pin anything on him. In desperation, Parliament passed a special Act in 1718 designed to make it easier to catch Wild: it stated that any profit from a crime was as serious a matter as the crime itself. Wild lasted another seven years before finally being captured, tried and sentenced to death in 1725. He was so frightened of the public humiliation he knew he could expect on the way to the gallows that he tried to take his own life with laudanum, but drank so much that he was violently sick, and survived to be jeered and pelted all the way to Tyburn.

charmingly Heath Robinson **clock** above the Neal's Yard Wholefood Warehouse. A tube marking off the minutes slowly fills with water. Then, on the hour, the water races into watering cans which tip into a gutter filled with flowers mounted on floats. The flowers rise into view as though they have just grown, then subside as the water drains away.

Seven Dials T9

Tube Covent Garden, Leicester Square.

The 'Neal' of Neal St refers to Thomas Neale, Master of the Royal Mint in the late

17th century, who dabbled unwisely in property speculation. Neale's number one priority was to squeeze every last penny out of his investment, and he felt that building a square would be a waste of precious leasable land. So instead he constructed a star-shaped development with seven streets leading off from an ornamental Doric pillar in the centre. The pillar had a sundial on each of six sides, as well as acting as a sundial itself – hence the name Seven Dials. Neale's stinginess caught up with him: the narrow maze of streets he constructed may have saved space, but it was also an ideal meeting place for criminals. The area degenerated into an appalling slum frequented only by street vendors scraping for a living.

In the late 18th century, rumours circulated that the Seven Dials monument concealed a vast treasure in its base. The authorities, worried that a riot might break out, took the pillar down in 1773 and only dared to re-erect it a century later, well away from London on the green at Weybridge in Surrey. It returned here in the late 1980s.

St Giles-in-the-Fields T8

Flitcroft St; **tube** *Covent Garden, Leicester Square, Tottenham Court Rd. Rarely open.*

This once-elegant church is now in desperate need of a good scrub. Queen Matilda established a leper colony here in 1101 (hence the dedication to St Giles, patron saint of outcasts and lepers), and the church later handed out a cup of charity to condemned prisoners who passed on their way to the gallows at Tyburn.

The present church, heavily influenced by St Martin-in-the-Fields (*see* p.108) with its classical Portland stone portico and tall spire, was built in 1753 by Henry Flitcroft, the son of William of Orange's gardener. Unfortunately the church is rarely open. If you do get in, look for the stone commemorating the Restoration poet Andrew Marvell, who died in 1678.

Photographer's Gallery T9

5–8 Great Newport St, **t** *(020) 7831 1772;* **tube** *Leicester Square; wheelchair accessible.* **Open** *Mon–Sat 11am–6pm, Sun noon–6pm.*

This excellent venue for photographic exhibitions is in the former home of Sir Joshua Reynolds, founder of the Royal Academy. There's also a good specialist shop and café.

CHARING CROSS ROAD

Tube Leicester Square, Tottenham Court Rd.

Foyle's (Nos.119–125) is the most famous bookshop on a street full of them. Don't be deluded by its reputation, however: it is a chaotic, antiquated mess. Foyle's fame largely rests on the boast that you can find any book at all on its well-thumbed shelves. Sure you can, as long as you have 36 hours to spare and the patience of a saint. On the left about three-quarters of the way down the narrow road alongside Foyle's, **Manette St**, notice the small sculpture in the wall of a goldbeater's arm. This, along with the street's name, is a folly taken straight from Dickens' *Tale of Two Cities*. One of the characters in that novel, Dr Manette, is described as living 'in a quiet street-corner not far from Soho Square' near a goldbeater's workshop. The street, originally Rose St, was duly renamed in 1895 and this curious ornament erected.

Charing Cross Rd's charm lies in higgledy-piggledy secondhand bookshops such as **Quinto** (think *84 Charing Cross Road*). Also have a look at **Zwemmer's**, at Nos.76–80, and **Shipley**, at No.70, for every kind of art book.

At Cambridge Circus, admire the swirling terracotta façade of the **Palace Theatre** (1891), built as an opera house and now semi-permanent home to the permanently booked-out hit musical *Les Misérables*, which opened here originally in 1985. In the south-eastern corner of the Circus is a curious **clock** held up by a sculpted naked woman.

TO THE EMBANKMENT

The Savoy U10

The Strand, t (020) 7846 4343, w www.savoy-group.com; tube Charing Cross, Embankment, Temple; wheelchair accessible.

When the Savoy opened in 1889, it was the most modern luxury hotel in the world, with electric lifts and lights and an unusually high number of bathrooms per floor. César Ritz was the first general manager and Auguste Escoffier first head chef; the pair of them absconded nine years later to found the Ritz Hotel in Paris. With them they took the Savoy's enviable guest list, as well as such recipes as Peach Melba, which they concocted for the delectation of the Australian opera singer Nellie Melba. Cars heading into the hotel drive on the right rather than the left; this is the only street in Britain where traffic conforms to the rest of Europe.

In the Middle Ages the Savoy hotel, and much of the ground to the east of it, was the site of the Savoy Palace, an imposing fortified waterside residence occupied at various times by the Black Prince and John of Gaunt, regent for the infant Richard II. The only vestige is the **Savoy Chapel** on Savoy St, which now bears little resemblance to the original. Some of the walls date from 1502, but the rest is mid-19th century. Once popular for society weddings, partly because it tolerated the remarriage of divorcees, it is now the Chapel of the Royal Victorian Order.

Victoria Embankment Gardens U11–V10

Tube Charing Cross, Embankment.

These gardens are part of the land reclaimed when Sir Joseph Bazalgette's Metropolitan Board of Works built the Embankment in the 1860s as a buffer against flooding and disease. It's a pleasant park, full of worthy statuary, but its main attraction is its view over one of London's more unusual landmarks, Cleopatra's Needle.

Cleopatra's Needle V11

Tube Charing Cross, Embankment.

A 60ft granite obelisk probably wasn't the most practical present the Turkish Viceroy of Egypt, Muhammad Ali, could have offered as a mark of his esteem for the British back in 1819. It took the British a staggering 59 years to get it back home, and even then the best place they could think to put it was here between the river and a four-lane highway. The French, given a similar monument by Ali at the same time, gave theirs pride of place in the Place de la Concorde.

Cleopatra's Needle has always been a bit of a joke. It's almost impossible to get close enough to admire the carvings and symbols dating back to 1450 BC which honour not just Cleopatra but Pharaohs Tethmosis III and Ramses II too. When the British were first presented with the obelisk in Alexandria, it was lying helplessly in the sand, having toppled over. For decades nobody could work out how to move it. Then in 1877 the engineer John Dixon built an iron pontoon and towed it out to sea, where it was nearly lost in a gale. The original site planned for the Needle, in front of the Houses of Parliament, turned out to be no good because of ground subsidence. When it finally went up on the present site in 1878, it was realized in horror that the contractor had planted the sphinxes at its base the wrong way around. A contemporary piece of graffiti read:

This monument one supposes
Was looked upon by Moses
It passed in time from Greeks to Turks
And was stuck up here by the Board of Works.

The Board of Works took it very seriously and buried mementoes beneath it for posterity. Somewhere under the 186 tons of granite are a selection of newspapers, some coins, a razor, a box of pins, four Bibles in different languages, Bradshaw's *Railway Guide* and photographs of the 12 best-looking Englishwomen of the day.

The Strand, Holborn and Fleet Street

09

1 Lunch

Seven Stars, *53–4 Carey St*, **t** *(020) 7242 8521;* **tube** *Chancery Lane*. **Open** *for food Mon–Fri 11am–11pm*. **Inexpensive**. This small pub is hidden away behind the Royal Courts of Justice and has been going since 1602. Not much seems to have changed since then.

2 Tea and Cakes

Indigo, *One Aldwych Hotel, 1 Aldwych,* **t** *(020) 7300 0400;* **tube** *Charing Cross, Embankment, Holborn*. **Open** *daily 6.30–11am, noon–3pm and 6–11.15pm*. A very stylish coffee shop in the One Aldwych Hotel.

3 Drinks

Ye Olde Cheshire Cheese, *145 Fleet St,* **t** *(020) 7353 6170;* **tube/train** *Blackfriars*. **Open** *Mon–Fri 11am–11pm, Sat 6–11pm, Sun noon–3pm*. Dr Johnson's old haunt, with atmospheric beams and good beers.

The Strand, Holborn and Fleet Street

'Sir,' said Dr Johnson to one of his visitors, 'if you wish to have a just notion of the magnitude of this great City you must not be satisfied with seeing its great streets and squares but must survey the innumerable little lanes and courts.' Johnson spoke from the heart: he lived around Fleet St and the Inns of Court for most of his adult life and was addicted to the furtive clubbishness of the labyrinthine narrow backstreets. Everyone knows Fleet St as the original home of British journalism, and the Inns of Court as the cradle of the English legal system. But the main thoroughfare, from the Strand to Ludgate Circus, has only the faintest signs – a bookshop or an appropriately named pub – of these two professions. The real activity, or what's left of it, goes on in the warren of quadrangles on either side, which resemble not so much the heart of a big city as a medieval university town.

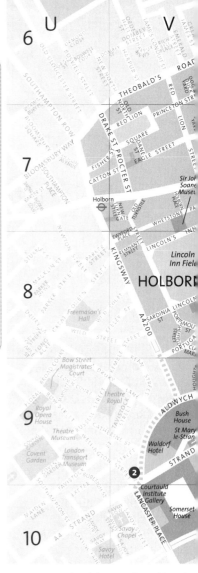

The topography of the area gives a hint of its atmosphere. The Inns of Court have always shrouded themselves in secrecy and ritual as a way of asserting their place in the social order. There is no less a mythology surrounding the great printing presses and journalists' pubs that once characterized Fleet St. But they have almost all gone, victims of new technology which has pushed the newspapers out to Docklands, and most of their old office buildings have been demolished or taken over by accountancy firms. But this is still very much a working area, so come during the week to see it at its best.

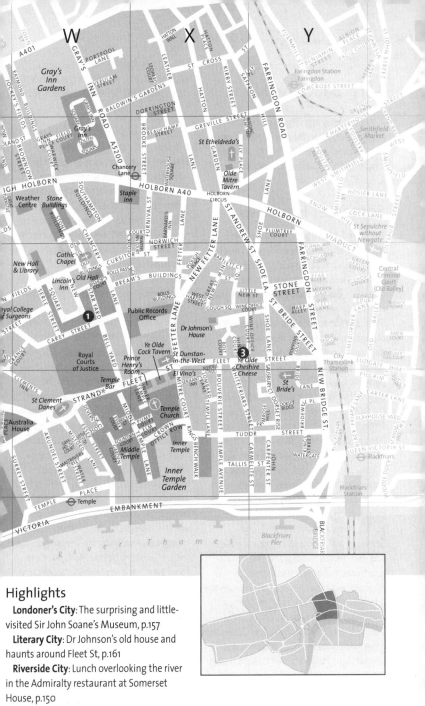

Highlights

Londoner's City: The surprising and little-visited Sir John Soane's Museum, p.157

Literary City: Dr Johnson's old house and haunts around Fleet St, p.161

Riverside City: Lunch overlooking the river in the Admiralty restaurant at Somerset House, p.150

Outdoor City: A picnic in the tranquil Inner Temple garden, p.155

Indoor City: Somerset House's museums, with priceless collections of art, mosaics or snuff boxes, p.150

THE STRAND

This is a noisy and largely soulless thoroughfare which, as the name implies, once formed the riverfront. For sights along its western end, *see* 'Covent Garden and Around', p.146.

Somerset House V10

The Strand, t (020) 7845 4600, e info@ somerset-house.org.uk, w www.somerset-house.org.uk; tube Temple (closed Sun), Charing Cross, Embankment; wheelchair accessible. Guided tours covering the highlights of Somerset House are available Tues, Thurs and Sat at noon (times are subject to change, call first for information); £2.75. Restaurant, café and giftshop.

Somerset House was the first Renaissance palace in England, built for one of the biggest thugs in the country's history. In 1547 the Duke of Somerset was named Lord Protector for the new king, nine-year-old Edward VI, and set about building a home grand enough to match his overweening ambitions. He knocked down two bishops' palaces, an Inn of Chancery and a church to make room for his super-palace, and pillaged two more churches to provide the stone. Such a man could not last long, and Somerset was executed in 1552. His palace was demolished in the 1770s. The replacement, used to house a succession of Royal Societies, various public records and now the Inland Revenue service, is a fine Georgian building by William Chambers.

In 1990, the Courtauld Institute Gallery was moved here, and then the buildings were spectacularly refurbished in 2000 to house the Gilbert Collection and the Hermitage Rooms. As part of the dramatic makeover, the central courtyard has been filled with a sea of ethereal fountains, which leap into an elaborate dance twice an hour and flicker with different-coloured lights at dusk. In winter, the courtyard becomes an outdoor ice-rink, one of the prettiest and most popular in London. The courtyard also sometimes becomes a venue for concerts, from classical to country.

The Courtauld Institute Gallery

Entrance to the right on the way into Somerset House, t (020) 7848 2526, e gallery info@courtauld.ac.uk, w www.courtauld .ac.uk; wheelchair accessible. Open Mon–Sat 10am–6pm, Sun noon–6pm, last adm 5.15pm; closed 1 Jan and 24–26 Dec; adm £4 or £7.50 for an annual ticket, concessions and children free, part-time and overseas students £3, free Mon 10am–2pm. Café.

This is Somerset House's chief attraction, with an exquisite collection of paintings, particularly of Impressionists and Postimpressionists. Most of the paintings were a bequest by the philanthropist Samuel Courtauld, who also set up a school of fine art affiliated to London University.

An elegant staircase leads to 11 smallish rooms spread over two floors. There is a magnificent *Adam and Eve* by **Lucas Cranach the Elder**, some fine **Rubens** including his early masterpiece *The Descent from the Cross*, and a roomful of unusual 18th-century Italian art including a series of **Tiepolos**. The Impressionists include a copy by the artist of **Manet**'s *Le Déjeuner sur l'Herbe* (the original being in the Musée d'Orsay in Paris), some wonderful **Degas** studies of dancers, and moody **Cézanne** landscapes. Highlights from the 20th century include **Modigliani** and some excellent British works donated in the early 1980s.

The Gilbert Collection

South Building, t (020) 7420 9400, w www.gilbert-collection.org.uk; wheelchair accessible. Open Mon–Sat 10am–6pm, Sun noon–6pm, last adm 5.15pm; closed 1 Jan and 24–26 Dec; adm (including audioguide) adults £4 or £7 including admission to the Courtauld Gallery, concessions £3, free to full-time students and the unemployed. Guided tours Thurs and Sat at 2.30pm; adults £6.50, concessions £6; bookings t (020) 7420 9410, e tours@gilbert-collection.org.uk. Giftshop.

Somerset House's restored South Building houses the Gilbert Collection of Decorative Arts. This spectacular collection is a gift to the nation from evening-gown maker and real-estate developer Arthur Gilbert, whose rags-to-riches tale is told in a series of exhibits which culminates in a rather odd waxwork of the man wearing yellow shorts. The collection is displayed in 17 gilded galleries, all crammed with an eye-popping collection of dazzling treasures – 'enough jewels to crown a decent-sized kingdom', as one reviewer put it, and valued at a startling £100 million.

The collection of **mosaics** includes Roman 'micromosaics' with up to 1,500 glass tesserae per square inch, and a beautiful collection of Florentine hard mosaics, such as a necklace and ear-ring set. There's a spectacular assortment of **gold- and silverwork** from the 15th to the 19th centuries, which includes one of the richest collections of gold snuffboxes in the world, once the property of such luminaries as Napoleon. You can take a closer look at the exquisite craftsmanship of the objects in the **Workshop Gallery**, where touchscreen computers explain some of the methods used.

Hermitage Rooms

South Bulding, t (020) 7845 4630, w www.hermitagerooms.com; wheelchair accessible. Open Mon–Sat 10am–6pm, Sun noon–6pm, last adm 5pm; closed 1 Jan and 24–26 Dec; adm adults £6, concessions £4, under-5s free. Tickets are sold for timed slots (on the hour and half-hour) on site or in advance from Ticketmaster on t (020) 7413 3398 (24 hours), w www.ticketmaster.co.uk, at all Ticketmaster ticket centres, including selected branches of Waitrose, HMV and Tower Records nationwide, and at the Virgin Megastore, Piccadilly (Ticketmaster charge a £1 booking fee per ticket). Giftshop.

The Hermitage Museum in St Petersburg, Russia, has more than 10km of gallery space, and yet can show barely a fraction of its vast collection. A partial solution to the problems of space and funding was to display part of their collection here. The galleries have been painstakingly refurbished to give some sense of the imperial interiors of the palaces of St Petersburg; Russian craftsmen laboured over the intricately worked marquetry floors (ladies are specifically requested not to wear pointed heels) and all the fittings and wall coverings have been carefully chosen to reflect the imperial opulence of Tsarist Russia. The temporary exhibitions held here have all proved enormously successful, and you should try to book well in advance.

St Mary-le-Strand V9

The Strand, t (020) 7836 3126; tube Temple (closed Sun), Charing Cross, Embankment. Open Mon–Fri 11am–4pm, Sun 10am–2pm.

Now in an island in the middle of the road, this church was James Gibbs's (*see* p.53) first full church commission in 1724, and borrows heavily from classical models. The round porch, for example, is a straight steal from Santa Maria della Pace in Rome, where Gibbs had studied, and the steeple is pure Wren. Still, it won Gibbs a handsome reputation as the English vogue for classicism took off. Originally, the church stood on the north side of the street, but turned into an island in 1910 as the advent of the motor car prompted the broadening of the Strand. The interior of the church was refitted in the 19th century and is unremarkable except for the thick unornamented interior walls, made that way to keep out traffic noise. St Mary is now dedicated to the women of the Royal Navy.

St Clement Danes W9

The Strand, t (020) 7242 8282; tube Temple (closed Sun), Chancery Lane, Holborn, Blackfriars. Open Mon–Fri 8.30am–4pm, Sat 8.30am–3.30pm, Sun 8.30am–12.30pm.

Christopher Wren's recently renovated church (1682) belongs to the Royal Air Force, which paid for the restoration of its elegant steeple after the Second World War. The place contains several war memorials and lists of

Oranges and Lemons

Every March, the pupils of St Clement Danes Primary School come here to receive an orange and a lemon in a ceremony echoing the words of a famous London nursery rhyme about the city's church bells:

Oranges and lemons
Say the bells of St Clement's.

In fact the ceremony is phoney, since the church in the rhyme is almost certainly St Clement's Eastcheap, near the wharves where citrus fruit used to arrive from the Mediterranean. The tune is played on the church carillon.

honour for the men who died fighting Nazi Germany.

Outside the church are **statues** to Air Chief Marshal Lord Dowding, hero of the Battle of Britain, and Arthur 'Bomber' Harris, who masterminded the bombing campaign which destroyed Dresden and other German cities. At the unveiling of the statue in 1992, a crowd of protesters gathered to voice their disapproval at the description of Harris as 'a great commander' and tried to daub the figure in spraypaint.

Royal Courts of Justice W8

Information **t** *(020) 7947 6000;* **tube** *Temple (closed Sun), Chancery Lane, Holborn, Blackfriars; wheelchair accessible.*
Open Mon–Fri 9.30am–4.30pm (no court cases in the August recess); adm free. Leave bags and cameras at the entrance.

The architect of this gargantuan Gothic extravaganza, George Edmund Street, had always wanted to build a cathedral, and it shows. The building is an astonishingly complex work of high vaulted ceilings, ornately carved halls, burrow-like corridors and crazy spires and towers. There are more than 1,000 rooms, including 79 chambers for court hearings, and 3 miles of corridors. The 230ft-long **Great Hall**, which you see as you come in, looks like the nave of a great church with its high vaulted arches and ornamented windows. This is one of the grandest exam-

ples of English Victorian Gothic. The effort of building it stretched Parliament's budget to breaking point, harried and alienated several groups of workers, and so exhausted poor old George Street that he died of a stroke shortly before his masterpiece was completed in 1882.

Fourteen years earlier, Street had been chosen from a ferociously competitive group of architects, including George Gilbert Scott, E.M. Barry and Alfred Waterhouse, to build a permanent site where civil cases could be heard in the High Court. (Criminal cases are tried at the Old Bailey; *see* p.219.) At the time, the legal profession was busy reforming itself into something close to its modern shape. Only a few years earlier, Dickens had published *Bleak House*, a rousing indictment of the bureaucratic, self-serving, expensive muddle surrounding legal suits, and the injustice meted out to innocent parties as a result. In 1875 the Supreme Court of Judicature replaced the old superior courts and established the Court of Appeal and the High Court as they are known today. The High Court is divided into three sections – the Family Division, which deals with divorce and private property disputes; the Chancery Division, which covers company law; and the Queen's Bench Division, which handles major libel and other prominent suits.

Street's ambition was, like the judiciary's, very much one of moral improvement. The grand figures gazing down from the **roof** as you walk in are Solomon (left), Alfred the Great (right) and Jesus Christ (centre, on the highest point of the upper arch). At the back, above the **northern entrance** to the Courts, is a fourth figure, that of Moses, the ultimate lawgiver. Inside, at the far end of the Great Hall and halfway up the **staircase**, Street deliberately left out one column as a sign to the Almighty that he acknowledged his own imperfections. Clearly, the architect hoped to impart some of his Christian idealism to the legal profession.

Despite Street's lofty ideals, little of the bureaucratic fog cleared as a result of the reorganization of the judiciary. Indeed

Street's grandly elaborate building, for all its architectural merits, could not have better expressed the Byzantine complications of the legal process. It is imposing, but ultimately expresses only the supreme self-confidence of the Lord Chancellors and Lord Chief Justices whose statues line the Grand Hall. To find the most appropriate symbol in this building, you should look not to those grand figures on the roof, but the emblem above the **judges' entrance** on the northern side of the law courts. It shows a cat and a dog tussling with all the base animal instincts of litigants.

You can see an **exhibition of legal costumes**, from the workaday to the ceremonial, to the right as you walk into the Great Hall. Back in the 18th century, wigs were common among many of the professions. Only three groups kept wearing them for any length of time – lawyers, clergymen and coachmen. Today it is only the lawyers (plus the coachmen of the royal household) who persist in the tradition, although there are occasional campaigns to scrap them. Perhaps wigs lend an air of *gravitas* that the law desperately needs. Sit in on one of the hearings (they are all open to the public – just ask at the information desk for advice on which to attend) and you get the feeling that advocates and judges are glorified actors playing out their roles on a privileged stage.

Temple Bar W9

Tube Temple (closed Sun), Blackfriars, Chancery Lane, Holborn.

In a traffic island in the middle of the road, this monument marks the edge of the City of London. In the Middle Ages the Bar was quite literally a barrier to control comings and goings into the City. So independent and powerful were the City fathers that any unwelcome visitors were simply slung into the jail that stood on the site. The unlucky ones had their heads and pickled body parts displayed on spikes. Even the sovereign had to ask permission to pass this way, a tradition that has lasted in ritualistic form into the modern era. If the Queen wants to enter the City on official business, she stops here to request entry from the Lord Mayor. The Lord Mayor then agrees and offers his sword as a demonstration of loyalty. The sword is immediately returned to show that the sovereign is in the City under the mayor's protection and she continues on her way. This is not a frequent ceremony: the last time it took place was during the Queen's Silver Jubilee celebrations in 1977.

For 200 years a Wren gateway marked this spot, but in 1878 it was removed because of traffic congestion and replaced with the present monument by Horace Jones. The **bronze panels** depict Queen Victoria and Edward, Prince of Wales, entering the City of London. The **bronze griffin** on top is one of the City's emblems, introduced by the Victorians, who remembered that the griffins of mythology guarded over a hidden treasure of gold. They presumably forgot, however, that griffins also tore approaching humans to pieces as a punishment for their greed.

THE INNS OF COURT

Tube Temple (closed Sun), Blackfriars, Chancery Lane, Holborn.

Sometimes it is hard to tell whether the four Inns of Court – Middle Temple, Inner Temple, Lincoln's Inn and Gray's Inn – are lawyers' associations or the meeting grounds of some quietly cabalistic sect. Their practices seem strange, if not incomprehensible, to anyone not fully initiated, and their history is steeped in semi-secret ritual.

History of the Temple

The first people to occupy the site of the Inns were the Knights Templar, the most fervent of all the Crusaders, who moved here halfway through the 12th century and set up a lucrative trading business along the River Thames. These fighting monks took their name, and the name of this area, from

Jerusalem's holiest of holies, Temple Mount, where shrines to Judaism, Christianity and Islam co-exist on the same site. One of those shrines, the Dome of the Rock, was the inspiration for the knights' trademark round churches (*see* 'Temple Church', below). The Knights Templar had peculiar customs and secret initiation rites which gave them an air of mystery similar to the one surrounding the lawyers today. Some of the folklore was passed on directly. Lawyers' briefs, for example, are still signed with a kind of loop that evolved from the Templars' special sign of the cross.

The wealth and power of the Templars incited the envy of secular authorities, who violently suppressed the order in 1307 and handed over the Temple buildings to their rivals, the Knights Hospitaller. The place fell into decline, and lawyers began renting the empty space. The legal profession organized itself much as the knights had done, with a division between the Middle and Inner Temples (the Outer Temple, to the west, was never occupied). The two Inns developed distinct identities. You can tell immediately which building belongs to which Inn because each is stamped with the appropriate emblem: a pascal lamb and flag of innocence to denote Middle Temple, a winged horse or Pegasus for Inner.

The knights were thrown out after the dissolution of the monasteries in 1539 but the lawyers did not gain full control of the Temple until 1609, when James I offered it to them on condition that they guarantee the upkeep of its buildings. This the lawyers did, though to judge by the wild revelries that went on it is scarcely believable that the church and master's house stayed in one piece. The students were forever putting on music and dance shows (in fact these were part of the curriculum). By the 16th century the Temple elders felt constrained to appoint Lords of Misrule to impose some semblance of order. The lawyers were not much more diligent in subsequent centuries. Often they would go fishing in the Thames all afternoon and had to be called in by a horn blast.

Fleet St's Apollo Club (now long gone) used to have a sign above its kitchen clock which barristers heeded with deep reverence: 'If the wine of last night hurts you, drink more today and it will cure you.'

If life is more civilized nowadays, it is probably because of the pressing need to earn a living and meet the Inns' astronomically high rents. Many barristers have moved out altogether, while some of the rooms on the upper floors have been taken over by individuals or small private companies unconnected with the law. You still see plenty of lawyers around, though, their black gowns flapping in the breeze as they scurry around the courtyards and up the poky staircases.

Middle Temple V–W9

Middle Temple Lane.

Walk down Middle Temple Lane, after passing under the 16th-century **wooden gateway** from Fleet St, and you'll pass several buildings and squares where the barristers have their offices or 'chambers'. Each entranceway is numbered and has a painted wooden board indicating the names of the occupants inside. The ground floor is usually occupied by a clerk who does administrative work for all the barristers on the staircase.

Brick Court (first on the right, walking down Middle Temple Lane) was once occupied by the playwright and occasional lawyer Oliver Goldsmith; now the court has been partly converted into a car park. **Pump Court** (first left) is one of the oldest parts of the Inn, whose deep wells were used to provide water for fighting fires during the bombing of the Second World War; the pump itself was destroyed and never replaced. **Fountain Court** (second right) still has the single water jet that gives it its name.

Middle Temple Hall

Corner of Fountain Court and Middle Temple Lane. Entry only by permission – with lashings of charm – at the Security Office.

This magnificent Tudor dining hall, completed in 1573, perfectly expresses the fulsome self-confidence of the legal profession. Admiring the grandeur of the double **hammerbeam roof** and the beautiful **screen**, both fashioned from solid English oak, it is easy to understand how Ben Jonson could describe the Inns of Court as 'the noblest nurseries of humanity and liberty in the kingdom'.

The **high table**, where the senior members of the Inn traditionally sit, was made from a single oak tree donated by Queen Elizabeth I. Since it's 29ft long, it was easier to build the hall around the table than to try to manœuvre the table into the hall; it hasn't moved since. The smaller table in front of it, known as the **Cupboard**, was cut from the wood of the *Golden Hinde*, the ship that Sir Francis Drake led against the Spanish Armada in 1588. The remaining 26 tables and pairs of benches were an economical and ecological brainwave made by recycling the original floorboards when they were first replaced in 1792. Sadly the benches may, by popular demand, soon be replaced by chairs which are a little less taxing on the behinds of these distinguished diners. Above the high table are the **portraits** of monarchs from Charles I through to William III. The other walls are emblazoned with the **coats-of-arms** of the Middle Temple's Readers, or senior lecturers. Everything is heavy with the weight of tradition, and yet is effortlessly elegant and light at the same time.

In Tudor and Stuart times the hall was used for lavish entertainments, particularly plays; Shakespeare's *Twelfth Night* had its première here in 1601. This was also where students would gather for their gambling sessions; when workmen replaced the floor in 1730, they discovered hundreds of dice beneath the old wooden planks. A century earlier James I had sanctioned dice-playing to allow students a break from the tedium of studying their dusty casebooks.

Middle Temple Garden

The garden, which stretches out behind the library towards the river, is according to tradition the place where the Wars of the Roses

> ### The US Declaration of Independence
>
> There is a copy of the Declaration of Independence in Middle Temple Library. The Middle Temple enthusiastically supported the end of British rule in America, and several of its members, notably Edmund Burke, were involved in drawing up both the Declaration of Independence and the US Constitution. A special relationship with the United States continues to this day.

started in 1455. The beginning of hostilities, at least as recounted in Shakespeare's *Henry VI*, came as the warring houses of Lancaster and York plucked their respective emblems, a red and white rose, from the Temple flower beds.

Inner Temple x9

Off Crown Office Row.

Notice the **Pegasus symbol** on the entrance gate. The magnificent lawns of the Inner Temple's **garden** are an ideal picnic spot in good weather, tranquil and surrounded by fine buildings. On the eastern side is **King's Bench Walk**, a fine brick terrace designed by Christopher Wren. Many of the Inner Temple's buildings, including its dining hall, were destroyed by wartime bombs.

Temple Church x9

*Inner Temple Lane, **w** www.templechurch .com; wheelchair accessible. **Open** Wed–Sat 10am–4pm, Sun services Oct–July at 8.30am and 11.15am. Note that the church is currently under restoration and so opening hours can be erratic.*

More or less intact, this is London's only surviving round church, dating back to 1185. It's a fine example of English Transitional style: the circular western end is Romanesque, while the nave (completed in around 1240) is Gothic. One of its charms is the way in which the semicircular **arches** of the earlier style intersect to form the peaked arches of the later. It is a simple design that

Barristers vs Solicitors

The Inns are not open to all lawyers, only the part of the profession known as barristers. English law divides lawyers into two groups: the majority who deal with clients directly and advise them on points of law, as well as representing them in the lower courts, known as solicitors; and the barristers, who alone are entitled to go to the High Court to plead a case. Historically the difference between the two kinds of lawyer was one of class. For centuries only the independently wealthy could afford to study at an Inn, or read for the bar. Becoming a solicitor was a vocation just for the more lowly orders.

Things have changed in as far as solicitors, especially in the City, have attained far higher status over the years and command equally high salaries. The Inns have also broadened the social range of their intake. Where once it was forbidden to take employment while reading for the bar, nowadays it is perfectly normal. Scholarships are available, especially for overseas students. But the old hierarchical division between barristers and solicitors is still felt, if only because the traditions of the Inns continue very much as before: for example, during the year spent reading for the bar, students still have to eat formal dinner exactly 12 times in the dining hall of their Inn. Another one of the great peculiarities of the barristers' professional code is that they are not allowed to form associations or companies; each one must be self-employed and, nominally, independent (the idea being that they are less corruptible this way). What makes this notion so curious is that the Inns are so manifestly a kind of association. Formal dinners and staircase camaraderie ensure constant contact between members of the profession, and it is still usually through friends or mentors that young barristers get their first jobs.

has been much tinkered with over the years, notably by Wren, who added the **buttresses** and the carved **reredos**, and by the 19th-century architects Sydney Smirke and Decimus Burton, who ensured, in the words of Walter Godfrey, that 'every surface was repaired away or renewed'. The gravest damage was wrought in the Second World War, when incendiary bombs brought down the roof, cracked the Purbeck marble columns and crashed into the nine **effigies of Crusader knights** at the western end of the church. The damage is now largely repaired, and there is a memorial commemorating the bombing in a choir window.

When James I handed over the church to the lawyers in 1609, he made Middle Temple responsible for the northern half, Inner Temple for the southern. They still sit that way today. They have not had recourse recently to the Templars' **penitential cell**, on the northern side towards the back. Prisoners in the 12th and 13th centuries would be left in the tiny room for weeks, fed only with bread and water left in a recess at the bottom. They could follow services through the slit at the front. Many succumbed to the hardship and were carried out of the cell feet first.

The **gateway to Fleet St** (*see* p.160) from Inner Temple Lane is a magnificent piece of 17th-century half-timber work, one of the few surviving examples of pre-Fire construction in wood in London.

Lincoln's Inn V–W8

Tube *Holborn, Chancery Lane.*

In many ways this is the most beautiful of the Inns of Court, with its broad meadows and grand buildings.

New Square

This is the heart of the Inn. You'll have to ask permission to see the **Old Hall**, built in 1492, which has a fine arch-braced roof, panelled walls and carved screen. It also boasts a large Hogarth painting, *Paul Preaching before Felix*, commissioned by the Inn in 1750. Next door is the **Gothic Chapel**, which looks medieval but in fact dates back only to the early 17th century – an indication of how backward English architecture was before Inigo Jones came to shake it up. To reach the interior, which has been largely refurbished, you have to climb a stone staircase. Beneath is a fine undercroft where, under the arches, students at the Inn used to meet and hold classes.

Further up on the same side is a fine Palladian ensemble known as the **Stone Buildings**, built by Robert Taylor in 1774 (note the scars left on the stonework by a German Zeppelin raid in 1917). On the other side of the lawn are the **New Hall** and **Library**, built in red brick in neo-Tudor style by Philip Hardwick in 1843–5.

A magnificent Tudor **Gatehouse** (1518) leads from the east side of the Inn into Chancery Lane; above the heavy oak doors are the arms of two distinguished members of Lincoln's Inn, Thomas More and Thomas Lovell, as well as those of the Inn's founder, the 14th-century Earl of Lincoln. On Chancery Lane is the Victorian Tudor Revival **Public Records Office**.

Lincoln's Inn Fields

This square was Inigo Jones's second attempt, after Covent Garden, at piazza architecture in London. Like its predecessor, though, it fell out of fashion almost as soon as it had been built, in the early 1640s. Only one of the original mansions, **Lindsey House** at Nos.59–60, has survived, albeit with a stuccoed façade added in the 18th century. The grassland in the centre of the square was never properly developed and soon turned into a brawling ground and general rubbish dump. Nowadays it is little more than a nondescript field, the allure of its greenery marred by ugly wire fencing to prevent the homeless from sleeping there.

Try to see the **Royal College of Surgeons** at Nos.35–53, a classical building revamped by Charles Barry in the 1830s, which has an extraordinary collection of anatomical specimens. It is not officially open to the public, but ask nicely and they may let you in. The collection, started by the 18th-century physician John Hunter, includes the skeleton of Jonathan Wild, the notorious thief-taker (*see*

p.144), plus a giant of 7ft 8in and a dwarf measuring just 20 inches.

Sir John Soane's Museum v7

*13 Lincoln's Inn Fields, **t** (020) 7405 2107, **w** www.soane.org; tube Holborn, Chancery Lane; ground floor wheelchair accessible. **Open** Tues–Sat 10am–5pm; closed all public hols and 24 Dec; **adm** free but any donations are gratefully accepted. **Guided tour** Sat at 2.30pm; £3, free to students. **Visits by candlelight** on the first Tues of each month 6–9pm.*

John Soane (1753–1837) was a great English eccentric and one of the great architects of his age, a fanatical student of antiquity and one of the towering figures of the Neoclassical movement in Britain. His greatest single achievement was the Bank of England, which fell victim to the philistinism of the City in the 1920s (*see* p.224). For the most part, Soane's works were too idiosyncratic or fantastic to win public competitions. A contemporary described him as 'personal to the point of perversity'. Soane did not seem unduly bothered by the relative paucity of high-profile commissions; he stayed busy throughout his professional life and won a formidable reputation as a lecturer on the architecture of his contemporaries.

In later life he bought up and converted these three adjacent houses in Lincoln's Inn Fields, adapting each room to his quirky style and filling them with objects from his remarkable art collection. In 1833 (four years before his death), Soane saw through a private Act of Parliament in which he bequeathed the whole collection to the public, leaving money for upkeep and payment of staff, with the stipulation that the museum be maintained forever as it was on the day of his death. It is a unique monument to one man's fertile imagination.

Every room yields surprises, whether it is the enormous collection of plaster casts Soane made from classical models, or the classical colonnade running along the upstairs corridor, or simply the amazing ambiguities of light, which Soane manipulated intriguingly in every area of the house with the aid of concave and then convex mirrors. Above the picture room on the first floor is a beautiful glass dome; in the basement you suddenly come across catacombs, or an atmospheric Monk's Parlour that looks like the setting for a Gothic horror novel.

One of the highlights is the **Picture Room** on the ground floor, containing two great satirical series of paintings by Hogarth: *The Rake's Progress*, which follows the rise and fall of a degenerate young man from the moment he comes into his inheritance to his untimely end in the madhouse, and *The Election*, four scenes satirizing the greed and corruption surrounding political ambition. Nowhere will you see better examples of Hogarth's unfailing eye for the grotesque and the debauched. The Picture Room also includes studies by Piranesi and architectural drawings by Soane himself. Soane ingeniously accommodated this sizeable collection into a minuscule room by hanging the whole lot on a series of false walls which he called 'picture planes'. These open out one after the other, until eventually they reveal a window looking down to the basement and a small alcove containing a plaster cast from Castle Howard of a nymph, gently undraping herself.

Soane's other prized exhibit is the **sarcophagus** of the Egyptian Pharaoh Seti I (1303–1290 BC) in the Sepulchral Chamber in the basement. This is the finest example of a sarcophagus you can see outside Egypt, beautifully preserved and covered in hieroglyphics honouring Osiris and Ra and adorned with a painted figure of the goddess Nut, to whom Seti had pledged allegiance, on the inside. The sarcophagus came originally from the Valley of the Kings, from which it was plundered by an interesting character called Giuseppe Belzona, a former circus strongman and tomb robber who eventually died in the jungle trying to find the source of the Niger. Initially, Belzona offered the sarcophagus to the British Museum, but the curators dithered and tried to haggle over its expensive price tag. In 1824 Belzona took it to

Soane, who snapped it up for the full asking price, a princely £2,000.

In the **Drawing Rooms** upstairs you see the plans Soane made to transform London into a rational city, including one proposal for a giant royal palace in Hyde Park and another for a new Neoclassical Parliament building. Try to imagine Westminster with this understated, elegant architecture instead of the actual neo-Gothic extravagance by Barry and Pugin. London would be quite a different city altogether.

Gray's Inn W6–7

Tube Chancery Lane, Holborn.

This, the last of the four Inns of Court, suffered most from wartime bomb damage and has largely been rebuilt in unimaginative imitation of the graceful brick original. The first open space you come to, **South Square**, has one elegant older building left at No.1. This was where Dickens began his working life, as a 15-year-old legal clerk. The **Chapel** contains some original 17th-century stained glass, and the **Hall** has managed to preserve its 16th-century wooden screen. The greatest pleasure is the long **garden** at the back, first planted by Francis Bacon in 1606 and popular ever since for lunchtime strolls and picnics.

Staple Inn W–X7

High Holborn; tube Chancery Lane.

One of the few pre-Great Fire shop frontings left in London leads from High Holborn into a former Inn of Chancery, one of nine so-called Inns which acted as a sort of overflow for the main Inns of Court. Lawyers had their offices here, and some students would pursue their studies while waiting for admission to the Temple, Lincoln's Inn or Gray's Inn. All the Inns of Chancery have now disappeared, and Staple Inn's quiet squares and graceful brick houses are occupied by the Institute of Actuaries. This is a postwar reconstruction of the original 14th-century buildings. Enjoy it as surreptitiously as you can: Staple Inn is not officially open to the public, but nobody will stop you wandering quietly in.

Furnival's Inn X7

High Holborn; tube Chancery Lane.

Across High Holborn from Staple Inn, the Victorian Gothic extravaganza in red brick and terracotta used to be Furnival's Inn, another Inn of Chancery. The present building, designed by Alfred Waterhouse and completed in 1879, was constructed for an insurance company which had offices here until 1999. It is a surprisingly graceful, if somewhat overstated, Victorian palace, leading you through a series of fine court-yards and elaborately arcaded passages.

HOLBORN

The area around and just east of Lincoln's and Gray's Inn is Holborn, a district of un-exciting offices and only occasionally exciting shops sandwiched in between the City and the more obvious delights of Bloomsbury. The only consolation of this nondescript corner of London is that it was a lot worse in the 17th and early 18th centuries, when the River Fleet was a notorious open sewer, filled with dead cats and rotten meat from Smithfield Market as well as all the stinking ordure of the City. The Fleet was eventually filled in in 1747; the Victorians then tried to jolly up the district, none too success-fully, by building **Holborn Viaduct**, a brightly decorated bridge over Farringdon Rd, and adorning it with allegorical statues of Com-merce, Agriculture, Science and Fine Arts.

Hatton Garden X6–7

Tube Chancery Lane, Farringdon.

This street is the centre of London's diamond trade and perfect for window-shopping. Jewellers have been here since the 1830s, but the street is also known for its curious inhabitants. The Italian revolutionary

Giuseppe Mazzini lived at No.5 in the early 1840s, while at No.57 a Mr Hiram Maxim perfected the world's first automatic gun in 1884.

Ely Place X7

Tube Chancery Lane, Farringdon.

The alley next to No.8 Hatton Garden leads past the **Olde Mitre Tavern**, with its low, cherry-panelled rooms dating back to Tudor times, and into a beautifully unspoilt street of smart Georgian townhouses, Ely Place, a private road, closed to traffic, with a fine **gatehouse**.

St Etheldreda's

*14 Ely Place. **Open** daily 8am–6.30pm.*

This is Holborn's most intriguing and beau-tiful church. Etheldreda was a 7th-century Anglo-Saxon princess who had the distressing habit of marrying and then refusing to sleep with her husbands. When husband number two, Prince Egfrith of Northumbria, finally lost patience with her and made unseemly advances, she withdrew into holy orders and founded a double monastery at Ely in Cambridgeshire. Seven years later, in 679, she was stricken with a tumour on her neck and died. None mourned Etheldreda more than her sister, the unfortu-nately named Sexburga, who campaigned ardently to have her sanctity recognized. In 695, Sexburga had Etheldreda's coffin opened and found that the tumour had vanished. Her skin was now quite unblem-ished. A miracle!

Etheldreda became Ely's special saint and was the obvious choice of patron for this double-storey church, built in the 13th century as part of the Bishop of Ely's London palace. It was by all accounts a sumptuous residence, with stunning gardens, but after the dissolution of the monasteries it went into decline. Elizabeth I leased part of the property to her favoured chancellor, Christopher Hatton, to whom we owe the name Hatton Garden, for an annual rent of £10, plus – a romantic touch, this – ten bales of hay and a red rose plucked at midsummer. Of all the palace buildings, only the church survived the double onslaught of the Civil War and the Great Fire. Today it is one of the oldest surviving buildings in the City and one of its few Roman Catholic churches (it was taken over by the Rosminian Order in the late 19th century).

The Interior

The Gothic **upper church** is a warm, lofty room with a fine wooden-beamed ceiling and huge **stained-glass windows** at each end. The east window, behind the altar, is particularly striking, with its depiction of the Holy Trinity surrounded by the apostles and Anglo-Saxon and Celtic saints including Etheldreda herself. The west window is much starker, portraying the martyrdom of three Carthusian priors at Tyburn in 1535 with Christ hovering over them. Both windows date from after the Second World War; their predecessors were shattered by German bombs.

Downstairs, the **lower church** or crypt is much simpler, no more than a room with a plain altar and little decoration. Round the walls are stone engravings depicting the stations of the cross, while in one of the alcoves on the south side is a statue of St Blaise, the patron saint of throat diseases (he once saved a boy who had swallowed a fishbone), who is commemorated in an annual ceremony.

FLEET STREET

Tube Temple (closed Sun), Blackfriars.

Until the mid-1980s Fleet St was the epicentre of the British press. The stench of newsprint emanated from the very bowels of the buildings where the presses ran all night. At the crack of dawn the first pubs and cheap cafés opened to feed the typesetters, printers and early-shift reporters. But nowadays Fleet St has all but died; the newspaper offices have been taken over by accountants and solicitors or, in the case of the downmarket *Sun* and *News of the World*, turned into a multi-storey car park. Meanwhile, most of the pubs and restaurants have either closed down or become sterile and expensive. The major titles which once all huddled around this small area are now scattered across London. Only Reuters, the international news and information agency, soldiers on at No.85.

From the 1970s onwards, it became clear that computerization was going to transform the newspaper industry. There was considerable resistance to modernization, particularly from the powerful print unions who correctly foresaw disaster for thousands of their members. For a while, newspapers struggled on with antiquated machinery and whole armies of surplus staff. Then in 1986 the Australian media baron Rupert Murdoch, who had bought up a number of struggling titles over the previous 20 years, simply fired all his unionized workers and moved the offices of *The Times, Sunday Times, Sun* and *News of the World* to a new site with state-of-the-art technology in Wapping. It was the end of an era, and everybody knew it. Within three years the *Daily Telegraph* had moved to Docklands, the *Daily Express* to Vauxhall and the *Evening Standard* and *Daily Mail* to Kensington.

Prince Henry's Room X9

First floor, 17 Fleet St, t (020) 8294 1158.
Open *Mon–Sat 11am–2pm; closed hols;*
adm *free, donations welcome.*

Henry was the son of James I, and this room was built on the occasion of his being named Prince of Wales in 1610. The site was scarcely grand, however, merely the upstairs room of an inn, but it became his 'committee room' from which he oversaw his vast estates. The chief attraction is the beautifully preserved **oak panelling** and the ornamentation on the **moulded plaster ceiling** – the oldest in the City of London – bearing the letters P.H. The room also houses a collection of memorabilia of the celebrated 17th-century diarist **Samuel Pepys**, who used to do a fair amount of his drinking around here.

Ye Olde Cock Tavern x9

*22 Fleet St. **Open** Mon–Fri 11am–11pm.*

One of Samuel Pepys's drinking haunts, the tavern still has fine wood panelling (unfortunately painted over in the last makeover), although it was rebuilt in the late 19th century. In Pepys's day it was a much-frequented chop house. His diary entry for 23 April 1668 describes in a macaronic mixture of languages how he turned up for an assignation with an actress called Mrs Knipp. He got well tanked up, 'did tocar her corps all over and besar sans fin'.

El Vino's x9

*47 Fleet St, **t** (020) 7353 6786. **Open** Mon–Fri 11am–10pm.*

Ironically, one of the street's more objectionable establishments is still going strong. Historically El Vino's wine bar must be one of the most reactionary drinking holes in London. Women were only served – reluctantly – after an appeal court ruling upheld their customer rights in 1982.

St Dunstan-in-the-West x8

*Fleet St, **t** (020) 7242 6027; wheelchair accessible. Closed most of the time.*

The first thing you'll notice is the church's **clock**, which looks like something out of *The Flintstones*, with its two muscular figures in gold loincloths who beat a gong every 15 minutes with their hefty clubs. Believe it or not, this dates from the 17th century, when it was erected by the parishioners of St Dunstan as a token of thanks for surviving the Great Fire along with their church. Nobody knows who the two figures are meant to represent, the best guess being Gog and Magog, the legendary giants of the City. The church dates back to the 13th century, but was completely rebuilt in the 19th and is now shut most of the time.

Notice the **memorial bust** on the outside to Lord Northcliffe, pioneer of the trashy downmarket newspaper and spiritual father of today's powerful press barons. Northcliffe never believed what he read in the papers and never particularly cared to. He used to tell his journalists: 'Never lose your sense of the superficial.'

Ye Olde Cheshire Cheese x8

*145 Fleet St. **Open** Mon–Fri 11am–11pm, Sat 6–11pm, Sun noon–3pm.*

The dark, low passage next to the pub is called Wine House Court, which, as the name suggests, was one of the great drinking haunts of the 18th century. One contemporary records that 'nothing but a hurricane' would have induced Dr Johnson to drink anywhere else. Ye Olde Cheshire Cheese retains much of the atmosphere of that era with its oak décor and hearty menu. Unfortunately the Cheese has become a little too touristy for its own good, but the beer, if not the food, is still to be recommended. At the turn of the 20th century its star attraction was a parrot named Polly who did impressions. On Armistice Night in 1918 Polly imitated the sound of a champagne cork popping 400 times before fainting from exhaustion. When she died in 1926, obituary notices appeared in more than 200 newspapers.

Dr Johnson's House x8

*17 Gough Square, **t** (020) 7353 3745, **e** curator@drjh.dircon.co.uk, **w** www.drjh.dircon.co.uk. **Open** May–Sept Mon–Sat 11am–5.30pm, Oct–April Mon–Sat 11am–5pm; closed all hols and 24 Dec; **adm** adults £4, concessions £3, children £1. **Giftshop**.*

This is the elegant 17th-century house where the good doctor lived from 1748 to 1759. For many of those years he was busy compiling his famous dictionary, the first of its kind in the English language. He worked in the attic, sitting in a rickety three-legged chair that somehow supported his vast bulk, and ordering about his six clerks, who must have had a tough time keeping up with his boundless energies and inexhaustible wit. Boswell said the attic looked like a counting house. Now it's of interest more for its atmosphere than its contents. The furniture is from the right period, but little of it ever belonged to Johnson. There is, of course, a first edition of the dictionary, along with portraits of Johnson and his friends, a chair on which the doctor sat when he drank at the Cock Tavern and – most bizarrely – a lump of rock said to be part of the Great Wall of China.

The chief legacy of the dictionary to lexicographers is its scrupulous references to literary texts. But it is also full of jokey definitions that poke fun at anyone and everyone, including Johnson himself: a lexicographer is defined as 'a writer of dictionaries, a harmless drudge'. The dictionary, published in 1755, made Johnson's reputation as both a serious academic and a great wit. His wife Tetty, however, did not live to see his moment of glory. Described by Joshua Reynolds as 'always drunk and reading romances in her bed', she died here in 1752.

St Bride's Y9

St Bride's Av, t (020) 7427 0133; wheelchair accessible (not crypt). **Open** *daily 8am–4.45pm; sung Eucharist with choir Thurs at 1.15pm except in Aug.*

This is the journalists' church, where Fleet St's association with newsprint began.

William Caxton's apprentice Wynkyn de Worde moved his printing press to a site next to St Bride's in 1500. All the lawyers and priests in the area meant he had the perfect market for his books on his doorstep. Fleet St became a literary haunt, attracting such figures as Dryden and Milton, and encouraging Christopher Wren to rebuild St Bride's after the Great Fire. In 1701 he finished off his renovation with the impressive **spire**, made up of four arched octagons of diminishing size, which inspired a local pastry cook called Mr Rich to make the world's first tiered wedding cake.

The body of the church was destroyed by a German bomb in December 1940, and has since been fully if unspectacularly repaired. In the **crypt** archaeologists have unearthed stones dating back to Roman times, including the remains of no fewer than seven previous churches built on the site. For centuries the land here was used as a burial ground. The display gives an excellent history of Fleet St, from its origins as the main artery of Saxon Loudenwic up to the trauma of the fruitless 1980s print union strike. One of the objects on display is an iron coffin with a sprung lid dating from 1818. The lid was a defence against 'resurrectionists', medical students who snatched bodies from graveyards to further their illicit studies of anatomy.

Bloomsbury
and Fitzrovia

Bloomsbury and Fitzrovia

Bloomsbury, according to William the Conqueror's survey *The Domesday Book*, started life as a breeding ground for pigs, but it has acquired a rather more refined pedigree since. Home to the British Museum, the new British Library, London University and countless bookshops and cafés, it is the intellectual heart of the capital. George Bernard Shaw, Mazzini, Marx and Lenin all found inspiration among the tomes of the Reading Room in the British Library. Bertrand Russell and Virginia Woolf helped form an intellectual movement here, the Bloomsbury Group, whose members invited each other for tea and gossip in the area's Georgian townhouses.

Separated from Bloomsbury by the traffic stream on Tottenham Court Rd, Fitzrovia is a bit like a more downmarket version of the same. In the 1950s and 60s, it became a kind of 'Soho North', with a great many pubs that were frequented by the likes of Dylan Thomas. This identity continues today, with an increasingly trendy mix of media and advertising offices, and lively eating and drinking places.

1 Lunch

Abeno, *47 Museum St*, *t (020) 7405 3211*; *tube* Holborn, Tottenham Court Rd. **Open** *daily noon–10pm*. ***Inexpensive***. A little treasure right by the British Museum. Specialises in *okonomi-yaki* (Japanese-style tortilla) individually cooked on a giant hotplate, a *teppan*, set into each table. The process is pure theatre and the result is surprisingly filling.

2 Drinks

Fitzroy Tavern, *16 Charlotte St*, *t (020) 7580 3714*; *tube* Goodge St. **Open** *Mon–Sat 11am–11pm, Sun noon–10.30pm*. Dylan Thomas's main drinking haunt, with literary mementoes on the walls downstairs.

Highlights

Londoner's City: Making conversation with the stuffed body of Jeremy Bentham, p.172

Literary City: The fascinating manuscripts in the British Library, from the Lindisfarne Gospels to *Finnegan's Wake*, p.173

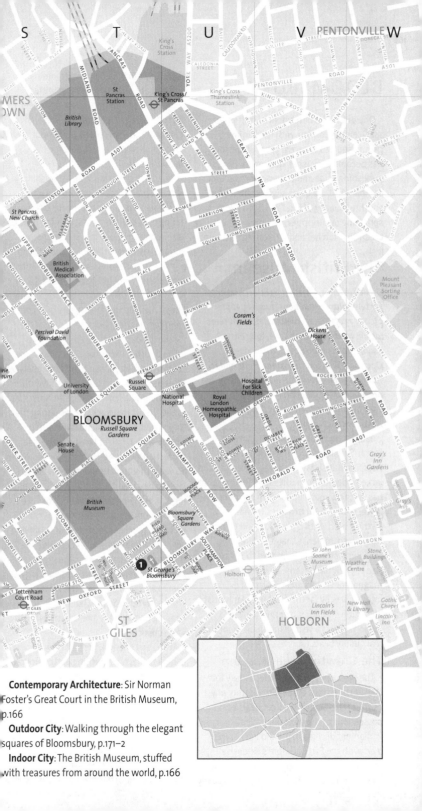

Contemporary Architecture: Sir Norman Foster's Great Court in the British Museum, p.166

Outdoor City: Walking through the elegant squares of Bloomsbury, p.171–2

Indoor City: The British Museum, stuffed with treasures from around the world, p.166

BLOOMSBURY

One of the classic residential districts of 18th-century London, with its intimate private squares, in recent years Bloomsbury has become a favoured location for the publishing trade and television production companies. It is a quiet, slightly shabby but youthful quarter of London, with a good sprinkling of curiosities, including some eccentric churches and interesting museums.

The British Museum T7

*Great Russell St, t (020) 7323 8000, booking for temporary exhibitions (10am–5.30pm) t (020) 7323 8181, w www.thebritishmuseum .ac.uk; wheelchair accessible; **tube** Russell Square, Tottenham Court Rd, Goodge St. **Open** Sat–Wed 10am–5.30pm, Thurs and Fri 10am–8.30pm; **adm** free, although donations are appreciated. Temporary exhibition prices vary, but are generally around £7 for adults, £3.50 for concessions.*

Back in the 1770s, the grumpy novelist Tobias Smollett complained that the fledgling British Museum was too empty and lacked a decent book collection. The museum has certainly made up for both deficiencies since. Stuffed with treasures from the farthest reaches of civilization, and boasting a library so immense that it outgrew the museum and had to be moved to St Pancras (*see p.173*), it has become an irresistible magnet for visitors and scholars of every interest. It is by far the most popular tourist attraction in London, catering to over six million visitors a year: triumphant proof that real quality beats tackiness any day.

The Growth of the Museum

The museum started as a depository for the art collections of the 18th-century physician Sir Hans Sloane, who bequeathed his possessions to the state on his death in 1753. Parliament decided to put Sloane's *objets d'art* with the Earl of Oxford's extensive collection of manuscripts in Montagu House, the predecessor to the present building. Early

visitors had to undergo an extraordinary bureaucratic procedure to be admitted, applying ahead of time in writing to seek the approval of the chief librarian, who allowed no more than 10 people in at a time. It was not until 1879 that access became free and unrestricted.

The collections grew at an astonishing pace. In 1757 George II donated the entire royal library, containing some 10,500 books dating back to Tudor times; over the next 50 years, books, manuscripts, state papers, antique vases, Egyptian relics and Oriental pottery came flooding in. In 1801 the British armed forces brought back some of Napoleon's priceless booty after defeating him at Alexandria. Fifteen years later Lord Elgin carried the celebrated friezes of the Parthenon back from Athens.

The British Museum was bursting at the seams. The man chosen to build a new, larger museum was Robert Smirke, an adventurer who had disguised himself as an American to see the art treasures of Paris during the Napoleonic Wars and who later toured Greece with a mob of hired gangsters for protection. His design, which took more than 20 years to complete, pioneered what was later to be called the Greek Revival. His ultra-regular, many-pillared building looks like a temple from antiquity spruced up with Victorian touches: the pediment contains a very classical-looking relief depicting that most 19th-century concern, the progress of civilization. Originally, Smirke's building had a large and airy courtyard, then in 1854 Smirke's brother Sydney built the Round Reading Room on the site, covering it with a vast copper dome.

At the end of 2000, the museum completed its most exciting and complicated reshuffle. It began with the removal of the British Library to new premises in St Pancras. This liberated Smirke's vast Greek Revival courtyard at the heart of the museum for redevelopment into what is now called the Great Court. In a scheme devised by Sir Norman Foster, this vast space (hidden to the public since 1857) has been transformed into

Finding Your Way Around the British Museum

There is more in the museum than can possibly be described; this chapter is a guide to its most famous and appealing artefacts. The best strategy is to pick up a floor plan from the information desk and make up your own mind what to see. Roughly speaking, the highlights are as follows.

Ground floor: The Great Court (including the Reading Room), Western Asia (Assyrian sculptures including the royal lion hunt reliefs from Nineveh), Egypt (Rosetta stone) and Greece (Parthenon Sculptures).

Upper floor: Egypt (mummies), Rome (Portland vase), Romano-British collection (Lindow Man, Mildenhall Treasure) and Medieval (Lewis chessmen).

The museum publishes three **guides** to the collections: a small guide (£2.50) which features a couple of suggested itineraries for the first-time visitor, a souvenir guide (£6), and an A–Z of the museum's collections (£12). You could also pick up an **audioguide** of the museum's highlights (£2.50, from the main entrance) and there is a special audioguide to the Parthenon Sculptures (suggested donation £3/£2) available just by the entrance to the Parthenon galleries.

Free guided 'Eye-opener' **tours** are available (a donation is gratefully received) which last 50mins. The Focus tours (adults £5, concessions £3), focusing on the most important objects in the museum's collections, last for 60mins and depart daily at 11.30am and 12.30pm, as well as 5.30pm amd 7pm on Thursday and Friday. The Highlights tours (adults £7, concessions £4) provide an introduction to the most famous objects in the collection and take place daily at 10.30am, 1.30pm, 2.30pm and 3.30pm. Book in advance for all tours.

London's first covered public square, which was officially opened by the Queen on 6 December 2000. Filled with light from its vaulted glass canopy, the Great Court is dominated by the gleaming white walls and dome of the Round Reading Room. This has been opened to the public for the first time, and is elegantly surrounded by new restaurants, shops and galleries, including the return of the ethnography collections from the now defunct Museum of Mankind. Beneath the Great Court two large staircases lead down to a new Centre for Education.

There are more projects planned for the 250th anniversary of the museum in 2003. The King's Library (just off the Great Court) is to be refurbished, and the new Wellcome Gallery of Ethnography is due to open with exhibitions exploring 'ideas of well-being and misfortune'.

Ground Floor
The Round Reading Room

This is one of the best-loved rooms in the world, with a beautiful cavernous dome bigger in diameter than those of St Paul's or St Peter's in Rome. Although designed by Sydney Smirke, it was the brainchild of Sir Antonio Panizzi, an Italian exile who invented the systems for labelling and cataloguing that are used in libraries to this day. A steady stream of the world's political thinkers and revolutionaries came to this room, among them Marx (who wrote *Das Kapital* in Row G), Mazzini and Lenin. Other writers who have found inspiration, consolation and even, occasionally, love among its 18 million tomes include Macaulay, Thackeray, Hardy, Dickens and Yeats.

It was with considerable reluctance that scholars and researchers gave up their seats of learning here in 1997, bemoaning not only the wonderful architecture they left behind, but also the acoustics: reading here was like reading in a fishtank – no sudden crashes, and all conversation reduced to a sweet-sounding blur. But now the original azure, cream and gold décor has been dramatically restored. Three-quarters of the floor space is taken up with a new information centre featuring the very latest in modern technology. The remaining quarter is the Paul Hamlyn Library, a new open-access library of 25,000 books.

Egypt
Room 4.

Many of the riddles of the ancient Egyptian world were solved through the **Rosetta Stone**, a slab of black basalt discovered by Napoleon's army in the Nile Delta in 1799, which by extraordinary good fortune reproduces the same text in three languages: Greek, demotic and Egyptian. The subject of the stone is not exactly inspiring: it is a decree issued at a general council of priests meeting in Memphis in 196 BC. But it offered the first opportunity for modern scholars to crack the code of Egyptian hieroglyphics. The man who takes the greatest credit is the French Egyptologist Jean François Champollion. But, as the patriotically minded museum display points out, he was greatly helped by the British scholar Thomas Young, who was the first to realize that hieroglyphs could have phonetic as well as symbolic value.

Western Asia
Rooms 6–10.

Western Asian treasures are spread throughout the British Museum, but the most accessible, the **Assyrian relics** of Nineveh, Balawat and Nimrud, are here on the ground floor. The Assyrians, occupying an exposed area in what is now northern Iraq, had a civilization essentially built on war with their neighbours, especially the Babylonians, between the 9th and 7th centuries BC. Their palaces are decorated with figures of wild animals, mythical creatures and magic symbols as well as depictions of conical-helmeted soldiers at arms with their chariots, battering rams and pontoons.

Nimrud was the stronghold of Ashurnasirpal II (883–859 BC). His palace doorway was flanked by two huge stone lions with human heads and wings, which have survived almost intact. There is a statue of the king himself, and stone reliefs illustrating his campaigns. The apotheosis of Assyrian civilization, though, was at **Nineveh** under King Ashurbanipal (668–627 BC). The reliefs from his palace show him routing the Arabs and defeating the Elamites at the Battle of the River Ulai (note the detail of the palm trees and musical instruments in the royal victory parade). The most extraordinary artwork depicts a **royal lion hunt**: the dying animals, shot through with arrows, are sculpted with great emotional force.

Greece
Rooms 11–23.

The Greek collections are dominated by the **Nereid Monument** (room 17) and the Parthenon Sculptures (popularly but now controversially known as the Elgin Marbles; see 'The Parthenon Sculptures aka The Elgin Marbles'). The Nereid Monument is a reconstruction of a vast tomb found at the Greek colony of Xanthos in Asia Minor. Built like a temple with a pediment supported by Ionic columns, it is a stunning tribute to the Lycian chieftains who are buried there; it also features remarkable frieze sculptures of men in battle, noblemen at court, an animal sacrifice and a hunting expedition. Dating from around 400 BC, the monument was destroyed at some stage by an earthquake and only rediscovered during an expedition by the archaeologist Charles Fellows in 1838. It has been painstakingly put back together and reached its present state only in 1951.

Oriental Collections
Ground floor rooms 33–4, upper floor rooms 92–4.

These rooms cover a huge amount of ground, from Chinese Tang dynasty glazed tomb figures to Turkish and Syrian ceramic work, by way of Thai banner painting and religious monuments from India and Nepal. Perhaps the most impressive section for the non-specialist are the rooms devoted to **South and Southeast Asia** (rooms 33–34). There is some magnificent filigree work in a 19th-century altar screen from Nepal; doors to a Balinese palace made of jackfruit wood, with gilded leaf motifs on red lacquer; beautiful stone figures of Vishnu, Shiva and other gods from 11th-century central India; and, at the end of room 33, large chunks of the 3rd-century Great Stupa at Amaravati in Andhra Pradesh. This is a grand domed Buddhist

The Parthenon Sculptures aka The Elgin Marbles (Room 18)

The Parthenon Sculptures have aroused so much controversy for being in Britain rather than Greece that their artistic merit is sometimes entirely overlooked. To set the record straight: Lord Elgin, the British Ambassador to the Ottoman Empire, discovered the stones lying forlornly on the ground when he visited Athens in 1800. The Parthenon, from which the marbles came, had been half wrecked in a skirmish between the Turks and a Venetian fleet besieging them in 1687, when a supply of gunpowder kept in the building exploded and brought many of the colonnades crashing to the ground. Elgin obtained a licence from the Ottoman Sultan in 1802 and proceeded to transport the treasures back home.

The British are probably right to assert that the marbles would not have survived if they had stayed in Greece: the Ottomans never lifted a finger to restore the Acropolis and at one stage ground down some of the stones that Elgin left behind to make cement. The Greek government states that its own national sentiments should be taken into consideration; fair enough, though the Parthenon Museum in Athens already has many of the best relief sculptures (the remainder being in Paris and Copenhagen). The British government has shown no sign of giving in to the Greek demands, and is not likely to in the foreseeable future.

The stones are frieze reliefs from the Parthenon, the temple to Athena on top of the Acropolis, and are considered some of the finest sculptures of antiquity. Depicting a Panathenaic festival to commemorate Athena's birthday, they reveal a remarkable mastery of detail and human feeling. The British Museum has them displayed in a vast room giving an idea of the scale of the Parthenon itself.

The best way to view the sculptures is as a kind of cartoon strip. The grand procession includes riders in their chariots, city elders, musicians, pitcher-bearers, attendants, sacrificial victims, beautiful girls carrying libation bowls, tribal heroes and, in the east frieze, the gods Hermes and Dionysus. On the south side is a depiction of a brawl between the Lapiths of Thessaly and their guests the Centaurs, who have got drunk and attempted to drag off the Lapith women. The exhibition also includes fragments of the east pediment, depicting the birth of Athena, and of the west front, showing the battle between Athena and Poseidon for control of Attica, the region around Athens.

temple, with narrative scenes of the life of Buddha decorated with lotus motifs.

Upper Floor
Egypt
Rooms 61–6.

The display of Egyptian **mummies and sarcophagi**, the most popular section of the British Museum (no doubt for its gruesomeness), was entirely refurbished in 1999. Here is the Egyptian way of death in all its bizarre splendour: rows and rows of spongy bodies wrapped in bandages and surrounded by the prized belongings and favourite food of the deceased. It took 70 days to prepare a body for interment in ancient Egypt. The body was either dried out or soaked in a solution of natron and water. The viscera were then cut out or dissolved with chemicals; the brain was extracted through the nostrils with the help of an iron hook. Only the heart, which the ancient Egyptians believed to be the centre of understanding, remained in the corpse at burial. After disembowelling, the bodies were washed with palm wine and sewn up, bandaged and strewn with valuables. Most unsettling of all is the body of a man from 3400 BC in a reconstructed grave pit.

Western Asia
Rooms 51–9.

The collection is more eclectic here than downstairs: Bronze Age tools from Syria, a mosaic column from Tell-al-Ubaid, reliefs from Kapara's palace in Tell Halaf (now in northeastern Syria) as well as further relics from Nimrud (ivory carvings) and Nineveh (tablets from the royal library). The two highlights are a collection of magnificently preserved **funerary busts from Palmyra** dating from the 1st and 2nd centuries AD, and the extraordinary sculpture *The Ram in the Thicket* from Ur (room 56), the birthplace of Abraham. Made of gold and lapis lazuli, this delicate figure dates back to 2600 BC, when Ur was part of Chaldea in southern Babylonia.

The Italy of the Greeks, Etruscans and Romans
Rooms 69–73.

These rooms are a bit of a mixed bag: Greek red-figure vases found in Lucania and Apulia in southern Italy (1400–1200 BC), a carved stone Etruscan sarcophagus found at Bomarzo north of Rome (3rd century BC), plenty of bronze heads of Roman emperors, and terracotta reliefs that once decorated the Pantheon, with orgiastic depictions of Cupid, Bacchus and satyrs.

The highlight of the Roman collection is the **Portland Vase** (room 70), so called because the Barberini family sold it to the Dukes of Portland. The vase, made around the time of the birth of Christ, is of cobalt-blue glass and coated in an opaque white glaze depicting the reclining figures of Peleus and Thetis, with Cupid and his love arrows hovering overhead. The vase has had a traumatic time of it since arriving in England: first a rival of the Portland family did his best to smash it, and then in 1845 a drunken visitor succeeded in breaking it into 200 pieces. He was later charged, not with criminal damage to a priceless treasure, but with the comparatively harmless offence of glass breakage. The vase has been lovingly put back together, though, and you would scarcely notice the difference.

Prehistoric and Roman Britain
Rooms 49–50.

The oldest and most gruesome exhibit here is **Lindow Man** (room 50), the shrivelled remains of an ancient Briton preserved down the centuries in a peat bog. The body, which has been dated to between 300 BC and AD 100, shows evidence of extreme violence. Evidently he was the victim of ritual slaughter, perhaps by Druids, who stripped, garotted and bled him, put his body in a bag and threw him into a bog at Lindow, near the town of Moss in Cheshire. There he lay until 1984, when a digging machine rooting around in the peat became entangled in the lower half of his body. All you see is his torso and crushed head, freeze-dried like instant coffee, with a reconstruction giving you a better idea of what he originally looked like.

Excavations in Britain have provided more pleasant surprises, notably the **Mildenhall Treasure**, 34 remarkably well-preserved pieces of 4th-century silver tableware dug up from a field in Suffolk in 1942. There are some beautiful mosaics, the largest of them a 4th-century **floor from Hinton St Mary** in Dorset which appears to be Christian in inspiration. The fish symbol much used by the early Christians features prominently, and the figures representing the four winds at the edges of the mosaic could also stand for the four gospels.

Medieval Antiquities
Rooms 40–48.

Here are more finds from digs around the British Isles. An excavation at **Sutton Hoo** (room 41) on the Suffolk coast brought to light an extraordinary haul from a burial ship loaded up in homage to an early 7th-century Anglo-Saxon king, possibly Raedwald, who died in 624. In the manner of the ancient Egyptians, the king's courtiers piled up everything he could possibly want for the afterlife: gilded ivory drinking horns, lyres, maplewood bottles, silver platters, gold jewellery, coins.

You should not miss the **Lewis chessmen** (room 42), a collection of 78 pieces in walrus ivory discovered in the Outer Hebrides in 1831. The farmer who first came across them fled thinking they were elves, and it was only the fortitude of his wife that persuaded him to go back for another look. The figures do not make up complete chess sets and are thought to have been left by a travelling salesman, possibly from Scandinavia, some time in the 12th century.

Prints and Drawings

Room 90.

The museum's vast collection is displayed in a continuing programme of special exhibitions. On a good day you might find Michelangelo's sketches for the Sistine chapel, etchings and sketches by Rembrandt, and a large selection of anatomical studies by Albrecht Dürer. Look out, too, for William Hogarth's satirical engravings, notably *Gin Lane*, which castigates the corrupting influence of drink on 18th-century London.

Bloomsbury Square U7

Tube *Holborn, Tottenham Court Rd, Goodge St, Russell Square.*

This was the original London housing development based on the leasehold system (*see* pp.51–3), and the model for the city's phenomenally rapid growth throughout the 18th and 19th centuries. Nowadays it is one of the more elegant squares in central London, with a ring of stately Georgian homes surrounding a flourishing garden.

The square also has a plaque commemorating the **Bloomsbury Group**, a movement that included Virginia Woolf, her husband Leonard, E.M. Forster, John Maynard Keynes, Bertrand Russell and the essayist Lytton Strachey. The group had no manifesto or specific aim: it was a loose association of like-minded intellectuals (most of them politically on the soft left) who met to exchange ideas. Following the teachings of the philosopher G.E. Moore, they believed that the appreciation of beautiful objects and the art of fine conversation were the keys to social progress – an admirable if somewhat elitist outlook. You can see plaques on their houses around Bloomsbury.

St George's Bloomsbury T7

Bloomsbury Way; tube *Holborn, Tottenham Court Rd.* **Open** *Sun–Fri 9.30am–5pm.*

This eccentric Baroque church is the work of Nicholas Hawksmoor, 18th-century specialist in the spooky and bizarre. The portico presents a sober classical façade, its plain pediment supported by two rows of Corinthian columns; but behind is an extraordinary stepped **steeple** that looks a bit like an elongated pyramid, topped by a wobbly statue of George I in a toga. The steeple, which is in fact based on Pliny's description of the mausoleum at Halicarnassus in Crete, prompted ridicule as soon as it was unveiled in 1731. Horace Walpole captured the mood of disdain for both the church and the exclusively German-speaking king in the following lines:

When Henry VIII left the Pope in the lurch
The Protestants made him head of the
Church
But George's good subjects, the Bloomsbury
people,
Instead of the Church, made him head of
the steeple.

The interior is a model of sobriety, typical of the plain open style pioneered by Wren. For a taste of Hawksmoor's more lugubrious side, you should walk round the outside to the left where a meandering alley ducks under arches and weaves around the church's blackened contours.

Dickens' House V5

49 Doughty St, **t** *(020) 7405 2127,* **w** *www .dickensmuseum.com; tube Russell Square.* **Open** *Mon–Sat 10am–5pm;* **adm** *adults £4, concessions £3, children £2, families £9.*

This is the only one of Dickens' many London homes to survive. The furnishings have been drafted in from other Dickens homes; there is little atmosphere, merely an accumulation of hallowed objects. The exhibits include first editions of some of his works, portraits and mementos.

University of London S5–T6

For the first 1,800 years of its history, London had no university at all, and only acquired one because non-Anglicans were not admitted to Oxford, Cambridge and the other British universities. From the time that University College opened in 1828, London has been a relatively progressive and unusually secular centre of learning. In 1878 London became the first British university to let women sit for degrees, and in 1912 was the first to appoint a woman professor.

Senate House S–T6

*Malet St, **w** www.ull.ac.uk, **t** (020) 7862 8500; **tube** Russell Square, Goodge St; wheelchair accessible.*

In 1936 the architect Charles Holden built the Senate House on the west side of Russell Square, a terrifyingly inhuman white hulk of a building. It looks better suited to bureaucrats than academics, and during the Second World War was taken over by the Ministry of Information. George Orwell turned it into the Ministry of Truth in his totalitarian nightmare *Nineteen Eighty-Four*. Now it contains the university library, as well as several smaller departments.

Petrie Museum of Egyptian Archaeology University Collection S5

*Malet Place, **t** (020) 7679 2884, **e** petrie .museum@ucl.ac.uk, **w** www.petrie.ucl.ac.uk; **tube** Euston Square, Warren St; wheelchair accessible (not to 2nd gallery). **Open** Tues–Fri 1–5pm, Sat 10am–1pm; **adm** free. **Giftshop**.*

If the mummies at the British Museum have whetted your appetite for all things Egyptian, this surprisingly little-known museum is well worth a look. It houses around 80,000 objects, which makes it one of the most extensive collections of Egyptian and Sudanese archaeology in the world. Among the highlights are the **world's oldest dress** (c. 2800 BC), with the world's oldest underarm sweat stains, and an extraordinary series of **Roman funerary portraits**. The museum is named after Professor William Flinders Petrie (1853–1942), who excavated dozens of major sites, including the first true pyramid at Meydum, where he uncovered some of the earliest evidence for mummification.

University College R5

*Gower St, **w** www.ucl.ac.uk; **tube** Euston Square, Warren St; wheelchair accessible.*

The college is a fine, if rather heavy, example of the Greek Revival style by William Wilkins, the architect of the National Gallery. Visitors should head straight for the South Cloister in the far right-hand corner: not far from the doorway is the glass cabinet containing the stuffed **body of Jeremy Bentham**, the utilitarian philosopher and political reformer, who died in 1832. Bentham had helped set up University College, and asked for his body to be preserved in this way. It is a surprisingly jolly monument. The skeleton, dressed in flamboyant clothing, is entirely the original article apart from the skull, which has been removed to the college safe and replaced with a smiling wax model topped with an eccentric straw hat. Once a week Bentham is carted off to attend meetings of the board of governors, where he is registered as 'present but not voting'. He is also invited to university parties.

Percival David Foundation of Chinese Art S5

*53 Gordon Square, **t** (020) 7387 3909, **w** www.soas.ac.uk/pdf; **tube** Euston Square, Goodge St, Russell Square; wheelchair accessible. **Open** Mon–Fri 10.30am–5pm; **adm** free but donations gratefully accepted. **Giftshop**.*

Overlooking one of the handsomest squares in Bloomsbury, this museum houses a fine collection of imperial porcelain and is named after the philanthropic collector who acquired its treasures. The vases, which are beautifully documented and dated, range from the Sung dynasty of the 10th century up to the Qing dynasty of the 18th.

Woburn Walk T5

***Tube** Euston, Euston Square.*

This short pedestrian street of beautifully preserved bow-fronted buildings dates from

1822. Look out for the plaque marking W.B. Yeats's house.

St Pancras New Church S4

Upper Woburn Place; tube King's Cross.

This rather splendid Greek Revivalist building was completed at great expense in 1822 by the father and son team of William and Henry William Inwood. Inspired in part by the Erechtheion in Athens, the church boasts a broad pediment propped up by an Ionic porch, and a fine two-tiered octagonal tower. The interior is long, dark and brooding. Round the back, there are pavilions at either side of the church supported by caryatids.

The British Library S–T3

96 Euston Rd, t (020) 7412 7000, w www.bl.uk; tube King's Cross, Euston; wheelchair accessible. Open Mon and Wed–Fri 9.30am–6pm, Tues 9.30am–8pm, Sat 9.30am–5pm, Sun 11am–5pm; adm free. Guided tours Mon, Wed, Fri 3pm, Tues 6.30pm, Sat 10.30am and 3pm, Sun 11.30am and 3pm; adm adults £5, concessions £3.50; book ahead on t (020) 412 7332; Tues and Sat tours include a visit to one of the reading rooms (adults £6, concessions £4.50). Workshops, bookshops, café (open Mon–Thurs 9.30am–6pm, Fri and Sat 9.30am–4pm, Sun 11am–4.30pm) and restaurant (open Mon–Fri 9.30am–5pm, Sat 9.30am–4pm).

Construction work on Colin St John Wilson's building began in 1978 and took 20 years, longer than the building of St Paul's Cathedral. By the time it was completed, Wilson had overspent by £350 million, his practice had dissolved, and the building itself had been exposed to that peculiarly violent brand of venom that the British reserve for new architectural projects. Prince Charles called it a 'collection of brick sheds groping for significance'. But even the building's most vicious critics were stunned and delighted by the spectacular interior, with its vast scale, open tracts of white travertine marble, and complex spaces flooded with light.

The entrance to the library is through the large piazza dominated by Edward Paolozzi's **sculpture of Isaac Newton** – a 3D version of William Blake's grim depiction.

The Collection

The big attraction is the library's vast number of manuscripts, from the sacred to the profane, from the delicate beauty of illuminated Bibles to the frenzied scrawl of Joyce's first draft of *Finnegan's Wake*. Among the greatest treasures are the **Lindisfarne Gospels**, the work of a monk named Eadfrith who wrote and illuminated them, on the island of Lindisfarne off the northeastern coast of England, in honour of St Cuthbert. The decorative pages look like Oriental carpets with their bright colours and attention to detail. In the text itself, look out for the English words scrawled in between the lines of Latin during the 10th century by Aldred, Bishop of Durham.

There is an extensive collection of **literary manuscripts**, including an illuminated version of Chaucer's *Canterbury Tales* and – arguably the highlight – Lewis Carroll's beautifully neat handwriting and illustrations in the notebook version of *Alice in Wonderland* (then called *Alice's Adventures Under Ground*), which he gave to his young friend Alice Liddell for Christmas in 1864. Look out, too, for Lenin's reapplication for a reader's ticket, which he made under the pseudonym Jacob Richter.

Stamp-lovers should head for the **Philatelic Collections**, which include first issues of nearly every stamp in the world from 1840 to 1890, and an extraordinary range of those issued since. The **British Library National Sound Archive** is a wonderful collection that includes early gramophones and record sleeves, and a series of priceless historical, literary and musical recordings: Florence Nightingale and Gladstone, James Joyce reading from *Ulysses*, and Charlie Parker's club performances (recorded on wire).

The other star exhibit is the **Magna Carta**. The British Library has two of the four surviving copies of this document, one of the founding texts of the modern democratic system, signed by King John at Runnymede in 1215 under pressure from his barons. Its 63 clauses are written in a fine if somewhat illegible hand.

St Pancras Station T2–3

*Euston Rd; **tube** King's Cross.*

This fabulously imposing 1874 Gothic Revival building by Sir George Gilbert Scott was in fact built as a hotel, with the station stretching behind.

FITZROVIA

In the 1940s and 50s this was a villagey extension of Soho with plenty of cheap food and drink and a colourful cast of literary eccentrics. Dylan Thomas, Theodora Fitzgibbon, Julian MacClaren Ross, George Orwell and Augustus John all drank at the Fitzroy Tavern on Charlotte St, which gave its name to the area.

Charlotte Street Q6–R7

Tube Goodge St, Tottenham Court Rd.

The centre of Fitzrovia, this was one of the key addresses of 1940s and 50s London. The television and advertising crowd moved in during the 1980s, pushing the area several notches upmarket. There are several good restaurants and the street is a popular place to eat and drink in the evenings. On the right as you head north is the **Fitzroy Tavern**, which displays pictures of Dylan Thomas, George Orwell and friends in the Writers and Artists bar in the basement. 'What will you have to drink?' the landlord used to ask the permanently sozzled Dylan Thomas. 'Anything that goes down my throat,' came the reply.

As you walk northwards up Charlotte St you are gradually overshadowed by the **Telecom Tower**, a sparkplug skyscraper built in 1965 to redirect London's telephone, radio and TV signals; unfortunately, it's closed to the public.

Fitzroy Square Q5–6

Tube Warren St.

George Bernard Shaw and Virginia Woolf lived at No.29 (though not, of course, at the same time), and another Bloomsbury Group acolyte, the artist Roger Fry, set up his Omega Workshops here. Some of the elegant Georgian houses, designed by the Adam brothers, survive.

Pollock's Toy Museum R6

*1 Scala St, **t** (020) 7636 3452, **w** www.pollocks web.co.uk; **tube** Goodge St, Tottenham Court Rd. **Open** Mon–Sat 10am–5pm; closed hols; **adm** adults £3, 3–18s £1.50. **Shop**.*

Benjamin Pollock was the leading Victorian manufacturer of toy theatres, and this small but very attractive museum is based on the collection that he left. It's an atmospheric place, the four narrow floors connected by creaky staircases. The theatres are on the top floor, and exhibits also include board games, tin toys, puppets, wax dolls, teddy bears and dolls' houses. Not least among the museum's attractions is an excellent shop which sells beautiful toy theatres, which children assemble out of wood and card and use to stage their own plays.

All Saints Margaret Street Q7

*Margaret St; **tube** Oxford Circus, Goodge St; wheelchair accessible.*

Ruskin once said of this church that it was 'the first piece of architecture I have seen built in modern days which is free from all signs of timidity and incapacity'. That was probably an understatement. William Butterfield's church, completed in 1859, is the apogee of the Victorian Gothic Revival: a riot of colour, decoration and rather sinister charm. Its arches, pillars and vaulted ceiling are almost aglow with coloured granite, marble, alabaster and painted tiles. Its tall spire (227ft) is spooky enough to warrant an appearance in a horror film.

Marylebone
and Regent's Park

Marylebone and Regent's Park

Marylebone has everything a village needs: a string of small specialist shops, a couple of delightful teashops, even a village green – if you count the manicured gardens of Regent's Park. No one really noticed it for years, but then Madge and Guy (otherwise known as Madonna and husband) moved in, bringing celebs and organic delis in their wake, and all of a sudden Marylebone is hot property. It's just a hop, skip and a jump away from the crowds and shops of Oxford St – and yet a world apart. It's bounded to the north by the traffic-clogged Marylebone Rd, where patient queues wait outside Madame Tussaud's and the Planetarium. Beyond it lies Regent's Park, filled with rose gardens and elegant prom-enades, and home to London's original Zoological Gardens.

Highlights

Londoner's City: Hire a rowing boat on the lake in tranquil Regent's Park, p.182

Literary City: The very believable Sherlock Holmes Museum, p.180

Outdoor City: London Zoo, where the word 'zoo' originated, p.181

Indoor City: The Wallace Collection, for a glimpse into the 18th century, p.178

---

1 Lunch

Ibla, *89 Marylebone High St,* **t** *(020) 7224 3799;* **tube** *Baker St, Bond St.* **Open** *Mon–Sat noon–2.30 and 7–10.15, Sun noon–2.30pm.* **Moderate**. A tempting variety of modern and classic Italian dishes in a contemporary but not consciously trendy restaurant.

2 Tea and Cakes

Pâtisserie Valerie at Sagne, *105 Marylebone High St,* **t** *(020) 7935 6240;* **tube** *Baker St, Bond St.* **Open** *Mon–Fri 7.30am–7pm, Sat 8am–7pm, Sun 9am–6pm.* Old-fashioned gilded tea and cake shop complete with chandeliers.

OXFORD STREET

Tube Oxford Circus, Bond St, Marble Arch.

The stretch of Oxford St west of Oxford Circus towards Marble Arch is forever packed with shoppers and tourists, for whom its wide pavements and large department stores symbolize the very essence of the big city. This rather puzzling mystique is not at all borne out by the reality, which is impersonal, uniform and unremittingly grey. The most prestigious address is **Selfridge's**, which for sheer size and range of goods is the closest rival in London to Harrods. The other department stores, such as Debenhams and John Lewis, are not nearly as much fun (or as cheap) as the specialist shops dotted around more intimate parts of London.

Off and behind Oxford St are a few side streets with interesting small stores: at the Selfridge's/Bond St end, try walking down South Molton St, Davies St, St Christopher's Place, James St, Duke St and, parallel to Oxford St, Wigmore St; just east of Oxford Circus there's Great Portland St and Argyll St, and pedestrianized Carnaby St (*see* p.135).

MARYLEBONE

Marylebone is London's most central village. It's hard to believe that the relentless crowds of Oxford St are just a few hundred yards away. Marylebone's pace of life is very different: the shops along Marylebone High St are human-sized, and you'll still find the odd butcher and grocer, as well as one of the loveliest bookshops in all London (Daunt's). It's an affluent neighbourhood, and there are strings of chi-chi boutiques, exclusive spas and dozens of restaurants that cater to the kind of clientele who boast a year-round tan.

The Wallace Collection N7

Hertford House, Manchester Square, t (020) 7593 9500, w www.wallace-collection.com; tube Bond St, Marble Arch; wheelchair accessible. Open Mon–Sat 10am–5pm, Sun noon–5pm; closed 1 Jan, Good Fri and 24–26 Dec; adm free but donations welcome. Guided tours Mon–Fri 1pm, plus Wed and Sat 11.30am, Sun 3pm; free; sometimes replaced by specialist gallery talks covering aspects of the collection; call or check the Web site for details of lectures. Audioguide available. Giftshop and café.

One could not hope for a more perfect monument to 18th-century aristocratic life than the Wallace Collection, a sumptuous array of painting, porcelain and furniture housed in a period mansion. It is the location that makes it, the wonderfully uplifting feeling as you glide up the staircases with their gilded wrought-iron banisters and wander from one elegant, well-lit room to another.

The collection is the result of several generations of accumulation by the Hertford family, who moved to Manchester Square in 1797 because of the excellent duck-shooting in the fields behind. The family's link with the art world had already begun in the mid-18th century, when the first Marquess of Hertford patronized Joshua Reynolds. The third Marquess had a penchant for Sèvres porcelain and 17th-century Dutch painting, while the fourth lived in Paris and spent his time buying up the works of Fragonard, Boucher and Watteau. Richard Wallace, who gave his name to the collection (as well as designing the Paris drinking fountains that still bear his name), was the bastard son of the fourth Marquess and acted as agent for his father in all his transactions. He later bequeathed the whole lot to the state, on condition that it remain on public view in central London.

Highlights include works by **Frans Hals** (*The Laughing Cavalier*), **Rembrandt** (*Titus*), **Rubens** (*Christ's Charge to Peter* and *The Holy Family*), **Poussin** (*Dance to the Music of Time*) and **Titian** (an extraordinary rendition of *Perseus and Andromeda* in which the Greek hero tumbles towards the open jaws of the sea monster with only his sword and shield to save him). Take your time around the rest of the collection to take in the finely carved wardrobes inlaid with tortoiseshell and gilt bronze, the delicate porcelain and any number of eccentric *objets d'art*.

Royal Institute of British Architects P6

*66 Portland Place, **t** (020) 7580 5533, **w** www.architecture.com; **tube** Great Portland St, Regent's Park, Oxford Circus; wheelchair accessible. **Open** Mon–Fri 8am–7pm, Sat 9am–5pm; **adm** free. Lectures.*

The elegant Art Deco institute has an excellent year-round exhibition programme focusing on contemporary architectural projects both here and abroad.

Broadcasting House P7

*Portland Place, **t** 0870 603 0304, **w** www.bbc.co.uk; **tube** Oxford Circus; wheelchair accessible. **Shop** and **café**.*

This rather grim 1930s building was long the nerve centre of the British Broadcasting Corporation, better known as the BBC, the Beeb or Auntie. Nowadays, most of the real business takes place in the huge, glassy complex out on Wood Lane in Shepherd's Bush (if you want backstage tours or tickets to BBC shows, contact the number or Web site above). This old building no longer runs tours, but you can visit the shop and café. On the façade, note the fine 1932 **sculptures** of Ariel (a pun on the word 'aerial') and Prospero by the sculptor and designer Eric Gill, who also created the Stations of the Cross in Westminster Cathedral. The story goes that scandalized 1930s BBC governors asked Gill to lop a few inches off Ariel's manhood.

All Souls P7

*Langham Place; **tube** Oxford Circus; wheelchair accessible. **Open** Sun–Fri 9.30am–6pm.*

Langham Place was one of the wiggles that John Nash had to contend with when building Regent St (*see* p.54). The problem was Sir James Langham, who agreed with some reluctance to have his house demolished but refused to sell his back garden. Nash was forced to steer his thoroughfare to the left, but graced the turn with the round church of All Souls, whose façade and curious spire guides the eye easily round the corner. Nash's church was much ridiculed at the time of its construction (1822–4), and often likened to an exclamation mark, but is now loved for its warm yellow stone and temple-like appearance.

BAKER STREET

Baker St may have romantic connotations if you're a fan of Sherlock Holmes, but the reality is much more mundane. It's now a broad urban artery full of whizzing traffic and with little character, but it's still home to a couple of London's most popular attractions. Among the ferociously competitive businesses picking over the spoils of Conan Doyle's celebrated detective are a Sherlock Holmes pub and a memorabilia shop at No.230 selling tea mugs and the like.

Madame Tussaud's and the Planetarium M6

*Marylebone Rd, **t** (020) 7935 6861, **w** www.madame-tussauds.com; **tube** Baker St; wheelchair accessible (phone ahead as limited capacity). **Madame Tussaud's open** May–Sept daily 8.30am–5.30pm, Oct–April daily 9am–5.30pm; **adm** adults £12, concessions £9.50, 5–16s £8.50, under-5s free. **London Planetarium open** June–Aug daily 10.20am–5pm, Sept–May daily 12.20–5pm; **adm** adults £7, concessions £5.60, under-16s £4.85. **Joint tickets** adults £14.45, concessions £11.30, children £10. Buy tickets in advance online or on the credit card hotline **t** 0870 400 3000.*

The world's most famous waxworks take some getting into. Unless you've planned ahead, there is no escaping the horrendous queues, which are little shorter in the winter than in high season. Get in line as soon after 8.30am as possible and take plenty of consolatory sustenance (i.e. chocolate, or whatever else keeps you and your children smiling). Nearly three million people put themselves through the crush each year, although it is hard to see why – the only thing you can say in the end about a waxwork is whether it's lifelike or not, and most of the film stars, politicians and famous villains here fare pretty indifferently on that score.

Back in the 19th century, of course, waxworks made more sense as they provided the only opportunity for ordinary people to catch a glimpse of the rich and famous, albeit in effigy. Marie Tussaud was a Swiss model-maker who trained with her uncle by making death masks of the victims of the Revolutionary Terror in France. By the time she came to England in 1802, she had 35 wax figures to her name, which she exhibited not far from here on Baker St (the show has occupied the present site since 1885). The Duke of Wellington was a particular fan and came often to admire the likeness of his vanquished foe, Napoleon. Madame Tussaud's hallmarks were her attention to detail, particularly in the costumes, and her efforts to keep the exhibition up to date with the latest celebrities. She even bought up George IV's coronation robes for a cool £18,000.

One of her most inspired ideas, the **Chamber of Horrors**, survives to this day. Down in the basement you'll find a gruesome array of crooks and murderers from Vlad the Impaler to Jack the Ripper. The final section of Madame Tussaud's is called the **Spirit of London**, a funfair-type ride in a modified black cab featuring illustrations of London's history from the Great Fire to the swinging 1960s. Strictly for kids only (and even then...).

If you have children, you might do better next door at the green-domed **Planetarium**, with its exciting and informative laser, sound and light show projected over a vast dome-shaped auditorium via a high-tech projector. The show explains how the solar system works, what the galaxy and the Milky Way are (apart from the chocolate bars you chomped in the queue), how earthquakes and volcanoes happen, and more.

Sherlock Holmes Museum L–M5

*239 Baker St, t (020) 7935 8866, **w** www .sherlock-holmes.co.uk; **tube** Baker St. **Open** daily 9.30am–6.30pm; closed 25 Dec; **adm** adults £6, children £4, under-7s free. **Giftshop**.*

The museum says its address is 221b Baker St, and certainly looks convincing enough to be the supersleuth's consulting rooms (there is even a fake Blue Plaque commemorating him above the door). Unfortunately, though, it is really No.239; the building encompassing No.221b (which never actually existed as a self-contained address) is the glass-and-concrete headquarters of the Abbey National Building Society.

The museum is a lot of fun, if you enter into its spirit of artifice. You are greeted at the door by either a housekeeper or a policeman. The rooms have been lovingly filled with late Victorian furniture, artefacts and sculptures of the characters from the Holmes stories. Most entertaining of all is the folder containing Sherlock Holmes' fan mail. Evidently schoolchildren in the United States are asked to write to Holmes as part of their homework; as a result some of the letters have a tone of almost surreal facetiousness. One begins: 'Dear Mr Dead Sherlock Holmes, I feel stupid writing to you because I know you are six feet under.'

REGENT'S PARK

*Park Information Office: The Store Yard, Inner Circle, t (020) 7486 7905; **tube** Baker St, Regent's Park, Great Portland St, Mornington Crescent, Camden Town, St John's Wood. **Open** daily 5am–sunset.*

Regent's Park is the most ornate of London's open spaces, a delightful mixture of icing-sugar terraces, wildlife, lakes and broad expanses of greenery. It is the most rigorously planned of the city's parks, the brainchild of George IV's favourite architect, John Nash, who conceived it as a landscaped estate on which to build several dozen pleasure palaces for the aristocracy. It was meant to be the culmination of a vast city rebuilding project, of which the centrepiece was Regent St. As detailed elsewhere (*see* p.54), Nash's dreams of a new London, endowing the city with aristocratic majesty, were tempered by a succession of objections and financial problems; Regent's Park, however, perhaps comes closest to embodying the spirit, if not quite the letter, of his plans. His stuccoed terraces around the perimeter of the park are at once imposing and playful; the handful of grand mansions inside the park exude an air of nonchalant, summery elegance; and the park itself is beautifully manicured, giving it a curious air of exclusivity even though it is open to all.

Originally, Regent's Park was part of the vast Forest of Middlesex that occupied much of North London. Once a royal hunting area, then farmland, it was a major source of hay, milk and butter for the city right up to the end of the 18th century. The development of the Portland estates to the south, however, made farming a poor prospect, and in 1811 the Prince Regent invited Nash to build a park based on a series of concentric rings dotted with mansions and fine terraces. With the Napoleonic Wars dragging on public finances, Nash's original 56 mansions were reduced to a paltry 8, and some of his terraces, particularly on the north side, had to be abandoned altogether. Nash's loss, though, may be our gain: the park is more accessible and less cluttered as a result.

London Zoo M1–N2

Outer Circle, Regent's Park, t (020) 7722 3333, w www.zsl.org; tube Camden Town, then 10min walk or bus No.274; wheelchair accessible. Open daily 10am–5.30pm, last adm 4.30pm; closed 25 Dec; adm adults £11, concessions £9.30, 3–15s £8; Lifewatch Season Ticket (free access for a year) around £30. Daily events (check the Web site), include feeding time (around 1.30pm) and Animals in Action at 2pm (leaving plenty of time to get a seat).

The London zoo is an animal microcosm of London, and even the lions, as a rule, behave as if they have been born in South Kensington.

Leonard Woolf

If Leonard Woolf was right to compare the zoo to London society, then it is also true that the fortunes of the gardens mirrored those of the British Empire. The Zoological Society of London was founded in 1826, and the zoo itself was created two years later on a plan drawn up by Decimus Burton. As the Empire stretched into the furthest corners of the earth, so the animals grew more exotic: monkeys, bears, emus, kangaroos and llamas at first, followed in due course by elephants, alligators, boas and anacondas, and joined eventually by bison, hippos, koalas and pandas. When giraffes first appeared in 1836, they created a fashion vogue for women's dresses patterned like their skin. A few years later disaster struck when the keeper of the new reptile house was bitten between the eyes by a cobra and died. A further calamity occurred in the 1870s when Alice the African elephant mysteriously lost the end of her trunk. Mostly, though, the zoo has nurtured and encouraged the British love of animals; its Chinese pandas, in particular, took more than their fair share of the newspaper headlines during the 1970s when the whole nation waited with bated breath to see whether they would mate or not (they did).

The Zoological Gardens in Regent's Park were where the term 'zoo' originated. The abbreviation, which first surfaced in the late 1860s, was immortalized in a music-hall song of the time beginning 'Walking in the zoo is the OK thing to do'. In these post-colonial, animally correct times, zoos are not quite as OK as they used to be, but London Zoo has responded to debate about its role with some energy. The Bear Mountain, once horribly overcrowded and a place of abject misery, has been redeveloped, and houses just three bears. The delightful **Children's Zoo** is built entirely out of sustainable materials, with a Camel House whose roof is planted with wild flowers and grass seed, a wonderful touch-paddock, barn and pet-care centre. Continuing the ecological theme, the zoo's latest and greatest project is the **Web of Life**, with fun, interactive exhibits colourfully demystifying the ecosystem and biodiversity. The 'environmentally progressive' glass building allows visitors not only to contribute to the natural heating and cooling system (by producing most of the heat), but to watch ants creeping along ropes showing off their superorganism strength, squirm at swarms of locusts crawling over a half-buried jeep and, coming full circle, admire the only giant anteaters in the UK.

One of the main attractions of visiting the zoo is the fine array of well-designed **animal houses** – the penguin pool by Lubetkin and Tecton (1936), Lord Snowdon's spectacular polygonal aviary (1964), Hugh Casson's elephant and rhino pavilion (1965) or the macaw aviary (1994).

On your way round you will be invited to 'adopt' any animal that takes your particular fancy. Pay £25 for an exotic breed of cockroach or seahorse, £6,000 for an elephant, or £35 for a part share in any animal, and you are assured the beast will be fed and nurtured for a year. Your name will also go on a plaque beside the animal's enclosure – you'll see plenty of these already in place.

Nash's Terraces O5–P2

One of the most successful of Nash's terraces is **Park Crescent**, just to the south of the Marylebone Rd. Its position at the top of Portland Place, the continuation of Regent St, gives you an idea of Nash's overall vision in his rethink of central London. Originally Nash wanted to continue the Neoclassical crescent around 360 degrees, but had to give up after his backer went bankrupt just six houses in. For a view of more terraces, all built in the same grandiose Neoclassical style, cross the Marylebone Rd and head up the eastern side of Regent's Park on or near the Outer Circle. First comes **Cambridge Terrace**, then the outrageously over-stuccoed **Chester Terrace**, followed by the magnificent **Cumberland Terrace**, with its portico of Ionic columns. On top is a bright blue and white pediment depicting Britannia and allegorical emblems of the arts, sciences and commerce.

The Inner Circle M3–N4

Within the Inner Circle is **Queen Mary's Rose Garden**, a magnificent array of flowers and plants of all kinds. At the north end is the **Open Air Theatre** (t *(020) 7486 2431; open late May–Sept; book well in advance*), a magical sylvan setting for summer productions of *A Midsummer Night's Dream* (plus a musical and one other Shakespeare each season). On the west side (find the path next to the Open Air Theatre) is the **Boating Lake**, a romantic stretch of water where you can rent boats of all kinds for a balmy summer afternoon's idle dreaming.

Around the outside of the Circle are some Nash-era mansions – such as Decimus Burton's **The Holme** – plus a few modern Georgian imitations by Quinlan Terry and others. These are among the most exclusive addresses in London, and well protected from prying eyes by imposing gates and state-of-the-art security systems. The US Ambassador is among the chosen few to live here.

London Central Mosque K3

146 Regent's Park Rd, t (020) 7724 3363, w www.islamicculturalcentre.co.uk; tube Baker St, Marylebone, St John's Wood; wheelchair accessible.

This rather remarkable mosque was built in 1978 as a study centre and place of worship for the city's growing Muslim population (easily the largest religious minority). The arcaded concrete outer buildings contain a rather plain grey minaret as well as the mosque itself. Take off your shoes and enjoy the sheer sense of space and light beneath the dome. There are few furnishings other than a large chandelier and thick decorated carpet, but the place exudes a feel of peace and calm.

South Kensington
and Knightsbridge

Highlights

Londoner's City: London's kids love pushing buttons and pulling levers at the Science Museum, p.193

Outdoor City: Looking for cheap works of art on the railings along Bayswater Rd, p.196, or listening to cranks at Speakers' Corner, p.197

Indoor City: The incredibly rich and varied collection at the Victoria and Albert Museum, p.186

1 Lunch

Orangery, *Kensington Palace, **t** (020) 7376 0239; **tube** High St Kensington. **Open** winter daily 10am–5pm, summer daily 10am–6pm. **Inexpensive**. Elegant café in Kensington Palace with a delightful summer terrace.*

2 Drinks

Iso-Bar, *145 Knightsbridge, **t** (020) 7838 1044; **tube** Knightsbridge. **Open** daily 5pm–midnight. Seriously stylish bar for shoppers.*

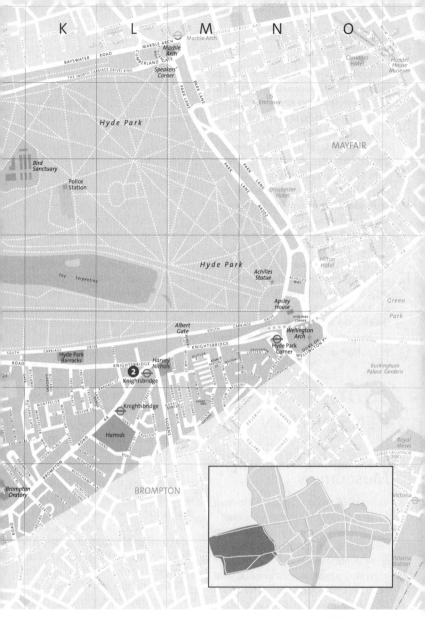

South Kensington and Knightsbridge

1851 was the year that everything happened in South Kensington. The present-day museum complex has its roots firmly in the Great Exhibition, the gargantuan Victorian trade fair that put Britain on the map scientifically, commercially and culturally, thanks to the encyclopedic ambitions of its sponsors, Henry Cole and Prince Albert. It was the idea of these two men to blend the arts and the sciences into a huge international show; they were also the originators of the collections which form the basis of today's Victoria and Albert, Science and Natural History Museums. Albert's name is everywhere – the Albert Hall, the Albert

Memorial, the Victoria and Albert Museum; indeed the district is sometimes referred to as Albertopolis. Before Albert and Cole, this was a distant outpost of the city, the haunt of highwaymen, duellists and hardened drinkers. After them, it turned into one of London's most desirable neighbourhoods.

The Victoria and Albert is the most remarkable of the museums for the sheer variety and value of its treasures. The Science Museum is the most immediately entertaining for kids, although the Natural History Museum gives its fair share and, whatever else you do, you should take a look at its outrageous neo-Gothic architecture. This chapter also explores the pleasant greenery of Hyde Park and Kensington Gardens, and the exclusive addresses of Knightsbridge, including the doyen of luxury department stores, Harrods.

SOUTH KENSINGTON

The Victoria and Albert Museum I–J15

Cromwell Rd, t 0870 442 0808, w www.vam .ac.uk; tube South Kensington; wheelchair accessible, with special leaflets. Open Thurs–Tues 10am–5.45pm, Wed 10am–10pm, last Fri of the month 10am–10pm (Friday Late View offers live performances and guest DJs, food and a bar, t (020) 7942 2000); closed 24–26 Dec; adm free, with free museum guide, but charges for some special exhibitions. Guided tours daily, hourly; free; call in advance. Activities on Sat for kids (backpacks and discovery trails) and all ages (demonstrations from shoe-making and Indian floor-painting to Islamic calligraphy and carpet-weaving), call t (020) 7942 2000. Restaurant on Level A at the entrance to the Henry Cole Wing.

This huge, sprawling museum is nominally dedicated to applied art and design, but in fact even such a broad definition does not sufficiently cover the sheer vastness of its collections. For half a century after its foundation in the 1850s, the museum was housed in a temporary eyesore of corrugated iron, cast-iron and glass which leaked, earning it the nickname 'the Brompton Boilers', because of its location in what was then the market-garden suburb of Brompton. The building was replaced in 1872, and in 1899 Queen Victoria laid the cornerstone for the last of its five extensions and agreed to give the museum its present name. Back in 1863, the museum was instructed to confine its purchases to 'objects wherein Fine Art is supplied to some purpose of utility'. The instructions were totally ignored and today it is filled with all manner of Indian, Oriental, European and American art, glass, silver, porcelain, textiles, tapestries, ironwork, armour, plaster casts and paintings.

After much controversy, the V&A has received planning permission to go ahead with its most daring building project ever. Architect Daniel Libeskind has designed a revolutionary seven-storey structure, variously described as 'shocking', 'an explosion in a cardboard box factory' and 'a brilliant aesthetic balancing act', intended to transform the Exhibition Rd entrance into a 'gateway to the 21st century'. Known as the Spiral, its walls will rise in a series of overlapping, sloping planes covered in ivory-coloured hand-crafted tiles. There will be no need for internal columns or supports, so light will filter freely through the glazed roofs. The uncluttered interior will host a range of new galleries both intimate and monumental, an online resource centre, a 'learning lab', a new auditorium and a stylish café.

Neither the museum guides nor this book would be foolhardy enough to undertake an exhaustive description of the whole place: what follows is a broad-brush and personalized account of what to expect.

Level A (Ground Floor)
The Dress Collection
Room 40.

An enthralling starting point is the room dedicated to European fashion across history.

The Great Exhibition

The Great Exhibition of the Works of Industry of All Nations by rights should never have happened at all. It required imagination, audacity, bureaucratic indulgence and inventive flair, all qualities that the city's authorities have usually lacked utterly. London in 1851, though, was lucky enough to have an imaginative royal patron, Prince Albert, an outstanding organizer in Henry Cole, and a designer of genius, Joseph Paxton. Albert first conceived of the show as a monument to free trade and the might of the British Empire, but also as a forum for the scientific and aesthetic achievements of the whole world. The young prince worried that Britain would recede as an industrial nation unless it became more familiar with the very latest in scientific innovation and artistic endeavour. It was a very un-British idea, coming from a prince who had been born and brought up in continental Europe, and it was not exactly greeted with universal glee.

But Albert had the support of Henry Cole, one of the few enlightened bureaucrats of the Victorian age and the closest thing to a renaissance figure the era could claim. Cole had reformed the public record office, helped establish the penny post and fought for a standard railway gauge. He was a painter, an industrial designer, a journalist and magazine editor; he even published the world's first Christmas card in 1843. Together, Cole and the Prince persuaded Parliament to set up a special commission to organize the Exhibition. Hyde Park was agreed upon as a venue, and a competition was launched to find the best architect for a suitable building. Nearly 250 designs were submitted. At first, the 27 commissioners tried to blend the merits of all of them, resulting in a disastrous hotchpotch, taller than St Peter's in Rome, that would have required 15 million bricks and years to construct. In the ensuing debate, the project almost foundered over the old elm trees along Rotten Row, which the commissioners wanted to cut down. It seemed the Exhibition would end, like so many London projects, in squabbling and penny-pinching.

Providence intervened in the shape of Joseph Paxton, a man of whom the Duke of Wellington said: 'I would have liked him for one of my generals.' Paxton was a brilliant gardener who had built glasshouses and arboreta for the Duke of Devonshire at Chatsworth, successfully protecting all manner of tropical plant species. In 1849 he

---

The flamboyant clothes of the 17th and 18th centuries gradually grow more restricted by corsets and bodices, then become blander and fussier in the 19th century, and turn morose in the 1930s and 1940s before exploding in new-found freedom and colour in the 1960s and beyond. Don't miss Vivienne Westwood's outrageous electric-blue **platform shoes**, which are so tall that they made supermodel Naomi Campbell fall over on the Paris catwalk when she revealed them to the world in 1993. The display cabinets have detailed descriptions of the rise of fashion, explaining how the Paris *haute couture* tradition was established by an Englishman, Charles Worth, who was personal dressmaker to Empress Eugénie of France. The collection also pays great attention to wigs, gloves, hats, buttons and shoes.

Musical Instruments
Room 40A.

Up a spiral staircase from the dress section are a range of music boxes, virginals and a Dutch giraffe piano with six percussion pedals, as well as the usual strings, wind and brass. The most impressive piece hangs unmissably in the stairwell: an **Italian double bass** dating from around 1700 which looks big enough to house an entire string orchestra.

The Renaissance in Italy
Rooms 11–20.

The V&A calls this disparate assortment the greatest collection of Renaissance art outside Italy. There are rood sculptures and reliefs, and beautifully decorated *cassones* in gilt and gesso, a *Neptune and Triton* by

hit upon the design formula that was to be the basis of the Crystal Palace. To protect a rare water plant, he constructed a glasshouse based on the ribbed skeletal leaf structure of the lily. His hollow cast-iron columns doubled as rain-water pipes, while a system of ridge-and-furrow roof lights provided heat, light and ventilation. After reading about the Exhibition project, Paxton approached Henry Cole saying he could build a suitable structure that would overcome the speed and cost problems, and spare the elm trees to boot. His plan was endorsed, and less than nine months later his Crystal Palace – 1,848ft long by 408ft wide, covering 18 acres and enclosing a staggering 33 million cubic feet of space – was complete.

The palace was essentially a glorified greenhouse, but on an astonishing scale. Its centrepiece was a 27ft-high fountain fashioned from four tons of pure crystal glass. For the first time London was using the most up-to-date building materials, glass and iron. The Crystal Palace was also the first major pre-fabricated building ever erected. All the parts could be made elsewhere using the latest machine tool technology. To Londoners used to the painfully slow construction of the past, the fast-rising apparition of the

Crystal Palace in Hyde Park must have been extraordinary.

The exhibition, which opened to great fanfare on 1 May 1851, was a huge and largely unexpected popular success. In the 140 days that it stayed open, over six million entries were recorded. People came by omnibus, by coach and by train from London, the countryside and the world. A young man by the name of Thomas Cook specialized in organized trips and made his name as the world's first tour operator. Rooms in London could not be had for love or money.

In all, the exhibition had some 100,000 objects on display. They included such innovations as the first cotton-spinning machines, cigarette rollers and wrappers, and the first soda siphon. The British section boasted the largest mirror in the world, a pioneer model alarm clock known as a 'servant's regulator', and a collapsible piano for gentlemen's yachts. The Germans sent stuffed animals, while the Canadians supplied a giant piano with room for four players at once. The Philosophical Instruments section was a treasure trove of the eccentric; there was a special walking stick with room inside for medical instruments, including materials to perform an

Giovanni Bernini, and *Samson Slaying a Philistine* by Giovanni Bologna. The greatest treasures are two delicate **reliefs by Donatello**, the *Ascension With Christ Giving the Keys to St Peter*, which may have been commissioned for the Brancacci Chapel in Santa Maria della Carmine in Florence, and a *Dead Christ Tended by Angels*, which may have been intended for Prato cathedral. Look out, too, for some glazed terracotta reliefs by **Luca and Andrea della Robbia**, particularly Luca's allegorical series *The Labours of the Months*, executed for the Medici Palace in Florence, and Andrea's *Adoration of the Magi*.

Poynter, Gamble and Morris Rooms

Access through rooms 13 and 15.

On your way through the Italian section you pass the world's first museum café-restaurant, where early visitors could drop in for refreshments. Each of the stunning rooms is a rich, highly decorated example of Victorian design. The **Poynter Room**, originally the grill room, is decked out in blue tiles depicting idyllic country harvest scenes in between allegories of the seasons and the months of the year. The **Gamble Room**, used for the cold buffet, is a throwback to the Renaissance with its gold and blue tiles, enamelled metal ceiling and apt quotation from Ecclesiastes around the walls: 'There is nothing better for a man than to eat and drink.' The last room is the work of **William Morris**. The theme here is nature and greenery, with plant motifs worked into the plasterwork beneath a ceiling stencilled with gold and white patterns. All three rooms highlight the Victorian taste for bright

enema. Among the more useless exhibits were a vase made entirely of lard and mutton fat, and a specially sprung bedstead that hurled its occupants onto the floor at a preset hour. The museum organizers provided a few innovations of their own, not least the world's first public toilets, known in gloriously euphemistic parlance as Comfort Stations.

Unfortunately, succeeding generations failed to carry on where Albert and Henry Cole had left off. The biggest crime was dismantling the Crystal Palace. Paxton had actually drawn up plans to expand it and keep it as a permanent winter garden. Parliament, for reasons best known to itself, voted to pull it down, and the giant structure was eventually reassembled, in modified form, at Sydenham in southeast London. Here it fell into slow decline, was converted into a naval depot during the First World War and eventually burnt down on 30 November 1936. The blaze was spectacular and could be seen as far away as Brighton.

Exhibition fever continued in London for another decade after the doors closed in November 1851. Prince Albert arranged for the purchase of nearly 90 acres of land just south of Hyde Park, with a view to building a science and museum park. A second International Exhibition was planned, and the architect Francis Fowke, a brilliant captain in the Royal Engineers, was commissioned to start work on the permanent buildings. The plans began to go seriously off course when Prince Albert died in 1861 at the age of 42. The International Exhibition was directly affected, and proved neither a popular nor a commercial success. Further misfortune followed with the untimely death of Francis Fowke in 1865, which put back the whole building programme. The Albert Hall opened in 1871 and the Albert Memorial shortly after, but the museums and great centres of learning had to wait years or even decades for completion. The Natural History Museum, mooted as early as 1860, was not opened until 1881; the V&A, meanwhile, had to content itself with temporary headquarters until 1909. Buildings to house Royal Colleges of Music and Art popped up towards the end of the century in Prince Consort Rd and Kensington Gore, but were not integrated into the whole. Albert's plans for a landscaped museum city thus gave way to the usual London mixture of bodge and compromise. The result is a higgledy-piggledy collection of buildings dotted between the park and Cromwell Rd.

colours, the reworking of ideas from the past, and a fascination for the rediscovery of nature.

Raphael Gallery

Room 48A.

Continuing the Italian theme, though on the other side of the Dress Collection, this vast room houses a hugely important Renaissance collection. The series of **cartoons** was painted by Raphael in 1514–15 by order of Pope Leo X as designs for tapestries to be hung in the Sistine Chapel, the private chapel of the Popes. They depict the acts of Sts Peter and Paul, the two pillars of the Catholic Church, and it is thought that their beauty and strength are in direct relation to the force felt by Raphael of Michelangelo's newly completed Sistine Chapel ceiling.

Plaster Casts and Fakes and Forgeries

Rooms 46, 46A and 46B.

The Fakes and Forgeries Hall contains *objets d'art* which were intended to deceive for various nefarious reasons, but which, in the light of modern times, have been more or less accepted as finely executed pieces. On either side of the hall, two cavernous galleries are devoted to near-perfect copies of some of the most famous sculptures and monuments in the world. The effect is altogether surreal: how can you get your mind around seeing Michelangelo's *David* and *Moses*, Ghiberti's *Gates of Paradise*, Trajan's Column from Rome, the Puerta de la Gloria from Santiago de Compostela and chunks of Bordeaux, York and Nuremberg cathedrals all in one place? The irony is that you can view many of these masterpieces better here than you would in situ. **Michelangelo's Moses** sits higher here than in San Pietro in Vincoli in Rome, subtly altering the effects of perspective; this version also omits the chip in Moses' knee which according to legend Michelangelo inflicted upon his own supremely realistic work to see if it would cry out in human pain. The real treat is his *David* – sneak round to the back of the pedestal and you'll see, hanging in a glass case, the plaster fig leaf the museum authorities used to hide the genitals when royal visitors came to the V&A. Such prudish protocol only stopped in the 1950s.

Asian and Islamic Art

Rooms 41, 42, 44, 45 and 47A–G.

The central section of Level A is devoted to art from the Islamic world, India, China, Japan and Korea. The Nehru Gallery of Indian Art (room 41) is divided into three sections which reveal the vast cultural history of the subcontinent in understandable gulps. The most famous piece here is **Tipu's Tiger**, a wooden sculpture dating from 1790 in which a tiger mauls the neck of an English soldier. There are Indian sculptures of deities dating back to the 1st century BC, and paintings and artefacts giving an overview of two millennia of Indian decoration. Up the marble steps through a colonnade from northern India, the Mughal Treasury is filled with masterpieces. The Mughal Empire, which lasted from 1526 until it was replaced by the British Raj in 1857, was an outstandingly rich period in all forms of art. Some of the highlights here include a late 16th-century manuscript illustration of the **life of Babu**, founder of the Mughal Empire; the perfectly formed white nephrite jade **drinking cup of Shah Jehan**; and the jewel-encrusted **spoon of Emperor Akbar**. From the 17th century on you can see the European influence, both in the figures depicted and in the styles adopted.

The Toshiba Gallery of Japanese Art (room 45) boasts some particularly fine **lacquer work**: tables, trays and some amazing playing-card boxes. Look out for the ornate **wicker baskets** and then compare them to the late 19th-century stoneware pots fashioned in imitation of them. There are also some interesting ceramics, including a huge **porcelain disc** originally shown in Europe at the 1878 Paris Exhibition. The Chinese Art section (rooms 44 and 47E) focuses principally on fine objects used in everyday life, particularly ceramics, and a collection of ornaments and figurines used in burial ceremonies. Grander pieces include a large **Ming dynasty canopied bed** and a **Qing dynasty embroidered hanging** for a Buddhist temple. The Korean Art gallery (room 47G) also focuses on everyday objects, including some ancient metalwork, and ceramics from the Koryo and Choson dynasties that go back to the 9th century. Finally the section on Art in the Islamic World (rooms 42 and 47C) contains a pot-pourri of carpets and prayer mats from Egypt and Turkey and finely decorated bowls and earthenware from Persia.

The Medieval Treasury

Room 43.

Sandwiched in the middle of the Asian and Islamic Art galleries is this magnificent collection of mainly religious artefacts from the 5th to the 15th centuries. The reliquaries and reliquary caskets boast highly intricate silver- and goldwork and delicate alabaster carving (look out in particular for the famous 13th-century **Eltenberg reliquary** from Cologne). There is beautifully patterned **clothwork** in a number of tapestries, altar covers and two elaborate English copes, ceremonial cloaks worn by the priesthood, from the 14th century.

The Pirelli Gardens

The central courtyard of the museum is open to the elements, and has plenty of benches and views up to the V&A's brick and terracotta turrets.

The British Galleries

1500–1714 in rooms 56–8, 1714–1837 in rooms 54 and 118–20, and 1837–1900 in rooms 122–5.

In November 2001, the V&A finally opened the doors of the new British Galleries, its most ambitious project for half a century.

The 15 galleries contain the most comprehensive collection of British design and art (from 1500 to 1900) anywhere in the world. There are more than 3,000 objects on display but the highlights are **Henry VIII's writing desk**, **James II's wedding suit** and the famous vast **Great Bed of Ware**, which was made for an inn and became instantly famous – Shakespeare and Ben Jonson both mentioned it in their plays. All of the top British designers are featured here – Morris, Gibbon, Macintosh and Adam – as well as famous manufacturers like Chippendale, Morris, Mackintosh, Wedgwood and Liberty. One of the most elaborate pieces is an elegant **18th-century tea table**, carved in the days when tea-drinking was an expensive hobby enjoyed only by the very wealthy. It is delicately inlaid with brass and mother-of-pearl and the legs have been painstakingly carved with men's stockings, a shoe and buckles. As well as individual objects, there are also some handsomely **re-created rooms**. The galleries have interactive computer terminals to learn more about the displays, and lots of touchy-feely exhibits.

Level B (First Floor)

20th-century Study Gallery
Rooms 103–6.

This series of rooms is as engaging a history of 20th-century design as you'll see. The focus is on household furniture, but within that remit is everything from Marcel Breuer's pioneering **Bauhaus chair** to Salvador Dalí's totally frivolous lipstick-pink **sofa** in the shape of one of Mae West's kisses.

Silver Galleries
Rooms 65–9.

This gallery boasts the latest hi-tech cabinets and lively interactive displays for its collection of 500 years of British silver.

Tapestries
Room 94.

Most outstanding here is the medieval series known as the **Devonshire Hunting Tapestries**. Famed for their beauty, wealth of detail and high standard of preservation,

these tapestries were commissioned in the 15th century for Hardwick Hall, a country mansion in Derbyshire. Each of the six pieces, displayed in subdued light, illustrates a different kind of hunt: boars and bears in one, otters and swans in another, and so on. Rather than dwelling on the gore, however, they are a joyous celebration of country life, blending figures of people and animals with a lush profusion of plants and trees. In the Boar and Bear Hunt, notice the emblem in mirror writing on one woman's sleeve. It reads *'Monte le désir'*, underpinning the delicately erotic themes of the tapestries; the mirror effect suggests the weavers worked from the back of the cloth and forgot that the lettering would come out back to front.

Henry Cole Wing

On the second floor of this wing (named after the museum's founding director) is the **Frank Lloyd Wright Gallery** (room 202), a series of rooms dedicated to the great 20th-century American architect and figurehead of the modern movement. A series of displays explains Wright's predilection for prairie-style houses with low roofs and horizontal window banding. There is a mock-up of one of his interiors, the general manager's office at Kaufmann's department store in Pittsburgh, all warm woods and rational geometry. Architectural plans and photographs give a quick overview of his main works, including his masterful spiral design for the Guggenheim Museum in New York.

Floor four features an exquisite collection of 15th–16th-century English miniatures by **Holbein**, court painter to Henry VIII, and of **Hilliard** and **Oliver**, court painters to Elizabeth I. Among the other watercolours and oils, try to pick out **Courbet**'s moody seascape *L'Immensité* or **Degas**'s depiction of a scene from Meyerbeer's *Roberto Il Diavolo*.

On floor six you come to a light, airy exhibition of some of the best of British painting, including a clutch of **Turners** and a broad selection of the work of **John Constable**. Most people only know Constable's *Hay Wain* and his other romantic country idylls displayed in the National Gallery; here you will find watercolours of rural scenes, soft-focus portraits and even the odd pastoral view of London from Hampstead, where the artist lived for a time. There is also a sketch in oils for the *Hay Wain*. If you've seen the original, you may notice that the boy on a horse, included here, was removed.

Brompton Oratory J15

Thurloe Place, **t** *(020) 7808 0900;* **tube** *South Kensington; wheelchair accessible.* **Open** *daily 6.30am–8pm.*

Behind the double-decker white stone classical façade of this heavily Catholic church is a gaudy Baroque interior based on the Chiesa Nuova in Rome. The Oratory, like its Roman model, is dedicated to San Filippo Neri, one of the leading lights of the Counter-Reformation in the 16th century. Neri founded an informal order called the Institute of the Oratory, in which priests and lay believers were encouraged equally to observe basic rules of piety and worship. Cardinal Newman, who was responsible for bringing the Oratory tradition to Britain during the Catholic revival in the Victorian age, also encouraged the building of this church, designed by Herbert Gribble and completed in 1884.

There is something oddly appealing about the very Italian coloured marble and relief figure work in the nave, perhaps because it seems so out of place in staid, largely Protestant London. The **dome** is a stunning 200ft high, and the nave, at 51ft, a good bit wider even than St Paul's Cathedral. The Oratory has always been popular with the city's Catholics, who tend to prefer it to Westminster Cathedral, built 20 years later. It is nevertheless a derivative piece of work. The **statue of St Peter** on the right-hand side of the nave is a copy of the figure in St Peter's in Rome. The marble **statues of the Apostles**, by Mazzuoli, were taken from Siena Cathedral. And the **portrait of *San Filippo*** by Guido Reni, hanging over the altar, is a copy of one in the saint's rooms in the Chiesa Nuova.

The Natural History Museum H–I15

Cromwell Rd, **t** *(020) 7942 5000,* **w** *www.nhm .ac.uk;* **tube** *South Kensington, Gloucester Rd; wheelchair accessible.* **Open** *Mon–Sat 10am–5.50pm, Sun 11am–5.50pm; closed 23–26 Dec;* **adm** *free, with charges for some temporary exhibitions.*

This museum looks for all the world like a cathedral. The interior is composed of a series of vast rounded arches in brick and terra-cotta and its floors are linked by a labyrinthine network of staircases worthy of the grandest of Gothic structures. Alfred Waterhouse, the architect who replaced Captain Fowke (*see* 'The Great Exhibition', above), drew his inspiration from the 11th- and 12th-century church-building styles of the Rhineland. It shows. His object was to induce an appropriate sense of awe in visitors coming to admire the wonders of creation. The result is way over the top, but quite glorious.

The Collection

You are soon jolted out of any notion that this is a place of worship by the giant skeletal **dinosaur** in the central hall. This 150-million-year-old plant-eating diplodocus looks very impressive indeed; the trouble is, like many of the dinosaurs on display, he's just a cast. There are animatronic models too: notice the amazingly lifelike unlabelled little psittico-saurus quietly sleeping on your left as you leave the exhibition. One display gives an intriguing list of theories on why prehistoric monsters died out: they drowned in their own dung, they developed cataracts in their eyes, slipped too many discs, were hit by a meteor, they suffered deep depression or else, Jim Jones-like, they committed mass suicide. Maybe they were just told they would have to appear in a film one day alongside the histrionically challenged Laura Dern, and they all expired from shame.

Elsewhere in the museum there are games explaining **human perception and memory**, interactive displays on **creepy-crawlies**, and, from October to March each year, the highlight of the whole museum, the **Wildlife Photographer of the Year** exhibition. The **Bird Gallery** features a remarkable collection of stuffed birds and wild animals from the 18th century onwards, and the section known simply as **Mammals** allows a closer peek at elephants and giraffes than you're ever likely to get in a zoo. The **Earth Galleries**, the geological section, are filled with beautiful stones and gems, and you can step into the 'Earthquake Experience' amidst the rattling bottles of a reconstructed Japanese supermarket.

At the end of 2002, the museum will open the first phase of its **Darwin Centre**: 22 million zoological specimens including fish, reptiles, crustaceans and amphibians, all stored in alcohol, will be shifted into the new building (already complete) and will be part of a new exhibit displayed with all the newest interactive computer technology.

The Science Museum H–15

Entrance on Exhibition Rd just above the side entrance to the Earth Galleries of the Natural History Museum, t (020) 7942 4455, IMAX advance booking line t 0870 870 4771, w www.sciencemuseum.org.uk; tube South Kensington; wheelchair accessible. Open daily 10am–6pm; adm free, although there are charges for the IMAX, the Simex simulator, the Virtual Voyage and the Motion Ride. **Activities**: *Science Night for kids (an after-hours tour of the building, with a choice of workshops and bedtime stories before lights out), t (020) 7942 4000; children must be between 8 and 11, accompanied by an adult in groups of five and bring a sleeping bag.* **Giftshop**, **restaurant** *and* **cafés**.

For sheer fun, the Science Museum is hard to beat and, since it opened its doors in 1928, it has done perhaps more than any other institution in London to make itself accessible and popular, undergoing constant updating and improvement.

Ground Floor

If you're planning a grand tour of the whole museum it may be best to start in the main building with the **Synopsis** (which takes you up to 1914, when the rest of the museum takes over) on the mezzanine above the ground floor. Here you can disabuse yourself of a few basic misconceptions: Jethro Tull was not just a bad 1970s rock band but also an 18th-century agricultural pioneer who introduced rowcrop farming. Here too is the Davy lamp, which warned miners about the presence of methane gas. Nearby, the **Power** section gives a brief history of engines, including pioneering models by Boulton and Watt from the 1780s. By the telephones is a modern reworking of Foucault's pendulum, the device which first illustrated the rotation of the earth. Then comes a great **Space** section, complete with rockets, and a recreation of the historic moment in 1968 when Neil Armstrong walked on the moon for the first time. Beyond, the **Land Transport** section traces the history of automobiles from Stephenson's Rocket to the Morris mini, the latter bisected from top to bottom. A **Making the Modern World** exhibition charts the rise of our industrial society over the last 250 years with iconic and ground-breaking objects like the Apollo 10 Command Module, a VW Beetle and the first genetically modified (now stuffed) mice.

Wellcome Wing

In 2000, the fantastic, ultra-modern Wellcome Wing was opened and the museum gained three floors of new galleries, an IMAX cinema, a new virtual-reality simulator, and another restaurant and shops. The wing dwells less on the achievements of yesterday than on what scientists are working on today and striving for in the future. State-of the-art interactive displays allow visitors to engage with the latest developments in science and information technology – everything from how the 'love bug' which brought down countless computer systems in 2000 was created, to the effects of the male contraceptive pill.

Basement

Here is one of the highlights for children, a gallery full of interactive games called the

Launch Pad, which has been given a bit of extra zip recently. Children are teamed up with an 'explainer' and helped through the rudiments of such diverse phenomena as bicycle gears and hangovers.

First Floor

A recent addition is the exhibition named **Challenge of Materials**, whose centrepiece is one of the state-of-the-art pods designed for the London Eye, as well as a spectacular glass and steel bridge spanning the main hall of the museum. The exhibits here celebrate British industry, manufacturing and design with such intriguing objects as a Bakelite coffin, a paper armchair and a dressing gown in Axminster carpet by Vivienne Westwood. **Time Measurement** traces the technology of clocks from the first Egyptian timepieces, based on water, to modern quartz and atomic clocks. Next is **Food for Thought**, which explains everything you wanted to know about nutrition (and a few things you didn't – a group of see-through plastic vats, for example, demonstrating all too graphically the quantity of urine, faeces and sweat that a 10-year-old boy produces in a month).

Second Floor

The highlight here is the **Chemistry** section, exploring the history of the science through the discoveries of such pioneers as Priestley, Dalton, Davy and Faraday. Under **Living Molecules** you'll find Crick and Watson's metal-plate model of the structure of DNA.

Third Floor

Over-12s can spend hours queuing and then learning to record and edit music in **On Air**, a nearly lifelike recording studio with interactive terminals for playing at being a DJ. Younger children head for the **Flight Lab**, featuring a simulator (usually switched to rollercoaster mode), a wind tunnel and a mini hot-air balloon. The main **Flight** section is a display of historic aircraft, a collection of models and an ingenious air traffic control display. Equally intriguing is **Optics**, a collection of spectacles, telescopes, microscopes and the like, leading up to such modern developments as lasers and holograms.

Fourth and Fifth Floors

These floors are devoted to **medicine**. The main curiosity is a series of 43 full-scale mock-ups depicting key developments in medical science – one of the first antiseptic hospital wards, surgery in a First World War trench, a 1930s dentist's office and a modern operating theatre equipped to perform open-heart surgery.

The Royal Albert Hall H13

Main entrance Kensington Gore, t (020) 7589 8212, w www.royalalberthall.com; tube South Kensington, Gloucester Rd, Knightsbridge; wheelchair accessible. Call or visit the Web site for details of concert programmes and events.

The Albert Hall is the one building designed by the unfortunate Captain Fowke (*see* 'The Great Exhibition', p.187) that actually made it into bricks and mortar, but it is unlikely, had he lived, that he would have been pleased with it. As a concert venue it has one unforgivable flaw, an echo that has been the butt of jokes ever since it opened. There is some truth in what the wags say: this is probably the only place where modern British composers can be sure of hearing their work in performance twice. Modern acoustics specialists have been trying to correct the problem with mushroom-shaped roof hangings since the late 1960s, with partial success.

For all its failings, the Albert Hall is still well-loved. Visually, it is one of the more successful Victorian buildings in London, both an echo of the colosseums of antiquity and a bold 19th-century statement on progress and learning. The high **frieze** around the outside depicts the Triumph of Arts and Sciences – a most Albertian theme. The hall is huge (capacity 7,000 or more) and remarkably versatile: through the year it hosts symphony orchestras, rock bands, conferences, boxing matches and tennis tournaments. Every summer it becomes the headquarters of the Proms, a series of low-priced concerts widely broadcast on radio and television. 'Prom' is short for promenade:

originally the concerts were held in the open air and were open to all comers; now the promenaders pay a small charge to stand in a special open area in the front stalls. The Last Night of the Proms in early September is a national institution; the orchestra plays the most patriotic of British tunes and the high-spirited audience, waving Union Jacks and banners, sings boisterously along. The Albert Hall is quietly undergoing restoration at the moment, but the only thing that won't change is the dreadful acoustics.

The Albert Memorial H13

*Just off Kensington Gore; **tube** South Kensington, Gloucester Rd, Knightsbridge. If you want a close-up view and a 45min tour, Sun at 2pm and 3pm, by very knowledgeable guides, ring **t** (020) 7495 0916.*

The notion of honouring Albert with a memorial was mooted even before the prince's untimely death in 1861. His over-eager homage-payers had to bide their time, though, if only because Albert himself was adamantly opposed to the idea. 'It would disturb my rides in Rotten Row to see my own face staring at me,' he said, 'and if (as is very likely) it became an artistic monstrosity, like most of our monuments, it would upset my equanimity to be permanently ridiculed and laughed at in effigy.' As it turned out, the prince's fears were well founded. The widowed Queen Victoria launched a competition for a memorial the year after her husband's death and was personally responsible for picking George Gilbert Scott, nabob of neo-Gothic excess, as the winner.

The 175ft-high monument he built is an over-decorated stone canopy housing an indifferent likeness of Albert reading a catalogue from the Great Exhibition by John Foley: a ponderous pickle of allegorical statuary and religious imagery decked out in marble, mosaic panelling, gilt, enamel and polished stone. The wonder is that anyone ever liked it. In fact, it was a big hit with the Victorians and remained popular well into the 20th century. It took a writer as cynical as

Norman Douglas to puncture the myth. 'Is this the reward of conjugal virtue?' he wrote in 1945. 'Ye husbands, be unfaithful!'

KENSINGTON GARDENS

***Tube** High St Kensington, Queensway, Lancaster Gate.*

This large expanse of park is divided from Hyde Park by the Serpentine, and has more trees. George Frampton's famous **statue of Peter Pan** is by the lakeside towards the Bayswater Rd end of the gardens. Just behind the statue is an attractive area of bushes and flowering plants known as the **Flower Walk**.

Kensington Palace F12

***t** (020) 7937 9561, **w** www.hrp.org.uk; Royal Ceremonial Dress Collection and Orangery wheelchair accessible. **Open** March–Oct daily 10am–6pm, Nov–Feb daily 10am–5pm, last adm 1 hour earlier; closed 1 Jan, Good Friday and 22–26 Dec; **adm** adults £8.80, concessions £6.90, children £6.30, families £26.80, including audioguide. **Orangery café**.*

Since the death of Princess Diana, Kensington Palace has become something of a shrine to her memory; this was where she lived after the failure of her marriage to Prince Charles. You won't be able to visit her private apartments, but the palace offers other attractions in their place.

William of Orange originally moved here in 1689 because he thought Whitehall Palace, being near the river, would be bad for his asthma. He appointed Christopher Wren to spruce up what was then a relatively modest Jacobean mansion, and took on the design of the grounds, including the elegant sunken garden, himself. Two of the more embarrassing royal deaths of the 18th century took place here: Queen Anne succumbed to apoplexy in 1714 after an extended bout of overeating, while George II had a violent stroke while squatting on his toilet in 1760.

The Interior

The audioguide tour is divided into two sections: the historic state apartments (hung with masterpieces from the royal collection), and an exhibition of royal ceremonial dress including the coronation robes worn by monarchs from George II onwards. The most interesting aspect of the apartments is the **decoration by William Kent**: a beautifully patterned ceiling in the Presence Chamber, some *trompe l'œil* murals of court scenes on the King's Staircase, and painted episodes from the *Odyssey* on the ceiling of the King's Gallery. The Cupola Room plays optical tricks to make you believe the ceiling is taller and more rounded than it is. From the King's Drawing Room there is a fine view over Kensington Gardens, the Serpentine and Hyde Park.

The fashions in coronation garb charted by the **ceremonial dress exhibition** indicate the changing status of the monarchy itself. The over-confident Georges wore ermine galore, particularly the profligate George IV, who sported a ludicrously flamboyant white feather hat and a train as thick as a shag-pile carpet. William IV and Victoria, whose coronations went almost unnoticed by a populace more interested in democratic reform than regal pomp, were sober almost to the point of blandness. Edward VII, who helped restore the monarchy's image, showed confidence with his bright military uniform and ermine mantle braided with gold.

The Diana Memorial Walk

t (020) 7298 2000. Send a stamped addressed envelope to the Royal Parks Information Office, The Old Police House, Hyde Park, London W2 2UH, if you'd like a leaflet describing the walk.

Kensington Palace is along the route of the 7-mile Diana Memorial Walk, which circles the four central royal parks – Kensington Gardens, Hyde Park, Green Park and St James's Park. The route is clearly marked with a rose symbol.

Serpentine Gallery I12

t (020) 7402 6075, w www.serpentinegallery .org; wheelchair accessible; closed Christmas. Open daily 10am–6pm.

This former tea pavilion hosts temporary exhibitions of contemporary art and has an excellent bookshop.

HYDE PARK

Tube Hyde Park Corner, Knightsbridge, Marble Arch, Lancaster Gate.

Hyde Park started out as part of the Westminster Abbey estate, a breeding ground for deer, boar and wild bulls. When Henry VIII dissolved the monasteries, he decided to keep it as a private hunting ground; it was not opened to the public until the beginning of the 17th century. William III hung lamps along **Rotten Row** (the sandy horse path running along the southern edge; its name is a corruption of the French *route du roi* – royal road) to deter highwaymen while he made his way from Kensington Palace to St James's, instituting the idea of street-lighting in London. The park was a favourite hangout for crooks of all kinds, and even George II was once robbed of his purse, watch and buckles while out walking. In the course of the 18th century it also became London's most popular duelling ground.

In 1730 Queen Caroline created the **Serpentine** by having the underground River Westbourne dammed. The L-shaped lake is still the park's most prominent feature, famous for its New Year's Day swims, which are open to anyone foolhardy enough to jump into the freezing winter water (some years the swimmers have to break the ice before they start).

The **railings** on the Hyde Park side of Bayswater Rd, to the north, are famously used to display cheap paintings for sale on Sunday afternoons.

Speakers' Corner L9

Tube *Marble Arch.*

The northeastern end of Hyde Park remains the only place in Britain where demonstrators can assemble without police permission, a concession made in 1872 in a truce between the Metropolitan Police and a succession of angry demonstrators. The spot is known as Speakers' Corner, and every Sunday afternoon you can hear impassioned crackpots droning on for hours about the moral turpitude of the world. Despite the fame of Speakers' Corner, it is hardly an impressive symbol of free speech. Microphones are banned, and most of the words are drowned out by the traffic on Park Lane. Nobody takes the place seriously any more, particularly in this media-saturated era. You can talk all you like, Speakers' Corner says, but nobody will hear you.

Marble Arch M9

Park Lane; **tube** *Marble Arch.*

The arch was designed in 1827 by John Nash as the entrance to Buckingham Palace. It turned out to be too narrow for carriages, however, and was moved here in 1851. Nearby is the site of the Tyburn gallows, in use until 1783.

Hyde Park Corner N13

Tube *Hyde Park Corner.*

Hyde Park Corner, now one of London's more impossible traffic junctions, abruptly separates Green Park from Hyde Park. The planners got their teeth into Hyde Park Corner at around the same time that they came up with the idea for Trafalgar Square, and both projects were intended for the same purpose: to glorify Britain's victories in the Napoleonic Wars. While Trafalgar Square honoured the country's great naval commander Horatio Nelson, who died in the heat of battle, Hyde Park Corner gave pride of place to the hero of Waterloo, the Duke of Wellington, who was still very much alive and climbing the political ladder towards the Prime Minister's office. Wellington was unfortunately one of the bigger bores in history, which might go some way to explain why he allowed such a dog's breakfast to be made of this collection of memorials to him.

Wellington Arch N13

w *www.english-heritage.org;* **adm** *£2.50.*

Originally the arch, designed by Decimus Burton, was topped by a vast statue of the duke astride Copenhagen, the horse he rode at Waterloo. The bronze monster, built by Matthew Cotes Wyatt and his son James, was 30ft high, weighed 40 tons and by all accounts was revoltingly ugly. One Frenchman who saw it exclaimed: 'We have been avenged!' So reviled was the statue that it was taken down in 1882 and eventually replaced with the present quadriga depicting four horses harnessed to a chariot of peace. The architect of the quadriga, Adrian Jones, held a dinner party for eight people in the open carcass of one of the bronze horses shortly before the ensemble was completed in 1912. Wellington, meanwhile, was compensated for the loss of one statue by the arrival of another: a replacement **equestrian figure** was erected next to the victory arch, rather closer to terra firma this time, in 1888. The Wellington Arch has just been opened to visitors after a £1 million facelift – a lift swoops to the top for fabulous views, and there is a fascinating exhibition of old photographs.

Decimus Burton also designed the **Greek Revival screen** at the entrance to Hyde Park.

Apsley House N12–13

149 Piccadilly, **t** *(020) 7499 5676,* **w** *www .apsleyhouse.org.uk; wheelchair accessible.* **Open** *Tues–Sun 11am–5pm;* **adm** *adults £4.50, concessions £3, under-18s free.*

Wellington was given this house, his London residence, as a reward for his victories against the French, and he modestly dubbed it No.1, London (its real address being the more prosaic 149 Piccadilly). Robert Adam had built it half a century earlier for Henry Bathurst, a man generally reckoned to be the most incompetent Lord Chancellor of the 18th century. The Iron Duke succeeded in defacing Adam's original work, covering the brick walls with Bath stone, adding the awkward Corinthian portico at the front and ripping out much of the interior with the help of the architects Benjamin and Philip Wyatt. It's a slightly sterile place now, but among the military memorabilia and unexciting portraits you will find some superb examples of work by **Goya**, **Velázquez** and **Rubens**. You can feel the coldness of a man who terrified most who met him and who, according to legend, once defused a riot in Hyde Park with a single crack of his whip. The museum has at least one pair of Wellington's boots, but not so much as a glimpse of an actual Wellington, the man's greatest legacy. The highlight is indubitably Canova's double-life-size **sculpture of Napoleon**, which Wellington stole from the Louvre after its megalomaniac subject rejected it. No, it wasn't that Napoleon found it too small: he was offended because the winged victory figure on the palm of one of the hands faced away from the sculpture, suggesting (so Napoleon thought, rightly as it turned out) that victory would finally elude him.

KNIGHTSBRIDGE

There is nothing very grand about the houses of Knightsbridge, but the confident late-Victorian mansions fetch astronomical rents. It was not always thus: for a long time it was a small village far from London noted mainly for its taverns, particularly the Fox and Bull, where Joshua Reynolds went boozing in the 18th century. It was the Great Exhibition that turned Knightsbridge into the birthplace of the department store.

Harvey Nichols L13

109–25 Knightsbridge (corner of Sloane St and Knightsbridge), **w** *www.harveynichols.com;* **tube** *Hyde Park Corner, Knightsbridge; wheelchair accessible.* **Restaurants.**
'Harvey Nicks' is probably the most stylish and upmarket of the Knightsbridge

department stores. It's justly famous for its weird and wonderful window displays, and fifth-floor food halls, where swishly packaged exotica of every description are sold under an equally exotic steel-panelled corrugated canopy with views over Knightsbridge.

Harrods L14

87–135 Brompton Rd, **t** *(020) 7730 1234,* **w** *www.harrods.com;* **tube** *Knightsbridge; wheelchair accessible.* **Open** *Mon, Tues, Sat 10am–6pm, Wed–Fri 10am–7pm.*
The most famous department store of all, Harrods is often mentioned in the same breath as its owner, Mohammed Al Fayed, infamous business tycoon and father of Dodi, last companion of Princess Diana. But Harrods' pedigree stretches back to the glory days of the 19th century. Henry Charles Harrod was an Eastcheap tea merchant who set up shop in Knightsbridge in 1849. Harrod's real coup, ironically, was a fire that destroyed the premises in December 1883. With impeccable *sang-froid*, Harrod wrote to his best customers that 'in consequence of the above premises being burnt down, your order will be delayed in the execution a day or two'. He made all his Christmas deliveries on time, so impressing the clientèle that in 1884 his turnover more than doubled.

The vast, terracotta-fronted palace that Harrods now occupies was built in the first five years of the 20th century, at much the same time as the first modern luxury hotels like the Savoy and the Ritz. Indeed Harrods is itself in some ways more like a five-star hotel than a mere shop: service and indulgence towards the customer are paramount, and no request is ever too much trouble. The place is kitted out to provide a fitting welcome to the noblest of princes; particularly striking are the **Food Halls** with their beautiful food displays and Edwardian Art Nouveau tiles in the Meat Hall depicting hunting scenes. As you wander around, you are serenaded alternately by a harpist and a piano player. You'll find just about anything on its six floors, as long as money is no object.

The South Bank

13

Highlights

Londoner's City: Londoners have a taste for the gruesome – learn about pre-anaesthetic operations at the Old Operating Theatre, p.211

Literary City: See a Shakespeare play 'in the round' at the Globe Theatre, p.206

Contemporary Architecture: The striking London Eye, with views for 25 miles, p.202

Riverside City: Walk by the river all the way from County Hall past London Bridge, along the 'Millennium Mile', *see map*

Outdoor City: Bounce over the not-so-wobbly Millennium Bridge, p.206

Indoor City: The fantastic collection of international modern art at Tate Modern, p.205

1 Lunch

Neat, *2nd Floor, Oxo Tower*, **t** *(020) 7928 5533*; **tube** *Southwark*. **Open** *Mon–Fri noon–2 and 7–10, Sat 7–10pm*. **Luxury**. Richard Neat's new restaurant and brasserie in the Oxo Tower. The brasserie is considerably cheaper than the restaurant.

2 Drinks

Anchor, *1 Bankside*, **t** *(020) 7407 1577*; **tube** *London Bridge*. **Open** *Mon–Sat 11am–11pm, Sun noon–10.30pm*. Excellent river views in this ancient institution, where fugitives from the Clink prison used to hide in cubby holes.

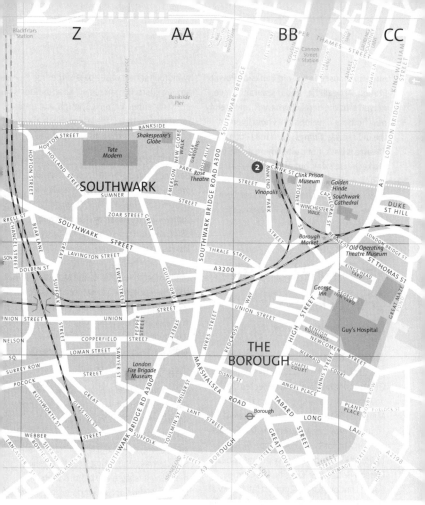

The South Bank

For centuries, London's South Bank conjured up images of poverty and grime, of wharves and raucous backstreet bars. The poor relation of the City, and unfashionably 'south of the river', it was a general dumping ground for undesirable persons, trades and pastimes. Southwark, the London borough stretching from Waterloo Bridge to the other side of Tower Bridge, has seen it all: butchers, tanners, whores, corrupt bishops, coach-drivers, actors, bear-baiters, railwaymen and dockers. Shakespeare's Globe Theatre was here, as was the notorious Marshalsea debtors' prison. It is one of the most atmospheric parts of London, used over and over by the city's novelists, particularly Dickens.

But more than for anywhere else in London, the turn of the millennium has been a time of frenzied refurbishment, rebuilding and planning for the South Bank. The river walk from County Hall to the Design Museum (*see* p.260) has been dubbed the Millennium Mile, and the area's 'Millennium Project' has produced some of the most exciting things to happen in London for more than a century. Be prepared to see a lot of new and surprising apparitions, and a good number of cranes, diggers and hard hats as the building works continue well into the new century. Biggest and most striking of all is the Millennium Wheel, officially known as the British Airways London Eye, an electric-powered observation wheel that arcs up 450ft into the London sky. And of course there's Tate Modern, a truly modern museum housed in the old Bankside Power Station. Art galleries and restaurants have moved into the derelict wharves, and trendy new housing developments now liven up the old railway sidings. Even the Globe Theatre is back, not quite where it was in Shakespeare's day, but almost.

For a walk around the Southwark of the past, taking in old inns and markets, turn to the 'Taverns, Stews and Players' walk on p.279.

THE SOUTH BANK

County Hall V13

Tube Waterloo, Westminster.

This grand grey-stone public building in the pompous Edwardian 'Wrenaissance' style was until 1986 the headquarters of the Greater London Council, the elected city government that proved such a threat to Margaret Thatcher that she abolished it. London's new city government, the Greater London Authority or GLA (*see* p.46), is building extraordinary new premises near London Bridge (*see* 'Outside the Centre: South London', p.259). County Hall is now a multi-purpose centre for residential housing, hotel accommodation and conferences. In the basement are the London Aquarium and the Dalí Universe exhibition, while at the time of writing Charles Saatchi was negotiating to open a gallery on the second floor. There is also a tacky and unpleasant development including amusement arcades.

London Aquarium

Basement, t (020) 7967 8000, e info@london aquarium.co.uk, w www.londonaquarium .co.uk; wheelchair accessible. Open daily 10am–6pm, last adm 5pm; closed 25 Dec; adm adults £8.75, concessions £6.50, 3–14s £5.25, families £25.

Here, in spectacular three-storey fish tanks set in long, lugubriously dark corridors, you can say hello to sharks, stingrays, octopi, cuttlefish, umbrella-like jellyfish and wondrous shoals of sea bass slithering among kitsch Roman ruins. The aquarium is primarily entertainment, though, and unfortunately fails to tell the visitor much about either the fish or the environment.

Dalí Universe

Basement, t (020) 7620 2720, w www.dali universe.com; wheelchair accessible via entrance on Queen's Walk. Open daily 10am–5.30pm; closed 25 Dec; adm adults £8.95, concessions £6.95, 10–16s £4.95, families £24.

There may be a lot of interesting stuff for Dalí fans here – copies of the Mae West lips sofa, the backdrop Dalí painted for the dream sequence in Hitchcock's film *Spellbound*, as well as a large collection of paintings and sculptures from the end of his life – but, sadly, it's badly laid out and very expensive.

The Saatchi Gallery

Second floor. Opening hours to be confirmed but likely to be similar to those of the London Aquarium and Dalí Universe; adm.

At the time of writing in early 2002, the advertising mogul and art collector Charles Saatchi was negotiating to open a gallery here. It will feature works from Saatchi's large collection of contemporary art as well as high-profile temporary exhibitions. The opening exhibition will show new work by Damien Hirst.

British Airways London Eye V12

Jubilee Gardens, bookings t 0870 5000 600, bookings and information w www.ba- londoneye.com; tube Waterloo, Westminster, Embankment; wheelchair accessible but only two wheelchairs per pod. Open May–Sept daily 9.30am–10pm, Oct–April daily 9.30am–8pm; closed 25 Dec; adm adults £9.50, concessions £7.50, 5–16s £5, under 5s are free but must have a booked place. Advance and on-the-day tickets are also available from the ticket office behind the London Eye, but the queues are very long and you should book well in advance. 'Flight times' are 30mins and you should arrive 30mins in advance to pick up advance-booked tickets.

The brainchild of husband and wife architects David Marks and Julia Barfield, this was originally meant to be a huge PR coup for British Airways and one of the highlights of London's Millennium celebrations. Perhaps not surprisingly given the magnitude of the undertaking (it is the highest structure with public access in London and it took two major attempts a month apart, 24 hours and the tallest A-crane in the world to pull it up to standing), the project was so dogged by delays and safety glitches that on Millennium Night the wheel was still not turning, much less taking passengers.

Since then, however, it has become one of London's most popular attractions, its elegant silhouette now a permanent (well, at least for now) part of the London skyline. Queues snake for miles as visitors queue for hours at peak times to be one of the 25 orbiting gawpers in each of the 32 pods to make the gentle, 30-minute revolution. The views stretch for 25 miles over London – at least on fine days, but the trip can be worth it even on rainy days, when rainbows seem to skitter along the rooftops.

The **Jubilee Gardens** behind the London Eye were laid out in 1977 to commemorate the Queen's Silver Jubilee. Sadly, the gardens are under threat from developers who are hoping to move the National Film Theatre (*see* 'The South Bank Centre', below) and build an enormous underground car park here. The local community, fed up with seeing their green spaces being swallowed up by the money men, have mounted a campaign which seems to be staving off the developers – at least for the moment.

The South Bank Centre V–W11

Tube *Waterloo, Embankment; wheelchair accessible.*

The South Bank Centre grew out of the 1951 Festival of Britain, the government's attempt to boost the nation's morale after the war with a broad range of public works projects and cultural events. The Royal Festival Hall, the South Bank's main concert venue, opened the same year. The National Film Theatre followed in 1958; the Hayward Gallery, Queen Elizabeth Hall and Purcell Room (for concerts) in the late 1960s; and the three-stage National Theatre (now Royal National Theatre) in 1976.

The Festival of Britain harked back to the Great Exhibition which had taken place exactly a century earlier, but it set a very different tone. Where the Victorian extravaganza was essentially a trade fair designed to generate revenue, the Festival of Britain was a government-sponsored jamboree primarily intended to give people a good time. One was profoundly capitalist in inspiration, the other essentially socialist. The South Bank Centre, with its faithful and diverse audience, high artistic standards and willingness to experiment, was the product of a collectivist spirit that almost entirely disappeared from British public life after the Thatcher revolution of the 1980s.

But the Lottery-funded Millennium Project is set to make great changes for the South Bank Centre. From the outside, the buildings lying at the heart of the South Bank Centre have always looked rather forbidding – lumps of dirty grey concrete streaked with rain, and proof if ever it was needed that concrete does not suit the English climate. With any luck this will all be remedied by a giant masterplan affecting each of the centre's venues, except the Royal National Theatre, which has gone solo and spent a £32 million Lottery grant on a refurbishment all of its own.

Aesthetics apart, the South Bank Centre has always worked remarkably well as a cultural complex. Everything is easily accessible, well signposted and free of traffic. The concerts and plays are subsidized and tickets relatively cheap – and there is always plenty going on in the foyers and elsewhere for free. People enjoy coming not just for the scheduled events, but also to hang out in the spacious halls with their plentiful cafés, occasional musicians, bookstalls (both inside and out), piers and river views.

The **Royal National Theatre** foyers have excellent bookshops, particularly for drama, as well as free live concerts in the early evenings; the recent Lottery grant has created a new foyer extension and an outdoor performance space for the pick of street theatre, linking the theatre to the riverside. The **Hayward Gallery** has no permanent exhibition, but puts on top-class temporary shows. The **Royal Festival Hall** has a varied programme of free lunchtime concerts. The **National Film Theatre** boasts the nicest of the centre's many eateries, the Film Café on the riverfront. Irritatingly, the best venue of all, the **Museum of the Moving Image**, will remain closed throughout the rebuilding works and is not due to reopen until 2003. The merits of the various venues are dealt with in detail in the 'Entertainment' chapter.

SOUTHWARK

Back in the 17th century, Bankside and the whole borough of Southwark were bywords for a raucous good time. The boisterous character of the area is easily explained by history. When the Romans first built London Bridge in AD 43, Southwark naturally developed as a small colony and market town opposite the City of London. As the City grew in wealth and importance, Southwark attracted some of the dirtier, more unpleasant trades that might have offended the rich merchants across the river. In 1392, for example, a decree was passed giving butchers the right to dump animal skins here, thus giving rise to the leather trade south of the river. In subsequent centuries, travellers often had to spend the night here because the bridge was only open at certain times. Southwark therefore developed a secondary role as a transport hub: Londoners would cross the bridge and wait for a coach to take them southwards on their journey.

With all this waiting around to do, particularly in the evening hours, inns and whorehouses (also banned in the City) were soon doing brisk business. Such brisk business, in fact, that in the 12th century the Bishops of Winchester built their palace here and took over the brothels as a lucrative sideline that they ran with extreme cruelty. For centuries much of Bankside was an unconsecrated graveyard for dead prostitutes; many of them perished in the neighbourhood's numerous private jails.

In 1556 Southwark came directly under the City's jurisdiction and cleaned up its act somewhat. The dissolution of the monasteries and the arrival of syphilis from America put paid to the Bishop of Winchester's little whoring scam. The theatres made the available entertainment a little more thought-provoking, if only for a brief period. And then local industries sprang up: Bankside bustled with wharves, breweries, foundries and glassworks.

Southwark remained a promising, if still raucous, area until the mid-18th century, when the construction of Westminster Bridge and the first Blackfriars Bridge diminished its importance as the most accessible of London's southern satellites. The arrival of the railways in the Victorian era made it even more isolated, reducing it to no more than a row of warehouses stuck between the noisy train tracks. Further decline came after the Second World War, as the London docks became obsolete and the area's wharves and warehouses closed. Today, like so many neglected areas of London, it has only its past to turn to as a source of income. Southwark is busy devoting itself to the heritage industry, with a flood of new museums and renovated historical landmarks.

Gabriel's Wharf X11

w www.gabrielswharf.co.uk; tube Waterloo.
Gabriel's Wharf, an odd little enclave of handicraft shops and restaurants overlooked by a huge painted frieze, is a cheerful island of colour. It's always full at weekends and

during the summer Salsa Festival in early July, but sadly the land is slated for redevelopment. At least at the moment, you can hire bikes for some very enjoyable (and flat) cycling along the riverbank.

Oxo Tower X11

Tube Waterloo; wheelchair accessible.

This elegant Art Deco tower, whose top windows are shaped to spell the name of the famous stock cubes, was magnificently restored in 1996 and now houses 30 designer and **jewellery** workshops, as well as a couple of **restaurants** and **bars**. In the tower you can buy work from the highest-quality designers and craftsmen at prices that are significantly cheaper than in galleries and shops in central London. Work on show includes designer-made lights and blinds, 'painterly' carpets, hand-painted silk scarves and ties, one-off chairs and tables and, in Studio Fusion, the best enamelled jewellery and silverwork you can see anywhere in the country. At the very top of the building, on the eighth floor, is a free public viewing gallery.

Tate Modern Z11

Bankside Power Station, t (020) 7401 5120, e information@tate.org.uk, w www.tate.org .uk; tube Southwark; wheelchair accessible. Open Sun–Thurs 10am–6pm, Fri and Sat 10am–10pm; closed 24–26 Dec; adm free, but charges for some special exhibitions. Giftshop and cafés.

The dark apparition that is Bankside Power Station was originally designed by Sir Giles Gilbert Scott (of red telephone box fame) as a companion piece to the power station at Battersea and built in two phases in 1937 and 1963. Now it has been dramatically transformed by Swiss architects Herzog & de Meuron to become London's most exciting museum of modern art. Its soaring central chimney is still a focal point, but the most striking new feature is the glass canopy running the length of the roof and adding two floors of vast new galleries with spectacular views across the river to the City.

The Jubilee Line Extension

Work on the Jubilee Line extension started in 1991, but, in typical British fashion, was not completed until 1999. The extension links Green Park in the west with Westminster, Greenwich, the financial centre of Canary Wharf and Stratford, in the northeast. Several of the new stations are worth a visit in themselves, particularly the monumental, awe-inspiring Canary Wharf by Foster Associates, North Greenwich by Will Alsop, Southwark by MacCormac Jamieson Pritchard, and Ian Ritchie's simple Bermondsey Station. All the extension stations have glass doors between the platform and the train tracks, a much needed safety feature that functions nearly without hitch. Unfortunately but rather predictably, delays on the line seem to have increased rather than decreased since the extension.

In its old home at Millbank, the Tate Gallery's modern collection, its most popular by far, was in dire need of more space to do justice to its 5,000 works of art. Now with seven new floors at Bankside, a much higher proportion of them will be on display at any one time. Tate Britain (*see* p.96) across the river at Millbank now focuses on British art from 1500 to the present, while Tate Modern houses the national collection of international 20th-century and new art. As in Tate Britain, the emphasis here is on exhibiting works in themed groups rather than the usual chronological approach. Some rooms go into greater depth exploring the historical and artistic context of an individual work. Less familiar works have taken their place alongside some of the Tate's best-known works of art, creating interesting juxtapositions.

It's impossible to give a blow-by-bow account of the gallery's works, as they change regularly; the themes, though, remain loosely the same. Among the pieces you can expect to see are **Henri Matisse**'s experiment with paper cut-outs, *The Snail* (which one of the guards used to insist is so called because a tiny nick at the very top of the picture looks exactly like a snail making its way slowly across the picture); and **Francis Bacon**'s contorted, all-too-human forms, especially the horrifying and hallucinatory *Three Studies for Figures at the Base of a Crucifixion*, and the series of pictures of his friend George Dyer; **Giacometti**'s gravely pessimistic series of stick-like figures; **Claude Monet**'s *Waterlilies*; **Magritte**'s disturbing dreamscapes; and the desolate cities of **Giorgio de Chirico** (*Uncertainty of the Poet*). Positively infamous is **Carl André**'s *Equivalent VIII*, a stack of 120 firebricks which caused such a furore when the Tate bought it for a six-figure sum in 1986 that it qualifies as the gallery's most crowd-pulling acquisition ever.

Well-represented artistic movements include **German Expressionism** (the nightmare visions of Kirchner, Kokoschka, Nolde and Grosz, with his grim *Suicide*, a red-stained view of a man shooting himself while a prostitute looks on apathetically), **Abstract Expressionism** (particularly Jackson Pollock and Mark Rothko) and **Pop Art** (Roy Lichtenstein's comic-book *Whaam!* and Andy Warhol's *Marilyn Diptych*, which parodies the movie superstar's transformation into a vulgar commodity).

Level 4 of Tate Modern is the venue for three major loan exhibitions each year, which include film, video and sculpture by artists such as Matthew Barney, Rebecca Horn, Cornelia Parker and Bill Viola.

The Millennium Bridge Z10

Tube Southwark, Blackfriars.

Norman Foster's 'Blade of Light' opened to rapturous applause on 10 June 2000. The bridge was the first to cross the River Thames in more than a century and was built to provide a pedestrian link between St Paul's and the South Bank. It's a slim, elegant swoop of glass supported by horizontal steel cables in a sophisticated version of a suspension bridge – but, like all suspension bridges, it was subject to 'wobbles'. The bridge bounced so alarmingly that it was closed down after just two days of service. Two

years of disputes, delays and redesign followed. In early 2002, the bridge reopened – after 2,000 volunteers and a host of computers agreed that the 'wobble' had been corrected.

Shakespeare's Globe AA11

21 New Globe Walk, box office t (020) 7401 9919, w www.shakespeares-globe.org; tube Southwark, London Bridge. Performances May–Sept; tickets £5. Shakespeare's Globe Exhibition (t (020) 7902 1500) open Oct–April daily 10am–5pm, May–Sept 9am–noon for exhibition and guided tour of the theatre, 12.30–4pm for exhibition and virtual tour of the theatre; adm adults £7.50, concessions £6, children £5, families £23. Shop, restaurant and café.

The original Globe was in fact a few hundred feet away from this site, on the corner of present-day Park St and Southwark Bridge Rd. When London's first playhouse, The Theatre, was forced to move off its premises in Finsbury Fields, just north of the City, in 1598, its manager Richard Burbage had it dismantled and reassembled here on Bankside, where the Rose Theatre had taken root 12 years earlier. Shakespeare helped finance Burbage's enterprise and had many of his plays, including *Romeo and Juliet*, *King Lear*, *Othello*, *Macbeth* and *The Taming of the Shrew*, performed for the first time in its famous O-shaped auditorium. Bankside was the perfect location for theatrical entertainment: all manner of pursuits not deemed proper across the river in the stiff-collared City had moved here, and the area was already notorious, among other things, for its taverns and brothels.

The Globe never properly recovered from a fire in 1613 and was finally demolished during the Civil War. This reconstruction was the brainchild of the late actor Sam Wanamaker, who devoted most of his retirement to realizing the scheme, which remained unfinished when he died in December 1993 at the age of 72. The theatre finally opened for business four years later, following a

Bear-baiting

The site of the Globe, if not the site of the original theatre, has a historical link with another aspect of Elizabethan Bankside: this was where crowds came to watch bears tear each other's limbs apart. Bear-baiting was highly popular in Shakespeare's time, and only stopped briefly during a ban imposed by the Puritans at the same time as they closed the theatres. 'The Puritans hated bear-baiting,' wrote Macaulay somewhat mischievously in the early 19th century, 'not because it gave pain to the bear, but because it gave pleasure to the spectators.' It was only towards the end of the 17th century that the barbarities of this sport impressed themselves on the authorities sufficiently to move them to ban it for good. John Evelyn describes in his diary his disgust on seeing cock-fighting, dog-fighting, bear- and bull-baiting in Bankside in 1670: 'One of the bulls tossed a dog full into a lady's lap as she sat in one of the boxes at a considerable height from the arena. Two poor dogs were killed, and so all ended with the ape on horseback, and I most heartily weary of the rude and dirty pastime.'

If you're in London during the summer you should try to see a performance to appreciate the peculiarities of Elizabethan theatre. The huge stage, with its vast oak pillars holding up a canopy roof, juts out into the open area holding up to 500 standing members of the audience (known as groundlings). The rest of the public is seated on wooden benches in the circular galleries, giving a peculiar sense of intimacy and audience involvement. Scenery is restricted to the brightly painted curtains at the back of the stage, so actors make full use of the architecture of the theatre itself to hide, run and do battle. Again, there are a few concessions to modern sensibilities: the seating is more spacious and comfortable than in Shakespeare's day, and performances take place in the evening as well as the traditional afternoon slot, with the help of discreet electric lighting.

Whether or not you come for a play, you can visit the **Shakespeare's Globe Exhibition**, which charts the building of both the original and the reconstructed theatre and offers a guided tour around the auditorium itself. At the time of writing, work is in full swing on The Cockpit, a second, indoor theatre, based on an unrealized project by Inigo Jones.

remarkable fund-raising effort in which actors, politicians and members of the general public volunteered to sponsor every last paving-slab and brick.

The construction is remarkably faithful to the original, from the distinctive red of its brickwork to its all-wooden interior and thatched roof (the first of its kind to appear in London since the Great Fire of 1666). There are a few postmodern retro flourishes, such as the theatrical masques incorporated into the design of the wrought-iron gates. And a few concessions had to be made to the 20th century, particularly when it came to fire-proofing: the thatch sits on an insulating layer of fibreglass and is painted with special fire-proof chemicals and dotted with sprinkler nozzles that form a curious pattern along the roof edge.

The Rose Theatre AA11

56 Park St, t (020) 7593 0026, w www.rose theatre.org.uk; tube London Bridge.
Open daily 10am–5pm; adm adults £3, concessions £2.50, children £2, families £8.

Until all the millennium redevelopments you could look through the ground-floor windows of this office block on the corner of Rose Alley to see the ruined foundations of the Rose Theatre, the first Bankside playhouse (1587), which was rediscovered here in 1989. Now you pay a small admission price to see them from inside, along with a multimedia presentation narrated by Sir Ian McKellen.

Vinopolis BB11

1 Bank End, **t** *0870 241 4040,* **w** *www.vinopolis*
.co.uk; tube London Bridge; wheelchair acces-
sible. **Open** *Tues–Fri and Sun 11am–6pm, Sat*
11am–8pm, Mon 11am–9pm; last adm 2hrs
before closing; closed 1 Jan and 24–26 Dec;
adm *adults £11.50, concessions £10.50, children*
£5, including vouchers for five tastings and, if
you have the time, a four-hour audioguide;
£2 art exhibition only; discounts for advance
booking online or on **t** *0870 4444 777 (24*
hours). **Wine bar** *serving tapas, smart*
brasserie, *informal but elegant* **refectory** *for*
light lunches and speciality pizzas.

This wine lover's paradise opened in July
1999, an apt celebration of Southwark's
wine-soaked past, and the multimedia invention of Duncan Vaughan Arbuckle, a London
wine merchant. He has transformed two and
a half acres of 19th-century railway arches
into 21 high-vaulted cellar-type rooms, each
giving a sketchy, often witty, impression of a
different wine-growing country or region of
the world. Prepare to spend a couple of hours
here as you weave through the hills of
Chianti on a Vespa, tour Australia's vineyards
in the front five rows of a jet plane, and
sample any of the 200 wines on offer (the
first five are free). All roads lead to Vinopolis
Vaults, a wine store run by Majestic, and the
in-house shop with everything for the
drinker from 43 different corkscrews to glassware and fine cigars.

Clink Prison Museum BB11

Clink St, **t** *(020) 7378 1558,* **w** *www.clink.co.uk;*
tube London Bridge. **Open** *Sept–mid-June*
daily 10am–6pm, mid-June–Aug (exact dates
depend on the weather) daily 10am–9pm;
closed 25 Dec; **adm** *adults £4, concessions and*
children £3, families £9.

This is one of London's more offbeat, not to
say macabre, small museums, on the site of
the notorious medieval jail. The Clink was the
Bishop of Winchester's private prison, where
anyone who dared to challenge the extortion
rackets he ran on Bankside would be locked

up in gruesome conditions. For 400 years
successive bishops acted as pimp to the local
prostitutes, known as Winchester Geese, and
used the prison as dire punishment for any
who tried to conceal their earnings, or work
for somebody else. Incredibly, the scam was
sanctioned by royal licence under Henry II;
not until the Reformation did anybody see fit
to question the moral standards that the
bishop set his flock.

The name Clink is familiar enough nowadays as a synonym for jail; it derives from a
Latin expression meaning, roughly speaking,
'kick the bucket', which gives a good indication of the fate a prisoner could expect
inside. Inmates had to pay their own way;
they even had to pay the costs of being fitted
with a ball and chain (a bit like modern car
wheel-clamping). The only food they could
buy was rotten and grossly overpriced. Well-
connected prisoners could expect a certain
alleviation from the suffering, but the
poorest were thrown into a rat-infested
dungeon called The Hole, from which few
emerged alive. Not surprisingly, the Clink was
a much detested institution that frequently
became a target for city mobs. It was only
after the Gordon Riots of 1780, in which the
Clink was destroyed for the fourth time in its
history, that the authorities decided it would
be best not to rebuild it.

The exhibition highlights the cruelty of life
in medieval Bankside, particularly the
barbaric treatment of women both in prison
and outside. In 1537 Henry VIII ruled that
women who murdered their husbands were
to be boiled in a vat of oil; it was up to the
executioner whether or not to boil the oil in
advance. Bankside women risked more than
judicial punishment. One intriguing room in
the exhibition (an X-rated section not open
to children) focuses on the risks of working in
the whorehouses, or 'stews' as they were
known. Many women believed the best way
to avoid conception was to pee as hard as
they could into a pot after intercourse
(there is a marvellous Rowlandson print
depicting this).

The *Golden Hinde* BB11

*Clink St, **t** (020) 7403 0123, **w** www.golden hinde.co.uk; **tube** London Bridge. **Open** May–Sept daily 10am–6pm, Oct–April daily 10am–5pm; **adm** adults £2.50, concessions £2.10, children £1.75. **Guided tours** booked in advance with entertaining guides dressed as the crew.*

This full-size reconstruction of a galley captained four centuries ago by Francis Drake is nowadays staffed by an extremely entertaining crew of actors dressed in Elizabethan costume. Although it looks unsailable, it has crossed the Pacific and Atlantic Oceans several times since it was built in 1973.

Southwark Cathedral CC11

*Montague Close, **t** (020) 7367 6700, **w** www.dswark.org; **tube** London Bridge; wheelchair accessible. **Cathedral open** daily 8.30am–6pm; **adm** free but donations gratefully accepted. Lunchtime and evening **concerts** take place regularly, call for details. **Visitors' centre open** Mon–Sat 10am–5.30pm, Sun 11am–4pm.*

Southwark Cathedral has a past almost as chequered as the neighbourhood, suffering fire, neglect and patchwork reconstruction over a history stretching back to the 7th century. It started life as the parish church of St Mary Overie (which merely means 'St Mary over the river'), built according to legend by the first boatman of Southwark to ferry gentlemen to and from the City. It burnt down at least twice before being incorporated into a priory belonging to the Bishop of Winchester sometime around 1220. In the Civil War it was a bastion of Puritanism where preachers denounced the Bankside playhouses. By the 19th century it had largely fallen to pieces, and the nave was rebuilt – twice as it turned out, since the first attempt was considered an appalling travesty. By the 20th century, with help from the restorers, Southwark was elevated to the rank of cathedral for the whole of south London.

The architecture is still predominantly Gothic, particularly the **choir**, fine **retro-choir** and **altar**, making it something of a rarity in London. The oldest relic is the **wooden effigy** of a 13th-century knight in the north choir aisle. In a pillar in the south transept you can see a **carving** of the hat and coat-of-arms of Cardinal Beaufort, the 13th-century Bishop of Winchester responsible for the bulk of the building work. The **tower** is 15th-century, although the battlements and pinnacles weren't completed until 1689. The nave is the only significant portion from a later era, although there are Victorian statues atop the reredos behind the altar. Shakespeare's youngest brother Edmund is buried in the churchyard. In the north aisle is the brightly painted medieval tomb of the poet John Gower (d. 1408). John Harvard, the founder of the Massachusetts university, was born in the parish of St Mary Overie in 1607 and has a chapel dedicated to him on the north side.

The cathedral's new annexe, which includes an education centre, **visitors' centre** and refectory, was opened in late 2001 and contains a wonderful café with tables outside in summer. The centre offers interactive tours of Southwark, past and present.

Borough Market BB11

*Off Borough High St, **w** www.borough market.org.uk; **tube** London Bridge. **Farmer's market** Fri noon–6pm, Sat 9am–4pm, some stalls and fruit and veg Thurs noon–6pm.*

A fruit and vegetable market started on the southern end of London Bridge as early as 1276, but was chased away to the present site in the 18th century because it caused too much traffic congestion. Curiously, the market is a non-profit organization run by the local parish; proceeds from renting out the stalls are used to give poorer residents a discount on their community taxes. Set under the lacy Victorian railway arches, it's a very atmospheric spot even when there are no stalls set up. Most recently, it's become one of the best organic and farmer's markets in London; on Fridays and Saturdays, dozens

London Bridge

'London Bridge is falling down,' goes the old nursery rhyme. Too right. London Bridge has fallen down so often that there's nothing left to see. No, it's not the one on all the postcards that opens in the middle (that's Tower Bridge), although God knows there are enough tourists who haven't realized this yet (and one American who, back in the 1960s, bought the previous incarnation of London Bridge and had it reconstructed stone for stone back home in Lake Havasu, Arizona – how disappointed his friends must have been). London Bridge stopped being interesting some time around 1661, when the spikes used to display the severed heads of criminals were finally removed. It ceased to be London's one and only river crossing about a century later with the construction of Westminster and Blackfriars Bridges. Now London Bridge is nothing more than a cantilevered lump of concrete with four busy lanes of traffic on top, just one nondescript bridge among many. And it hasn't fallen down for centuries.

Time was when London Bridge burnt or fell down once every 10 years or so, cutting off all contact between the City and the South Bank. For the first thousand years of its history the bridge was made of wood, and back in the Dark Ages London was full of arsonists, rabble-rousers and general no-goods. It fell down most spectacularly in 1014 when London was besieged by the Danes and a spineless King Ethelred had fled into the countryside. Ethelred's ally, Olaf of Norway, sailed a fleet of ships up to the bridge, attached ropes to the piles and pulled the whole structure down by rowing away as vigorously as possible. The Danes, who were

of small producers set up their stalls here selling everything from cakes to wild boar sausages, fresh juices to crisp, tart English apples. The biggest market of the month always takes place on the third Saturday.

Bramah Tea and Coffee Museum BB12

40 Southwark St, t (020) 7403 5650, w www.bramahmuseum.co.uk; tube London Bridge; wheelchair accessible. Open daily 10am–6pm; adm adults £4, concessions and children £3, families £10. Café and tea and coffee shop.

This museum, the brainchild of a lifelong commodity broker called Edward Bramah, gives an engaging account of coffee and tea both as drinks and as commodities. It also shows off an astonishing collection of 400 biscuit barrels and Bramah's collection of coffee- and teapots. They come in all shapes and sizes: monsters, hedgehogs, petrol pumps, Sherlock Holmes! Biggest and most impractical of all is the world's largest hand-thrown teapot, which would make 800 cups of tea if anyone had the strength to pour them.

Borough High St AA13–BB12

Tube London Bridge, Borough.

You'll notice some of the alleys off Borough High St have names like King's Head Yard and White Hart Yard after the pubs that used to stand here. George Inn is the only coaching inn that still survives (*see below*); many of the other famous landmarks of Borough High St are no more. Tabard Inn, which once stood on the site of modern-day Talbot Yard, was where Chaucer's fictional pilgrims gathered to tell their Canterbury Tales. The Queen Inn was owned by John Harvard until he sold up and went to the United States to found his famous university, while the White Hart is mentioned both in Shakespeare's *Henry VI* and in Dickens' *Pickwick Papers*.

Borough High St was also the site of several of Southwark's seven prisons, most notorious of which was the Marshalsea just off the eastern side of the High St. The list of its inmates reads like a roll of eminent alumni at an Oxford or Cambridge college: Ben Jonson, Tobias Smollett, Leigh Hunt (who libelled George IV by calling him, with perfect accuracy, a 'portly Adonis') and Dickens'

holed up on the South Bank, realized they had lost their only means of entering the city and withdrew.

The first stone bridge was started in 1176 and took 33 years to complete. Its broad columns caused the river to freeze in winter and created treacherous currents in summer, making it a hazardous obstacle to navigate. All but the smallest vessels had to negotiate their way through a narrow passage in the middle where a drawbridge could be raised. On top were houses, shops and a chapel to St Thomas à Becket. As a saying of the time went, 'London Bridge was made for wise men to go over and fools to go under.' Accidents were commonplace: in 1428 the Duke of Norfolk and several of his henchmen were drowned when their barge overturned.

Because of the bridge's strategic importance, it was frequently attacked by rebel leaders and riot mobs. The rebel baron Simon de Montfort took it briefly in 1264 (though he could not penetrate the City walls themselves), as did Wat Tyler and his peasant revolters in 1381. The bridge provided little defence for itself other than as a deterrent: in 1305 the head of the Scots patriot William Wallace (hero of Mel Gibson's *Braveheart*) appeared, parboiled and coated in tar, above the portico of the gatehouse as an example to other would-be plotters. Plenty more heads followed, sometimes scores of them at a time. After Jack Cade's rebellion in 1450 there were so many heads on display that the authorities had to call a temporary halt. The practice stopped for good when Charles II came to the throne, the restored monarch being understandably nervous about severed heads given what had happened to his father, Charles I.

bankrupt father. Dickens himself used the prison as the fictional birthplace of his heroine Little Dorrit.

The George Inn BB12
George Inn Yard, off Borough High St.

The coaching inns were like the railway stations that eventually superseded them, each one providing a transport service to a specific group of destinations. Unlike railway stations, however, the inns had no fixed timetable but functioned according to demand. As a result there was often a great deal of waiting to do, and the inns made up for this by ensuring a ready supply of draught ale for waiting passengers. The George Inn goes back to the 16th century, although the present buildings date from shortly after the Great Fire. It is an elegant terrace of small interconnecting wooden bars looking out on a quiet courtyard, where during the summer you can see morris dancing (an old English ritual which involves wearing folklore costumes festooned with bells) and open-air productions of Shakespeare. Take a look at the 18th-century **clock** on the right-hand wall of the bar at the western end of the inn: this was the brainwave of one particularly parsimonious landlord fed up with coach passengers gawping through his window to find out the time. Not only did he put the clock on a side wall where it could not be seen from the courtyard, he also charged passers-by a penny for the right to look at it.

Old Operating Theatre, Museum and Herb Garret CC12

9A St Thomas's St, t (020) 7955 4791, w www.thegarret.org.uk; tube London Bridge; wheelchair access can be arranged with plenty of notice. **Open** *6 Jan–14 Dec daily 10.30am–5pm;* **adm** *adults £3.75, concessions £2.75, under-16s £2.25, families £9. Note that it's a stiff climb up a spiral staircase.*

First of all, the old church tower which houses the museum deserves a little explanation. It used to be attached to the chapel of St Thomas's, one of the biggest hospitals in London, founded on this site back in the 12th century. The hospital moved to Lambeth in the 1860s to make way for London Bridge railway station, and all the old buildings except this one were destroyed. For a century the chapel was considered a mere curiosity, an unspectacular relic from a bygone age. Then, in 1956, a historian named Raymond Russell noticed a curious hole above the tower belfry. He squeezed through and discovered a garret containing a 19th-century operating theatre, the only one of its kind to have survived in the whole country. It was restored and in 1968 turned into a museum charting the tower's history, first as a medieval garret devoted to herbal remedies, then as an operating room attached to a women's ward in the next building. It is a fascinating, if grim place; nowhere else in London will you get such a graphic insight into the horrors of medicine before the modern age.

The Museum

The centrepiece of the museum is the operating theatre itself, built in 1821 and used up until 1862 when St Thomas's moved to Lambeth. You can still see the bloodstains on the floor, and the mop and bucket used to clear up the mess. It looks like a lecture hall, with rows of seats on three sides for students and colleagues to watch the proceedings: in the days before dead bodies became widely available, watching operations was the only legal way doctors and medical students could carry out anatomical research.

Back in the early 19th century, surgeons had no proper notion of hygiene and performed their operations in frock coats 'stiff and stinking with pus and blood', as the museum explains. They washed their instruments only after the operation (to wipe the blood off), but did not think to do so beforehand. The patient, who was usually tanked up on ale (for years the daily allowance was three pints per patient), would be held down by six or seven people as the knife or saw penetrated the flesh; the surgeon would then kick a box of sawdust to the appropriate spot beneath the operating table to catch the blood. The trick was to get the whole thing over with as quickly as possible: one surgeon at Guy's Hospital, Alfred Poland, once managed to amputate a leg in 37 seconds.

The museum also gives a lightning account of the history of apothecaries and of herbal and surgical medicine in London, accompanied by a display of gynaecological instruments that would not look out of place in a torture chamber. For a long time St Thomas's actually had a reputation for showing great indulgence towards women. In the 15th century Mayor Dick Whittington established eight rooms where unmarried mothers could stay and deliver their offspring out of the public eye to save their reputations. Unfortunately such enlightenment did not last and in 1561 the hospital banned unmarried pregnant women, saying its job was the relief of 'honest persons, and not of harlots'. The most famous woman in the hospital's history was Florence Nightingale, the legendary nurse of the Crimean War who set up London's first nursing school at St Thomas's in 1858.

London Bridge Tower CC11

Tube London Bridge.

The London Bridge train station is not remarkable at the moment. It's a busy commuter station which pipes all the workers from South London into the City. But it might become the site of one of London's most daring buildings: the 'London Bridge Tower', a tall, metallic pyramid which would cap the station and soar up for 80 storeys to become the tallest building in Europe. Designed by Italian architect Renzo Piano, it is the latest in a line of skyscraper projects for London, which have included the Midland Bank Tower out by Canary Wharf. Historically, tall buildings have been tucked away on the fringes of London, but this was to create a new precedent. The project was already causing controversy before the events of 11th September, and, in the wake of that, it may be put on ice for the foreseeable future.

The City

1 Lunch

Sweetings, *39 Queen Victoria St*, **t** *(020) 7248 3062*; **tube** *Cannon St.* **Open** *Mon–Fri noon–3pm.* **Moderate.** This traditional and excellent fish restaurant is an old favourite.

2 Drinks

Tower 42; **tube** *Liverpool St.* **Open** *Mon–Fri 9am–11pm.* Try the 42nd-floor oyster bar.

Highlights

Londoner's City: Every Londoner's favourite building, St Paul's Cathedral, p.216

Contemporary Architecture: Richard Rogers''inside-out' Lloyd's of London, p.228

Riverside City: Find out about Tower Bridge at the Tower Bridge Experience, *see* p.232

Indoor City: The unmissable medieval Tower of London, p.229

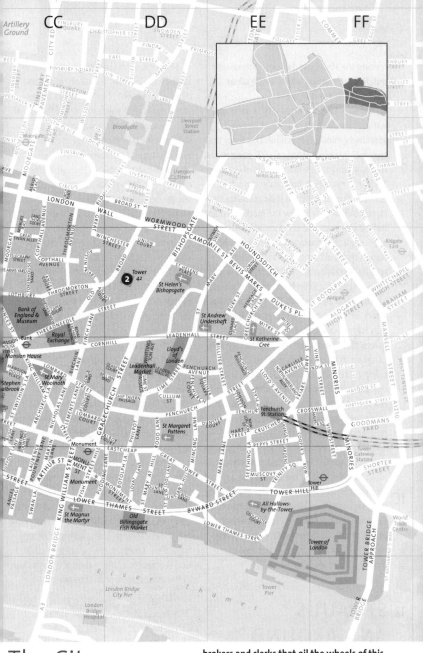

The City

The City is the heart of London, the place where the whole heaving metropolis began, and yet there is something so strange about it that it scarcely seems to be part of London at all. Tens of thousands of commuters stream in each morning, the bankers,

brokers and clerks that oil the wheels of this great centre of world finance, spilling out of Liverpool St or crossing over London Bridge towards their jumble of gleaming high-rise offices. During the lunch hour, you can see them scurrying to their local sandwich bar or expense-account lunch. By early evening they have all vanished again, back to their townhouses and dormitory communities, leaving the streets and once-monumental buildings to slumber eerily in the silent gloom of the London night.

This is T.S. Eliot's 'Unreal City', a metropolis without inhabitants, a place of frenzied, seemingly mindless mechanical activity that the poet, back in the apocalyptic early 1920s, thought worthy of the lost souls of Limbo. And yet it remains oddly fascinating, full of echoes of the time when it *was* London. Its streets still largely follow the medieval plan. Its fine churches and ceremonial buildings express all the contradictory emotions of a nation that built, and then lost, an entire empire. Its business is still trade, as it was in the 14th century, even if it is trade of a most abstract and arcane sort. The great exchange floors for commodities, shares and bonds may have disappeared in this computer-driven global marketplace, but the City still clings on to its curious traditions and colourful ceremonies. The Guildhall, the epicentre of City power down the centuries, is a shrine to such ritual, where the fathers of commerce dress up in gaudy robes and nod reverentially to the past.

Wren's churches, and St Paul's Cathedral in particular, grace the skyline, but the area is also characterized by the bloody carcasses of Smithfield meat market and the grim legacy of Newgate prison, now converted into the Central Criminal Court – a reminder that until the 17th century the City was a place not only of wealth-creation but also of poverty, blood and disease.

ST PAUL'S AND AROUND

St Paul's Cathedral Z–AA9

t (020) 7236 6883, w www.stpauls.co.uk; tube St Paul's; wheelchair accessible. Open Mon–Sat 8.30am–4pm; adm adults £5, concessions £4, children £2.50. Service Sun 11am. Guided tours at 11am, 11.30am, 1.30pm, 2pm; adults £2, children £1. Audioguide £3.50.

St Paul's is more than just a cathedral or famous landmark: it is an icon for a whole city. Get to know St Paul's and you understand many of the ambitions and failings of London itself. For nearly 1,400 years, successive buildings on this site have sought to express the material confidence of a powerful capital while at the same time delineating its spiritual aspirations. Back in the 7th century, St Paul's was England's first major Christian temple; in its medieval incarnation it was the largest single building in the land. In the hands of Christopher Wren, who rebuilt it from scratch after the Great Fire, it was hailed as an architectural masterpiece. Since then St Paul's has dutifully propped up all the myths of the nation: as the burial place for heroes during the glory days of empire, as a symbol of British endurance during the Second World War when it miraculously survived the Blitz, or as the fairy-tale setting for Prince Charles's marriage to Lady Diana Spencer in 1981.

Yet St Paul's has often shared more with the commercial world outside its doors than with the spiritual world celebrated within. In the Middle Ages the cathedral was itself a kind of market, with horses parading down the nave and stallholders selling beer and vegetables to all comers. Even today, the first thing to confront the visitor is a cash register, a sign of St Paul's peculiar ease in reconciling religious faith with the handling of money. St Paul's is a monument to wealth first, and God second. No wonder, then, if it has a little of the atmosphere of the counting-house.

History

There had already been two St Paul's, dating back to the earliest days of Christianity, but it was the third St Paul's that made everyone sit up and take notice. It was a monster, 585ft long with a 450ft spire, making it the largest building in England and bigger by far than Wren's cathedral. It was not so much a church as a mini-city all of its own, incorporating ecclesiastical buildings, schools and colleges. It was the focus of all processions and ceremonies in the city, and a popular meeting place for citizens of all classes. By 1385 the cathedral had become so rowdy that the bishop issued a formal ban on ball games and beer-selling and introduced fines for window breakages. A century later an order went out banning wrestling on the premises.

The Reformation brought further decadence. The nave became known as Paul's Walk, a convenient thoroughfare for market stallholders bringing their food, beer and animals through from Carter Lane (to the south) to Paternoster Row (to the north). In 1554 a vain order was issued to ban horses and shooting inside. Services were little more than a diversion, and restricted to the choir.

Not surprisingly, the building started falling to pieces. When the spire was struck by lightning and collapsed in 1561, it was not replaced. In 1634 Inigo Jones started revamping the building in classical style, but never got beyond a new portico at the western end. During the Civil War the roof fell in, the windows were smashed and most of the statuary vandalized beyond repair. Wren, commissioned to consider the cathedral's future in 1663, called it 'defective both in beauty and firmness... a heap of deformities that no judicious architect will think corrigible by any expense that can be laid out upon it.'

He did not have to lobby long for the merits of demolition. On 4 September 1666, the first flames of the Great Fire reached St Paul's and proceeded to engulf it entirely.

Nothing was easy about the rebuilding. Wren initially used gunpowder to clear the wreck of old St Paul's but had to resort to battering rams instead after terrified locals complained of rogue pieces of stonework flying through their living-room windows. As for the design, Wren set his heart on building a dome in the manner of the great Italian Baroque churches. That idea, too, met stiff resistance – it was considered excessively Popish in those religiously sensitive times. You can see his magnificent 20ft oak replica of the Great Model (plan number two, and a longer, sleeker version of the present

building) on display in the crypt. Eventually the dome problem was solved through a mixture of guile and compromise. Wren submitted a third plan dispensing with a dome in favour of a steeple, and had it approved in 1675; in return the royal warrant giving him the go-ahead granted him the liberty 'to make some variations rather ornamental than essential, as from time to time he should see proper'. By the time the cathedral opened 35 years later, the dome was back, as were many of the architect's other rejected ideas.

The Cathedral

The sheer imposing scale of St Paul's is apparent as soon as you approach the entrance at the **west front**. The broad staircase leads up to a two-tiered portico upheld by vast stone columns and flanked by two clocktowers. Dominating the high pediment in the centre is a statue of St Paul, with St Peter to his left and St James to his right. It is surely no coincidence that these three figures look down on the sovereign of the day, Queen Anne, whose statue stands on the ground outside the entrance. The ensemble, the work of a single artist, Francis Bird, forges a clear mystical link between the City, the Crown and the Church.

The **nave** is vast but remarkably simple in its symmetries; concentrate on the harmony of the architecture and try to blank out the largely hideous statuary and incidental decoration added well after Wren's time. As you walk beneath the dome look down at the marble floor and you'll see the famous **epitaph to Wren**, added by his son after his death in 1723, 'Lector, si monumentam requiris, circumspice' (Reader, if you seek a memorial, look around you).

Look, in particular, up towards the magnificent **dome**. This is something of an optical illusion, nowhere near as big on the inside as it is on the outside. In fact, Wren built a smaller second dome inside the first to keep the interior on a manageable scale. The story goes that the first stone used to construct the dome was a relic from the old St Paul's which by coincidence bore the Latin word *resurgam* (rise up). Wren took it as a good portent and had the word inscribed in the pediment above the south door, adorning it with an image of a phoenix rising from the ashes.

You can climb up into the dome, or domes, from a staircase on the south side of the cathedral. The first stopping-off point is the **Whispering Gallery** 100ft up, so-called because you can murmur with your face turned towards the wall and be heard with crystal clarity on the other side of the dome, 107ft away. You can also admire James Thornhill's series of **frescoes** on the life of St Paul which stretch all the way around the gallery. Vertigo permitting, you can continue on up to the Stone Gallery, the Inner Golden Gallery and the Outer Golden Gallery, offering **panoramic views** over London from just below the ball and cross at a height of 365ft. In the latter stages of building, the septuagenarian Wren used to be hoisted up here in a basket every Saturday to inspect the work. In deference to his age, however, he left it to his son to lay the final and highest stone. The solidity of the dome more than proved its worth during the Blitz. An incendiary bomb made a direct hit on 29 December 1941, but by good fortune it fell out on to the Stone Gallery, where further damage was prevented by the swift action of the volunteer fire-fighting group, the St Paul's Watch. Throughout the war, St Paul's offered a symbol of resistance to the nation as time and again it evaded the German bombing.

Back on terra firma, you can explore all the junk added to St Paul's in the generations following Wren. Until 1795 there were no monuments inside the church, its greatest ornaments being the magnificent **organ**, built by Wren himself, and the attractively carved **choir stalls** by Grinling Gibbons. **Henry Moore's statue** *Mother and Child*, on the north side behind the choir, is also worth admiring. Oh, but what a disaster the rest is, particularly the execrable Victorian mosaics of the Creation and the grotesque

monuments to General Gordon of Khartoum and the Duke of Wellington. The baldacchino in front of the altar is a shameless steal from St Peter's in Rome, built as a war memorial in 1958. **Holman Hunt**'s fine pre-Raphaelite painting *The Light of the World*, a lush depiction of Christ opening the door to a man's soul, hangs on the north transept – but only reluctantly is it admitted that this is not the original, which is in Keble College, Oxford.

And so down to the **crypt** (entrance near the south door), whose highlight is undoubtedly Wren's Great Model (*see* 'History', above) and the fine exhibition that accompanies it. Most of the space, though, is taken up with tombs commemorating Britain's military leaders. Among the rows and rows of unknowns you can find the Duke of Wellington (again) in his pompous porphyry casket and, directly beneath the dome, the black marble sarcophagus honouring Horatio Nelson.

St Paul's Churchyard

The churchyard is no more than an alleyway and, besides housing the cathedral **Chapter House** (a red-brick building designed by Wren in 1712) and **Deanery**, has never been particularly religious in purpose. Before the Great Fire it was the centre of the London book trade. It was also the site of St Paul's Cross, a kind of popular gathering place which Thomas Carlyle described as '*The Times* newspaper of the Middle Ages'. The cross was a bizarre combination of speaking platform, pulpit and gallows. It was finally dismantled and destroyed in 1673; an unremarkable memorial **statue of St Paul** on a tall column was erected in its place in 1910.

St Mary-le-Bow BB8

Cheapside, **t** *(020) 7248 5139;* **tube** *Bank, St Paul's, Mansion House.* **Open** *Mon–Thurs 6.30am–6pm, Fri 6.30am–4pm.* **Café.**

One of the most impressive of Wren's churches, St Mary-le-Bow is famous for two reasons: first for its massive, distinctive **steeple**, which soars 217ft into the sky, and secondly for its **Bow Bells**, which have formed part of the mythology of London for centuries. It was their resounding peal that persuaded the fairy-tale Dick Whittington to turn again and return to London in search of fame and fortune. Ever since, the tradition has been that anyone born within earshot of the bells can call themselves a true Londoner. The bells no doubt owe their reputation to the fact that for a long time they were the loudest in the City. In the 14th century they were rung to signal a curfew. During the Second World War, the BBC used them to introduce its radio news broadcasts. Now, unfortunately, they are rarely used and survive largely as a folk memory.

There is a third, less well-known, reason why you should visit St Mary-le-Bow: its magnificently preserved **Norman crypt**. Along with the Guildhall's, it is one of the few left in London. This was where William Fitzosbert, nicknamed Longbeard, took refuge and was finally smoked out after the failure of his rebellion against Richard the Lionheart's war taxes in 1196. The round arches of the crypt probably gave the church its name; the space is now used as a café with tasty home-cooked food.

St Nicholas Cole AA9

Distaff Lane; **tube** *St Paul's.*

St Nicholas Cole Abbey was the very first church Wren worked on; it was completed in 1677 and has a conical steeple.

Christ Church Greyfriars Z8

King Edward St; **tube** *St Paul's.*

In the Middle Ages this was the second-largest church in the City after St Paul's. It became popular for funerals after Henry III buried the heart of his wife Eleanor of Provence here in 1291; the dead were often interred in monk's habits to speed their passage to heaven. Gutted in the Great Fire and then destroyed again in the Blitz, Christ Church can now only boast its steeple, decorated with urns, and the ruined shell of the nave.

The Old Bailey Z8

Old Bailey, **t** *(020) 7248 3277;* **tube** *St Paul's; accessible only via a highly uninviting public entrance in Warwick Passage and several flights of stairs.* **Open** *Mon–Fri 10.30–1 and 2–4.30; closed all hols;* **adm** *free. Strictly no cameras, large bags, drink, food, mobile phones/pagers, radios, gas canisters, etc; no children under 14; note that there is no cloak-room for bags.*

The soaring gilt statue of Justice rising from the roof of the Old Bailey has become such a potent symbol of temperance in the English legal system that it has eradicated virtually all memory of the barbarity once associated with this site. Until 1902 this place was Newgate Prison, one of the most gruesome of all jails. Generations of prisoners were left here quite literally to rot; to this day judges wear posies of sweet-smelling flowers on special occasions as a grim reminder of the stench that used to emanate from the cold, filthy cells.

The mood now could not be more different. The nickname 'Old Bailey' conveniently avoids all reference to the old prison. Ask about the place's history and you will be given a list, not of the horrors of incarceration, but of the famous names whose trials have taken place here: Oscar Wilde; the Edwardian wife-murderer Dr Crippen; and William Joyce, known as Lord Haw-Haw, who broadcast enemy propaganda from Nazi Germany during the Second World War.

You are welcome to attend a court hearing in one of the public galleries, although the tightly arranged wooden benches are not exactly designed for comfort. The rituals are similar to those of the civil courts (*see* p.152), although the mood is inevitably more sombre. Over the years, the system's confidence has been shaken by a spate of miscarriages of justice, particularly in cases involving IRA bombings and police murders.

Newgate

Newgate became the City jail as early as the 12th century, although its notoriety grew only after the Great Fire, when it was entirely rebuilt. On arrival prisoners were regularly bullied and robbed by the governor and his warders. They were then slung into dark underground dungeons without ventilation or running water. The only way to avoid starvation was by bribery. Jail fever, a virulent strain of typhoid, was rife, and the whole place stank of disease and human flesh. Many of the prisoners had little to look forward to except one last walk on the way to the gallows at Tyburn (now called Marble Arch). The unluckiest were pressed to death in their cells for failing to confess their crimes.

Few ever hoped to escape from such a place, yet in the 18th century the burglar and highwayman Jack Sheppard managed to do so twice. The first time Sheppard picked the lock of his condemned cell with a nail file. The second time he made his getaway, quite incredibly, from a third-floor cell in a bell-tower where he had been handcuffed, manacled and chained to the floor. As a result he became an overnight celebrity, an unfortunate side-effect for a man on the run and one that precipitated his recapture. Back

in prison he was visited by an eminent former inmate of Newgate, Daniel Defoe, who wrote one of several contemporary accounts of his life, and by James Thornhill, the king's portraitist, who painted him. When he was finally carted off to Tyburn in 1724, a large crowd came out to cheer him. Just before the hangman pulled the rope over his neck, a penknife was found concealed in his clothing. Even in extremis, Sheppard had been planning another escape.

Gradually a campaign started to reform Newgate, and in the 1770s the prison was entirely rebuilt to a design by George Dance the Younger. It did not stand for long, since it was one of the targets of the Gordon Riots of 1780. When the prison was rebuilt, for the second time in 10 years, one of its first new inmates was the riot leader himself, the anti-Catholic fanatic Lord George Gordon, who died there of jail fever in 1793. Conditions scarcely improved, and indeed the prison only gained in notoriety as the gallows were moved from Tyburn to a site just outside the front door in Newgate St.

But eventually Newgate's reputation proved its undoing. The public hangings came to an end in 1868 and the prison itself was demolished in 1902 to make way for the criminal courts you see today.

Fortunately for the released prisoners, the death sentence was abolished in Britain in 1965.

The legend above the entrance to the Old Bailey reads: 'Defend the children of the poor and punish the wrongdoer'. On both these counts, the place has been less successful than it thinks.

St Sepulchre without Newgate Z8

Corner of Giltspur St and Holburn Viaduct, **t** *(020) 7248 3826,* **w** *www.st-michaels.org.uk/ sepulchre;* **tube** *St Paul's; wheelchair accessible.*

When the condemned prisoners of Newgate heard the great Bell of Bailey inside the tall tower of this church ring out at

dawn, they knew that their final hour had come and that they were soon to begin the final journey to Tyburn. Back in 1605 a parishioner by the name of Robert Dowe thought he would give the prisoners a little more notice of their fate and paid for a handbell to be rung at midnight along a tunnel which connected St Sepulchre to the prison. He also wrote a few lines for the bellman to recite:

All you that in the condemned hole do lie
Prepare you for tomorrow you shall die
Watch all and pray; the hour is drawing near
That you before the Almighty must appear.
Examine well yourselves, in time repent,
That you may not to eternal flames be sent.
And when St Sepulchre's Bell in the morning tolls
The Lord have mercy on your souls.

The bellman would approach the condemned cell and shout the last lines through the keyhole, just to make sure the message got through. No doubt they told him to shut up and keep his bad poetry to himself. The **bell** itself is now locked in a glass case on the south side of the church.

St Sepulchre is an interesting mixture of styles. Its 15th-century **fan-vaulted porch** and part of the tower survived the Great Fire; the rest, largely rebuilt in the 1670s, has been tinkered with and restored right up to the present day. St Sepulchre is now known as the musicians' church and prides itself on its lunchtime concerts. The **Musician's Chapel** on the north side includes a stained-glass window dating from the early 1960s which depicts Dame Nellie Melba as Mimi in *La Bohème*.

OUTSIDE THE OLD CITY WALLS

St Bartholomew's Hospital Z7

*Giltspur St, **t** (020) 7601 8152, **t** 7601 8033; **tube** Barbican; museum wheelchair accessible by arrangement. **Museum open** Tues–Fri 10am–4pm, but call ahead to check as it's staffed by volunteers and opening hours may vary; **adm** free. **Guided tours** Fri at 2pm; meet at the Henry VIII Gate on West Smithfield; £4.*

St Bartholomew's, or Bart's as it is known, is the oldest hospital in London, dating back to 1123. It was founded, somewhat improbably, by Henry I's court jester Henry Rahere, who made a vow to help the sick after catching malaria on a pilgrimage to Rome. For the first 400 years it was more of a priory than a serious hospital, offering little more than prayer by way of medical help to its patients.

Medieval medicine was a haphazard affair at the best of times; pioneers such as John of Gaddesdon, who practised at Bart's in the early 14th century, administered live beetles and crickets as well as revolting mixtures of chemicals and human spittle. Few of the patients who entered Bart's ever came back out again. It was not until the 16th century, after the dissolution of the priory by Henry VIII, that Bart's devoted its full energies to medicine and employed full-time physicians. Its early practices seem horrific nowadays: the beds were infested with lice and invariably occupied by more than one patient, the windows were kept shut at all times and there was no access to hot water. It took several centuries to iron out all these problems; the hospital itself was entirely rebuilt in the 1730s by James Gibbs. In the 18th century Bart's became a pioneer in medical science and developed a prestigious teaching college. Until the mid-19th century, when medical research finally won government sanction, students and surgeons who wanted to increase their knowledge of anatomy had to resort to body-snatching.

The highlight of the guided tour is a visit to the **Great Hall** and staircase with its two **Hogarth paintings** on medical themes commissioned for the hospital. The main church located inside the complex is **St Bartholomew-the-Less**, a small octagonal structure by George Dance the Younger (1789); most of its furnishings were destroyed by wartime bombing.

Finally, in the North Wing there is the **Museum of St Bartholomew's Hospital**, which contains a mixture of exhibits on the history of medicine and the history of Bart's. There are fascinating displays of amputation instruments, early syringes and stethoscopes.

St Bartholomew-the-Great Z7

*Little Britain, **t** (020) 7606 5171, **w** www.great stbarts.com; **tube** Barbican; wheelchair accessible. **Open** Tues–Fri 8.30am–5pm (4pm mid-Nov–mid-Feb), Sat 10.30am–1.30pm, Sun 8.30–1 and 2.30–8; closed around 26–28 Dec. **Concerts.***

A 13th-century **stone arch** topped by a Tudor timber gateway leads to the only remaining part of Rahere's original priory, the church of St Bartholomew-the-Great. The original Norman church was 300ft long and included the whole area now taken up by the churchyard. By the time Henry VIII's wreckers had finished with it, only about one-third of the original building was left. It is nevertheless an impressive place. Most of the Norman arches are original, as are the vaulted wooden ceiling, font and Gothic cloister bays on the right as you come in. Much of the rest, including the porch and choir screen, was refurbished in the late 19th century.

Look out for a stone commemorating the 17th-century citizen **Edward Cooke** on the south wall. There used to be a noticeable damp patch directly below: legend had it that the stone shed real tears, although the installation of a radiator underneath seems to have proved a great consolation. There is also a touching memorial on the northern side of the church to **Margaret and John Whiting**, who both died in 1681. The verse tells the story: 'Shee first deceased, Hee for a little Tryd/to live without her, likd it not and dyd.'

Just north of the church is a street whose name, **Cloth Fair**, is a reminder of the festive trade markets that took place here for 700 years. A few houses in the street survived the Great Fire, notably No.41, which has been carefully restored. The poet laureate and London conservationist John Betjeman lived at No.43, which is now a pub.

Smithfield Market Y7–Z8

Tube Farringdon. Open Mon–Fri 5–9am.

Smithfield has come a long way since the 14th century, when cattle were slaughtered in front of the customers and witches boiled alive for the entertainment of the populace. Nowadays it is a civil, sanitized sort of place: the carcasses arrive ready-slaughtered and are stored in giant fridges so you'll barely see a speck of dirt or blood. The covered market halls have been refurbished and are surrounded by restaurants and pubs.

Smithfield was originally a jousting field within easy reach of the city walls. The annual Bartholomew Cloth Fair started in the 12th century, and shortly afterwards

drovers began bringing cattle and horses to a weekly market. After the Black Death of 1348–9, Smithfield was the city's main mortuary. The meat market proper did not get going until the 17th century, but it rapidly became a major London institution. As late as the 1830s, bulls were regularly seen stampeding down major roads, goring terrified residents and occasionally killing them. Around Smithfield itself, the streets were filled with the stench of blood and entrails which blocked up the gutters and infiltrated the water system.

Finally, in 1855, the Victorians decided enough was enough. Cholera epidemics were becoming all too common and, under the influence of such reformers as Edwin Chadwick, the authorities started thinking seriously about hygiene. Live animals were banned from coming further into the city than Islington. The City architect Sir Horace Jones built the first covered market halls at Smithfield and linked them to London's new railway stations by underground passageway. Since Jones's overhaul, the market has continued in more or less the same form. Unlike other food wholesale markets such as Covent Garden or Billingsgate, there seems to be no pressure on Smithfield to move out to the suburbs.

Charterhouse Square Z6

*Tube Barbican. **Guided tours** of the monastery April–Aug Wed 2.15pm, Sat 11am, booking essential, on **t** (020) 7251 5002; **adm** £3.*

This delightfully leafy square was the site of a magnificent Carthusian monastery founded in 1370. Seventy years after the dissolution of the monasteries, it became a private boys' school, so successful that in 1872 it had to move to the lush expanses of Surrey. The buildings are still privately owned, and little survives of the original monastery except the cloisters, the 14th-century chapel and the somewhat war-damaged 17th-century library.

Museum of London AA7

*150 London Wall, **t** (020) 7600 3699, recorded information **t** 7600 0807, **w** www.museum oflondon.org.uk; **tube** Barbican, St Paul's; wheelchair accessible via lifts in Aldersgate St. **Open** Mon–Sat 10am–5.50pm, Sun noon–5.50pm; last adm 5.30pm; closed 24–26 Dec; **adm** free. **Giftshop** and **café**. The museum is being expanded (call or check the Web site for details in advance as some sections may be temporarily closed) over several years.*

This ambitious and fast-changing museum sets out to tell the story of London from prehistoric times to the present, drawing on a vast collection of documents and historical relics. It is an ideal place to come if you want to familiarize yourself with the basic facts about the city.

In the **Roman** section, a cleverly angled window gives a view down onto a piece of Roman wall (AD 200) in the grounds outside. Three room settings – the dining room of a wealthy Roman, a slightly simpler living room and a well-equipped kitchen – give an unusual insight into everyday Roman life. Some of the most beautiful relics of the period come from the Temple of Mithras, a shrine to a Persian deity much invoked by Roman soldiers (*see* 'St Stephen Walbrook', p.226).

More recent treasures include two stupendously ornate 1928 lift cars originally installed in Selfridge's and, dotted about the museum, a selection of **well-reconstructed rooms and buildings** from London's history: a Victorian grocer's shop and pub, an F.W. Woolworth counter, a cell at Newgate Prison, a Second World War 'bedroom' in an Anderson shelter. **World City: London 1789–1914** uses more than 2,000 objects to re-create one of the most dynamic periods of London's history. Visitors can take a virtual trip through Victorian London using early film clips and photographs. **London Now** is an innovative and continually evolving exhibition; semi-permanent displays include a chunk of concrete from the notorious Ronan Point tower block in Newham (which collapsed in the 1970s) and a model of squatter houses in the East End.

The museum also has a magnificent range of **clothing**, giving an insight into changing fashions since the 17th century. The undisputed centrepiece, though, is the **Lord Mayor's Coach**, which has pride of place at the bottom of the main staircase in full view as you descend from level to level. Built in 1757 in blazing red and burnished gold, the coach is still used every November for the investiture of the new Lord Mayor. For all its splendour, though, you might not want to travel in it: it has no springs, only leather braces, which must make any ride distinctly bumpy. Until 1951 it also had no brakes.

Barbican Arts Centre AA6

*Silk St, **t** (020) 7638 8891, **w** www.barbican .org.uk; **tube** Barbican; wheelchair accessible. **Open** Mon–Sat 9am–10.30pm, Sun and hols noon–11pm.*

The City's only residential area worthy of the name, rebuilt after extensive wartime bombing, would not be out of place in a 1960s television escape drama. There are some advantages to living here: the leafy balconies, the forecourts and fountains. But the development is not exactly on a human scale. Friendly-sounding buildings like the Shakespeare Tower or Defoe House are in fact monolithic skyscrapers. The main reason for coming, apart from the dubious pleasure of gaping and shuddering, is a trip to the Arts Centre, home to two **theatres**, an **art gallery** (*open Mon–Sat 10am–5.45pm, Sun noon–6.45pm; adm*), three **cinemas**, a **concert hall** and a semi-tropical **conservatory** (*Level 3, **t** (020) 7638 4141; open daily noon–dusk*).

On Fore St, you pass **St Giles Cripplegate** (*open Mon–Fri 9.30am–5.30pm*), where John Milton was buried in 1674. The church itself, mostly built in the 16th century, escaped the 1666 fire but was destroyed by wartime bombs and then faithfully rebuilt in the 1950s. A stretch of the **Roman city wall** can be seen just behind it.

AROUND THE BANK OF ENGLAND

The Bank of England CC8

*Threadneedle St; **tube** Bank.*

Up to the time of the Great Fire, most of London's banking needs were serviced by the Company of Goldsmiths, in a primitive system which was only as good as the immediate creditworthiness of its customers. When Charles II reneged on a large debt in 1672, five banks went out of business. Sixteen years later, when James II declared war against France, the government suddenly found itself unable to raise the funds necessary to finance its armed forces. In 1694 a Scottish merchant, William Paterson, proposed the creation of a new joint-stock bank that would lend £1.2 million to the government in the first instance at an interest rate of 8% and with no fixed term for repayment. The proposal was an instant success; the money was raised in less than three weeks and soon afterwards the Bank was recognized by royal charter. As time went on, the Bank became the undisputed manager of the national debt: this rose from its initial £1.2 million to £12 million in 1700 and £850 million by the end of the Napoleonic Wars in 1815. This was when token money evolved, occasioned by an acute shortage of gold; banknotes became commonplace in the 19th century and the Bank of England became sole issuer in 1921 – before then any bank could issue notes.

The Bank has had a tough time of it in recent years, particularly since the abandonment of worldwide currency controls in the 1970s. The rise of virtually unfettered currency speculation has severely limited its control over the value of sterling, while the changing nature of international capital made it increasingly hard for the Bank to monitor the activities of the commercial houses. In the 1990s, following a number of financial scandals, the Bank lost its regulatory powers to the new Financial Services Authority, though it gained responsibility for setting interest rates. The creation of a single currency for Europe challenged the Bank to help ensure that London's wholesale financial markets were ready from the outset. They'll have an even greater challenge if and when the UK ever joins EMU.

Architecturally, the Bank has a distinctly mixed record. At the end of the 18th century, Sir John Soane, that most quirky and original of English architects, came up with a magnificently intricate Neoclassical design, a veritable treasure trove of interconnecting rooms, each with its own peculiarities of light and decoration. But Soane's design proved too good for the people it was built for. In 1925 the Bank governors decided they needed more space, and instead of considering an extension or a new building they simply demolished Soane's work and replaced it with an unimaginative multi-storey patchwork by Sir Herbert Baker. All that remains of Soane's original work is the secure curtain wall on the outer rim of the building and, thanks to a postwar reconstruction, the first room in the museum, the Bank Stock Office.

Bank of England Museum

*Entrance on Bartholomew Lane, **t** (020) 7601 5545, **w** www.bankofengland.co.uk; wheelchair accessible by prior arrangement. **Open** Mon–Fri 10am–5pm; closed hols; **adm** free. **Audioguide** £1.*

Beneath Sir John Soane's vaulted roof in the **Bank Stock Office**, illuminated naturally through a series of domed skylights, the museum's displays recount the architectural fortunes of the Bank. The original mahogany counter-tops and oak ledger-rests are casually leant on by glassy-eyed bank clerk mannequins dressed in their 1798 finery. You are then led through a series of rooms that give an account of the Bank's history culminating in Herbert Baker's 1925 Rotunda. Here, amidst utmost security, you can attempt to lift one of the two genuine **gold bars** in the museum. Other hands-on activities have recently been introduced and include interactive computer terminals and a foreign exchange game in which you can play at being a dealer without necessarily growing the ulcers.

The Royal Exchange CC8–9

*Threadneedle St; **tube** Bank. Closed to the public.*

Eight huge Corinthian pillars give this building a sense of importance to which it can no longer lay claim. The Royal Exchange was once the trading centre of the City par excellence, home to all of London's stock and commodity exchanges; it now houses company offices. This is the third Royal Exchange building to occupy the site. London's first exchange was built by the merchant and Lord Mayor Sir Thomas Gresham in the 1560s; before that, traders conducted their business in the open air in Lombard St. In Gresham's building the commodity traders still gathered in a central open courtyard (the covered parts being occupied by shopkeepers), but at least they could repair to the arcades on rainy days. Gresham's exchange, generally reckoned to be one of the finest Tudor buildings in London, burnt down in the Great Fire of 1666; fire also claimed its successor, which housed the first offices of Lloyd's of London. The present building, designed by Sir William Tite, dates from 1844, a rare example of Neoclassical architecture from the Victorian era. The pediment at the front nevertheless indulges in a characteristically Victorian taste for allegory: the 17 figures depicted there are all heroic portrayals of the merchant classes, with an embodiment of Commerce in the very centre.

Mansion House BB–CC9

*Main entrance on Walbrook, **t** (020) 7626 2500; **tube** Bank. Unfortunately not open to the public for most of the year. **Guided tours**; book six months in advance, parties of 15–40 only (call the number above or contact the Museum of London, which organizes tours around the time of the Lord Mayor's Show in November); free.*

The official residence of the Lord Mayor, this was intended to be something of a trend-setter, the first project of the Georgian era to be designed in Palladian style (mayors had previously lived in their own houses). The building ended up being delayed not just for years but for decades. In the end George Dance's building, on the site of the old Stocks Market, was completed in 1752, nearly 40 years after the project was first put forward. The end result is not a tremendous success: the awkward shape of the surrounding square does not allow the eye to be drawn towards its grandiose portico, which in any case is top-heavy and unwieldy with its six Corinthian columns. Its stained-glass windows depict scenes from London's history, including the signing of the Magna Carta and the stabbing of Wat Tyler, the leader of the Peasants' Revolt, by Mayor William Walworth.

St Stephen Walbrook BB9

*Walbrook, **t** (020) 7283 4444; **tube** Bank. **Open** Mon–Thurs 10am–4pm, Fri 10am–3pm; **adm** free.*

St Stephen's is widely considered Christopher Wren's masterpiece, a sort of mini-St Paul's that is all nave and no transepts, a bit like the giant cathedral down the road. Wren in fact used this church, built in 1672–9, to test out some of his ideas for St Paul's. St Stephen's benefits from the smaller scale: the interior has a graceful intimacy as well as an architectural flamboyance often missing from Wren's coolly geometrical designs. St Stephen's was badly damaged in the war and restored a number of times since; now it has been rearranged as a single open space, circled by Corinthian columns, with Henry Moore's cream-coloured **altar**, irreverently nicknamed the Camembert, as its centrepiece. Note the florid **pulpit** with its impressive black wrought-iron canopy. Note, also, the emphasis on natural light supplied from the windows around the base of the dome – this typical Wren touch was obscured for years by some thoroughly unnecessary stained glass.

From Walbrook, take Bucklersbury and turn left on Queen Victoria St. On the left just before Budge Row is the site of the **Temple of Mithras**, the Roman shrine whose treasures are stored in the Museum of London (*see* p.223). The site is wedged in a corner of an office block.

St Mary Woolnoth cc9

Corner of Lombard St and King William St; **tube** *Bank.*

St Mary Woolnoth is an intriguing design by Nicholas Hawksmoor based on a series of squares within squares. The interior is based on the same design by Vitruvius as the Banqueting Hall at Mansion House. **Lombard St**, by the church, is named after the Italian bankers who taught Londoners the rudiments of financial transaction in the 13th century.

Guildhall bb8

Gresham St, **t** *(020) 7606 3030 ext 1463,* **w** *www.cityoflondon.gov.uk;* **tube** *St Paul's, Bank; wheelchair accessible.* **Open** *Mon–Fri 10am–4pm; frequently closed for events, so phone;* **adm** *free.* **Guided tours** *of the hall, crypt and library; call in advance; free.* **Art gallery open** *Mon–Sat 10am–5pm, Sun noon–4pm; last adm 30mins earlier; closed 1 Jan and 25–26 Dec;* **adm** *adults £2.50, concessions £1, under-16s free, free Fri and after 3.30pm.* **Clock Museum open** *Mon–Fri 9.30am–4.45pm; closed hols and till July 2002.*

The Guildhall is the seat of the City's government, headed by the Lord Mayor and his Sheriffs and Aldermen and composed principally of the 12 Great Livery Companies, or guilds, that nominally represent the City's trading interests. The governing body, known as the Corporation of London, is now basically a powerful borough council for the City, but back in the Middle Ages it wielded near-

absolute power over what was then the whole of London. Even kings could not touch it, since the guilds generated much of the nation's wealth and made sure everyone knew it. Henry III tried to impose direct rule on London in the 13th century but eventually gave up, describing the City fathers as 'nauseously rich'.

The Guildhall, first built in the 15th century, has preserved its medieval identity to a remarkable degree, despite the calamities of the Great Fire and the Blitz. The old oak beams proved remarkably resilient on both occasions, glowing from the heat but remaining solidly in place. The building nevertheless bears the marks of countless renovations. The pinnacled façade looking onto Guildhall Yard is a bizarre 18th-century concoction of classical, Gothic and even Indian styles.

The public entrance leads to the western end of the magnificent **old hall**, giving a spectacular view of the 152ft room draped with the banners of the 12 Great Livery Companies – Mercers, Grocers, Drapers, Fishmongers, Goldsmiths, Skinners, Merchant Taylors, Haberdashers, Salters, Ironmongers, Vintners and Clothworkers. On the wall behind each banner is the coat-of-arms and motto of each company. They are lined up in order of importance, starting at the far end on the left and moving in criss-cross fashion up towards the western door. The recesses of the hall are dotted with monuments to famous British leaders. Most eccentric are the large painted limewood figures perched on the musician's gallery at the west end. These are **Gog and Magog**, giants so mythical that nobody is quite sure where they come from; one theory has it that they represent the antagonistic forces of ancient Britain and Troy. They cropped up regularly as floats in the midsummer pageants of the 15th and 16th centuries. Since 1708 they have also stood in the Guildhall; the present models, erected after the war, are 9ft high.

The **crypt** is divided into two: the eastern half, split into 12 bays propped up by blue

Purbeck marble pillars, and the western half, which has a magnificent vaulted ceiling. The western half is presumed to be the cellar of the original Guildhall, dating back to the 15th century or possibly earlier. It is lit by 19 stained-glass windows depicting the arms of the livery companies. Somewhere beneath the floor are the foundations of the amphitheatre that the Romans built. Excavations in 1988 revealed that the foundations of the medieval Guildhall were in fact the Roman ruins; the arena is presumed to cover the area now taken up by Guildhall Yard.

The **art gallery** contains the Corporation's own collection, including many Victorian works and some Pre-Raphaelite paintings. Around the corner (on Aldermanbury) is the **Guildhall Clock Museum**, with more than 600 clocks reverently, if unmemorably, displayed by the Worshipful Company of Clockmakers.

St Helen's Bishopsgate DD8

Great St Helen's; tube Liverpool St; wheelchair accessible. Open Mon–Fri 9am–5pm, ring the bell on the south side of the rectory.

In the Middle Ages St Helen's was a Benedictine nunnery popular with the daughters of the rich and well-connected. As such, it was more of a career monastery than a place of great religious inspiration; indeed in 1439 the prior had to issue an order banning dance and revelry and scolding the nuns for 'kissing secular persons'. The nunnery was dissolved in 1538, and although the church survived intact it went into a long decline that lasted right up to the time of the IRA Bishopsgate bombs of 1992 and 1993 (in which three people were killed and the 15th-century church of St Ethelburga within Bishopsgate was blown clean away). Ah, but what wonders have been achieved by restoration in the face of adversity. A rather dark, dingy church has been transformed into something approaching its original medieval splendour. St Helen's always was

The Perils of Writing Guidebooks

The Perpendicular Gothic church of St Andrew Undershaft, on the corner of St Mary Axe and Leadenhall St, is notable for one curious feature, a memorial to London's first historian, John Stow. A 16th-century tailor with a lifelong passion for literature, Stow was already well advanced in middle age when he embarked on the original London guidebook, *A Survey of London*, an astonishingly detailed record of the buildings of the City as he found them. It was a labour of love, and one that brought him pitiful reward. On its publication in 1598, he was paid just £3, and although the book was reprinted within a year he never enjoyed a further share of the profits. 'It hath cost me many a weary mile's travel, many a hard-earned penny and pound, and many a cold winter's night study,' he wrote. By 1603 he was reduced to leaving begging bowls in the street outside his house and two years later he was dead. Stow's widow shared her late husband's tenacity and, despite her severely straitened circumstances, had a marble statue of him erected inside this church where he was buried. The City belatedly recognized Stow's contribution and initiated an annual ceremony in which the Lord Mayor removes and replaces the quill pen in Stow's right hand. The ritual continues to this day. By 1905 the original statue had become so dilapidated that the Merchant Taylors' company paid for a replacement.

remarkable for its unusual **twin nave**; now the floor has been raised, the windows scrubbed clean, and the interior rearranged to allow every corner to reveal its unassuming beauties – the Jacobean **pulpit**, the 15th-century **choir stalls**, the **window** dedicated to Shakespeare and the many **brass-covered tombs**, including that of Sir Thomas Gresham, founder of the Royal Exchange. The **organ**, which once blocked the 13th-century beams and stonework of the south transept, has been moved to a new upstairs gallery, a decision that has enhanced both areas of the church.

St Katherine Cree EE8

*Leadenhall St; **tube** Aldgate; wheelchair accessible. **Open** Mon, Tues, Thurs and Fri 10.30am–4.30pm.*

This was one of the few church buildings in the City to survive the Great Fire. Built in the 1620s in Renaissance style, with Tuscan columns and rounded arches, St Katherine's has no qualms about the morality of making money: it is dedicated 'to commerce, industry and finance'. Its distinctive blue-ribbed **plaster ceiling** is adorned with the crests of City livery companies. The **Rose Window** is a copy from the medieval incarnation of St Paul's, and the 18th-century **altar** is attributed to Robert Adam.

Lloyd's of London DD9

*1 Lime St, **w** www.lloydsoflondon.co.uk; **tube** Monument. Closed to the public.*

This is the City's most innovative and challenging building, designed by Richard Rogers for the world's biggest insurance market. Insurance did not begin at Lloyd's – the Lombards introduced the idea to England in the 16th century – but Lloyd's was where it became a market. Edward Lloyd was the owner of one of London's first and most fashionable coffee-houses in the 1680s and attracted a clientèle of ships' captains, shipowners and merchants. Soon the customers were doing business, and the coffee house gradually gained recognition as the centre for marine insurance worldwide. It was a pleasant, clubbish sort of place that grew more impersonal only as the weight of business became larger. In the late 18th century the show moved away from the lingering aroma of coffee beans and into more conventional offices, first in the Royal Exchange and then, in 1925, in the first of two addresses of its own on Leadenhall St.

In the late 1970s the British architect Richard Rogers, fresh from his success with the hi-tech Pompidou Centre in Paris, was commissioned to design a new building next door here in Lime St. It opened in 1986. Like the Pompidou Centre, this building has all its innards – heating ducts, ventilator shafts and so on – on the outside to permit greater flexibility of space on the inside. The fuss over this idea was very similar in both Paris and London: one joke goes that Lloyd's started out as a coffee house and ended up as a percolator. This is nevertheless a sober building, a tall, narrow edifice, the inside an uncluttered atrium where brokers and underwriters can get on with making money undistracted. Indeed, as another joke has it, it may be the only building in London with all the guts on the outside and the arseholes on the inside. Its most endearing features are the exterior lifts, which offer dramatic views over the City, and the famous Lutine Bell, a relic from a 19th-century shipping disaster, which is rung once for bad news and twice for good.

Leadenhall Market DD9

***Tube** Monument, Aldgate. **Open** Mon–Fri 7am–4pm.*

Leadenhall Market is a whiff of real life among the office blocks. It has considerable charm, plenty of bustle and excellent food, particularly meat, fish and cheese. For centuries it was just another City market, but went upmarket in the 1880s when Horace Jones, who had previously cleaned up Smithfield, designed the present covered arcades. The prices match the clientèle, many of them businessmen doing some inexpert and usually extravagant housekeeping; hence the popularity of game and exotic fish. It's worth a good sniff around, though, and makes an ideal stopping point for lunch.

St Margaret Patten's DD9

*Rood Lane and Eastcheap; **tube** Monument. **Open** Mon–Fri 8am–4pm; closed Christmas.*

Wren's church of 1684–7 was named after a locally made overshoe (patten). Its uncharacteristically plain lead steeple is strikingly reflected in the mirror glass of an office building opposite.

Monument cc10

*Monument St, t (020) 7626 2717; **tube** Monument. Viewing platform, accessible by spiral staircase, **open** daily 10am–6pm, last adm 5.30pm; closed 1 Jan and 25–26 Dec; **adm** £1.50.*

The Monument commemorates the Great Fire of London. On its completion in 1677 it was the tallest free-standing column in the world. Parliament charged Christopher Wren and his assistant Robert Hooke with the task of erecting a memorial on or near the bakery in Pudding Lane where the fire had broken out. In the end they built a monument the same height (202ft) as the distance between its pedestal and Mr Farynor's burnt-out shop one street over to the east. The Monument is a simple Doric column in Portland stone. The only symbol of the Fire itself is the **bronze urn** spouting metallic flames at the very top. The Latin inscription on the north panel of the base describes the course of the Great Fire; the other panels glorify Charles II and the rapid rebuilding of the late 1660s. The **view** from the top is obscured by office buildings but enjoyable nonetheless, particularly at dusk. In the late 18th and early 19th century this was a favourite spot for suicides; the authorities put an end to this in 1842 by enclosing the gallery in an iron cage.

St Magnus the Martyr cc10

*Lower Thames St; **tube** Monument. **Open** Tues–Fri 10am–4pm, Sun 10.30am–2pm.*

T.S. Eliot reckoned this was one of the finest of Wren's interiors but that may be overstating it. It is another elegant Wren rectangle, topped with a tallish spire and filled with statues, gilded sword rests and other heroic paraphernalia. The church also has a fine organ built in 1712.

Old Billingsgate Fish Market DD10

*Lower Thames St; **tube** Monument, Tower Hill.*

'Famous for fish and bad language,' remark Christopher Hibbert and Ben Weinreb in their *London Encyclopedia*. Since when was bad language the preserve of fishermen? It is too late to argue: there's nobody left inside Horace Jones's elegant pseudo-Renaissance building because the effing fishmongers moved out to the Isle of Dogs in the early 1970s. Citibank bought up the building in the late 1980s and the Richard Rogers partnership managed an elegant conversion. The original arcaded frontage is now glazed in plate glass and the fish and bad language have been replaced with state-of-the-art offices.

AROUND THE TOWER

The Tower of London FF10

*Tower Hill, t (020) 7709 0765, **w** www.hrp .org.uk; **tube** Tower Hill; Jewel House wheelchair accessible. **Open** March–Oct Mon–Sat 9am–6pm, Sun 10am–6pm, Nov–Feb Tues–Sat 9am–5pm, Sun and Mon 10am–5pm; last adm an hour before closing; closed 1 Jan and 24–26 Dec; **adm** adults £11.50, concessions £8.75, children £7.50, families £34. Colourful **pageants** and **festivals** throughout the year; **Ceremony of the Keys** daily at 9.30pm, write 6 weeks in advance. **Shop**, **snackbars** and **restaurant** serving lunch and Victorian teas.*

The Tower is a sight that everyone from out of London is compelled to visit, but that Londoners only ever go to once. Ever since the monarchy moved out in the early 17th century, the Tower has existed principally as a stronghold of historical nostalgia, a place that owes its appeal more to romantic notions of the past than to real past events.

So what is the big attraction? First of all the site, which is undoubtedly one of the best preserved medieval castles in the world. Take your time wandering around **the outside of the Tower**, with its formidable ramparts, walls and turrets, and broad grassed-over moat. The **White Tower**, the keep at the centre of the complex, dates back to William

A Bloody History

The Tower's known royal history began with William the Conqueror. Keen to show the people of London that he meant business soon after his arrival in 1066, William ordered the building of a castle to help secure his new conquest. The first tower, built just to the east of the city walls, was a temporary structure made of wood; the stone keep (later called the **White Tower** because it was whitewashed under Henry III) took about 50 years to complete. It was and is a phenomenally sturdy building, with walls up to 15ft thick and 90ft high. The Tower has changed hands many times but, to its credit, has never been taken by storm.

In the 1140s the Tower's Constable, Geoffrey de Mandeville, conspired with Queen Mathilda to overthrow her husband, King Stephen, and nearly succeeded. Half a century later, Richard the Lionheart entrusted the Tower (and the kingdom) to William of Longchamp while he went away on the Crusades. Longchamp built two new towers, erected a fortifying wall and dug a ditch around the perimeter. It was not enough to prevent Richard's brother John seizing power; Longchamp surrendered after a three-day siege and went into exile in France. By this time the Tower had also become the kingdom's most important jail, usually housing a rather upmarket clientele of enemies to the throne. Its very first prisoner, Bishop Ranulf Flambard of Durham, escaped in 1101 by getting his guards drunk and lowering himself out of his window on a rope smuggled into his cell in a wine casket. In 1244, the Welsh prince Griffith tried a similar ruse by tying his bedclothes together, but his rope broke and he died in the fall.

Under Henry III, the Tower expanded considerably and included for the first time a menagerie, complete with lions, leopards, a polar bear and an elephant. Prisoners were brought in from the river through **Traitor's Gate**, which you can still see today. During the Montfort revolt of the 1260s Henry found the Tower invaluable to protect himself from the wrath of Parliament. Indeed the decision to bring the Crown Jewels here in 1303 was prompted by concern for their security at Westminster. The Tower was seemingly impenetrable; the closest anyone ever got to breaching it was during the Peasants' Revolt, when the mob ransacked the kitchen, armoury and bedchambers, mockingly pulled the beards of the guards and made unseemly advances towards the Queen Mother. Four of the king's ministers were caught off guard at prayer, dragged out on to Tower Hill and beheaded. Once the revolt was over, their heads were displayed on London Bridge as an official rebuke for their carelessness.

This was the first of many bloody incidents in the Tower, culminating in the mayhem of the Wars of the Roses in the mid-15th century. Henry VI, who spent much of his reign either in the Tower or on the battlefield, was almost certainly murdered in the **Wakefield Tower** in 1471, although his rival and successor Edward IV claimed he died of 'pure displeasure and melancholy'. In 1478 Edward's brother, the Duke of Clarence, was arrested for treason and then died in the Tower under mysterious circumstances. Finally, and most notoriously, Edward's 12-year-old son and successor, also called Edward, was murdered along with his 10-year-old brother in the Garden Tower (since called the **Bloody Tower**) in 1483. The culprit was probably the

the Conqueror and includes the magnificent heavy round arches and groin vaults of the 13th-century **St John's Chapel**.

More importantly, the Tower corresponds to every myth ever invented about England. Its history is packed with tales of royal pageantry, dastardly plots, ghoulish tortures and gruesome executions; it doggedly maintains its quaint, quasi-historic traditions. The Tower is still guarded by liveried figures known as **Beefeaters** (the official title is Yeoman Warder). At precisely 9.53 each evening they conduct their 700-year-old Ceremony of the Keys, seven minutes of key-clanking and praise of the monarch as the chief warder requests the opening of the

boy king's protector, Richard of Gloucester, who went on to seize the throne for himself. The story is familiar to anyone who knows Shakespeare's history plays *Henry VI* and *Richard III*. Several historians contest this version of events, arguing that Richard was not a hunchbacked villain but a well-meaning Lord Protector who fell victim to machinations within the House of York and then to the propaganda machine of the Tudor dynasty which took the crown from him. There is no conclusive evidence either way.

The dissolution of the monasteries and the rejection of the Catholic Church by Henry VIII sparked a positive orgy of blood-letting and cruelty. Victims included the scholar bishop John Fisher (so ill-treated in his prison cell he had to be carried to the scaffold), two of Henry's wives (Anne Boleyn and Catherine Howard, both accused of adultery), the teenage royals Jane Grey and Guildford Dudley (who posed a nominal threat to Queen Mary), the plotters who tried to put Mary Queen of Scots on the throne in the 1580s, and the luckless courtier and explorer Walter Raleigh, who never quite managed to side with the right conspiracy and whose wife carried his severed head around in a red leather bag for years after his death. One of the most virtuous victims was the humanist thinker Sir Thomas More (who was eventually canonized by Pope Pius XI). On the way up to the scaffold he quipped that he might need some help, but 'on the way down, let me shift for myself' and he urged the executioner to 'Pluck up thy spirits, man. My neck is very short'. His cell has recently been opened to the public for the first time.

James I put an end to this reign of political terror when he took the throne in 1603. The Tower ceased to be a royal residence and lost some of its notoriety as a prison. But it still had great symbolic value as the repository of the Crown Jewels. During the Civil War Charles I tried desperately to retain control of the Tower, but the man he appointed Constable, Thomas Lunsford, was denounced by Parliament as a cannibal and the jewels were eventually seized and most of them destroyed. The new jewels fashioned at the Restoration became the object of a bizarre plot by an Irishman called Captain Blood. Blood disguised himself as a priest and befriended the Jewel House Keeper, who was foolish enough to sell him his pistols. Blood and a group of friends then launched a raid, but were discovered in the act when the keeper's son turned up unannounced. One man shoved the orb down his breeches, while Blood flattened the crown with a mallet and tried to run off with it. The Tower guard caught up with them and hauled Blood before the king. Charles was so taken with Blood's cheek that, far from punishing him, he gave him estates in Ireland and a fat annual pension. Blood became a national celebrity. When he died, his body had to be exhumed to persuade the people that his death was not just another trick.

The Tower never really played much of a role again. The animals (apart from the ravens, who remain to this day) were moved to London Zoo in 1835 after one of the lions attacked a guard. Prisoner numbers dwindled as the rise of democracy made treason less fashionable, although the Tower still played host to the occasional spy in wartime. Hitler's deputy Rudolf Hess spent some time here before starting his lifelong confinement in Spandau jail in Berlin.

gates of Byward Tower from a sentry. There are also the famous **ravens**. Traditionally birds of ill omen, it is their absence rather than their presence which is feared, ever since Charles II decreed that at least six ravens must be kept at the Tower to protect his Kingdom from disaster. Accordingly the ravens enjoy an exalted status and a luxurious diet of raw meat, biscuits soaked in blood, a weekly egg and the occasional whole rabbit. And of course the Tower is home to the Crown Jewels.

The Crown Jewels

You'll probably have to share the Jewels with the entire population of Cleveland, Ohio, but at least there is an attempt at crowd control, thanks to the conveyor-belt system. Most of the collection dates from 1660 onwards, although the **ampulla** and **anointing spoon**, used to bless the new sovereign's head with oil, managed to survive the Civil War. There are two main crowns: **St Edward's Crown**, a heavy, somewhat unwieldy piece used only during the coronation ceremony itself; and the golden **Crown of State**, encrusted with 3,000 gems, originally made for Queen Victoria and still used for grand occasions such as the state opening of Parliament. Next are the **jewelled sword and spurs**, also used to anoint the new monarch, followed by the **orb, bracelets and two sceptres** which symbolize the sovereign's secular and divine mission. The orb represents the spread of Christianity around the world, the sceptres forge the link between the monarch and his or her subjects, while the bracelets are an emblem of Britain's link to the Commonwealth. The **Ring of Kingly Dignity** is a sapphire mounted with rubies, while the **Great Sword of State**, the sovereign's symbolic personal weapon, is decorated with a lion and unicorn as well as the royal arms. You'll notice that many of the items were made in the 19th century or later; it was in the late Georgian and Victorian era, when the monarchy lost most of its real power, that it sought its legitimacy instead in ceremony.

Tower Bridge FF11

Recorded bridge lift information **t** *(020) 7378 7700.* **Tower Bridge Experience,** *southern tower,* **t** *(020) 7378 1928,* **e** *enquiries@tower bridge.org.uk,* **w** *www.towerbridge.org.uk;* **tube** *Tower Hill, London Bridge; wheelchair accessible.* **Open** *April–Oct daily 10am–6.30pm, Nov–March daily 9.30am–6pm; last adm an hour and a quarter before closing; closed 1 Jan and 24–26 Dec;* **adm** *adults £6.25, concessions and children £4.25.*

Tower Bridge is one of the great feats of late Victorian engineering, half suspension bridge and half drawbridge, linked to two

neo-Gothic towers. Designed by an engineer, John Wolfe-Barry, and an architect, Horace Jones, working in tandem, it has become one of London's most recognizable landmarks. Its fame was not exactly instant; indeed, at its opening in 1894, the critics founds its evocation of medieval style crude. Its two bascules, the arms that rise up to let tall ships through, weigh an astonishing 1,000 tonnes each. Despite the decline of river freight traffic, the bridge still opens at least once a day.

The **Tower Bridge Experience** is a hi-tech retelling of the history of the bridge, plus a chance to enjoy the view from the overhead walkways and admire the giant Victorian hydraulic engines that once operated the bridge (it is now done with electric power).

All Hallows-by-the-Tower EE10

Byward St; **tube** *Tower Hill.* **Open** *Mon–Fri 9am–5.30pm, Sat and Sun 10am–5pm; closed 26 Dec–2 Jan.*

The 7th-century church of All Hallows was where Samuel Pepys first came to watch the Great Fire engulf the City. All Hallows survived, but it had less luck thereafter and was bombed to pieces during the Blitz. The church nevertheless possesses some remarkable remains, including a **Saxon arch** at the entrance to the choir and a beautifully carved **font cover by Grinling Gibbons**.

Trinity Square EE10

Tube Tower Hill.

Trinity Square is dominated by the old **Port of London Authority** building, a striking example of Edwardian Baroque, now occupied by an insurance broking company. According to ancient custom, the first five yards of the building belong to the Crown because they can be reached by bow and arrow from the Tower of London; the insurance company pays a special tribute every year by way of rent. At the south end of the square, next to the Tube station, is a chunk of **Roman wall** dating from the 3rd century.

Outside the Centre: North London

15

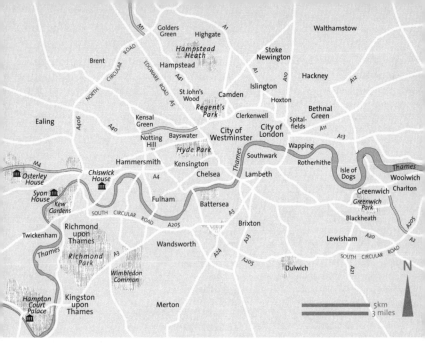

North London has some of the city's most delightful urban villages, a wild and beautiful heath, and a legendary cricket ground. Crooked, cobbled Hampstead is famously the stomping ground of literati and psychoanalysts, with museums to Keats and Freud; suave, sophisticated Islington oozes liberal media types and designer bars; and genteel Highgate with its teashops and quiet parks is the last resting place of writers and philosophers from Marx to George Eliot.

St John's Wood Off maps

Anyone familiar with the cover of the Beatles' *Abbey Road* album, the one where they walk across a zebra crossing, will know what St John's Wood looks like; if you want to follow in their footsteps, **Abbey Rd** itself, former home to the EMI studios where most of the classics were recorded, is a 5-minute walk from the tube up Grove End Rd.

The Saatchi Collection

*98A Boundary Rd, **t** (020) 7624 8299; **tube** St John's Wood, Swiss Cottage; **bus** 139, 189. **Open** Thurs–Sun noon–6pm; **adm** adults £5, concessions £2.*

Advertising magnate Charles Saatchi began buying up art in the 1980s, starting with early forays into Postmodern Neo-expressionist artists like Schnabel and Anselm Kiefer, and moving on to conceptual art by little-known British artists (many of them graduates from Goldsmith's College). The relationship has been a sound investment for Saatchi, who has cornered the market in works by Fiona Rae, Jenny Saville, Gary Hume, the Chapman Brothers, Damien Hirst and Sarah Lucas, whose value has soared as conceptual art has continued to tighten its vice-like grip on all Britain's art institutions. There are three shows here a year and Saatchi's pot-luck approach to buying ensures that most exhibitions will be a stimulating mix of the excellent and the execrable.

Lord's Cricket Ground

*St John's Wood Rd, **t** (020) 7432 1033, **t** 7289 1611; **tube** St John's Wood; **bus** 139, 189; wheelchair accessible (not 2nd floor of museum). **Museum open** during play on match days; closed on major match days; **adm** adults £6.50, concessions £5, children £4.50. **Guided tours** April–Sept daily at 10am, noon and 2pm, Oct–March daily at noon and 2pm; book in advance.*

This mecca for lovers of the world's most eccentric sport and headquarters of its soul in England, the Marylebone Cricket Club, is not a place to come with naïve questions about overs, innings and lbw. Highlights of the small **museum** include the Ashes, the trophy contested in matches between England and Australia (actually the remains of a bail ritually burnt after a meeting of the two sides in 1882); and a sparrow – now stuffed – which was killed by a particularly vicious delivery at Lord's in 1936.

Clerkenwell Off maps

Just north of the City, Clerkenwell was by turns a centre for monks, clockmakers, gin manufacturers and Italian labourers. It has the feel of a cosy village, with its squares, winding streets and pretty churches. Its proximity to the City made it an ideal headquarters for the Knights of the Order of St John, who stayed here until the dissolution of the monasteries in the 1530s. In the 19th century much of Clerkenwell was slumland, and the Victorians built forbidding prisons here to cope with the overflow from the City jails. After decades of neglect, it has undergone something of a revival, its once grimy backstreets now filled with slick new offices, converted lofts and cheap, attractive cafés.

There are no major sights here, but in the streets around Clerkenwell Green you will come across some interesting historical nuggets.

The Marx Memorial Library

37–8 Clerkenwell Green, t (020) 7253 1485, w www.marxmemoriallibrary.sageweb.co.uk; tube Farringdon; bus 55, 243. Open Mon 1–6pm, Tues–Thurs 1–8pm, Sat 10am–1pm; non-members are welcome to look around for free but cannot use the library or its lending facility unless they pay a membership fee.

This library has the best private collection of radical literature in the city. Lenin wrote radical pamphlets here in 1902–3.

St John's Gate

St John's Lane, t (020) 7324 4070, w www .sja.org.uk; tube Farringdon, Barbican; bus 55, 63, 143, 221, 170, 243; museum wheelchair

*accessible. **Museum open** Mon–Fri 10am–5pm, Sat 10am–4pm; closed bank hol weekends; **adm** free. **Guided tours** Tues, Fri and Sat 11am and 2.30pm; minimum donation adults £5, concessions £3.50; book in advance, t (020) 7324 4074. **Shop**.*

The Knights of St John were Crusaders. Like the Templars, they set up a priory in London and built a round church inspired by the Dome of the Rock in Jerusalem. Visitors were welcome, especially the sick and the poor, who were invited to receive three days' board and lodging free of charge. Much of the original priory was burnt down in the Peasants' Revolt. This crenellated stone gatehouse, dating from 1504, is all that remains of the rebuilding work. Now it is a small museum containing relics and armour of the medieval knights, and exhibits celebrating the work of the St John's Ambulance charity, a modern incarnation of the crusading order. You can visit the remains of **St John's Church** as part of a tour. The 15th-century altar paintings were looted during the dissolution and only returned in 1915; the 12th-century crypt, part of the original church structure, is also well worth a visit, for itself and for its alabaster effigies.

Camden Off maps

Camden's exotic if downtrodden air was captured in the paintings of Walter Sickert, Augustus John and other members of the so-called Camden Town Group at the time of the First World War. The area's modern identity as a haven for artists and small shopkeepers was established in the 1970s, when the market started and the Victorian warehouses were slowly converted into artists' studios, music venues and restaurants.

Camden Market

Off Chalk Farm Rd; tube Camden, Chalk Farm; bus 24, 29, 31, 253. Some stalls and shops open Mon–Fri 9.30am–5.30pm, but the best time to visit is Sat and Sun 10am–6pm.

Camden is above all its open-air market, or rather a series of markets, that have sprung up around the canal and the surrounding streets, which are a magnet for multinational crowds every weekend. The nerve centre of the market is at Camden Lock, just next to the canal off Chalk Farm Rd (the extension of Camden High St). In the middle of the market is a three-storey building with narrow staircases and passages selling jewellery and crafts; around it are stalls selling clothes, antiques, books and records. The stalls continue for about 500 yards up the Chalk Farm Rd, in an area known as The Stables. Some of the most interesting shops are on Camden High St, which is really a market unto itself; the Electric Ballroom nightclub doubles on Sundays as a bazaar for cheap designer fashions and jewellery.

Jewish Museum

129–31 Albert St, between Parkway and Delancey St, t (020) 7284 1997, e admin@ jmus.org.uk, w www.jewmusm.ort.org; tube Camden Town; bus 274, C2; wheelchair accessible. Open Mon–Thurs 10am–4pm, Sun 10am–5pm; closed bank holidays and Jewish festivals. Temporary exhibitions.

This celebration of Jewish life in England from the Middle Ages onwards is notable mostly for its collection of old ritual objects from London synagogues. The centrepiece is an elaborately carved 16th-century Venetian Synagogue Ark. There are also attractive illuminated marriage contracts and some Torah bells fashioned by the 18th-century silversmith Abraham Lopes de Oliveira. The museum has another site up in Finchley at 80 East End Rd, N3, t (020) 8349 1143, e *jml.finchley@lineon.net*, w *www.jewmusm .ort.org*; tube Finchley Central. That site focuses on the social history of London Jews.

Islington Off maps

Tube Angel, Highbury and Islington; bus 19 (from Piccadilly), 38, 73 (from Victoria).

In the 1950s you wouldn't have found much in Islington apart from a clapped-out old music hall, a few eel and pie shops and an extended series of slummy terraced houses. How times have changed. Now it is one of the liveliest and trendiest districts in the capital, a Mecca for liberal-minded professionals, particularly writers and broadcasters, who live in attractively refurbished Georgian townhouses and eat out in expensive ethnic restaurants. The place is packed with pubs, cafés, designer bars and shops, and alternative theatres. Every night its streets are full to bursting with young people. Many of the once sad backstreets, particularly those overlooking the Grand Union Canal and the New River, have been scrubbed clean of their industrial-era grime.

In the 1950s and 60s this was the unfashionable home of the playwright Joe Orton and his lover Kenneth Halliwell. **No.25 Noel Rd**, where they shared a dingy second-floor bedsit, has become something of a pilgrimage site, especially since Stephen Frears' film *Prick Up Your Ears*, which told the story of their extraordinary life and violent death, when Halliwell beat Orton to death with a hammer before killing himself with an overdose of barbiturates.

Camden Passage

Off Upper St; tube Angel. Antiques shops and stalls best visited Wed 10am–2pm or Sat 10am–5pm. Farmers' market held Sun am.

Camden Passage, just off Islington Green, is a cobbled row of elegant antiques shops and stalls. Most of the stalls and smaller shops open on Wednesday mornings and Saturdays only, but the larger antique furniture shops may open at other times if you ring the bell. Dealers are adept at shipping overseas and will deduct VAT (UK sales tax). The market itself is a browser's paradise since everything looks perfect and most of the prices are too high to consider seriously for purchase. If you're tenacious and prepared to haggle (which you must), you can sometimes find the odd bargain, especially amongst the Victorian silverware and out-of-the-ordinary prints.

Canonbury Tower

Canonbury Place; tube Highbury and Islington; bus 4, 19, 30, 43.

Canonbury is one of the most unspoilt areas of Georgian housing in North London.

Its name recalls Islington's roots as the burgh, or district, of the canons of the priory of St Bartholomew at Smithfield. Then, as now, the most imposing building in the neighbourhood was Canonbury Tower, a building of mythical reputation whose history goes back to pre-Roman times; no fewer than 24 ley lines meet at the point where the central pillar of its main staircase stands.

Once part of the priory, the square tower passed into the hands of a rich cloth merchant called John Spencer some years after the dissolution of the monasteries. Spencer disinherited his daughter after she escaped from the tower in a basket in 1599 to elope with her penniless lover Lord Compton; he was, however, tricked into readopting her by Queen Elizabeth, who asked him to sponsor a poor child she knew. Spencer consented, realizing too late the child was his own grandson. Lord Compton eventually took over the running of the manor, and began a tradition of leasing it out to eminent tenants. The statesman Sir Francis Bacon lived here in the 17th century, and the playwright Oliver Goldsmith in the 18th. Now it is home to the **Tower Theatre**, a popular repertory venue with a strong local following. Inside you can see some Elizabethan wall panelling, and plasterwork on the ceilings dating back to the end of the 16th century.

Estorick Collection of Italian Art

Northampton Lodge, 39A Canonbury Square, **t** *(020) 7704 9522,* **e** *curator@estorick collection.com,* **w** *www.estorickcollection .com;* **tube** *Highbury and Islington;* **bus** *271 to door, 4, 19, 30, 43 to Upper Street/Canonbury Lane, 38, 56, 171a to Essex and Canonbury Rds; wheelchair accessible.* **Open** *Wed–Sat 11am–6pm, Sun noon–5pm;* **adm** *adults £3.50, concessions £2.50.* **Library, café** *and* **giftshop.**

This is a fascinating private collection of Italian art, featuring mainly Futurist painters such as Balla, Boccioni and Carra. There are also pieces by Giacometti and Giorgio Morandi. The square on which the museum stands, Canonbury Square, is one of the finest ensembles of Georgian housing in the area. Evelyn Waugh and George Orwell each lived here at different times.

Crafts Council Gallery

44A Pentonville Rd, **t** *(020) 7278 7700,* **w** *www.craftscouncil.org.uk;* **tube** *Angel;* **bus** *30, 73, 214, 394; wheelchair accessible.* **Open** *Tues–Sat 11am–6pm, Sun 2–6pm; closed 1 Jan and 25–26 Dec;* **adm** *free.*

An excellent exhibition of modern British crafts.

London Canal Museum

12–13 New Wharf Rd, King's Cross, **t** *(020) 7713 0836,* **w** *www.canalmuseum.org.uk;* **tube** *King's Cross;* **bus** *17, 91, 259, 274.* **Open** *Tues–Sun 10am–4.30pm, last adm 3.45pm;* **adm** *adults £2.50, concessions £1.25.*

This museum covers the development of London's canals, once vital trade routes, housed in an 1850s ice cream warehouse (blocks of ice were brought from Norway to Limehouse and thence along the canal to the wells beneath this warehouse).

Highgate Map p.284

Tube *Archway, Highgate;* **bus** *271 (from Liverpool St via Archway), 210, C11 (from Hampstead).*

Highgate has been a genteel hilltop village, protected from the hubbub of the capital, since the 13th century. It's a very pleasant place for a drink and people-watch, with some old-fashioned pubs. For a walk through Hampstead and Highgate, *see* p.283, where you'll also find a map of the area.

The Whittington Stone

At the foot of Highgate Hill, near Archway Station; **tube** *Archway.*

This statue of a cat marks the spot where, according to the fairy tale, a dejected young Dick Whittington stopped on his way out of London and was persuaded to return by the chimes of the Bow Bells prophesying his rise to Lord Mayor (*see* 'Turn Again, Whittington' for a dissection of that myth). Highgate Hill was an obvious place for storytellers to set

Turn Again, Whittington

The Whittington Stone is inscribed with the words:

Sir Richard Whittington
Thrice Lord Mayor of London
1397 Richard II
1406 Henry IV
1420 Henry V

This is the spot where, as little more than a boy, the future Lord Mayor Dick Whittington is supposed to have heard the bells of St Mary-le-Bow calling him back to the City of London, just as he was about to give up hope of ever making his fortune there. Dick Whittington is in many ways the emblematic Londoner, and his story is known to every London schoolchild through storybooks and Christmas pantomimes. It is a touching tale of a poor boy made good, a salutary lesson teaching us never to give up hope and that even the most modest of us can rise to the top of the social ladder. Unfortunately the story bears no relation to the way medieval London worked, and certainly has nothing in common with the life of the real Richard Whittington.

The fable – with apologies to those who know it – runs something like this. Young Dick makes his way to London with no other possession in the world except his cat, persuaded that he will find the streets paved with gold. His dreams are quickly dashed, and he finds employment only as a kitchen-boy in the house of a well-to-do merchant. The merchant is about to embark on a trading voyage to Barbary, and generously invites each of his servants to contribute something to the cargo so they can benefit from the profits of the trip. Poor Dick has nothing to give but his cat, who is duly dispatched upon the high seas. Subject to abuse in the kitchen and left with no friends in the world, Dick grows increasingly desperate and resolves to leave London. As he reaches Highgate, however, he hears the loud peal of the Bow Bells ringing out to him with the words:

Turn again, Whittington
Thrice Lord Mayor of London

Dick heeds the bells' advice, and on his return to the merchant's house discovers that he is rich beyond his wildest imaginings. Evidently the king of Barbary had a severe problem with rat infestation, and was delighted to buy Dick's cat for a fantastic sum. Dick marries his master's daughter, Alice, and eventually fulfils the prophecy of the bells.

such a scene, since it was the site of the last toll-gate in London; the precise location a little way up the hill may have coincided with that of a medieval cross outside a leper's hospice (now superseded by the Whittington Hospital). Having been fortuitously picked as the location of a fairy tale, Highgate has taken great pains to honour its famous would-be wayfarer. The stone has been replaced at least twice, has been adorned with a special railing and a lamp-post, and has acquired this statue representing Whittington's faithful cat.

Waterlow Park

Off Highgate High St.

This little-known park, off the villagey row of shops and small cafés which is Highgate High St, affords one of the best views over London. On a clear day you can see not only the skyscrapers of the City and Docklands, but the woods and suburban jungle of South London. From here, London looks uncharacteristically romantic, an impression helped by the grandiose Victorian architecture of Highgate Cemetery in the foreground. Waterlow Park itself is pleasant enough but remarkable mostly for **Lauderdale House**, a Tudor-framed mansion, home to the first Lord Mayor of London and used as a summer residence by Charles II's mistress Nell Gwynne. It was here that she is reputed to have dangled her infant son from a window until King Charles made him Duke of St Albans. Now an arts centre and café, Lauderdale House hosts art exhibitions, outdoor summertime concerts, children's shows and workshops.

The real Richard Whittington was not poor at all, but the third son of a well-to-do merchant. Thanks to his father's connections he became apprenticed to a mercer's company in the City of London and worked his way up to become one of the richest men of his times. He was Master of the Company of Mercers three times before attaining the office of Lord Mayor, which he in fact held four times. He was never knighted, so the 'sir' is also erroneous. His wife, who was indeed called Alice, was the daughter of the City merchant Sir Ivo Fitzwaryn. As for the 'cat', that was a medieval word for a trading boat; Whittington had a fleet of them which made his fortune by carrying wares to and from the continent. He was a generous philanthropist: he refurbished Newgate Prison, provided a ward for unmarried mothers at St Thomas's Hospital, and founded the College of Priests next to St Michael Paternoster Royal, where he was buried in 1423. He made his real mark, however, by increasing the economic and political power of the City through the expansion of the wool trade and the wider use of bills of exchange. He was the first London mayor to be called Lord, and his riches went a long way to paying for the magnificent Guildhall (see p.226).

Interestingly, the fairy-tale version of the Whittington story only evolved in the early 17th century, a moment of great social flux when a fable about social mobility was a convenient foil for the burgeoning mercantile order. On closer inspection, however, it undermines its bogus promise of social mobility. It suggests that he was called to high office by a supernatural force (speaking through bells), the inference being that the rich deserve their riches because they have been chosen from on high. One can draw a perverse parallel between the Whittington tale and the story of St Peter, who was scurrying away from Rome when Christ appeared to him in a vision and called him back with the words *Quo vadis?* Both stories are about men losing their nerve and then, after a supernatural revelation, finding new inner strength. The difference, of course, is that Peter was fleeing persecution, not poverty, and returned to a martyr's death, not untold riches. The parallel, which would have been clear to 17th-century audiences, certainly has disturbing implications. In the City of London's curious system of thought, it seems making money is a virtue, even a form of redemption, on a par with the crucifixion of one of Christ's apostles.

Highgate Cemetery

Swains Lane, **w** *highgate-cemetery.org/index.asp; surfaces uneven, parts of tour are uphill.* **Western cemetery open** *for guided tours only, April–Oct Mon–Fri noon, 2pm and 4pm, Sat and Sun 11am–4pm hourly, Nov–March Sat and Sun 11am–3pm hourly; closed 25 and 26 Dec;* **adm** *£3 plus camera permit; book in advance on* **t** *(020) 8340 1834; no children under 8.* **Eastern cemetery open** *April–Sept daily 10am–5pm, Oct–March daily 10am–4pm; closed 25 and 26 Dec;* **adm** *£1. Note that the cemetery is still an active burial ground and visitors should treat it as such.*

Highgate Cemetery has been a tourist attraction ever since it opened in 1839, both for its magnificent funereal Victorian architecture and for its views. 'In such a place the aspect of death is softened,' wrote the *Lady's Newspaper* in 1850. The **western side** is the older and more splendid of the two halves, with a maze of winding paths that lead to the so-called Egyptian Avenue, which you enter through an arch flanked with obelisks and mock-Egyptian columns. This avenue leads beneath a bridge to the Circle of Lebanon, a hemicycle of tombs on either side of a circular path constructed around a magnificent cedar of Lebanon. The spire of St Michael's parish church looms above at the top of Swains Lane. Guides are wonderfully well informed and will point out the eminent dead occupying these hallowed tombs; they include the chemist Michael Faraday and the poet Christina Rossetti.

The **eastern cemetery** opened in 1857 to cope with the overload of coffins from across the road and here you can still roam around at will. Most people head straight for the large black bust of Karl Marx marking the place where the much maligned philosopher was buried in 1883. The bust, with its two inscriptions, was erected in 1956, the year when the crushing of the Hungarian uprising turned many Western liberals off the whole idea of communism. The visitors have kept coming regardless, admiring the two epitaphs: 'Workers of the world unite' (from the *Communist Manifesto*) and 'The philosophers have only interpreted the world in different ways; the point, however, is to change it' (from the *Theses on Feuerbach*). The eastern cemetery contains a sprinkling of other left-wing revolutionaries, mainly from the Developing World, plus the remains of novelist Mary Ann Evans (a.k.a. George Eliot) and the radical conservative thinker Herbert Spencer, who died in 1903. The combination of Marx and Spencer has always seemed an odd one, but thanks to the department store chain of (almost) the same name it makes a good joke.

Hampstead Map p.284

Tube Hampstead; *bus* 46 *(from King's Cross), 210, C11 (from Highgate). On a fine day, the best way to reach Hampstead from Highgate is to walk across the Heath.*

In 1814 John James Park described Hampstead as 'a select, amicable, respectable and opulent neighbourhood'. So it has remained, a pretty hilltop village of Georgian rows and Victorian mansions, inhabited by wealthy if liberally inclined families and surrounded by the vast expanse of the Heath. John Constable came here and painted some distant cityscapes that were barely distinguishable in tone from his great rural idylls. No wonder: the air is so pure and the Heath so big and wild you can easily feel you are lost in the deep heart of the English countryside. For a walk through Hampstead and the Heath, *see* p.283, where you will also find a map of the area.

Everything in Hampstead is carefully planned and lovingly looked after, from the window boxes in the Georgian houses on Holly Hill to the inverted white-on-black street signs. The dress code, for the most part, is one of effortless chic. Spot the hordes of designer teenagers driving Daddy's Porsche into the village in the early evening to hook up with their equally glamorous friends for a night on the town. Hang around any of the cafés on Hampstead High St of an afternoon to earwig on the conversations of the 'ladies who lunch' and see if you can spot any of the rich and famous – they're never far away here. Have a look in the estate agents' windows for a laugh and a taste of how the other half live.

The real pleasure of Hampstead village is in getting lost in the winding dead-end back-streets lined with Georgian houses and backed by woodland. For example, take Hollybush Hill, opposite the exit to the Tube; just off it, on Hollybush Mount, lined with lovely small houses, is the 17th-century **Hollybush pub**, so called because landlords used to hang a bush outside the door to advertise their wine and beer. Just after the pub is a steep staircase plunging back down towards Heath St. Better, however, to head down **Holly Walk** (bear left at the large hospital building and then double back left down Mount Vernon, which becomes Holly Walk), another delightful cobbled path flanked by fine houses and a small flower-filled cemetery. At the bottom of the hill is **St John's**, an attractive 18th-century church with a tall tower and, inside, a balustraded gallery and a bust of Keats beside the lectern. Constable is buried in the churchyard. The road from the church back to Heath St, called **Church Row**, is one of the most elegant lines of Georgian housing in London, with large, shimmering bay windows, discreetly deco-rated red-brick façades and ornate wrought-iron frontings.

Heath St is one of two Hampstead thor-oughfares lined with fine shops, delicatessens, cafés and restaurants. The other, the **High St**, can be reached through **Oriel Passage**, which has an old oak tree growing in a minuscule patch of ground halfway along. Cross the High St and you come into **Flask Walk** with its secondhand bookshops, elegant restaurants with handwritten menus, and posh tea merchant Keith Fawkes. Along with its continuation, **Well Walk**, this is where fashionable folk came to take the Hampstead spa waters back in the 18th century.

Keats' House

Keats Grove, t (020) 7435 2062, e keats house@corpoflondon.gov.uk, w www .cityoflondon.gov.uk, w www.keatshouse.org .uk; tube Hampstead; bus 24, 46, 168, 268; wheelchair accessible by prior arrangement. Open April–Nov Tues–Fri 1–5pm, Sat 10–1 and 2–5, Sun 2–5pm; adm adults £3, concessions £1.50, under-16s free. Call in advance to check opening hours, which can be erratic because of building works.

The main attraction of Keats' House is in fact the plum tree in the garden, under which Keats wrote 'Ode to a Nightingale' in 1819 (if you think it looks a bit young, you are right – it is a replacement). The house, called Wentworth Place and completed in 1816, was in Keats' time split into two halves. In all, Keats lodged here for only two years. It was nevertheless an eventful time. He produced some of his best and most famous work, fell in love with Fanny Brawne, who lived in the other half of the house, and contracted the consumption that was to kill him two years later, at 25. The house's attractions are somewhat limited. Keats used one living room downstairs and one bedroom upstairs. Memorabilia have nevertheless been strewn in every room; these include a lock of Keats' hair and some of his manuscripts and books.

2 Willow Road

2 Willow Rd, t (020) 7435 6166; tube Hampstead; bus 24, 46, 168, 268; ground floor wheelchair accessible (film tour of rest of house). Open April–Oct Thurs–Sat noon–5pm, March, Nov and Dec Sat 10am–5pm; adm £4.20 (free to members of National Trust). Guided tours of 1hr every 45mins.

This house is part of a small terrace built by architect Ernö Goldfinger, the designer of the now fashionable but once despised Trellick Tower in West London (*see* 'Portobello Market', p.245). Designed in 1937, it's a typically sleek, pared-down Modernist take on the terraced Georgian houses close by. Inside, the furniture (also designed by Goldfinger) is complemented with Modernist art, including pieces by Henry Moore, Bridget Riley and Marcel Duchamp. It remained Goldfinger's family home until 1994 and still has a family feel – there are all kinds of odds and ends turned up by his children, and there are pieces of furniture designed by his daughter. Ian Fleming, author of the James Bond books, lived close by and disliked both the house and its owner. He showed his contempt by giving the architect's name to one of his most famous villains.

Fenton House

20 Hampstead Grove, t (020) 7435 3471, recorded info t 01494 755563, w www .nationaltrust.org.uk; tube Hampstead; ground floor wheelchair accessible. Open end March–Oct Wed–Fri 2–5pm, Sat, Sun and bank holiday Mons 11am–5pm; adm adults £4.30, children £2.15, families £10.50.

This is a splendid brick mansion dating from 1693. Aside from the elegant rooms and fine garden, the house has collections of early keyboard instruments and fine porcelain. Some of the quiet streets nearby, particularly **Admirals Walk**, are well worth a look for their lovely housing.

Kenwood House

Hampstead Lane, t (020) 8348 1286; tube Highgate, then bus 210, or walk across the Heath; mostly wheelchair accessible. House open April–Sept daily 10am–6pm, Oct daily 10am–5pm, Nov–March daily 10am–4pm; closed 24 and 25 Dec; adm free. Grounds open summer daily 8am–8pm, winter daily 8am–4pm. Outdoor concerts in summer, to book tickets call IMG on t (020) 8233 7435, or visit w www.picnicconcerts.com.

The unpretentious atmosphere at Kenwood is a breath of fresh air after the stuffily earnest stately homes dotted around the rest of London. The location makes it, what with the expanse of the Heath rolling away to the south and its breathtaking views over Highgate and central London. Kenwood is famous for its summer concerts held by the lake at the bottom of the garden; the orchestra sits under a white awning and the audience watches from across the water. If you can't make it for an evening concert, bring a picnic and come to a rehearsal in the afternoon. The atmosphere is almost as magical, the children can run around – and it's free.

The house itself dates back to 1616 but was given a near-total facelift by Robert Adam in the 1760s. He stuck on the white Neoclassical façade, an elegantly simple affair in stucco adorned with slim pilasters, and reworked most of the interiors, including the remarkable **library** with its elegant curved ceiling and fluted Corinthian columns. The **pictures**, bequeathed by Lord Iveagh, who bought the house in 1925, are dotted around the main house and library extension; they include works by Rembrandt (a remarkable self-portrait), Vermeer (*The Guitar Player*), Van Dyck, Gainsborough, Guardi, Reynolds, Landseer and Turner.

Hampstead Heath
Tube Hampstead, Belsize Park.

At the southern end of the Heath, **Parliament Hill** is the site of an ancient barrow where the rebel queen Boudicca is rumoured to have been buried. The view from the top of the hill, no more than a bump compared to the heights of Kenwood, isn't too bad, though it's not a patch on Primrose Hill; it's a favourite spot for ornithologists and kite-flyers. At the bottom of the hill are **Highgate Ponds**, a series of open-air pools segregated by sex to encourage nude bathing. The ladies' pool, discreetly hidden behind some thick bushes, is nearest the top just off Millfield Lane; the men's pools are alongside the path nearer Highgate Rd. There's also a mixed pond on the Hampstead side of the Heath where teenage boys come to meet girls.

Spaniards Inn
Spaniards Rd, t (020) 8731 6571;
tube Hampstead/Highgate, then bus 210.
Open Mon–Sat 11am–11pm, Sun noon–10.30pm. Pub food.

This 16th-century inn, named after two Spanish proprietors who killed each other in a duel, owes its fame to the 18th-century highwayman Dick Turpin, who used to stop for drinks here in between coach hold-ups. During the Gordon Riots of 1780, a group of mobsters dropped by on their way to Kenwood, then belonging to the Lord Chancellor Lord Mansfield, which they intended to destroy. The publican offered the rioters pint after pint of free beer as an inducement to stay out of trouble. Soon the men weren't in a fit state to walk to Kenwood, let alone burn it down, and when the army arrived they were disarmed without incident. You can see their muskets hanging on the wall in the saloon bar.

The Freud Museum
20 Maresfield Gardens, t (020) 7433 2002,
t 7435 5167, w www.freud.org.uk;
tube Finchley Rd, Swiss Cottage; bus 46 (from Hampstead or Swiss Cottage); wheelchair accessible. Open Wed–Sun noon–5pm; adm adults £5, concessions and children £3.

This is the house where Freud set up his last home after fleeing the Nazis in Vienna in 1938. Six rooms have been left untouched since the founder of psychoanalysis died of throat cancer here on the eve of the Second World War. Of greatest interest is the **couch** where his patients lay during sessions – if, that is, it is not on loan to another museum. You can also see Freud's collections of furniture and archaeological and ethnographical artefacts, including some extraordinary phalluses, and watch the home movies he made of his family and dog at home in Vienna in the increasingly dark days of the 1930s.

Outside the Centre: West London

16

Much of West London is affluent, fashionable (if perhaps slightly stuffy) and delightfully green. Notting Hill is the city's trendiest suburb, made famous by the eponymous film and the antique-cum-fleamarket which spills down Portobello Rd. Chelsea, after a few decades of bohemian debauchery, has settled down to enjoy its privileged position on the riverbank. Further west, the river curls through sleepy suburbs and expansive parklands, including Britain's largest and loveliest urban park, in Richmond. Stately homes and Palladian mansions are scattered thickly across West London, and there's also the magnificent royal palace at Hampton Court and the vast botanical gardens at Kew.

For an overview of West London, *see* the map on p.234.

Notting Hill Map pp.306–7

Tube Notting Hill; **bus** 12, 94 (from Oxford St).

Notting Hill conjures up many images: antiques dealers pulling a fast one on the southern end of Portobello Rd; dancing in the streets during the annual Carnival; arty types queueing outside the Gate cinema; young people rifling through secondhand records and cheap jewellery underneath the A40 flyover; Moroccans and Portuguese chatting in the cafés of Golborne Rd; affluent families relaxing in their gardens in Lansdowne Rise. But, much to the annoyance of local residents and small shopkeepers (being put out of business by the soaring leases), the overriding image of recent times is of Hugh Grant and Julia Roberts.

Once considered irredeemably out of fashion, Notting Hill now risks becoming as exclusive as the posh villas on Campden Hill on the south side of the main road. The process began in the 1980s with a period of rapid gentrification. The once-thriving drug culture waned into insignificance, but it also created barriers of class and status that hadn't existed since the neighbourhood became an emblem of multiculturalism after the big immigrant waves from the Caribbean

in the 1950s. The motorway flyover creates a divide between the spruced-up pastel-painted Victorian houses to the south (Notting Hill proper), and the high-rise 1960s council estates to the north (dismissively described as North Kensington).

The area derives its name from the Danish King Knutt, who built an encampment in the district around AD 700. For centuries Knottynghull was nothing more than fields and gravel pits, and as late as 1849 the cows outnumbered humans three to one. In the late 1870s, the Victorians decided to make it 'the centre of a new prosperous and refined district', building a hippodrome to attract residents. But for some reason the place did not catch on and by the end of the 19th century it was considered distinctly passé. After the Second World War it was, like Soho and Brixton, a rundown inner-city area where immigrants could find plenty of cheap housing. Notting Hill became a mini-Caribbean, a fresh antidote to the sleepy calm of most of London's Victorian suburbs.

For a map of the area, *see* pp.306–7.

Portobello Market B8–C10

Bus 28, 31, 52, 70, 328 (from Notting Hill). **Antiques market** Sat 7am–5.30pm; **fruit and vegetable market** Mon–Wed, Fri and Sat 9am–5pm, Thurs 9am–1pm.

The market first appeared in the 1870s, when gypsies came to sell horses for the nearby hippodrome. Westbourne Grove forms a neat dividing line between the touristy **antiques market**, which takes place on Saturdays at the southern end of Portobello Rd towards Notting Hill, and the shabbier furniture, food, jewellery, cheap records, books, postcards and funky bric-a-brac on sale up towards the flyover and beyond. The whole street offers a view onto a tight-knit and resolutely individual local community. Broadly speaking, the crowd gets more unorthodox and eclectic the further down the street you go. Anybody in London who has had any silver stolen goes to the **silver market** just north of Westbourne Grove on Saturday mornings to see if their

The Notting Hill Carnival

After an explosion of racial tension in the summers of 1957 and 58, community leaders resolved to put on an annual show to vaunt the attractions of Caribbean culture; by the mid-1960s the Notting Hill Carnival, held on the last weekend in August, had become a permanent fixture. For two days each year, on the Sunday and Bank Holiday Monday, the streets throb with steel bands and soca music. The crowds dance while balancing glasses of Jamaican Red Stripe – and of course many people are getting pleasantly high on choice Caribbean weed. People of all ages and nationalities from all over London come along for the party. Everywhere is the tangy smell of saltfish, goat curry, fried plantain and patties. Floats cruise by with dancers in fantastical outfits.

In the past, the tension between residents and the police occasionally boiled over at the Carnival. But in recent years the police have got things just about right, and are generally to be photographed limboing with revellers in an embarrassed sort of way. The all-PC Metropolitan Police now treats it as an exercise in PR rather than a potential riot to be confronted. The Carnival has been occasionally marked by gang violence on the backstreets, but, as a visitor, you are highly unlikely to see any of this first hand. You're far more likely to have a great time, make a few new friends, get a samosa stuck to your shoe, and go home with a headache from too much beer and sun.

wares have turned up there. Under the flyover is a **bric-a-brac** and cheap **clothes market**, as well as an indoor arcade packed with home-crafted **jewellery**. Further north, among the ugly modern brick housing estates, you stumble across small **art dealers**, the excellent jazz shop **Honest Jon's** and the authentic Spanish restaurant **Galicia**.

Finally, off to the right is **Golborne Rd**, a bustling short street divided between Portuguese and Moroccan communities. Each has its own cafés and restaurants; the **Lisboa Patisserie**, with its homemade

pastries and pavement seating, is famous for its custard tarts. The Iberian connection goes back to the 18th century and a local farm named after Porto Bello in Mexico, taken from the Spaniards by the British army in 1739.

Towering above Golborne Rd, and the whole area, is the once-hated and now deeply trendy 1960s **Trellick Tower**, by the architect Ernö Goldfinger.

Kensal Green Cemetery Off maps

*Harrow Rd, **t** (020) 8960 1030; **tube** Kensal Green; **bus** 52, 70 (from Notting Hill Gate). **Open** April–Sept daily 8am–6pm, Oct–March daily 9am–5pm; **adm** free. **Guided tours** of cemetery and catacombs first and third Sun of the month at 2pm; £4; call in advance.*

This Victorian 'garden of the deceased' was a popular place for 19th-century celebrities to be buried, partly due to its extraordinary Greek Revival architecture. The large entrance arch frames an avenue leading to the **Anglican Chapel**, itself adorned with Doric pillars and colonnades. The chapel stands atop a layered cake of underground burial chambers, some of which used to be served by a hydraulic lift. Around the rest of the cemetery are extraordinary testimonies to 19th-century delusions of grandeur: vast ornate tombs worthy of the Pharaohs, decorated with statues, incidental pillars and arches. What made Kensal Green such a hit was a decision by the Duke of Sussex, youngest brother of George IV, to eschew royal protocol and have himself buried among the people, so to speak. Eminent fellow-occupants include Thackeray, Trollope, Wilkie Collins, Leigh Hunt and the father and son engineering duo Marc and Isambard Kingdom Brunel. A personal favourite is the fantastically named Ermintrude Alert.

Holland Park Map pp.306–7

*Tube Holland Park; **bus** 94 (from Notting Hill).*

This is one of the most attractive residential areas in London, especially in the springtime when the small private gardens and trees are in bloom. It is also dotted with good restaurants and pubs. For the park itself, *see* p.379.

Leighton House A12

12 Holland Park Rd, t (020) 7602 3316, w www.rbkc.gov.uk/leightonhousemuseum; tube High St Kensington; bus 9, 10, 49, 52, 70. Open Wed–Mon 11am–5.30pm; adm free.

This apparently straightforward red-brick house opens into a grand extravaganza of escapist late Victorian interior design. Lord Leighton, a Victorian painter of historical and exotic fantasy themes, used his imagination and the inspiration of a number of friends to create an astonishing, totally over-the-top Oriental palace here in his London home. The highlight is undoubtedly the **Arab Hall**, completed some 14 years after the rest of the house, in 1879, which has a stained-glass cupola, a fountain spurting out of the richly decorated mosaic floor, and glorious painted floral tiles which Leighton and his friends picked up in Rhodes, Cairo and Damascus. Dotted around the downstairs reception rooms, among the paintings of Leighton and his contemporaries Millais and Burne-Jones, are highly ornate details including Cairene lattice-work alcoves and marble columns decorated in burnished gold. It's the Victorian dream of Oriental exotica made flesh, a re-creation of the *Arabian Nights* in grey northern Europe. One wonders what it would have been like to live in: even Lord Leighton's studio has a gilded dome above its broad north-facing windows.

Little Venice Off maps

Tube Warwick Avenue. If you want to reach Little Venice by boat from Camden or Regent's Park, call the London Waterbus Company on t (020) 7482 2550, t 7480 2660; services run on the hour between Little Venice and Camden, April–Oct daily 10am–5pm, Nov–March Sat and Sun 10am–3pm from Little Venice, 11am–4pm from Camden Lock.

Little Venice is an unexpectedly tranquil and atmospheric corner of London, an area of tree-lined streets, understated Victorian townhouses and, above all, the canal with its colourful array of houseboats. The best way to explore it is to walk down the towpath from Regent's Park through the lower end of St John's Wood. The most colourful area is around Blomfield Road and Maida Av, where pretty iron bridges cross the canal.

Chelsea

Chelsea was an attractive riverside community long before it was integrated into Greater London. The humanist and martyr Thomas More made the district fashionable by moving here in the 1520s, and soon every courtier worth his salt, and even Henry VIII himself, was building a house near his. The attractions of this 'village of palaces' were obvious: close to Westminster and only a short boat-ride away from the City, and yet at the same time safely concealed from the general hubbub behind a large bend in the river. By the mid-19th century, Chelsea had turned into a bustling little village of intellectuals, artists, aesthetes and writers as well as the so-called Chelsea Pensioners in the Royal Hospital.

The almost rural calm of the district was shattered in the late 19th century, when big, brash building developments began to crowd out the intimate townhouses of Cheyne Walk and the streets just behind the river. The construction of the Chelsea Embankment in 1871–4 was particularly damaging, a disruption only exacerbated by the motor car. In the 1950s and 60s, Chelsea became the refuge of the dying aristocracy, as films like Joseph Losey's *The Servant* (shot in Royal Av) showed to withering effect. In the 1980s, the young of these last-ditch aristos mutated into a social animal known as the Sloane Ranger, a special kind of upper-class twit that lived off Daddy's allowance, threw food around in chic restaurants and went to the country at weekends for a spot of polo or shooting. The pre-marital Princess Diana was the prototype Sloane Ranger – giggly, not very bright and constantly on the look-out for the Ideal Husband.

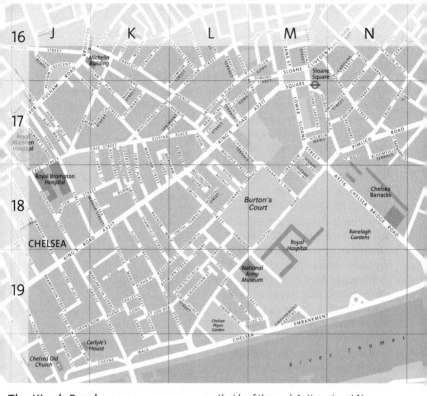

CHELSEA

Michelin Building

Royal Marsden Hospital

Royal Brompton Hospital

Burton's Court

Chelsea Barracks

Royal Hospital

Ranelagh Gardens

National Army Museum

Chelsea Physic Garden

Carlyle's House

Chelsea Old Church

River Thames

The King's Road J19–M17

Tube Sloane Square, then walk; bus 11, 22, 19, 211, 319 (from Sloane Square).

Chelsea's artistic streak flourished with a vengeance along the King's Rd in the 1960s and early 70s. Like Carnaby St in Soho, the King's Rd let its hair down and filled with cafés and fashion shops selling mini-skirts and cheap jewellery. Old-fashioned shops, including the delightfully named toilet-maker Thomas Crapper, were superseded by the likes of Terence Conran, who opened the first of his then ground-breaking chain of household stores, Habitat, opposite the Chelsea Town Hall. The **Royal Court Theatre**, on Sloane Square, came into its own as a venue for avant-garde writers like John Osborne (the original Angry Young Man), Edward Bond and Arnold Wesker. Mods, later replaced by punks, set the fashion tone for whole generations of young people.

In recent years most of the boutiques have either gone upmarket or been replaced by generic high-street chainstores. Some of the 1960s spirit lives on, however, in the delightfully sprawling **antiques markets** on the south side of the road: Antiquarius at No.137, the Chenil Galleries at Nos.181–3, and the Chelsea Antiques Market at No.253. You might also want to take a look at the **Chelsea Farmers' Market**, with its cafés and craft shops, just off the King's Road on Sydney St. Terence Conran has not abandoned the district either, expanding his restaurant empire with one knock-out location after another: at the World's End end of the street is his **Bluebird** food emporium, and a couple of blocks north of here, on the restaurant-lined Fulham Rd, is the remarkable Art Nouveau **Michelin Building** (No.61), which he renovated in the 1980s, complete with glass cupolas and mosaics, to create offices, a Conran Shop and the Bibendum restaurant.

The Royal Hospital M18–19

Royal Hospital Rd, t (020) 7881 5204; tube Sloane Square, then walk; bus 11, 19, 22, 211, 319 (from Sloane Square). Open Mon–Sat 10–noon and 2–4, Sun 2–4pm (closed Sun in winter); adm free. Museum and shop open April–Sept.

Charles II took a leaf out of Louis XIV's book and created his very own Invalides for war veterans here in Chelsea. Christopher Wren (who else?) was set to work in 1682, and 10 years later he came up with this graceful building made up of three courtyards. The **main block** to the north contains a simple panelled chapel adorned with flags captured in battle down the centuries, and a Great Hall featuring a large painting of Charles II on horseback by Antonio Verrio.

The real stars, however, are the Pensioners themselves, a 400-strong group of lucky veterans whose every need is attended to from the age of 55 or so until they die. Their day-to-day uniform is navy blue, and they wear a peaked cap inscribed with the letters RH for Royal Hospital. They are generally rather eccentric and some are very old indeed. 'I keep fit by routine,' 97-year-old Sergeant Jones once told a television reporter. 'A pint of beer mid-morning and evening, same as everyone else, and always have a bath on Monday.' On special occasions they parade in scarlet frock coats and three-cornered hats; every 29 April, for example, known as Oak Apple Day, they commemorate the Battle of Worcester, from which Charles II escaped by hiding in an oak tree, by covering his statue in the south courtyard with oak sprigs.

The highlight of a visit is the graceful **chapel**, which has barely changed since it was built in 1692. For the most part, it's elegantly restrained, with plenty of natural light pouring in through the windows (Wren didn't believe in stained glass in such a small space), but the huge, blowsy fresco of *Christ Rising from the Dead* (1710–12) strikes an almost comic note – Christ flies out of the tomb brandishing the English flag.

The gardens are used every May to host the exclusive **Chelsea Flower Show**, a week-long display of blooms and garden design which brings out the very deep-seated English love of gardening. The eastern end of the grounds leading up to Chelsea Bridge Rd, **Ranelagh Gardens**, was once the most fashionable place for a stroll in 18th-century London.

National Army Museum L–M19

Royal Hospital Rd, t (020) 7730 0717, w www .national-army-museum.ac.uk; tube Sloane Square; bus 11, 19, 22, 211, 319 (from Sloane Square); wheelchair accessible. **Open** *daily 10am–5.30pm;* **adm** *free.*

Unusually, this military museum chronicles the history of the British army from the perspective of the soldiers themselves. From the archers at the Battle of Agincourt to an abseiling SAS trouper, both the horrors and glories of war are brought to life with personal and often touching relics and exhibits: the skeleton of Napoleon's horse, Marengo; the saw used to amputate the Earl of Uxbridge's leg at Waterloo; a stuffed cat rescued from Sebastopol by a sentimental British officer. You can try on a Civil War helmet, feel the weight of a cannon ball and set yourself a computer challenge to test your skill at jungle survival.

Chelsea Physic Garden L19

Swan Walk (off Royal Hospital Rd), t (020) 7352 5646, w www.chelseaphysicgarden .co.uk; tube Sloane Square; bus 11, 19, 22, 211, 319 (from Sloane Square); wheelchair accessible. **Open** *April–Oct Sun 2–6pm;* **adm** *adults £4, children £2, free to carers and the disabled. Open throughout the year to Friends of the Garden (£12).*

This wonderfully unusual garden of rare trees, plants, herbs and seeds has a history stretching back to 1676, when it was founded by the Apothecaries' Company. The statue in the garden is of Sir Hans Sloane, the physician and philanthropist who saved it from bankruptcy in 1722. Sir Hans owned large tracts of Chelsea (hence the number of streets named after him) and built up a huge collection of art and antiquities that were bequeathed to the nation after his death and formed the basis of the British Museum.

Cheyne Walk K20

Tube Sloane Square; bus 11, 19, 22, 211, 319 (from Sloane Square).

Just behind the Chelsea Embankment are the delightful 18th-century brick houses of

Cheyne Walk, one of London's most fashionable addresses for the past 200 years. Among the famous residents have been George Eliot, who died at **No.4**; Henry James, who spent the latter years of his life in **Carlyle Mansions**, a Victorian house standing just beyond the King's Head and Eight Bells pub; Whistler, who was living at **No.101** when he produced some of his most extraordinary paintings of the Thames; Hilaire Belloc, the writer of children's cautionary tales, at **No.104**; and Turner, who used **No.119** as a retreat where he lived under the pseudonym Admiral or 'Puggy' Booth. The **Queen's House** at No.16 was shared during the 1860s by a trio of poets, Dante Gabriel Rossetti, Algernon Swinburne and George Meredith, who kept a whole bestiary of animals, including noisy peacocks that upset the neighbours no end.

Carlyle's House J20

*24 Cheyne Row, t (020) 7352 7087; **tube** Sloane Square; **bus** 11, 19, 22, 211, 319 (from Sloane Square). **Open** April–Oct Wed–Sun 11am–5pm; **adm** adults £3, children £1.75, free to members of the National Trust.*

Few houses in London evoke such a strong sense of period or personality as this red-brick Queen Anne building, where the historian Thomas Carlyle, author of *The French Revolution* and *Frederick the Great*, lived with his wife from 1834 until his death in 1881. It has been kept almost exactly as the Carlyles left it. Even the old man's hat still hangs on the peg in the entranceway. What strikes you about the place is how extraordinarily impractical it must have been. The staircases and corridors were horribly dark – an effect enhanced by the fact that electricity has never been installed – and Carlyle's study was a small windowless room at the top of the house. There was no running water on the upper floors, only a hand pump and a system of pulleys to bring buckets up. One imagines the couple, Jane Carlyle in particular, being sticklers for cleanliness, hard work and thrift.

Chelsea Old Church J20

*Old Church St (off Cheyne Walk), t (020) 7795 1019; **tube** Sloane Square; **bus** 11, 19, 22, 211, 319 (from Sloane Square); wheelchair accessible. **Open** daily 9.30–1 and 2–4.30.*

This church preserves the memory of Sir Thomas More, author of the humanist tract *Utopia* and the most famous man to lose his head for standing up to Henry VIII over his break with the Pope. The church's history goes back to Norman times, but most of it was rebuilt in classical style in the 17th century. The best-known, and oldest surviving, part is the **south chapel**, which More built in 1528 for his own private use. In the **sanctuary** is a monument to More as well as a tomb containing the remains of his first wife. He originally intended to be buried here himself, as the inscription on his monument testifies, but after his execution his head was eventually interred at Canterbury Cathedral.

Outside the church is a colourful **statue of More** (sculpted in 1969), sitting in his Lord Chancellor's robes and gazing piously across the river towards Battersea. The churchyard has been converted into a small park called Roper Gardens (after More's daughter Margaret Roper and her husband William).

Chiswick House Off maps

*Entrance on Burlington Lane, t (020) 8995 0508, **w** www.english-heritage.org.uk; **tube** Turnham Green; **train** Chiswick (from Waterloo); **bus** 267 (from Hammersmith, also past Syon Park); wheelchair accessible by prior arrangement. **Open** April–Sept daily 10am–6pm, Oct daily 10am–5pm, Nov–March Wed–Sun 10am–4pm; last adm half an hour before closing; closed first two weeks of Jan; **adm** adults £3.30, concessions £2.50, children £1.70. Audioguide, introductory video and exhibition are included in the ticket price.*

This was one of the first Palladian mansions in London, built by Lord Burlington with his friend William Kent in 1725–9. Modelled closely on Palladio's Villa Rotonda in Vicenza (which also inspired Thomas

Jefferson's Monticello), Chiswick House is built around a central octagonal room in a series of classically inspired geometric patterns, and topped by a shallow dome. The interior decorations, including some spectacular plaster ceilings and the sumptuous Blue Velvet Room, are by William Kent. Kent also helped design the garden, one of the first in England to break away from the formal Dutch style. It is packed with classical follies including an Ionic temple, a Doric column, an avenue of urns, two obelisks and statues of Caesar, Pompey and Cicero.

Syon Park Off maps

Main entrance on London Rd, with another off Park Rd near the riverfront, t (020) 8560 0881, w www.syonpark.co.uk; tube Gunnersbury, then bus 237 or 267; train Kew Bridge, then bus 237 or 267; bus 267 (from Hammersmith, also past Chiswick House); gardens wheelchair accessible only. House open March–Oct Wed, Thurs, Sun 11am–5pm, other times by arrangement; adm £6 including adm to gardens. Gardens open daily 10am–dusk.

Syon Park stretches down to the river, with a fantastic **butterfly house**, a vintage **car museum**, a **mini-zoo**, a **trout fishery**, a wholefood **shop** and a **gardening centre**, housed beneath an impressive Victorian domed conservatory made of gunmetal and Portland stone.

Syon House itself, built in crenellated stone around a quadrangle, was once part of a monastery, but was seized by Henry VIII for his own private use after his break with the Roman Church. He locked up his fifth wife, Catherine Howard, in Syon House before her execution on adultery charges. Since 1594 Syon Park has belonged to the Percy family, holders of the Duchy of Northumberland. In 1762 Robert Adam was commissioned to rework the interior, and the landscape architect Capability Brown was set to work on the grounds. The house is particularly successful, using only the bare bones of the original structure to create a sumptuous classical

atmosphere. The highlights are the Great Hall, which makes up for the unevenness of the floor with a series of small steps embellished with Doric columns, and the anteroom, which has a lavishly gilded plasterwork ceiling and a multicoloured marble floor. Osbert Sitwell said this room was 'as superb as any Roman interior in the palaces of the Caesars'.

Osterley Park House Off maps

Entrance from Jersey Rd near Osterley Tube, t (020) 8568 3164; tube Osterley; wheelchair accessible. Park open daily 9am–7.30pm; adm free. House open April–Oct Wed–Sun 1–4.30pm, last adm 4pm; closed Good Fri; adm £4.20.

About a mile to the north of Syon Park is another stately home decorated by Robert Adam. Originally the country home of Sir Thomas Gresham, the 16th-century financier and founder of the Royal Exchange, it came into its own in the 18th century when the Child banking family commissioned Adam to convert the turreted Tudor villa into a work of classical splendour. The state rooms are rich in plaster ceilings, friezes, decorated pilasters, painted ornaments and fine contemporary furniture. Horace Walpole was overwhelmed, saying the drawing room alone was 'worthy of Eve before the Fall'. The vast **gardens**, sadly cut in two by the M4 motorway, are full of old oak and cedar trees, and even a lone, very ancient mulberry. The lake is pretty in summer and has been adorned with a floating pagoda donated by a Japanese company.

Kew Off maps

Kew, like nearby Richmond, has long enjoyed royal patronage. Green, affluent and tranquil, it sits on the south bank of the Thames and seems a world away from the hubbub of the city centre. The nicest way to reach Kew is by river: there are countless river trips offered between Charing Cross or Westminster piers upriver to Hampton

Court; the journey to Kew takes about an hour and a half (*see p.71*).

Kew Gardens

Most useful entrance is Victoria Gate on Kew Rd, t (020) 8332 5000, w www.kew.org; tube Kew Gardens; train Kew Bridge (from Waterloo); bus 65, 391 (from Richmond); wheelchair accessible. Gardens open daily 9.30am–dusk; closed 1 Jan and 25 Dec; adm adults £6.50, concessions £4.50, under-16s free. Glasshouses and other buildings open daily 9.30am–5.30pm. Guided tours in the summer at 11am, 12.30pm and 2pm from Victoria Gate; call t (020) 8332 5633 in advance. Victoria Gate visitor centre stocks guidebooks and free maps. Take sturdy shoes as there are around 300 acres of gardens to explore.

The Royal Botanical Gardens at Kew have always been more than a collection of trees, flowers and plants: they are more like a giant vegetable laboratory, sucking up new information about the botanical world and, through the power of their research, influencing the course of human history in all sorts of unexpected ways. It was a commission from Kew to bring examples of breadfruit back from the South Seas that set the ill-fated HMS *Bounty* on its way to Tahiti in 1789. In the 19th century, Kew's laboratories first isolated quinine and, realizing it was an efficient natural antidote to malaria, recommended putting it in the tonic water with which the colonial administrators of India and Malaya diluted their gin. Kew was also involved in the development of commercial rubber and helped produce artificial fibres like rayon and acetate.

For the visitor, Kew is a place of many wonders: 38,000 different plant species, some of them entirely extinct in the wild; vast glasshouses showing off some of the best of Victorian architecture; historic houses and buildings including Kew Palace and the Chinese Pagoda; and, above all, acres and acres of beautifully tended parkland, some of it wonderfully wild and remote, with views up and down the Thames and across to Syon

Park on the riverbank opposite. All year round, Kew provides a glorious array of colours: flowering cherries and crocuses in spring; roses and tulip trees in summer; belladonna lilies, heather and darkening leaves in autumn; strawberry trees and witch hazels in winter.

Development

In the 18th century, Kew was part of the royal estates that stretched down as far as Richmond. Princess Augusta, the mother of George III, first had the idea of laying a botanical garden in the grounds of Kew Palace where she lived. The botanical garden was at first of only incidental importance; George III spent his energies commissioning a series of follies and outhouses from the architect William Chambers. These included three pseudo-classical temples, a ruined Roman arch, the handsome Wren-like Orangery, and – most striking of all – the Pagoda.

The botanical garden began to grow thanks to the enthusiasm of its keeper, Sir Joseph Banks, who organized Kew's first foreign plant-hunting expeditions and set about cultivating rare species. A cycad called *Encephalartos altensteinii*, which was sent to Kew from South Africa in 1775 and now sits in the Palm House, is the oldest glasshouse plant in the world. Near the Orangery is a beautiful maidenhair tree planted as far back as 1761. Banks's was nevertheless a small-scale enterprise, and Kew did not really take off until 1840, when it was handed over from the royal family to the state, opened to the public and expanded to more than 200 acres.

The first director of the new public gardens, Sir William Hooker, put Kew on a firm scientific and research footing and founded the discipline known as 'economic botany' – botany in the service of people. His most lasting architectural influence was his commission of two great glasshouses from Decimus Burton, the Palm House and the Temperate House. William Hooker's son Joseph, a veteran of plant-hunting expeditions to Antarctica, New Zealand and Nepal, took over as director in 1865 and established the Jodrell Laboratory to enhance Kew's research credentials. Since the 1970s a number of new glasshouses have been added to the garden, including the Princess of Wales Conservatory in 1985.

Around the Gardens

The **Palm House** (1844–8) is a wondrous structure of curvilinear iron and glass, reminiscent of Joseph Paxton's ill-fated Crystal Palace, with a two-storey dome as its centrepiece. It used the latest techniques of water heating and ventilation to provide a home for palms and other exotic plant life, and had the coal for its basement furnaces supplied by underground railway from the Campanile built by Decimus Burton 100 yards away to the south. Now that the Palm House basement is no longer needed for coal burning, it has been converted into a display of marine life, including algae, coral and exotic fish.

The **Temperate House**, built in the early 1860s and modified right up to 1898, is far bigger but more conventional in structure, using straight panes and iron rods to achieve its great height and width. Covering nearly 48,000 sq ft, the Temperate House is ideal for growing rare and exotic trees. Its oldest specimen is a Chilean wine palm brought to Kew as no more than a seed in 1846.

Kew Palace, an elegantly gabled two-storey Jacobean mansion, is currently closed for renovations (*closed until 2004; call Hampton Court on t (020) 8781 9500 for new opening times*). William Chambers' **Pagoda**, a ten-storey octagonal tower, was inspired by a visit to China in his youth. When finished in 1762, it was the most accurate rendering of Chinese architecture in Europe, although to be completely accurate it should have had an odd number of storeys. Queen Charlotte's pretty thatched **summer cottage** (*open April–Sept daily 10.30am–5pm; adm free*) is tucked away in the woods of the south-western section of the gardens. There's little to see inside, but the best time to visit is in spring, when it is surrounded by a thick carpet of bluebells.

To the left of the Victoria Gate is the **Marianne North Gallery**, displaying her

collection of 832 botanical paintings based on her travels around the globe between 1871 and 1885.

Since the 1970s a number of new glasshouses have been added to the garden, including, in 1985, the **Princess of Wales Conservatory** containing Kew's collection of tropical herbaceous plants, not least of which is the incredible *Titan Arum*, which at 2m high is one of the largest flowers in the world. In 1996 the *Titan* blossomed for the first time, exuding a terrible stink which clung to the clothes of photographers; since then its supposed bi-annual flowering has been a bit erratic, but rumours are still festering for a July or August blooming any year now.

Princess Anne opened the **Museum No.1** opposite the Palm House in May 1998. This is where Kew shows off its fascinating 'economic botanic collection' of wood and plant materials which have been made into useful materials for man – a 200-year-old shirt made out of pineapple fibres from the Caribbean, an incredible collection of Japanese lacquer boxes, a fishing net collected by explorer David Livingstone, and a walking stick brought home by Kew's own Sir Joseph Banks. After a recent refurbishment, it's now got an interactive 'Plants and People' exhibition which is a big hit with kids. It shows how people rely on plants for all sorts of surprising reasons, from weapons to medicine and personal hygiene.

Kew Bridge Steam Museum

Green Dragon Lane, t (020) 8568 4757, w www.kbsm.org; tube Gunnersbury, then bus 237 or 267; train Kew Bridge; mostly wheelchair accessible. Open daily 11am–5pm; closed Christmas week and Good Fri; adm adults £4, concessions £2, children £2, families £7; adm drops one pound during the week. Shop and café (weekends only).

An exhibition of functioning steam pumps in an old Victorian water-pumping works, complete with tall brick chimney and a new exhibition on water and public sanitation with 'lucky holes' for viewing the London sewer system.

Richmond Off maps

Tube Richmond; train Richmond (from Waterloo); boat trips (see p.71); bus 65, 391 (from Kew).

Richmond is a tranquil, affluent riverside community of attractive Georgian and neo-Georgian houses, flanked on all sides by wide expanses of greenery – Kew Gardens and the Old Deer Park golf course to the north, Marble Hill Park across the river in Twickenham, and Richmond Park to the south and east. On a sunny day it is an ideal place to walk along the river.

In medieval times, the focal point of the district was Shene Palace, a relatively modest manor house used as a lodge for hunting in the surrounding hills. All that remains is a **stone gateway** off Richmond Green, bearing Henry VII's coat of arms, and the **palace wardrobe**, or household office, to the left just inside Old Palace Yard. In Old Palace Yard is **Trumpeters' House**, an elegant mansion built by a pupil of Christopher Wren. Further fine Georgian houses are to be found in all the neighbouring streets, such as **Old Palace Terrace** and **Maids of Honour Row**. Today, as ever, the biggest attraction of Richmond is the riverside, which boasts, amongst other things, the elegant five-arched **Richmond Bridge** dating from the 1770s.

Richmond Park

Bus 371 (from Richmond Station). Open March–Sept 7am–dusk, Oct–Feb 7.30am–dusk.

At 2,470 acres, Richmond Park is the largest urban park in Britain and one of the least spoilt in London. A few medieval oaks survive, as do many of the varieties of wildlife that medieval royal parties hunted. The **deer** are what make Richmond Park famous – around 350 fallow deer and 250 red deer, which do so well in the heart of London that there is an annual cull – but there are also hares, rabbits, weasels and parakeets (*see* above). Richmond Park also has two ponds for anglers, five cricket pitches, two golf courses, no fewer than 24 football grounds and numerous cycle paths.

The Parakeets of Richmond Park

It's not just an urban myth: there really are flocks of green parakeets in Richmond Park, and in parks throughout southwest and southeast London. The birds are in fact the ring-necked parakeet (*Psittacula krameri*), the world's most common parrot. The birds' arrival is the subject of several urban myths, involving their having escaped about 30 years ago from quarantine at Heathrow or from a film set at Shepperton Studios. But the birds were in fact first seen in Britain in 1855, although they appear to have then died out and only re-established themselves around 1970. At the moment their presence seems limited to Greater London, but they're breeding, have no natural predators and can live to be as old as 20 – there were 2,000 to 3,000 in 1997 but that figure may now have doubled. Ornithologists are concerned that the birds could grow to be a major pest if they establish themselves in agricultural areas, as they feed on crops. Strange but true.

Ham House

Ham St, t (020) 8940 1950, e shhgen@smtp .ntrust.org.uk; bus 65, 371 (from Richmond Station); ferry to Marble Hill (see below); wheelchair accessible by prior arrangement. Grounds open Sat–Wed 11am–6pm; adm free. House open April–Oct Sat–Wed 1–5pm; tearoom open Sat and Sun 11am–4pm; adm adults £6, concessions and children £3, families £15, free to members of the National Trust. Lecture lunches and recitals all year; call for details. Shop and restaurant open all year.

Ham House is one of the grandest surviving Jacobean mansions in London, a magnificent three-storey red-brick house that has recently been restored to something approaching its original splendour. Built in 1610 and nicknamed the 'sleeping beauty' for its tranquil position, it became the home of William Murray, a friend of Charles I, who as a child had acted as the future king's whipping boy: when Charles was naughty, he was the one who was beaten.

The highlight is the **Great Hall**, a wonderfully airy room decorated in blue, with a gallery overlooking the black and white checked floor. The rest of the house boasts a profusion of tapestries, velvet drapes, and plaster ornamentation on the staircases and ceilings. The **gardens** have retained their original 17th-century formal layout; the hedges and trees conceal the house from the river, lending an air of mystery and anticipated pleasure as you approach from the ferry stop. In 2001, a delightful 18th-century **dairy** was opened to the public; even the marble slabs are supported by cast-iron cows' legs. It will be the site of an introductory video to the house from late 2002, when visitors to the restaurant will also be able to taste the products of the new 17th-century kitchen garden.

Twickenham Off maps

Marble Hill House

Richmond Rd, **t** *(020) 8892 5115,* **w** *www .english-heritage.org.uk;* **train** *St Margaret's (from Waterloo or Victoria);* **bus** *33, 90, 290, R68, R70 (from Richmond Station);* **ferry** *(a one-man company, Hammerton's,* **t** *(020) 8892 9620; Feb–Oct daily, Nov–Jan Sat and Sun) for foot passengers only from Ham House to Marble Hill (adults 50p, children and bikes 30p); ground floor wheelchair accessible.* **Open** *April–Sept daily 10am–6pm, Oct daily 10am–5pm, Nov–Mar Wed–Sun 10am–4pm; closed 24–26 Dec;* **adm** *adults £3.30, concessions £2.50, children £1.30. For* **concert** *tickets, contact IMG on* **t** *(020) 8233 7435,* **w** *www.picnicconcerts.com.*

This simple white Palladian villa was built in 1729 for Henrietta Howard, the 'exceedingly respectable and respected' mistress of George II. The house is rather empty, having been neglected for 200 years and stripped of most of its furniture. But the park is open and very green, affording a broad view of the river. A series of annual open-air concerts is staged here every summer; it is a delightful venue when the weather holds.

Orleans House

Orleans Rd, **t** *(020) 8892 0221,* **e** *leisure@ richmond.go.uk,* **w** *www.guidetorichmond .co.uk/orleans.html; for transport, see 'Marble Hill House', above; partly wheelchair accessible.* **Open** *Tues–Sat 1–5.30pm, Sun and bank hols 2–5.30pm (Nov–March closes at 4.30pm); closed Good Fri and 24–26 Dec;* **adm** *free.* **Shop**.

Twickenham was briefly fashionable at the turn of the 19th century as a refuge for royalists fleeing the French Revolution. One, the Duke of Orléans, later King Louis Philippe, set up home next to Marble Hill Park in Orleans House and lived there from 1800 to 1817. The house, attractively set in a woodland garden, had been built a century earlier for one of William III's ministers. Its best feature, and the only one to survive, is James Gibbs's Neoclassical **Octagon Room**, which has some fine plasterwork and a black and white checked floor now used as an outsize chess board. The room, plus a modern extension, has been turned into an art gallery with a variety of temporary exhibitions including contemporary crafts.

Strawberry Hill

Waldegrave Rd; **train** *Strawberry Hill (from Waterloo);* **bus** *33 (from Richmond).* **Open** *April–Oct Sun 2pm for 90min guided tours, and by appointment the rest of the year on* **t** *(020) 8240 4224;* **adm** *adults £5, concessions £4.25.*

This is generally believed to be the earliest building of the Gothic Revival in England. For 50 years after he bought the property in 1749, Horace Walpole set about building what he himself termed 'a little plaything of a house, the prettiest bauble you ever did see'. He stole ideas and ornaments from any Gothic source he could lay his hands on – exterior battlements, Tudor chimneys, quatrefoil windows and fireplaces based on archbishops' tombs. For the Long Gallery he copied the fan-vaulted ceiling of the Henry VII chapel at Westminster Abbey. Much altered, Strawberry Hill is now a Roman Catholic college called St Mary's.

Rugby Football Museum

Rugby Rd Stadium, t (020) 8892 2000,
e museum@rfu.com, w www.rfu.com;
train Twickenham (from Waterloo or Victoria);
wheelchair accessible. Open Tues–Sat
10am–5pm, Sun 2–5pm, on match days 11am
until kick off and for one hour after the game;
adm adults £4, concessions £3, joint price for
museum and stadium tour, adults £6, conces-
sions £4, families £19. Shop and café.

The museum offers a guided tour of the
changing rooms and field, a history of the
game and an array of trophies.

Hampton Court
Palace Off maps

Hampton Court, t (020) 8781 9500,
w www.hrp.org; train Hampton Court (from
Waterloo); river trips (see p.71); bus R68 (from
Richmond via Marble Hill), 267 (via Syon Park
and Chiswick House, May–Sept Sun only);
wheelchair accessible. Open 25 March–
27 Oct Mon 10.15am–6pm, Tues–Sun 9.30am–
6pm, 28 Oct–24 March Mon 10.15am–4.30pm,
Tues–Sun 9.30am–4.30pm; last adm 45mins
before closing; closed 24–26 Dec; adm adults
£11, concessions £8.25, 5–16s £7.25, families £33;
joint tickets with Tower of London available.
Free audioguide, orientation tours and
costumed guided tours. Gardens open daily
7am–dusk.

Hampton Court Palace is one of the finest
Tudor buildings in England, a place that
magnificently evokes the haphazard pleasures and cruel intrigues of Henry VIII's court.
We are lucky to have it. Oliver Cromwell
meant to sell off its treasures and let it go to
pieces, but then fell in love with it and
decided to live there himself. Christopher
Wren intended to raze it to build a new
palace; only money problems and the death
of Queen Mary prevented him from wreaking
more damage than he did. He replaced many
of the original Tudor features with a boring
series of royal apartments built in the same
workaday, if well-proportioned, style that he
adopted for his legal buildings at Middle

Temple and Lincoln's Inn. Now Hampton
Court is, stylistically speaking, a palace at war
with itself; Wren's classicism sits awkwardly
in its Tudor surroundings, the result of a
hostile but unsuccessful takeover bid.

A Chronological Tour

Hampton Court started as the power base
of Henry VIII's most influential minister.
Cardinal Thomas Wolsey bought the property from the Knights of St John in 1514, one
year before he became Lord Chancellor of
England. As his influence grew, so did the
palace: at its zenith it contained 280 rooms
and kept a staff of 500 busy, constantly
entertaining dignitaries from around Europe.
Seeing the grandeur to which his chief
minister was rapidly allowing himself to
become accustomed, Henry VIII grew
nervous and threatened to knock Wolsey off
his high perch. Wolsey responded in panic by
offering Hampton Court to the monarch;
Henry at first snubbed him by refusing to
take up residence there. Wolsey was then
given the impossible task of asking the Pope
to grant Henry a divorce from his wife,
Catherine of Aragon. When he failed, his
possessions were seized by the Crown and he
was arrested for high treason. It seems
Hampton Court haunted him to the end. All
his life, Wolsey had refused to set foot in
Kingston, the town across the river from the
palace, in the belief that it would bring him
bad luck. As he lay on his deathbed in
Leicester, he found out to his consternation
that the constable of the Tower of London
where he was headed was a certain
Mr Kingston.

Henry first got interested in Hampton
Court as a love nest for himself and his new
flame, Anne Boleyn. The two of them moved
here even before Henry had annulled his first
marriage, and they set about effacing every
possible trace of Wolsey. They removed his
coat-of-arms, since restored, from the main
entrance arch and renamed it **Anne Boleyn's
Gateway** – a magnificent red-brick structure
with octagonal towers at either end. In 1540,
Henry added a remarkable **astronomical**

clock, and renamed the main courtyard within Clock Court.

Hampton Court was where Henry retreated to block out the dark consequences of his bruising politics. While Thomas More, the main opponent to Henry's break with the Catholic Church, languished in the Tower on the night before his execution in 1535, Henry was living it up at his new palace watching Anne Boleyn dance her heart out. More predicted, with devastating accuracy: 'These dances of hers will prove such dances that she will spin our heads off like footballs, but it will not be long ere her head will dance the like dance.' Anne lasted just one year before succumbing to the intrigues at Hampton Court and ending up on an executioner's block on trumped-up charges of adultery. Henry did not seem unduly perturbed, and the night after her death he supped at Hampton Court with his prospective third wife, Jane Seymour, wearing a feather in his cap.

The mid-1530s were Hampton Court's heyday. Henry built the **Great Hall**, with its 60ft-high hammerbeam roof and its stained-glass windows, amended right up to the end of his life to include the crests of each of his wives, even the ones he executed. The king also established the gardens, planting trees and shrubs, notably in the **Pond Garden**, and built a **real tennis court** (*closed in winter*) which still survives in the outhouses at the northeastern end of the palace. Hampton Court began to turn sour for him after Jane Seymour died in 1538 giving birth to his much anticipated son and heir, Edward. Thereafter Henry grew cantankerous and paranoid, a mood not exactly lifted when he began suffering from ulcerations in his legs and found it difficult to walk. Edward led the greater part of his unhappy short life at Hampton Court; it is said that his mother's ghost appears occasionally on the east side of Clock Court, dressed in white and holding a lighted taper.

For a century after Henry's death, Hampton Court continued to thrive. The Great Hall became a popular theatrical venue, and the state rooms were filled with fine paintings, gold-encrusted tapestries, musical instruments and ornaments. Charles I built the gardens' fountains and lakes as well as the long waterway, cut to provide the palace with water at the expense of local communities. Charles also accumulated a vast **collection of art** including the wonderfully restored *Triumph of Caesar* series by Mantegna, which hangs in its own gallery at the south end of the palace.

By the time William and Mary came to the throne, appreciation of Tudor architecture had waned. The apartments at Hampton Court were considered old-fashioned and uncomfortable, and Christopher Wren was drafted in to build a new palace to rival Louis XIV's extravaganza at Versailles – a project that, perhaps fortunately, never saw the light of day. The bulk of Wren's work is at the eastern end of the palace and centres on the cloisters of **Fountain Court**. The new apartments were decorated by the likes of Antonio Verrio, James Thornhill, Grinling Gibbons and Jean Tijou in sumptuous but stilted fashion; the **Chapel Royal** was also rebuilt, with only the Tudor vaulted ceiling surviving.

The best work carried out under William III was in the **gardens**, notably the lines of yew trees along the narrow strips of water, the herb garden (now beautifully restored) and the famous **maze**. Originally the maze was a religious penance to impress upon ordinary mortals the labyrinthine complications of a life in the service of Christ. Now it is an enormously popular diversion, particularly for children too small to peer over the hedges.

Once you've had your fill of the palace, there's a lovely walk beside the **river**, where you can also hire rowing boats.

Outside the Centre: South London

North Londoners rarely venture south of the river, but there's plenty to entice them – and more is springing up all the time, from the psychedelic new Fashion and Textile Museum to the vast glassy 'testicle' being built to house London's mayor. Downriver is the gracious maritime village of Greenwich, spliced by the Meridian line; to the south is the light-filled, elegant picture gallery in Dulwich, and the Wimbledon Lawn Tennis Museum, where you can find out exactly how many strawberries are eaten every year at the celebrated tennis tournament.

For an overview of South London, *see* the map on p.234.

Lambeth

In popular folklore, Lambeth is known for spawning the word 'hooligan' (the Fagin-like pickpocket Patrick Houlihan, also called Hooligan, thrived here in the 1890s along with his band of young apprentices) and for inspiring the famous music-hall number 'Doing the Lambeth Walk', which comes from Lupino Lane's folklore musical about Cockney life, *Me and My Girl.* You can still visit Lambeth Walk, a quiet street market off Lambeth Rd near the junction with Kennington Rd, although the Victorian music halls that used to thrive here are long gone.

Imperial War Museum Off maps
*Lambeth Rd, **t** (020) 7416 5000, **w** www.iwm .org.uk; **tube** Lambeth North, Elephant and Castle; wheelchair accessible. **Open** daily 10am–6pm; closed 24–26 Dec; **adm** free. **Giftshop** and café.*

Until the First World War this was the site of the notorious Bethlehem Royal Hospital for the Insane, better known as Bedlam, where inmates were kept like zoo animals in cages and cells. In the 17th and 18th centuries the public was admitted free of charge to laugh at the lunatics, a barbaric practice that was curbed when it emerged that the king himself, George III, was going mad. The building is now used to illustrate Britain's wartime experiences from 1914 to the present day.

Despite the intimidating pair of artillery cannon at the entrance, this museum does everything it can to illustrate the human side of war, not just the military hardware. Certainly there are plenty of Zeppelins and Cruise missile launchers along with lashings of patriotic fervour, but there are also sound and light shows illustrating the terrors and privations of life in a First World War trench, exhibits on rationing and air raids, and artworks including Henry Moore's drawings of London during the Blitz. A new five-storey extension was opened in June 2000, dedicated primarily to the **Holocaust**. This is a harrowing but excellent exhibition which was four years in the making; it focuses primarily on the Jews of Europe, but the stories of the Romanies, Soviet POWs, prisoners of conscience and disabled and homosexual victims are also recounted.

In the basement of the main building a **clock** counts down the lives which have been lost in wars all over the world, a number which currently increases at the rate of two per minute and reached a sickening 100 million at the turn of the millennium.

Lambeth Palace V15
*Lambeth Palace Rd; **tube** Waterloo. Currently closed to the public.*

Lambeth Palace, the Archbishop of Canterbury's official residence, dates back to 1190 but was largely rebuilt in neo-Gothic style by Edward Blore in the 19th century. The most interesting visible feature is the red-brick Tudor gatehouse, completed in 1501.

Museum of Garden History V15
*Parish Church of St Mary-at-Lambeth, Lambeth Palace Rd, **t** (020) 7401 8865; **tube** Waterloo; wheelchair accessible. **Open** March–mid-Dec Sun–Fri 10.30am–5pm; **adm** free. **Shop** and café.*

The plants on display here were first gathered by Charles I's gardener John Tradescant, who is buried in the church with his son. You can also see **gardening tools** dating back to the ancient world. The **church**, largely rebuilt in 1852 but still based on its 14th-century predecessor, is curious for other reasons too:

it contains the only full-immersion font in London, and is the last resting place of Captain Bligh, of *Mutiny on the Bounty* fame. In the south chapel is a stained-glass window commemorating a medieval pedlar who grew rich when his dog unearthed great treasure while scratching around one day on a piece of wasteland in the area. The pedlar left an acre of land to the parish when he died, but asked for the window for him and his dog in return. The intricate little '**knot garden**' is surrounded by benches – a delightful oasis for when museum fever sets in.

Florence Nightingale Museum V13
*St Thomas's Hospital (entrance on the right as you go in), **t** (020) 7620 0374, **w** www .florence-nightingale.co.uk; **tube** Waterloo, Westminster; wheelchair accessible. **Open** Mon–Fri 10am–5pm, Sat, Sun and most bank hols 11.30am–4.30pm, last adm one hour before; **adm** adults £4.80, concessions and children £3.60, families £10.*

You won't learn much more about the founder of modern nursing here than at the Old Operating Theatre (*see* p.211), but the museum nevertheless builds up a vivid image of her life and times. Here are the letters, childhood books and personal trophies that the 'Lady with the Lamp' brought back from the Crimean War. You can also see a reconstructed ward from the Crimea, contemporary nurses' uniforms and some of the equipment they used.

'Pool of London' Map pp.280–81

For sights in nearby Southwark, *see* pp.204–12.

The London Dungeon DD12
*28–34 Tooley St, **t** (020) 7403 7221, **w** www.the dungeons.com; **tube** London Bridge; wheelchair accessible. **Open** daily 10am–5.30pm, last adm 4.30pm; closed 25 Dec; **adm** adults £11.95, concessions £10.50, 4–14s (must be accompanied by an adult) £7.95.*

'Enter at your peril,' says the sign above the door. It is an appropriate warning for a museum that strives to make a spectator sport out of medieval torture but can only manage the ketchup-splattered inauthenticity of a Hammer horror movie. There is scarcely a genuine historical artefact in the place: it is all bad waxworks, for which no amount of ghoulish music or spooky lighting can compensate. Go to the Clink (*see* p.208) instead.

HMS *Belfast* DD11
*Morgan's Lane, off Tooley St, **t** (020) 7940 6300, **w** www.iwm.org.uk/belfast; **tube** London Bridge; quarterdeck, boat deck and café wheelchair accessible. **Open** March–Oct daily 10am–6pm, Nov–Feb daily 10am–5pm; last adm 45mins earlier; closed 24–26 Dec; **adm** adults £4.70, concessions £3.60, under-16s free.*

A bit of a special interest item, this. The *Belfast* was built in 1938, saw active service throughout the Second World War, took part in the D-Day landings and was 'saved for the nation' in 1971. You are free to roam its seven floors and admire its gun turrets, instrument decks and boiler room. If you've ever seen one of those old stiff-upper-lip British war films like *The Cruel Sea*, you won't need any introduction. If you are one of those people who starts behaving like a six-year-old at the sight of military hardware, then this will be right up your alley. If not, the experience falls somewhat short of a thrill a minute.

Fashion and Textile Museum DD13
*83 Bermondsey St, **t** (020) 7403 0222, **f** 7403 0555; **tube** London Bridge; wheelchair accessible. **Café** and **giftshop**.*

The former warehouses and factories which line Bermondsey St are now loft-apartments; the area's rapid regeneration is partly due to the startling pink and orange Modernist building which has been dropped into the middle of it. This is the new Fashion Museum, conceived by the equally colourful fashion designer Zandra Rhodes and due to open to the public at the end of 2002.

The GLA Building Off maps
***Tube** Tower Hill, London Bridge, Bermondsey.*
London's Mayor, Ken Livingstone (better known to the tabloids as 'Red Ken'), and the

Greater London Authority are soon to be housed in the gleaming building which is rising at an astonishing pace next to Tower Bridge. It has already been nicknamed the 'Testicle' thanks to its odd, elliptical shape. The councils of London's 33 boroughs have local responsibilities, but the GLA and the Mayor deal with strategic issues which affect London as a whole. The complex will include housing, shops and restaurants and is set to be completed in 2003.

Design Museum Off maps

28 Shad Thames, t (020) 7940 8790, w www .designmuseum.org; tube Tower Hill, London Bridge, Bermondsey; wheelchair accessible. Open daily 11.30am–6pm, last adm 5.15pm; closed 24–26 Dec; adm adults £5.50, concessions and children £4, families £16. Temporary exhibitions, café, the Conran-owned Blueprint Café and an excellent giftshop.

The museum's abiding and always thought-provoking theme is the aesthetics of mass-produced objects. The car, the record-player, the telephone, the vacuum cleaner are all here, and their design history is lovingly traced from the 1920s to the present day. The museum also hosts temporary exhibitions on contemporary design issues and well-known movements such as Bauhaus. The museum shop tries to keep up with what's most practical, aesthetic and outlandish in 21st-century design.

As recently as the 1950s, **Butler's Wharf** was a hive of trade in commodities from tea and coffee to rubber, spices, wines and spirits. The rise of container shipping sounded the wharf's death knell; now it's a chi-chi little enclave of expensive restaurants (mostly part of the Conran empire), fabulously expensive apartments, and smart boutiques.

Rotherhithe Off maps

Tube Rotherhithe; bus P11 (from Waterloo Station and London Bridge).

Rotherhithe was one of the places from which the Pilgrim Fathers set out for America in the *Mayflower* in 1620. You might think

hordes of Americans would come to pay homage to their forefathers, but in fact Rotherhithe is a delightfully unspoilt, relatively unknown part of riverside London and one of the most successful of the Docklands redevelopments. The old warehouses have been repaired but not tarted up, and the streets have been kept narrow.

The departure of the Pilgrim Fathers is commemorated in the **Mayflower pub**, at 117 Rotherhithe St, which is partly built out of the broken-up segments of the original ship and has a model of the vessel hanging outside its front door. Because of its tourist clientèle, the pub is allowed to sell postage stamps. This was probably the tavern where Captain Christopher Jones and his crew spent the night before their departure for the Americas. Within two years, the ship came back from its expedition, and Jones was eventually buried, along with the three co-owners of the *Mayflower*, in the churchyard of **St Mary's** opposite. The church itself, which was attractively rebuilt in the 18th century, contains a plaque to Jones as well as remains of the *Fighting Téméraire*, the man-of-war whose demise was captured by Turner in his famous painting (in the National Gallery).

Greenwich Map opposite

Ferries and cruise boats run from Waterloo, Embankment, Tower and Westminster piers; tube North Greenwich (for the Dome), then bus 188, M2 into town; DLR Greenwich, Greenwich Cutty Sark; train (from Charing Cross, Waterloo East, Cannon St and London Bridge) Greenwich (from the station's main entrance turn left into Greenwich High Rd and it's three minutes to the centre), Maze Hill (for the National Maritime Museum); bus 188 (from Waterloo and Bermondsey); walk through the tunnel from the Isle of Dogs. Tourist office: Pepys Building, 2 Cutty Sark Gardens, t 0870 608 2000, for excellent information and guided walks.

Greenwich has been a place of pleasure since the 15th century, when Henry V's brother, Duke Humphrey of Gloucester, built

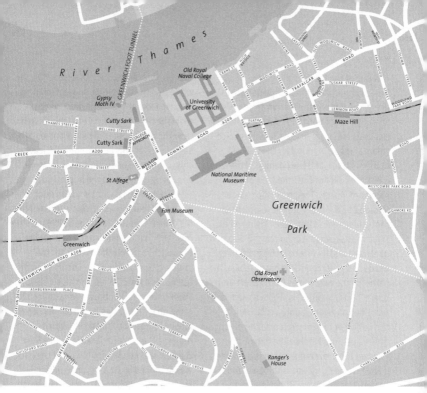

the first royal palace. While neighbouring districts like Deptford and Woolwich have always had to live by their wits and the hard graft of building and unloading ships, Greenwich has concentrated on idle pleasures like hunting and jousting, or rarefied pursuits like astronomy. Thanks to the contributions of Jones, Wren, Hawksmoor and Vanbrugh, it also boasts a remarkable architectural heritage, evident from the moment you look up from the ferry pier. In the foreground is Wren's Royal Naval College, once a hospital for retired seamen; behind it is the Queen's House, the first of Inigo Jones's experiments in Palladianism; and behind that, up on the hill in the park, is Wren's Royal Observatory with its elegant octagonal central tower.

Duke Humphrey's palace, Bella Court, was replaced by a fine red-brick construction named Placentia in 1427. It was popular with the royal family because of the excellent hunting in the forests behind. Henry VIII was born at Greenwich and, after a boyhood spent jousting, hunting and attending pageants, never lost affection for the place. The latter half of Henry's reign, when

Hampton Court took over as the 'in' palace, saw a decline at Greenwich. But Queen Elizabeth I liked the place; it was here that Sir Walter Raleigh magnanimously threw his cloak on a 'plashy place' (a puddle) so Her Majesty would not get her feet muddy. Placentia survived until the Civil War, when the Parliamentarians used it to stable their horses. But it was the Stuarts who breathed new life into Greenwich with the fine buildings we see today.

A good day to visit Greenwich is the weekend, when the market is in full swing.

The *Cutty Sark* and the *Gipsy Moth*

*By Greenwich Pier, **t** (020) 8858 3445, **w** www.cuttysark.org.uk; **DLR** Greenwich Cutty Sark (see main Greenwich entry); main exhibition wheelchair accessible. **Cutty Sark open** April–Sept Mon–Sat 10am–6pm, Sun noon–6pm, Oct–March 10am–5pm, Sun noon–5pm; **adm** £3.50. Gipsy Moth IV closed to the public.*

Much is made of the **Cutty Sark** as the last of the great tea clippers that plied the route from England to the Far East. Built in 1869, it was one of the fastest sailing ships of its time, winning the annual clippers' race in 1871 when it made the journey from Shanghai to London in 107 days. Its commercial usefulness was limited, however, since steam ships soon took over the bulk of maritime trade, and the opening of the Suez Canal took a lot of the time pressure off merchant vessels. The greatest pleasure afforded by the *Cutty Sark* now is its magnificent gilded teak fittings, the rigging on its three masts (capable of holding 30,000 sq ft of canvas) and its fine collection of figureheads and other maritime memorabilia. The name, by the way, comes from Robert Burns' poem 'Tam O'Shanter', in which a witch is described as wearing only a cutty sark, a corruption of the French *courte chemise*, or 'short shirt'. You'll notice the female figurehead on the prow is dressed in this manner.

Next to the *Cutty Sark* is the **Gipsy Moth IV**, the ketch in which the British mariner Sir Francis Chichester made his solo round-the-world voyage in 1966–7, completing the trip in nine months and one day. That may not sound very impressive in these days of hi-tech boats and 80-day circumnavigations of the globe, but back in the 1960s the feat made Chichester famous, especially as he was 66 years old at the time, and earned him the distinction of being knighted with the same sword that Elizabeth I used to honour her great sea captain Francis Drake.

The Old Royal Naval College

King William Walk, recorded information **t** *0800 389 3341,* **w** *www.greenwichfoundation.org.uk;* **transport** *see main Greenwich entry; wheelchair accessible by prior arrangement.* **Chapel and Painted Hall open** *Mon–Sat 10am–5pm, Sun 12.30–5pm, last adm at 4.15pm;* **adm** *adults £3, concessions £2, under-16s free, free Sun and after 3.30pm.*

The Royal Naval College is on the site of the old Palace of Placentia (*see* 'Greenwich', above). Charles II's first thought when he restored the monarchy was to rebuild Placentia, but he didn't have the money and gave up soon after the foundation stone was laid. Queen Mary had another idea after she witnessed the terrible wounds inflicted on British sailors at the battle of La Hogue in 1692: she commissioned Christopher Wren to clear the ruins of the old palace and build a naval hospital. This he promptly did, leaving only a Jacobean undercroft, used for wine and coal storage, from the original structure.

Mary and Wren did not enjoy an altogether happy collaboration, since Mary insisted that the Queen's House should be visible from the river, and that the path of the Deptford to Woolwich road, which ran through the middle of the building site, should be undisturbed. As a result, Wren and his successors, Hawksmoor and Vanbrugh, were obliged to come up with a design based on four separate buildings. The final result, with its majestic Neoclassical façades overlooking the river and pepper-pot towers at the back, was described by Dr Johnson as admirable but 'too much detached to make one great whole'. The naval pensioners grew to dislike it, too, though not for its architecture so much as the corruption of its administrators. 'Columns, colonnades and friezes ill accord with bully beef and sour beer mixed with water,' complained one Captain Baillie in 1771. The hospital was eventually closed, and the Royal Naval College, which had been based in Portsmouth, moved here in 1873, where it remained until the late 1990s. In 1999, the University of Greenwich successfully negotiated to take 150-year leases on Queen Anne Court, Queen Mary Court and King William Court. The remaining building, King Charles Court, was let to Trinity College of Music.

The Chapel and Painted Hall

Only the Chapel and Painted Hall are open to the public and remain in the possession of the Greenwich Foundation for the Royal Naval College. The university hopes to open some other parts of the building, but plans are as yet undecided. The **Chapel** is based on a design by Wren, but was entirely refurbished by James Stuart after a fire in 1779. It has an intricate plaster-moulded ceiling, and a fine painting of *St Paul at Melita* by Benjamin West above the altar.

The **Painted Hall** is a magnificent ensemble of three rooms painted in opulent style by James Thornhill, the man who also decorated the cupola of St Paul's. Greenwich is the overall theme, whether expressed in allegorical depictions of warships, or in portraits of the great astronomers – Tycho Brahe, Newton and the first Astronomer Royal, John Flamsteed. The culmination of Thornhill's work is the rather absurdly patriotic ceiling in the first of the rooms, the Great Hall, which shows William and Mary, all temperance and dignity, handing a cap of liberty to the prostrate figure of a conquered Europe. Thornhill was paid £1 per foot for the walls and £3 per foot for the ceilings, so he can't have done badly out of it. Nevertheless, he painted a rather tongue-in-cheek self-portrait at the foot of one of the walls with one hand held out – presumably for more money.

The Queen's House and the National Maritime Museum

Trafalgar Road, t (020) 8858 4422, w www.nmm.ac.uk; transport see main Greenwich entry; wheelchair accessible. Open daily 10am–5pm; adm free.

The **Queen's House** was Inigo Jones's first experiment in Palladian architecture after his return from Italy in 1615. James I's wife, Anne of Denmark, was the queen in question, who wanted her own private villa as an extension to the Palace of Placentia. For years after Anne's death in 1619 the house languished unfinished, but the project was taken up again by Queen Henrietta Maria in 1629. So happy was she with the final result, completed in 1640, that she nicknamed it her 'house of delights' and returned to live in it as the Queen Mother after the Restoration. The building is a textbook exercise in Palladian classicism – simple and sober on the outside, and full of 'licentious imaginacy', as Jones put it, on the inside. We can't entirely appreciate Jones's intentions, since his original H-shape was filled in with the addition of a couple of first-floor rooms in 1662. Not all the interior decoration was completed by the time of the Civil War, and

many of the fittings that were already in place – including paintings by Rubens, Raphael and Van Dyck – were sold off by the Roundheads. Much of the decay that the Queen's House suffered in the 18th and 19th centuries has been reversed, however, thanks to a recent restoration, bringing the building back to something close to its 1660s state.

The centrepiece is the **Great Hall**, a perfect 40ft cube immediately inside the main entrance, with an elegant gallery at first-floor level. At first sight it looks as though the original ceiling fresco, *The Arts of Peace* by Gentileschi, has been re-instated after a long exile at Marlborough House. In fact it is a computer-enhanced photographic copy: the original can't be moved back because bits of it are missing. What is genuine is the **Tulip Staircase** at the eastern end of the hall, a wrought-iron helix staircase which twists its way up to the Queen's Bedroom. This was the first open-well staircase to be built in England, or as Jones put it, the first with 'a vacuum in ye middle'. The floral decorations on its banister are not in fact tulips but fleurs-de-lys in honour of Henrietta Maria, who was daughter of Henry IV of France.

The Queen's House is now at the centre of the **National Maritime Museum**, whose side wings are connected to the main house by colonnades constructed in 1807 to commemorate Nelson's victory over the French at Trafalgar two years earlier. It recently reopened after a £20,000,000 overhaul and is now one of the most up-to-date museums in the UK. A whole floor is devoted to interactive learning, ostensibly for kids, but everyone seems to enjoy shooting water pistols or blowing hair-dryers at model ships. The courtyard has been glassed over and airily accommodates 16 new galleries with the larger exhibits: an enormous propeller, a container, even a yacht. Historical memorabilia, particularly that of Napoleon's era, still feature, but the focus has shifted from past history to an engagingly energetic portrayal of the high-tech world of modern shipping.

One gallery is devoted to **Nelson**: the uniform in which he was killed at Trafalgar, his watch, his shoe buckles, his stockings and his chair. Pictures depict episodes of his life, including a rather touching one of him as a 15-year-old midshipman trying to kill a polar bear with his musket. Nelson planned to claim the hide as a trophy to give to his father, but his musket jammed and only a cannon blast fired by one of his shipmates saved him from a mauling.

Among the many **paintings** are a vast Venetian School depiction of *The Battle of Lepanto* (1571), and Turner's account of Trafalgar, called *Victory*. The only note of humour is struck in Hogarth's portrait of *George Graham*, commander of the warship *Bridgewater*: in the background you can see the cook spilling his brew down the ship chaplain's neck.

St Alfege

Greenwich Church St, t (020) 8853 2703, w www.st-alfege.org; transport see main Greenwich entry; wheelchair accessible by prior arrangement.

Greenwich's first mention in the history books was in 1011 when invading Danes kidnapped Alfege, Archbishop of Canterbury, and held him to ransom for 3,000 pieces of silver. Alfege refused to let the ransom be paid, and after a year in captivity he was beaten to death with the left-over bones of the Danes' feasts. He was canonized for his pains, and commemorated at this church. Unfortunately, the church has not had much more luck than poor Alfege himself. First consecrated soon after its namesake's death, it was rebuilt twice during the Middle Ages and again, after the nave fell in, in 1712–18 by Nicholas Hawksmoor. Hawksmoor's thick **columns** and **pediment** topped with urns have survived, but the interior had to be completely overhauled after the church was bombed in the Blitz. Only the gilded wrought-iron **altar railings** by Jean Tijou have survived intact. A sinister story is of a 17th-century woman who used to stand throughout Sunday service with a sign saying: 'I stand here for the sin of fornication.' Nobody ever found out who she was.

The Fan Museum

12 Croom's Hill, t (020) 8305 1441, w www.fan-museum.org; transport see main Greenwich entry; wheelchair accessible. Open Tues–Sat 11am–5pm, Sun noon–5pm; adm adults £3.50, concessions £2.50, under-7s free. Tea served Tues and Sun. Shop.

This is a delightful collection of 2,000 fans from the 17th century to the present, housed in two immaculate Georgian houses. Nearby, the finest house on Croom's Hill is **The Grange**, outside which is a gazebo overlooking Greenwich Park built by a 17th-century Lord Mayor of London, Sir William Hooker.

Greenwich Park

Transport see main Greenwich entry.

The park, along with Blackheath beyond, was the hunting ground that attracted Duke Humphrey to Greenwich back in the 15th century. It has been tamed considerably since then, particularly under Charles II, who hired the great French landscape gardener André Le Nôtre, of Versailles fame, to help lay it out in the 1660s. There is no evidence Le Nôtre ever visited the site; indeed, to judge from the way the park falls away abruptly at the bottom, it looks as though he didn't even realize it was on a hill. It is nevertheless an elegant place, unusually continental in its formality. Sadly, the deer that once roamed freely are confined to The Wilderness on the southeastern edge; they were isolated after a 19th-century stroller was gored and killed.

The Ranger's House

Chesterfield Walk, just beyond Croomshill Gate, t (020) 8853 0035, w www.english-heritage.org.uk. Open April–Sept daily 10am–6pm, Oct daily 10am–5pm, Nov–March Wed–Sun 10am–4pm; adm adults £2.80, concessions £2.10, under-16s £1.40.

This elegant mansion dating from 1699 holds a collection of musical instruments and 17th-century portraits. There's also a new gallery with changing art exhibitions, and the Architectural Study Centre is a treasure-trove of fragments salvaged from long-demolished London houses.

The Old Royal Observatory

Greenwich Park, t (020) 8858 4422, recorded information t 8312 6565; transport see main Greenwich entry. Open daily 10am–5pm; closed 23–26 Dec; adm free.

Greenwich is, of course, a time as well as a place: Greenwich Mean Time, as measured at this observatory, has synchronized the world's watches and guided the world's ships since 1884. The first two things you see on approaching the museum entrance are the metal plaque marking 0° longitude and, next to it, a large red ball on a stick that lowers every day at 1pm precisely as a symbol of the accuracy and universality of GMT.

Why Greenwich? First, because this was where England's first Astronomer Royal, John Flamsteed, decided to build his home and observatory in 1675. And secondly, because Flamsteed and his successors did more than anyone to solve the oldest navigational problem in the book: how to measure longitude (*see* 'To Find Longitude'). The **museum** gives an engaging account of all this, and takes the history of both navigation and time up to the present, including the landmark 1884 Washington conference that selected Greenwich as the Prime Meridian, and the invention of atomic clocks based on the nine billion vibrations per second of a caesium atom. The observatory itself is also worthy of note, particularly Flamsteed's original observatory, the **Octagon Room**, which was designed by the professional astronomer and architect Christopher Wren. The room, where Flamsteed kept his telescopes and tested the rotation of the earth with a 13ft pendulum, is one of Wren's finest achievements, a model of geometric simplicity and airy beauty which by his own admission was built 'for the observer's habitation and a little for pomp'.

The Millennium Dome

Tube North Greenwich; bus 188, M2 (from Greenwich centre).

The Dome cost £758m to build, partly paid for by the public via the National Lottery. It is made of Teflon and fibreglass and supported by 12 steel masts attached to 70km of wire

To Find Longitude

As a seafaring nation, Britain had more interest than most in ensuring that its ships did not continue to run into trouble because they could not find their way. Measuring latitude was relatively easy, as it could be ascertained from the angle of the Pole Star to the horizon. But longitude was something else. Scientists knew what they needed: a dependable and portable watch or clock with which to work it out. But for anything other than the shortest journeys no such timepiece existed (watches either lost or gained time while at sea). So acute did the problem become that 'to find longitude' became a synonym for an impossible task.

In 1754, Parliament issued a Longitude Act, offering a reward of £20,000 to the person who could crack the problem. The first proposals ranged from the sublime to the ridiculous. One was to line barges around the world and have them set off flares simultaneously every night at midnight. Another was to sprinkle a special magic 'powder of sympathy' on a pack of dogs who were to be sent to the four corners of the world; one of them would be stabbed in London every day at noon, and all the others would then howl in vicarious pain.

It was a Yorkshire clockmaker called John Harrison who eventually broke the impasse. He constructed his first marine clock, based on a double pendulum, in 1730, and continued perfecting it all his life. Each of his four prototypes took years to produce, and by the time he came up with the prizewinning model in 1772 – complete with bimetallic strip to compensate for temperature changes, caged roller bearing and grid-iron pendulum – he was already 79 years old. Captain Cook took Harrison's clock to Australia and called it his 'trusty friend'.

cable. It is big enough to hold two Wembley Stadiums and as tall as Nelson's Column. Throughout 2000 it hosted Britain's grand exhibition to mark the millennium, the most popular attraction in the UK for that year. The Dome's future remains uncertain.

The Millennium Village

Tube North Greenwich; **bus** 188, M2 (from Greenwich centre).

This 'model village' is made up of 1,400 sustainable and beautifully designed homes, a large proportion of which are classified as 'affordable'. The village has the first ever **low-energy foodstore** in Britain. It has natural light; is surrounded by earth mounds to insulate and prevent heat gain and loss; and the heat generated by the refrigeration is re-used.

Thames Barrier Visitor Centre Off maps

Unity Way, SE18, **t** (020) 8854 1373; **train** Charlton (from Charing Cross); wheelchair accessible. **Open** Mon–Fri 10am–5pm, Sat and Sun 10.30am–5.30pm; closed 25 and 26 Dec; **adm** adults £1, concessions and children 75p.

The barrier in question was constructed between 1972 and 1984. London has always been prey to flooding – hundreds were killed in floods as recently as 1953. The barrier is best seen from the river (the exhibition is rather dull), and is reminiscent of a row of little Sydney Opera Houses. Not just pretty baubles, they constitute a truly remarkable engineering feat. The gates between the fins regulate the water flow, ensuring London's safety; if you call ahead, you can watch the barrier being raised during its monthly tests.

Dulwich Picture Gallery Off maps

College Rd, **t** (020) 8693 5254, **w** www.dulwich picturegallery.org.uk; **train** North Dulwich (from London Bridge), West Dulwich (from Victoria); wheelchair accessible. **Open** Tues–Fri 10am–5pm, Sat and Sun 11am–5pm; closed hols exc. bank hol Mons; **adm** adults £4, senior citizens £3, free to children and on Fri.

This elegant Neoclassical building, built by Sir John Soane in 1811–14, was the first public picture gallery in England. Built to house Dulwich College's extensive collection of Old Masters, it includes Rembrandts, Rubens, Van Dycks, Poussins, Watteaus, Canalettos and Raphaels. Curiously, the gallery's founders, Sir Francis Bourgeois and Noel Desenfans, chose to have their mausoleum placed among the pictures. It is based on an engraving of an Alexandrian catacomb. The new annexe features exhibitions by artists such as Howard Hodgkin and David Wilkie.

Horniman Museum Off maps

100 London Rd, Forest Hill, SE23, **t** (020) 8699 1872, **e** enquiry@horniman.demon.co.uk, **w** www.horniman.co.uk; **train** Forest Hill (from Charing Cross); wheelchair accessible by prior arrangement. **Museum open** Mon–Sat 10.30am–5.30pm, Sun 2–5.30pm; closed 24–26 Dec; **adm** free, but donations appreciated. **Garden open** daily 7.30am–dusk.

This delightfully engaging museum is set in a rambling Arts and Crafts-style building designed by Charles Harrison Townsend, and named after a Victorian tea trader who established the museum here in 1901. It houses a series of permanent and temporary exhibits covering everything from a natural history section (with a giant walrus as its centrepiece) to London's first permanent gallery devoted to African and Caribbean culture. The Living Waters Aquarium has just been refurbished, and there's a nature trail and animal enclosure out in the gardens.

Wimbledon Lawn Tennis Museum Off maps

Church Rd, SW19, **t** (020) 8946 6131, **w** www .wimbledon.org/museum; **tube** Southfields; wheelchair accessible. **Open** Tues–Sat 10.30am–5pm, Sun 2–5pm; closed 1 Jan, Good Fri, 25 Dec and during championships exc. to ticketholders; **adm** adults £5.50, concessions £4.50, 5–16s £3.50. **Shop** and **café**.

This museum covers the history of the famous tennis tournament, including the quantity of strawberries consumed by spectators and the ever-changing fashion in hemlines.

Outside the Centre: East London

18

Jack the Ripper and the Kray twins probably wouldn't recognize London's East End nowadays: the streets and squares of Shoreditch and Hoxton are riddled with more artists' studios, galleries, hip clubs and slick designer bars then you could shake a pickled shark at. No longer synonymous with poverty and violence, the East End has become the spiritual home of Brit Art. It's also home to some of London's best markets: Spitalfields, with its quirky fashions and cafés; Petticoat Lane, for its smooth-talking Cockneys; and, best of all, the colourful Columbia Road Flower Market. Along the river, the former docklands on the Isle of Dogs have been converted into offices and apartments, and a pair of glassy towers have shot up to flank the city's tallest skyscraper, Canary Wharf.

For an overview of East London, *see* the map on p.234.

Spitalfields

Spitalfields was, as the name implies, originally the grounds of a medieval hospital, and remained more or less rural until the mid-17th century. It first drew attention to itself as a centre for religious nonconformity; the first Baptist chapel popped up in the district in 1612, a trend encouraged when some 60,000 French Protestants settled in the area after 1685. Under the French influence, Spitalfields became established as a centre for fine silks, and its prosperity was enhanced by Huguenot investment in the Bank of England, which was set up in 1694 largely to cover the costs of war against the Protestants' foe, Louis XIV. Today the only relics of the French presence in Spitalfields are the street names – Fournier St, Fleur-de-Lys St or Nantes Passage – and the fine Georgian brick houses in which the silk merchants lived. Silk-weaving declined dramatically as a trade in the 19th century, partly because of the unsuitability of the English climate for sericulture, but mostly because of the advent of machine-woven cotton. The 50,000 weavers engaged in the trade in 1824 had dwindled to just 3,300 by 1880. Cloth is still an important trade in Spitalfields, but nowadays it is mostly worked on by Bangladeshis labouring for slave wages in backstreet sweatshops.

The area's gone upmarket recently; artists moved in to take advantage of the industrial spaces, and some of them (like Tracey Emin) have become famous, attracting celebrity-seekers and hangers-on. On the streets, poverty goes hand-in-hand with expensive designer showrooms, and gleaming Vespas are parked next to battered old bikes held together with string.

Spitalfields Market EE–FF6
Tube Liverpool St. **Open** *Mon–Fri 9am–4pm, Sun 8am–7pm.*

This charming covered market is forever threatened with redevelopment, but currently specializes in organic products, plus crafts, junk and antiques; it's best on Sundays. A fashion market is held on Thursdays (10am–5pm) – it's great for unusual, cheap clothes.

Christ Church Spitalfields FF6
Corner of Fournier St and Commercial St, t (020) 7247 7202, w www.spitalfields.org.uk; tube Liverpool St, Aldgate East. **Open** *Mon–Fri noon–2.30pm (but usually open most of the day).* **Early Music Festival** *in July,* **Winter Festival** *in Dec; festival hotline t (020) 7377 1362.*

Nicholas Hawksmoor's imposing church was built in 1714 under the Fifty New Churches Act, with the specific aim of providing an Anglican counterweight to the increasingly nonconformist atmosphere of Spitalfields. For sheer impressiveness he succeeded triumphantly. The tall spire sits atop a massive portico of four Tuscan columns connected by a central barrel-vaulted arch. Inside is a deceptively simple floorplan, based on a rectangular classical basilica but offset by small tricks of proportion played by the side aisles and the never-completed gallery, which occupies only the western end below the wooden-cased organ. Christ Church was struck by lightning in 1841 and then badly tampered with in the

Roots of the East End

Back in the 1880s and 90s, the East End was almost entirely cut off from the rest of the city. Victorian maps tended to leave the area out, like uncharted territory in a god-forsaken corner of the Empire. In 1902, the visiting American novelist Jack London could not find a cab to take him there and was told by an agent for Thomas Cook: 'We are not accustomed to taking travellers to the East End.' The district was an ugly secret that London tried to forget about, a place so destitute it was beyond charity. The only time it was mentioned in polite society was in connection with the Jack the Ripper murders, which in many ways were the embodiment of the bad conscience of late Victorian London (*see p.272*).

The East End acted as a repository for immigrants and working-class Londoners from the 17th century onwards. Spitalfields filled with Protestant Huguenot silk-weavers fleeing France after the revocation of the Edict of Nantes in 1685; Limehouse was the site of the kilns used to extract lime from the chalk of the Kent hills, and the centre of the first Chinese community in London. The construction of the docks at the beginning of the 19th century prompted the biggest spurt in growth, as jerry-builders covered the remaining fields with shoddy houses for the dockers. The property speculators soon went bust, and the area turned into a slum of narrow streets, shady back-alleys and dilapidated houses. A whole alphabet soup of immigrants spilled into the neighbourhood in the late 19th and early 20th centuries: Chinese, North Africans, Malays, Lascars, Swedes, Native Americans, Russians and Tatars. Most significant, perhaps, were the thousands of Jews who fled the Russian and Polish pogroms, landing for the most part at Irongate Stairs near St Katharine's Dock.

Unlike New York's offering of the uplifting vision of the Statue of Liberty, there was no special welcome for these people, no poems exhorting the tired, poor, huddled masses to struggle for their freedom. Instead there was just dirt, hunger and deprivation, the tyranny of the workhouse and the rancid chill of

course of reconstruction; in the 20th century it was allowed to fall into an advanced state of dilapidation and is only now being put back together in the form that Hawksmoor originally intended. The repairs to the exterior have been completed, and the next stage is to rebuild the original Baroque galleries in the interior. Homeless people sleep in the churchyard, and alcoholics come to the rehabilitation centre in the crypt.

Petticoat Lane Market Off maps

Middlesex St; tube Aldgate, Aldgate East.
Held Sun 9am–2pm.

Keep your eyes out for rip-offs: the traders of Petticoat Lane are some of the smoothest talkers in London. The market trades unashamedly off the romantic image of the charming, sly Cockney, ready to crack a joke but also happy to pull a fast one on you at the first opportunity. Get here early, as the market, with its 850 stalls spilling far and wide into the surrounding streets, quickly turns into a crush. Historically, Petticoat Lane has been the preserve of the rag trade (the market dates back to the mid-18th century), as the name implies, and it still does brisk business in leather coats. You'll find all sorts of other bric-a-brac as well – furniture, books, old lamps – and plenty of Jewish snacks (bagels and salt beef) to keep you going.

Brick Lane Off maps

Tube Shoreditch, Aldgate East. Market held
Sun dawn–noon.

This is the high street of the Bengali community, an intriguing mixture of textile sweatshops, clothes stores selling cheap saris, halal butchers, record shops and cheap Indian restaurants – all slowly being infiltrated by City yuppies and artists. The **Truman Brewery** has been converted into a cutting-edge art gallery, as well as a series of painfully trendy boutiques, and there's a hip café where you can lounge around on cushions and listen to DJ sessions.

home. Racism, too, held sway over the East End (as it still does). In the 1930s, Oswald Mosley marched his blackshirts through the area as a deliberate provocation. On one occasion, known as 'the Battle of Cable Street', an anti-fascist counter-demonstration succeeded in stopping Mosley's mob; the following week, however, the windows of every Jewish shop on Mile End Rd were smashed in retaliation.

From the 1880s to the 1980s, the population declined from around 900,000 to 140,000. The collapse of the British Empire and the advent of container shipping turned vast chunks of the East End and the Docks into wasteland. Even the arrival of a wave of Bangladeshi immigrants in the 1970s did little to reverse the trend. Only when Margaret Thatcher decided to rebuild the docks as an upmarket office and residential development (*see* p.273) did the East End show any signs of new life. But what a strange new life it was. The imposition of a yuppie culture jarred completely with the East End's working-class roots. The old traditions were either squashed by the developer's ball and chain, or sweetened and packaged as a kind of nostalgic quaintness. The myth of the crafty Cockney that had been invented in the music halls was resuscitated to provide local colour at Petticoat Lane Market, and to provide entertainment for 16 million television viewers a week through the BBC soap opera *EastEnders*.

Once upon a time, the border between the City and the East End seemed so impenetrable you could have built the Berlin Wall there, complete with sniffer dogs and searchlights, and not noticed the difference. Now sections of the East End have been virtually co-opted by next door's wealthy traders and stockbrokers. The office blocks and wine bars have spilled over into Aldgate; the street signs have been repainted green and gold (with the names written in Roman and Urdu script for local colour); and the once cheap, unlicensed Bengali restaurants of Brick Lane have long since tarted themselves up with venetian blinds and American Express signs in the windows.

The place comes into its own on Sunday mornings, when the lane and neighbouring streets become a **market** selling cheap bric-a-brac, clothes, fruit and veg, and every kind of secondhand goods. The cultural make-up of Brick Lane is not entirely Bengali: Jewish establishments are dotted around the neighbourhood. Brick Lane has always been a strange hodge-podge of people and cultures: the **Jamme Masjid** at the bottom end was built in 1743 as a Huguenot chapel, and served as a synagogue and Methodist hall before turning into one of the main Muslim places of worship in London.

Whitechapel Art Gallery Off maps

Whitechapel High St, t (020) 7522 7878, w www.whitechapel.org; tube Aldgate East; wheelchair accessible. Open Tues and Thurs–Sun 11am–5pm, Wed 11am–8pm; closed 1 Jan and 25–26 Dec; adm free. Giftshop and café.

This is a lively gallery focusing on contemporary and avant-garde work, housed in an interesting Art Nouveau building designed by Charles Harrison Townsend at the turn of the 20th century. It was the brainchild of Samuel Barnett, a local vicar who believed education could help eradicate the appalling poverty in the East End. Jackson Pollock and David Hockney both held exhibitions here early in their careers.

Bethnal Green Museum of Childhood Off maps

Cambridge Heath Rd, t (020) 8983 5200; tube Bethnal Green; wheelchair accessible. Open Sat–Thurs 10am–5.50pm; closed 1 Jan, May Day and 24–26 Dec; adm free. Take plenty of 20p pieces to work the old-fashioned automated machines.

This extension of the Victoria and Albert Museum is housed in the building once known as the Brompton Boilers where the decorative arts collections were kept during the 1850s – it was dismantled and moved here from South Kensington (you'll notice the very Victorian mosaic frieze on the outside depicting Agriculture, Art and Science). Inside are some extraordinarily intricate children's toys, notably dolls' houses – a whole floorful, dating back to the 1690s – train sets, puppet theatres and board games; a shame, however, that they are displayed in such gloomy cabinets.

Shoreditch and Hoxton Off maps

Shoreditch was traditionally a seedy East End neighbourhood, with strip clubs and dreary clothes' wholesalers. But it has recently become the latest haunt for artists, designers and anyone involved in the rise and fall of the dotcom bubble. **Hoxton Square** is the centre of the fashionable wave of bars and galleries which have hit the otherwise rundown neighbourhood; here you'll find the British Film Institute's new **Lux Arts Cinema**, which has its own trendy bar and restaurant, and the painfully cool **White Cube Gallery** (**w** *www.whitecube.com*), which shows artists of the spiky Brit Pack kind. If you're planning to make a night of it in this neighbourhood (*see* 'Nightlife' for bars and clubs), think hard about what to wear in order to wheedle your way past the bouncers.

Columbia Road Flower Market

Off Hackney Rd about 1.2km north of Liverpool St Station; tube Liverpool St, Old St, Shoreditch. Open Sun 8am–1pm.

Columbia Market was set up in 1869 as a covered food market in a vast neo-Gothic palace. The traders preferred to do their business on the street, however, and the venture failed. The shortlived market building was knocked down in 1958 to make room for the lively, modern, highly successful flower market. As well as a wide range of cut flowers and pot plants, you can buy home-made bread and farmhouse cheeses, and enjoy the small cafés that line the street.

Geffrye Museum

Kingsland Rd, E2, t (020) 7739 9893, e info@ geffrye-museum.org.uk, w www.geffrye-museum.org.uk; tube Liverpool St, then bus 242; train Dalston Kingsland (on North London Line, two stops from Highbury and Islington); wheelchair accessible. Open Tues–Sat 10am–5pm, Sun and bank hol Mons noon–5pm; closed 1 Jan, Good Fri and 24–26 Dec; adm free. Giftshop and restaurant.

A thoroughly absorbing series of reconstructions of British living rooms from Tudor times to the present, housed in a row of former almshouses, with a newer extension focusing on design. It's got a great café, and a series of concerts in the gardens in summer. There are also some fantastic and very cheap Vietnamese restaurants in the area (*see* 'Eating Out', p.338).

Wapping Off maps

Wapping has almost always been poor: John Stow described Wapping High St in his *Survey of London* (1598) as 'a filthy strait passage, with alleys of small tenements or cottages'. Sailors made up the bulk of its modest population, later replaced by dockers, whose community was hemmed in by a thick wall protecting the warehouses of the London Docks. The waterfront near Wapping Wall known as **Execution Dock** earned its name because pirates and smugglers used to be hanged there and then displayed in chains for as long as it took for three tides to wash over them.

Wapping is where some of the first failed luxury flats of the 1980s were built. Some of the architecture is truly dire, and, although the area is now more or less fully inhabited, Wapping still has no soul. The ambitious and attractively converted Tobacco Dock on The Highway, for example, was supposed to be a thriving new shopping centre, but is forlorn and virtually empty. The most successful ventures in Wapping are tourist ones, such as St Katharine's Dock, next to the Tower of London, and some great riverside pubs. Also here is 'Fortress Wapping', the heavily

Everybody's Favourite Serial Killer

He is the most famous criminal in the universe, and yet nobody has ever found out who he was. Jack the Ripper really needs no introduction – the man who terrorized prostitutes in the East End of the 1880s, the world's first sex murderer to be labelled as such, the Hannibal Lecter of old London Town. Certainly, his is a grim legacy. But what is it about him that captures the imagination so? To read some accounts of his handiwork, you would have thought that crime never existed in London until he invented it.

In fact, old Jack was remarkable neither for the heinousness of his crimes, nor even for his targeting of prostitutes. In the East End of the time, prostitution was rife, and many unfortunate women also came to appalling ends at the hands of pimps or customers.

What made Jack special was not so much his psychotic behaviour as his appeal to newspaper editors. In 1888, the year of the Ripper murders, the popular press was just beginning to hit the big time; circulation of the leading paper, the *Lloyd's Weekly News*, was edging towards the one million mark. Every newspaper loves a good story, and Jack the Ripper had it all – sex, violence, mystery, squalor and the possibility of endless speculation about suspects.

There were deeper reasons, too, why Jack the Ripper appealed to late Victorian audiences. The senseless violence he perpetrated was a startling expression of the urban alienation of the age. The Jack the Ripper saga presented an opportunity for people to exorcise, at a safe distance, their anxieties and feelings of responsibility for the chaos of the city. The sex angle was also cathartic in its way, sending a frisson of guilt-ridden excitement down the spine of every buttoned-up Victorian prude.

The facts of the case, it's true, are pretty gruesome. The Ripper first struck on 31 August, slitting the throat and abdomen of Mary Ann Nichols in Buck's Row in Whitechapel. The next victim was Annie Chapman, mutilated and decapitated on 8 September at the back of a lodging house

guarded centre of the Murdoch Empire. Murdoch was the first to make the break from Fleet St, moving here in 1986 and firing all the printers and journalists in his workforce in one fell swoop.

St Katharine's Dock
Tube Tower Hill; **DLR** Tower Gateway.

St Katharine's Dock looks benign enough now, with its yachts and cafés, but it was once one of the most callous of riverside developments. To build the docks and commodity warehouses here in the 1820s, the authorities knocked down 1,250 houses and made more than 11,000 people homeless. For all that, the dock was not a great financial success and lost money until its closure in 1968. Now prettified with boats and bright paint, its walkways are linked with a series of attractive iron bridges. Tourists love it, perhaps because it is an obvious lunch spot after a hard morning's sightseeing at the Tower of London (*see* p.229), along a sign-posted walkway. At the fake (and awful) 19th-century Dickens Inn and the other local watering holes, sightseers make strange drinking companions for the brokers who work in Commodity Quay, home of the London futures and options market.

St George in the East
*Pennington St, t (020) 7481 1345; **tube** Tower Hill, Shadwell; **DLR** Tower Gateway, Shadwell. **Open** daily 9am–5pm.*

Nicholas Hawksmoor's early 18th-century church, with its broad, tall tower with pepperpot turrets, was the site of an unholy row in the 19th century between a High Church rector and the Low Church Bishop of London who disagreed about the liturgy. The congregation joined in the mayhem by blowing horns, whistling and bringing vicious dogs into Sunday service, forcing the rector to resign. The docks were heavily bombed during the Blitz, when the interior of St George was destroyed. It has now been

in Hanbury St. Murders three and four took place on 30 September – Elizabeth ('Long Liz') Stride in Berner St, and Catherine Eddowes in Mitre Square in the City, the latter found with her intestines pulled out. More than a month went by, and then the killer struck for a final time, killing Mary Jane Kelly in Miller's Court off Dorset St.

By now every bar room in the country was discussing who the killer might be, speculating what his motives were and suggesting how to catch him. Among the intriguing ideas for tracking down the culprit was a plan to place springed dummies of women in dark alleyways that would sound an alarm as soon as they were touched. Just as all this gossip reached fever pitch, however, the killings suddenly stopped. Nobody knows why.

So who was Jack the Ripper? At first the most popular theory was that he was a doctor, since the mutilations betrayed a knowledge of anatomy and seemed to have been carried out with medical instruments. But soon the wildest conspiracy theories grew up, linking the murders to everyone from Oscar Wilde to the Queen herself. The most likely (and therefore, to Ripperologists, the least interesting) suspect was a Dr Montague John Druitt, a doctor of law who disappeared soon after Mary Kelly's murder and whose corpse was subsequently found floating in the Thames with stones in his coat pockets. But another possible is a Liverpudlian businessman called James Maybrick whose trips to London coincided with the killings; some fairly convincing diaries and other artefacts linking him to the case have been found (or created).

The fascination of the Ripper case has only increased with the years, and every literary, criminological and scientific school has come up with its own theory. Conspiracy theorists have become convinced there was an official cover-up, particularly since Scotland Yard mysteriously closed the files on the case in 1992. By now the Ripper is not just a historical figure, but an icon of popular culture. He has starred in the parodic musical *Eine kleine Rippermusik*, and inspired a play (Frank Wedekind's *Lulu*) and numerous films.

---

redesigned as an intriguing hybrid – part church, part block of flats, part courtyard.

St Anne Limehouse Off maps

Off the Commercial Rd, **t** *(020) 7987 1502;* **DLR** *Limehouse, Westferry.* **Open** *Mon–Fri 2–4pm, Sat and Sun 2.30–5pm.*

The chunky tower of Hawksmoor's church has been a guide to ships coming into London ever since it was completed in 1724. It has also been the subject of diabolical rumours. Why was it not consecrated for six years after its completion? Why is there a pagan symbol, a pyramid, in the churchyard? Hawksmoor's surviving papers provide no clues, and speculation still rages. The interior of the church, a rectangle containing an elongated Greek cross, is intact, although many of the fittings were added after a fire in 1850.

Limehouse, named after the lime kilns which used to operate here, bears the vestiges of the mini-Chinatown it was before the 1980s property bonanza, and it has a little-publicized reputation for good cheap Chinese restaurants. In the 19th century the area was considered an iniquitous den of vice; this was where Oscar Wilde set the opium-smoking scene in his novel *The Picture of Dorian Gray*.

The Isle of Dogs Off maps

DLR *Westferry or Poplar stations through to Island Gardens (good views from the train);* **ferry** *West India Dock Pier;* **walk** *via foot tunel from Greenwich Pier.*

The Isle of Dogs is a peninsula defined by a tight loop in the river and criss-crossed by artificial waterways. There is no hard evidence that it ever had any association with dogs, although there are folktales that the royal kennels were once kept here. Most likely, 'dogs' is a corruption of 'docks'; after all, that was what provided the area's livelihood from 1802 until the second half of the 20th century. The bright new developments around Canary Wharf are striking and even beautiful, and a conversation point at the very least. Take the **Docklands Light Railway** (DLR) through the area, for revealing views of council estates and dilapidated warehouses interspersed with shining new buildings. The southern end of the Isle of Dogs is littered with upmarket residential estates as well as a sprinkling of older council houses. You get a keen sense here of the social dislocations brought about by the redevelopments; most troubling is the rise of the extreme right-wing British National Party. At the southern end of the Isle is the entrance to the rather spooky **Greenwich foot tunnel**.

Canary Wharf

Tube Canary Wharf; DLR Canary Wharf.

There's no mistaking the main attraction around here. The 812ft glass and steel tower block at the centre of Canary Wharf soars over the Docklands skyline, the flashing light atop its pyramidal apex winking 40 times a minute. Cesar Pelli's monster tower, officially known by its address One Canada Square and completed in 1991 after just 18 months under construction, is the tallest building in London by far, and the second tallest in Europe after the Messeturm in Frankfurt (which pips it to the post with a flagpole banned by London's air traffic controllers). This is, though, Europe's largest single property development. The tower is closed to visitors, which is a shame because the view from the 50th floor is quite stunning. The striking **Jubilee Line station** here is worth the trip in itself (*see* 'The Jubilee Line Extension', p.205). In 2001, two more enormous towers (built to house the offices of HSBC and Citigroup) rose up on either side of Canary Wharf.

In the early evening of 9 February 1996 a huge IRA bomb explosion at Canary Wharf killed two people. A million square feet of office space were damaged and repair works have taken years.

Museum in Docklands

*West India Quay, t (020) 7001 9800, e info@museumindocklands.org.uk; DLR West India Quay; wheelchair accessible. **Due to open** from summer/Sept 2002, from when daily 10am–6pm; closed 1 Jan and 25 Dec; **adm** adults about £5.*

This new museum, created by the Museum of London's curators and archaeologists, documents the massive upheavals to London's historic port area and the Docklands. The story of London's river, port and people is told through a variety of exhibits.

Storm Water Pumping Station

*Stewart St; **DLR** South Quay, then 10mins' walk along Marsh Wall.*

Built by John Outram in 1988, the enormous pump station looks like an outsized Chinese temple, and is one of the most successful buildings in the Docklands. Inside the 'terrorist-proof' station, storm water from the Isle of Dogs flows into an underground chamber, and is pumped into a massive concrete surge tank from where it drains into the Thames. At the same time a propeller fan in the apex of the pediment rotates at 16 rpm to expel any sewer gases that build up inside the station.

William Morris Gallery Off maps

*Lloyd Park, Forest Rd, E17, t (020) 8527 3782, w www.lbwf.gov.uk/wmg; tube Waltham- stow Central; ground floor (main collections) wheelchair accessible. **Open** Tues–Sat 10–1 and 2–5, plus first Sun in the month 10–noon and 2–5; closed all hols and 24 Dec; **adm** free.*

Walthamstow is a long way to go, but William Morris's childhood home and this exhibition on his life and work are fascinating. Beautifully presented exhibits are arranged carefully in this elegant Georgian house and include Arts and Crafts wallpaper, stained glass, tiles and carpets. There's also a collection of pre-Raphaelite paintings and drawings by Burne-Jones and Rossetti, plus a few Rodin sculptures.

Walks

19

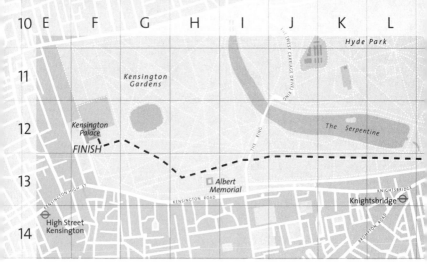

ROYAL LONDON

Only 10 European monarchs have survived into the 21st century, and none has managed it with quite the same resolution as Queen Elizabeth II. The year 2002 marks the 50th anniversary of her coronation, but, parades and processions aside, the milestone has brought the vexing question of exactly what the royal family is for bubbling to the surface – perhaps partly because 2002 also marked the end of an era with the death of the Queen Mother, and of course also of her daughter, Princess Margaret. According to a recent poll, the Queen is considered a good ambassador for the country by 81% of Britons, but a quarter of the population also believe that a president should be elected on her death – possibly because the nation has largely lost patience with the Queen's troublesome offspring and her tactless husband.

Start: Westminster Tube.
Finish: Kensington Palace (nearest Tube High St Kensington.
Distance: 4 miles.
Walking time: To take in all the stops at the Abbey and palaces, leave a full day.
Suggested day: Any day but Sunday.
Lunch and drinks stops: The Portrait Restaurant, *see p.315*; ICA Café, *see p.315*; Quilon, *see p.315*; Orangery, *see p.326*; Phoenicia, *see p.334*.

While entertainment and not government has been the monarchy's *raison d'être* for more than a century now, the revelations of affairs, divorce, toe-sucking, under-age drinking, and appalling social gaffs are the stuff of soaps, not fairy tales. The hoi polloi may approve of the Queen, doggedly Doing Her Duty in twin-sets and pearls, but they fell in love with the late Princess Diana, who exposed the truth behind the royal myths. The mystique of the monarchy, so carefully cultivated for so long, lies in tatters, but the tabloids prove that the daily dramas of the royal princes, or the relationship between Prince Charles and Camilla Parker Bowles, can still shift a paper or two, so perhaps the magic hasn't quite disappeared yet.

Note that many of the sights on this walk are closed on Sundays – with the notable exception of Spencer House, which is only open on Sundays, when Westminster Abbey is only open for services. It's worth booking tickets for the Houses of Parliament and Buckingham Palace (open only in July and August) in advance rather than face the endless queues. As part of the Jubilee celebrations in 2002, extended opening hours are promised, but can't be relied upon.

As you leave Westminster Tube, you'll find yourself at the foot of **Big Ben** (*see p.90*), and facing the **Palace of Westminster** (better known as the Houses of Parliament; *see p.89*) and Westminster Abbey. Westminster became the heart of London's royal and

MAYFAIR

N O P Q R S T U

TRAFALGAR SQUARE

Charing Cross

Admiralty Arch

Embankment

Institute of Contemporary Arts

Green Park

Queen's Chapel

Banqueting House

Spencer House

ST JAMES'S

River Thames

St James's Palace

Apsley House

Clarence House

St James's Park

Banqueting House

Hyde Park

Hyde Park Corner

Wellington Arch

Buckingham Palace Gardens

CONSTITUTION HILL

Buckingham Palace

Cenotaph

DOWNING ST

Westminster START

The Queen's Gallery

St James's Park

PARLIAMENT SQUARE

Big Ben

Royal Mews

St Margaret's Westminster

Houses of Parliament

Westminster Abbey

Green Park

PICCADILLY

PARK LANE

Broad Walk

religious life in the 11th century, when Edward the Confessor established his court and began the construction of a new abbey here. Cross the street and keep walking straight down St Margaret St, and, if you haven't already arranged for an entrance ticket (see p.89), join the queue waiting patiently outside St Stephen's entrance and prepare for a long wait. The palace was the permanent seat of all the English monarchs after Edward until 1532, when a fire forced Henry VIII up the street to Whitehall.

Although it was almost entirely rebuilt in the 19th century, the medieval Westminster Hall survives on the northern side. First built as a banqueting chamber in 1097 by King William Rufus, its crowning glory, the magnificent oak hammerbeam ceiling, was added at the end of the 14th century by Richard II. Until 1821 the hall was used for coronation banquets, when the Royal Champion would ride in full armour into the hall to confront anyone who dared challenge the new ruler's right to the throne. For six centuries, it was also the highest court of law, where Guy Fawkes, Charles I and Cromwell were among those tried; the unfortunate Fawkes was hanged, drawn and quartered outside in the Old Palace Yard. Now it is only used for the lying-in-state of members of the royal family, including most recently the Queen Mother.

When you leave the Houses of Parliament, cross St Margaret St to the white stone church which gives the street its name. **St Margaret's** (see p.93) is overshadowed by the presence of the Abbey next door, but it's still the preferred setting for society marriages among the minor royals. Beyond it lies the splendour of **Westminster Abbey** (see p.86), which holds a powerfully symbolic place in English culture; this is where monarchs are christened, crowned and buried, where the Anglican church derives its deepest inspiration, and where the nation commemorates its greatest politicians, artists and scientists.

The main entrance faces Parliament Square, next to the church of St Margaret. The Abbey was consecrated on 28 December 1099, just days before the death of its founder, Edward the Confessor, who was canonized here in 1161 and whose shrine remains the epicentre of the Abbey. The Abbey has become a giant mausoleum and contains more than 3,000 tombs, including those of the Tudor monarchs Henry VII, Henry VIII, Edward VI, Mary and Elizabeth I, buried with elaborate pomp in the magnificent Lady's Chapel, better known as Henry VII's Chapel. In the Abbey's museum (access via the cloisters, off the south choir aisle), you can gaze at the royal coronation and funerary regalia, including the eerie wax effigies and royal death masks of monarchs such as Edward III and Henry VII.

Return to Parliament Square, negotiate the traffic around it (the square has the dubious distinction of being London's first traffic roundabout), and walk down Parliament St, which becomes Whitehall. Pass the **Cenotaph**, the nation's memorial to those who died in the two World Wars, then **Downing St** (*see* p.94) on your left, and you'll come to the **Banqueting House** (1615–22; *see* p.94), almost overwhelmed by the monolithic headquarters of the Ministry of Defence behind it.

Banqueting House is all that remains of the medieval Whitehall Palace which went up in flames in 1698, and was the first building erected by Inigo Jones, Palladio's biggest fan, on his return from Italy. In 1635, Rubens was commissioned by Charles I to paint the beautiful ceiling frescoes in the main dining hall on the first floor; they celebrate the union of England and Scotland under James I, and the Divine Right of the Stuart kings. It's a bitter irony that it was under this vainglorious display that Charles I prepared himself for his execution in 1649, clothing himself in several shirts so he wouldn't shiver with cold and allow his enemies to whisper that he died in fear.

Almost opposite the Banqueting Hall, on the other side of Whitehall, is **Horse Guards Parade** (*see* p.95), the embodiment of royal pomp and pageantry. The role of the guards is nominally to guard the Queen, but in reality to perpetuate the mystique which surrounds the royals; stiffly resplendent in their immaculate uniforms and plumed helmets, they must be the most photographed people in London. If you want to catch the rooty-toot ceremony of the Changing of the Guard, be here at 11am.

Continue walking up Whitehall towards **Trafalgar Square**, where Nelson perches high on his column. Just to the left as you approach the square is **Admiralty Arch** (*see* p.117), the grand triple entrance to the Mall. Walk through it and onto the processional route which sweeps up to Buckingham Palace. On your left is **St James's Park**, one of London's quietest and loveliest, where you can stroll in peace, feed the ducks and pelicans at the lake, or pitch a deck chair for a

picnic. It's one of the four central London royal parks, once used for the royal pastimes of hunting and rumpy-pumpy.

To your right, Carlton House Terrace (now the home of the **ICA**; *see* p.117) flanks the Mall with a rank of gleaming columns. George IV moved here from St James's Palace round the corner, fed up with its dirty little rooms. Turn right down Marlborough Rd (next to Carlton House). At the top of the road on the right is the **Queen's Chapel** (*see* p.122), a small but perfectly formed Neoclassical church which was built to celebrate the marriage of the future Charles I to the Infanta of Spain. In fact the marriage never took place, but the church retains its royal connections and it was here that both Princess Diana's and the Queen Mother's coffins were laid before their funerals.

Turn left at the top of Marlborough Rd onto Cleveland Row, where you'll find the main entrance to **St James's Palace** (but won't be able to get in, at least not without friends in very high places). This Tudor palace was built by Henry VIII, and became a royal residence when Whitehall Palace burnt down in 1698. Several royals live here, including Prince Charles, who was ousted from Kensington Palace after he separated from Princess Diana. The Queen Mother used to live in Clarence House next door. St James's was largely remodelled by Nash (who built Clarence House at the same time) in the early 19th century, but two Tudor towers still stand at the bottom of St James's St.

Walk up St James's St and take the second left onto St James's Place; at the end, on the left, is the graceful Palladian **Spencer House** (*see* p.123), built for the ancestors of Princess Diana. Inside, eight of its opulent rooms have been opened to the public – but only on Sundays and only by guided tour.

Return to the Mall (down St James's St and back down Marlborough Rd) and turn right. The grand sweep of the Mall will deposit you at the entrance to **Buckingham Palace** (*see* p.114), the royal residence since Queen Victoria moved in with her entourage in 1837. Built in 1702 as the city residence of the Duke of Buckingham, it has been substantially and chaotically remodelled several times since, most recently in 1913. Since 1993, the palace has been opened to the public for two months of the year; the Queen moves out, the carpets are rolled away, the valuables tucked behind tasselled ropes, and the hoi polloi snake through. It's an expensive and largely unrewarding experience for any but the most committed royalist. For a glimpse into the ceremonial side of royal life, stroll down Buckingham Gate (which flanks the southern side of Buckingham Palace) and visit the **Royal Mews** (*see* p.116), where the ornamental carriages and coaches are kept.

Return to the main gates of Buckingham Palace, and walk down Constitution Hill towards the flamboyant **Wellington Arch** (*see* p.197), marooned in an island of traffic. It's just been reopened after an expensive renovation, and a lift will swoop you up for fantastic views across **Hyde Park**. Leave the traffic behind you and enter Hyde Park via the **Queen Elizabeth Gate** (just behind Apsley House, which overlooks the horrible knot of traffic here at Hyde Park Corner); the gates are a frilly, wrought-iron monstrosity erected in honour of the late Queen Mother in 1993.

Once through the gates, you can soak up the atmosphere of central London's largest and best-loved park. Henry VIII snatched it from the Church after the dissolution of the monasteries in the 1530s and turned it into a private hunting ground. It didn't open to the public until the beginning of the 17th century, when you could refresh yourself with 'milk from a red cow'. On the left is a pretty rose garden, and just beyond it leads the paved former carriageway called **Rotten Row** (a corruption of the French *route du roi* – 'royal road'); this was London's first lit street, after William III had lanterns hung along its length to deter highwaymen while he made his way from Kensington Palace to St James's Palace. Follow the royal route until it meets the broad, paved promenade called The Ring, cross it and continue along the footpath directly opposite. This delightful

stretch is called Flower Walk, which edges past the huge gilded **Albert Memorial** (*see* p.195) erected by Queen Victoria in memory of her husband. From here, you can take any of the small paths to the right, which all lead eventually to **Kensington Palace**.

The palace gates are still strewn with bouquets in memory of Princess Diana, who lived here until her death in 1997. In the late 17th century, the formerly modest Jacobean mansion was converted into a residence for William of Orange, who decided that living so close to the river in Whitehall was bad for his asthma. Wren and Hawksmoor were called in to make it a palace fit for kings, and William Kent later finished off the job. It was a royal residence for just 50 years, and now holds apartments for the Duke and Duchesses of Kent and Gloucester as well as those of the late Princess Margaret. Nowadays it is the connection with Diana that draws the crowds, even though her former apartments are not open to the public. The delightful café in the Orangery is a good spot for a cream tea and to finish the walk. For the nearest Tube, walk down Kensington High St.

TAVERNS, STEWS AND PLAYERS

The fortunes of the borough of Southwark have long been moulded by its proximity to the Thames and to the City of London just across the river. Situated at the southern end of London Bridge – for centuries the only way into the City from the south – it rapidly filled up with coaching inns and brothels catering to travellers and pilgrims preparing for their journey south. Hospitals, prisons and the smellier industries like tanning and brewing were pushed out here, followed by the great Elizabethan playhouses in the 16th century. The area became London's wildest and most scurrilous entertainment district, famous for its stews (brothels), inns, theatres and blood sports. Its industrial

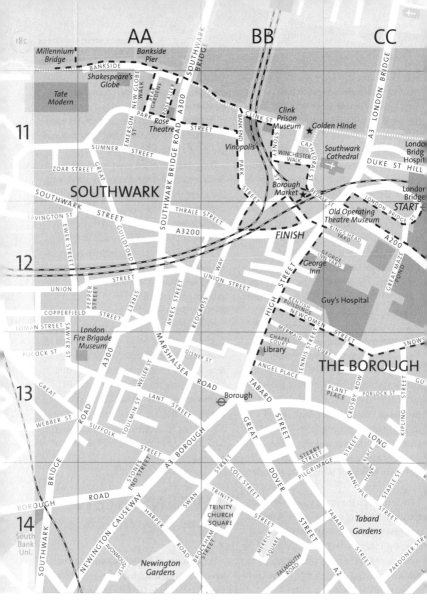

Map labels:

AA BB CC

Millennium Bridge
Bankside Pier
BANKSIDE
Shakespeare's Globe
SOUTHWARK BRIDGE
LONDON BRIDGE
Tate Modern
NEW GLOBE WALK
PARK STREET
ROSE ALLEY
BEAR GARDENS
A300
Rose Theatre
Clink Prison Museum
Golden Hinde
London Bridge Hospit
EMERSON STREET
CLINK STREET
STONEY ST
CATHEDRAL ST
Southwark Cathedral
DUKE ST HILL
SUMNER STREET
Vinopolis
WINCHESTER WALK
London Bridge
ZOAR STREET
PARK STREET
BOROUGH HIGH ST
London Bridge
START
SOUTHWARK
Borough Market
Old Operating Theatre Museum
SOUTHWARK STREET
GREAT GUILDFORD STREET
THRALE STREET
A200
KING'S HEAD YARD
LAVINGTON ST
A3200
FINISH
GREAT MAZE POND
EWER STREET
George Inn
11
12
13
14

WAY
UNION STREET
GEORGE INN YARD
George Inn
UNION
STREET
PEPPER STREET
AYRES STREET
REDCROSS WAY
KENISH BUILDINGS
NEWCOMEN STREET
Guy's Hospital
COPPERFIELD STREET
SAWYER ST
MERMAID COURT
SNOWS
LOMAN STREET
London Fire Brigade Museum
DISNEY ST
CHAPEL COURT
Library
TENNIS STREET
THE BOROUGH
POCOCK ST
MARSHALSEA ROAD
ANGEL PLACE
GU
GREAT
PLANT PLACE
CROSBY ROW
PORLOCK ST
KIPLING STREET
LONG
WEBBER STREET
BRIDGE ROAD
WELLER ST
LANT STREET
TOULMIN STREET
Borough
TABARD STREET
GREAT DOVER STREET
STERRY STREET
PILGRIMAGE
MANCIPLE STREET
BLACK HORSE CT
STAPLE ST
South Bank Uni.
SUFFOLK STREET
STONES END STREET
A3 BOROUGH
SWAN STREET
COLE STREET
PILGRIMAGE
Tabard Gardens
BOROUGH ROAD
NEWINGTON CAUSEWAY
HARPER ROAD
AVONMOUTH ST
BROCKHAM STREET
TRINITY CHURCH SQUARE
TRINITY STREET
MERRICK SQUARE
FALMOUTH ROAD
A2
TABARD STREET
PARDONER STR
Newington Gardens
SOUTHWARK
BRIDGE ROAD

---

importance rose in the 18th and 19th centuries, when raw goods for the factories were transported by boat, unloaded at the wharves, and stacked in the huge warehouses which still pepper the neighbourhood. When the docks closed down in the 1970s, the area slumped into decline, but things are finally looking up as the riverside regeneration continues apace.

This is the London of Chaucer, Shakespeare and Dickens but, besides its literary monuments, this walk will take you to an 18th-century operating theatre, an antiques

market where you can legally flog stolen goods, past the grandiose Victorian exchanges for raw goods, and leave you sipping a well-earned pint at a fine local pub.

If you arrive by Tube at London Bridge, take the Borough High St exit. Turn right onto Borough High St, and then right again into St Thomas St. This street is named for the monastery and hospital founded here in the 13th century. On the left is the **Old Operating Theatre, Museum and Herb Garret** (*see p.211*). The operating theatre, the oldest in Britain, had been closed down when the hospital

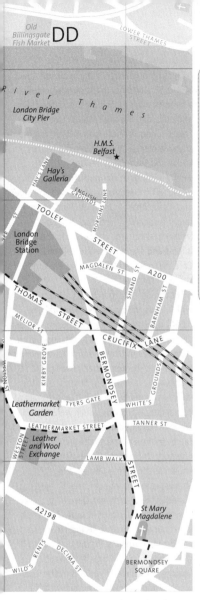

Old Billingsgate Fish Market

DD

River Thames

London Bridge City Pier

H.M.S. Belfast ★

Hay's Galleria

London Bridge Station

TOOLEY STREET

MAGDALEN ST   A200

THOMAS STREET

MELIOR ST

CRUCIFIX LANE

KIRBY GROVE

BERMONDSEY

Leathermarket Garden   TYERS GATE   WHITE'S

LEATHERMARKET STREET   TANNER ST

Leather and Wool Exchange

LAMB WALK

A2198

WILD'S RENTS   DECIMA ST

St Mary Magdalene †

BERMONDSEY SQUARE

> **Start**: London Bridge Tube.
>
> **Finish**: Borough Market (nearest Tube London Bridge).
>
> **Distance**: About 3 miles.
>
> **Walking time**: Anything from a couple of hours to a full day, if you take in some of the museums.
>
> **Suggested day**: Friday morning for the antiques market; Thursday, Friday or Saturday for Borough Market.
>
> **Lunch and drinks stops**: Honest Cabbage, *see* p.327; Delfina, *see* p.327; Manze's, *see* below; George Inn, *see* p.346; Borough Café, *see* below; Southwark Cathedral Refectory, *see* below; Anchor, *see* p.346; Market Porter, *see* below.

Bermondsey St, still lined with the 19th-century warehouses which were once piled high with goods brought by boat along the river. This area was the heart of London's leather trade from the Middle Ages; tanning is a smelly business and was kept as far as possible from the city. The street names – Tanner St, Morocco St, Skin Market Place – still echo the past, but the tanneries and factories were all closed down by the 1970s. Bermondsey St is now becoming very fashionable as the warehouses are converted into chic loft apartments and galleries; the blazing pink and orange building on the left is the **Fashion and Textile Museum** (*see* p.259), slated to open in late 2002. The **Honest Cabbage**, set in a former Victorian pub, or the arty **Delfina** café, are both good lunch stops.

At the bottom of the street on the left is the pale, serene church of **St Mary Magdalene**, established in the 13th century and the oldest building in Bermondsey, although it was substantially rebuilt in the 1830s. On Friday mornings, Bermondsey Square (across Long Lane at the bottom of Bermondsey St) is packed with a famous **antiques market**, where an urban myth has it that stolen goods can be sold between 6 and 8am. The square is surrounded with antique and bric-a-brac shops which are always good for a rummage. Just beyond the square is

moved to new premises in the mid-19th century and was discovered by chance tucked away in the garret of St Thomas's Church in 1957. It's now a fascinating – if gruesome – little museum, stuffed with surgical saws and bleeding cups. The tiny theatre itself offers a toe-curling glimpse into the horrors of undergoing surgery before anaesthetics were invented.

Leave the theatre and continue down St Thomas St, keeping the towering complex of Guy's Hospital on your right. Turn right down

Tower Bridge Rd, where you'll find **Manze's** tiled traditional pie and mash shop (at No.87, **t** (020) 7407 2985) and the brave can try jellied eels.

Retrace your steps back up Bermondsey St and turn left down Leathermarket St, passing the graceful, curved **Morocco Store** on your left and the attractive **Leathermarket Garden** on your right. On the left, at the corner with Weston St, is the old **Leather and Wool Exchange**, where traders would come to buy the raw materials for the factories. There's a pub and a café here now, but much of the exchange has been turned into offices. Turn right onto Weston St, then left onto Snowfields, and keep walking until you reach Borough High St again.

Turn left down Borough High St and stop by the modern Southwark Library. It wasn't just noxious factories that were pushed south of the river: prisons were established here, too. Charles Dickens, whose family was incarcerated in **Marshalsea Debtors' Prison** in 1824, described its miserable conditions in *Little Dorrit*. The prison was closed in 1842 and nothing remains except a stretch of wall in the small garden next to the library. Little Dorrit was baptised and married in the gloomy church of **St George the Martyr** which overlooks the garden, and is depicted kneeling in a modern stained-glass window here.

Walk back up Borough High St. On the right is **Tabard Yard**, named for the inn where Chaucer's pilgrims departed for the shrine of Thomas Becket in his famous *Canterbury Tales*. The street was once crammed with inns catering for travellers preparing for the journey south, but the only surviving inn – and the only surviving galleried coaching inn in London – is the **George Inn** (*see* p.211), down George Yard on the right. It's a handsome black and white pub built in 1676 which now shares its courtyard with a tatty modern eyesore. Still, the outdoor tables make it very popular in summer. Before the theatres were built, performances took place in the inn courtyards, with the spectators watching from the galleries.

Cross Borough High St and walk left down Stoney St. Underneath the railway arches are a handful of higgledy-piggledy shops, cafés and pubs, and **Borough Market** (*see* p.209). This is London's finest food market; traditionally a wholesale fruit and veg market, on Friday and Saturday it fills up with stalls selling all kinds of wonderful gourmet produce. Time seems to have stood still here, and it's become a popular film location – you might recognize it from *Lock, Stock and Two Smoking Barrels*. You can tuck into the best bubble and squeak in London at the **Borough Café**, just down Park St, a very picturesque corner of the city.

Cut through the market to Cathedral St, which leads to **Southwark Cathedral** (*see* p.209), a surprisingly harmonious mish-mash of genuine Gothic and Victorian neo-Gothic styles. There has been a church here since at least the 7th century, when it was called St Mary Overie (a distortion of Mary Over the River), and long before that it was the site of Roman burial grounds, which were turned up when the recent annexe was being built and can be glimpsed next to the (very nice) new refectory. During the Elizabethan age, it was known as the Actor's Church, and Shakespeare's younger brother Edward is buried in the churchyard. Despite its elevation to cathedral status in 1905, the church has retained a small-scale, local feel.

Return to Cathedral St, and turn right. At the end of the street are the ruins of **Winchester Palace**, of which only the rose window and west wall have survived the centuries. This was the notorious abode of the Bishops of Winchester, who held court here for 400 years, running a lucrative – and officially sanctioned – prostitution racket in the surrounding 'stews', or brothels. The 'Winchester Geese', as the prostitutes were known, were thrown into the Bishop's private prison, **The Clink** (*see* p.208), if they attempted to conceal their earnings or tried to work for anyone else. There's a gruesome museum on the site of the Clink right next to the former palace on Clink St. It gives a mind-boggling glimpse into Elizabethan notions of contraception and the terrible fate of prisoners condemned to The Hole.

Head left out of The Clink, past the wine museum of **Vinopolis** (*see* p.208), and snake right to meet the river. There's a popular riverside pub here, the **Anchor**, the sole survivor of the 22 taverns which once stretched along Bankside. In Elizabethan times, this area became the raffish entertainment district of the City of London; boatmen would ferry visitors across the river for the seedy delights of the brothels, inns and playhouses. There were four theatres here: the Rose, the Swan, the Hope and the Globe. None survive, although the remnants of the **Rose Theatre** (*see* p.207) were discovered beneath a modern office block on Rose Alley. In 1997, a reconstruction of the **Globe Theatre** (*see* p.206), the largest of Bankside's theatres, rose up on New Globe Walk, about 200 metres from its original site on Park St. The 'sharers' of the original Globe were the eight leading players of the Lord Chamberlain's Men, including Shakespeare, who wrote *Hamlet*, *Macbeth*, *Othello* and *King Lear* for this playhouse. Try to catch a play 'in the round', or visit the 'Shakespeare Experience', which includes a tour of the circular auditorium.

Just beyond the Globe is Cardinal Cap Alley, former site of another famous inn, and beyond it is the magnificently converted power station, now **Tate Modern** (*see* p.205). Opposite it stretches the beleaguered **Millennium Bridge**, a sleek pedestrian bridge designed by Norman Foster which opened in 2000 and closed again almost immediately when it was discovered how much it bounced when people walked along it. Foster's so-called 'Blade of Light' was quickly re-nicknamed the 'Wobbly Bridge'; now reopened, it's worth sauntering across towards the great dome of St Paul's if only to check out if the new stabilisers work.

Retrace your steps back along Bankside, past the Globe, and turn right down **Bear Gardens**. It wasn't just the taverns and brothels that enticed the city gents from north of the river: among the most pernicious activities that took place here was the cruel sport of bear-baiting. Bears were tied to a stake and ripped apart by vicious dogs as spectators placed bets. The sport wasn't just popular with commoners – Queen Elizabeth I brought the French ambassador by barge to watch the gory display. The last bear garden was closed down in 1682 and nothing remains except the name.

Turn left at the bottom of Bear Gardens onto Park St, which passes under Southwark Bridge Rd. Just after the bridge, a small plaque marks the site of the original Globe Theatre. Continue along Park St as it curves to the right, and turn right down Redcross Way. This meets the broad expanse of Southwark St, where just to the left you'll see the imposing **Hop Exchange**, built in 1866. Southwark was the centre of the English brewing trade from the Middle Ages; the Miller in Chaucer's *Canterbury Tales* warned his fellow pilgrims, 'If the words get muddled in my tale/Just put it down to Southwark ale.' The Hop Exchange is now an office building but, if you can wheedle your way inside, there's a beautiful light-filled courtyard with a glass roof, designed so that the hops could be examined by natural light.

Contemplating hops is thirsty work. The inns of Bankside and Borough High St may have largely disappeared, but plenty of pubs have sprung up in their place. To try out some good English ales, walk down Southwark St back to Borough High St, where you should turn left onto Stoney St. The **Market Porter** pub, just by the market, has a particularly fine selection and is as good a place as any to finish up this walk.

HAMPSTEAD AND HIGHGATE

Hampstead and Highgate are two peaceful, hill-top villages in the north of the city, huddled on either side of the vast Heath, one of London's wildest and most beautiful parks. Chic, affluent Hampstead

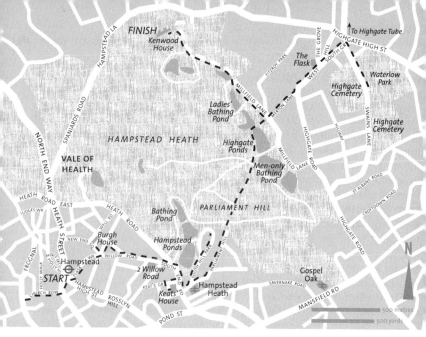

has long been the favoured retreat of writers, artists and intellectuals from Freud to Keats, many of whom came to take the waters at the spa which was established here at the end of the 17th century. It's long gone now, but the cobbled alleys lined with Georgian terraces and crooked Victorian mansions are still some of the most picturesque in London. The Heath spreads across several hundred acres, scattered with woods, bathing ponds and quiet paths where you can lose yourself for an hour or two. On the eastern flank of the Heath is genteel Highgate, with a smattering of teashops and pubs, and a staggeringly ornate Victorian cemetery.

The walk winds up at Kenwood House, a Neoclassical mansion in the northern part of the Heath, where – if you've remembered to book in advance (see p.361) – you can enjoy an outdoor concert by the lake in summer. This walk is best enjoyed during the summer, when you can wander about the gardens, take a dip in the ponds, and enjoy a pint or two out on the terrace of an old inn. If you want to have a picnic on the Heath, make sure you pick up provisions on Hampstead High St or Heath St.

The exit from Hampstead Tube is on the corner of Hampstead High St and Heath St; almost opposite the station on the High St is

a wonderful French pâtisserie, **Maison Blanc**, which is a great place to pick up provisions if you want to have a picnic on the Heath. Cross the High St and walk left down Heath St (passing the wonderful Hungarian tearooms of the **Louis Pâtisserie** on your left at No.32), then turn right onto **Church Row**. This broad, handsome enclave of Georgian townhouses is one of the few survivors from the glory days of the Hampstead spa, when the city gents would come with their families to take the waters.

Return to the Tube, and turn down Hampstead High St. Turn left again down narrow Ginsberg Yard, which becomes Flask Walk; the name recalls the days when the (supposedly) beneficial spring waters were sold in threepenny flasks along this alley. If ale is more to your taste, you can stop off at the **Flask Inn** at No.14, a cheerful, old-fashioned boozer with Victorian trimmings where the local spring water was once bottled. It does decent, if unexceptional, pub grub.

Continue down Flask Walk, which opens out onto Well Walk, where the Victorian **Chaleybeate Well** commemorates the springs. On the left (just off New End Square) is an elegant Queen Anne mansion covered with creepers and squeezed behind a hodge-podge of council housing; this is

Burgh House, which now contains a local museum with a motley assortment of paintings and oddities, and a delightful tearoom (the Buttery) in the basement with outdoor seating in a plant-filled courtyard in summer.

Stroll down Well Walk and turn right down Church Hill, which meets Willow Rd. At the end of this street on the right is the sleek Modernist house simply called **No.2 Willow Road** (see p.241). Designed in 1937 by the Hungarian-born architect Ernö Goldfinger, it is elegantly slotted into a trim Georgian terrace. Despite Hampstead's reputation for liberality, not all of Goldfinger's neighbours were impressed: Ian Fleming hated it so much that he gave one of his most despicable villains the architect's name in revenge. Inside, the light-filled, elegant rooms are decorated with Modernist paintings and sculptures, including works by Barbara Hepworth, who lived here in the 1930s.

Willow Rd drops down to meet South End Rd, where peaceful Keats Grove leads off to the right. On the left is the tranquil **home of John Keats** (1795–1821; see p.241), one of Hampstead's most famous residents. The consumptive poet languished here before heading to Rome to die. He fell in love with the girl next door, Fanny Brawne, and both houses have been converted into a quiet, slightly dull museum, where the ghoulish might enjoy a glimpse of the bed where Keats first coughed blood, confiding to a friend 'that drop of blood is my death warrant'. The small gardens are pretty and contemplative, and the sickly plum tree is a successor to the one beneath which Keats is said to have composed his 'Ode to a Nightingale'.

Return to South End Rd and turn right towards Hampstead Heath train station. The restored **Victorian lavatory** which sits just opposite the train station at the bottom of South End Rd on the left was long used for cottaging (cruising for gay sex); the playwright Joe Orton would regularly come here to pick up young men before he was bludgeoned to death by his jealous lover, Kenneth

Start: Hampstead Tube (Northern Line).
Finish: Kenwood House, from where it's a lengthy walk back across the Heath to Hampstead, or the No.210 bus will take you to Highgate Tube (Northern Line).
Distance: 4–5 miles, not including walking around Highgate Cemetery or any detours on the Heath.
Walking time: Leave a whole day to fully explore Highgate Cemetery, Kenwood House and to picnic on the Heath.
Suggested days: The summer is best for this walk. Highgate Cemetery is open only at the weekend in winter but daily in summer; check the opening times of Keats House and 2 Willow Rd if you want to visit them (p.241).
Lunch and drinks stops: Maison Blanc (for picnic provisions), see below; Louis Pâtisserie, see p.330; Flask Inn, see below; Burgh House Buttery, see below; The Flask, see p.348; Lauderdale House, see below; Kenwood House Pub and Brasserie, see below.

Halliwell. This isn't the only grim tale associated with this corner of Hampstead: it was at the bottom of South Hill Park (cross South End Rd and keep the train station on your right) that Ruth Ellis shot her lover David Blakely five times in 1955; she was subsequently executed in Holloway, the last woman to be hanged in Britain.

South Hill Park forks at **Parliament Hill**; take the right fork and walk up Parliament Hill, which becomes a pathway onto the Heath, and keep going until you reach the top of the hill. This is a favourite spot for families and kite-fliers (it's often called Kite Hill), and offers stunning views out over London. It's the perfect picnic spot, too.

Several paths lead from the top of the hill; take the paved one which heads northeast and is a continuation of the path you came up by. It meanders gently towards the **bathing ponds** on the eastern side of the Heath. If you've brought a swimming costume (and have a sturdy constitution) you can take your pick. The path will deposit you next to the men-only pond, or you can turn left and walk north towards the ladies' pond (the mixed pond is back on the western side of the Heath, but both the water and the clientele are decidedly suspect).

Another paved path cuts between two of the ponds and leads off the Heath onto Millfield Lane, part of the village of Highgate. Walk straight up the hill along Merton Lane, turn left at the top, and continue along Highgate West Hill, where you'll find the fine old pub **The Flask** at No.77. Keats would stroll across the Heath to this inn, which has changed little in the last couple of centuries, and still boasts its low, beamed ceilings and wood-panelled walls. Nowadays it also has a very popular outdoor terrace in summer and offers surprisingly good food. Highgate West Hill becomes South Grove, which flanks Pond Square, a prim little square lined with a couple of cafés.

Swains Lane leads off Pond Square; Highgate's celebrated cemetery sprawls on either side of the road, but first, take a little stroll into **Waterlow Park** (on the left), a quiet and little-known corner of London which offers spectacular views over the flamboyant mausoleums in the adjoining cemetery and far out across the city. At the centre is **Lauderdale House**, now an arts centre but once the home of Charles II's mistress Nell Gwynne. It's another good coffee stop, with outdoor seating in summer.

Back on Swains Lane, you can't miss the arched entrance to the western part of **Highgate Cemetery** (*see* p.239) on the right. This side of the cemetery is the most magni- ficent – stuffed with splendid mausoleums dripping with weeping angels, and an eye- popping mock-Egyptian City of the Dead – but is only open for guided visits. The eastern side, across the road, is less ornate but still atmospheric. Karl Marx is buried at the back,

along with his grandson, wife and housekeeper, Helene Delmuth, with whom he had an affair. When she fell pregnant, Engels was forced to accept paternity in order to avoid scandal. The tomb is now topped with a brash bronze bust, erected by the Communist movement in the 1950s with blithe disregard for Marx's own wishes for a simple burial monument. Nearby is the grave of Mary Ann Evans (better known by her pen name George Eliot), and behind it is that of her lover, George Henry Lewes.

Head back to the Heath (it's easiest just to retrace your steps along Swains Lane and Highgate West Hill). When you get to the bottom of Merton Lane, turn right along Millfield Lane, which becomes a walkway heading northwest through the Heath. It leads to **Kenwood House** (*see* p.241), a Neoclassical mansion which was beautifully remodelled in the late 18th century by Robert Adam. It has a fairy-tale setting overlooking the Heath, and is famous for the concerts held on summer evenings by the pretty lake in the gardens. It's well worth trying to book tickets for one of these events, but, if not, the house itself contains a small but excellent collection of European artworks, including paintings by Gainsborough, Reynolds, Turner, Vermeer and Van Dyck, all handsomely displayed in airy galleries. There's a pub and a brasserie, with outdoor seating overlooking the gardens in the summer, and a pathway strewn with Henry Moore sculptures just in front of the house.

This is where the walk ends. If, after an hour or two of lounging on the lawns here, you can't muster the energy to trek back to Hampstead across the Heath, the No.210 bus from outside Kenwood House will deposit you close to Highgate Tube Station.

Day Trips

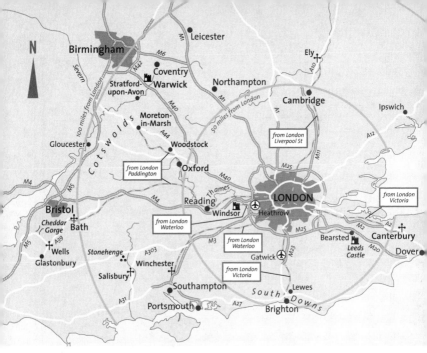

England is so small that you arrive just about anywhere in three or four hours. In the time it takes to cross London, you could be most of the way through a train journey to Manchester or York at the other end of the country. So the notion of a day trip is a flexible one. Here are a few brief suggestions for places no more than an hour and a half away; a complete run down would fill another book.

WINDSOR

Windsor Castle

t (01753) 869 898, *e* information@royal collection.org.uk, *w* www.royal.gov.uk. **Open** March–Oct daily 9.45am–5.15pm, last adm 4pm, Nov–Feb daily 9.45am–4.15pm, last adm 3pm; closed 21 April noon–5.15pm, 2 June 9.45am–1pm, 17 June and 25–26 Dec; **adm** adults £11.50, over-60s £9.50, 5–17s £6, families £29.

A fire at Windsor Castle in November 1992 was the culmination of what Queen Elizabeth II called an 'annus horribilis' of scandal and misfortune. Now the castle has been meticulously restored for millions of pounds and is back on its feet – a medieval fortress inhabited and embroidered by the monarchy for the last 900-odd years. The highlight is the castle itself, a vast complex of crenellated towers, turrets and loopholes. Inside you can tour some of the royal apartments, decorated with Holbeins, Rembrandts and Van Dycks from the Royal Collection;

Getting There

Trains leave from Waterloo or Paddington and take 35–50 mins. There are also **Green Line buses** from Eccleston Bridge behind Victoria Station.

Tourist Information

Royal Windsor Information Centre, 24 High St, Windsor, *t* (01753) 743900, *w* www .windsor.gov.uk. *Open* Sun–Fri 10am–4pm, Sat 10am–5pm.

Lunch

Bexley Arms Pub and Restaurant, Vansittart Rd, *t* (01753) 865552. Local pub, with good ales, darts and pool. Very friendly owners and decent home-cooking.

Cornucopia Bistro, 6 High St, Windsor, *t* (01753) 833009. Friendly bistro just 200m from the castle gates, with sunny décor and tasty Mediterranean-style dishes.

St George's Chapel, with its magnificent Perpendicular vaulted ceiling, where 10 sovereigns including Henry VIII are buried; and the extraordinary Queen Mary's Dolls House. Arguably the most intricate in the world, it took 1,500 craftsmen three years to build it for the future Queen Mary at the end of the 19th century.

Eton College

Down the road from the castle, near the River Thames, is Eton College, the most exclusive private boys' school in the country. The 15th-century buildings are fine, but the real attraction is the sight of adolescent boys who talk like Prince Charles and run around in tailcoats and bow ties. In 2002, the gardens will open to visitors to mark the Queen's Golden Jubilee (see p.394).

OXFORD

The home of England's oldest university is a wondrous cluster of soft yellow sandstone buildings and 'dreaming spires' that rise romantically out of the mist on damp autumn mornings. Oxford is a bustling town, a place of many facets and diverse culture.

Oxford University

The university, which dates back to the 12th century, is a surprisingly unacademic place. For centuries, its main function was as a meeting place for the sons of the influential and the wealthy; exams were not introduced until the early 19th century, and even today many students spend a disproportionate amount of time on the river, acting in student plays or debating in the Oxford Union, a misleadingly named private club that fancies itself as a mini-parliament. Terms are short (just eight weeks), lectures are optional, and the only structured teaching in many subjects is a weekly one-on-one session between student and tutor.

Getting There

Trains leave from Paddington and take an hour. The best bus is the **Oxford Tube**, which leaves from Grosvenor Gardens near Victoria.

Tourist Information

Tourist Information Centre, *The Old School, Gloucester Green, Oxford, t (01865) 726871, w www.visitoxford.org.* **Open** *Mon–Sat 9.30am–5pm, Sun and hols 10am–3.30pm.*

Lunch

The Kings Arms, *40 Holywell St, t (01865) 242369.* A 17th-century coaching inn and one of Oxford's most popular drinking dens. Good range of ales, wines and whiskies and decent pub grub.

Le Petit Blanc Brasserie, *71–2 Walton St, t (01865) 510999.* Marco Pierre White's upmarket brasserie does a great *prix fixe* lunchtime menu.

The White Horse, *Broad St, t (01865) 728318.* Another old pub, known for attracting the university's most eccentric characters. Also does reasonable pub food.

The university is split into colleges, fortified mini-monasteries that are medieval in inspiration if not always in architecture. All have a chapel, student lodgings, courtyards and well-manicured lawns. The most beautiful include **Magdalen** (very romantic), **Merton** (idyllic by the riverside), **Christ Church** (imposing if a little flashy), **New College** (with a winding alley leading to the main gate, gargoyles and a great Epstein sculpture in the chapel) and **All Souls** (especially Hawksmoor's superb north quadrangle and old library, which you can see through the railings in Radcliffe Square even if the college is shut).

You should also visit the **Bodleian Library**, particularly the Divinity School, one of the most beautiful examples of Perpendicular style; admire the views up and down the **High St**; and take a **punt** – a flat boat propelled by a long pole – along the Thames, known locally as the Isis. The **Ashmolean** (**w** *www.ashmol.ox.ac.uk*) is one of the finest museums in Britain, with a huge collection spanning several millennia. At the other end of the spectrum is **Moma** (**w** *www.moma .org.uk*), Oxford's trendy museum of modern art.

Blenheim Palace

t *(01993) 811091*, **w** *wwwblenheimpalace.com.* **Palace open** *11 March–Oct daily 10.30am– 5.30pm;* **park open** *daily 9am–5pm;* **Marlborough Maze and Butterfly House open** *mid-March–Oct daily 10am–6pm;* **adm** *£10, concessions £7.50, 5–15s £5.*

Eight miles north of Oxford in Woodstock is John Vanbrugh's Blenheim Palace, built for the ancestors of Winston Churchill. The slightly forced Versailles-like splendour of its buildings is more than compensated for by the lush and vast landscaped park.

STRATFORD-UPON-AVON AND THE COTSWOLDS

Stratford

Stratford is one of the bigger tourist cons in the world; all it boasts, apart from its excellent theatre run by the **Royal Shakespeare Company**, is a handful of pretty cottages that have been shamelessly exploited as a Shakespeare heritage trail. The Bard was certainly born in Stratford, but whether he was really raised in the so-called **Birthplace Museum** is open to question. Come for the theatre, and perhaps for Anne Hathaway's attractive thatched cottage at **Shottery** one mile out of town; but otherwise you would do better to explore the surrounding countryside.

The Cotswolds

These gently rolling hills, known as the Cotswolds, are dotted with pretty sandstone

Getting There

There are **trains** from Paddington to Stratford and Moreton-in-Marsh (although these may involve changing trains, usually at Oxford, Didcot, Banbury or Leamington Spa), and **National Express coaches**, which take nearly four hours from Victoria Coach Station. There are trains from Marylebone to Warwick (1hr 45mins). To see this area properly, you really need a **car**.

Tourist Information

South Warwickshire Tourist Office, *Bridgefoot,* **t** *(01789) 293127,* **w** *www.stratford-upon-avon.co.uk.* **Open** *Easter–Oct Mon–Sat 9am–5pm, plus Sundays either side of Xmas 11am–4pm, Nov–Easter Mon–Sat 9am–6pm, Sun 11am–5pm.*

Lunch

Marlowe's Restaurant and Georgie's Bistro, *18 High St, Stratford-upon-Avon,* **t** *(01789) 204999.* Choose between the relaxed ground-floor bistro and elegant first-floor gourmet restaurant. This is a favourite with the actors from the RSC and has friendly staff, wooden beams and plenty of olde-worlde charm.

Badger's Hall, *High St, Chipping Campden,* **t** *(01386) 840839.* Homemade scones with strawberry jam and clotted cream in one of the prettiest villages in the Cotswolds. B&B available.

villages with names like Broadway, Stow-on-the-Wold, Upper and Lower Slaughter and Chipping Campden, which date back to Tudor and Jacobean times. Tourism has made them a bit too twee for their own good in recent years, but they nevertheless make a delightful day out.

Warwick Castle

t *(01926) 406600,* **w** *www.warwick-castle .co.uk.* **Open** *April–Sept daily 10am–6pm, Oct–March daily 10am–5pm, last adm 30mins before closing; closed 25 Dec;* **adm** *(depending on month) adults £10.75–13, concessions*

£7.70–9.50, children £6.55–7.60, families £30–34. Shop, restaurant, café and picnic area.

North of Stratford is Warwick Castle. Dating back to the Norman conquest, it has an atmospheric dungeon and torture chamber, complete with horrifying instruments, and an extensive park landscaped by the ubiquitous Capability Brown.

CAMBRIDGE

Cambridge University

Founded by renegade students from Oxford and still known by its rival as 'the other place', central Cambridge consists almost entirely of its university and is rather quiet and cerebral as a result (although it is becoming increasingly known as a centre for computer technology). Its most beautiful colleges – made of whiter stone than Oxford's – are lined in a row, with gardens rolling down towards the bank of the River Cam. The **riverside**, with its views of St John's, Trinity, Caius (pronounced 'Keys') and King's, is known as The Backs; it has a special magic that makes the trip to Cambridge worthwhile all on its own.

King's College has a 15th-century Perpendicular chapel of extraordinary beauty, a riot of fan vaulting illuminated by elegant tall windows. The chapel choir, which performs regularly, is one of the most famous in the world. Other worthwhile sights include the brick and stone buildings of **Jesus College**, on the other side of town, and the **Fitzwilliam Museum**, which has some valuable Roman and Greek artworks.

Ely Cathedral

Northeast of Cambridge is Ely, with its fine cathedral. Behind the Norman front is a unique and extraordinary octagonal tower in the Decorated style. There are also traces of the vast Saxon abbey where St Etheldreda (*see* p.159) made her name.

Getting There

Trains leave from King's Cross and Liverpool St and take 45mins to one hour. **Buses** leave from Victoria Coach Station but can get stuck in the North London traffic. There are frequent trains (15mins) and buses between Ely and Cambridge.

Tourist Information

Tourist Information Office, *The Old Library, Wheeler St, Cambridge, t (01223) 322640, e tourism@cambridge.gov.uk, w www .cambridge.gov.uk/leisure/tourism. Open Mon–Fri 10am–5.30pm, Sat 10am–5pm, Sun 11am–4pm (closed Sun in winter); closed 1 Jan and 25–26 Dec.*

Lunch
Cambridge
Auntie's Tea Shop, *1 St Mary's Passage, t (01223) 315 641.* Old-fashioned tearooms with a nice line in fairy cakes and other teatime staples.

Venue, *66 Regent St, t (01223) 308 100.* Fashionable new restaurant and bar, serving excellent modern European cuisine.
Ely
The Fire Engine, *25 St Mary's St, t (01353) 662 582.* Well-known contemporary art gallery and restaurant with decent, if pricey, food and a pretty courtyard garden.

Waterside Tea Rooms, *52 Waterside, t (01353) 66757.* Pretty tearooms in a 15th-century house near the marina; B&B also available.

BATH

Bath has the finest array of Regency architecture in the country, the result of the town's popularity as a spa and gambling retreat in the latter half of the 18th century. It is a place of elegance and refinement, set in beautiful rolling countryside. The balming effects of the local spring water were first appreciated by the Romans, who built the baths (Aquae Sulae) that give the town its

Getting There

Trains leave from Paddington and take 80 minutes. **National Express buses** leave from Victoria Coach Station and take up to three hours. You really need a **car** to explore the countryside and towns around Bath in a day trip.

Tourist Information

Tourist Information Centre, *Abbey Chambers, Abbey Church Yard*, **t** *(01225) 477 101*, **e** *tourism@bathnes.gov.uk*, **w** *www .visitbath.co.uk (official Web site)*, **w** *www .bath.co.uk (useful local Web site)*. **Open** *May–mid-Oct Mon–Sat 9.30am–6pm, Sun 10am–4pm, mid-Oct–April Mon–Sat 9.30am–5pm, Sun 10am–4pm; closed 1 Jan and 25–26 Dec*.

Lunch

You'll be spoilt for choice in Bath.

The Circus Restaurant, *34 Brock Street*, **t** *(01225) 318 918*. Delicious modern European cooking, good-value lunch menus, and friendly owners.

The Pump Room, *Stall St*, **t** *(01225) 477 785*. The original fancy tearooms: enjoy a proper cream tea served by unctuous waiters.

Sally Lunn's Refreshment House and Museum, *4 North Parade Passage*, **t** *(01225) 461 634*. Apparently the oldest house in Bath (1492) and the former home of the creator of the Sally Lunn bun – only available in the tearoom here.

name. You can visit the bubbling underground source as well as the **Roman baths** and Georgian **Pump Room** built on top (entrance on Stall St).

Next door is the magnificent 16th-century **cathedral**, with two Jacob's ladders on either side of the main façade (note that some of the angels of the ladder are upside down, this being the only way the sculptor could think of showing them in descent). The rest of the town is a remarkably unified ensemble of 18th-century architecture, much of it the work of John Wood. **Royal Crescent** at the top of the town is a majestic sweep of 30 curved houses incorporating 114 Ionic columns. The

Avon **riverside** is also delightful, notable for Robert Adam's splendid **Pulteney Bridge**.

The biggest event to hit Bath in recent years is the **Bath Spa Project**, due for completion in October 2002. Once again, visitors will be able to take the waters, albeit in a slick new contemporary building, which will boast an open-air thermal rooftop pool, steam rooms, and an indoor thermal pool with water naturally hot at 35°C.

Around Bath

Near Bath is the picture-postcard village of **Castle Combe**, with its old stone houses and rickety tearooms alongside a babbling brook. The countryside of Wiltshire, Avon and Somerset is enchanting in general. If you have a car you might want to combine Bath with **Wells** (great cathedral), **Glastonbury** (famous for its ancient ruins and music festival) and the **Cheddar Gorge** (where the cheese originally came from). East of Bath is **Salisbury**, with another fine cathedral much painted by Constable, and **Stonehenge**, the celebrated prehistoric stone ring, atmospherically situated in the middle of Salisbury Plain.

WINCHESTER

Winchester was the capital of Wessex in Saxon times, growing rich on the wool trade, and at one stage even took over from London as the most important city in England. The city is now dominated by its magnificent **cathedral** (**w** *www.winchester-cathedral .org.uk*), at 556ft the longest medieval church in Europe. Begun in 1079, it was worked on over several centuries; the original Norman arches of the nave are concealed behind an elaborate web of 14th-century Perpendicular tracery. The high point of the interior is the choir, with its lovely wooden stalls. The stained-glass window in the north aisle pays homage to Jane Austen, who had a house in College Street and died there in 1817.

From the cathedral it is a short walk to the other main attraction of Winchester, its prestigious private **school** (*guided tours available*), which dates back to 1382, when the then bishop, William of Wykeham, first accepted boys for religious and secular instruction. Now it is one of the most exclusive fee-paying 'public' schools in the country.

The gateway in College St leads to a series of medieval and Gothic Revival courtyards where pupils work and live. The school's brightest pupils, known as scholars, dress up in shirt, tie and academic gown, while non-scholars wear straw hats and conventional jackets. The chapel, in Chamber Court, has a remarkable fan tracery roof built by Hugh Herland, the late 14th-century craftsman who also worked on Westminster Hall in the Houses of Parliament. The grounds, where pupils play cricket, soccer and a weird mud-spattered game called Winchester football, extend to the south towards some **Saxon barrows** around St Catherine's Hill.

BRIGHTON

Brighton is a city of many facets. On the one hand, it is an old-fashioned English seaside resort of grand hotels on the front, ice-cream vans, hurdy-gurdy players, old men with rolled-up trousers on the pebble beach and lovers strolling along the pier; on the other, its cafés and nightclubs have an unmistakably young and trendy feel. For years Brighton was where married men used to come for dirty weekends with their lovers; they still come, although the town is now better known for its large gay community. Brighton is a town of more innocent pleasures, too. One speciality, evoked in the famous novel by Graham Greene, is **rock**, a hard, coloured stick of peppermint-flavoured sugar candy.

The streets behind the waterfront, **the Lanes**, have been attractively pedestrianized and make for pleasant strolling. Further inland, John Nash's Taj Mahal-esque

Royal Pavilion, was built for George IV as a kind of Regency Disneyland. Spurned by the Victorians, it is now fully restored and open to the public. The conglomeration of Brighton and Hove got city status in 2001 and is extremely proud of the fact, and, as the icing on the cake, it was chosen to be a European City of Culture in 2002.

The Sussex Downs

Try, too, to explore the beautiful countryside of the Sussex Downs in Brighton's hinterland. **Lewes** (pronounced 'Lewis'), the county capital, is particularly picturesque, as are smaller villages like **Steyning**. Near Lewes is **Glyndebourne**, an attractive country house famous for its outstanding (but very expensive) summer opera season.

CANTERBURY

Canterbury is the cradle of the Anglican Church, the place where St Augustine came to convert King Ethelbert of Kent in 597. The **cathedral** bears traces of every medieval style from Norman to Perpendicular. Two tremendous towers at the western end lead you into the nave, which was entirely rebuilt by Henry Yevele in the 14th century. In the northwest transept is a slab in the pavement marking the spot where Archbishop Thomas à Becket, Henry II's 'turbulent priest', was murdered in 1170. Other attractions include a fine **Roman mosaic floor** in Butchery Lane, the Saxon remains of **St Augustine's Abbey**, the Norman **King's School** and some well-preserved sections of medieval wall, especially the **Westgate**.

LEEDS CASTLE

*t 0870 600 8880, **w** www.leeds-castle.com; take a **train** from Victoria to Bearsted (the castle is in the southern county of Kent, not in the northern city of Leeds), from where a coach will take you to the castle; **National**

Getting There

Trains for Canterbury leave from Victoria and Charing Cross and take around one hour 20 minutes. **National Express coaches** take even longer (around two hours).

Tourist Information

Tourist Information Centre, *34 St Margaret's St, Canterbury, t (01227) 766 567, **w** www.canterbury.co.uk. Open April–Oct Mon–Sat 9.30am–5.30pm, Sun 10am–4pm, Nov–March Mon–Sat 9.30am–5pm, Sun 10am–4pm (closed Sun Jan–March); closed 1 Jan and 24–26 Dec.*

Lunch

Lloyds, *89–90 St Dunstans St, t (01227) 76822. Laid-back, stylish restaurant serving fine food at reasonable prices. The menu changes every 4 weeks, depending on what's in season.*

The Moat Tea Rooms, *67 Burgate, t (01227) 784 514. Wooden beams, old sideboards stuffed with crockery, and plenty of chintz – the perfect spot for a cream tea.*

*Express also runs a bus service from Victoria Coach Station. **Castle** open March–Oct daily 10am–5pm, Nov–Feb daily 10am–3pm; closed for open-air concerts (phone for details) and 25 Dec; **adm** adults £11, concessions £9.50, 4–15s £7.50. Joint train and admission tickets are available from Victoria and all other stations on the way (call t 0870 603 0405 for details).*

If you visit only one of the many stately homes dotted around London, this is where you should head. Its **Norman ramparts** are built, Chenonceaux-like, over two islands in a lake formed by the River Len, surrounded by verdant meadows and trees. For hundreds of years Leeds was a favourite royal residence; it now boasts an elegant series of **state rooms**; an eccentric collection of medieval **dog collars**; a **park** landscaped by Capability Brown with lakes, waterfalls, nature reserves and herb gardens; and, best of all, an enchanting **maze** (bigger and better than Hampton Court's) with an intricately carved underground grotto at its centre.

Where to Stay

There are several pitfalls to avoid when choosing the ideal hotel for your stay in London. For one thing there is no universal rating, and the star and crown systems fall well below the standards of their counterparts in other countries. However, while some hotels still rest on their wildly out-of-date laurels, others, both new and traditional, are as appealing and competitively priced as any in the world.

If at all possible, try to arrange accommodation from your home country. Flight and accommodation packages cover a wide price range and can work out to your advantage. If booking independently, you can usually confirm your booking by giving a credit card number or sending a fax. The **London Tourist Board** also operates a telephone credit card booking service (**t** (020) 7604 2890; open Mon–Fri 9.30am–5.30pm). If you turn up in London without a room in your name and you get nowhere ringing the tourist offices (see p.81), you can line up outside a tourist office and try your luck there. Try Victoria Station forecourt, Liverpool St station or the Underground concourse at Heathrow Terminals 1–3. Commission rates vary from a small one-off fee to a percentage of the room rates, included in the prices quoted. The following internet address may also be useful: **w** www.demon.co.uk/hotel-uk/excindex.html.

If you're not travelling in summer, try haggling a bit and you might negotiate your own discount. Weekend rates are common, and if you stay for a week you might get one night free. You may be able to save your pennies by declining breakfast or by asking for a room without a bath. In the cheaper establishments, the corridor bathrooms are usually better than the en suite kind, so this is not much of a sacrifice.

Most hotels are in the West End or around Kensington, Chelsea, Earl's Court and West London. Try to avoid streets which, like Sussex Gardens in Bayswater, are just long strips of touristy hotels and lack true London charm. Finding somewhere quiet can be a problem, especially in the busy summer months, but as a broad rule of thumb you will be disturbed less the further you are out of the centre. The best places to stay are in districts like Notting Hill, Fulham and Holland Park, or else by the river – don't forget the newer hotels in the Docklands. Having said that, Bloomsbury offers some excellent bargains.

Remember that space is tight, so book as far in advance as possible, whatever the category of accommodation.

Price Categories

Prices given are for a normal double room for one night, with bathroom and without breakfast, but find out about discounts before dismissing a place as too dear. The categories are:

luxury	£200 and over
expensive	£120–199
moderate	£80–119
inexpensive	under £80

Westminster, Victoria and Pimlico

Luxury

Hilton London St Ermin's R14
Caxton St, W1, **t** *(020) 7222 7888,* **f** *7222 6914,* **e** *stermins@jolly hotels.it,* **w** *www.jollyhotels.it;* **tube** *St James's Park.*
Glossy hotel in a plush Edwardian mansion close to St James's Park.

Expensive

Dolphin Square Hotel R18
Chichester St, SW1, **t** *(020) 7834 3800,* **t** *0800 616 607,* **f** *(020) 7798 8735,* **e** *reservations@dolphin squarehotel.co.uk,* **w** *www.dolphin squarehotel.co.uk;* **tube** *Pimlico.*
A pristine modern hotel set among its own gardens, with a

mind-boggling range of spa and excercise facilities. Designed with the business traveller in mind, all rooms have their own kitchens and some have separate sitting rooms. The hotel restaurant is the acclaimed Rhodes in the Square.

Map Key

P	Q	R	S	T

Westminster, Victoria and Pimlico Hotels

The Goring P15

Beeston Place, SW1, **t** *(020) 7396 9000,* **f** *7834 4393,* **e** *reception@ goringhotel.co.uk;* **w** *www.goring hotel.co.uk;* **tube** *Victoria; wheelchair accessible.*

Exquisite family-run hotel, which succeeds in blending its traditional Edwardian roots and values with a light, welcoming and highly individual atmosphere. £185–225.

The Rubens at the Palace P14

39–41 Buckingham Palace Rd, SW1, **t** *(020) 7834 6600,* **f** *7828 5401,* **e** *reservations@rubens.red carnationhotels.com,* **w** *www.red carnationhotels.com;* **tube** *Victoria.*

Perfect location close to the Palace and the Royal Mews should the Queen invite you for tea. Traditional and very comfortable.

Tophams Belgravia O15

28 Ebury St, SW1, **t** *(020) 7730 8147,* **f** *7823 5966,* **e** *tophambelgravia@ compuserve.com;* **tube** *Victoria, Sloane Square.*

This long-established neighbourhood favourite is contemporary and colourful. The staff are keen and friendly.

Moderate

Sanctuary House Hotel S14

33 Tothill St, SW1, **t** *(020) 7799 4044,* **f** *7799 3657,* **e** *sanctuary house@fullers.co.uk,* **w** *www .fullers.co.uk;* **tube** *St James's Park.*

Cheerful Fuller's pub with 34 en suite bedrooms upstairs decked out with fake Victoriana. Fantastic location and decent pub food. From £70 (good weekend deals).

Winchester Q16

17 Belgrave Rd, SW1, **t** *(020) 7828 2972,* **t** *7798 5685;* **tube** *Victoria, Pimlico.*

Smart, welcoming B&B with good facilities and smooth service. All rooms are newly decorated and have en suite bathrooms and TV.

Windermere Hotel P17

142–4 Warwick Way, SW1, **t** *(020) 7834 5163,* **f** *7630 8831,* **w** *www .windermere-hotel.co.uk;* **tube** *Victoria, Sloane Square.*

Delightful little hotel with a small restuarant and bar. Quiet and unassuming but very well located.

Inexpensive

Carlton Hotel R17

90 Belgrave Rd, SW1, **t** *(020) 7976 6634,* **f** *7821 8020,* **e** *info@city hotelcarlton.co.uk,* **w** *www.city*

hotelcarlton.co.uk; *tube Victoria, Pimlico*.

Another decent choice in Belgravia: all rooms have en suite bathrooms, as well as tea- and coffee-making facilities. From £60.

Collin House O16
104 Ebury St, SW1, t/f (020) 7730 8031, e collin.house@faxvia.net; tube Victoria, Sloane Square.
Clean, hospitable bed and breakfast behind Victoria Station. Homey but fresh. £65–80.

Enrico Q17
77–9 Warwick Way, SW1, t (020) 7834 9538, f 7233 9995, e enrico hotel@hotmail.com; tube Victoria.
Basic but comfortable rooms in Pimlico. £40–60 inc. breakfast.

Huttons Hotel Q17
55 Belgrave Rd, SW1, t (020) 7834 3726, f 7834 3389, e reservations@ huttons-hotel.co.uk, w www .huttons-hotel.co.uk; tube Victoria, Pimlico.
Dapper, family-run B&B which has recently been renovated. From £55.

Oak House P16
29 Hugh St, SW1, t (020) 7834 7151; tube Victoria.
Small rooms with basic catering facilities for only £46. Breakfast in your room. No advance booking (unless you want to stay for a few days), so roll up early in the day.

Trafalgar Square and Around

Luxury

St Martin's Lane T10
45 St Martin's Lane, WC2, t (020) 7300 5500, f 7300 5515, e stmartins lane@compuserve.com; tube Charing Cross, Leicester Square.
Ultra-stylish glass-fronted celebrity magnet. There are three expensive restaurants for die-hard fashionistas who don't mind paying through the nose for the privilege of dining with a TV personality.

Expensive

Trafalgar Square Thistle S10
Whitcomb St, WC2, t (020) 7930 4477, f 7925 2149, e trafalgar .square@thistle.co.uk; tube Leicester Square, Piccadilly Circus, Charing Cross.
Bland, smoothly efficient chain hotel. The location couldn't be more central.

Moderate

Manzi's S10
1–2 Leicester Square, WC2, t (020) 7734 0224, f 7437 4864; tube Leicester Square, Piccadilly Circus, Charing Cross.
Set above the famous fish restaurant, the 15 rooms offer excellent value and a slightly ramshackle charm – bang in the centre of London. Doubles £83–92, triples £107, quads £116.

St James's, Mayfair and Regent Street

Luxury

Brown's P10
Albermarle St, W1, t (020) 7493 6020, f 7493 9381, e brownshotel@ brownshotel.com, w www.browns hotel.com; tube Green Park, Piccadilly Circus.
Old-fashioned English establishment, with the air of a country house, and impeccable, stiff-collar service. Attractive if smallish rooms. From £275.

Claridges O9
Brook St, W1, t (020) 7629 8860, f 7499 2210, e info@claridges.co.uk, w www.claridges.co.uk; tube Bond St, Oxford Circus.
There are Art Deco bedrooms, a black and white marbled foyer and a touch of royal class at London's most celebrated smaller luxury hotel. Prices range from £395 to £4,115 (the latter for a two-floor penthouse).

Connaught O10
16 Carlos Place, W1, t (020) 7499 7070, f 7495 3262, e info@the-connaught.co.uk, w www.the-connaught.co.uk; tube Green Park, Bond St; wheelchair accessible.
Attentive service commands a troupe of loyal devotees. An air of calm exclusivity presides. Outstanding restaurants. Book in writing well in advance. From £335.

Dorchester N11
53 Park Lane, W1, t (020) 7629 8888, f 7409 0114; tube Hyde Park Corner, Marble Arch; wheelchair accessible.
Triple-glazed rooms (to foil the Park Lane traffic) and views over Hyde Park, plus a spa, a dazzling choice of fine restaurants and acres of gold and marble. From £345.

Dukes Q12
35 St James's Place, SW1, t (020) 7491 4840, f 7493 1264, e enquiries @dukeshotel.co.uk; tube Green Park, Piccadilly Circus.
Discreetly tucked down a quiet sidestreet, Dukes is popular with the kind of people who are usually hunting and shooting on their estates. Or at least they like to look as though they are. The martinis are purportedly the best in the city.

London Hilton O12
22 Park Lane, W1, t (020) 7493 8000, f 7208 4142, w www.hilton .com; tube Marble Arch, Hyde Park Corner.
Swish modern tower overlooking the park. The kitsch Hawaiian theme bar, Trader Vic's, mixes one of the meanest martinis in the city. The restaurant – Windows – offers spectacular views from the 28th floor.

Le Meridien Piccadilly R10
21 Piccadilly, W1, t 0870 400 8400, f (020) 7437 3574, e impicc@forte-hotels.com; tube Green Park, Piccadilly Circus.
One of the classiest and grandest hotels in the Meridien chain, this has very luxurious rooms,

impeccable service and the prestigious Marco Pierre White Oak Room restaurant. Despite the sumptuous décor, it's hard to forget that this is a chain hotel. From £320.

Metropolitan O12

19 Old Park Lane, W1, t (020) 7447 1000, f 7447 1100, e res@ metropolitan.co.uk, w www .metropolitan.co.uk; tube Hyde Park Corner, Green Park.

Cool hip minimalism permeates; the young staff wear DKNY and each room has its own CD player, VCR, fax, Kiehl's toiletries and a minibar stocked with all the usual plus an instamatic camera. The ultra-fashionable Nobu restaurant and Met bar are located here. From £270.

The Ritz Q11

Piccadilly, W1, t (020) 7493 8181, f 7493 81 81, e enquire@theritz london.com, w www.theritz london.com; tube Green Park, Piccadilly Circus; wheelchair accessible.

Marble galore, gorgeous rococo carpets, plus glorious views over Green Park if you pick your room right. *Ancien régime* luxury. From £380.

Covent Garden and Soho

Luxury

Kingsway Hall U8

Great Queen St, WC2, t (020) 7309 0909, f 7309 9696, e kingsway hall@compuserve.com, w www.kingswayhall.co.uk; tube Holborn, Covent Garden.

Brand-new hotel with well-equipped rooms and excellent service. Inside the hotel, you could be in any city in the world, but Covent Garden is on your doorstep. Interesting weekend deals.

Savoy U10

Strand, WC2, t (020) 7836 4343, f 7240 6040, e info@the-savoy .co.uk, w www.the-savoy.co.uk; tube Charing Cross, Embankment.

Sleek, businesslike luxury. The *fin de siècle* dining room is a favourite for afternoon tea. Many bars and restaurants with discreet good service. From £380 (£500 for a view of the Thames).

West Street T9

13–15 West St, WC2, t (020) 7010 8700; tube Covent Garden, Leicester Square.

The restaurant may not be everyone's cup of tea but above it are the three most fabulous rooms in central London. Choose from the White Room, with marble floors and an enormous white leather-padded bed; the Stone Room, with a delicious private terrace; or the Loft Room, with floor-to-ceiling windows. Space NK toiletries in the bathrooms and a full English breakfast in bed add to the perfection. From £250 including breakfast.

Expensive

Hazlitt's S8

6 Frith St, W1, t (020) 7434 1771, f 7439 1524, w www.hazlitts hotel.com; tube Tottenham Court Rd, Leicester Square.

Small Georgian rooms with some four-posters and claw-footed iron baths in the former home of essayist William Hazlitt. Palm trees and classical busts complement the old-fashioned hospitality. Winner of the Caesar Hotel of the Year award 2002. From £190.

Moderate

Fielding U9

4 Broad Court, Bow St, WC2, t (020) 7836 8305, f 7497 0064, e reservations@the-fielding-hotel.co.uk, w www.the-fielding-hotel.co.uk; tube Covent Garden, Holborn.

Attractively decorated, the smallish rooms and tiny reception are well compensated for by the friendly staff and location opposite the Royal Opera House.

Holborn

Luxury

One Aldwych V9

1 Aldwych, WC2, t (020) 7300 0500, f 7300 1001, e sales@onealdwych .co.uk, w www.onealdwych.co.uk; tube Holborn, Temple (closed Sun), Charing Cross, Embankment.

Contemporary chic at its most sophisticated. Opened in 1998, this has become a bolthole for the stars. From £300.

Waldorf V9

Aldwych, WC2, t 0870 8484, f (020) 7836 7244; tube Holborn, Temple (closed Sun), Charing Cross, Embankment.

Opulence from another age: there are still tea dances in the elegant Palm Court, painted a restful *eau-de-Nil*. The rooms don't quite match up to the promise of the gilded public area, but are splendidly equipped all the same.

Bloomsbury and Fitzrovia

Luxury

Charlotte Street Hotel R7

25 Charlotte St, W1P, t (020) 7806 2000, f 7806 2002, e charlotte@ firmdale.com, w www.charlotte streethotel.com; tube Tottenham Court Rd, Goodge St.

Chic little boutique hotel which has proved a big hit with the media crowd thanks to its glamorous 75-seat screening rooms. Rooms are stylishly decorated with a charming mix of the traditional – embroidered cotton quilts – and the contemporary – CD and DVD players in all rooms. The staff are perhaps the nicest in all London. The restaurant is a treat even if you aren't staying.

Grange White Hall V7

2 Montague St, WC1, t (020) 7580 2224, f 7580 5554, w www.grange hall.co.uk; tube Holborn, Russell Square.

Newly and comfortably renovated, with a bit too much squeaky-

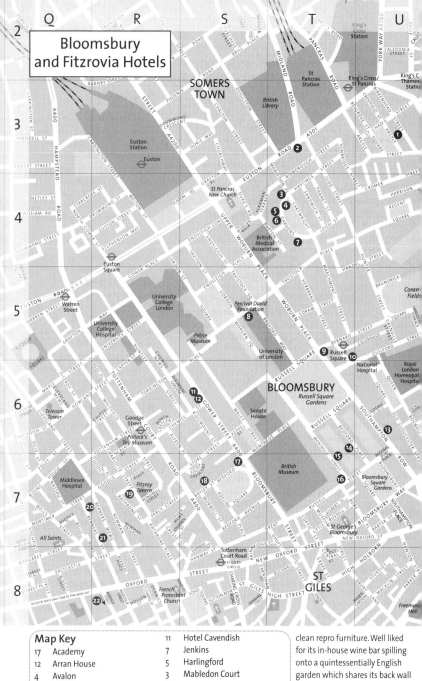

Bloomsbury
and Fitzrovia Hotels

clean repro furniture. Well liked for its in-house wine bar spilling onto a quintessentially English garden which shares its back wall with the British Museum. Some rooms have four-poster beds. £190–230.

myhotel Bloomsbury S7
11–13 Bayley St, WC1, **t** *(020) 7667 6000,* **f** *7667 6044,* **e** *guest_services@myhotels.co.uk,* **w** *www*

Health studio, Yo Sushi bar, smart restaurant, champagne bar and a fleet of immaculately kempt staff.

Sanderson Q7
50 Berners St, W1, t (020) 7300 9500, e sandersonsuk@ virginnet.co.uk; tube Tottenham Court Rd, Oxford Circus.
The team behind St Martin's Lane – Ian Schrager and Philippe Starck – have given a 60s office block the minimalist makeover. It's terrifyingly fashionable, and priced to match. Still, it's handy for shopping, theatres and Soho. Look out for weekend deals.

Expensive

Academy S7
The Bloomsbury Town House, 17–21 Gower St, WC1, t (020) 7631 4115, f 7636 3442, e res-academy@ etontownhouse.com; tube Goodge St, Tottenham Court Rd.
Five original Georgian townhouses in the heart of Bloomsbury. Cosy library and small paved garden. An antique charm.

Berners Hotel R7
10 Berners St, W1A, t (020) 7666 2000, t 7666 2001, e berners@ berners.co.uk, w www.theberners hotel.co.uk; tube Tottenham Court Rd, Oxford Circus.
Just north of Oxford St, a stone's throw from Soho. Elegantly restored Edwardian mansion with a slightly stuffy atmosphere. £170–250.

Bonnington U6
92 Southampton Row, WC1, t (020) 7242 2828, f 7831 9170, e sales@ bonnington.com, w www .bonnington.com; tube Holborn, Russell Square; wheelchair accessible.
Friendly Edwardian hotel which has been recently refurbished. £100–150.

Melia White House P5
Albany St, NW1, t (020) 7387 1200, f 7388 0091, e melia.white.house@ solmelia.es, w www.solmelia.es; tube Great Portland St; wheelchair accessible.
Huge modern hotel in the Spanish chain. From £180.

Montague on the Gardens T7
15 Montague St, WC1, t (020) 7637 1001, f 7636 6498, e sales@ montague.redcarnationhotels.com, w www.redcarnationhotels.com; tube Holborn, Russell Square.
Chintzy, lush and comfortable; a stone's throw from the British Museum.

Russell T5
Russell Square, WC1, t (020) 7837 6470, f 7837 2857, w www.principal hotel.co.uk; tube Russell Square.
Extravagant Victorian Gothic establishment now run by Principal Hotels and undergoing a major and long overdue revamp.

Moderate

Harlingford T4
61–3 Cartwright Gardens, WC1, t (020) 7387 1551, f 7387 4616, e book@harlingfordhotel.com; tube King's Cross, Euston.
Simple B&B rooms with access to tennis courts. Loyal clientèle and friendly Australian staff.

Jenkins T4
45 Cartwright Gardens, WC1, t (020) 7387 2067, f 7383 3139, e reservations@jenkinshotel .demon.co.uk, w www.jenkins hotel.demon.co.uk; tube King's Cross, Euston.
The pick of the bunch on this hotel-lined crescent. Clean and light, with a friendly family atmosphere. No smoking. Book two months ahead.

St Margaret's T6
26 Bedford Place, WC1, t (020) 7636 4277, f 7323 3066; tube Russell Square, Holborn.
Clean, fresh B&B with plenty of flowers and large, well-proportioned rooms. Extremely nice staff. Only £62 with a shared bathroom, and prices drop if you stay more than one night.

Inexpensive

Arran House S6
77–9 Gower St, WC1, t (020) 7636 2186, f 7436 5328, e arran@dircon .co.uk, w www.london-hotel.co.uk; tube Goodge St, Euston Square.

.myhotels.co.uk; tube Goodge St, Tottenham Court Rd.
Designed by the Conran partnership, this is a cool, clean hotel where you are sent a questionnaire in advance asking for your pillow (feather or foam) and music (country or pop) preferences. Lots of Aveda goodies in the bathroom and waffle slippers – look down and they say 'my my'.

Wonky floors and a lovely rose garden add charm to this otherwise no-frills guest house. In-house laundry and use of kitchen including microwave. Internet facilities. Vidoes on request. £75 en suite, £55 with shared bathroom.

Avalon T4
46–7 Cartwright Gardens, WC1, **t** *(020) 7387 2366,* **f** *7387 5810,* **e** *reception@avalonhotel.co.uk,* **w** *www.avalonhotel.co.uk;* **tube** *King's Cross, Euston.*
No-frills cheapie: the most basic of the B&Bs on this crescent. £49–69.

Celtic T6
61–3 Guildford St, WC1, **t** *(020) 7837 9258;* **tube** *Russell Square.*
Simple family-run B&B. Ask for a room at the back as street rooms can be noisy. £55.

Crescent T4
49–50 Cartwright Gardens, WC1, **t** *(020) 7387 1515,* **f** *7383 2054,* **e** *general.enquiries@crescenthotel oflondon.com,* **w** *www.crescent hoteloflondon.com;* **tube** *King's Cross, Euston.*
Use of the garden and public tennis courts a big plus here. A no-frills B&B. £80 inc. breakfast.

Elmwood U3
19 Argyle Square, WC1, **t** *(020) 7837 9361;* **tube** *King's Cross.*
Basic but very cheap, in a lovely square near the new British Library and not far from King's Cross. £35–40.

Hotel Cavendish S6
75 Gower St, WC1, **t** *(020) 7636 9079,* **w** *www.hotelcavendish.com;* **tube** *Goodge St, Euston Square.*
Friendly, charmingly ramshackle B&B set in two Georgian townhouses which have preserved some original features. Comfortably disordered gardens and lovely, welcoming owners. £60.

Mabledon Court T4
10–11 Mabledon Place, WC1, **t** *(020) 7388 3866,* **f** *7387 5686,* **e** *book@ mabledonhotel.com;* **tube** *King's Cross, Euston.*
Clean but unexciting hotel near King's Cross. £80 inc. breakfast.

Tavistock S5
Tavistock Square (southeast side), WC1, **t** *(020) 7278 7871,* **f** *7837 4653,* **e** *info@imperialhotels.co.uk,* **w** *www.imperialhotels.co.uk;* **tube** *Euston, Euston Square, Russell Square.*
Large rooms in a good location. Art Deco finishes but impersonal atmosphere and tour-group clientèle. Views over Tavistock Square garden a plus. £80 inc. breakfast.

Marylebone and Regent's Park

Expensive

Dorset Square L6
39–40 Dorset Square, NW1, **t** *(020) 7723 7874,* **f** *7724 3328,* **e** *dorset@ firmdale.com;* **tube** *Baker St, Marylebone.*
Elegantly restored Regency building between Madame Tussaud's and Regent's Park. Stylish décor, delightful staff and a strong cricket theme because of the nearby Lord's ground.

Durrants N7
George St, W1, **t** *(020) 7935 8131,* **f** *7487 3510,* **e** *enquiries@durrants hotel.co.uk;* **tube** *Marble Arch, Baker St; wheelchair accessible.*
A former 18th-century coaching inn preserving many old-fashioned touches, including silver plate-covers in the restaurant. Rooms are simple but spotless and staff are very pleasant.

Moderate

Bentinck House Hotel O8
20 Bentinck St, **t** *(020) 7393 9141,* **f** *7724 5903;* **tube** *Bond St.*
Very friendly, family-run hotel handy for shopping in the West End. Compact but pleasant rooms. £80.

Blandford M6
80 Chiltern St, W1, **t** *(020) 7486 3103,* **f** *7487 2786,* **e** *blandford hotel@dial.pipex.com,* **w** *www .capricornhotels.co.uk;* **tube** *Baker St, Bond St.*
Simple B&B-style hotel, offering decent rooms and a copious

morning meal, in a quiet side-street near Baker St station.

Bryanston Court L8
56–60 Great Cumberland Place, W1, **t** *(020) 7262 3141,* **f** *7262 7248,* **e** *info@bryanstonhotel.com;* **tube** *Marble Arch; wheelchair accessible.*
Efficient hotel with few frills but a pleasant atmosphere and an open fire in winter. Plans are afoot for a major expansion.

Edward Lear M8
28–30 Seymour St, W1, **t** *(020) 7402 5401,* **f** *7706 3766,* **e** *edwardlear@ aol.com,* **w** *www.edlear.com;* **tube** *Marble Arch.*
Named after the nonsense-verse writer. Small efficient hotel with a homey feel. £90 en suite, £65 with shared bathroom.

Georgian House Hotel M7
87 Gloucester Place, W1, **t** *(020) 7935 2211,* **f** *7486 7535,* **e** *info@ georgian-hotel.demon.co.uk;* **tube** *Baker St, Marylebone.*
Spacious rooms with personality. £90 but there are generous discounts for staying three nights and for taking rooms three or four flights up.

Hart House Hotel M8
51 Gloucester Place, W1, **t** *(020) 7935 2288,* **f** *7935 8516,* **e** *reservations@harthouse.co.uk;* **tube** *Marble Arch, Baker St, Marylebone.*
Well-run Georgian mansion overlooking Portman Square, with remarkably large rooms for the area.

Inexpensive

Concorde L8
50 Great Cumberland Place, W1, **t** *(020) 7402 6169,* **f** *7724 1184,* **w** *atconcorde-hotel.com;* **tube** *Marble Arch.*
A cheery, no-frills establishment under the same good management as Bryanston Court (see above). In need of some renovation at the time of writing and indeed big changes are planned. Self-catering options. £70–85.

South Kensington and Knightsbridge

Luxury

Basil Street Hotel L14
Basil St, SW3, **t** *(020) 7581 3311,* **f** *7581 3963,* **e** *info@thebasil.com,* **w** *www.thebasil.com;* **tube** *Knightsbridge.*
Pleasant, family-owned hotel with a friendly atmosphere and good, old-fashioned service, located just 90 seconds from Harrods. And it's got a women-only bar – the Parrot Club.

The Berkeley M13
Wilton Place, SW1, **t** *(020) 7235 6000,* **f** *7235 4330,* **e** *info@the berkeley.co.uk;* **tube** *Hyde Park Corner.*
Classic, luxurious hotel which prides itself on its service. Among the sumptuous trimmings is a rooftop swimming pool. From £310.

Blakes Off maps
33 Roland Gardens, SW7, **t** *(020) 7370 6701,* **f** *7373 0442,* **e** *blakes@easynet.co.uk;* **tube** *South Kensington.*
Sumptuous and exotic hotel. Idiosyncratic rooms, some with four-poster beds and antique lacquered chests. Birdcages and carved giraffes to boot. £155–310.

Cliveden Town House M16
26 Cadogan Gardens, SW3, **t** *(020) 7730 6466,* **f** *7730 0236,* **e** *reservations@clivedentown house.co.uk,* **w** *www.clivedentown house.co.uk;* **tube** *Sloane Square.*
A very elegant, refined hotel set in a quietly opulent townhouse overlooking Cadogan Gardens. Exceptionally smooth service. £160–310.

Halkin N13
5 Halkin St, SW1, **t** *(020) 7333 6000,* **f** *7333 1100,* **e** *info@theberkeley .co.uk;* **tube** *Hyde Park Corner; wheelchair accessible.*
Luxury at its most understated and expensive. Sleek, contemporary décor, an award-winning

Italian restaurant, and an excellent Thai restaurant. From £285.

Hyatt Carlton Tower M16
2 Cadogan Place, SW1, **t** *(020) 7235 1234,* **f** *7235 91 29;* **tube** *Knightsbridge.*
Deluxe mod cons and marble bathrooms, a stone's throw from Harrods, with a well-equipped health club, swimming pool and spacious rooms. £325–350.

Lanesborough N13
Hyde Park Corner, SW1, **t** *(020) 7259 5599,* **f** *7259 5606;* **tube** *Hyde Park Corner.*
Country house elegance and utmost luxury – personalized stationery awaits each guest on arrival.

Expensive

Aster House I17
3 Sumner Place, SW7, **t** *(020) 7581 5888,* **e** *asterhouse@btinternet .com,* **w** *www.asterhouse.com;* **tube** *South Kensington.*
Sophisticated English townhouse hotel, even more sumptuous after a recent facelift.

Claverly K14
13–14 Beaufort Gardens, SW3, **t** *(020) 7589 8541,* **f** *7584 3410,* **e** *reservations@claverlyhotel.co.uk;* **tube** *Knightsbridge.*
Lovingly detailed hotel, with attractive rooms and an imaginative breakfast featuring waffles and fresh juices as well as bacon and eggs.

Diplomat M15
2 Chesham St, SW1, **t** *(020) 7235 1544,* **f** *7259 6153,* **e** *diplomathotel@ btintnernet.com;* **tube** *Knightsbridge, Sloane Square.*
Comfortable rooms up and down a glass-domed stairwell. Copious buffet breakfast and just a short walk to Beauchamp Place and Harrods.

Five Sumner Place I17
5 Sumner Place, SW7, **t** *(020) 7584 7586,* **f** *7823 9962,* **e** *reservations@ sumnerplace.com,* **w** *www.sumner place.com;* **tube** *South Kensington.*
The feel of a country home in the heart of London, with a stunning

conservatory-style breakfast room. Smart but unpretentious and quiet. £100–140.

The Gore H14
189 Queen's Gate, SW7, **t** *(020) 7584 6601,* **f** *7589 8127,* **e** *sales@gore hotel.co.uk;* **tube** *Gloucester Rd.*
Gothic and Edwardian décor, old prints, *objets d'art,* and a lush, upbeat atmosphere.

Knightsbridge Green Hotel L13
159 Knightsbridge, SW3, **t** *(020) 7584 6274,* **f** *7225 1635,* **e** *thekghotel @aol.com,* **w** *www.thekghotel.co .uk;* **tube** *Knightsbridge.*
Right in the thick of Knightsbridge, virtually opposite Harrods. A mix of traditional and modern décor. Excellent value. Non-smoking. Breakfast is brought to your room.

Number Sixteen I16
16 Sumner Place, SW7, **t** *(020) 7589 5232,* **f** *7584 8615,* **e** *reservations@ numbersixteenhotel.co.uk,* **w** *www.numbersixteenhotel.co.uk;* **tube** *South Kensington.*
Four charming Victorian townhouses with lovely gardens and fountains, large reception areas and comfortable rooms with balconies. Posh B&B.

Moderate

Hotel 167 Off maps
167 Old Brompton Rd, SW5, **t** *(020) 7373 0672,* **f** *7373 3360,* **e** *enquiries @hotel167.com;* **tube** *South Kensington.*
Attractively decorated Victorian corner house with young clientèle.

The South Bank and Southwark

Luxury

London Mariott Hotel County Hall V13
The County Hall, SE1, **t** *(020) 7928 5200,* **w** *www.mariott.com/ mariott/lonch;* **tube** *Waterloo, Westminster.*
The rooms here have the most spectacular views in London – out across the river to the Houses of

Parliament in one direction and back to St Paul's in the other. The luxury facilities also include an excellent gym with a full-size swimming pool. Prices range from £200 to £250.

Expensive

London Bridge Hotel CC12
8–18 London Bridge St, SE1, **t** *(020) 7855 2200,* **w** *www.london-bridge-hotel.co.uk;* **tube** *London Bridge.*
Grand old 19th-century hotel opposite the station with newly refurbished rooms and a largely corporate clientèle.

Novotel London Waterloo V15
113 Lambeth Rd, SE1, **t** *(020) 7793 1010,* **f** *7793 0202,* **e** *h1785@accor-hotels.com,* **w** *www.novotel.com;* **tube** *Waterloo, Lambeth North.*
New, modern chain hotel with all mod cons. Impersonal staff, but well located. Find out about weekend deals.

Moderate

Holiday Inn Express Z11
103–109 Southwark St, SE1, **t** *(020) 7401 2525,* **f** *7401 3322,* **w** *www.expresssouthwark.co.uk;* **tube** *Southwark.*
Formulaic chain hotel which nonetheless gets booked months in advance. Good facilities including Internet access and an incredible location just a few minutes from Tate Modern and the river. £90.

Inexpensive

London County Hall Travel Inn V13
Belvedere Rd, SE1, **t** *0870 238 3300,* **t** *(020) 7902 1619,* **e** *ti_county hall@whitbread.com,* **w** *www.travelinn.co.uk;* **tube** *Waterloo, Westminster.*
A chain hotel in a prime location – very reasonably priced rooms close to the river. Sadly the views are reserved for the expensive Mariott hotel round the corner. An excellent choice for families. £70.

Mad Hatter Y11
3–7 Stamford St, SE1, **t** *(020) 7401 9222,* **e** *madhatter@fullers.co.uk;* **tube** *Southwark.*
Pleasant if unmemorable rooms above a Fullers pub. Great location just a stone's throw from the Tate Modern and London Eye. £60–80.

The City and Around

Luxury

Great Eastern Hotel DD7
Liverpool St, EC2, **t** *(020) 7619 5000,* **f** *7618 5001,* **e** *sales@great-eastern-hotel.co.uk,* **w** *www.great-eastern-hotel.co.uk;* **tube** *Liverpool St.*
The Grande Dame of railway hotels has had the Conran treatment. Now packed with minimalist Japanese restaurants and designer-clad staff, it still retains a whiff of a more romantic age, especially in some of the panelled sitting rooms.

Threadneedles DD8
5 Threadneedle St, EC2, **t** *(020) 7432 8451,* **t** *(020) 7289 4878,* **e** *simon_tyrie@etontownhouse.com,* **w** *www.etontownhouse.com;* **tube** *Bank.*
Sleek new boutique hotel in an old bank, which has retained its stained-glass dome and other original fittings. The rooms are elegant and contemporary, and there's a bar, restaurant, meeting rooms and well-equipped gym. £265–2,795!

Expensive

Thistle City Barbican Off maps
120 Central St, EC1, **t** *(020) 7956 6000,* **f** *7253 1005,* **e** *barbican@thistle.co.uk,* **w** *www.thistle hotels.com;* **tube** *Old St, Barbican.*
Another bland chain hotel in a strikingly ugly building. Still, facilities are pretty good and there just isn't much choice near the City. Weekend deals can be surprisingly good value.

Tower Thistle FF11
St Katharine's Way, E1, **t** *(020) 7481 2575,* **f** *7488 4106,* **e** *tower.business centre@thistle.co.uk,* **w** *www .thistlehotels.com;* **tube** *Tower Hill; wheelchair accessible.*
Not a beauty, but ideally placed next to the Tower overlooking the river. Modern fittings and every conceivable comfort. Geared towards business travellers. £170–250.

Moderate

City Hotel Off maps
12 Osborn St, SE1, **t** *(020) 7247 3313,* **e** *info@cityhotellondon.co.uk;* **tube** *Aldgate East.*
Modern chain hotel close to Brick Lane and Spitalfields Market. Nothing special, but it has some family rooms which can make the price very attractive. From £110.

Hampstead

La Gaffe Off maps
107 Heath St, NW3, **t** *(020) 7435 4941,* **f** *7794 7592,* **e** *lagaffe@msn .com,* **w** *www.lagaffe.co.uk;* **tube** *Hampstead.* **Moderate.**
Charming bed and breakfast above an Italian restaurant in an 18th-century shepherd's cottage. Bedrooms (some of them small) are reached via a precipitous stairway. A happy, upbeat place to stay. Hampstead is great for restaurants and an easy commute to the West End. £90.

Hampstead Village Guesthouse Off maps
2 Kemplay Rd, NW3, **t** *(020) 7435 8679,* **f** *7794 0254,* **e** *info@ hampsteadguesthouse.com;* **tube** *Hampstead.* **Moderate–inexpensive.**
Dutch family household just a step away from Hampstead Heath. Lots of books and pot plants, plus there's a fridge and phone in all rooms. £72–84. There's also a studio flat for £120 per night.

Camden and Primrose Hill

Hampstead Britannia Hotel Off maps
*Primrose Hill Rd, NW3, t (020) 7586 2233, f 7722 8558, e hampstead@ britannia-hotels.co.uk, w www .britannia-hotels.co.uk; tube Chalk Farm. **Moderate.***
A chain hotel in a 70s block. The restaurant and bar has a pretty, leafy terrace and the park is close by. Primrose Hill is a wealthy and pleasant area with some good restaurants.

Camden Lock Hotel Off maps
*89 Chalk Farm Rd, NW1, t (020) 7267 3912, f 7267 5696, w www .camdenlockhotel.co.uk; tube Chalk Farm. **Inexpensive.***
Small, modern hotel with very helpful and friendly staff. It's geared towards business travellers but offers excellent weekend deals. Handy for Camden Market. £54–74 (lowest price is for July and August weekends).

Swiss Cottage

Swiss Cottage Off maps
*4 Adamson Rd, NW3, t (020) 7722 2281, f 7483 4588, e reservations@ swisscottagehotel.co.uk; tube Swiss Cottage. **Expensive–moderate.***
Part of the Best Western group, with olde-worlde atmosphere – lots of antiques, reproduction furniture and even a grand piano. Easy transport to the centre, and there are plenty of good restaurants in Swiss Cottage. £105–155.

Notting Hill, Holland Park and Bayswater

Luxury

Halcyon A12
81 Holland Park, W11, t (020) 7727 7288, f 7229 8516, e saleskensington @hilton.com; tube Holland Park.
Modern but traditional, in a large, renovated Holland Park mansion

house. Popular with showbiz and media people. Rated restaurant (the Aix en Provence) and bars.

Hempel G10
31–5 Craven Hill Gardens, W2, t (020) 7298 9000, f 7402 4666, e reservations@the-hempel.co.uk, w www.the-hempel.co.uk; tube Paddington, Lancaster Gate.
Luxury hotel designed by Anouska Hempel in 1997. Takes minimalism to its logical, most exotic extreme. Pure white foyer interrupted only by other-worldly flames and Thai ox-carts. Each room is unique, with mundane objects like electric sockets and bath plugs sublimely invisible.

Pembridge Court D10
34 Pembridge Gardens, W2, t (020) 7229 9977, f 7727 4982, e reservations@pemct.co.uk; tube Notting Hill Gate.
Elegant Victorian townhouse, fastidiously deconstructed with flourishing vegetation, and a quirky collection of Victoriana and antique clothing. Next to Portobello Market.

Portobello B9
22 Stanley Gardens, W11, t (020) 7727 2777, f 7792 9641, e info@ portobello-hotel.co.uk; tube Holland Park.
Victorian Gothic furniture juxtaposed with modern comfort and access to a local health club. Idiosyncratic rooms: some splendid, others a touch poky. £160–260.

Thistle Hyde Park Hotel H10
90 Lancaster Gate, W2, t (020) 7262 2711, f 7262 2147, e hyde.park@ thistle.co.uk, w www.thistlehotels .com; tube Queensway, Lancaster Gate.
Overlooking Kensington Gardens, the stucco palace façade disguises a thoroughly modern interior. Formerly well known as Whites, it's now part of the Thistle chain.

Expensive

Mornington G10
12 Lancaster Gate, W2, t (020) 7262 7361, US toll free t 1800 528 1234, f 7706 1028, e peter.elmquist@

mornington.co.uk, w www .mornington.se; tube Queensway, Lancaster Gate.
Scandinavian-run hotel with serious but professional staff. Nice library bar. Next to the Football Association, so lots of soccer types around.

Posthouse Kensington E14
Wright's Lane, W8, t 0870 400 9000, f (020) 7937 8239, w www.posthouse-hotels.co.uk; tube High St Kensington.
Large, featureless modern hotel. Nonetheless, it offers excellent facilities including gym, sauna and indoor pool. Weekend rates are exceptionally good and in the moderate category.

Moderate

Byron F10
36–8 Queensborough Terrace, W2, t (020) 7243 0987, f 7792 1957, e byron@capricornhotels.co.uk; tube Queensway, Bayswater.
Young, smart hotel full of sunshine and flowers, just a stone's throw from Kensington Gardens.

Delmere I8
130 Sussex Gardens, W2, t (020) 7706 3344, f 7262 1863, e delmere hotel@compuserve.com, w www.delmerehotels.com; tube Paddington.
Smart building on an otherwise dowdy street of hotels. Some tiny rooms, but others are spacious and comfortable.

Gate C10
6 Portobello Rd, W11, t (020) 7221 0707, f 7221 9128, e enquiries@gate hotel.com; tube Notting Hill Gate.
Pleasant, no-nonsense hotel in plum location among the antique shops of Portobello Rd. Rooms are tiny but well-appointed. £85–95 inc. continental breakfast.

Kensington Gardens E9
9 Kensington Gardens Square, W2, t (020) 7221 7790, f 7792 8612; tube Queensway, Bayswater.
Attractive rooms and some very nice bathrooms make this simple B&B a good mid-range choice. £85.

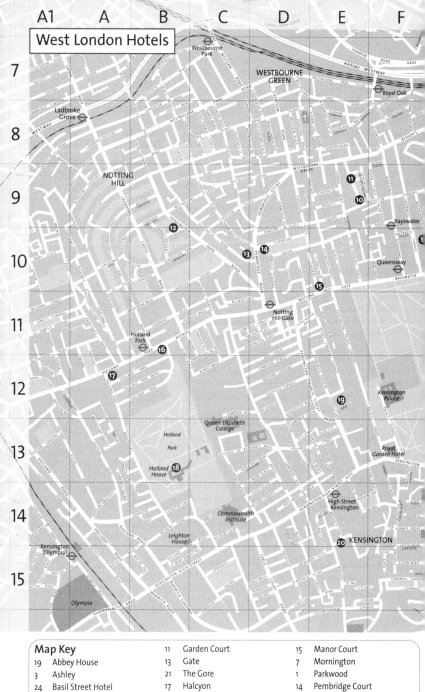

Map Key

19	Abbey House	11	Garden Court	15	Manor Court
3	Ashley	13	Gate	7	Mornington
24	Basil Street Hotel	21	The Gore	1	Parkwood
23	The Berkeley	17	Halcyon	14	Pembridge Court
4	Border	8	Hempel	12	Portobello
9	Byron	18	Holland House YHA	20	Posthouse Kensington
25	Claverly	10	Kensington Gardens	16	Ravna Gora
2	Delmere	22	Knightsbridge Green Hotel	6	Thistle Hyde Park
26	Diplomat	5	Lancaster Hall (German YMCA)		Hotel

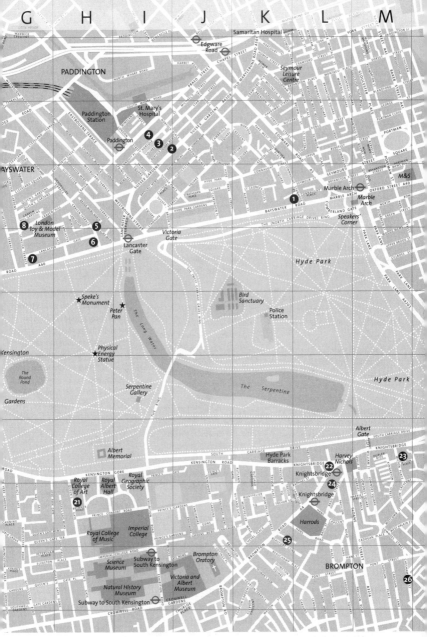

Parkwood L9
4 Stanhope Place, W2, **t** *(020)
7402 2241,* **f** *7402 1574,* **e** *pkwd
hotel@aol.com,* **w** *www
.parkwoodhotel.com;*
tube *Marble Arch.*
This is a small, family-run hotel in
a charming Georgian mansion
situated near the welcome
greenery of Hyde Park.

Inexpensive

Abbey House E12
11 Vicarage Gate, W8, **t** *(020) 7727
2594,* **f** *7727 1873,* **e** *abbeyhouse
desk@btconnect.com,* **w** *www
.abbeyhousekensington.com;*
tube *High St Kensington, Notting
Hill Gate.*
Simple, spacious rooms in this
delightful Victorian townhouse in

a quiet leafy square. Friendly
service. Shared bathrooms. Good
value at £74 (rates drop for longer
stays).

Ashley I8
15–17 Norfolk Square, W2, **t** *(020)
7723 9966,* **f** *7723 0173,* **e** *ashhot@
btinternet.com;* **tube** *Paddington.*
Maniacally clean and quiet hotel,
ideal for families or business

people looking for peace. Party animals stay away. The bulletin board has hints on sightseeing. £75.

Border I8
14 Norfolk Square, W2, **t** *(020) 7723 2968;* **tube** *Paddington.*
No-nonsense hotel with simple facilities, in a square full of similar hotels. £69 en suite, £59 with shared bath.

Garden Court E9
30–31 Kensington Gardens Square, W2, **t** *(020) 7229 2553,* **f** *7727 2749,* **e** *info@gardencourthotel.co.uk;* **tube** *Bayswater, Queensway.*
Simple bed and breakfast with nice views over the square at the front and gardens at the back. Well located next to Queensway and not far from Portobello. £88 en suite inc. breakfast, £58 with shared bath.

Lancaster Hall (German YMCA) H10
35 Craven Terrace, W2, **t** *(020) 7723 9276,* **f** *7706 2870,* **e** *info@ lancaster-hall-hotel.co.uk;* **tube** *Lancaster Gate, Paddington.*
Sounds grim and looks awfully generic, but the rooms (twin only) are clean, and the location excellent. £60–75.

Manor Court E10
7 Clanricarde Gardens, W2, **t** *(020) 7792 3361,* **w** *www.visitbritain.com;* **tube** *Notting Hill Gate.*
Simple, friendly B&B offering basic accommodation close to Kensington Palace. There are seven family rooms which are remarkably good value. £45–65.

Ravna Gora B11
29 Holland Park Av, W11, **t** *(020) 7727 7725,* **f** *7221 4282;* **tube** *Holland Park.*
Palatial Holland Park mansion turned slightly dilapidated bed and breakfast, with a talkative Serbian owner. £54–64.

Earl's Court

Hogarth E16
35–7 Hogarth Rd, SW5, **t** *(020) 7370 6831,* US toll free **t** *1800 528 1234,* **f** *7373 6179,* **e** *sales@marston*

hotels.com; **tube** *Earl's Court.* **Expensive.**
Part of the Best Western chain. Not a thing of beauty but friendly and with full amenities near Earl's Court Exhibition Centre. £130.

Twenty Nevern Square Off maps
20 Nevern Square, SW5, **t** *(020) 7565 9555,* **f** *7565 9444,* **e** *hotel@ twentynevernsquare.co.uk,* **w** *www.twentynevernsquare.co.uk;* **tube** *Earl's Court.* **Expensive.**
Small but perfectly formed town-house hotel. Each room is differently decorated, from Indonesian to Chinese, though all have marble bathrooms. Lots of rich natural fabrics and four-poster beds. Sumptuous buffet breakfast included. £175.

Beaver Off maps
57–9 Philbeach Gardens, SW5, **t** *(020) 7373 4553,* **f** *7273 4555,* **e** *hotelbeaver@hotmail.com,* **w** *www.smoothhound.co.uk/ hotels/beaver.html;* **tube** *Earl's Court.* **Inexpensive.**
Simple, attractive establishment on a lovely street, with a pool table and cheap car parking. There's a plush lounge with polished wooden floors. £40–80.

Heathrow

Comfort Inn Off maps
Shepiston Lane, Hayes, Middx UB3, **t** *(020) 8573 6162,* **w** *www .comfortheathrow.com;* **shuttle bus** *to Heathrow terminals 1, 2 and 3;* **train** *Hayes and Harlington (from Paddington).* **Moderate.**
Newly refurbished three-star hotel with modern furnishings.

Crowne Plaza Off maps
Stockley Rd, West Drayton, Middx UB7, **t** *(01865) 445555,* **f** *(01895) 867790,* **w** *www.london-heathrow .crowneplaza.com;* **shuttle bus** *to all Heathrow terminals;* **train** *West Drayton (from Paddington).* **Moderate.**
Glassy, modern four-star hotel with 24-hour leisure club and swimming pool. Standard room rates mean an excellent deal for families. All rooms £114.

Harmondsworth Hall Off maps
Summerhouse Lane, Harmonds-worth Village, West Drayton, Middx UB7, **t** *(020) 8759 1824,* **e** *elain@harmondsworth hall.com,* **w** *harmondsworthhall .com;* **pick-up and drop-off service** *from Heathrow;* **train** *West Drayton (from Paddington).* **Inexpensive.**
Lovely, ivy-covered old stone hall close to Heathrow but thankfully not on the flight path. Good-value family rooms, welcoming owners and delicious English breakfasts. Doubles £55–65, family rooms £75.

Gatwick

Melville Lodge Off maps
15 Brighton Rd, Horley, Surrey RH6 7HH, **t** *(01293) 784951,* **f** *785669,* **e** *melvillelodge.guesthouse@tesco .net;* **w** *www.smoothhound.co.uk/ hotels/mellodge.html;* **train** *Horley (from Victoria).* **Inexpensive.**
Pleasant little B&B which goes out of its way to be welcoming. All rooms have hospitality trays and tea- and coffee-making facilities. £38–45.

Waterhall Country House Off maps
Prestwood Lane, Ifield Wood, Crawley, West Sussex RH11 0LA, **t** *(01293) 520002,* **f** *539905,* **e** *info@waterhall.co.uk,* **w** *www .smoothhound.co.uk/hotels/water hal.html;* **train** *Crawley (from Victoria).* **Inexpensive.**
Handsome country house with very comfortable rooms and a sunny conservatory. £45.

B&B Agencies

The bed and breakfast is a British (and Irish) tourist institution: you get to stay in someone's house, enjoy their company and eat a slap-up breakfast for a fraction of the cost of a hotel. In London the system works less freely than in the rest of the country, but you will have noticed that some of the hotels listed above have a distinctly B&B flavour to them. Try finding one through one of the following agencies:

Bulldog Club

14 Dewhurst Rd, W14, **t** (020) 7371 3202, **f** 7371 2015, **e** jackson@bull dogclub.u-net.com, **w** www.bull dogclub.com.

Will fix you up in palatial surroundings – at a price of course. £85 for a single room, £105 double.

Host and Guest Service

103 Dawes Rd, SW6, **t** (020) 7385 9922, **f** 7386 7575, **e** acc@host-guest.co.uk, **w** www.host-guest.co.uk.

3,000 homes all over London from as little as £16.50 per person per night.

London Bed and Breakfast Agency Ltd

71 Fellows Rd, Hampstead, NW3, **t** (020) 7586 2768, **f** 7586 6567, **e** stay@londonbb.com, **w** www.londonbb.com.

B&Bs in central London and the near suburbs. £20–60 per person per night double occupancy or £23–60 for the visitor travelling alone.

London Homestead Services

3 Coombe Wood Rd, Kingston, Surrey, **t** (020) 8949 4455, **f** 8949 5492, **e** lhs@netcomuk.co.uk.

Minimum stay three nights. From £16. Book early.

Uptown Reservations

41 Paradise Walk, SW3, **t** (020) 7351 3445, **f** 7351 9383, **e** inquiries@up townres.co.uk.

Offers homes in Knightsbridge, Chelsea, Notting Hill and similarly smart neighbourhoods. £65–85 per person per night.

Worldwide Bed and Breakfast Association

PO Box 2070, London W12 8QW, **t** (020) 8742 9123, **f** 8749 7084, **e** bestbandb@atlas.co.uk.

Offers rooms in upmarket private homes in central and southwest London. £30–75 per person per night.

Student Halls of Residence

A number of university halls of residence throw open their doors to visitors during the long summer holiday from July to September. They can be excellent value (from £25 for a double room per night). Conditions are obviously a bit spartan, and you won't be able to cancel bookings very easily. Try this agency:

King's Campus Vacation Bureau

t (020) 7848 1700, **f** 7848 1717, **e** vac.bureau@kcl.ac.uk, **w** www.kcl.ac.uk/servicesforsociety.

Agency for four halls of residence all over London.

Or contact the following direct:

International Students House P5

229 Great Portland St, W1, **t** (020) 7631 8300, **f** 7631 8315, **e** accom@ish.org.uk, **w** www.ish.org.uk; **tube** Great Portland St.

Excellent value for money, with access to a whole range of student amenities. No upper age limit. Prices per person: in a single (£31), twin (£25), 3–4 sharing (£18) or dormitories (£12).

John Adams Hall S4

15–23 Endsleigh St, WC1, **t** (020) 7387 4086; **tube** Euston Square, Russell Square.

From £25 per person per night.

Ramsey Hall Q6

20 Maple St, W1, **t** (020) 7387 4537, **f** 7383 0843; **tube** Warren St.

Mainly singles and a few twins. Approx. £24 per person for B&B. Longer stays are cheaper.

Walter Sickert Hall Off maps

29 Graham St, N1, **t** (020) 7477 8822, **f** 7040 8825, **e** wxh@city.ac.uk, **w** www.city.ac.uk/ems; **tube** Angel.

£30–60 per person per night.

Youth Hostels

Not that much cheaper than the cheapest B&Bs. You can get a full list of addresses by calling the YHA Head Office in St Albans on **t** (01727) 855215.

City of London YHA Z9

36 Carter Lane, EC4, **t** 0870 770 5764, **f** 0870 770 5765, **e** city@yha.org.uk; **tube** St Paul's.

Right by St Paul's Cathedral. A few singles and doubles but most accommodation is in 4–8-bed dorms. B&B £19.90 for under-18s, £23.50 for adults.

Earl's Court YHA Off maps

38 Bolton Gardens, SW5, **t** 0870 770 5804, **f** 0870 770 5805, **e** earls court@yha.org.uk; **tube** Earl's Court.

This is real backpacker territory. Mainly 6–10-bedded rooms. B&B £16 for under-18s, £18.50 for adults.

Hampstead Heath YHA Off maps

4 Wellgarth Rd, **t** 0870 770 5846, **f** 0870 770 5847, **e** hampstead@yha.org.uk; **tube** Golders Green.

Another good bet, though, despite its name, not actually on the Heath. B&B £17.70 for under-18s, £19.90 for adults.

Holland House YHA B13

Holland Walk, Kensington, **t** 0870 770 5866, **f** 0870 770 5867, **e** hollandhouse@yha.org.uk; **tube** Holland Park.

Without doubt the most scenic location, slap bang in the middle of Holland Park in a converted Jacobean mansion. B&B £18.50 for under-18s, £20.50 for adults.

Oxford St YHA R8

14 Noel St, **t** 0870 770 5984, **f** 0870 770 5985, **e** oxford@yha.org.uk; **tube** Oxford Circus, Tottenham Court Rd.

Right in the heart of Soho. B&B £17.50 for under-18s, £21.50 for adults.

Rotherhithe YHA Off maps

20 Salter Rd, SE16, **t** 0870 770 6010, **f** 0870 770 6011, **e** rotherhithe@yha.org.uk; **tube** Rotherhithe.

Off the beaten track, but fairly handy for Greenwich. B&B £19.90 for under-18s, £23.50 for adults.

St Christopher's Inn BB12

161–3 Borough High St, **t** (020) 7404 1856 (for all branches),

w www.st-christophers.co.uk;
tube London Bridge.
Clean and cheerful backpacker's
hostel very close to London Bridge.
Discos at weekends, Internet
access, four 12-bed dormitories at
a bargain price. Other locations
are Greenwich, Shepherd's Bush
and Camden. £10 per person
per night.

St Pancras YHA T3
79–81 Euston Rd, t 0870 770 6044,
f 0870 770 6045, e stpancras@
yha.org.uk; tube Euston, King's
Cross.
Opposite the British Library.
Central but seedy neighbourhood.
B&B £19.90 for under-18s, £23.50
for adults.

Self-Catering

Only really worth it if you're
with a large group, or if you're
staying for several weeks. Try the
following agencies:

Aston's
31 Rosary Gardens, South
Kensington, SW7, t (020) 7370 0737,
f 7590 6060, e sales@astons-
apartments.com, w www.astons-
apartments.com.

Court Apartments
26 Trebovir Rd, SW5, t (020) 7370
0991, f 7370 0994, e mayfhotel@
aol.com, w www.mayflowerhotel
andapartments.co.uk.
From standard studios to luxury
flats, in and around Earl's Court.

Kensbridge Hotel Group Flat
Rentals
t (020) 7589 2923, f 7373 6183.
Flats available all over South
Kensington.

Camping

Naturally, this condemns you to
staying far from the centre, but it
is certainly the cheapest way to
stay in (or, rather, near) London.
Here are some sites:

Abbey Woods Caravan Club
Site Off maps
Federation Rd, Abbey Wood, SE2,
t (020) 8311 7708, f 8311 1465;
train Abbey Wood (from Charing
Cross, London Bridge).
Woodland camping near the
Dartford Tunnel and the A2
motorway.

Caravan Club Site Off maps
Crystal Palace Parade, SE19, t (020)
8778 7155, f 8676 0980;
train Crystal Palace, Sydenham Hill
(from Victoria, London Bridge,
Clapham Junction).
Adjacent to the park at Crystal
Palace.

Lee Valley Leisure
Centre Off maps
Meridian Way, N9, t (020) 8345
6666, f 8803 6900; train Ponders
End (from Liverpool St).
Plenty of leisure and sports facili-
ties close by.

Eating Out

Food, Glorious Food

The English system of cooking it would be impertinent for me to describe; but still when I think of that huge round of par-boiled ox flesh, with sodden dumplings, floating in a saline, greasy mixture, surrounded by carrots looking red with disgust, and turnips pale with dismay, I cannot help a sort of inward shudder, and making comparisons unfavourable to English gastronomy.

The Memoirs of A Stomach, Anon, 1853

Nice manners, shame about the food: nothing about the English has traditionally left foreigners so aghast as their dining habits. The horror stories are legion: of wobbly, green-tinged custard, of vegetables boiled until they're blue, of rice pudding so sickly and overcooked it makes you gag. No wonder visitors from abroad often contemplate packing a few home goodies to keep the wolf from the door. But, in fact, you can put away your prejudices: London is now one of the great gastronomic centres of the planet. Never in its history has the city been so cosmopolitan, and never has there been such a wide variety of cuisines to sample. Its cutting-edge chefs are treated like superstars as they vie to reproduce and improve the best that world cooking can offer. London boasts the best Indian food outside India, and the best Chinese food in Europe. There are excellent Caribbean restaurants, Lebanese restaurants, Italian, Greek and Spanish restaurants, Polish, Hungarian and Russian restaurants. Even the British restaurants aren't bad, and some are outstanding.

Getting historical, London's food started to experience problems during the Industrial Revolution in the mid-18th century. London's population rocketed, and food couldn't be transported fast enough, or kept fresh long enough, to cope with demand. Standards plummeted and food adulteration became rife. In his novel *Humphrey Clinker*, Tobias Smollett described the bread as 'a deleterious paste, mixed up with chalk, alum and bone-ashes'; lamb was 'pale, coarse and frowzy', poultry was 'rotten', game could not be had 'for love or money' and the veal was 'bleached by repeated bleedings'. Food historians have confirmed that these rantings are only too well rooted in fact. But while the poor subsisted on porridge, gruel, suet, boiled meats and these gruesome additives, the rich continued to eat rather well. French and Italian dishes, introduced into aristocratic households early in the century, were much appreciated – apart from garlic, which was considered vulgar and smelly.

Food turned into a full-scale political and economic crisis in the early 19th century. The Corn Laws of 1815 protected middle-class farmers to the detriment of smaller land-owners, and a run of poor harvests in 1817–19 compounded the problem. Food prices soared, and violent anti-government demonstrations multiplied. Then the advent of canned food in the 1820s deprived working people of fresh vegetables and fruit.

The quality of food slowly improved after the repeal of the Corn Laws in 1846. But by this time many ordinary city-dwellers had simply forgotten how to cook, and standards of preparation plummeted – hence all those overboiled joints of meat and vegetables. Working-class Londoners munched their way through a lot of ready-made pies, industrial sliced bread and fish and chips. The middle and upper classes also lost their interest in food, as the new gentlemen's clubs (*see* p.124) fostered male chumminess above gastronomic excellence.

The two world wars of the 20th century instilled a Spartan attitude to food across most of the social spectrum. The dizzy spirit of national pride following the Battle of Britain and the Blitz led people to believe that the strictures of rationing were good for the character and that decent food was a sign of decadence. A certain kind of Englishman actually relished spaghetti rings and wobbly processed jelly, and terrorized children who showed reluctance to eat up. Eating out, even in the prosperous decades after 1945, was considered a luxury only the very rich could afford. At best people would grab a pie or a sandwich at lunchtime, or pop out for a quick Indian or Chinese takeaway. Restaurant standards were abysmally low: all rubbery meat and soggy vegetables, served up by rude waiters. The shops were not much better, taking forever to stock basic items: dried pasta was first seen circa 1960, and fresh fruit juice only became widely available around 1982.

The last 30 years, however, have seen a revolution in eating habits in London. Britain's entry into the European Economic Community (as it then was) in 1973, and the subsequent boom in foreign travel, woke people up to the possibilities of good healthy eating. This is now a country where cookery programmes on television are beginning to outnumber detective serials and soap operas. London's trendier neighbourhoods are filling to bursting point with new cafés, lunch-spots and designer eateries. The opening of a high-profile new restaurant is a full-blown media event, the fads and fancies of modern cuisine a constant subject of society gossip. The fusty old establishments have been forced to change or die. Spaghetti houses, bistros, vegetarian cafés and tapas bars (as well, unfortunately, as fast-food burger joints) have made eating out accessible to a far broader range of people than ever before; at the same time, at the upper end of the market, top-class chefs have developed a new brand of British cuisine that improvizes, occasionally brilliantly, on ideas taken from around the world. The standard of restaurant food in London is now higher overall than in Paris, and far more varied than anywhere else except perhaps New York.

In the midst of all the changes, traditional English food has become something of a sideshow, and perhaps deservedly so given its shoddy history. You are most likely to encounter it over breakfast, particularly if you stay in a hotel or guest house. A **full English breakfast**, if you can face it first thing in the morning, will keep you going all day: a deceptively harmless-looking glass of fruit juice to start, followed by cereal or porridge, followed by a huge fry-up of bacon, egg, sausage, tomato and fried bread, followed by oodles of toast and marmalade washed down with a limitless supply of tea. In some of the classier establishments you might also get offered **black pudding**, **kippers** (smoked herring) or **kedgeree** (a mixture of smoked fish, rice and hard-boiled eggs). This is an intimidating prospect minutes after you've rolled out of bed, and not one, you might be relieved to know, that most Londoners can face – they usually opt for a bowl of cereal or a couple of slices of toast, with perhaps a fry-up at the weekend to recuperate after a hard night.

The menu for the rest of the day depends on where you choose to eat. Pubs or cheap cafés might offer **shepherd's pie** (minced meat and mashed potatoes), a variety of pastry **pies** (steak and kidney being a typical filling), fry-ups, or a **ploughman's lunch** (salad, pickle and cheese). Traditional restaurants may offer the much loved **Sunday-lunch roasts**: roast beef with horseradish sauce and **Yorkshire pudding** (a crisp, hollow batter cake), or roast lamb with **mint sauce** and **redcurrant jelly**, or pork with **crackling** (roasted lumps of pork skin) and **apple sauce**. Dessert could be a heavy **steamed pudding** served with custard, or **rice pudding**.

Teashops and hotels offer traditional **afternoon tea**: cucumber sandwiches, scones with strawberry jam and cream, crumpets, muffins and a large variety of cakes. In the East End you can still find **jellied eels**, **cockles** and **whelks**, often served at street stalls. Dotted all over town are the inevitable **fish and chip shops**, where Britain's most famous dish really does come wrapped in newspaper (although it is usually covered in separate sheets of greaseproof paper first).

All this can be rather heavy and unappetizing; curiously, though, London's new chefs have taken up such traditional fare as a challenge and succeeded in producing surprisingly good de luxe versions of it. They make their own pork pies and sausages; they use fresh, not frozen, fish and coat it in a crisp batter rather than dousing it in grease; and above all they make sure their mashed potato is smooth and creamy, not full of dubious brown lumps.

There are a number of chains spreading across London: Café Rouge, Caffè Uno, Dôme. These are so-so, tending towards bland and clichéd menus. Among pizza chains, Pizza Express stands out and is always a good bet.

The listings below give a good idea of the sheer variety of food on offer. Don't leave London without having at least one good Indian meal; for something more unusual, try one of the Caribbean or African restaurants. And try, too, to sample some of the new trends in British cuisine, either at a family-run café, or at one of the high-class establishments run by the likes of Alastair Little or Marco Pierre White. You have a treat in store.

Practicalities

London restaurants tend to take lunch orders between 12.30 and 2pm, and dinner orders between 7 and 10pm, although you'll find cafés and brasseries that stay open all afternoon and accept orders until 11pm or later.

The one drawback is **money** – eating out in London is an expensive pleasure. There are some incredible bargains to be had, but overall you are lucky to get away with much less than £20–30 per head for a decent evening meal. One reason for this is the wine, which can be cripplingly expensive without being especially reliable: watch out. Meal prices should be inclusive of **tax** (VAT), but an extra **cover charge** may be added in swankier places. Look carefully to see if **service** is included. If not, leave an extra 10–15 per cent of the total, preferably in cash.

All but the cheapest establishments will take cheques or **credit cards**. If you are paying with plastic, the total box will inevitably be left for you to fill, in anticipation of a fat tip. Don't feel under any pressure, especially if service is already included.

Note on payment: when we state in the listings that a restaurant takes 'all cards', we mean AmEx, Diners Club (DC), MasterCard (MC) and Visa (V). When one of these credit cards is not accepted, we state its absence. 'TC' means sterling travellers' cheques are accepted.

Price Categories

The listings below divide restaurants into the following categories, according to the price of a three-course meal without wine and service:

luxury	more than £60
expensive	£25–60
moderate	£15–25
inexpensive	under £15

Westminster

Restaurants

Expensive

The Atrium T15
*4 Millbank, **t** (020) 7233 0032; **tube** Westminster. **Open** Mon–Fri noon–3 and 6–1, Sat and Sun noon–3pm. **Payment**: all cards; TC. **Set menus**: three courses inc. coffee £28.50–30.50.*
Elaborate Mediterranean-Asian dishes which manage successfully to negotiate the pitfalls of most fusion cuisine. Politicians and media moguls love this stylish restaurant set underneath the glass atrium of the Millbank building.

The Cinnamon Club S14
*Old Westminster Library, Great Smith St, **t** (020) 7222 2555, **w** www.cinnamonclub.com; **tube** St James's Park. **Open** Mon–Fri 7.30–10am, noon–3pm and 6–10.30pm, Sat 6–10.30pm, Sun noon–4pm. **Payment**: AmEx and DC not accepted. **Set menus**: (Mon–Fri lunch) two courses £15, three courses £18.*
The hushed library atmosphere still lingers in this excellent new Indian restaurant. The owner spent years tracking down the very best chefs from India, and as a result the food is simply outstanding.

Ken Lo's Memories of China O16
*67–9 Ebury St, **t** (020) 7730 7734; **tube** Sloane Square, Victoria; wheelchair accessible. **Open** Mon–Sat noon–2.30 and 7–11, Sun 7–11pm. **Payment**: all cards; TC. **Set menus**: (Mon–Sat noon–2.30pm, minimum two people) £22–27.50; (7–11pm, minimum two people) £24.50–40.*
Minimalist décor, but maximalist cooking. Ken Lo, one of Britain's best-known Chinese restaurateurs, offers a stunning gastronomic tour of China.

Olivo O15
*21 Eccleston St; **tube** Victoria. **Open** Mon–Fri noon–2.30 and 7–11, Sat*

Vegetarian Food

Being vegetarian is not a problem in London: most, if not all, restaurants offer veggie choices these days. When a non-vegetarian restaurant offers particularly interesting veggie alternatives, we say so in the listings. The following are exclusively vegetarian restaurants and cafés:
Bah Humbug (*see* p.337), **Beatroot** (*see* p.321), **The Gate** (Hammersmith; *see* p.336), **The Gate** (Swiss Cottage; *see* p.328), **Mildred's** (*see* p.319), **The Place Below** (*see* p.328), **The Quiet Revolution** (*see* p.325).

---

*and Sun 7–11pm. **Payment**: DC not accepted; TC. **Set menus**: (lunch) two courses £15, three courses £17.*
A very pretty yellow- and blue-painted Italian restaurant serving stunning Sardinian cuisine. There's a great selection of local wines and perhaps the best tiramisu in London.

Moderate

Boisdale O16
*13–15 Eccleston St, **t** (020) 7730 6922; **tube** Victoria. **Open** for food Mon–Fri noon–2.30 and 7–10.30, Sat 7–10.30pm. **Payment**: all cards; TC. **Set menus**: two courses £14.90, £17.45.*
Half 'speakeasy', half aristocratic drawing room in the Scottish Highlands, this is a wonderfully eccentric experience. The modern Scottish menu (with a noggin of whisky here and there) is an added bonus. Jazz from 10pm Mon–Sat.

Inexpensive

Jenny Lo's Tea House O16
*14 Eccleston St, **t** (020) 7259 0399; **tube** Victoria. **Open** Mon–Fri 11.30–3 and 6–10, Sat noon–3 and 6–10. **Payment**: no cards; TC.*
Building on her father Ken Lo's inspiration, Jenny Lo has established a delightful Chinese soup and noodle eatery with therapeutic herbal teas and a warm atmosphere.

Pubs, Wine Bars and Cafés

Paviours Arms T16
*Neville House, Page St, **t** (020) 7834 2150; **tube** Pimlico, St James's Park. **Open** for food Mon–Sat noon–2.30 and 5.30–9.30. **Payment**: DC not accepted.*
Lovely Art Deco pub with a spectacular sinuous black bar. Decent pub food is served at lunchtimes and evenings.

Trafalgar Square and Around

Restaurants

Expensive

The Criterion R10
*224 Piccadilly, **t** (020) 7930 0488; **tube** Piccadilly Circus; wheelchair accessible. **Open** Mon–Sat noon–2.30 and 5.30–11.30, Sun 5.30–11.30pm. **Payment**: all cards; TC. **Set menus**: (lunchtime and 5.30–6.30), two courses £14.95, three courses £17.95. **Booking advised**.*
A magnificent Art Deco gold mosaic interior, originally opened in 1870. Marco Pierre White's expensive brasserie food draws big crowds; service tends to be swift, almost impatient.

J. Sheekey T10
*St Martin's Court, **t** (020) 7240 2565; **tube** Leicester Square. **Open** Mon–Sat noon–3 and 5.30–midnight, Sun noon–3.30 and 5.30–midnight. **Payment**: all cards; TC. **Set menus**: (Sat and Sun lunch) two courses £10.75, three courses £14.50, plus £1.50 cover charge.*
This elegant suite of wood-panelled rooms is now the youngest sibling of The Ivy, with all the trendy elegance that that implies. The emphasis is still on fish (beautifully executed, from Dover sole to blue-fin tuna with Italian barley and herb salsa), plus particularly fine desserts. You can also eat at the bar.

Moderate

The Portrait Restaurant T10
National Portrait Gallery, 2 St Martin's Place, t (020) 7312 2490; **tube** *Leicester Square, Charing Cross.* **Open** *Mon–Fri noon–2.30 and 5.30–8.30, Sat and Sun 11.30–2.30 and 5.30–8.30.* **Payment**: *DC not accepted.*
Right at the top of the new extension to the National Portrait Gallery, with a glass wall giving heart-stopping views down Whitehall. Excellent, ungimmicky food too – modern European dishes like salt cod fishcake with artichoke, or goat's cheese fritter, all served in generous portions.

Inexpensive

Melati R9
21 Great Windmill St, t (020) 7437 2745; **tube** *Piccadilly Circus.* **Open** *Mon–Thurs and Sun noon–11.30pm, Fri and Sat noon–12.30am.* **Payment**: *DC not accepted.* **Set menus**: *(minimum two people) £16.50–25.*
Lively and authentic Indonesian restaurant with a cosy wooden interior. Good portions and a reliable menu including soups, satays, coconut desserts and exotica such as *cumi cumi istimewa* (stuffed squid in dark red, sweet soy sauce).

Pubs, Wine Bars and Cafés

Photographer's Gallery Café T9
5 Great Newport St, t (020) 7831 1772, w www.photonet.org.uk; **tube** *Leicester Square.* **Open** *daily noon–6pm.* **Payment**: *no cards.*
A real oasis, this relaxing café is right in the middle of the gallery. Entrance is free and the cakes and light snacks are homemade and delicious.

Portrait Café T10
National Portrait Gallery, 2 St Martin's Place, t (020) 732 2465; **tube** *Leicester Square, Charing Cross.* **Open** *Mon–Wed, Sat and Sun noon–6pm, Thurs and Fri 10am–8.30pm.* **Payment**: *AmEx and DC not accepted; TC.*

Nothing special, but perfectly decent, the gallery café is tucked away in the basement. Light pours in through the unusual glass roof (at least on sunny days). Fresh sandwiches and snacks.

Buckingham Palace and the Royal Parks

Restaurants

Expensive

Quilon R14
St James's Court Hotel, 41 Buckingham Gate, t (020) 7281 1899; **tube** *St James's Park.* **Open** *Mon–Fri noon–2.30 and 6–11, Sat 6–11pm.* **Payment**: *all cards; TC.* **Set menus**: *(lunch) £12.95 for two courses, £15.95 for three courses.*
Very swish hotel restaurant serving Indian and particularly Keralan specialities, with the emphasis on seafood.

Moderate

Noura O14
16 Hobart Place, t (020) 7235 9444, w www.noura-brasseries.co.uk; **tube** *Victoria.* **Open** *daily noon–midnight.* **Payment**: *all cards; TC.* **Set menus**: *(noon–6pm) £12.50 for meze, main course and coffee, (6pm–midnight) £18–28 for meze, main course and coffee.*
Sleek, modern Lebanese brasserie with a delicious range of meze. Don't miss out on the homemade ice cream. Snacks are served all day.

Pubs, Wine Bars and Cafés

Café Internet P14
22–4 Buckingham Palace Rd, t (020) 7233 5786; **tube** *Victoria.* **Open** *daily 8am–10pm.* **Payment**: *DC not accepted; TC.*
Surf the Net while you lunch – sandwiches and snacks all day.

ICA Café S11
ICA, The Mall, t (020) 7930 8619; **tube** *Piccadilly Circus, Charing Cross.* **Open** *for food Mon noon–4*

and 6–10, Tues–Sat noon–4 and 6–11, Sun noon–4pm. **Payment**: *DC not accepted; TC.*
You have to pay the £1.50 day membership fee to get in, but it's worth it. Exhibitions at the ICA are almost always good for a look anyway, and the bar is worth remembering because it has a late-night licence. The food is (almost always) good and attractively presented, and always very reasonably priced. It's much quieter at lunchtimes – at night it can overrun with wannabe Brit Packers.

Tiles Wine Bar P15
36 Buckingham Palace Rd, t (020) 7834 7761; **tube** *Victoria.* **Open** *for food Mon–Fri noon–2.30pm, with a light evening menu 5.30–10pm.* **Payment**: *DC not accepted; TC.*
Welcoming wine bar with a pretty first-floor restaurant (the decorative floor tiles give the place its name). Very friendly staff, comfy sofas in the lounge bar, and a simple but good menu. The homemade chips are fantastic.

St James's, Mayfair and Regent Street

Restaurants

Luxury

Le Gavroche M10
43 Upper Brook St, t (020) 7408 0881, w www.le-gavroche.co.uk; **tube** *Marble Arch.* **Open** *Mon–Fri noon–2 and 7–11.* **Payment**: *all cards; TC.* **Set menus**: *lunch inc. half-bottle of wine, mineral water and coffee £38.50.*
Albert Roux is one of the most revered cooks in Britain, the first this side of the Channel to win three Michelin stars (Le Gavroche currently has two stars). He has now delegated much of the cuisine to his son, Michel, but standards are still de luxe. Extraordinary creativity, from the sautéed scallops to the coffee cup dessert. It doesn't come cheap – a

customer once reputedly spent £13,500 on dinner for three.

The Square P10

6–10 Bruton St, **t** (020) 7495 7100, **e** squarethe@aol.com; **tube** Bond St, Green Park. **Open** Mon–Fri noon–2.45 and 6.30–9.45. **Payment**: all cards; TC. **Set menus**: lunch two courses £20/£45, three courses £25/£55; dinner three courses £55, eight courses £75.

Sleek, modern, top-calibre French restaurant (which also boasts a couple of Michelin stars). Constantly changing menu, luxury ingredients and a strong emphasis on fish. Outstanding wine list. Service borders on the starchy with the bias firmly on the superb quality of the food.

Expensive

Al Hamra O11

31–3 Shepherd's Market, **t** (020) 7493 1954; **tube** Green Park, Hyde Park Corner. **Open** daily noon–11.30pm. **Payment**: all cards; TC.

Sophisticated if overpriced Middle Eastern restaurant in the cosmopolitan chic of Shepherd's Market, where you can sit out in the summer months. Select a meze of different dishes from the 48 delicacies – batrakh (fish roe with garlic and olive oil) and makdoue (aubergines stuffed with walnuts and spices) are particularly recommended.

Le Caprice Q11

Arlington House, Arlington St, **t** (020) 7629 2239; **tube** Green Park. **Open** Mon–Sat noon–3 and 5.30–midnight, Sun noon–4 and 5.30–midnight. **Payment**: all cards; TC. **Booking essential.**

Eternally fashionable (despite the slightly dated décor) with impressively high standards of cuisine and exceptional service. Essentially 'modern British' food with some imaginative Middle Eastern twists. A pianist tinkles away nightly from 7pm.

The Greenhouse O11

27A Hay's Mews, **t** (020) 7499 3331; **tube** Green Park; wheelchair accessible. **Open** Mon–Fri noon–2.30 and 5.30–11, Sat 5.30–11pm, Sun 5.30–9pm. **Payment**: all cards. **Set menus**: three courses inc. water and coffee £22.

The idea behind this restaurant was to resurrect stale old English recipes. Liver and bacon or sponge pudding may sound dull, but they come to life here. Signature dishes include fillet of smoked haddock with Welsh rarebit on a tomato and chive salad.

Nobu O12

Metropolitan Hotel, 19 Old Park Lane, **t** (020) 7447 4747; **tube** Hyde Park Corner. **Open** Mon–Thurs noon–2.15 and 6–10.15, Fri noon–2.15 and 6–11, Sat 6–11pm, Sun 6–9.30pm. **Payment**: all cards; TC. **Set menus**: lunch chef's selection £50, bento box £23.50, sushi box £25; dinner chef's selection £70.

Dark glasses and a fat wallet are de rigueur at this glamorously minimalist New Wave Japanese. Exquisite menu, from meltingly delicious sushi and crisp tempura to unique Japanese dishes with South American touches. The excellent cocktails and saké list should not be missed.

Quaglino's Q11

16 Bury St, **t** (020) 7930 6767, **w** www.conran.com; **tube** Green Park; wheelchair accessible. **Open** Mon–Thurs noon–3 and 5.30–midnight, Fri and Sat noon–3 and 5.30–1, Sun 5.30–11pm. **Payment**: all cards; TC. **Set menus**: (daily lunch and 5.30–6.30pm) two courses £12.50, three courses £15.

Modern, designer restaurant in a converted sunken ballroom, which is beginning to look a little tired. Another outpost of the Conran empire. The menu is mainly Italian and equally design-conscious, although otherwise unremarkable.

Zen Central O11

20–22 Queen St, **t** (020) 7629 8103; **tube** Green Park. **Open** daily noon–2.15 and 6.30–11.30. **Payment**: all cards; TC. **Booking advised.**

More inventive and glitzy than your average Chinese and more expensive, too. An interesting, unusual range of Beijing, Cantonese and Szechuan specialities.

Moderate

Momo Q10

25 Heddon St, **t** (020) 7434 4040; **tube** Piccadilly Circus; wheelchair accessible. **Open** Mon–Sat noon–2.30 and 7–11, Sun noon–2.30 and 6–10.30. **Payment**: all cards; TC. **Set menus**: lunch two courses £17.

Stylish Moroccan restaurant filled with antiques, rich carpets and fabrics. It's quiet during the day, but packs out with a glamorous crowd in the evenings. Its bohemian little sister next door, **Mô**, is an equally trendy Moroccan tearoom decked out with all kinds of bazaar finds (which are for sale). It's less pricy and offers a small but exquisite menu.

Mulligans' Q10

13–14 Cork St, **t** (020) 7409 1370; **tube** Green Park, Piccadilly Circus. **Open** for food Mon–Fri noon–3 6.30–9.30. **Payment**: all cards; TC.

Hearty Irish cooking (beef cooked in Guinness, and other favourites), as well as lighter dishes (blue cashel cheese and artichoke and spinach salad), especially at lunch. Wicked puddings, particularly the black and white one with apple and ginger chutney. Very friendly staff. Bar food also available.

Sofra Bistro O11

18 Shepherd's Market, **t** (020) 7493 3320; **tube** Green Park, Hyde Park Corner. **Open** daily noon–midnight. **Payment**: all cards; TC. **Set menus**: meze noon–6pm £8.95, 6pm–midnight £9.95.

Turkish food with all the usual meze dishes, a crushed wheat salad and delicious sticky filled pastries. An emphasis on fresh ingredients ensures high quality at reasonable prices – most of the time. Eternally popular; seating can be cramped and service often downright poor. There are branches at St Christopher's Place, W1, **t** (020) 7224 4080, and 36 Tavistock St, WC2, **t** (020) 7240 3773.

Riverside City

The following restaurants are renowned for their river views: **Admiralty** (*see* p.323), **Baradero** (*see* p.338), **Blue Print Café** (*see* p.336), **Chez Lindsay** (*see* p.336), **Mem Saheb on Thames** (*see* p.338), **Neat** (*see* p.326), **Le Pont de la Tour** (*see* p.336), **The River Café** (*see* p.336).

Zinc Bar and Grill Q10
*21 Heddon St, t (020) 7255 8899;
tube Piccadilly Circus. Open for food Mon–Wed noon–11pm, Thurs–at noon–11.30pm. Payment: all cards. Set menus: (Mon–Sat noon–7pm) two courses £11.50.*
Just off Regent St, this is yet another outpost of the Conran empire. Still, it's not too pretentious, the staff are friendly and helpful, and the food (modern European) is very good indeed. There are also tables outside in summer.

Inexpensive

Condotti's P9
*4 Mill St, t (020) 7499 1308;
tube Oxford Circus, Piccadilly Circus. Open Mon–Sat noon–midnight. Payment: all cards; TC.*
A smart pizza parlour full of lunchtime businesspeople and well-heeled shoppers; in the evening it jollies up. Modern art on the walls, good food and delightful service.

Pubs, Wine Bars and Cafés

Browns Hotel P10
*Dover St or Albermarle St,
w www.brownshotel.com; tube Green Park. Tea served Mon–Fri 3–5.45pm, Sat and Sun 2.30–5.45pm. Set teas: £23, £29 (winter tea), £33 (with champagne).*
Very snobbish traditional English hotel serving tea to all comers, as long as you dress to fit the part. Bookings are not accepted.

La Madeleine Q10
5 Vigo St, t (020) 7734 8353; tube Piccadilly Circus. Open Mon–Sat 8am–8pm, plus in summer Sun 11am–7pm. Payment: AmEx not accepted; TC.
Delightful, relaxing spot serving heavenly cakes and pastries, as well as great coffee. There are some light meals available too, and very friendly staff.

The Ritz Q11
*Piccadilly, W1, t (020) 7493 8181,
w www.theritzhotel.co.uk;
tube Green Park. Tea sittings daily at 1.30pm, 3.30pm and 5pm. Set teas: £27.*
The fanciest, most indulgent tea in town, served in the sumptuous Edwardian Palm Court. Worth splashing out, but you'll definitely need to book well in advance.

Soho and Chinatown

Restaurants

Expensive

Alastair Little S9
*49 Frith St, t (020) 7734 5183;
tube Tottenham Court Rd, Leicester Square. Open Mon–Sat noon–3 and 6–11, Sun noon–3.30pm. Payment: DC not accepted; TC. Set menus: lunch three courses £27; dinner three courses £35.*
One of the first and also the best of British *nouvelle cuisine* restaurants. There are generally six main courses; fish and shellfish feature prominently. The menu changes according to what's fresh in the market. Spartan décor, which, at the time of writing, is looking decidedly tatty.

**L'Escargot
Marco Pierre White** S9
*48 Greek St, t (020) 7437 2679;
tube Tottenham Court Rd, Leicester Square. Open Mon–Fri 12.15–2.15 and 6–11.30, Sat 6–11.30pm. Payment: all cards; TC. Set menus: (12.15–2.15 and 6–7) two courses £14.95, three courses £17.95; (6–11.30pm) three courses £42.*
A new chef and a spectacular refurbishment have given this old favourite a new lease of life. Classic French food under the gaze of high modern art: Picassos upstairs; Mirós and Chagalls downstairs. A speciality is *feuilleté* of snails served with bacon.

Quo Vadis S9
*26–9 Dean St, t (020) 7437 9585;
tube Leicester Square, Tottenham Court Rd. Open Mon–Fri noon–2.30 and 5.30–11.30, Sat 5.30–11.30pm. Payment: all cards; TC. Set menus: (noon–2.30 and 5.30–6.45) two courses £14.95, three courses £19.95.*
Marco Pierre White's fine modern French food in a beautiful room with impeccable service.

Richard Corrigan at Lindsay House S9
*21 Romilly St, t (020) 7439 0450,
w www.lindsayhouse.co.uk; tube Leicester Square, Piccadilly Circus. Open Mon–Fri noon–2.30 and 6–11, Sat 6–11pm. Payment: all cards; TC. Set menus: pre-theatre dinner (Mon–Sat 6–6.45pm) two courses £24, three courses £29.50; dinner five courses £44; tasting menu eight courses £65.*
In a suite of elegantly ramshackle 18th-century rooms, the expertly executed modern Irish menu is exciting and rewarding. Cosy, eccentric atmosphere with entry by doorbell.

The Sugar Club Q10
*21 Warwick St, t (020) 7437 7776;
tube Oxford Circus, Piccadilly Circus; wheelchair accessible. Open Mon–Sat noon–3 and 6–10.30, Sun 12.30–3 and 6–10.30. Payment: all cards; TC. Set menus: (Sat and Sun lunch) two courses £15, three courses £18.*
Spectacularly innovative fusion fare in a cool, creamy ambience. Most weird and wonderful combinations – roast kangaroo with beetroot, duck with vanilla-scented flageolets – delight even the most discerning taste-buds. Expensive, but not over-priced.

Zilli Fish R9
*36–40 Brewer St, t (020) 7734 8649;
tube Piccadilly Circus, Leicester Square. Open Mon–Sat noon–11.30pm. Payment: all cards; TC.*
Fashionable haunt with comfy chairs, slow service and mostly superb fish (and prices to match).

Moderate

Andrew Edmunds R9
*46 Lexington St, **t** (020) 7437 5708;*
***tube** Oxford Circus, Piccadilly
Circus.* **Open** *Mon–Fri 12.30–3.30
and 6–10.45, Sat and Sun 1–3pm.*
Payment*: DC not accepted.*
Well-priced and well-prepared
modern Mediterranean dishes in a
strangely old-fashioned (but
perennially popular) setting with
wooden benches and gloopy
candles. Very busy: service can be
a bit frenzied and the room
smoky. Menus change daily and
the wine list is well judged.

Aurora R9
*49 Lexington St, **t** (020) 7494 0514;*
***tube** Oxford Circus, Piccadilly
Circus.* **Open** *daily noon–3.30 and
6–11.* **Payment***: all cards.*
This bijou café remains a
delightful refuge from the
clamour of Soho: easy
Mediterranean food and relaxed,
cosy atmosphere.

Il Forno S8
*63–4 Frith St, **t** (020) 7734 4545;*
***tube** Tottenham Court Rd.* **Open**
*Mon–Fri noon–2.45 and 6–10.45,
Sat and Sun 6–10.45pm.* **Payment***:
all cards; TC.* **Set menus***: (summer
only) two courses £10, three
courses £12.50.*
The latest in a long line of restaurants in this spot, this is an urbane
and fashionable Italian with lots
of bleached wood and pale
colours. There are excellent pizzas
made with very fresh ingredients,
and a delicious polenta dish,
topped with porcini mushrooms.

French House Dining Rooms S9
*49 Dean St, **t** (020) 7437 2477;* ***tube**
Leicester Square, Piccadilly Circus.*
Open *Mon–Sat 12.30–3 and
6.30–10.* **Payment***: all cards.*
Dark, worn wooden rooms above
a pub of the same name.
Atmospheric, 1920s ambience,
much frequented by literati.
Excellent French food, sometimes
with British influences.

Fung Shing S10
*15 Lisle St, **t** (020) 7437 1539;* ***tube**
Leicester Square, Piccadilly Circus.*
Open *daily noon–11.30pm.*

Payment*: all cards; TC.* **Set menus***:
(minimum two people) £16.50
per person.*
Delicate, mainly Cantonese food,
served with style in a bright
lemon dining room; there is also
an airy veranda at the back. There
is a boosted vegetable section, but
one of the classic dishes is braised
suckling pig.

Kettners S9
*29 Romilly St, **t** (020) 7734 6112;*
***tube** Leicester Square, Piccadilly
Circus, Tottenham Court Rd.* **Open**
Mon–Sat 11am–11pm. **Payment***: all
cards; TC.*
A quirky Soho institution; decent if
overpriced pizzas in respectably
shabby 18th-century-style
surroundings. Full of 'luvvies' and
raucous hen nights.

Little Italy S9
*21 Frith St, **t** (020) 7734 4737;* ***tube**
Leicester Square, Tottenham Court
Rd.* **Open** *Mon–Sat noon–4am,
Sun noon–11.30pm.* **Payment***: all
cards; TC.*
An offshoot of the famous Bar
Italia, with authenticity that some
of the more fashionable places
lack. Photos of boxers adorn the
walls. A long menu, with unusual
dishes of the day, like meatloaf
steamed in tomato sauce, as well
as regular dishes. A big favourite
with office parties – partly thanks
to the late-night bar downstairs.

Livebait Café Fish S10
*36–40 Rupert St, **t** (020) 7287
8989;* ***tube** Leicester Square,
Piccadilly Circus.* **Open** *Mon–Sat
noon–11pm, Sun noon–10.30pm.*
Payment*: all cards; TC.* **Set menus***:
two courses £11.50, three courses
£15.50.*
This is a buzzy café and informal
restaurant. Fish and shellfish chargrilled, steamed, *meunière*, fried,
marinated, or in breadcrumbs
with chips if you, like many
English people, prefer your
aqueous creatures unrecognizable.

Poon's S9
*27 Lisle St, **t** (020) 7437 4549;* ***tube**
Leicester Square, Piccadilly Circus.*
Open *daily noon–11.30pm.*
Payment*: AmEx and DC not

accepted.* **Set menus***: (minimum
two people) £15–17.50 per person.*
Famous for being cheap and for its
hearty soups and high-quality
'wind-dried' duck.

Randall & Aubin R9
*16 Brewer St, **t** (020) 7287 4447;*
***tube** Piccadilly Circus, Leicester
Square; wheelchair accessible.*
Open *Mon–Sat noon–11pm, Sun
4–10.30pm.* **Payment***: all cards.*
An old Victorian butcher's shop
converted into an oyster and
champagne bar, with a rôtisserie.
The original tiled interior has been
preserved, along with the uncomfortable seats. Specializes in
seafood and spit-roasts – ingredients can be made into sandwiches
to order. (It can easily jump a price
bracket depending on what
you order.)

Saigon S9
*45 Frith St, **t** (020) 7437 7109;* ***tube**
Leicester Square, Tottenham Court
Rd.* **Open** *Mon–Sat noon–11.30pm.*
Payment*: all cards.* **Set menus***:
(minimum 2 people) £33.30 for 2.*
A long-established Soho favourite
serving Vietnamese food, well
presented and served amid
pleasant décor. The set meals are a
great introduction to the food.

Satsuma R9
*56 Wardour St, **t** (020) 7437 8338;*
***tube** Piccadilly Circus, Leicester
Square, Tottenham Court Rd.*
Open *Mon and Tues noon–11pm,
Wed, Thurs and Sun noon–11.30pm,
Fri and Sat noon–midnight.*
Payment*: all cards; TC.*
Slick and trendy Japanese diner
with bench seating, good sushi
and a range of luxurious bento
boxes. Friendly, sometimes efficient service.

Soho Spice R9
*124–6 Wardour St, **t** (020) 7434
0808, **w** www.sohospice.co.uk;*
***tube** Oxford Circus, Tottenham
Court Rd.* **Open** *Mon–Thurs
noon–midnight, Fri and Sat
noon–3am, Sun 12.30–10.30pm.*
Payment*: all cards; TC.* **Set menus***:
lunch £7.50; dinner £15.*
Radiant blue and magenta and
wooden tables make for a modern

Indian look. Good standard food, although choice can be limited. A hint of Thai influence. Also a late-night bar. There's a sister restaurant, the **Red Fort**, at 77 Dean St, **t** (020) 7437 2115.

Spiga R9
84–6 Wardour St, **t** *(020) 7734 3444;* **tube** *Leicester Square, Piccadilly Circus, Tottenham Court Rd.* **Open** *Mon, Tues and Sun noon–3 and 6–11, Wed–Sat noon–3 and 6–midnight.* **Payment:** *all cards; TC.*
A fine, imaginative modern Italian noteworthy for its thin-crust pizzas with toppings from classic to innovative (swordfish and rocket, a fine combination). Airy setting and swift service, too.

Sri Siam S9
16 Old Compton St, **t** *(020) 7434 3544;* **tube** *Leicester Square, Piccadilly Circus.* **Open** *Mon–Sat noon–3 and 6–11, Sun 6–10.30pm.* **Payment:** *all cards.* **Set menus:** *three courses £14.95–24.95.*
Modern, minimalist and hip, a combination unusual in a Thai restaurant. The sleek, cream walls host throngs of diners in the evening, although it can be empty at lunch. Service can be almost over-attentive.

Vasco and Piero's Pavilion R8
15 Poland St, **t** *(020) 7437 8774,* **w** *www.vascosfood.com;* **tube** *Oxford Circus.* **Open** *Mon–Fri noon–3 and 6–11, Sat 6–11pm.* **Payment:** *all cards; TC.* **Set menus:** *pre-theatre dinner (Mon–Fri 6–7pm) two courses £12.50; (Mon–Sat 6–11pm) two courses £18.50, three courses £22.50.*
Sophisticated, friendly Italian serving immaculately presented dishes, e.g. grilled breast of guinea-fowl with juniper berries. Truffles from Umbria available in season and heavenly desserts.

Inexpensive

Bali Bali T9
150 Shaftesbury Av, **t** *(020) 7836 2644;* **tube** *Leicester Square.* **Open** *Mon–Sat noon–2.30 and 5.45–11.30, Sun 5–10pm.* **Payment:**

all cards; TC. **Set menus:** *lunch £5.50–6.75.*
A reasonable Indonesian place with a varied menu of light and well-spiced food. Incredibly cheap set lunches and dinners, too.

Café España S9
63 Old Compton St, **t** *(020) 7494 1271;* **tube** *Leicester Square.* **Open** *Mon–Sat noon–midnight, Sun noon–11pm.* **Payment:** *AmEx and DC not accepted.*
A plain, authentic little Spanish restaurant – a far cry from the un-Spanish tapas bars that have cropped up all over London. Generous portions of Galician and Castilian dishes, emphasizing fish. Popular even among Spaniards. Especially delicious paella.

Golden Harvest S10
17 Lisle St, **t** *(020) 7287 3822;* **tube** *Leicester Square, Piccadilly Circus.* **Open** *Mon–Thurs and Sun noon–12.45am, Fri and Sat noon–1.45am.* **Payment:** *AmEx and DC not accepted.* **Set menus:** *£6.95–25.*
Outstandingly good low-priced Chinese food in a modest, low-lit setting. The owners are Chinatown's fishmongers, so fresh fish is easily guaranteed, including pomfret and carp.

Hing Loon S9
25 Lisle St, **t** *(020) 7437 3602;* **tube** *Leicester Square, Piccadilly Circus.* **Open** *Mon–Sat noon–11.30pm, Sun noon–11pm.* **Payment:** *all cards; TC.* **Set menus:** *£5.80, £7.50, £9.50.*
Despite miniature quarters, the food can be very good, though the menu is so vast (including spiced duck's kidneys) that a few dishes don't come up to scratch. The 'specials' of the day are usually delightfully done.

Jimmy's S9
23 Frith St, **t** *(020) 7437 9521;* **tube** *Leicester Square, Tottenham Court Rd.* **Open** *Mon–Wed noon–3 and 5.30–11, Thurs–Sat noon–3 and 5.30–11.30.* **Payment:** *no cards.*
Moussaka and chips, as eaten by the Rolling Stones in the 1960s, is a mainstay of this basement Soho institution. Better loved for its

history and low prices than for gastronomic prowess.

Kulu Kulu R10
76 Brewer St, **t** *(020) 7734 7316;* **tube** *Piccadilly Circus.* **Open** *Mon–Fri noon–2.30 and 5–10, Sat noon–3.45 and 5–10.* **Payment:** *AmEx and DC not accepted; TC.*
Sushi is handmade at this tiny, congested Japanese eating spot. A conveyor belt runs along the counter and the food is served on colour-coded plates. Also non-sushi dishes.

Mildred's R9
45 Lexington St, **t** *(020) 7494 1634;* **tube** *Tottenham Court Rd.* **Open** *Mon–Sat noon–11pm.* **Payment:** *no cards; TC.*
Eclectic wholesome vegetarian fare in one small room. The menu changes weekly but always includes a stir fry and falafel. There are also vegan and organic specials and organic wines. Good Sunday brunch. Swift, friendly service.

Pollo S9
20 Old Compton St, **t** *(020) 7734 5917;* **tube** *Leicester Square, Tottenham Court Rd.* **Open** *daily noon–midnight.* **Payment:** *no cards; TC.*
Cheap Italian pasta dive. Extremely popular and frenetic: students come in droves and bunch up on scuffed benches in wooden booths.

Tokyo Diner S9
2 Newport Place, **t** *(020) 7287 8777;* **tube** *Leicester Square.* **Open** *daily noon–midnight.* **Payment:** *DC not accepted; no cheques.* **Set menus:** *(noon–5pm) £4.70–7.90.*
One of the earlier Japanese fast-food houses: good sushi and Japanese noodle dishes at low prices. Brisk, friendly service.

Wagamama R9
10A Lexington St, **t** *(020) 7292 0990,* **w** *www.wagamama.com;* **tube** *Oxford Circus, Piccadilly Circus.* **Open** *Mon–Sat noon–11pm, Sun 12.30–10.30pm.* **Payment:** *all cards.* **Set menus:** *£8.50–9.50.*
Sister to the original in Bloomsbury, now with several

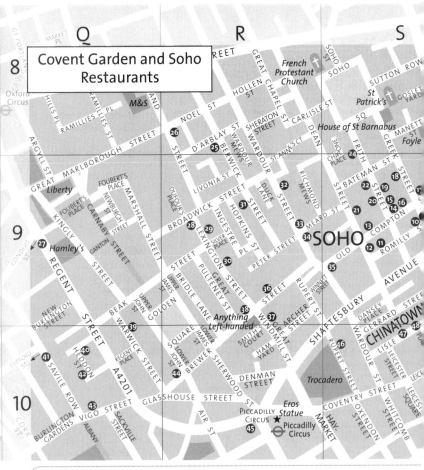

Map Key

22	Alastair Little	24	Il Forno	2 Mode
29	Andrew Edmunds	12	French House Dining Room	40 Momo
28	Aurora	47	Fung Shing	1 Mon Plaisir
8	Bali Bali	49	Golden Harvest	41 Mulligan's
25	Bar Chocolate	48	Hing Loon	57 Orso
15	Bar Italia	6	The Ivy	13 Pâtisserie Valerie
31	Beatroot	56	Joe Allen	54 Paul
5	Bertorelli's	61	J. Sheekey	52 Photographer's Gallery Café
4	Café des Amis du Vin	14	Jimmy's	17 Pollo
35	Café España	10	Kettners	50 Poon's
55	Calabash	44	Kulu Kulu	62 Portrait Café
58	Christopher's	19	Little Italy	63 The Portrait Restaurant
27	Condotti's	46	Livebait Café Fish	53 Prospect Grill
45	The Criterion	43	La Madeleine	21 Quo Vadis
18	L'Escargot Marco Pierre White	9	Maison Bertaux	36 Randall & Aubin
		37	Melati	11 Richard Corrigan at Lindsay House
		28	Mildred's	

branches across the city. The philosophy of this Japanese noodle bar is 'positive eating, positive living'. There's hi-tech, efficient, fast service on long communal tables. The long queues move fast.

Pubs, Wine Bars and Cafés

Bar Chocolate R8
26–7 D'Arblay St; **tube** Oxford Circus, Tottenham Court Rd. **Open** Mon–Sat 10am–11pm, Sun noon–10.30pm. **Payment:** AmEx not accepted.

A very funky café-bar with good-value food, comfy sofas and friendly staff. It's much quieter during the day – at night it packs out.

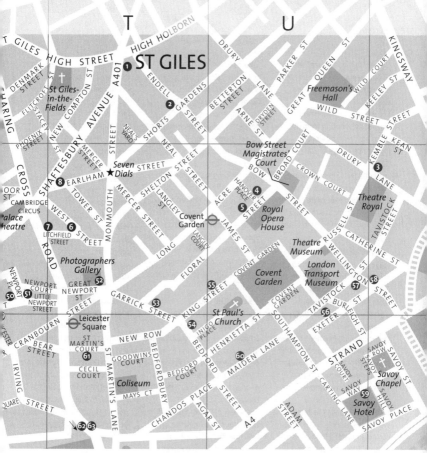

Bar Italia S9

*22 Frith St; **tube** Leicester Square, Piccadilly Circus, Tottenham Court Rd. **Open** Mon–Sat 24 hours, Sun 7am–4pm. **Payment**: no cards.*
The café reputed to have the best coffee in town, and it knows it. The mirrored bar, complete with TV showing Italian soccer games, could have come straight from Milan. The seating's a bit cramped, but at least there are tables on the pavement. Better to stand. The place to come after clubbing.

Beatroot R9

*92 Berwick St; **tube** Oxford Circus, Leicester Square, Piccadilly Circus, Tottenham Court Rd. **Open** Mon–Sat 9am–6.30pm. **Payment**: no cards; TC.*
Cheerful, down-to-earth vegetarian eat-in/takeaway café where you choose your food box and have it filled with any selection of hot dishes and salads from the food bar. Great puddings, too.

Maison Bertaux S9

*28 Greek St; **tube** Leicester Square, Piccadilly Circus, Tottenham Court Rd. **Open** daily 9am–8pm. **Payment**: no cards; TC.*
Mouthwatering pastries in a slightly cramped, but delightfully old-fashioned, upstairs tearoom which is always crowded.

Pâtisserie Valerie S9

*44 Old Compton St; **tube** Leicester Square. **Open** Mon–Fri 7.30am–8pm, Sat 8am–7pm, Sun 9am–6pm. **Payment**: DC not accepted; TC.*
Divine French cakes, light snacks including an excellent *croque monsieur*, and coffee. You may have to wait for a seat (share one of the dark wooden tables).

Covent Garden and Around

Restaurants

Expensive

The Ivy T9

*1 West St, **t** (020) 7836 4751; **tube** Leicester Square; wheelchair accessible. **Open** Mon–Sat noon–3 and 5.30–midnight, Sun noon–3.30 and*

5.30–midnight. **Payment**: all cards; TC. **Set menus**: (Sat and Sun lunch) three courses £16.50. **Booking essential**.

The moody oak panels and stained glass dating from the 1920s are offset by vibrant modern paintings. The menu caters for elaborate as well as tamer tastes. Salmon fishcakes on a bed of leaf spinach is a signature dish. This is the ultimate celebrity haunt, which means that you have to book well (preferably months) in advance.

Christopher's V9
18 Wellington St, **t** (020) 7240 4222, **w** www.christophersgrill.com; **tube** Covent Garden, Charing Cross. **Open** for brunch Mon–Sat 11.30am–4.30pm, lunch daily noon–3pm, dinner daily 5pm–midnight. **Payment**: all cards; TC. **Set menus**: pre-theatre dinner (Mon–Sat 5–7pm) two courses £14.50, three courses £18.50.

The opulent curved stone staircase in the foyer recalls a 19th-century pleasure dome – this was once London's first licensed casino and later a high-class brothel. The American menu emphasizes steaks and grills, but there's also seafood (crab chowder or fried oysters) and beautiful roasts. There's a very romantic, quiet bar downstairs.

Orso U9
27 Wellington St, **t** (020) 7240 526; **tube** Covent Garden, Charing Cross. **Open** daily noon–midnight. **Payment**: DC not accepted; TC. **Set menus**: (Sat and Sun noon–5pm) two courses £15, three courses including a glass of champagne or a bloody Mary £17; pre-theatre dinner (Mon–Sat 5–6.45pm) two courses £15, three courses inc. coffee £17.

Mainly Tuscan food, interestingly and daringly interpreted, like pizza with goat's cheese and roasted garlic and oregano, or puntarelle with anchovy dressing. Osso buco is another speciality. The walls are covered with photographs of the great and the good who frequent the place.

Rules U10
35 Maiden Lane, **t** (020) 7836 5314, **w** www.rules.co.uk; **tube** Covent Garden, Charing Cross. **Open** Mon–Sat noon–11.30pm, Sun noon–10.30pm. **Payment**: all cards; TC. **Set menus**: (Mon–Fri 3–5pm) two courses £19.95.

The oldest restaurant in London (established 1798). Formal and determinedly old-fashioned (apart from the odd laminated menus), panelled in dark wood and decorated with hunting regalia. Specializes in game of the season (from their own estate): even rarities such as snipe, ptarmigan and woodcock. Dress smart and book in advance.

Savoy Grill U10
The Savoy Hotel, The Strand, **t** (020) 7420 2065; **tube** Embankment, Charing Cross. **Open** Mon–Fri 12.30–2.30 and 6–11.15, Sat 6–11.15pm; closed Aug. **Payment**: all cards; TC. **Set menus**: (Mon–Fri 6–7pm) two courses £22, three courses £29.75.

Resolutely old-fashioned and none the worse for it, the Savoy Grill may be stuffy, but nothing can compare when it comes to a sense of luxury.

Moderate

Bertorelli's U9
44A Floral St, **t** (020) 7836 3969; **tube** Covent Garden, Leicester Square; wheelchair accessible. **Open** Mon–Sat noon–11pm. **Payment**: all cards.

Conveniently located for opera-goers, 'Bert's' serves a broad range of proven Italian favourites, but also a more radical catalogue of Italian dishes, from maltagliati served with pumpkin, cream, chorizo and grated chilli cheese, to antipasti of deep-fried mozzarella, roasted peppers and smoked eel.

Café des Amis du Vin U9
11–14 Hanover Place, **t** (020) 7379 3444; **tube** Covent Garden; wheelchair accessible. **Open** Mon–Sat 11.30am–11.30pm. **Payment**: all cards; TC. **Set menus**: (11.50am–7pm and 10–11.30pm) two courses £12.50, three courses £15.

French brasserie, favoured by theatre- and opera-goers. Broad menu from simple omelettes to roast halibut with scallions or lamb with pumpkin-seed couscous. Solid and dependable though service can be dicey.

Joe Allen U9
13 Exeter St, **t** (020) 7836 0651, **t** 7497 2148; **tube** Covent Garden, Charing Cross. **Open** Mon–Fri noon–12.45am, Sat 11.30am–12.45pm, Sun 11.30am–11.15pm. **Payment**: all cards; TC. **Set menus**: (lunch) two courses £13, three courses inc. coffee £15; pre-theatre dinner (Mon–Fri 5–6.45pm) two courses £13, three courses £15; brunch (Sat and Sun 11.30am–4pm) two courses £14.50, three courses inc. a drink £16.50.

Started out as an American restaurant, serving hamburgers and steaks, but now embraces modern British and European, too. The long menu lacks character, but there are some delights, particularly the monster puddings. Joe Allen's is a venue to be seen in, good for star-gazers. Rollicking atmosphere.

Mon Plaisir T8
21 Monmouth St, **t** (020) 7836 7243, **w** www.monplaisir.com; **tube** Leicester Square, Covent Garden. **Open** Mon–Fri noon–2.15 and 5.45–11.15, Sat 5.45–11.15pm. **Payment**: all cards; TC. **Set menus**: (Mon–Fri noon–2.15pm) two courses £13.95, three courses £15.95; pre-theatre dinner (Mon–Sat 5–7.15pm) two courses £12.95, three courses inc. a glass of wine and coffee £15.95.

Some of its ramshackle, bohemian charm has been lost, but still a safe bet for appetizing, well-presented French provincial dishes, especially French seafood. Signature dishes include coquilles St-Jacques meunière, gratinée à l'oignon, steak tartare, crème brûlée, and also homemade foie gras.

Prospect Grill T9
4–6 Garrick St, **t** (020) 7379 0412; **tube** Covent Garden, Leicester

Square. **Open** Mon–Sat 11.45–3.30 and 5.45–1.45, Sun 11.45am–3.30pm. **Payment**: DC not accepted. **Set menus**: lunch or pre-theatre dinner (available until 7pm) two courses £13.95, three courses £15.95. Low key but very stylish. Elegant leather-covered benches, deep-red walls and attentive staff. The food is excellent: crisp North American dishes like a perfectly chargrilled steak and chips, or fresh asparagus dusted with parmesan.

Sarastro V9

126 Drury Lane, **t** (020) 7836 0101, **w** www.sarastro-restaurant.com; **tube** Covent Garden, Holborn. **Open** daily noon–12.30pm. **Payment**: all cards; TC.
An over-the-top opera-themed restaurant, where you eat surrounded by stage props. Professional opera singers every Monday. Reasonable Mediterranean menu.

Souk T9

27 Litchfield St, **t** (020) 7240 1796; **tube** Leicester Square. **Open** daily noon–11.30pm. **Payment**: AmEx and DC not accepted; TC.
Set menus: three courses inc. mint tea £15.
Atmospheric North African basement restaurant, made cosy with lots of knick knacks and fabrics. It can get a bit stuffy in summer, but in winter it's the perfect escape.

Inexpensive

Calabash U9

Africa Centre, 38 King St, **t** (020) 7836 1976; **tube** Covent Garden, Leicester Square. **Open** Mon–Fri 12.30–2.30 and 6–10.30, Sat 6–10.30pm. **Payment**: all cards; TC.
Dishes from all over Africa. An institutional feel pervades, partly because of the collegey canteen. Nigerian egusi (stew of beef, melon and shrimps cooked in palm oil), couscous from the Maghreb, dioumbre (okra stew) from the Ivory Coast, or yassa chicken (grilled with lemon and pepper) from Senegal, with lots of fried plantain. African music on Fri and Sat nights.

Pubs, Wine Bars and Cafés

Mode T8

57 Endell St, **t** (020) 7240 8085; **tube** Covent Garden, Tottenham Court Rd. **Open** Mon–Fri 8am–11pm, Sat 9am–9pm. **Payment**: AmEx and DC not accepted.
This is a cosy, welcoming café with a vaguely bazaar-like atmosphere thanks to the scattered lanterns and rugs. There are good salads, pasta dishes and sandwiches, and smiley Italian staff.

Paul T10

29 Bedford St, **t** (020) 7836 5324; **tube** Covent Garden, Charing Cross, Leicester Square. **Open** Mon–Fri 7.30am–9pm, Sat and Sun 9am–9pm. **Payment**: all cards; TC.
Part of the plush French chain, this elegant café offers superb bread, cakes and pastries to eat in or take away.

Holborn and Fleet Street

Restaurants

Expensive

Admiralty V10

Somerset House, The Strand, **t** (020) 7845 4646, **w** www .gruppo.co.uk; **tube** Charing Cross, Embankment, Holborn. **Open** Mon–Sat noon–2.45 and 6–10.45. **Payment**: all cards. **Set menus**: lunch four courses inc. glass of champagne £28, five courses (vegetarian) £39, £45.
Set in the newly refurbished Somerset House, this beautiful newcomer to London's restaurant scene has been snapping up awards left, right and centre. And justly too: the views and the elegant décor are more than matched by the exquisitely prepared French cuisine. Unusually, the restaurant also offers a spectacular five-course vegetarian set menu.

Bank Aldwych V9

1 Kingsway, **t** (020) 7379 9797; **tube** Holborn; wheelchair accessible. **Open** Mon–Fri 7.30–3 and 6–11.30, Sat 11.30–3.30 and 5–11.30, Sun 11.30am–3.30pm. **Payment**: all cards.
Set in a converted bank, this is a big, cheerful, stylish restaurant serving assured modern European cuisine. It's difficult when the food is this good, but try to leave room for dessert.

City Rhodes X8

1 New St Square, **t** (020) 7583 1313; **tube** Chancery Lane, Blackfriars. **Open** Mon–Fri noon–2.30 and 6–9, Sat noon–2.30 and 7–10.30. **Payment**: all cards.
Renowned modern British fare served in smart, unfussy surroundings that ensure you keep your attention on the food. Popular with suited professionals and much quieter in the evenings. The desserts are spectacular.

Indigo V9

One Aldwych Hotel, 1 Aldwych, **t** (020) 7300 0400; **tube** Charing Cross, Embankment, Holborn. **Open** daily 6.30–11am, noon–3pm and 6–11.15pm. **Payment**: all cards. **Set menus**: (Mon–Sat 6–7pm and 10–11.15pm) two courses £15.50, three courses £19.50.
This is the very stylish coffee shop, breakfast bar and restaurant for the glossy One Aldwych hotel. It's pricey, but very elegant, and the food (fashionable modern European) is generally of a high standard.

Pubs, Wine Bars and Cafés

Gordon's Wine Bar U11

47 Villiers St, **t** (020) 7930 1408; **tube** Embankment, Charing Cross. **Open** daily 11am–11pm. **Payment**: all cards.
A dusty, old-fashioned wine bar with brick vaults and spluttering candles. An interesting selection of often unusual wines are on offer, and food – light meals and sandwiches – is served all day until 10pm.

Old Bank of England X9
*194 Fleet St, **t** (020) 7430 2255;*
***tube** Chancery Lane, Blackfriars.*
***Open** for food Mon–Fri 11am–8pm.*
***Payment**: all cards.*
This former bank is a spectacular place, with high ceilings, a gallery and massive windows. It's big and noisy (which would also describe a lot of the people who drink here), but it does serve reasonably decent pub grub and good ales.

Seven Stars W8
*53–4 Carey St, **t** (020) 7242 8521;*
***tube** Chancery Lane. **Open** Mon–Fri 11am–11pm. **Payment**: all cards.*
This small pub is hidden away behind the Royal Courts of Justice and has been going since 1602. Not much seems to have changed since then and it's refreshingly free of background music and fruit machines. Pub food and sandwiches are served all day.

Waldorf Meridien Hotel V9
*Aldwych, **t** (020) 7836 2400; **tube** Covent Garden. **Tea served** Mon–Fri 3–5.30pm £18, £21 and £28. **Tea dance** Sat 2pm, Sun 4pm £25, £28 inc. champagne.*

Bloomsbury and Fitzrovia

Restaurants

Luxury

Pied à Terre Q6
*34 Charlotte St, **t** (020) 7636 1178;*
***tube** Goodge St, Tottenham Court Rd. **Open** Mon–Fri 12.30–2.30 and 7–11, Sat 7–11pm. **Payment**: all cards; TC. **Set menus**: (Mon–Fri 12.30–2.30pm) two courses £19.50, three courses £23; (Mon–Sat 7–11pm) two courses £39.50, three courses £50, eight courses £65.*
The neutral setting is a fine foil for Tom Aiken's virtuoso modern French cuisine. The food is just as magnificent at lunchtime, with the added bonus of generous set menus.

Expensive

Archipelago Q5
*110 Whitfield St, **t** (020) 7323 9655, **f** 7323 9616; **tube** Warren St. **Open** Mon–Fri 12.30–2.30 and 7–11, Sat 7–11pm. **Payment**: all cards; TC.*
This weird and wonderful Oriental fantasy restaurant (the menu an origami snake in a basket, the bill delivered in a birdcage) is rescued by the food from being a load of pretentious nonsense. The tone is playful and the innovative and spicy fusion fare is as dreamy as the surroundings.

Nico Central P7
*35 Great Portland St, **t** (020) 7436 8846; **tube** Oxford Circus. **Open** Mon–Fri noon–2.30 and 6.30–10.30, Sat noon–2.30 and 7–10.30. **Payment**: all cards. **Set menus**: (lunch) two courses £16.75, three courses £19.50.*
No longer run by Nico Ladenis, this can be a bit hit and miss. When it's on form, the set menus are a good way to try the Provençal-inspired menu with occasional exotic twists such as apple galette and red snapper with couscous.

Moderate

Alfred T8
*245 Shaftesbury Av, **t** (020) 7240 2566; **tube** Tottenham Court Rd. **Open** Mon–Fri noon–3.30pm. **Payment**: all cards; TC. **Set menus**: two courses £13.90, three courses £17 (Mon £10).*
A modern angle on old British favourites. Stark, no-nonsense décor and formica tabletops underline the delicacy of the cooking. Straightforward dishes like roast pork, with imaginative accompaniments like marinated artichoke.

Elena's L'Etoile R7
*30 Charlotte St, **t** (020) 7636 7189; **tube** Goodge St, Tottenham Court Rd. **Open** Mon–Fri noon–2.30 and 6–10.45, Sat 6–10.45pm. **Payment**: all cards; TC. **Set menus**: pre-theatre deal (Mon–Sat 6–8pm) gives a 20% discount on total bill.*
Gracefully faded grandeur and old photographs of fêted regulars serve as the backdrop in this favourite Fitzrovian brasserie. Good classic French fare with a number of modern, even Eastern twists.

Inexpensive

Abeno T7
*47 Museum St, **t** (020) 7405 3211; **tube** Holborn, Tottenham Court Rd. **Open** daily noon–10pm. **Payment**: DC not accepted; TC. **Set menus**: lunch £6–16.*
A little treasure right by the British Museum. Specialises in *okonomi-yaki* (Japanese-style tortilla) individually cooked on a giant hotplate, a *teppan*, set into each table. The process is pure theatre and the result is not only delectable but surprisingly filling. Only organic ingredients. Exquisite starters and delightful service.

La Brasserie Townhouse T7
*24 Coptic St, **t** (020) 7636 2731; **tube** Tottenham Court Rd, Holborn. **Open** Mon–Fri 8.30–3 and 6–11, Sat and Sun 9–3 and 6–11. **Payment**: all cards; TC. **Set menus**: (noon–2 and 5.30–7) two courses £7.95, three courses £9.95.*
A fusion of modern French and international cooking. Depending on your mood it can seem cramped or just cosy and cheerful, with very friendly service and huge portions. Full English breakfast or full continental breakfast with home-baked croissant, and homemade jam. Wide choice on the set menus.

Wagamama T7
*4 Streatham St, **t** (020) 7323 9223; **tube** Holborn, Tottenham Court Rd. **Open** Mon–Sat noon–11pm, Sun 12.30–10.30pm. **Payment**: all cards. **Set menus**: £8.50–9.50.*
The first branch of this popular noodle-bar chain. See p.319.

Pubs, Wine Bars and Cafés

October Gallery Café U6
*24 Old Gloucester St, **t** (020) 7242 7367; **tube** Holborn, Russell Square. **Open** Tues–Sat 12.30–2.30pm. **Payment**: no cards.*

Eclectic inspiration from around the world; busy, cosy and friendly. A limited choice – but usually a vegetarian option. There's a delightful plant-filled courtyard.

Marylebone and Regent's Park

Restaurants

Moderate

Blandford St Restaurant N7
5–7 Blandford St, **t** (020) 7486 9696; **tube** Baker St, Bond St, Marble Arch. **Open** Mon–Fri noon–2.30 and 6.30–10.30, Sat 6.30–10.30pm. **Payment**: DC not accepted. **Set menus**: (lunch) two courses £21.50, three courses £25.
Beautifully presented, inventive modern European cuisine at this low-key restaurant. Excellent service and an unusually good range of vegetarian options.

Giraffe N7
6–8 Blandford St, **t** (020) 7935 2333; **tube** Baker St, Bond St, Marble Arch. **Open** Mon–Fri 8–4 and 5–11, Sat and Sun 9–5 and 6–11. **Payment**: DC not accepted.
See Hampstead branch, p.330.

Ibla N7
89 Marylebone High St, **t** (020) 7224 3799; **tube** Baker St, Bond St. **Open** Mon–Sat noon–2.30 and 7–10.15, Sun noon–2.30pm. **Payment**: all cards. **Set menus**: (lunch) two courses £15, three courses £18; (dinner) three courses £30, four courses £35.
The excellent set-price menu changes regularly but includes a tempting variety of modern and classic Italian dishes: tagliolini with artichokes and smoked ricotta, monkfish with aubergine purée and courgette, lamb fillet with broad beans and leek. Décor is contemporary but not consciously trendy; service is relaxed and friendly.

Levant N8
Jason Court, 76 Wigmore St, **t** (020) 7224 2992, **w** www.levant restaurant.co.uk; **tube** Bond St. **Open** for food Mon–Fri noon–

11.30pm, Sat and Sun 5.30–11.30pm. **Payment**: all cards. **Set menus**: (Mon–Fri noon–6pm) two courses £8.50; (dinner) meze £19.50, meze and main course £28.
An exotic, candle-lit Lebanese bar-restaurant with long tables and little nooks with silky cushions scattered around low tables. Very tasty food and a good selection of Lebanese wines. There's even a belly-dancer at weekends.

Maroush L9
21 Edgware Rd, **t** (020) 7723 0773; **tube** Marble Arch. **Open** daily noon–2am. **Payment**: all cards.
The best of the Middle Eastern restaurants on Edgware Rd. A fun atmosphere with lively décor. Wonderfully spiced dishes and excellent meze. Stuffed lamb is a favourite off the lengthy menu. Beware though: if you arrive to eat after 10pm the minimum charge is a startling £48 per person. There are now four restaurants in the Maroush chain, but this remains the best.

Singapore Garden L5
154–6 Gloucester Place, **t** (020) 7723 8233; **tube** Baker St. **Open** Mon–Thurs and Sun noon–2.45 and 6–10.45, Fri and Sat noon–2.45 and 6–11.15. **Payment**: all cards; TC. **Set menus**: (Mon–Fri noon–2.45pm) two courses £7; (minimum 2 people) £17.50. **Booking advised**.
A spacious, light basement venue under Regent's Park Hotel, serving Singaporean Chinese food. The (sometimes very hot) seafood dishes are especially good. Busy lively atmosphere and very friendly service.

Union Café & Restaurant N7
96 Marylebone Lane, **t** (020) 7486 4860; **tube** Baker St, Bond St. **Open** Mon–Sat 12.30–3 and 6.30–10.30. **Payment**: DC not accepted; no cheques.
Preaches simplicity with great verve. Delicious salads; organic, free-range produce is guaranteed, where appropriate. Non-puritanical puddings. Sleek and popular with fashion-business diners.

Inexpensive

No.6 Brasserie N7
6 George St, **t** (020) 7935 1910; **tube** Marble Arch, Bond St. **Open** Mon–Fri 8am–5.30pm. **Payment**: AmEx and DC not accepted. **Booking essential**.
This is a combination of deli and a small dining room at the back which is always packed at lunchtimes. Simple, modern cooking (wild salmon fishcakes, leek and cheddar soufflé) using ultra-fresh ingredients is the secret of its success.

Patogh K7
8 Crawford Place, **t** (020) 7262 4015; **tube** Edgware Rd. **Open** daily 1pm–midnight. **Payment**: no cards; TC. **BYO**.
A fine, no-frills Iranian eatery offering huge amounts of good food (this is how kebabs should be). No charge for corkage.

Sea Shell K6
49–51 Lisson Grove, **t** (020) 7723 8703; **tube** Marylebone. **Open** Mon–Fri noon–2.30 and 5–10.30, Sat noon–10.30pm. **Payment**: DC not accepted; TC.
Arguably the best fish and chips in town, though becoming increasingly commercial. Fine homemade fish cakes and tartare sauce. Clean and attractive. Café-style eating as well as takeaway.

Pubs, Wine Bars and Cafés

Aveda/The Quiet Revolution N6
28–9 Marylebone High St, **t** (020) 7487 5683; **tube** Baker St, Bond St. **Open** Mon–Sat 9am–6pm. **Payment**: all cards.
Wonderful organic café next to the Aveda shop; big chunky shared wooden tables. Great soups, sandwiches and light snacks. Very chic.

Maison Blanc N7
7 Thayer St, **t** (020) 7224 0228; **tube** Baker St, Bond St. **Open** Mon–Sat 8.30am–6.30pm, Sun 9am–6pm. **Payment**: DC not accepted.
Mouthwatering French pâtisserie. Buy cakes or quiches to eat out in the park.

Pâtisserie Valerie at Sagne N7
*105 Marylebone High St, **t** (020)
7935 6240; **tube** Baker St, Bond St.
Open Mon–Fri 7.30am–7pm, Sat
8am–7pm, Sun 9am–6pm.
Payment: DC not accepted.*
Old-fashioned gilded tea and cake
shop complete with chandeliers,
serving creamy French cakes,
sandwiches and snacks.

South Kensington and Knightsbridge

Restaurants

Expensive

Bibendum J16
*Michelin House, 81 Fulham Rd,
t (020) 7581 5817; **tube** South
Kensington; wheelchair accessible.
Open Mon–Fri noon–2.30 and
7–11.30, Sat noon–3 and 7–11, Sun
7–10.30pm. **Payment:** all cards; TC.
Set menus: two courses £24, three
courses £28.50.*
Excelling in ultra-rich French
regional food, set in the sumptuous Art Deco Michelin building.
This is the flagship restaurant of
the Conran empire. The oyster bar
downstairs, with a shorter fish-
oriented menu, is cheaper though
less grand. A notch less snooty is
the coffee shop and sandwich bar.

Bombay Brasserie G16
*Courtfield Close, Courtfield Rd,
t (020) 7370 4040; **tube** Gloucester
Rd; wheelchair accessible. **Open**
daily 12.30–3 and 7.30–midnight.
Payment: AmEx not accepted; TC.
Set menus: buffet lunch inc. coffee
£16.95. **Booking essential.***
This is posh, with sumptuous colonial décor, and gastronomically
flawless. Largely north Indian
menu, including unusual tandoori
dishes. Beautiful veranda.

Salloo's M13
*62–4 Kinnerton St, **t** (020) 7235
4444; **tube** Hyde Park Corner,
Knightsbridge. **Open** Mon–Sat
noon–2.30 and 7.30–11.15, Sun
noon–2.30pm. **Payment:** all
cards; TC.*
Excellent succulent grilled meats
are the speciality at this Pakistani

restaurant – although you would
be advised to stick to them rather
than stray into other areas of the
menu. Well-prepared marinades
and terrific tandooris. Classy location and good wine list.

San Lorenzo L15
*22 Beauchamp Place, **t** (020) 7584
1074; **tube** Knightsbridge, South
Kensington. **Open** Mon–Sat 12.30–3
and 7.30–11.30, Sun 12.30–3pm.
Payment: all cards; TC.*
Fashionable celeb hangout since
the 1960s. Good, if over-priced,
Italian food with mouth-watering
desserts and perfect espresso.

Moderate

Cambio de Tercio Off maps
*163 Old Brompton Rd, **t** (020) 7244
8970; **tube** Gloucester Rd.
Open Mon–Sat 12.30–2.30 and
7–11.30, Sun 12.30–2.30 and 7–11.15.
Payment: DC not accepted.
Booking advised.*
Exuberant contemporary Spanish
cooking: delicate paella, skate
wings, salt cod, octopus. Intensely
popular. Some excellent real tapas
to start with – *jamón serrano* with
fino or manzanilla.

Caravela K15
*39 Beauchamp Place, **t** (020) 7581
2366; **tube** Knightsbridge, South
Kensington. **Open** Mon–Sat
noon–3 and 7–11, Sun 7–11pm.
Payment: all cards; TC. **Set menus:**
lunch two courses inc. a glass of
wine £7.95.*
Lively Portuguese restaurant with
a guitarist and singers to sere-
nade you as you eat your salt cod
or charcoal-grilled meats in a
cheerily nautical setting. Rich and
tasty puddings.

Inexpensive

Stockpot L14
*6 Basil St, **t** (020) 7589 8627; **tube**
Knightsbridge. **Open** Mon–Tues
11.30am–11.30pm, Wed–Sat
noon–11.45pm, Sun noon–11pm.
Payment: no cards. **Set menus:** two
courses £3.80–4.95.*
Cheap and cheerful with strains of
school dinners. Hardly has preten-
sions towards culinary art, but the
quality isn't actually bad.

Pubs, Wine Bars and Cafés

Orangery F12
*Kensington Palace, **t** (020) 7376
0239; **tube** High St Kensington.
Open winter daily 10am–5pm,
summer daily 10am–6pm.
Payment: DC not accepted.*
Elegant café with a delightful
summer terrace. Try the spiced
apple cake.

Orsini J15
*8A Thurloe Place, **t** (020) 7581 5553;
tube South Kensington.
Open Mon–Fri 8am–8pm, Sat
8am–7pm, Sun 10am–7pm.
Payment: DC not accepted.*
Friendly and unassuming
Neapolitan café with delicious
cakes and a good-value
lunch menu.

The South Bank and Southwark

For neighbouring areas, *see*
'South: Bermondsey'.

Restaurants

Luxury

Neat X11
*2nd Floor, Oxo Tower Wharf, Barge
House St, **t** (020) 7928 5533; **tube**
Southwark. **Open** Mon–Fri noon–2
and 7–10, Sat 7–10pm. **Payment:**
AmEx and DC not accepted. **Set
menus:** lunch three courses £29;
dinner three courses £49.*
Richard Neat's new restaurant and
brasserie in the Oxo Tower uses
the same formula as his equally
chi-chi restaurant in Cannes –
even down to the mauve suede
décor. Classy food, sumptuous
surroundings and breathtaking
views. The brasserie is considerably cheaper than the restaurant
if you don't want to splurge too
much, and the lunch menu is
remarkably good value.

Moderate

Champor Champor DD13
*Weston St, **t** (020) 7403 4600; **tube**
London Bridge. **Open** Mon–Sat*

12.30–2 and 6.30–midnight, last orders 10pm. **Payment:** all cards; TC. **Set menus:** two courses £19, three courses £22.50.

Entering this amazing new South East Asian restaurant is like walking into a jewel box: rich red walls, shimmering silks, paintings and ancient carvings are a world away from the grey street outside. A mixture of breads and grilled tofu skins is served in a gilded basket, and the menu is equally daring – try stir-fried crocodile tail, or Balinese lamb with lemongrass and galangal. A great deal of thought and care has gone into this new venture – and it shows in the exceptional quality of the cuisine and in the exquisite presentation of each dish. A very special little spot.

Delfina DD13

50 Bermondsey St, **t** (020) 7537 0244, **w** www.delfina.org; **tube** London Bridge; wheelchair accessible. **Open** for food Mon–Fri noon–3pm. **Payment:** all cards; TC.
Large, airy gallery-cum-café serving excellent and thoughtful cuisine. Dishes span the world, from spaghetti with scallops to chargrilled kangaroo. This street is becoming increasingly fashionable, so hopefully it won't be long before Delfina extends its opening hours.

The Fire Station X13

150 Waterloo Rd, **t** (020) 7620 2226; **tube** Waterloo; wheelchair accessible. **Open** for food Mon–Sat noon–11pm, Sun noon–9.30pm. **Payment:** all cards.
This former fire station has been converted into a packed, vibrant pub-like eatery, just opposite the Old Vic theatre. Easy-going modern British.

Honest Cabbage DD13

99 Bermondsey St, **t** (020) 7234 0080; **tube** London Bridge. **Open** Mon–Wed noon–3 and 6.30–10, Thurs and Fri noon–3 and 6.30–11, Sat 6.30–11pm, Sun noon–4pm. **Payment:** AmEx and DC not accepted; TC.
This is a laid-back restaurant set in an old Victorian pub, catering to

SE1's loft-dwellers and arty types. The thoughtful menu scrawled on the blackboard changes daily and always features a vegetarian option. Staff are very friendly, and Sunday brunch has become an institution. There's an equally good sister restaurant in Waterloo: the **Honest Goose**, 61 The Cut, SE1, **t** (020) 7261 1221.

RSJ X11

13A Coin St, **t** (020) 7928 4554, **t** 7401 2455; **tube** Waterloo. **Open** Mon–Fri noon–2 and 5.30–11, Sat 5.30–11pm. **Payment:** all cards; TC. **Set menus:** two courses £15.95, three courses inc. coffee £16.95.
Flamboyant, innovative French cooking, with a certain amount of global influence. Predominantly Loire wines. Delightful, sunny upper rooms. Very popular.

Waterloo Bar & Kitchen X13

131 Waterloo Rd, **t** (020) 7928 5086; **tube** Waterloo. **Open** Mon–Fri noon–2.45 and 5.30–10.30. **Payment:** all cards; TC. **Set menus:** (lunch) two courses £10.95, three courses £12.95; (dinner) two courses £12.95, three courses £15.95.
Serious modern European food, simple but well prepared, with dreamy carpaccio and a good wine list. Small, informal setting, with wooden floors, long tables and ochre walls, behind the Old Vic. Always busy and buzzy.

Inexpensive

Cubana W13

48 Lower Marsh, **t** (020) 7928 8778; **tube** Waterloo. **Open** Mon–Sat 10am–midnight. **Payment:** all cards; TC.
You can't miss this café – a huge Cuban beauty shimmies across the whole wall. Inside, it's equally loud and colourful; come for the big jugs of cocktails, the cheap (filling but unremarkable) food, and the rowdy party atmosphere.

Pubs, Wine Bars and Cafés

Konditor and Cooke Y12

Young Vic Theatre, The Cut; **tube** Waterloo. **Open** Mon–Sat 8.30am–

10pm, until 11pm when there's a show. **Payment:** AmEx and DC not accepted.
Excellent soups, sandwiches and light meals from the Konditor and Cooke bakery (which has a shop around the corner at 22 Cornwall Rd). Leave room for the cakes – among the best in London, especially the florentines. Evening meals are also served – like a delicious homemade pumpkin ravioli.

The City

For neighbouring areas, see 'Holborn and Fleet Street', 'North: Clerkenwell', 'East: Hoxton and Shoreditch' and 'East: Spitalfields and Whitechapel'.

Restaurants

Expensive

Club Gascon Z7

57 West Smithfield, **t** (020) 7253 5853; **tube** Barbican, Farringdon. **Open** Mon–Fri noon–2 and 7–11, Sat 7–11pm. **Payment:** all cards; TC. **Set menus:** five courses £30.
Still very fashionable, this serves very high-quality Gascon food (cassoulet, sweetbreads, smoked eel) in tapas-size portions, the idea being for each customer to order five or six. Lively, buzzy and extremely good.

Searcy's BB6

Level 2, Barbican, Silk St, **t** (020) 7588 3008; **tube** Barbican; wheelchair accessible. **Open** Mon–Fri noon–2.30 and 5–10.30, Sat 5–10.30pm, Sun noon–2.30 and 5–6.30. **Payment:** all cards; TC. **Set menus:** (lunch) two courses £19, three courses £22.50; (dinner) two courses £28.50, three courses £32.50.
The Barbican's in-house restaurant has generally good and beautifully presented modern European cooking, and the view over the water-filled central courtyard is great. However, prices are fierce and unless you're there for a pre-theatre meal the service can be slow.

Moderate

Alba BB7

107 Whitecross St, **t** (020) 7588 1798; **tube** Barbican, Moorgate. **Open** Mon–Fri noon–3 and 6–11, Sat and Sun noon–3pm. **Payment**: all cards. **Set menus**: dinner two courses £11, three courses £15.

Quietly good Italian restaurant, specializing in polenta, risotto and other northern or Piedmontese dishes. The only drawback is the location, next to the hideous labyrinthine quarters of the Barbican. Pink and minimalist inside.

Quality Chop House Off maps

94 Farringdon Rd, **t** (020) 7837 5093; **tube** Farringdon. **Open** Mon–Fri noon–3 and 6.30–11, Sat 6.30–11pm, Sun noon–4 and 7–11.30. **Payment**: AmEx and DC not accepted; TC. **Booking advised**.

Superior English specialities like fishcakes, game pie and roast lamb, with modern Mediterranean influences steadily appearing. It's all served in the highly atmospheric rooms of a former 19th-century working-men's club – hence the miserably hard wooden benches. It's extremely popular, especially for Sunday brunch.

Sweetings BB9

39 Queen Victoria St, **t** (020) 7248 3062; **tube** Cannon St. **Open** Mon–Fri noon–3pm. **Payment**: no cards.

This traditional and excellent fish restaurant is an old favourite in the City, but it's often hard to get a seat.

Inexpensive

The Place Below BB8

St Mary-le-Bow, Cheapside, **t** (020) 7329 0789; **tube** St Paul's, Bank. **Open** Mon–Fri noon–2.30pm. **Payment**: AmEx and DC not accepted; TC. **Unlicensed**.

A popular vegetarian restaurant set in the impressive crypt of St Mary-le-Bow.

North: St John's Wood and Swiss Cottage

Restaurants

Expensive

L'Aventure Off maps

3 Blenheim Terrace, NW8, **t** (020) 7624 6232; **tube** St John's Wood. **Open** Mon–Fri 12.30–2.30 and 7.30–11, Sat 7.30–11pm, plus Easter–Sept Sun 12.30–2.30 and 7.30–10. **Payment**: DC not accepted; TC. **Set menus**: lunch three courses £18.50; dinner three courses £27.50.

Utterly charming little restaurant, hidden behind a profusion of plants and flowers. Fresh, immaculately prepared French cuisine served by welcoming staff.

Moderate

The Gate Off maps

72 Belsize Lane, NW3, **t** (020) 7435 7733; **tube** Belsize Park, Swiss Cottage. **Open** Mon–Sat 10am–11pm, Sun noon–4pm. **Payment**: DC not accepted. **Set menus**: two courses £10.

The latest venture from the owners of the fabulous Gate restaurant in Hammersmith (see p.336), this is a cool, minimalist space serving excellent vegetarian dishes and a good range of snacks all day.

The Salt House Off maps

63 Abbey Rd, NW8, **t** (020) 7328 6626; **tube** St John's Wood, Swiss Cottage. **Open** for food Mon–Fri 12.20–3 and 6.30–10.30, Sat and Sun 12.30–4 and 7–10.30. **Payment**: DC not accepted; TC. **Set menus**: (Mon–Fri 12.20–3pm) three courses £9.75.

Restrained modern décor, excellent creative contemporary cuisine and very friendly service make this one of the best dinner options in town. The sitting area at the front, with big cosy sofas, is nicer than the dining room at the back.

Wakaba Off maps

122A Finchley Rd, NW3, **t** (020) 7586 7960; **tube** Finchley Rd. **Open** Mon–Sat 6.30–11pm. **Payment**: all cards. **Set menus**: inc. green tea, miso soup, rice and pickles £23.60–33.

One of the first Japanese restaurants in London, this is still one of the best, in an incredibly minimalist white setting. Good service, great sashimi, and excellent set menus for a special splurge. Worth the trip down the unappealing Finchley Rd.

Inexpensive

Zuccato Off maps

Top floor, O2 Complex, 225 Finchley Rd, NW3, **t** (020) 7431 1799; **tube** Finchley Rd. **Open** for food Mon–Sat noon–midnight, Sun 10.30am–11pm. **Payment**: all cards.

A chic Italian place, this is the best option in this shopping/cinema complex. Great presentation and service and very good food: the ravioli with peas is excellent, though the risotto can be a touch stodgy.

Pubs, Wine Bars and Cafés

Maison Blanc Off maps

37 St John's Wood High St, NW8, **t** (020) 7586 1982; **tube** St John's Wood. **Open** Mon–Sat 8.30am–6.30pm, Sun 9am–6pm. **Payment**: AmEx and DC not accepted.

Another branch of the excellent French pâtisserie. Chocolates, cakes and a pretty little terrace at the back in summer.

North: Clerkenwell

Restaurants

Moderate

Gonbei Off maps

151 King's Cross Rd, EC1, **t** (020) 7278 0619; **tube** King's Cross. **Open** Mon–Sat 6–10.30pm. **Payment**: AmEx and DC not

accepted. **Set menus:** *dinner five courses £19.80.*
One of London's few low-priced Japanese restaurants. The sushi is particularly recommended, as is the noodle soup with tempura.

Moro Off maps
*34–36 Exmouth Market, EC1, **t** (020) 7833 8336; **tube** Farringdon; wheelchair accessible. **Open** for food Mon–Fri 12.30–2.30 and 7.30–10.30, Sat 7.30–10.30pm. **Payment:** DC not accepted; TC.*
This fashionable restaurant on a fashionable street doesn't rest on its laurels; the food is every bit as stylish as its clientèle. Tangy North African and Spanish dishes are prepared with the freshest ingredient and beautifully presented.

The Peasant Off maps
*240 St John St, EC1, **t** (020) 7336 7726; **tube** Angel, Farringdon. **Open** for food Mon–Fri 12.30–3.30 and 6.30–11, Sat 6.30–11pm. **Payment:** all cards; TC.*
Attractive and pristine little room above a handsome Victorian pub. Inspiration for the sophisticated menu comes from around the world – chicken *paillarde* to an excellent choice of meze.

St John Off maps
*26 St John St, EC1, **t** (020) 7251 0848; **tube** Farringdon; wheelchair accessible. **Open** for food Mon–Fri noon–2.30 and 6–10.30, Sat 6–11pm. **Payment:** all cards; TC.*
A converted smokehouse, still with an industrial feel to it. Hearty, meaty, ingenious British cooking with a difference: every conceivable part of the animal (trotters, ox heart, bone marrow) is presented in interesting dishes. No fussiness, thin on sauces, crisp vegetables.

Inexpensive

Fish Central Off maps
*149–51 Central St, EC1, **t** (020) 7253 4970; **tube** Angel, Barbican, Old St. **Open** Mon–Fri 11–2.30 and 4.45–10.30, Sat 4.45–10.30pm. **Payment:** AmEx and DC not accepted; TC.*
A smart café in a grotty street serving fine basic fish 'n' chips as

well as more elaborate fresh fish dishes. There are some veggie options.

North: Camden

Restaurants

Moderate

Café Delancey Off maps
*3 Delancey St, NW1, **t** (020) 7387 1985; **tube** Camden Town. **Open** Mon–Sat 9am–11.30pm, Sun 9am–10pm. **Payment:** AmEx and DC not accepted; TC.*
Popular local French restaurant, with robust, attractively presented dishes. Caters for all types. Brasserie food: venison but also snacks and soups.

Cheng Du Off maps
*9 Parkway, NW1, **t** (020) 7485 8058; **tube** Camden Town. **Open** Mon–Thurs noon–3 and 6–11.30, Fri noon–3 and 6–2.30am, Sat 1pm–2.30am, Sun 1–10.30pm. **Payment:** AmEx and DC not accepted. **Set menus:** (minimum two people) two courses £13, £14.*
Spicy Chinese Szechuan cooking in the heart of Camden. Attentive service, quiet ambience and a friendly owner.

Mango Room Off maps
*10 Kentish Town Rd, NW1, **t** (020) 7482 5065; **tube** Camden Town. **Open** Tues–Sun noon–3 and 6–midnight, Mon 6pm–midnight. **Payment:** AmEx and DC not accepted.*
Very cool bar-restaurant with modern London-Caribbean cooking: excellent saltfish and desserts. There's a great range of cocktails, too.

Odette's Off maps
*130 Regent's Park Rd, NW1, **t** (020) 7586 5486; **tube** Chalk Farm. **Open** for food Mon–Fri 12.30–2.30 and 7–11, Sat 7–11pm. **Payment:** all cards. **Set menus:** lunch three courses £12.50.*
This Primrose Hill gem is cosy and romantic, twinkling in mirrors and serving faultless modern European cooking to a gentle and appreciative clientèle.

Inexpensive

Andy's Taverna Off maps
*81 Bayham St, NW1, **t** (020) 7485 9718; **tube** Camden. **Open** Mon–Fri noon–2.30 and 6–midnight, Sat 5.30pm–midnight, Sun 5.30–11.30pm. **Payment:** DC not accepted; TC.*
Highly thought-of Greek eatery with a flower-walled backyard. The menu looks standard Greek, but the ingredients are high quality and the cooking light.

Café Corfu Off maps
*7–9 Pratt St, N1, **t** (020) 7267 8088; **tube** Camden Town. **Open** Tues–Fri noon–10.30pm, Sat and Sun noon–11.30pm. **Payment:** AmEx and DC not accepted. **Set menus:** three courses £15–20.*
Cheerfully eccentric décor – lots of candles and old posters – and excellent, crisply presented Greek food. This is widely regarded as one of the best Greek restaurants in London. The wine list is superb and there are belly dancers at weekends.

North: Islington

Restaurants

Moderate

Granita Off maps
*127 Upper St, N1, **t** (020) 7226 3222; **tube** Angel, Highbury and Islington. **Open** Tues 6.30–10.30pm, Wed–Sat 12.30–2.30 and 6.30–10.30, Sun 12.30–3pm. **Payment:** AmEx and DC not accepted; TC. **Set menus:** (Sun 12.30–3pm) two courses £13.50, three courses £15.50.*
Highly esteemed, with an imaginative, well-prepared and eclectic menu.

Metrogusto Off maps
*11–13 Theberton St, N1, **t** (020) 7226 9400; **tube** Angel. **Open** Mon–Fri noon–2.30 and 6.30–10.30, Sat noon–3 and 6–11, Sun noon–3pm. **Payment:** AmEx and DC not accepted; TC.*
Cool, simple but sophisticated modern Italian food in this relaxed, welcoming restaurant.

Inexpensive

Le Mercury Off maps
140A Upper St, N1, **t** *(020) 7354
4088;* **tube** *Angel, Highbury and
Islington.* **Open** *Mon–Sat
11am–1am, Sun noon–11.30pm.*
Payment: *all cards.* **Set menus:**
*(lunch) two courses £5.45, three
courses £6.95.*
Delightful French restaurant
serving delicious and surprisingly
ambitious food at rock-bottom
prices. The décor is anything but
budget, and the staff are friendly.

North: Highgate

Sabor de Brazil Off maps
36 Highgate Hill, N19, **t** *(020) 7263
9066;* **tube** *Archway.* **Open**
Tues–Sun 7–11.45pm. **Payment:** *no
cards;* **TC.** **Inexpensive.**
Welcoming, family-run Brazilian
restaurant – don't miss the
coconut-milk blancmange. A band
often plays on Wednesday nights.

Café Mozart Map p.284
17 Swains Lane, N6, **t** *(020) 8348
1384;* **tube** *Highgate.* **Open** *daily
9am–10pm.* **Payment:** *AmEx and
DC not accepted.* **Inexpensive.**
Wonderful wood-panelled
Viennese café – try the shnitzel or
the goulash but make sure you
leave room for the mouth-
watering pastries.

North: Hampstead

Restaurants

Giraffe Map p.284
46 Rosslyn Hill, NW3, **t** *(020) 7435
0343;* **tube** *Hampstead.* **Open**
*Mon–Fri 8–4 and 5–11, Sat and Sun
9–5 and 6–11.* **Payment:** *DC not
accepted.* **Moderate.**
Bright colours, cheery staff and a
lively modern global menu with a
Middle Eastern slant make this all-
day place a pleasant option.

Jin Kichi Map p.284
73 Heath St, NW3, **t** *(020) 7794
6158;* **tube** *Hampstead.* **Open**
*Tues–Fri 6–11pm, Sat 12.30–2 and
6–11, Sun 12.30–2 and 6–10.*
Payment: *all cards;* **TC.** **Set menus:**
lunch £7–12. **Moderate.**
A cosy Japanese restaurant
serving delicious and reasonably
priced dishes. Watch the chef cook.

Pubs, Wine Bars and Cafés

The Coffee Cup Map p.284
74 Hampstead High St, NW3,
t *(020) 7435 7565;* **tube** *Hampstead.*
Open *Mon–Sat 8am–midnight, Sun
9am–midnight.* **Payment:** *no cards.*
A cosy 60s throwback, with red
leatherette banquettes, a small
outdoor terrace and a splendid
menu including delicious raisin
toast. Good for watching the
beautiful people walk by outside.

Louis Pâtisserie Map p.284
32 Heath St, NW3; **tube** *Hampstead.* **Open** *daily 9am–6pm.*
Payment: *no cards.*
Famous Hungarian tearoom
which has been a haunt of *mittel*-
European emigrés for decades.
Wonderful cheesecake and cream
cakes brought on a tray for you to
choose from.

North: Golders Green

Carmelli's Off maps
128 Golders Green Rd, NW11; **tube**
Golders Green. **Open** *Mon–Wed
6am–3pm, Thurs 6am until Fri one
hour before the sabbath, Sat 10pm
until 6am Mon.* **Payment:** *no cards.*
The best bagels (as well as a
wonderful range of cakes and
breads) in London, in the heart of
Jewish Golders Green, though you
can't eat them on the premises.

West: Notting Hill, Holland Park and Ladbroke Grove

Restaurants

Expensive

Alastair Little A8
136A Lancaster Rd, W11,
t *(020) 7243 2220;* **tube** *Ladbroke*

Grove. **Open** *Mon–Fri 12.30–2.30
and 6.30–11, Sat 12.30–3pm, Sun
noon–3pm.* **Payment:** *all cards;* **TC.**
Set menus: *lunch three courses £27,
dinner three courses £35.*
Sister branch of the famous Soho
establishment (*see* p.317). Even
more minimalist, but the food's
just as marvellous.

Bali Sugar B7
33A All Saints Rd, W11, **t** *(020) 7221
3844;* **tube** *Westbourne Park.* **Open**
*Mon–Fri noon–3 and 6.30–11, Sat
and Sun 11.30–3.30 and 6.30–11.*
Payment: *all cards.*
This is one of the hippest spots in
London. Clean, tangy globally
inspired dishes with a South
American bias, e.g. Peruvian rock
shrimp ceviche with lime, plantain
and tomato; charred tuna with
chopstick spinach, oyster
tempura and mustard-soy glaze.
Leafy garden.

Clarke's D11
124 Kensington Church St, **t** *(020)
7221 9225;* **tube** *Notting Hill Gate,
High St Kensington.* **Open** *Mon–Fri
12.30–2 and 7–10, Sat and Sun
12.30–2pm.* **Payment:** *all cards;* **TC.**
Set menus: *dinner inc. coffee £44.*
A Californian restaurant with an
emphasis on fresh produce. The
single-choice set menu changes
nightly (salad of roasted pigeon
with watercress, blood orange and
black truffle; chargrilled turbot
with chilli and roasted garlic
mayonnaise, sea kale and leaf
spinach). Small, intimate,
prissy corner; precise and professional cooking.

Dakota C8
127 Ledbury Rd, **t** *(020) 7792 9191;*
tube *Notting Hill Gate, Ladbroke
Grove.* **Open** *for food daily
noon–3.30 and 7–11.* **Payment:** *DC
not accepted;* **TC.**
Ever popular amongst the great
and the good of Notting Hill.
Modern US cuisine.

Kensington Place D11
201 Kensington Church St, W8,
t *(020) 7727 3184;* **tube** *Notting Hill
Gate, High St Kensington; wheel-
chair accessible.* **Open** *Mon–Fri
noon–3 and 6.30–11.45, Sat*

noon–3.30 and 6.30–11.45, Sun noon–3.30 and 6.30–10.15. **Payment:** all cards. **Set menus:** (Sun–Fri lunch) three courses £16. Sleek, glass-fronted, ultra-noisy, modern dining room with bold garden frescoes and high-quality 'eclectic European' cuisine: venison, sirloin steak, wild sea trout, sorrel omelette. Definitely not the place for a quiet, anonymous dinner.

192 B8

192 Kensington Park Rd, W11, **t** (020) 7229 0482; **tube** Ladbroke Grove. **Open** Mon–Fri 12.30–3 and 6.30–11.30, Sat 12.30–3.30 and 7–11.30, Sun 12.30–3.30 and 7–11. **Payment:** all cards; TC. **Set menus:** (Mon–Fri 12.30–3pm) two courses inc. coffee £11.50; (Sun 12.30–3.30pm) two courses inc. coffee £12.50.
Stuffed with media types and celebrities whom everyone is too cool to notice, the atmosphere in 192 is not for everyone. The food, however, is unfailingly good – simple Italian and Mediterranean dishes carefully prepared with fresh ingredients.

Orsino A10

119 Portland Rd, W11, **t** (020) 7221 3299; **tube** Holland Park. **Open** daily noon–11.30pm. **Payment:** DC not accepted; TC. **Set menus:** (noon–3pm, 5.30–7pm and 10–11.30pm) two courses £12.50, three courses £16.50.
The sister restaurant to Orso (see p.322) shares many of the latter's characteristics. Terracotta walls, Venetian blinds and sophisticated cooking with Tuscan roots: veal escalopes with sun-dried tomatoes, sage and white wine.

Pharmacy Bar and Restaurant C11

150 Notting Hill Gate, W11, **t** (020) 7221 7511; **tube** Notting Hill Gate. **Open** for food noon–3 and 6.45–midnight. **Payment:** DC not accepted; TC. **Set menus:** lunch three courses £28; dinner three courses £38.
The initial furore over the Damien Hirst-designed bar has long died

down, but there are still queues for this Notting Hill hangout. The bright and breezy first-floor restaurant serves creative European dishes from excellent fish and chips to suckling pig.

Moderate

Brasserie du Marché aux Puces A6

349 Portobello Rd, W10, **t** (020) 8968 5828; **tube** Ladbroke Grove, Notting Hill Gate. **Open** Mon–Sat 10am–11pm, Sun 11am–3.30pm. **Payment:** DC not accepted; TC. **Set menus:** (lunch) two courses £12.95, three courses £16.95. **Booking advised.**
Inventive, café-style restaurant. Eclectic, well-executed dishes such as roast scallop of venison with poached pear and rösti potatoes. Understandably popular.

The Cow Dining Room D7

89 Westbourne Park Rd, W2, **t** (020) 7221 0021; **tube** Westbourne Park. **Open** for food in upstairs restaurant Mon–Sat noon–3 and 7–10.30, Sun 1–4pm. **Payment:** DC not accepted.
The relaxed, almost countrified atmosphere at the upstairs rooms above this trendy pub (of the same name) belies the precision cooking. Modern British-Pacific Rim menu, perfect for Sunday lunch. Downstairs you can down some Guinness and oysters (there's plenty of choice on the bar menu) with the local trendies.

Galicia A7

323 Portobello Rd, W10, **t** (020) 8969 3539; **tube** Westbourne Park, Ladbroke Grove. **Open** Mon noon–3pm, Tues–Sun noon–3 and 7–11.30. **Payment:** all cards; TC. **Set menus:** lunch three courses £7.50.
Galicia jostles with a rum mixture of authentic 'Gallego' locals and a trendy crowd of Notting Hill Gate fashion fiends. But the tapas, the moody waiters and the 'feel' are uncannily real. Excellent paella and seafood options.

Geale's D11

2 Farmer St, W8, **t** (020) 7727 7528; **tube** Notting Hill Gate.

Open Mon–Sat noon–3 and 6–11, Sun 6–10.30pm. **Payment:** DC not accepted; TC.
Superior fish and chips (deep-fried in beef dripping for a touch of class). Very busy.

Osteria Basilico B9

29 Kensington Park Rd, W11, **t** (020) 7727 9372; **tube** Ladbroke Grove. **Open** Mon–Fri 12.30–3 and 6.30–11, Sat 12.30–4 and 6.30–11, Sun 12.30–3.30 and 6.30–10.30. **Payment:** DC not accepted.
Intensely popular, hence intensely noisy, restaurant with warm ochre walls. New-wave Italian dishes: spaghetti with fresh lobster and tomato, and linguini with spiced salami, parmesan, tomato and basil. Wooden kitchen tables and chairs, and echoey floors. Brazen staff.

Wiz A10

123A Clarendon Rd, W11, **t** (020) 7229 1500; **tube** Holland Park, Ladbroke Grove. **Open** for food Tues–Thurs noon–3pm, Fri noon–3 and 6.30–midnight, Sat noon–4 and 6.30–midnight, Sun noon–4pm. **Payment:** all cards.
Extending the Spanish tapas idea to include miniature dishes from every corner of the globe, Anthony Worrall Thompson's latest dining concept is new and fun. There's a full à la carte menu as well as a tapas menu.

Inexpensive

Calzone D10

2A Kensington Park Rd, W11, **t** (020) 7243 2003; **tube** Notting Hill Gate. **Open** daily 10am–11.30pm. **Payment:** DC not accepted.
Wide thin-crust pizzas. The antidote to Pizza Express, particularly if you dislike chain restaurants. Situated in an interesting, curved glass-fronted room overlooking the junction of four roads.

Casa Santana A6

44 Golborne Rd, W10, **t** (020) 8968 8764; **tube** Ladbroke Grove, Westbourne Park. **Open** Tue–Sun noon–11pm. **Payment:** AmEx and DC not accepted.
Neighbourhood Portuguese restaurant (Madeiran meat stews

Map Key

6	Alastair Little	13	The Cow Dining Room	22	Maroush
21	Al San Vincenzo	12	Dakota	23	Micro Kalamaras
4	Bali Sugar	15	40° at Veronica's	11	192
2	Brasserie du Marché des Puces	3	Galicia	32	Orangery
26	Calzone	29	Geale's	40	Orsini
39	Caravela	30	Kensington Place	8	Orsino
1	Casa Santana	17	Khan's	10	Osteria Basilico
33	Cibo	24	Mandarin Kitchen	20	Patogh
31	Clarke's	14	Mandola	27	Pharmacy Bar and Restaurant
		25	Manzara	34	Phoenicia
				28	Rôtisserie Jules

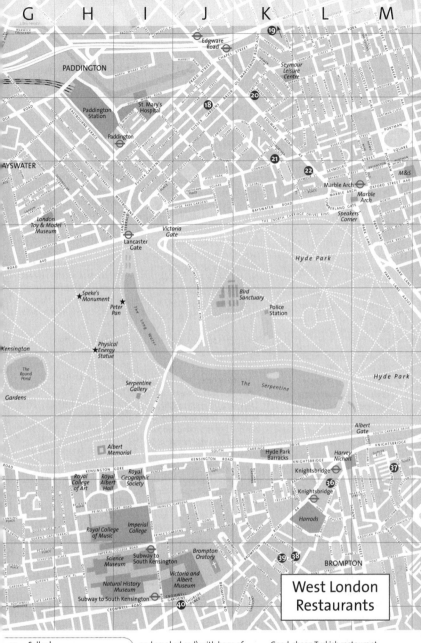

West London
Restaurants

37	Salloo's
38	San Lorenzo
18	Satay House
5	Sausage and Mash Café
19	Sea Shell
16	Standard Indian Restaurant
36	Stockpot
7	Wiz
35	Wódka

and smoked cod) with bags of character and good if somewhat inconsistent food. Triumphant desserts and Madeiran beers.

Manzara D10
24 Pembridge Rd, W11, **t** *(020) 7727 3062;* **tube** *Notting Hill Gate.* **Open** *Mon–Fri 8am–10pm, Sat 9am–8pm, Sun 11am–8pm.* **Payment:** *no cards.*

Good, cheap Turkish restaurant with a wide selection of meze dishes. Sometimes a little oily or overdone – but always good value and some tasty, fresh choices.

Mandola D9
139–41 Westbourne Grove, W11, **t** *(020) 7229 4734;* **tube** *Notting Hill Gate; wheelchair accessible.* **Open** *officially Mon–Sat noon–*

11.30pm, Sun noon–10.30pm (can be erratic during the day). **Payment**: *AmEx and DC not accepted; TC.* **Set menus**: *three courses £20.* **Booking essential.** **Unlicensed.**

Delightful, very popular Sudanese restaurant. Simple wooden décor with some African exotica. Strong Arabic overtones to the dishes: *filfilia* (vegetable stew), *addas* (lentil stew dressed with caramelized garlic) and *fule*.

Rôtisserie Jules C11
133A Notting Hill Gate, W11, **t** *(020) 7221 3736;* **tube** *Notting Hill Gate; wheelchair accessible.* **Open** *daily noon–11.30pm.* **Payment**: *DC not accepted; TC.*

Cheap but decent – and kids love it. Good free-range chicken and other meats, with huge portions. Three courses for a very modest bill.

Sausage and Mash Café B7
268 Portobello Rd, W10, **t** *(020) 8968 5828;* **tube** *Ladbroke Grove.* **Open** *Tues–Sun 11am–10pm.* **Payment**: *AmEx and DC not accepted.*

Trendy, cheap and cheerful. The excellent, good-quality sausages range from spicy Thai to vegetarian leek and blue cheese. Have them with mash and gravy (or veggie gravy) or make a sandwich to take out. It gets packed at weekends.

Pubs, Wine Bars and Cafés

Julie's A10
135–7 Portland Rd, W11; **tube** *Holland Park.* **Open** *for food Mon–Sat 12.30–2.45 and 7.30–11, Sun 12.30–3.30 and 7.30–10; afternoon tea served daily 3–7.30pm.* **Payment**: *DC not accepted; TC.*

Multi-level and multi-purpose establishment with eccentric décor that is part café, part wine bar and part restaurant. The place is at its best for afternoon tea when it is neither too expensive nor too pretentious.

West: High Street Kensington

Phoenicia C14
11–13 Abingdon Rd, W8, **t** *(020) 7937 0120;* **tube** *High St Kensington.* **Open** *daily noon–midnight.* **Payment**: *all cards; TC.* **Set menus**: *meze £16.80, £24.95; (Mon–Fri 12.15–3pm) two courses £9.95, three courses £11.95; buffet (Sat 12.15–2.30pm) £12.95, (Sun 12.15–3.30pm) £14.95; (daily noon–7pm) one course £7.95, two courses £9.95, three courses £11.95.* **Moderate.**

Swish, carpeted Lebanese restaurant attracting smart customers. Delicious meze selections: excellent *basturma* (smoked, cured Lebanese beef) and falafel. Portions can be modest. Makes much of puddings: a variety of fresh cream and pastry dishes doused in aromatic syrups.

Wódka F14
12 St Alban's Grove, W8, **t** *(020) 7937 6513,* **w** *ww.wodka .co.uk;* **tube** *Gloucester Rd, High St Kensington.* **Open** *Mon–Fri 12.30– 2.30 and 7–11.15, Sat and Sun 7– 11.15pm.* **Payment**: *all cards; TC.* **Set menus**: *(lunch) two courses £10.90, three courses £13.50.* **Moderate.**

The proprietor is intent on modernizing the image of Eastern European food in London. The interior's plain with a jazz backdrop. A list of 30 different vodkas and *eaux de vie*. The result is classy and professional.

West: Little Venice and Bayswater

Restaurants

Expensive

Al San Vincenzo K8
30 Connaught St, W2, **t** *(020) 7262 9623;* **tube** *Marble Arch.* **Open** *Mon–Fri noon–3 and 7–9.30, Sat 7–9.30pm.* **Payment**: *all cards.* **Set menus**: *two courses £27, three courses £33.*

Spicy southern Italian food prevails at this efficient and friendly establishment. Simple cooking, but some eccentric components are added to unlikely subjects, such as parmesan with lamb. Intimate, tiny room. Good wine list.

Moderate

40° at Veronica's E9
3 Hereford Rd, W2, **t** *(020) 7229 5079;* **tube** *Bayswater, Notting Hill Gate.* **Open** *Sun–Fri noon–3 and 6.30–10.30, Sat 6.30–10.30pm.* **Payment**: *all cards; TC.* **Set menus**: *(Mon–Fri) two courses £14.50, three courses £17.50.*

A restaurant that has succesfully and charmingly unearthed historical British dishes – spring lamb with crabmeat or calf's liver and beetroot – and even relaunched recipes that date from the 14th century, adapting them to more modern tastes.

Mandarin Kitchen F10
14–16 Queensway, W2, **t** *(020) 7727 9012;* **tube** *Bayswater, Queensway.* **Open** *daily noon–11.30pm.* **Payment**: *all cards.* **Set menus**: *(minimum two people) £10.50.* **Booking advised.**

Massively popular Chinese restaurant, with fish you can pick out of the fishtank. Mainly Cantonese food, in spite of its name. One of the best Chinese places outside Chinatown, hence the huge queues.

Red Pepper Off maps
8 Formosa St, W9, **t** *(020) 7266 2708;* **tube** *Warwick Av.* **Open** *Mon– Fri 6.30–10.45pm, Sat 12.30–2.30 and 6.30–10.45, Sun 12.30–3.30 and 6.30–10.30.* **Payment**: *AmEx and DC not accepted.*

Really excellent pizzas plus an interesting menu of fish and meat dishes in this classy, crowded place with a heated outdoor terrace. Good service.

Inexpensive

Ben's Thai Café Off maps
Above the Warrington Pub, 93 Warrington Crescent, W9, **t** *(020) 7221 3134;* **tube** *Maida Vale, Warwick Av.* **Open** *daily noon–1.20 and 6–9.30.* **Payment**: *AmEx and DC not accepted.*

Very reasonable Thai food, heavy on the seafood, and good service in this Warwick Av favourite. The pub is good, too.

Khans F8
13–15 Westbourne Grove, W2, t (020) 7727 5420; tube Bayswater; wheelchair accessible. Open daily noon–midnight. Payment: AmEx and DC not accepted.
Hectic Indian restaurant. Noise drowns intimacy, and yet the main dining room preserves its charm – painted clouds waft all about you and palm trees act as columns. Delicious food.

Micro Kalamaras F9
76–78 Inverness Mews, W2, t (020) 7727 9122; tube Bayswater, Queensway. Open Mon–Fri 5.30–11, Sat and Sun 12–3 and 5.30–11. Payment: all cards; TC.
Very friendly Greek basement restaurant which has been pleasing locals and going strong since 1961.

Satay House J8
13 Sale Place, W2, t (020) 7723 6763; tube Edgware Rd, Paddington. Open daily noon–2 and 6–11. Payment: DC not accepted; TC.
Small, intimate and colourful restaurant serving delicious Malaysian food – most of the customers appear to be Malaysian. Strong flavours and a broad range of delicious recipes, chargrilled, baked and marinated.

Standard Indian Restaurant E8
21–3 Westbourne Grove, W11, t (020) 7229 0600; tube Bayswater. Open daily noon–3 and 6– midnight. Payment: DC not accepted; TC.
First-rate tandoori restaurant with excellent pickles and good service.

West: Earl's Court and Olympia

Restaurants

Expensive

Cibo A14
3 Russell Gardens, W14, t (020) 7371 6271; tube Shepherd's Bush,

Olympia. *Open Mon–Fri noon–2.30 and 7–11, Sat 7–11pm, Sun noon–2.30pm. Payment: all cards; TC. Set menus: (Mon–Fri noon–2.30pm) two courses £14.50; (Sun noon–2.30pm) two courses £18.95, three courses £21.95.*
Imaginative pasta sauces (wild mushrooms and broad beans), and duck ravioli, as well as many other unusual interpretations of Italian food. Thick, multi-coloured, individualized porcelain, and naked Renaissance ladies on the walls. Be prepared to take your time.

Inexpensive

Lou Pescadou Off maps
241 Old Brompton Rd, SW5, t (020) 7370 1057; tube Earl's Court. Open Mon–Fri noon–2.30 and 7–11, Sat and Sun noon–2.30 and 6.30–11. Payment: all cards; TC. Set menus: (Mon–Fri noon–2.30pm) £9.90; (Sat and Sun) three courses £13.50.
Jolly atmosphere and friendly waiters. Reliably good Provençal-style fish: fish soup, mussels, monkfish, turbot, sea bream, langoustines with cream and garlic.

La Pappardella Off maps
253 Old Brompton Rd, SW5, t (020) 7373 7777; tube Earl's Court. Open daily noon–midnight. Payment: all cards; TC. Inexpensive.
Crowded, high-decibel, good-value, ultra-friendly Italian: 18 varieties of pizza, also pasta, veal and fish.

West: Chelsea

Restaurants

Luxury

Gordon Ramsay M19
68 Royal Hospital Rd, SW3, t (020) 7352 4441; tube Sloane Square, then long walk/taxi. Open Mon–Fri noon–2 and 6.45–11, Sat and Sun noon–2pm. Payment: all cards; TC. Set menus: lunch three courses £35; three courses £65, seven courses £80. Booking advised.
Gordon Ramsay's talent as a chef ensures his latest restaurant glittering success. Some of the finest

and most elaborate cuisine in London in an elegant and intimate atmosphere. Bookings taken no more than a month in advance. There are just two dinner sittings: 6.45pm and 9pm.

Moderate

Chutney Mary Off maps
535 King's Rd, SW10, t (020) 7351 3113; tube Fulham Broadway, then walk; bus 11, 22. Open Mon–Sat 12.30–2.30 and 6.30–11.30, Sun 12.30–3 and 6.30–10.30. Payment: all cards; TC. Set menus: (lunch and 6.30–7.15pm) two courses £11, three courses £14; brunch (Sun) three courses £15.
Anglo-Indian 'Raj' décor complements a terrific menu of unusual specialities. Good service and wine list.

Inexpensive

Chelsea Bun Diner Off maps
9A Limerston St, SW10, t (020) 7352 3635; tube Sloane Square, Fulham Broadway. Open Mon–Sat 7am–midnight, Sun 9am–7pm. Payment: AmEx and DC not accepted. BYO.
American-style all-day breakfasts, plus burgers and pasta from the 200-item-long menu. They have a selection of wine and beer, but you can bring your own wine if you prefer. Excellent value.

Chelsea Kitchen K18
98 King's Rd, SW3, t (020) 7589 1330; tube Sloane Square. Open Mon and Tues 11.30am–11.30pm, Wed–Sat noon–11.45pm, Sun noon–11pm. Payment: no cards. Set menus: two courses £3.80–4.95.
This venue has been known since the 1960s for slap-up Continental food at knock-down prices. Now part of the Stockpot chain, it's still a studenty haven of cheapness in the posh streets around.

Pubs, Wine Bars and Cafés

Pâtisserie Valerie J15
215 Brompton Rd; tube Sloane Square. Open Mon–Fri 7.30am–

8pm, Sat 8am–7pm, Sun 9am–6pm. **Payment**: DC not accepted; TC. Branch of the luscious Soho French pâtisserie.

West: Hammersmith

Restaurants

Expensive

River Café Off maps
Thames Wharf Studios, Rainville Rd, W6, t (020) 7381 8824; tube Hammersmith then 15min walk; wheelchair accessible. Open Mon–Sat 12.30–3 and 7–9.30. Payment: all cards.
You've bought the cook book, now taste the food. Simple, very tasty Italian food in a splendid riverside setting designed by Richard Rogers.

Moderate

The Gate Off maps
51 Queen Caroline St, W6, t (020) 8748 6932; tube Hammersmith. Open Mon–Fri noon–3 and 6–10.45. Payment: all cards.
First-rate vegetarian restaurant with mouth-watering fennel mousse, wild mushroom cannelloni and teryaki aubergine. Sunflower walls and a leafy courtyard make an attractive ambience. There's a branch in Belsize Park (see p.328).

Inexpensive

Spitfire Off maps
93 Fulham Palace Rd, W6, t (020) 8748 7272; tube Hammersmith. Open Tues–Sat noon–3 and 6–11, Sun noon–3 and 7–11. Payment: no cards.
Quiet, friendly, family-run local adorned with flying memorabilia. Hearty Polish cooking: *pierogis*, sweet red cabbage, meatballs, black pudding, potato pancakes, and *golonka* (pig's knuckle).

West: Chiswick

Christian's Off maps
1 Station Parade, Burlington Lane, W4, t (020) 8995 0382; train Chiswick (from Waterloo). Open Tues–Fri noon–2.30 and 7–10.30,

Sat 7–10.30pm. **Payment**: all cards; TC. **Moderate**.
Unpretentious, pretty French restaurant, serving up hefty portions of immaculately prepared Gallic cuisine. There's an airy little conservatory at the back.

West: Twickenham

Brula Off maps
43 Crown Rd, Middx, t (020) 8892 0602; train St Margarets (from Waterloo). Open Tues–Fri 12.30–2 and 7–10.30, Sat 7–10.30pm. Payment: no cards. Set menus: (Tues–Fri) two courses £8, three courses £10. Inexpensive.
Very pleasant bistro, with paddle fans whirring and a mirrored wall. Mediterranean dishes and amazing desserts.

West: Kew

The Glasshouse Off maps
14 Station Parade, Surrey, t (020) 8940 6777; train/tube Kew Gardens. Open Mon–Thurs noon–2.30 and 7–10.30, Fri and Sat noon–2.30 and 6.30–10.30, Sun noon–2.30pm. Payment: DC not accepted; TC. Set menus: lunch (Mon–Sat) three courses £19.50; dinner three courses £25; Sun lunch three courses £21.50. Moderate.
Highly regarded relative newcomer serving delicious modern European dishes like roast loin of pork with black pudding, and ravioli *paysanne* with cep broth. Light, elegant décor and friendly service make it a treat.

Kew Greenhouse Off maps
1 Station Parade, Surrey; train/tube Kew Gardens. Open daily 9am–dusk. Payment: no cards.
Cakes and pastries in a plant-filled conservatory near Kew Gardens.

West: Richmond

Ocean Off maps
100 Kew Rd, Surrey, t (020) 8948 8008; tube/train Richmond. Open Mon–Sat 6–11pm, Sun

noon–10.30pm. **Payment**: DC not accepted. **Moderate**.
Stylish seafood restaurant with plenty of outdoor seating in summer.

Chez Lindsay Off maps
11 Hill Rise, Surrey, t (020) 8948 7473; tube/train Richmond. Open Mon–Sat 11am–11pm, Sun noon–10pm. Payment: AmEx and DC not accepted. Set menus: two courses £5.99, three courses £10.99. Inexpensive.
Pretty Breton-style restaurant on the banks of the Thames. Delicious crêpes and galettes – the seafood fillings are particularly good.

South: Bermondsey

Le Pont de la Tour Off maps
Butlers Wharf, 36D Shad Thames, SE1, t (020) 7403 8403; tube London Bridge, Tower Hill, Bermondsey; wheelchair accessible. Bar and grill open Mon–Sat 11.30am–11.30pm, Sun noon–11pm. Restaurant open Mon–Fri noon–3 and 6–11.30, Sat 6–11.30pm, Sun noon–3 and 6–11. Payment: all cards; TC. Set menus: bar and grill lunch two courses £12.95, three courses £15.95; bar and grill brunch (Sat and Sun noon–3pm) two courses £16.95, three courses £19.95; restaurant lunch three courses £28.50. Luxury.
The flagship of Terence Conran's restaurant empire at Butlers Wharf is notable for its high prices and views of the river, Tower Bridge and the City. The less pricey bar and grill can be a great place to come for a well-shaken cocktail if you don't mind braying City types.

Blue Print Café Off maps
Design Museum, Butlers Wharf, Shad Thames, SE1, t (020) 7378 7031; tube London Bridge, Tower Hill, Bermondsey. Open Mon–Sat noon–3 and 6–11, Sun noon–3pm. Payment: all cards; TC. Set menus: two courses £19.50, three courses £22.50. Expensive.
French and Italian food at Pont de la Tour's slightly less expensive,

smaller and infinitely more appealing sister establishment. The conservatory allows a more intimate and no less spectacular view over the river. Friendly, professional staff and reliably good food.

Arancia Off maps
52 Southwark Park Rd, SE16, t (020) 7394 1751; tube Bermondsey. Open Mon–Fri 11am–11pm, Sat 8–11pm. Payment: AmEx not accepted; TC. Inexpensive.
Friendly, easy-going and surprisingly creative Italian restaurant with plenty of good vegetarian options. It's popular with the hip young City-workers who are moving into the neighbourhood in droves.

South: Greenwich

Restaurants

Moderate

Time Off maps
7A College Approach, SE10, t (020) 8305 9767; DLR Cutty Sark. Open for food Mon–Sat noon–2.30 and 7–10.30, Sun noon–2.30pm. Payment: DC not accepted.
Very cool bar with stripped floors, retro furniture and a gallery restaurant serving excellent global cuisine.

Inside Off maps
19 Greenwich South St, SE10, t (020) 8265 5060; train/DLR Greenwich. Open Tues–Fri noon–2.30 and 6.30–11, Sat 11–3 and 6.30–11, Sun 11am–3pm. Payment: DC not accepted.
This is a new, stylish (in a minimalism-meets-formica sort of way) neighbourhood restaurant. Well-prepared, global cuisine such as Scotch rib-eye with spinach polenta, and good vegetarian choices as well. Puds are fantastic – try dark-chocolate tart with white chocolate and Grand Marnier ice cream.

Inexpensive

Noodle Time Off maps
10–11 Nelson Rd, SE10, t (020) 8293 5263; DLR Cutty Sark. Open daily
11.30am–11.30pm. *Payment: no cards.*
Bargain-basement, very popular restaurant serving huge bowls of noodles for less than a fiver.

Pubs, Wine Bars and Cafés

North Pole Off maps
131 Greenwich High Rd, SE10, t (020) 8853 3020; train/DLR Greenwich; wheelchair accessible. Open for food Mon–Sat 6.30–10.30pm, Sun noon–10pm. Payment: DC not accepted.
Trendy gastro-pub. The upstairs dining area can get a bit too noisy on Saturday nights, when DJs are thudding in the bar, but the delicious Mediterranean cuisine is prepared with assurance and flair. The only downside is that it's surprisingly pricey.

Royal Teas Off maps
76 Royal Hill, SE10, t (020) 8691 7240; train/DLR Greenwich. Open daily 10am–6pm. Payment: no cards.
Delightful little teashop serving great breakfasts, proper tea in a tea pot, and yummy homemade cakes.

South: Brixton

Restaurants

Bah Humbug Off maps
The Crypt, St Matthew's Peace Garden, Brixton Hill, SW2, t (020) 7738 3184; tube Brixton. Open Mon–Thurs 5–11pm, Fri and Sat 5–11.30pm, Sun 11am–5pm. Payment: AmEx and DC not accepted. Moderate.
A buzzing vegetarian restaurant, with an unusual, inventive menu. Jazz on the first Sunday of the month.

Brixtonian Havana Club Off maps
11 Beehive Place, SW9, t (020) 7924 9262, w www.brixtonian.co.uk; tube Brixton. Open for food Mon–Thurs and Sun noon–3 and 7–10.30. Payment: DC not accepted; TC. Moderate.

A cheerful, lively place with excellent Caribbean and 'Black British' cooking, with frequently changing specials and unusual dishes, all well cooked. It's popular and great fun. DJ sets and open-mike sessions.

Pubs, Wine Bars and Cafés

Dogstar Off maps
389 Coldharbour Lane, SW9, w www.dogstarbar.co.uk; tube Brixton. Open Mon–Thurs noon–2.30am, Fri and Sat noon–4am, Sun noon–2am. Payment: all cards.
A big Bohemian Brixton bar, with flavoured vodkas, juices and reasonable bar food. Becomes a club at night with music and (occasionally) comedy. Busy: the Sunday-night knees-up is particularly popular.

East: Whitechapel and Spitalfields

Restaurants

Café Spice Namaste Off maps
16 Prescot St, E1, t (020) 7488 9242; tube Tower Hill; DLR Tower Gateway; wheelchair accessible. Open Mon–Fri noon–3 and 6.15–10.30. Payment: all cards; TC. Set menus: (minimum two people) £25–35. Moderate.
Unusual and modern twists on a variety of Indian cooking styles, including a number of Goan dishes. Delicious.

Sweet and Spicy Off maps
40 Brick Lane, E1, t (020) 7247 1081; tube Liverpool St, Aldgate East, Shoreditch. Open daily 8am–10pm. Payment: no cards. BYO. Inexpensive.
A couple of restaurants have managed to hang on but this is the only surviving Pakistani café on increasingly trendy Brick Lane. Huge quantities of good, well-spiced curry. No charge for corkage if you bring your own booze.

Pubs, Wine Bars and Cafés

Brick Lane

Beigel Bake Off maps

*159 Brick Lane, E1; **tube** Liverpool St.* ***Open** daily 24 hours.* ***Payment:** no cards.*

Famous round-the-clock bagels. Always crowded, even at three in the morning.

East: Hoxton and Shoreditch

Restaurants

Moderate

The Real Greek Off maps

*15 Hoxton Market, N1, **t** (020) 7739 8212; **tube** Old St; **bus** 26, 48, 55, 149, 242.* ***Open** Mon–Sat noon–3 and 5.30–10.30, Sun noon–3pm.* ***Payment:** AmEx and DC not accepted.* ***Set menus:** (Mon–Sat noon–3 and 5.30–7, minimum two people)* £14.50.

Best known as the location for the fight scene in *Bridget Jones' Diary*, this is one of the most fashionable restaurants in East London. A new *mezédes* bar has just opened next door.

Inexpensive

F. Cooke Off maps

*150 Hoxton St, N1, **t** (020) 7729 7718; **tube** Old St, Liverpool St.* ***Open** Mon–Thurs 10am–7pm, Fri and Sat 10am–8pm.* ***Payment:** no cards.*

This award-winning pie and mash shop was established 100 years ago. This is not the original branch.

Viet Hoa Café Off maps

*70–2 Kingsland Rd, E2, **t** (020) 7729 8293; **tube** Old St; **bus** 26, 48, 55, 67, 149, 242, 243.* ***Open** noon–3.30 and 5.30–11.* ***Payment:** AmEx and DC not accepted.*

First-rate Vietnamese food, from steaming bowls of soup to spicy prawn dishes, in a bustling studenty atmosphere. You have to share the long tables with other diners. Downstairs has become more upmarket, with waiters in dickie bows.

Pubs, Wine Bars and Cafés

The Blue Orange Off maps

*65 Columbia Rd, E2; **tube** Shoreditch; **bus** 22, 26, 48, 55.* ***Open** Thurs–Fri 10am–4.30pm, Sat 9.30am–5pm, Sun 7.30am–4pm.* ***Payment:** no cards.* ***Unlicensed.***

The perfect place for brunch after a visit to the Columbia Road Flower Market (*see* p.271). Ramshackle, plant-filled (of course) and quirky, this wonderful café has an outdoor courtyard and a great selection of cakes and pastries. The lovely tiled and wrought-iron furniture from Morocco is for sale.

The Quiet Revolution Off maps

*49 Old St, N1, **t** (020) 7253 5556; **tube** Old St.* ***Open** Mon–Fri 9am–4pm, Sat and Sun 10am–4pm.* ***Payment:** AmEx and DC not accepted.*

Excellent organic café with wooden tables, delicious soups and sandwiches and a great line of juices – try the wheatgrass if you need a boost.

East: The Isle of Dogs

Baradero Off maps

*Turnberry Quay, E14, **t** (020) 7537 1666; **DLR** Crossharbour, then left and left again; **bus** 6, D3, D8; wheelchair accessible.* ***Open** Mon–Fri 11am–11pm, Sat 8–11pm.* ***Payment:** DC not accepted.* ***Moderate.***

Big, airy Spanish restaurant and tapas bar with views out over the river and a popular waterside terrace. Very interesting selection of Spanish wines.

Mem Saheb on Thames Off maps

*65 Amsterdam Rd, E14, **t** (020) 7538 3008; **DLR** Crossharbour, then head east to the water.* ***Open** Mon–Fri noon–2.30 and 6–11.30, Sat and Sun 6–11.30pm.* ***Payment:** all cards.* ***Inexpensive.***

An Indian restaurant with a fantastic view across the water to the Millennium Dome and some innovative dishes.

Nightlife

Drunk for a Penny, Dead Drunk for Two

Drink suits the English: it relaxes them, unbuttons their inhibitions and tends to make them rather witty (or so they think). Unfortunately, it also makes them drunk. For as long as the ale has flowed, the country has been trying to decide whether it likes or abhors its high alcohol consumption. Puritans and reactionaries have periodically tried to blame all the ills of society on drink. At the same time, sozzled eccentrics have spent years of their lives contemplating the meaning of life through an alcoholic haze; most of London's great writers and poets have spent a large proportion of their free time down at the boozer.

Ale was the universal drink of the Middle Ages, more common and more widely available than water. This lukewarm form of beer was cheap and relatively weak – even hospital patients would down two or three pints a day without serious side-effects. In the 14th century, taverns would be inspected by so-called ale-conners, who would deliberately splash beer on their bench or chair before sitting down. If their cloak stuck to the bench, they knew the ale had been adulterated with sugar, and fined the landlord. Wine, which had to be imported from France or further afield, was restricted to the upper classes. Vintners, too, were often suspected of tampering with their produce; in 1350 a wine merchant called John Penroe was sentenced to drink as much of his adulterated wine as he could, then had the rest poured over his head.

London's real drinking problems began in the 17th century, with the introduction of Dutch *genever*, later known simply as gin. The spirit had a diabolical attraction to working people: it was very cheap, tasted better than beer (which

was often watered down or adulterated) and was less likely to make them ill in the short term than water, which came straight from the Thames and was polluted with excrement, animal carcasses and the effluent of the city's fledgling industries. Gin consumption soared, and quickly became an excuse for class prejudice. The politician William Temple went as far as to suggest that the best remedy for drunkenness would be to cut wages and increase working hours, thereby robbing workers of the time and the wherewithal to down their gin. At the end of the 17th century, Londoners were getting through 600,000 gallons of gin per year. In 1727 the figure had jumped to 3.5 million gallons, and by 1735 6.5 million gallons. In 1736 Parliament tried to impose a duty of one pound per gallon but the law was ignored. Bootleggers without licences undercut the official sellers, and anybody who informed on them was hunted down and killed by angry mobs. In 1751 the novelist Henry Fielding, then chief magistrate at Bow St, remarked: 'Should the drinking of this poison be continued in the present height during the next 20 years, there will by that time be few of the common people left to drink it.' The same year, the government finally succeeded in introducing duties on gin, and consumption began to level out.

It seems astonishing that Britain managed to create an empire at all in the 18th century, let alone start the Industrial Revolution. Aristocrats may have shunned gin but they went gaga over punch (favoured by the Whig party), claret (the Tories' tipple of choice) and cognac. The throne was occupied by one lush after another. The inaugural banquet for William of Orange and Queen Mary at Whitehall in 1689 turned into such an orgy of inebriation that, according to one French observer, 'there was not a single one that did not lose conscious-

ness'. Queen Anne was particularly partial to brandy, and eventually died of apoplexy brought on by excessive eating and drinking. George IV was also fond of a drop or two and spent his wedding night in a drunken stupor in a fireplace.

In their few sober moments, the authorities continued to worry about the gin problem and mounted a campaign, echoed in the newspapers, to bring back beer drinking for the sake of the nation's health. 'Beer and porter [an old word for dark ale] are the natural beverage of the Englishman,' opined *The Times* in 1829, 'the increase of gin-drinking and that of suicides, murders and all kinds of violence are contemporaneous.' The Duke of Wellington solved the problem in one go in 1830 with his Beer Act, which abolished all duty on beer and slashed the price of licences for beer retailers and inn-keepers. Within a year, 31,000 beer licences had been issued, and the nation's drinking habits changed for ever.

The pub as we know it today was a Victorian invention, a place riddled with class prejudice and moral overtones. Respectable gentlemen who a century earlier had happily eaten and drunk in chop-houses and taverns did not set foot in pubs at all. But even within the pub, there was a class divide between the lounge or saloon bar (for well-dressed patrons) and the public bar (for riff-raff). It was not long before the Victorian moralists barged in. In 1872, under the influence of the Temperance Society, strict licensing hours were introduced. The Society ensured that children would be kept out of pubs, whether for drinking or not, thereby encouraging the menfolk to get even drunker in the secure knowledge that their families couldn't see what they were up to.

The temperance crusaders held sway for much of the 20th century, and generations of drinkers had to suffer strictures imposed during the First World War to discourage munitions workers from getting drunk while handling high explosives. The licensing laws were not relaxed until the late 1980s, when at last it was possible to buy a drink in the afternoons. By that time cafés and wine bars had begun to challenge the traditional tippler's bastion, the pub, and pubs themselves had become less class-conscious and more welcoming to women and children. The partitions dividing the saloon from the public bar have nearly all been removed now, although you might still see the words in the glass of the door. By and large, the level of drunkenness has gone down and the atmosphere improved immeasurably.

At the same time, however, the health kick and the advent of mineral water have stripped alcohol of some of its appeal. You'll still find people downing five or six pints and calling it a quiet night, but they are becoming the exception rather than the rule. The recession of the early 1990s caused London boardrooms to ordain employee sobriety at lunchtime in the interests of a productive afternoon, and the habit has largely stuck. But pubs are still at the centre of most Londoners' social life – at least until the age of 40. Visitors will be struck by the lack of stigma associated with drunkenness, particularly, in fact, among young women, the new 'ladettes'.

Pubs

The London pub – gaudily decorated with gleaming brass, ornate mirrors and stained glass – is still an essentially Victorian establishment, at least to look at. Even some recently built pubs eschew modern décor in favour of mock-Tudor beams, leaded windows and reproduction hunting prints. Others follow the trend for sanitized theme-pubs in which creaky beams and sawdust are replaced with chrome, steel and acres of blond wood. The line between pubs and wine bars is

beginning to blur; once known and loved for serving beer and spirits, many pubs now boast not only an impressive wine list but better coffee than the café next door. Gone too are the days when the pubs closed just when you were feeling thirsty; you can now drink without interruption between 11am and 11pm (except in some outer London pubs which still take a break from 3 to 7pm, and in the City of London, where the nightly exodus of workers is mirrored by shorter opening hours).

Beer is still the traditional drink of choice. British beer ('bitter') can be an acquired taste – stronger, darker and flatter than lager and served lukewarm rather than cold – but many who persevere get hooked in time. In recent years, **lager** consumption has overtaken bitter, outraging the traditionalists and purists. However, while many pubs still serve an unimaginative line-up of generic multinational lagers, it is ever easier to find new and more rewarding types from around the world, both draft and bottled versions – Staropramen, Kirin, Cobra. Traditional local breweries continue to fight an energetic rearguard campaign for bitter and real ale with the help of CAMRA, the Campaign for Real Ale. CAMRA's influence has been greater in country pubs and England's northern cities than it has in London. Nevertheless, you can find many decent bitters like Fuller's London Pride and Young's, and creamy, full-bodied ales like Theakston's, Abbot and Ruddles.

Our list could go on and on for ever, so the following are generally included because they shine in some way – overlooking the river, maybe, or because of a particular historical association. You'll notice their eccentric names, which date from a time when most drinkers were illiterate and recognized pubs only by their signs. Hence the preponderance of coats-of-arms (King's Arms, Queen's Arms, Freemasons' Arms, etc) and highly

pictorial appellations (Dog and Duck, Nag's Head, Slug and Lettuce, etc). Look out for the name of the brewer that owns the pub. If the sign says 'Free House', that means the pub is independent and generally has a better range of beers. The growing trend for pubs to provide food a cut above traditional pub fodder has earned some the title of 'gastropub'; many of these are as good as any restaurant at the price and are also listed under 'Pubs, Wine Bars and Cafés' in the 'Eating Out' chapter.

Bars

Long gone are the days when all that London had to offer was the traditional boozer full of blokes downing beer. The Atlantic Bar marked the beginning of a new wave of designer bars, where style can sometimes seem more important than content. These are the places where the wannabes want to be seen and rub shoulders with Madonna or the stars of *Big Brother*. They have led a revolution in the kind of drinks on offer. Ask for a Screaming Orgasm or a Sloe Comfortable Screw, and you'll get a pitying look – these days it's all about caipirinhas and martinis made with fresh fruit and your choice of vodka from 17 different countries. But it's a fickle business and the crowd can soon move on. Bars come and go, but we list a few that have stayed the course or show promise.

Westminster and Victoria

Pubs

Paviours Arms T16
*Neville House, Page St, t (020) 7834 2150; tube St James's Park, Pimlico.
Open Mon–Sat 11am–11pm, Sun noon–7pm.*
A stunning 1930s Art Deco pub with a black bar running the length of the three drinking and dining areas; the carpet's artistic designs are a talking point.

Red Lion T13

48 Parliament Square, t (020) 7930 5826; tube Westminster. **Open** *Mon–Sat 11am–11pm, Sun noon–7pm.*

There's been a pub on this site since the 15th century, but the current Victorian building is best known as a hangout for politicians; look out for journalists getting a private briefing.

Bars

Page's Bar T16

Page St, t (020) 7834 6791, w www.pagesbar.com; tube St James's Park, Pimlico. **Open** *Mon–Fri 11am–11pm, Sat 5–11pm.*

A mecca for fans of the *X-Files, Star Trek* and *Dr Who.*

Zander R14

45 Buckingham Gate, t (020) 7379 9797; tube Victoria. **Open** *Mon–Sat noon–11pm, Sun noon–10.30pm.*

Acclaimed ultra-modern-style bar, boasting the longest bar in Europe at 48 metres.

Trafalgar Square, Leicester Square and Piccadilly Circus

Pubs

Chandos T10

29 St Martin's Lane, t (020) 7836 1401; tube Leicester Square, Charing Cross. **Open** *Mon–Sat 11am–11pm, Sun noon–10.30pm.*

A busy London pub serving traditional Yorkshire ales from Sam Smith's. Downstairs can get crushed but it's more relaxed in the spacious first-floor bar.

De Hems S9

11 Macclesfield St, t (020) 7437 2494; tube Leicester Square. **Open** *Mon–Sat noon–midnight, Sun noon–10.30pm.*

An 18th-century Dutch pub in the heart of the West End, specializing in Dutch and Belgian beers. Expanded onto two floors but still packs out.

Riverside City

The following pubs have riverside views, and several of them are also of great historical interest:

All Bar One (Shad Thames; *see* p.346), **Anchor** (*see* p.346), **The Angel** (*see* p.350), **Balls Brothers** (*see* p.346), **Doggetts** (*see* p.346), **The Dove** (*see* p.349), **Duke's Head** (*see* p.350), **London Apprentice** (*see* p.350), **Lots Road Pub** (*see* p.349), **The Mayflower** (*see* p.350), **The Prospect of Whitby** (*see* p.352), **Town of Ramsgate** (*see* p.352), **Trafalgar Tavern** (*see* p.350), **White Cross** (*see* p.350), **White Swan** (*see* p.350).

Ship and Shovel T11

1–3 Craven Passage, off Northumberland Av, t (020) 7839 1311; tube Embankment, Covent Garden, Charing Cross. **Open** *Mon–Fri 11am–11pm, Sat noon–11pm.*

Uniquely, this pub is split in half by the passage that runs between Villiers St and Northumberland Av, but both parts are a traditional and friendly London alehouse.

Bars

Cork & Bottle T10

44–6 Cranbourn St, t (020) 7734 7807; tube Leicester Square. **Open** *Mon–Sat 11am–midnight, Sun noon–10.30pm.*

For over 30 years, this basement wine bar has been a secret hide-away from the madness of the West End, offering an extensive wine list and bistro-style food.

Corney & Barrow T10

116 St Martin's Lane, t (020) 7655 9800; tube Charing Cross, Leicester Square. **Open** *Mon–Sat 11am–midnight, Sun noon–10.30pm.*

This West End outpost for the City wine bar chain offers two bars and a restaurant across three floors looking out towards Trafalgar Square.

Denim T9

44 Upper St Martin's Lane, t (020) 7497 0376; tube Leicester Square. **Open** *Mon–Wed 4pm–1am, Thurs–Sat 5pm–1.30am, Sun 5–11.30pm.*

Decorated in bold purples and oranges (maybe why some of the customers wear shades), this painfully stylish venue has a bar and dining area upstairs and a clubby bar in the basement.

Gordon's U11

47 Villiers St, t (020) 7930 1408; tube Charing Cross, Embankment. **Open** *Mon–Sat 11am–11pm.*

Wine has been sold on this site since 1364, and the current basement bar still serves sherry and port in beakers straight from the barrel.

On Anon R10

1 Shaftesbury Av, t (020) 7287 8008; tube Piccadilly Circus. **Open** *Mon–Sat 5pm–3am, Sun 5.30–11.30pm.*

Eight bars under one roof, all differently and amusingly designed, from fake hunting lodge to gentleman's library. A party venue that does good cocktails.

Rockwell T11

Trafalgar Hotel, 2 Spring Gardens, t (020) 7870 2959; tube Charing Cross, Embankment. **Open** *Mon–Sat 11am–1am, Sun 11am–12.30am.*

A chic cocktail bar offering views over Trafalgar Square.

Saint T9

8 Great Newport St, t (020) 7240 1551; tube Leicester Square. **Open** *Mon 5pm–1am, Tues–Thurs 5pm–2am, Fri 5pm–3am, Sat 7.30pm–3am.*

A cocktail bar that turns clubby as the night goes on: purple-bathed entrance and green sofas.

10 Room R10

10 Air St, t (020) 7734 9990; tube Piccadilly Circus. **Open** *Mon–Fri 5.30pm–3am, Sat 8pm–3am.*

Exclusive to the point of rudeness, this bar still manages to pull in the crowds to sip cocktails on purple sofas.

Tiger Tiger S10

29 Haymarket, t (020) 7930 1885; tube Piccadilly Circus. **Open** *Mon–Sat noon–3am, Sun noon–11.30pm.*

This party venue offers a lounge bar, cocktail bar and club under one roof, with décor ranging from North African to Eastern.

St James's and Mayfair

Pubs

Ye Grapes O11
16 Shepherd's Market; **tube** *Green Park.* **Open** *Mon–Sat 11am–11pm, Sun noon–10.30pm.*
Attractive and popular pub tucked into the corner of the market's main square.

Bars

Che Q11
23 St James's St, **t** *(020) 7747 9380;* **tube** *Green Park.* **Open** *Mon–Fri 11am–11pm, Sat 5–11pm.*
Award-winning style bar specializing in cocktails and cigars.

Claridge's Bar O9
55 Brook St, **t** *(020) 7629 8860;* **tube** *Bond St.* **Open** *Mon–Sat 11am–11pm, Sun 1–10.30pm.*
In one of the world's top hotels, this cocktail bar has been given a modern makeover but, with its leather chairs and marble fireplaces, retains its classic, traditional atmosphere.

Hanover Square Wine Bar P9
25 Hanover Square, **t** *(020) 7408 0935;* **tube** *Bond St, Oxford Circus.* **Open** *Mon–Fri 11am–11pm.*
A relaxed basement wine bar with a magnificent wine list and bistro-style food.

10 Tokyo Joe's P12
85 Piccadilly, **t** *(020) 7495 2595;* **tube** *Green Park.* **Open** *Wed–Sat 8pm–4am, Sun 8pm–12.30am.*
Chic and stylish basement bar, with private booths and friendly staff.

Trader Vic's O12
Hilton Hotel, Park Lane, **t** *(020) 7493 8000;* **tube** *Green Park.* **Open** *Mon–Thurs 5pm–1am, Fri and Sat 5pm–3am, Sun 5–10.30pm.*
Live hula music and piña coladas are part of the kitsch appeal of this world-famous Hawaiian theme bar – a little tacky and pricey, but an experience.

Zeta O12
Hilton Hotel, Park Lane, **t** *(020) 7208 4067;* **tube** *Green Park.* **Open** *Mon and Tues 11am–1am, Wed–Fri 11am–3am, Sat 5pm–3am.*
Acclaimed cocktail bar, with a Californian-style minimalist design.

Soho and Chinatown

Pubs

The Dive Bar S9
Gerrard St; **tube** *Leicester Square.* **Open** *Mon–Sat 5.30–11pm, Sun 6–10.30pm.*
A 1970s throwback in the heart of Chinatown: a bizarrely old-fashioned shabby pub upstairs; red vinyl banquettes below.

Dog & Duck S9
18 Bateman St, **t** *(020) 7494 0697;* **tube** *Tottenham Court Rd, Piccadilly Circus.* **Open** *Mon–Fri noon–11pm, Sat 5–11pm, Sun 6–10.30pm.*
Soho's smallest pub, on the site of the home of the Duke of Monmouth, who hunted in the area in the 17th century, crying 'So-Ho'. Customers spill out onto the pavement in the summer, and huddle round the charcoal fire in the winter.

The French House S9
49 Dean St, **t** *(020) 7437 2799;* **tube** *Leicester Square.* **Open** *Mon–Sat noon–11pm, Sun noon–10.30pm.*
Meeting-place for De Gaulle's Free French during the Second World War; now adorned with pictures of famous Frenchmen. The wine, of course, is excellent.

The Red Lion Q9
14 Kingly St, **t** *(020) 7734 4985;* **tube** *Piccadilly Circus, Oxford Circus.* **Open** *Mon–Sat 11am–11pm, Sun noon–10.30pm.*
Not terribly exciting – standard dark wood, old-fashioned look – but probably the cheapest pint in central London, and friendly staff, too.

Sun and Thirteen Cantons R9
21 Great Pulteney St, **t** *(020) 7734 0934;* **tube** *Oxford Circus, Piccadilly Circus.* **Open** *Mon–Fri noon–11pm, Sat 4–11pm.*
Busy traditional pub that attracts a young bohemian crowd, often spilling out into the street in the summer.

Toucan R8
19 Carlisle St, **t** *(020) 7437 4123;* **tube** *Tottenham Court Rd.* **Open** *Mon–Fri 11am–11pm, Sat 1–11pm.*
An ever-popular Irish bar without the shamrocks but with excellent whiskeys and Guinness.

Bars

Alphabet R9
61–3 Beak St, **t** *(020) 7439 2190;* **tube** *Leicester Square.* **Open** *Mon–Fri noon–11pm, Sat 4–11pm.*
Busy arty bar, good for cocktails. Basement lounge bar with DJs playing chilled-out sounds.

Amber R9
6 Poland St, **t** *(020) 7734 3094;* **tube** *Piccadilly Circus, Oxford St.* **Open** *Mon–Fri 11am–12.45am, Sat 4pm–12.45am.*
Sharply designed basement bar with booths and light wood panelling, below a ground-floor restaurant.

Atlantic Bar & Grill R10
20 Glasshouse St, **t** *(020) 7734 4888;* **tube** *Piccadilly Circus.* **Open** *Mon–Fri noon–3am, Sat 5pm–3am, Sun 6–10.30pm.*
The rich and famous have generally moved on, but the Atlantic retains much of its glamour – chandeliers, marble columns and fake leopardskin still have style.

Lab S9
12 Old Compton St, **t** *(020) 7437 7820;* **tube** *Piccadilly Circus.* **Open** *Mon–Sat noon–midnight, Sun 4–10.30pm.*
Award-winning cocktail bar attracting a style-conscious but laid-back crowd, on two floors – the basement bar is more spacious. Don't be scared of the razor blades embedded in the toilet seats.

Covent Garden and Around

Pubs

Lamb and Flag T9
*33 Rose St, t (020) 7497 9504;
tube Covent Garden, Leicester
Square. Open Mon–Thurs 11am–
11pm, Fri and Sat 11am–10.45pm,
Sun 11am–10.30pm.*
One of the few wooden-framed
buildings left in central London,
dating back to the 17th century,
with low ceilings and a lively
atmosphere. In the past, the pub
was for a long time nicknamed
the Bucket of Blood because it
staged bare-knuckle fights. Now
you just have to try to knuckle
your way past the crowds at
the bar.

Punch & Judy U9
*40 The Market, t (020) 7379 0923;
tube Covent Garden. Open Mon–
Sat 11am–11pm, Sun noon–10.30pm.*
Busy traditional London pub with
a terrace providing a fantastic
view of Covent Garden and its
street performers.

Bars

American Bar U10
*The Savoy, The Strand, t (020) 7836
4343; tube Charing Cross, Embankment. Open Mon–Sat 11am–11pm.*
Once the quintessential place for
cocktails, this hotel bar retains
some of the glamour of its past.

Detroit T9
*35 Earlham St, t (020) 7240 2662;
tube Leicester Square, Covent
Garden. Open Mon–Sat 5pm–
midnight.*
A low-ceilinged basement bar
famed for its cocktails and stylish
customers.

Freedom Brewing Company T9
*41 Earlham St, t (020) 7240 0606;
tube Leicester Square, Covent
Garden. Open Mon–Sat noon–
11pm, Sun noon–10.30pm.*
One of the first and most famous
of London's stylish microbrewery
bars, with a range of own-
brewed lagers.

Freud's T8
*198 Shaftesbury Av, t (020) 7240
9933; tube Covent Garden.
Open Mon–Sat 11am–11pm, Sun
noon–10.30pm.*
A small, unpretentious basement
bar in granite and gothic, with
an extensive cocktail list.

Langley T9
*5 Langley St, t (020) 7836 5005;
tube Covent Garden. Open Mon–
Sat 4.30pm–1am, Sun 4.30pm–
12.30am.*
This large basement bar offers a
loud party atmosphere with retro
décor and 1970s cocktails.

Navajo Joe's T9
*34 King St, t (020) 7240 4008;
tube Covent Garden, Leicester
Square. Open Mon–Sat noon–
11pm, Sun noon–10.30pm.*
A lively two-level bar specializing
in cocktails and tequila.

One Aldwych V9
*1 Aldwych, t (020) 7300 1070;
tube Covent Garden, Charing Cross,
Embankment. Open daily 9.30am–
11pm.*
The lobby bar of One Aldwych
hotel is one of London's most
essential meeting places, a
Manhattan-style cocktail bar filled
with the city's most fashionable.

Retox Bar U9
*The Piazza, Russell St, t (020) 7240
5330; tube Covent Garden.
Open Mon–Wed 5–11pm, Thurs
5–1pm, Fri and Sat 5pm–3am.*
Popular basement bar, known for
its cocktails, with DJs pumping
out club sounds for the late-
night crowd.

Holborn and Fleet Street

Pubs

Bleeding Heart Tavern X6
*Bleeding Heart Yard, off Greville St,
t (020) 7242 8238; tube Farringdon.
Open Mon–Fri 11am–11pm.*
This bloodily named pub has been
restored to its original 18th-
century design, with real ales and
an extensive wine list, It's linked to
a bistro offering fine dining.

> ## Literary City
> The following pubs were once
> the haunts of London's hard-
> drinking playwrights, poets or
> authors:
> **Fitzroy Tavern** (see p.345),
> **George Inn** (see p.346), **Ye Olde
> Cheshire Cheese** (see p.344), **Ye
> Olde Cock Tavern** (see p.344),
> **Punch Tavern** (see p.344),
> **Spaniards Inn** (see p.348).

Cittie of York W7
*22 High Holborn, t (020) 7242 7670;
tube Holborn, Chancery Lane.
Open Mon–Sat 11.30am–11pm.*
Once the longest bar in London,
originally built in the 15th century,
but this Gothic building dates
back to 1923. Cosy, separate
booths, ideal for the winter.

The Lamb V5
*94 Lamb's Conduit St, t (020) 7405
0713; tube Holborn. Open Mon–Sat
11am–11pm, Sun noon–4 and
7–10.30.*
Lovingly restored Victorian pub
serving real ales and good food in
a traditional atmosphere.

Ye Olde Cheshire Cheese Y8
*145 Fleet St, t (020) 7353 6170; tube
Blackfriars. Open Mon–Fri 11am–
11pm, Sat 6–11pm, Sun noon–3pm.*
Dr Johnson's old haunt, with
atmospheric beams but disappointing food.

Ye Olde Cock Tavern X9
*22 Fleet St; tube Temple. Open
Mon–Fri 11am–11pm.*
Roomy and historic pub with
traditional food and friendly
service.

Perseverence V6
*63 Lamb's Conduit Street, t (020)
7405 8278; tube Chancery Lane.
Open Mon–Sat noon–11pm, Sun
noon–10.30pm.*
Restored Victorian-style pub with
leather banquettes and a stag's
head on the wall; strong on food.

Punch Tavern Y8
*99 Fleet St, t (020) 7353 6658; tube
Blackfriars. Open Mon–Fri 11am–
11pm.*
Britain's satirical magazine *Punch*
was created in this small London
pub in 1841, which is why cartoons

cover the walls; there is also Punch and Judy memorabilia, ornate décor and plush furnishings.

Seven Stars W8

53–4 Carey St, **t** (020) 7242 8521; **tube** Chancery Lane. **Open** Mon–Fri 11am–11pm, Sat noon–11pm.

An upspoilt pub dating back to the time of Shakespeare (well, 1602), hidden behind the Royal Courts of Justice.

Bars

AKA T8

18 West Central St, **t** (020) 7836 0110; **tube** Holborn. **Open** Mon and Wed–Fri 6pm–3am, Sat 6pm–5am.

A modern late-night bar with industrial-style décor, specializing in cocktails, with a mezzanine restaurant. Club nights take over later on.

El Vino's X8

47 Fleet St, **t** (020) 7353 6786; **tube** Chancery Lane. **Open** Mon–Fri 11am–10pm.

This wine bar has been an integral part of the City since 1879 and remains an unpretentious place for City boys and girls to let their hair down.

Bloomsbury, Fitzrovia and Marylebone

Pubs

Duke of York V5

7 Roger St, **t** (020) 7242 7230; **tube** Russell Square. **Open** Mon–Fri noon–11pm, Sat 6–11pm.

Fashionable gastropub with a retro feel, real ales and reasonably priced modern European food.

Fitzroy Tavern R7

16 Charlotte St, **t** (020) 7580 3714; **tube** Goodge St. **Open** Mon–Sat 11am–11pm, Sun noon–10.30pm.

Dylan Thomas's main drinking haunt; see the literary mementoes on the walls downstairs.

O'Conor Don N7

88 Marylebone Lane, **t** (020) 7935 9311; **tube** Bond St. **Open** Mon–Fri 11am–11pm.

An Irish pub run by a genuine Irish family, with a basement bar offering respite from the often-crowded ground floor.

Bars

Jerusalem R7

33–4 Rathbone Place, **t** (020) 7255 1120; **tube** Tottenham Court Rd. **Open** Mon–Thurs noon–2am, Fri noon–3am, Sat 7pm–3am.

This is a truly chameleon bar, transformed from light and airy in the daytime to a club decked in red velvet at night.

Mash Q8

19–21 Great Portland St, **t** (020) 7637 5555; **tube** Oxford Circus. **Open** Mon–Tues 7am–1am, Wed–Fri 7am–2am, Sat noon–2am (licensed from 11am only).

One of the most well-known style bars, Mash has fun retro décor across three floors, including a basement lounge bar. Try its impressive cocktails or a beer from the on-site microbrewery.

Match P8

37–8 Margaret St, **t** (020) 7499 3443; **tube** Oxford Circus. **Open** Mon–Sat 11am–midnight.

A leading bar in the booming cocktail scene, Match attracts a stylish crowd with its chilled DJs, warm décor and private nooks.

The Social Q7

5 Little Portland St, **t** (020) 7636 4992; **tube** Oxford Circus. **Open** Mon–Fri noon–midnight, Sat 1pm–midnight.

A narrow bar often packed with stylish types drinking cocktails, with a larger, darker basement bar.

Truckles T7

Pied Bull Yard, off Bury Place, **t** (020) 7404 5338; **tube** Holborn, Tottenham Court Rd. **Open** Mon–Fri 11.30am–10pm, Sat 11.30am–3.30pm.

A modern wine bar, part of the Davy's chain. A secluded courtyard offers a summertime alternative to the gloomy but cosy interior.

South Kensington, Knightsbridge and Chelsea

Pubs

Admiral Codrington K16

17 Mossop St, **t** (020) 7581 0005; **tube** South Kensington. **Open** Mon–Sat 11.30am–11pm, Sun noon–10.30pm.

Once a hangout for the likes of Diana Spencer, this American-style bar attracts the beautiful young things of Chelsea.

Anglesea Arms J17

15 Selwood Terrace, **t** (020) 7373 7960; **tube** Gloucester Rd, South Kensington. **Open** Mon–Sat 11am–11pm, Sun noon–10.30pm.

Good beer in this local Chelsea haunt.

Builder's Arms K18

13 Britten St, **t** (020) 7349 9040; **tube** South Kensington. **Open** Mon–Sat 11am–11pm, Sun 11am–10.30pm.

Handsome modern pub with seriously tasteful décor, plenty of wines and good food.

Chelsea Ram Off maps

32 Burnaby St, **t** (020) 7351 4008; **tube** Fulham Broadway, Sloane Square. **Open** Mon–Sat 11am–11pm, Sun noon–10.30pm.

Stylish and modern gastropub with a good choice of wines.

King's Head and Eight Bells K20

50 Cheyne Walk, **t** (020) 7352 1820; **tube** Sloane Square. **Open** Mon–Sat 11am–11pm, Sun noon–10.30pm.

Enjoy the antiques displays as well as the beer in this 16th-century building with views of the Battersea peace pagoda.

Phene Arms K19

Phene St, off Oakley St, **t** (020) 7352 3294; **tube** South Kensington, Sloane Square. **Open** Mon–Sat 11am–11pm, Sun noon–10.30pm.

Small old pub with a courtyard garden in a quiet residential street, with surprisingly adventurous food.

Bars

Blue Bar M13
Berkeley Hotel, Wilton Place,
***t** (020) 7235 6000;* ***tube** Hyde Park
Corner.* ***Open** Mon–Sat 4–11pm.*
One of the new breed of hotel
bars offering serious style and
cocktails. The owners have taken a
panelled Victorian room within
the hotel, dipped it in blue and
added leather flooring and tassels.

Collection J16
264 Brompton Rd, ***t** (020) 7225 1212;*
***tube** South Kensington.*
***Open** Mon–Fri 5–11pm, Sat 11.30–
3.30 and 5–11, Sun 11.30–3.30 and
6.30–10.30.*
Exclusive style bar and restaurant;
a long glass corridor leads to a
minimalist bar of bamboo, brick
and sofas.

Crescent Off maps
99 Fulham Rd, ***t** (020) 7225 2244;*
***tube** South Kensington.* ***Open** Mon
11am–11pm, Tues–Sat 10am–11pm,
Sun 11am–10.30pm.*
A small minimalist wine bar with
a large basement area, frequented
by shoppers taking a break from
Jimmy Choo and Prada.

Eclipse K16
13 Walton St, ***t** (020) 7581 0123;*
***tube** South Kensington.*
***Open** Sun–Wed noon–midnight,
Thurs–Sat noon–1am.*
A small neighbourhood style bar,
good for cocktails and unusual
spirits.

Iso-Bar L13
145 Knightsbridge, ***t** (020) 7838
1099;* ***tube** Knightsbridge.* ***Open**
daily 5pm–midnight.*
Seriously stylish bar and restaurant for shoppers weary of
wandering round Harvey Nicks
and Harrods.

Mandarin Bar M13
*Mandarin Oriental Hyde Park, 66
Knightsbridge,* ***t** (020) 7235 2000.*
***Open** Mon–Sat 11am–1.45am, Sun
11am–10.30pm.*
A chic cosmopolitan bar with a
mammoth choice of drinks –
stylishness at its classiest.

Lambeth, the South Bank and Southwark

Pubs

All Bar One Off maps
34 Shad Thames, ***t** (020) 7940 9771;*
***tube** London Bridge.* ***Open** Mon–
Sat noon–11pm, Sun noon–10.30pm.*
Huge chain bar but in a great location, with a wooden deck and
benches facing the river.

Anchor BB11
1 Bankside, ***t** (020) 7407 1577;*
***tube** London Bridge.* ***Open** Mon–
Sat 11am–11pm, Sun noon–10.30pm.*
Superior food and excellent river
views in this ancient institution,
where fugitives from the Clink
prison next door used to hide in
cubby holes.

Fire Station X13
150 Waterloo Rd, ***t** (020) 7620 2226;*
***tube** Waterloo.* ***Open** Mon–Sat
11am–11pm, Sun noon–10.30pm.*
A highly regarded pub-restaurant
with the odd hose and fire bucket
to remind you that it's in a former
fire station.

George Inn BB12
*George Inn Yard, off Borough High
St,* ***t** (020) 7407 2056;* ***tube** London
Bridge, Borough.* ***Open** Mon–Sat
11am–11pm, Sun noon–10.30pm.*
The last surviving coaching inn in
London, the George goes back to
the 16th century, although the
present buildings date from
shortly after the Great Fire. It is an
elegant terrace of small interconnecting wooden bars looking out
on a quiet courtyard, where
during the summer you can see
morris dancing and Shakespeare.

Royal Oak BB13
44 Tabard St, ***t** (020) 7357 7173;*
***tube** Borough.* ***Open** Mon–Fri
11am–11pm.*
Acclaimed traditional pub,
restored to its Victorian grandeur,
offering good food and ales from
Sussex brewer Harvey's.

Bars

Balls Brothers DD11
Hay's Galleria, Tooley St, ***t** (020)
7407 4301;* ***tube** London Bridge.*
***Open** Mon–Fri 11.30am–9.30pm.*
One of the 12 bars and restaurants
owned by the Balls family, which
has been operating in the City for
five generations. This branch is in
a stone-floored basement but
there is seating in a small ground-
floor bar and in the paved Galleria
with views towards the Thames.

Wine Wharf BB11
Stoney St, ***t** (020) 7940 8335;*
***tube** London Bridge.* ***Open** Mon–
Sat 11am–11pm.*
Part of the wine-themed Vinopolis
attraction in the heart of the
historic Thames waterfront. You
can try any wines off the extensive list before you buy. Luxurious
leather sofas, loft-style décor and
a range of tasty (if pricey) tapas.

The City

Pubs

Doggetts Y10
1 Blackfriars Bridge, ***t** (020) 7633
9057;* ***tube** Blackfriars.* ***Open** Mon–
Sat noon–11pm, Sun noon–6pm.*
Named after an annual boat race
from London Bridge to Chelsea, a
large, rambling pub, renovated in
1999. So-so bar food, good beer,
excellent river views.

Bars

La Grande Marque Z8
47 Ludgate Hill, ***t** (020) 7329 6709;*
***tube** St Paul's, Blackfriars.*
***Open** Mon–Fri 11.30am–9.30pm.*
Drink some of the world's best
wines and champagnes beneath
the high-vaulted ceilings of this
former bank.

The Pavilion CC7
Finsbury Circus Gardens, ***t** (020)
7628 8224;* ***tube** Moorgate.*
***Open** Mon–Fri 11am–10/11pm.*
One of the most well-known wine
bars of the City, the Pavilion offers
diners and drinkers a peaceful
view over a bowling green.

Tower 42 DD8
25 Old Broad St, t (020) 7877 2424;
tube Liverpool St. Open Mon–Fri
9am–11pm.
There are two bars in the former
NatWest Tower, both offering
fantastic views of London.
TwentyFour on the 24th floor is
the better of the two, but you
can't fault the sights from the
circular champagne and oyster
bar on the 42nd floor.

North: Clerkenwell

Pubs

The Eagle Off maps
159 Farringdon Rd, EC1, t (020) 7837
1353; tube Farringdon. Open Mon–
Sat 11am–11pm, Sun noon–10.30pm.
One of the first pubs to set the
trend for less emphasis on
drinking and more on food – good
nosh, good atmosphere.

The Fox and Anchor Z6
115 Charterhouse St, EC1, t (020)
7253 5075; tube Barbican,
Farringdon. Open Mon–Fri
7am–11pm.
Comfortable market pub known
for serious breakfasts.

The Hope Z6
94 Cowcross St, EC1, t (020)
7250 1442; tube Farringdon.
Open Mon–Fri 6am–10.30am and
11.30am–9pm.
Pub with upstairs restaurant
serving champagne breakfasts
(£18.50) as well as more standard
morning nosh-ups (£7.50 for full
cooked breakfast) and a traditional British lunch of roasts and
Scottish steaks.

Jerusalem Tavern Y6
55 Britton St, EC1, t (020) 7490 4281;
tube Farringdon. Open Mon–Fri
11am–11pm.
This popular pub has a traditional
feel although it was created only
11 years ago by its owner, St Peter's
Brewery in Suffolk.

The Peasant Off maps
240 St John St, EC1, t (020) 7336
7726; tube Farringdon, Angel. Open
Mon–Fri noon–11pm, Sat 6–11pm.

A former boozer transformed into
a modern gastropub, with a good
range of wines and Belgian beers.

The Well Off maps
180 St John St, EC1, t (020) 7251
9363; tube Farringdon. Open Mon–
Sat 11am–11pm, Sun noon–10.30pm.
Unpretentious pub in a traditional
setting, with a good selection of
beers, wines and cocktails.

Bars

Clerkenwell House X6
23–7 Hatton Wall, EC1, t (020) 7404
1113; tube Chancery Lane. Open
Mon–Fri noon–11pm, Sat 1–11pm,
Sun 1–10pm.
Modern style bar with a clubby
feel over two floors, with pool
tables in the basement.

Dust Off maps
27 Clerkenwell Rd, EC1, t (020) 7490
5120; tube Barbican, Farringdon.
Open Mon–Wed noon–11pm, Thurs
and Fri noon–2am, Sat 7.30pm–
2am, first Sun of the month
5pm–midnight.
Style-conscious bar that becomes
more clubby as the night wears
on. One of the first to herald the
transformation of Clerkenwell
into a hip area – lots of cocktails
and speciality beers.

Smiths of Smithfield Y7
67–77 Charterhouse St, EC1, t (020)
7236 6666, w www.smithsofsmith
field.co.uk; tube Barbican,
Farringdon. Open Mon–Fri
7.30am–11pm, Sat 10.30am–11pm,
Sun 10.30am–10.30pm.
An impressive four-storey bar and
restaurant, with a cavernous
ground-floor bar and more intimate cocktail bar on the first floor.

North: St John's Wood and Swiss Cottage

Pubs

Clifton Off maps
96 Clifton Hill, NW8, t (020) 7372
3427; tube St John's Wood, Maida
Vale. Open Mon–Sat 11am–11pm,
Sun noon–10.30pm.

A former villa converted into a
pub, where Edward VII allegedly
wooed actress Lillie Langtry while
he was Prince of Wales in the late
19th century. The inside is intimate
and gothic; outside there's a small
garden.

Bars

Elbow Room Off maps
135 Finchley Rd, NW3, t (020) 7586
9888; tube Swiss Cottage. Open
Mon 6pm–1am, Tues–Thurs
noon–2am, Fri and Sat noon–3am,
Sun noon–11pm.
Part of the chain that brought the
style and chic back into pool, with
food and cocktails available.

North: Camden and Chalk Farm

Pubs

Crown and Goose Off maps
100 Arlington Rd, NW1, t (020) 7485
8008; tube Camden Town.
Open Mon–Sat 11am–11pm, Sun
noon–10.30pm.
Award-winning pub and wine bar
with real ale, good food and
friendly service.

The Engineer Off maps
65 Gloucester Av, NW1, t (020) 7722
0950; tube Chalk Farm. Open
Mon–Sat 9am–11pm, Sun 9am–
10.30pm.
Relaxed gastropub spilling over
with Camden's trendies. Modern
British menu with imaginative
use of fresh ingredients and
generous portions. Lovely
summer garden.

The Lansdowne Off maps
90 Gloucester Av, NW1, t (020) 7483
0409; tube Chalk Farm. Open Mon
6–11pm, Tues–Sat noon–11pm, Sun
noon–10.30pm.
This gastropub offers a terrific
choice of wines to accompany the
daily Mediterranean menu. Great
for Sunday lunch.

Lord Stanley Off maps
51 Camden Park Rd, NW1, t (020)
7428 9488; tube Camden Town;
train Camden Rd. Open Mon

6–11pm, Tues–Sat noon–11pm, Sun noon–10.30pm.
A comfortable pub serving Caribbean food in a shabby, bare but appealing wooden interior.

Queens Off maps
49 Regent's Park Rd, NW1, t (020) 7586 0408; tube Chalk Farm. Open Mon–Sat 11am–11pm, Sun noon–10.30pm.
A modern gastropub in a traditional neo-Georgian pub, with views of Primrose Hill from the restaurant area on the first floor.

Spread Eagle Off maps
141 Albert St, NW1, t (020) 7267 1410; tube Camden Town, Mornington Crescent. Open Mon–Sat 11am–11pm, Sun noon–10.30pm.
A mismatch of rooms, built from the mid-1850s onwards, creates an alehouse that remains popular with the fashionable locals – notable for appearing in the cult movie *Withnail and I*.

North: Islington

Pubs

Canonbury Tavern Off maps
21 Canonbury Place, N1, t (020) 7288 9881; tube Highbury and Islington; train Essex Rd, Highbury and Islington. Open Mon–Sat 11am–11pm, Sun noon–10.30pm.
Delightful garden pub.

Compton Arms Off maps
4 Compton Av, N1, t (020) 7359 6883; tube Highbury and Islington. Open Mon–Sat noon–11pm, Sun noon–10.30pm.
A country-style pub with low ceilings and an ivy-covered garden, an oasis in the urban sprawl.

Duke of Cambridge Off maps
30 St Peter's St, N1, t (020) 7359 3066; w www.singhboulton.co.uk; tube Angel. Open Mon 5–11pm, Tues–Sat noon–11pm, Sun noon–10.30pm.
An unappealing exterior hides a chic and spacious gastropub with good beers, some organic wines on a long list, and reasonable if expensive food.

King's Head Off maps
115 Upper St, N1, t (020) 7226 0364; tube Angel, Highbury and Islington. Open Mon 11am–midnight, Tues–Thurs 11am–1am, Fri and Sat 11am–2am, Sun noon–1am.
Popular Islington pub, where the money is still counted according to the old pre-decimal system of pounds, shillings and pence. The pub theatre is excellent.

Northgate Off maps
113 Southgate Rd, N1, t (020) 7359 7392; train Essex Rd. Open Mon–Fri 5–11pm, Sat noon–11pm, Sun noon–10.30pm.
A popular upmarket gastropub in a former backstreet boozer.

The Social Off maps
Arlington Square, N1, t (020) 7354 5809; tube Angel; train Essex Rd. Open Mon–Fri 5–11pm, Sat noon–11pm, Sun noon–10.30pm.
Upbeat, upmarket gastropub popular with a stylish crowd, still bearing its old name, the Hanbury, because of its listed status.

Bars

Medicine Bar Off maps
181 Upper St, N1, t (020) 7704 9536; tube Angel. Open Mon–Thurs 5pm–midnight, Fri 3pm–2am, Sat noon–2am, Sun noon–10.30pm.
A mix between a laid-back pub and a stylish cocktail bar, with an outside area in summer.

25 Canonbury Lane Off maps
25 Canonbury Lane, N1, t (020) 7226 0955; tube Highbury and Islington. Open Mon–Fri 5–11pm, Sat and Sun noon–11pm.
Small unpretentious café-bar in a former backstreet boozer, with excellent cocktails.

North: Highgate and Archway

Pubs

The Bull Off maps
13 North Hill, N6; tube Archway, Highgate. Open Mon–Sat 11am–11pm, Sun noon–10.30pm.

A large tree-lined garden and patio are the most attractive features of this former drinking haunt for painters such as Hogarth and Millais.

The Flask Map p.284
77 Highgate West Hill, N6, t (020) 8348 7346; tube Archway, Highgate. Open Mon–Sat 11am–11pm, Sun noon–10.30pm.
Friendly pub dating back to the 17th century at the top of Highgate Hill. Good food and winter heaters in the beer garden.

St John's Off maps
91 Junction Rd, N19, t (020) 7272 1587; tube Archway. Open Mon–Sat 11am–11pm, Sun 11am–10.30pm.
Acclaimed gastropub with a large relaxed restaurant offering gourmet dishes.

North: Hampstead

Pubs

Holly Bush Map p.284
22 Holly Mount, NW3, t (020) 7435 2892; tube Hampstead. Open Mon–Sat noon–11pm, Sun noon–10.30pm.
Idyllic pub with five low rooms grouped around an old wooden bar.

Freemasons Arms Off maps
32 Downshire Hill, NW3, t (020) 7433 6811; tube Belsize Park, Hampstead. Open Mon–Sat noon–11pm, Sun noon–10.30pm.
Huge garden and terrace, with a pitch to play the ancient game of pell mell. Gets crowded.

Spaniards Inn Map p.284
Spaniards Rd, Hampstead Heath, NW3, t (020) 8731 6571; tube Hampstead; bus 210 (from Hampstead or Highgate tubes). Open Mon–Sat 11am–11pm, Sun noon–10.30pm.
Reputed as a highwayman's pub patronized by Dick Turpin and a host of scurrilous scribblers including Byron and Shelley. Wonderful garden and, of course, the expanse of Hampstead Heath just across the road.

West: Notting Hill, Holland Park and Ladbroke Grove

Pubs

The Cow D7
89 Westbourne Park Rd, W2, t (020) 7221 5400; **tube** Royal Oak, Westbourne Park. **Open** Mon–Sat noon–midnight, Sun noon–10.30pm.
Busy and fashionable Irish-style pub and restaurant specializing in seafood.

Golborne House Off maps
36 Golborne Rd, W10, t (020) 8960 6260; **tube** Westbourne Park.
Open Mon–Sat noon–11pm, Sun noon–10pm.
Stylish gastropub.

Ladbroke Arms B11
54 Ladbroke Rd, W11, t (020) 7727 6648; **tube** Holland Park. **Open** summer Mon–Sat 11am–11pm, Sun noon–10.30pm, winter Mon–Fri 11–3 and 5.30–11, Sat 11am–11pm, Sun 11am–10.30pm.
Very popular pub with a flower-lined patio.

The Pelican B7
45 All Saints Rd, W10, t (020) 7792 3073; **tube** Notting Hill Gate, Westbourne Park. **Open** Mon 5–11pm, Tues–Sun noon–11pm.
Relaxed organic gastropub, with wooden tables and church pews.

Portobello Gold B9
95–7 Portobello Rd, W11, t (020) 7460 4900; **tube** Notting Hill Gate. **Open** Mon–Sat 10am–midnight, Sun 10am–10.30pm.
A modern pub serving cocktails and excellent food alongside ales to a sophisticated crowd.

The Westbourne D7
101 Westbourne Park Villas, W2, t (020) 7221 1332; **tube** Royal Oak, Westbourne Park. **Open** Mon 5–11pm, Tues–Fri noon–11pm, Sat 11am–11pm, Sun noon–10.30pm.
Busy fashionable gastropub with outside areas and distinctive décor, including an original Francis Bacon.

William IV Off maps
786 Harrow Rd, NW10, t (020) 8969 5944; **tube** Kensal Green.
Open Mon–Thu noon–11pm, Fri and Sat noon–midnight, Sun noon–10.30pm.
Smart and modern pub near Kensal Green Cemetery, with loud music, comfortable leather sofas, a beer garden and a trendy young crowd. The food is mainly Mediterranean.

Bars

Beach Blanket Babylon C9
45 Ledbury Rd, W11, t (020) 7229 2907; **tube** Notting Hill Gate.
Open Mon–Sat noon–11pm, Sun noon–10.30pm.
Once one of the trendsetters in the world of stylish cocktail bars, this venue still wows with its garish décor.

Julie's Wine Bar A10
135–7 Portland Rd, W11, t (020) 7229 8331; **tube** Holland Park.
Open Mon–Sat 9am–11pm, Sun 9am–10pm.
An intimate setting for sipping wine or cocktails, in the labyrinthine interior or crammed outside on the pavement tables.

Pharmacy C11
150 Notting Hill Gate, W11, t (020) 7221 2442; **tube** Notting Hill Gate.
Open Mon–Thurs noon–3 and 5.30–1, Fri noon–3 and 5.30–2, Sat noon–2am, Sun noon–midnight.
One of London's most well-known style bars, noted for its cocktails as well as its display cabinets of drugs and artwork by Damien Hirst.

West: Little Venice

Pubs

Prince Alfred Off maps
Formosa St, W9, t (020) 7286 302; **tube** Warwick Av. **Open** Mon–Sat 11am–11pm, Sun noon–10.30pm.
A traditional Victorian pub with a twist: half the space is sectioned into little booths with wooden dividers, in which the doors are so low that you have to bend double to creep through. Shabby but fun.

The Warrington Off maps
93 Warrington Crescent, W9, t (020) 7286 2929; **tube** Maida Vale. **Open** Mon–Sat 11am–11pm, Sun noon–10.30pm.
The faded Art Deco setting makes this pub special. Gets very busy on summer evenings. There's a good cheap Thai restaurant above it.

West: Fulham

Pubs

The Atlas Off maps
16 Seagrave Rd, SW6, t (020) 7385 9129; **tube** West Brompton.
Open Mon–Sat noon–11pm, Sun noon–10.30pm.
Friendly wood-panelled stylish pub, with good food and a small garden.

Lots Road Pub Off maps
114 Lots Rd, SW10, t (020) 7352 6645; **tube** Fulham Broadway, Sloane Square. **Open** Mon–Sat 11am–11pm, Sun 11am–10.30pm.
A relaxed atmosphere, an open kitchen and views over Chelsea Harbour make this one of the better of the new gastropubs.

West: Hammersmith

Pubs

The Dove Off maps
19 Upper Mall, W6, t (020) 8748 5405; **tube** Hammersmith, Ravenscourt Park. **Open** Mon–Sat 11am–11pm, Sun noon–10.30pm.
An unspoilt real-ale pub dating back 300 years, with a riverside terrace. It's noted for reputedly having the world's smallest bar, measuring 3.12 sq m.

Queen's Head Off maps
Brook Green, W6; **tube** Barons Court, Hammersmith. **Open** Mon–Sat 11am–11pm, Sun noon–10.30pm.
Old coaching inn overlooking a green, with a beer garden at the back.

Stonemason's Arms Off maps
54 Cambridge Grove, W6, **t** (020)
8748 1397; **tube** Hammersmith.
Open Mon–Sat noon–11pm, Sun
noon–10.30pm.
Busy, spacious gastropub
furnished with old wooden tables
and church pews; excellent food
such as kangaroo burgers and
sweet potato chips.

West: Chiswick

Pubs

Bollo House Off maps
13–15 Bollo Lane, W4, **t** (020) 8994
6037; **tube** Chiswick Park.
Open Mon–Sat noon–11pm, Sun
noon–10.30pm.
Acclaimed new gastropub in a
traditional but stylish open-
plan setting.

Old Packhorse Off maps
434 Chiswick High Rd, W4, **t** (020)
8994 2872; **tube** Chiswick Park.
Open Mon–Sat 11am–11pm, Sun
noon–10.30pm.
Although this pub was built in the
19th century, there has been a
hostelry on this site since Roman
times. A traditional pub with
modern touches, it offers real ales
and Thai food plus memorabilia
from the former Chiswick Empire.

West: Richmond and Twickenham

Pubs

London Apprentice Off maps
62 Church St, Isleworth, **t** (020)
8560 1915; **train** Isleworth.
Open Mon–Sat 11am–11pm, Sun
noon–10.30pm.
Built in the 17th century, with a
conservatory and river views.

White Cross Off maps
Water Lane, Riverside, Richmond,
t (020) 8940 6844; **tube/train**
Richmond. **Open** Mon–Sat
11am–11pm, Sun noon–10.30pm.
A pub that turns into an island at
high tide (well, for 20 minutes
or so). Enjoy the real fires and
good food.

White Swan Off maps
Riverside, Twickenham, **t** (020)
8892 2166; **train** Twickenham.
Open Mon–Sat 11am–11pm, Sun
noon–10.30pm (winter closes
3pm–5.30pm Mon–Thurs).
Dating back 300 years, with a beer
garden overlooking the river.

South: Putney

Pubs

Duke's Head Off maps
8 Lower Richmond Rd, SW15, **t** (020)
8788 2552; **tube** Putney Bridge.
Open Mon–Sat 11am–11pm, Sun
noon–10.30pm.
Fine views along the river, though
you have to put up with plastic
cups if you sit outside.

South: Rotherhithe

Pubs

The Angel Off maps
101 Bermondsey Wall East, SE16;
tube Rotherhithe. **Open** Mon–Sat
11–3 and 5.30–11, Sun noon–3 and
7–10.30.
The pub where Captain Cook had
his last drink before sailing to
Australia. Notable for its ship's
wheel, smugglers' trapdoor and
balcony overlooking Tower Bridge
and Execution Dock.

The Mayflower Off maps
117 Rotherhithe St, SE16, **t** (020)
7237 4088; **tube** Canada Water,
Rotherhithe. **Open** Mon–Sat
noon–11pm, Sun noon–10.30pm.
Inn from which the Pilgrim
Fathers set out for America, now
with a long jetty from which to
admire the river. Indifferent food.

South: Greenwich

Pubs

Trafalgar Tavern Off maps
Park Row, Greenwich, SE10, **t** (020)
8858 2437; **DLR** Cutty Sark Gardens;
train Maze Hill. **Open** Mon–Sat
11.30am–11pm, Sun noon–10.30pm.

Once famous for its Whitebait
Dinners, at which cabinet ministers and senior public figures
would hold informal chats over
seafood from the Thames – river
pollution ended the tradition in
1914, though you can still eat
whitebait as a bar snack. Riverside
views of the Millennium Dome.

South: Brixton

Pubs

Hope & Anchor Off maps
123 Acre Lane, SW2, **t** (020) 7274
1787; **tube** Brixton. **Open** Mon–Sat
11am–11pm, Sun noon–10.30pm.
Good homemade food and a
garden to enjoy a summer drink.

Bars

Dogstar Off maps
389 Coldharbour Lane, SW9, **t** (020)
7733 7515; **tube** Brixton. **Open** Sun–
Thurs noon–3am, Fri and Sat
noon–4am.
One of the reasons that Brixton
became up and coming, the
Dogstar continues to pack to
capacity with its loud clubby
atmosphere into the early hours.

South: Clapham

Pubs

Belle Vue Off maps
1 Clapham Common Southside,
SW4, **t** (020) 7498 9473;
tube Clapham Common.
Open Mon–Fri 5pm–midnight, Sat
noon–midnight, Sun noon–10.30pm.
Small popular pub painted in bold
colours. Sofas and pine tables
pack out for food evenings and
weekends.

Bread & Roses Off maps
68 Clapham Manor St, SW4, **t** (020)
7498 1779; **tube** Clapham Common,
Clapham North. **Open** Mon–Sat
11am–11pm, Sun noon–10.30pm.
Despite being run by a workers'
co-operative and being a base for
local radicals and artists, this is a
stylish upmarket pub serving real
ale alongside good-quality food.

Falcon Off maps
33 Bedford Rd, SW4, t (020) 7274 2428; tube Clapham North. Open Mon–Sat noon–11pm, Sun noon–10.30pm.
Spacious pub with even more spacious patio garden that fills up all year around, but especially when the sun shines.

Frog and Forget-Me-Not Off maps
32 The Pavement, SW4, t (020) 7622 5230; tube Clapham Common. Open Mon–Fri 4–11pm, Sat noon–11pm, Sun noon–10.30pm.
The shabby deep sofas and the sunny roof terrace fill up quickly. Eternally popular with young fashionable locals.

Landor Off maps
70 Landor Rd, SW9, t (020) 7274 4386; tube Clapham North. Open Mon–Sat noon–11pm, Sun noon–10.30pm.
Cosy traditional pub with a theatre upstairs.

Prince of Wales Off maps
38 Old Town, SW4, t (020) 7622 3530; tube Clapham North. Open Mon–Fri 5–11pm, Sat 1–11pm, Sun 1–10.30pm.
The oddities on the walls of this small local pub give it an alternative look and a young crowd.

Railway Off maps
18 Clapham High St, SW4, t (020) 7622 4077; tube Clapham North. Open Mon–Sat 11am–11pm, Sun noon–10.30pm.
Lively modern pub serving delicious Thai food.

Sun Off maps
47 Old Town, SW4, t (020) 7622 4980; tube Clapham Common. Open Mon–Sat 11am–11pm, Sun noon–10.30pm.
Friendly stylish pub on two floors where the outside patio packs out.

Windmill on the Common Off maps
Clapham Common Southside, SW4, t (020) 8673 4578; tube Clapham Common. Open Mon–Sat 11am–11pm, Sun noon–10.30pm.
Large traditional pub on the edge of the common serving pub grub and ales. Outside seating.

Bars

Sand Off maps
156 Clapham Park Rd, SW4, t (020) 7622 3022; tube Clapham Common. Open Mon–Sat 5pm–2am, Sun 5pm–1am.
A sophisticated sandy-coloured bar specializing in cocktails, offering a chilled-out atmosphere and comfy sofas.

So.uk Off maps
165 Clapham High St, SW4, t (020) 7622 4004; tube Clapham Common. Open Mon–Wed 5pm–midnight, Thurs–Fri 5pm–2am, Sat noon–2am, Sun noon–midnight.
A narrow, lushly furnished bar with décor and food from North Africa and strong on cocktails. Owned by ex-footballer Lee Chapman and wife Leslie Ash.

White House Off maps
65 Clapham Park Rd, SW4, t (020) 7498 3388; tube Clapham Common. Open Sun–Tues 6pm–midnight, Wed 6pm–1am, Thurs–Sat 6pm–2am.
Three storeys of lounge bar, restaurant and members' club, popular with a late-night clubby crowd.

South: Wimbledon

Pubs

Firestables Off maps
27–9 Church Rd, SW19, t (020) 8946 3197; tube/train Wimbledon. Open Mon–Sat 10am–11pm, Sun 10am–10.30pm.
Award-winning gastropub with modern décor and friendly service.

East: Old Street, Shoreditch and Hoxton

Pubs

The Fox Off maps
28 Paul St, EC2, t (020) 7729 5708; tube Moorgate, Old St. Open Mon–Fri noon–11pm.
Restored Victorian pub with a country feel. With a good restaurant upstairs and outside terrace.

Bars

Bluu Off maps
1 Hoxton Square, N1, t (020) 7613 2793; w www.bluu.co.uk; tube Old St. Open daily 10am–10pm.
Laid-back stylish bar in browns and creams with a retro feel, in the former home of the Blue Note jazz club.

Cargo Off maps
83 Rivington St, EC2, t (020) 7613 1250; tube Old St, Liverpool St. Open Mon–Fri noon–1am, Sat 6pm–1am, Sun noon–midnight.
A leading new venue for live music, with a restaurant and lounge bar thrown in.

Great Eastern Dining Room Off maps
54–6 Great Eastern St, EC2, t (020) 7613 4545; tube Old St. Open Mon–Fri noon–midnight, Sat 6.30pm–midnight.
A pre-club lounge bar with quirky décor in a former warehouse.

Home Off maps
100–106 Leonard St, EC1, t (020) 7684 8618; tube Old St. Open Mon–Fri 5pm–midnight, Sat 6pm–midnight.
One of the first bars to make Hoxton trendy – a chic basement lounge bar with a dining area.

Hoxton Square Bar and Kitchen Off maps
2 Hoxton Square, N1, t (020) 7613 0709; tube Old St. Open Mon–Sat 11am–midnight, Sun 11am–10.30pm.
At the heart of the ultra-fashionable Hoxton scene, this is a lounge bar where the sofas are always full. Allegedly modelled on an airport building.

Light Off maps
233 Shoreditch High St, E1, t (020) 7247 8989; tube Liverpool St. Open Mon–Wed 12.30pm–midnight, Thurs and Fri 12.30pm–2am, Sat 6.30pm–2am, Sun 12.30–10.30pm.
Converted from an electricity-generating station, this stylish bar

retains some industrial touches. A small terrace offers views over the City.

Shoreditch Electricity Showrooms Off maps
39A Hoxton Square, N1, **t** *(020) 7739 6934;* **tube** *Old St.*
Open *Sun–Thurs noon–midnight, Fri and Sat noon–1am.*
One of the mainstays of the Hoxton bar scene, this stylish bar with a retro feel still packs them in, especially with DJs in the basement bar at weekends.

Sosho Off maps
2 Tabernacle St, EC2, **t** *(020) 7920 0701;* **tube** *Moorgate, Old St.*
Open *Mon–Wed 11am–midnight, Thurs and Fri 11am–2am, Sat 7pm–2am.*
Award-winning cocktail bar, from the team behind the West End's Match, with DJs creating a clubby atmosphere in the basement bar.

East: Whitechapel and Spitalfields

Pubs

Pride of Spitalfields Off maps
3 Heneage St, E1, **t** *(020) 7247 8933;* **tube** *Aldgate, Shoreditch.*
Open *Mon–Sat 11am–11pm, Sun noon–10.30pm.*
A splendid locals' pub – where the locals include the designers and artists from nearby Brick Lane.

Ten Bells FF6
84 Commercial St, E1, **t** *(020) 7377 2145;* **tube** *Aldgate East.*
Open *Mon–Sat 11am–11pm, Sun noon–10.30pm.*
The original Jack the Ripper pub, with oodles of memorabilia. Marred by the tourist coaches who drop in during the evening but friendly enough at lunchtime.

East: Wapping

Pubs

The Prospect of Whitby Off maps
57 Wapping Wall, E1, **t** *(020) 7481 1095;* **tube** *Wapping.* **Open** *Mon–Fri 11.30–3 and 5.30–11, Sat 11.30am–11pm, Sun noon–10.30pm.*
A charming pub with loads of history, starting in 1520, and a hangman's noose to remind us of the executions once held here. There's a river terrace and great views, plus traditional pub grub.

Town of Ramsgate Z6
62 Wapping High St, E1, **t** *(020) 7264 0001;* **tube** *Wapping.*
Open *Mon–Sat noon–11pm, Sun noon–10.30pm.*
The pub where the merciless 17th-century Judge Jeffreys finally got his comeuppance. Friendly East End atmosphere, with a riverside garden and view of the post where smugglers and pirates used to be condemned to hang in chains for the duration of three high tides.

East: The Isle of Dogs

Bars

Beluga Café Off maps
West India Quay, E14, **t** *(020) 7537 4665;* **tube** *Canary Wharf;* **DLR** *West India Quay.* **Open** *Mon–Sat 11am–11pm, Sun noon–10.30pm.*
A champagne and oyster bar, with a broad wine list, in a converted warehouse.

Corney & Barrow Off maps
9 Cabot Square, E14, **t** *(020) 7512 0397;* **tube** *Canary Wharf;* **DLR** *West India Quay.* **Open** *Mon–Fri 8am–11pm (licensed from 11am), Sat noon–11pm.*
An ultra-modern wine bar, part of the Corney & Barrow empire, with an outside terrace and large windows overlooking the quay.

Jamies Off maps
28 Westferry Circus, E14, **t** *(020) 7536 2861;* **tube** *Canary Wharf;* **DLR** *Westferry Circus.* **Open** *Mon and Tues 11.30am–11pm, Wed–Sat 11.30am–midnight, Sun noon–10.30pm.*
Part of the Jamies Bar chain of wine bars, this features a waterfront terraces with doors and windows that can be folded away in the summer.

Clubs and Discos

From the hot and sweaty to the cool and sophisticated, London has about 150 clubs and discos providing anything from big-band swing to techno. The London club scene used to be hampered by the licensing laws, but now you can buy alcohol until 3am at most places and carry on dancing until dawn or beyond. The main handicap is price: it usually costs around £10 to get into a club, and £3 or more for a drink. Some clubs have dress codes, which may mean no jeans or trainers.

Things change fast in clubland: the following venues are all long-lasting, but opening times and music may change. Check a listings magazine.

Bagleys Studios Off maps
King's Cross Freight Depot, off York Way, **t** *(020) 7278 2777;* **tube/train** *King's Cross.* **Open** *Fri 10pm–6am, Sat 10.30pm–7.30am.*
This busy multiplex offers trancy techno on Friday, funky house and disco on Saturday.

Bar Rumba R10
36 Shaftesbury Av, **t** *(020) 7287 2715;* **tube** *Piccadilly Circus.* **Open** *Mon 10.30pm–3am, Tues 8.30pm–3am, Wed 10pm–3am, Thurs 10.30pm–3.30am, Fri 9pm–4am, Sat 10pm–6am, Sun 8pm–1am.*
Lively bar and club. Latin nights Mon/Tues, soul and R'n'B Sun, funk and house other nights.

Café de Paris S10
3 Coventry St, **t** *(020) 7734 7700;* **tube** *Piccadilly Circus.* **Open** *Mon–Wed 10pm–3pm, Thurs 8pm–3am, Fri and Sat 8pm–4am.*
Very glamorous 1920s ballroom, with lots of red velvet and Jacuzzis, but expensive.

Camden Palace Off maps
1a Camden High St, **t** *(020) 7387 0428;* **tube** *Mornington Crescent.* **Open** *Tues and Wed 10pm–2.30am, Fri 10pm–6am, Sat 10pm–8am.*
Huge main floor and balcony with a loyal, young crowd dancing to garage and techno.

The Cross Off maps
Goods Way Depot, off York Way,
t (020) 7837 0828; tube/train King's
Cross. Open Fri and Sat 11pm–6am.
Low brick arches add to the hot,
sweaty atmosphere. Three bars
and a chill-out garden. Friendly
crowd. Friday is mixed gay night.

The End T8
16A West Central St, t (020) 7419
9199; tube Holborn, Tottenham
Court Rd. Open Mon and Thurs
10pm–3am, Fri 11pm–5am, Sat
10pm–7am.
Classic house-party tunes at this
central venue, with gay night
on Thursdays.

Fabric Y7
77A Charterhouse St, t (020) 7336
8898; tube/train Farringdon.
Open Fri 10pm–5am, Sat
10pm–7am, Sun 10pm–late.
One of the new breed of super-
clubs, based in an old warehouse
in Smithfield, attracting huge
crowds for an all-night party.
Sunday is 'polysexual' night, with
Addiction to DTPM's mix of disco,
hip-hop and Latino house.

The Fridge Off maps
Town Hall Parade, Brixton
Hill, t (020) 7326 5100;
tube/train Brixton. Open Fri
and Sat 10pm–6am.
Funky music and a packed
dancefloor.

The Gardening Club U9
4 The Piazza, Covent Garden,
t (020) 7497 3154; tube Covent
Garden. Open Mon 10pm–3am,
Tues 5pm–3am, Wed 8pm–3am,
Thurs 8pm–late, Fri 8pm–5am, Sat
8pm–late, Sun 7pm–1am.
Varied music during the week;
house dominates at weekends.

G.A.Y. S8
London Astoria, 157 Charing Cross
Rd (Thurs, Fri, Sat), The Mean
Fiddler, 165 Charing Cross Rd (Mon),
t (020) 7734 6963; tube Tottenham
Court Rd. Open Mon and Thurs
10.30pm–4am, Fri 11pm–4am, Sat
10.30pm–5am.
Ever-popular superclub for mainly
younger lovers of pop and trash,
with chart-toppers on stage most
Saturdays.

Gossips S9
69 Dean St, t (020) 7434 4480;
tube Tottenham Court Rd.
Open Mon–Wed 10pm–3am, Thurs
and Fri 8pm–3.30am, Sat
10pm–3.30am.
Atmospheric dark cellar with a
wide range of music.

Hanover Grand P9
6 Hanover St, t (020) 7499 7977;
tube Oxford Circus. Open Wed and
Thurs 10.30pm–3.30am, Fri 9pm–
3.30am, Sat 10pm–3.30am.
A converted ballroom is the ideal
spot for glamorous girls and boys.

Heaven U11
Under the Arches, Craven St, t (020)
7930 2020; tube Charing Cross.
Open Mon 10pm–3am, Wed
10.30pm–3am, Thurs 8pm–3am, Fri
10pm–6am, Sat 10pm–5am.
Excellent club with multiple bars,
dancefloors, laser shows and crazy
lighting. The biggest gay club in
Europe, but some 'straight' nights.

Hippodrome T10
Cranbourn St, t (020) 7437 4311;
tube Leicester Square. Open Mon–
Thurs 9pm–3am, Fri and Sat
9pm–3.30am.
Vastly popular, tacky club
attracting a large crowd. Trapeze
artists and fire-eaters.

Home S10
1 Leicester Square, t (020) 7909 1111;
tube Piccadilly Circus.
A superclub on three floors, with
mainly house, trance and garage
and a variety of well-known
names. Closed while changing
ownership, so phone to check for
opening times.

Limelight S9
136 Shaftesbury Av, t (020) 7434
0572; tube Leicester Square. Open
Sun–Thurs 10pm–3am, Fri 10pm–
3.30am, Sat 9pm–3.30am.
A converted church blasting out
all kinds of music, especially
heavy rock.

Madame Jo Jo's R9
8–10 Brewer St, t (020) 7734 2473;
tube Piccadilly Circus. Open Mon–
Wed 10pm–2am, Thurs 9.30pm–
3am, Fri 10pm–3am, Sat 10.30pm–
3am, Sun 9.30pm–2.30am.

Outrageous transvestite cabaret.
Camp and colourful but a bit
touristy.

Ministry of Sound Off maps
103 Gaunt St, t (020) 7378 6528;
tube Elephant and Castle. Open Fri
10.30pm–6am, Sat midnight–9am.
Expensive, but very trendy and
always packed. A New York-style
club with lots of garage and house
music. Expect long queues.

The Scala U2
278 Pentonville Rd, t (020) 7833
2022 4480; tube/train King's Cross.
Open Thurs 9pm–3am, Fri
10pm–5am.
Excellent club and live-music
venue. Friday is gay indie night
Popstarz.

Stringfellow's T9
16 Upper St Martin's Lane, t (020)
7240 5534; tube Leicester Square.
Open Mon–Sat 7.30pm–3.30am.
Glamour models and footballers
come here, as do lots of tourists
dressed up in their smartest togs
for this expensive but tawdry
night spot. Decent food. They
describe their dress code
as 'corporate' …

Subterania Off maps
12 Acklam Rd (under Westway),
t (020) 8960 4590; tube Ladbroke
Grove. Open Mon–Thurs 10pm–
2am, Fri and Sat 10pm–3am, Sun
7pm–midnight.
Reggae and dub on Wednesday;
funk, jazz and hip-hop on Friday;
house on Saturday.

Tube S8
Falconberg Court, t (020) 7287
3726; tube Tottenham Court Rd.
Open Fri and Sat 10pm–4am.
Gay club with popular Wig Out on
Saturdays playing trash and
retro sounds.

Turnmills Off maps
63 Clerkenwell Rd, t (020) 7250
3409; tube/train Farringdon.
Open Fri 10.30pm–7.30am, Sat
9pm–1pm on Sun.
Everything from funky jazz to
house and techno at the home
of Trade, London's original gay
late-nighter from 4am
Sunday morning.

Entertainment

The indispensable guide to the week's events is the listings magazine *Time Out*, which appears on Wednesday morning; it provides addresses, descriptions and reviews of everything scheduled over the following week. It isn't perfect, tending to overhype celebrities and the latest fashion fads, but it has no serious competition, although look out for its smaller rival, *What's On in London*, and the London *Evening Standard*'s *Hot Tickets*.

Theatre

The London stage is where actors like Anthony Hopkins, Ralph Fiennes and Alan Rickman come home to roost when they aren't making megabucks in the movies. And these days it's where the Hollywood stars, from Kathleen Turner and Nicole Kidman to Macauley Culkin and Jason Priestley, come in an effort to prove they can pass muster in the land of Shakespeare. Those Californian casting directors know very well that London boasts the best serious stage acting anywhere, a reputation it has built up meticulously over several centuries. Its playwrights have pioneered no theatrical movements – England boasts no equivalent of Pirandello or Brecht – but have nevertheless turned out compelling and challenging dramas of a quality not seen in any other European city. Likewise, West End actors rarely become major international stars, but still command enormous respect on Broadway and in Hollywood.

What to See and Where to Go

The major commercial theatre companies are concentrated in the West End, just as the main New York stages are grouped together on Broadway. Two distinct traditions are forever jostling for attention, the straight play and the musical. Shakespeare is of course a perennial favourite, along with Chekhov, Shaw and Noël Coward, but in pure terms of seat numbers the darling of the British musical, Andrew Lloyd Webber, is way ahead in the popularity ratings. Lloyd Webber's shows, from *Cats* through to *Phantom of the Opera*, have been running without interruption in London for the past quarter-century. Lloyd Webber's flagship theatre, the Palace on Cambridge Circus, has for the past few years been showing a musical he didn't write himself, the smash hit *Les Misérables*. Just across the road at the St Martin's is the longest-running show in London, Agatha Christie's *The Mousetrap*, which has been on in one theatre or another since 1952. Longevity is no guarantee of quality, and you'd do well to give this wooden and outdated tourist attraction a wide berth.

Established playwrights, such as David Hare, Harold Pinter and David Mamet, are increasingly turning to the off-West End theatre companies to stage their work. The most consistent and reliable of these is the three-stage Royal National Theatre on the South Bank, which puts on superb versions of the classics as well as showcasing high-quality new writing. The RNT is followed closely by the Royal Shakespeare Company, which concentrates mainly on the Bard and his contemporaries. The Royal Court in Sloane Square and Lyric in Hammersmith are excellent venues for new work, while experimental shows and reworkings of established plays are the hallmark of the Almeida in Islington, the Hampstead Theatre or the Donmar Warehouse in Covent Garden.

The fringe is always active, and occasionally you can find first-rate shows in draughty halls or upstairs rooms in pubs. If you're in London during the summer, don't forget about open-air venues like the Globe Theatre, Regent's Park and Holland Park, where you can enjoy Shakespeare (particularly *A Midsummer Night's Dream*) and lively modern comedies.

There's not a lot of point recommending individual theatres, as the quality of each production can't be guaranteed, but the following addresses should give you some pointers as to where to look. The telephone numbers are for the box office.

Tickets

Most performances start at 7.30pm or 8.00pm, with matinées usually scheduled on Wednesdays and Saturdays. By far the best way to book is through the theatre itself. At most places you can pay by credit card over the phone, then pick up the tickets just before the curtain goes up. Booking details, times and seating plans are available on Web sites such as **w** *www.londontheatre .co.uk*. Ticket agents charge stinging commissions, usually 22%, although they can be a necessary evil to get into the big musicals (try Ticketmaster on **t** (020) 7344 4444, **w** *www.ticket master.co.uk*, or First Call on **t** (020) 7420 0000). The Royal National Theatre offers a limited number of cheap tickets from 10am on the day of the performance (get there early as there are often long queues), and the Society of London Theatre has a ticket booth in Leicester Square (*open 2.30–6.30pm, or noon–6pm on matinée days*) with half-price tickets for West End shows that night. If all else fails, you can try for returns in the hour before the performance starts; students can get a hefty discount this way.

The Big Two

Barbican Arts Centre AA–BB6 *Silk St, Barbican*, **t** *(020) 7638 8891*, **w** *www.barbican.org.uk*; *tube/train Barbican, Moorgate.* One of Europe's largest arts centres, the Barbican presents a year-round programme of art, music, film and theatre. It presents classical and modern drama on its two stages, the large, more conventional Barbican Theatre and the more intimate experimental Pit. Although the Royal Shakespeare Company no longer uses the Barbican as its London home, it continues to perform at the Barbican Theatre as well as at other London venues throughout the year. Many of its productions are transfers from its base in Shakespeare's birthplace, Stratford-upon-Avon. The Barbican is also the venue for BITE, an annual festival of international theatre.

Royal National Theatre W11
South Bank Centre, t (020) 7452 3000, w www.nationaltheatre .org.uk; tube/train Waterloo.
The National has three stages: the large apron of the Olivier, the conventional proscenium at the Lyttelton, and the smaller, cosier Cottesloe. You don't just get top-notch theatre: you can enjoy foyer concerts, browse through the bookshops and linger in the cafés with views out over the Thames. Highly recommended.

West End

Arts T9
Great Newport St, t (020) 7836 3334, w www.artstheatre.com; tube Leicester Square.
Once famous for its avant-garde productions, the theatre was the first home of the Royal Shakespeare Company. After suffering a decline, it has reopened as a modern venue, presenting mainstream plays with a quirky bent.

Donmar Warehouse T9
Earlham St, Covent Garden, t (020) 7369 1732, w www.donmar-ware house.com; tube Covent Garden.
In the shell of a 19th-century warehouse, the Donmar was set up by Sam Mendes, now an Oscar-winning film director, and has become an excellent venue where many distinguished young directors have cut their teeth.

Her Majesty's Theatre S11
Haymarket, t (020) 7494 5400, w www.stoll-moss.com; tube Piccadilly Circus.
Built in the style of an Italian opera house, this is one of the finest theatres in London, dating back to 1704 and, more recently, home to long-running musical *Phantom of the Opera*.

New Ambassadors T9
West St, t (020) 7369 1761, w www.theambassadors.com; tube Leicester Square.
After being saddled with Agatha Christie's *The Mousetrap* for 25 years until its transfer to St Martin's next door, the Ambassadors has become a leading venue for award-winning contemporary drama.

Players U11
The Arches, Villiers St, t (020) 7839 1134; tube/train Charing Cross.
Many leading actors of the past, such as Peggy Ashcroft, have trod these boards, but it is now famed for its revivals of Victorian music hall.

Playhouse U11
Northumberland Av, t (020) 7494 5372; tube/train Charing Cross.
After a history of presenting great plays by the likes of Shaw and the classic *Goon Show* radio broadcasts, the Playhouse fell into decline but was reopened in 1991 to become a venue again for mainstream quality drama.

St Martin's T9
West St, t (020) 7836 1443; tube Leicester Square.
For over half a century, some of Britain's most popular plays were produced in this lovely Edwardian theatre, until Agatha Christie's *The Mousetrap* was transferred from the neighbouring New Ambassadors and still refuses to budge.

Savoy U10
The Strand, t (020) 7836 8888; tube/train Charing Cross.
Originally built by Richard D'Oyly Carte as the home of Gilbert and Sullivan's Savoy Operas, it was the first theatre in London with electric lighting. It has been

remodelled twice since then after being ravaged by fires. It now presents the usual West End fare of musicals and popular shows.

Soho Theatre R8
21 Dean St, t (020) 7478 0100, w www.sohotheatre.com; tube Tottenham Court Rd.
One of London's newest theatres, offering a showcase for young playwrights.

Theatre Royal Drury Lane V9
Catherine St, t (020) 7494 5000, w www.stoll-moss.com; tube Covent Garden.
Despite numerous fires, this has the longest continuous history of any theatre in Britain. Among the many stars to perform here was Nell Gwynne, the mistress of Charles II. It is now one of the top venues for big crowd-pulling shows.

Theatre Royal Haymarket S11
Haymarket, t (020) 7930 8800, w www.trh.co.uk; tube Piccadilly Circus.
Unadventurous choice of plays, but impeccable production and acting standards in this early 19th-century theatre built by John Nash. Maggie Smith, Vanessa Redgrave and Ian McKellen are regular stars here.

Wyndham's T10
Charing Cross Rd, t (020) 7369 1746, w www.theambassadors.com; tube Leicester Square.
One of the more reliable West End addresses, with plenty of serious productions that attract big-name foreign actors like John Malkovich and Dustin Hoffman.

Outside the West End

All of the following are off our maps, unless stated otherwise.

Almeida
Almeida St (but see below), Islington, t (020) 7359 4404, w www.almeida.co.uk; tube Angel, Highbury and Islington; train Highbury and Islington.
The Almeida's Islington home is being completed refurbished, so it

is temporarily based in a disused coach depot in Omega Place, off Caledonian Rd, near to King's Cross Station, until spring 2003. It is a superb fringe theatre that has acquired a formidable reputation. Staging different productions every six or seven weeks, it often produces its own plays but also reworks classical pieces.

Apollo Victoria P15
Wilton Rd, **t** *0870 4000 651;* **tube/train** *Victoria.*
A monstrous Art Deco venue that has been home to some of London's top musicals for over 100 years.

BAC (Battersea Arts Centre)
176 Lavender Hill, **t** *(020) 7223 2223,* **w** *www.bac.org.uk;* **train** *Clapham Junction.*
Lively theatre venue south of the river in Battersea's former Victorian town hall. It has three theatre spaces that have been a platform for many new and experimental works.

Bridewell Y9
Bride Lane, **t** *(020) 7936 3456,* **w** *www.bridewelltheatre.co.uk;* **tube/train** *Blackfriars, St Paul's.*
This was once a Victorian swimming pool and laundry but is now an intimate venue best known for its excellent music theatre.

Drill Hall S6
16 Chenies St, **t** *(020) 7637 8270,* **w** *www.drillhall.co.uk;* **tube** *Goodge St.*
The Bloomsbury Rifles no longer practise their shooting here, but this is still the place for hard-hitting, often high-brow, drama.

Greenwich Theatre
Crooms Hill, **t** *(020) 8858 7755,* **w** *www.greenwichtheatre.co.uk;* **train** *Greenwich.*
Originally built as an extension of the adjoining pub, the theatre became a cinema and then closed for many years before being reopened by local enthusiasts to become a leading fringe venue.

Hampstead Theatre
Avenue Rd, **t** *(020) 7722 9301,* **w** *www.hampstead-theatre.co.uk;* **tube** *Swiss Cottage.*

Actors and audiences mingle in the bar after the show at this friendly neighbourhood theatre, which is often a springboard for prestigious West End productions.

ICA (Institute of Contemporary Arts) S11
Carlton House Terrace, The Mall, **t** *(020) 7930 3647,* **w** *www.ica.org.uk;* **train** *Charing Cross.*
The Queen lives just down the road, but that hasn't stopped the ICA's small theatre presenting some of the most avant-garde theatre in London.

Jermyn Street Theatre Q11
16B Jermyn St, **t** *(020) 7287 2875,* **w** *www.jermynstreettheatre.co.uk;* **tube** *Piccadilly Circus.*
Formerly the waiter's changing rooms above a restaurant, this is one of the more exciting places for contemporary drama, mainly run by volunteers and raising cash for charity.

Lyric Hammersmith
King St, **t** *(020) 8741 2311,* **w** *www.lyric.co.uk;* **tube** *Hammersmith.*
Hosts many regional and foreign theatre companies. Home also to the smaller, experimental Studio.

Old Vic X13
Waterloo Rd, **t** *(020) 7369 1722,* **w** *www.oldvictheatre.com;* **tube/train** *Waterloo.*
The former home of the National Theatre has come down in the world a bit, but still puts on good productions. Peter O'Toole caused a sensation here in the early 1980s by playing *Macbeth* for laughs in a near-incoherent drunken slur. The theatre was packed out every night, but the management was scandalized.

Richmond Theatre
The Green, **t** *(020) 8940 0088;* **tube/train** *Richmond.*
Sitting on Richmond Green, this is one of the most impressive theatres outside the West End and is a fine setting for revivals and new plays.

Riverside Studios
Crisp Rd, **t** *(020) 8237 1111,* **w** *www.riversidestudios.co.uk;* **tube** *Hammersmith.*

With three stages, this is a popular venue for small, often avant-garde productions.

Royal Court M16
Sloane Square, **t** *(020) 7565 5000,* **w** *www.royalcourttheatre.com;* **tube** *Sloane Square.*
The major venue for experimental or counter-cultural writing, made famous by Shaw and Granville-Barker in the 1920s and kept prominent by the likes of Edward Bond, Caryl Churchill, Howard Brenton and Hanif Kureishi. The Theatre Upstairs on the first floor is one of the better fringe venues.

Theatre Royal Stratford East
Gerry Raffles Square, Stratford, **t** *(020) 8534 0310,* **w** *www.stratfordeast.com;* **tube/train/DLR** *Stratford.*
High-quality drama in a crumbling Victorian palace in the midst of grey tower blocks. Worth the long trip out.

Victoria Palace P15
Victoria St, **t** *(020) 7834 1317;* **tube/train** *Victoria.*
This rather shabby former music hall once echoed to the sounds of revues, such as the *Black and White Minstrels*, but it's now ideal for big-budget musicals.

Young Vic X–Y12
66 The Cut, **t** *(020) 7928 6363,* **w** *www.youngvic.org;* **tube/train** *Waterloo.*
Near to the Old Vic, the studio theatre presents old and new plays, sometimes quite innovative, aimed mainly at younger audiences.

Open-air Theatre

Holland Park Theatre C13
Holland Park, **t** *(020) 7602 7856,* **w** *operahollandpark.com;* **tube** *High St Kensington.*
In the grounds of the 17th-century Holland House, the open-air theatre's season runs from June to August, but puts on all manner of productions, not just Shakespeare.

Regent's Park
Open Air Theatre M3–4
Inner Circle, Regent's Park, t (020) 7486 2431, w www.open-air-theatre.org.uk; tube Baker St, Regent's Park.
Open-air theatre from May to September, best known for its Shakespearean productions, in which some of the world's greatest actors have performed in the past. Bring a blanket and umbrella to keep the worst of the English summer at bay.

Shakespeare's Globe AA11
21 New Globe Walk, t (020) 7401 9919, w www.shakespeares-globe.org; tube Southwark, London Bridge; train London Bridge.
Opened for business in 1997, the Globe was the dream of the late director and actor Sam Wanamaker, who died before the theatre was fully opened. This lovingly reconstructed version of Shakespeare's original London theatre puts on three or four Elizabethan productions each year, most of them by the Bard, in a season that lasts from May until September. It's proving popular, so book early (box office opens around January once the programme has been fixed). Lots of audience participation and period high jinks (like jesters with firecrackers attached to their feet). Watch out for rain and cold, though, as the theatre is open to the skies (*see* p.206 for more on the theatre itself).

Pub Theatres

The Bush Off maps
Shepherd's Bush Green, t (020) 7610 4224, w www.bush theatre.co.uk; tube Shepherd's Bush.
With giant cushioned steps as seating, this is an intimate venue presenting modern, easy-going theatre. The seats now have more suitable wooden backing, but sometimes you still have to clamber over fellow theatregoers to find somewhere to sit.

Finborough Off maps
Finborough Arms, 118 Finborough Rd, t (020) 7373 3842, w www.finboroughtheatre.co.uk; tube Earl's Court.
A cramped theatre space specializing in new writing.

The Gate D11
11 Pembridge Rd, t (020) 7229 0706, e gate@gatetheatre.freeserve .co.uk; tube Notting Hill Gate.
Excellent pub theatre, above the Prince Albert, that features new plays and ambitious reworkings of classics, including Greek tragedy.

Grace Theatre Off maps
The Latchmere, 503 Battersea Park Rd, t (020) 7794 0022; train Clapham Junction.
The pub and the surrounding area may have smartened up over the years, but the Grace Theatre has long been worth seeking out for its revivals and new drama.

King's Head Off maps
115 Upper St, Islington, t (020) 7226 1916; tube Angel.
Eccentric pub with a popular theatre in a charming back room. Serves a three-course dinner in the theatre just before the curtain rises (metaphorically speaking, because there is no curtain).

Landor Theatre Off maps
The Landor, 70 Landor Rd, Clapham, t (020) 7737 7276; tube Clapham North.
A typical box of a theatre above a gothic local pub, specializing in music theatre.

Man in the Moon Off maps
392 Kings Rd, Chelsea, t (020) 7351 2876; tube Sloane Square.
Agents and producers come here because of its reputation for talented new writers and actors.

Music
Jazz Clubs

Jazz came to London in the 1950s, largely thanks to the effort of the late Ronnie Scott and his excellent club in Soho, and it has gone from strength to strength ever since. Venues used to be poky, smoky and cheap; now they are smartening up, perhaps a shade too much, since they are starting to offer fancy food and drink at extraordinarily high prices. The music has not suffered yet, however, and continues to flow until the not-so-early hours of the morning. Check *Time Out* for jazz concerts in pubs and foyers of the larger theatres. Note that many clubs charge a (usually nominal) membership fee. You may find it hard to book for the more popular shows at Ronnie Scott's, for example, if you're not already a member.

Bull's Head Off maps
373 Lonsdale Rd, Barnes, SW13, t (020) 8876 5241. Train Barnes.
Top-notch bands in a riverside setting.

Jazz After Dark S8
9 Greek St, t (020) 7734 0545; tube Tottenham Court Rd.
Jazz, Latin jazz and salsa, with a bar and restaurant (licensed to 2am, 3am at weekends). Admission free before 11pm on weekdays.

Jazz Café N13
5 Parkway, Camden, t (020) 7344 0044; tube Camden Town.
Typical of the new-style jazz club, a slick venue with plush dinner-table seating (food optional). The music is first rate.

100 Club R8
100 Oxford St, t (020) 7636 0933; tube Tottenham Court Rd.
Lively basement venue with an eclectic mix of trad and modern jazz, as well as blues, swing and rockabilly. The Sex Pistols gave one of their first performances here in the mid-1970s.

Pizza Express R8
10 Dean St, t (020) 7439 8722; tube Tottenham Court Rd.
Be-bop to accompany your pizza; an unlikely setting, but a congenial one which boasts its own resident band as well as many prestigious visitors. Branch at **Pizza on the Park**, 11 Knightsbridge, off Hyde Park Corner, t (020) 7235 5273.

Ronnie Scott's S9
47 Frith St, t (020) 7439 0747;
tube Leicester Square. **Open**
Mon–Sat 8.30pm–3am.
The prime jazz venue in town,
with a steady flow of big names
and a suitably low-key, laid-back
atmosphere. Book if you have
time, and get there early (around
9pm) to ensure a decent seat.

606 Club Off maps
90 Lots Rd, Fulham, t (020) 7352
5953; tube Fulham Broadway.
Open *daily 8.30pm–2am.*
Basement club featuring many
local musicians, with the
emphasis on contemporary jazz.
Late-night restaurant licence and
good modern food.

Vortex Off maps
Stoke Newington Church St, t (020)
7254 6516; train Stoke Newington.
Friendly first-floor jazz bar
featuring many local North
London bands.

Rock, Pop and World Music

By and large, the huge venues
are impersonal and have terrible
acoustics, while smaller, more
specialized clubs are infinitely
more rewarding and cheaper, too.
Posters and press adverts will tell
you how to buy tickets. You'll
probably have to go through a
ticket agency for the bigger acts;
otherwise go directly to the
venue. Once again, *Time Out* will
have all the details, including reliable recommendations on the
week's best shows.

Astoria S8
157 Charing Cross Rd, t (020) 7434
9592; tube Tottenham Court Rd.
Popular for bands of all types,
from obscure to chart-topping.

Brixton Academy Off maps
211 Stockwell Rd, Brixton, SW9,
t (020) 7771 2000; tube/train
Brixton.
A venue for the best indie and cool
bands, which is probably why
Madonna chose to play here to a
select crowd.

London Arena Off maps
Limeharbour, Isle of Dogs, E14,
t (020) 7538 1212; DLR Crossharbour.
One of the premier venues for big
pop and rock acts.

Shepherds Bush Empire Off maps
Shepherds Bush Green, W12, t (020)
7771 2000; tube Shepherds Bush.
Top rock and indie bands play the
BBC's former television theatre.

Wembley Arena Off maps
Empire Way, Wembley, t (020) 8902
0902; tube Wembley Park.
After the closure of Wembley
Stadium, its neighbour is still one
of the main venues for big acts,
with a capacity of 12,500.

Opera and Classical Music

London has classical music
coming out of its ears: two major
opera companies, five world-class
orchestras, lunchtime concerts,
summer festival concerts, open-air
concerts. For generations, classical
music in Britain was tinged with
class prejudice, being a pursuit of
the educated upper-middle
classes who turned up their noses
at the philistine hordes who
couldn't tell their Handel from
their Haydn. You'll still find the
snobs lurking in the foyers of the
Festival Hall and on the rarefied
airwaves of the BBC's classical
station Radio 3. But you'll also find
a wealth of unpretentious, dedicated young performers and
audiences, especially in smaller
concert venues like the Wigmore
Hall. London's weakness is
undoubtedly in contemporary and
avant-garde music; programmers
tend to play very safe, with a
preponderance of Mozart,
Beethoven and Brahms.

The following addresses are for
the main concert and opera
venues; again, you should check
Time Out to see what's playing.

Barbican Centre AA–BB6
Silk St, t (020) 7638 8891,
w www.barbican.org.uk;
tube/train Barbican, Moorgate.

Home to the London Symphony
Orchestra and English Chamber
Orchestra. Excellent acoustics
make up for the hard-to-find
venue. *See p.223.*

London Coliseum T10
St Martin's Lane, t (020) 7632 8300,
w www.eno.org; tube Charing
Cross, Leicester Square.
Home to the English National
Opera, which performs in English
to high musical standards and
with infectious enthusiasm. It is
less pretentious than Covent
Garden and tickets can be
cheaper, rising from £3 to around
£66. For weekday performances
and Saturday matinées, 37 seats in
the dress circle are on sale on the
day. Over 100 seats in the balcony
are available for all performances.
Day seats are sold from 10am to
personal callers, and by phone for
credit card bookings from midday
for matinees and 12.30pm for
evening performances. Tickets
may be restricted to two per
person. *See p.109.*

Royal Albert Hall H13–14
Kensington Gore, t (020) 7589 8212,
w www.royalalberthall.com;
tube South Kensington.
This imposing 19th-century landmark building hosts music events
throughout the year, but the highlight is the Henry Wood
Promenade Concerts (Proms)
every year from July to early
September. The Proms are an
eclectic platform for music old
and new, and for unknown as well
as established performers. The
seats are removed from the area
in front of the stage, leaving an
open space in which people either
stand or sit on the floor for as
little as £3 per person. Queues
form in the hours before the
performance begins; bring a
cushion to soften the bum-
numbing pavements. From
mid-May, you can also book
conventional seating in advance,
at regular concert prices (up to
around £30). There are elaborate
rules for buying tickets, but you
can find out more on the official
Web site at **w** *www.bbc.co.uk/*

proms. The Last Night of the Proms is a raucous affair at which the all-English orchestra plays all-English music, and the all-English audience sings along to the national anthem and 'Rule Britannia'. In 2001, this 50-year tradition was put aside to commemorate those who died in the terrorist attacks on the United States, replacing the all-English finale with Beethoven's *Choral Symphony*. *See p.194.*

Royal Opera House U9
Covent Garden, t (020) 7304 4000, w www.royalopera.org;
tube Covent Garden.
Britain's leading opera venue is up there with the Met and La Scala. It has recently undergone a long-overdue renovation and, under pressure to attract new audiences, tickets can be bought for as little as £3, although the best seats still cost over £150. *See also p.143.*

Sadler's Wells Off maps
Rosebery Av, t (020) 7278 8916, w www.sadlers-wells.com;
tube Angel.
Dating back to 1683, this is now a somewhat unfashionable venue for all kinds of music, including the infectious if silly late Victorian operettas of Gilbert and Sullivan performed by the D'Oyly Carte Company (April and May).

St John's Smith Square T15
Smith Square, t (020) 7222 1061, w www.sjss.org.uk;
tube Westminster.
The superb acoustics in this fine Baroque church have made it one of the best concert venues in London, particularly for choral and small orchestral performances.

St Martin-in-the-Fields T10
Trafalgar Square, t (020) 7839 8362, w www.stmartin-in-the-fields.org; tube Charing Cross, Leicester Square.
Since 1726, this landmark church has played host to some of the world's greatest musicians, from Handel to Mozart. Its evening and lunchtime concerts feature orchestras, chamber groups and choirs in the spectacular setting, sometimes lit only by candles.

South Bank Centre V–W11
South Bank, Belvedere Rd, t (020) 7960 4242, w www.sbc.org.uk;
tube/train Waterloo.
Three first-rate concert halls under the same roof: the Royal Festival Hall boasts its own organ and room for as many musicians and singers as any musical work might demand; the Queen Elizabeth Hall, which is smaller and a little more adventurous in its programming; and the Purcell Room, for chamber music only. The larger halls also host occasional jazz, rock, dance and even small-scale opera performances.

Wigmore Hall O8
36 Wigmore St, t (020) 7935 2141, w www.wigmore-hall.org.uk;
tube Bond St, Oxford Circus.
An intimate venue with excellent acoustics that is noted for its chamber concerts. It attracts solo performers like guitarist Julian Bream or prima donna Jessye Norman. The tickets are very cheap – between £6 and £20 – and sell out very fast.

Lunchtime Concerts

St John's Smith Square, St Martin-in-the-Fields, the Barbican, the Royal National Theatre and the Royal Opera House's Vilar Floral Hall, all listed above, host lunchtime concerts, but there are many other wonderful venues across London. Check *Time Out* and other listings for performances. Some charge admission; others are free but ask for donations. Some of those listed below also stage evening concerts.

St Anne and St Agnes BB8
Gresham St, t (020) 7606 4986; tube St Paul's, Bank.

St Bride's Fleet St Y9
t (020) 7427 0133; tube Blackfriars, St Paul's.

St Giles Cripplegate BB7
Fore St, t (020) 7638 1997; tube/train Moorgate, Barbican

St Helen's DD5
Great St Helen's, Bishopsgate, t (020) 7283 2231; tube Liverpool St, Bank.
Magnificently restored church.

St James Piccadilly R10–11
Piccadilly, t (020) 7381 0441; tube Piccadilly Circus.
Mondays, Wednesdays and Fridays at about 1pm.

St John's Waterloo X12
Waterloo Rd, t (020) 7928 2003, w www.stjohnswaterloo.co.uk, tube/train Waterloo.
Wednesday lunchtime concerts, along with occasional daytime and evening music events on other days.

St Magnus the Martyr CC10
Lower Thames St, t (020) 7626 4481; tube Monument.

St Mary-le-Strand V9
The Strand, t (020) 7836 3126; tube Temple.

St Michael's CC9
St Michael's Alley, Cornhill, t (020) 7248 3826, w www.st-michaels.org.uk; tube Mansion House.
There have been organ recitals here at 1pm every Monday since 1916.

St Sepulchre-without-Newgate Z7–8
Holborn Viaduct, t (020) 7248 3826; tube St Paul's.
Mainly piano recitals on Fridays.

Open-air Concerts

Greenwich Park Off maps
t (020) 8858 2608; train Greenwich.
London's oldest royal park is a spectacular platform for concerts throughout the summer, close to the Greenwich Royal Observatory and offering views over the Thames and London.

Marble Hill House Off maps
Richmond Rd, for tickets contact IMG on t (020) 8233 7435, w www.picnicconcerts.com; train St Margaret's (from Waterloo or Victoria).
Sunday evenings only. *See p.254.*

Holland Park Theatre C13
Holland Park, t (020) 7602 7856, w operahollandpark.com; tube High St Kensington.
The open-air season runs from June to August, with all manner of productions, including opera.

Kenwood House Map p.234
Hampstead Lane, **t** *(020) 7413 1443,*
tube *Hampstead, then bus 210.*
From June to September, enjoy
idyllic outdoor concerts beside a
lake at the top of Hampstead
Heath. *See p.241.*

Dance

London puts on everything from
classical ballet to performance
art. The **Royal Opera House** (*see*
'Opera and Classical Music', above)
is home to the highly accom-
plished Royal Ballet, which is
cheaper and much less snooty
than the Royal Opera in the same
building. The **London Coliseum**
(*see* above) hosts the English
National Ballet, at least for now.
Sadler's Wells (*see* above) used to
have its own ballet company too,
but it decamped to Birmingham
in 1990; the theatre nevertheless
puts on an eclectic dance
programme that has recently
included both the mime artist
Lindsay Kemp and the National
Ballet of Cambodia. Two other
addresses worth knowing about
are the **ICA** on the Mall (*see*
'Theatre' above), arguably the
most avant-garde address in
town; and **The Place Theatre** (*17
Duke's Road, Bloomsbury,* **t** *(020)
7380 1268,* **w** *www.theplace.org.uk;*
tube/train *Euston*), in The Place
building, which is also home to
the London Contemporary Dance
School. Every autumn, from mid-
October to early December,
London stages a festival called
Dance Umbrella, which provides a
showcase for performers from
around the world.

Comedy Clubs

Comedy has been all the rage in
London since the early 1980s.
Stand-up comedy was once
restricted to music halls or to
workingmen's clubs in northern
England. Performers were generally fat and male, and cracked
decidedly off-colour jokes. The
only 'sophisticated' comedy was

the zany brand pioneered by the
Footlights Revue at Cambridge
University and developed by the
likes of Peter Cook, Dudley Moore
and *Monty Python*. These were
middle-class performers
who, despite a strong anti-
establishment streak, appealed
mostly to their own kind. Comedy,
like so much else, was divided
along class lines.

All that changed with the
advent of the Thatcher government in 1979 as a new
counter-culture of politically
aware comedy sprang up.
Performers from a broader social
and racial spectrum, including
Lenny Henry, Rowan Atkinson,
Harry Enfield, Ben Elton, Rik Mayall
and Jo Brand, soon became established stars, both on television
and in some cases in feature films,
too. All of them started out in
London's comedy clubs, particularly the Comedy Store in Leicester
Square (now in new premises),
which opened in 1979, the year of
Thatcher's election. The comedy
club circuit has expanded considerably since then, and established
performers mingle easily with
new talent in more than 20 major
venues. Sit in the front rows at
your peril, as you are likely to be
roped into the act and insulted or
humiliated. Some of the humour
is a bit parochial, revolving around
British adverts and television
programmes, but many acts are
truly inspired. Usually several
artists will contribute to a single
evening, so if you don't like one
there's not long to wait for something better. Look out for hilarious
Boothby Graffoe, political radical
Mark Thomas, Al Murray's Pub
Landlord and Rob Newman; but
going to a good club to see acts
you've never heard of can be just
as rewarding as following the big
names. On the Web, look for sites
such as **w** *www.chortle.co.uk* for
the latest London listings.

Amused Moose Soho R9
Bar Code, 3–4 Archer St, **t** *(020)
8341 1341,* **w** *www.amusedmoose*

.co.uk; **tube** *Piccadilly Circus,
Leicester Square.*
Hidden away in the basement of a
gay bar, this has become a leading
venue for top acts. It's normally
open every night except Tuesdays.

Banana Cabaret Off maps
The Bedford, 77 Bedford Hill, **t** *(020)
8673 8904,* **w** *www.banana
cabaret.co.uk;* **tube/train** *Balham.*
Tucked away behind a pub is this
friendly, award-winning circular
venue with a balcony and
domed roof, hosting some of the
top names.

Bound and Gagged Off maps
*Tufnell Park Tavern, 162 Tufnell Park
Road;* **tube** *Tufnell Park; and The
Fox, 413 Green Lanes;* **tube** *Wood
Green. For both,* **t** *(020) 8450 4100,*
w *www.boundandgagged
comedy.com.*
Saturday night above-pub clubs
with unusual, interesting acts.
Many of today's top names, from
Lee Evans to Eddie Izzard, have
played at these venues.

Chuckle Club V9
*London School of Economics,
Houghton St,* **t** *(020) 7476 1672,*
w *www.chuckleclub.com;*
tube *Holborn.*
An unassuming student bar that
has somehow managed to attract
the top acts for many years for its
Saturday-night shows.

Comedy Café Off maps
66–8 Rivington St, **t** *(020) 7739
5706,* **w** *www.comedycafe.fsnet
.co.uk;* **tube** *Old St.* **Open** *Wed–Sat.*
More of a restaurant with comedy,
but no one seems to pay attention
to the 'Do Not Heckle' sign.

Comedy Store S10
1A Oxendon St, **t** *(020) 7344 0234,*
w *www.thecomedystore.co.uk;*
tube *Piccadilly Circus, Leicester
Square.*
Improv on Wednesday and Sunday
by the Comedy Store Players;
otherwise, it's stand-up. The most
famous comedy club of them all
has got a bit slick for its own good
and the hefty admission fee
(£8/12) reflects that. The standard
remains very high, however.

Downstairs at the King's Head Off maps
2 Crouch End Hill, t (020) 8340 1028; train/tube Finsbury Park.
Open *Thurs–Sun.*
A Bohemian basement club with a warm atmosphere encouraged by the very funny compères.

East Dulwich Cabaret Off maps
The Magdala, 211 Lordship Lane, t (020) 8855 0496; train East Dulwich, North Dulwich.
Open *Thurs–Sat.*
Pub venue.

Hackney Empire Off maps
291 Mare St, Hackney, t (020) 8985 2424; w www.hackneyempire .co.uk; train Hackney Central.
Comedy with a political edge in a fine Victorian theatre.

Hen & Chicken Off maps
109 St Paul's Rd, Highbury Corner, t (020) 7704 2001; tube/train Highbury & Islington.
Recently reopened, this friendly pub theatre is best known for its comedy.

Jongleurs Off maps
49 Lavender Gardens, Battersea; train Clapham Junction; Bow Wharf, 221 Grove Rd; tube Mile End; Camden Lock, Dingwalls Bldg, Middle Yard, Chalk Farm Rd; tube Camden Town. All three t 0870 78 70 707, w www.jongleurs.com.
One of the original comedy clubs, now the biggest, with venues across the UK. Top acts on Friday and Saturday nights. Book in advance, although you may still have to queue.

Meccano Club Off maps
The Dove Regent, 65 Graham St, Islington, t (020) 7813 4478, w www.globalspot.net/meccano; tube Angel.
Recently moved from a sweaty cellar to a trendy bar, this attracts some of the finest comics on the circuit. Always worth a visit.

Red Rose Comedy Club Off maps
129 Seven Sisters Rd, Finsbury Park, t (020) 7281 3051, w www.redrose comedy.co.uk; tube/train Finsbury Park. **Open** *Sat.*

Top acts at knock-down prices in a slightly iffy, but allegedly 'up-and-coming' area.

Up the Creek Off maps
302 Creek Rd, Greenwich, t (020) 8858 4581, w www.up-the-creek.com; tube/train Greenwich.
Open *Fri–Sun.*
This friendly, purpose-built comedy club is one of London's best comedy venues thanks to compère and owner Malcolm Hardee.

Cinema

London cinemas are a bit like the British film industry – bursting with potential, forever on the verge of a real breakthrough, but poorly looked after and often disappointing. The mainstream cinemas are on the whole very expensive (£8 or more for a ticket, regardless of whether the venue is a plush auditorium with THX Dolby sound or a cramped back room with polystyrene walls). The multiplex has hit London in a big way, for example at the Warner and Empire in Leicester Square or at Whiteleys in Queensway. For no discernible reason, seats tend to be numbered, which means confusion breaks out just as the main feature is starting, and the audience rarely settles down until 10 minutes into the first reel. There has been a flurry of interest in new British and independent cinema in recent years, but Hollywood blockbusters still grab more than their fair share of the market, and the work of some of the most challenging British directors – Mike Leigh, Nicolas Roeg or Ken Loach – might not make a first-run cinema at all.

On the plus side, the arthouse and repertory sector is reasonably healthy, showing subtitled foreign-language films as well as the classics of American and British cinema. Prices are lower than first-run cinemas – £4 to £5 is normal – and can be lower still if you pay a membership fee and return regularly. The National Film Theatre offers the broadest range, while clubs like the Everyman attract a fiercely loyal clientèle. If you want a break from the kids, look out for the increasing number of London cinemas, particularly outside the West End, which are re-creating the tradition of Saturday-morning film clubs for children.

Film censorship in general is very strict, and in some cases the British Board of Film Classification cuts out footage it finds offensive without alerting the audience. Films are graded U (family films), PG (parental guidance recommended), 12 (nobody under that age), 15 (ditto) or 18 (ditto). The system is governed by crazy pseudo-puritanical rules that border on paranoia – the very first film to be censored in Britain, back in 1898, was a close-up of a piece of Stilton cheese. Don't ask why. Steven Spielberg's dinosaur thriller *Jurassic Park* was given a PG rating despite its self-evidently disturbing effect on children, while an intelligent classic like Robert Altman's *McCabe and Mrs Miller* is lumped along with pornography in the 18 bracket.

Barbican Arts Centre AA–BB6
Silk St, Barbican, t (020) 7638 8891, w www.barbican.org.uk; tube/train Barbican, Moorgate.
Britain's biggest arts complex also has a two-screen cinema showing both mainstream releases and independent arthouse movies from around the world.

Chelsea Cinema I19
206 King's Road, t (020) 7351 3742; tube Sloane Square.
A small cinema that is particularly good for mainstream movies from across Europe and beyond.

Ciné Lumière H16
French Institute, 17 Queensberry Place, t (020) 7073 1350; tube South Kensington.
A good place to catch up on Gabin, Godard *et compagnie.*

Coronet D11
103–105 Notting Hill Gate, t (020) 7727 6705; tube Notting Hill Gate.

Mainstream releases on two screens in a converted Victorian theatre.

Curzon Mayfair O11
38 Curzon St, t 0871 871 0071; tube Hyde Park Corner.
Cinema showing art or foreign films. A more relaxed venue is its sister-cinema, the Curzon Soho (*93 Shaftesbury Av, t (020) 7439 4805; tube Leicester Square, Piccadilly Circus*).

Electric B9
191 Portobello Rd, t (020) 7727 9958; tube Ladbroke Grove.
A leading arthouse movie house, this is London's oldest purpose-built cinema, restored to how it looked nearly a century ago.

Everyman Off maps
5 Hollybush Vale, Hampstead, t (020) 7431 1777, w www.everyman cinema.com; tube Hampstead.
The oldest rep cinema in London, with an excellent bar. Lots of old favourites and a dedicated, studenty audience.

Gate D11
87 Notting Hill Gate, t (020) 7727 4043; tube Notting Hill Gate.
Classy West London cinema with lively Sunday matinée line-ups. First-run films and classic revivals.

Goethe-Institut I15
50 Princes Gate, Exhibition Rd, t (020) 7596 4000, w www.goethe .de/gr/lon; tube South Kensington.
Shows a broad range of German-language cinema, sometimes without subtitles.

ICA Cinematheque S11
Carlton House Terrace, The Mall, t (020) 7930 3647, w www.ica.org .uk; tube Charing Cross.
The wackiest film selection in town, with the emphasis on the avant-garde, especially feminist and gay cinema.

Metro S10
11 Rupert St, t (020) 7437 0757, w www.metrocinema.co.uk; tube Piccadilly Circus, Leicester Square.
Two-screen cinema that shuns Hollywood fare in favour of in-dependent productions.

National Film Theatre W11
South Bank Centre, t (020) 7928 3232, w www.bfi.org.uk; tube/train Waterloo.
The mecca of London's film junkies and the main venue for the annual London Film Festival each November. Lots of old and new films always showing in rep on its three screens, with special seasons, for instance of Iranian cinema.

Odeon Leicester Square S10
t 0870 5050 007, w www.odeon .co.uk; tube Leicester Square.
London's plushest venue, which premières major Hollywood productions, often with royals and film stars in tow. Even more expensive than the average main-stream cinema, with interminable adverts before the main feature. Odeon cinemas (on the same tele-phone number) are across London.

Prince Charles S10
Leicester Place, t (020) 7437 8181, w www.princecharlescinema.com; tube Leicester Square.
This former soft-porn cinema has smartened up its act and shows a constantly changing schedule of cult classics at £3.50 a seat. Surely this can't go on. Take advantage while you can.

Renoir U5
Brunswick Centre, Brunswick Square, t (020) 7837 8402; tube Russell Square.
The most adventurous of central London's cinemas, showing lots of foreign films and the best of British and American independents.

Ritzy Off maps
Brixton Oval, Coldharbour Lane, t (020) 7737 2121, w www.ritzy cinema.co.uk; tube/train Brixton.
Friendly arty cinema showing specialist arthouse movies along-side big mainstream releases on its five screens.

Riverside Studios Off maps
Crisp Rd, t (020) 8237 1111, w www.riversidestudios.co.uk; tube Hammersmith.
A popular rep cinema for classic revivals and world cinema.

Screen on the Hill Off maps
230 Haverstock Hill, Belsize Park, t (020) 7435 3366, w www.screen cinemas.co.uk; tube Belsize Park.
Popular first-run and art cinema with excellent coffee at the bar. Affiliated cinemas include the rather cramped Screen on Baker Street (*96 Baker St, t (020) 7486 0036; tube Baker St*) and the more commercial Screen on the Green (*83 Upper St, Islington, t (020) 7226 3520; tube Angel*).

Tricycle Off maps
269 Kilburn High Rd, t (020) 7328 1900; tube Kilburn.
Specialising in arthouse and world cinema, this theatre hosts an Irish film festival and a Black film festival annually, with various other mini film festivals during the year.

UCI Empire
Leicester Square S10
t 0870 010 2030, w www.uci-cinemas.co.uk; tube Leicester Square.
Three screens and the latest blockbusters. UCI also has an eight-screen multiplex in West London (second floor, Whiteleys Shopping Centre, Queensway, t 0870 010 2030; tube Queensway, Bayswater).

UGC Trocadero R10
13 Coventry St, t 0870 907 0716; tube Piccadilly Circus, Leicester Square.
Blockbusters within a leisure and retail complex. UGC also runs other mainstream movie theatres in Chelsea, Haymarket, Fulham, Hammersmith and Docklands.

Warner Village West End S10
Leicester Square, t (020) 7437 4347; w www.warnervillage.co.uk; tube Leicester Square.
The West End's biggest multiplex, showing big movies alongside more specialized shows across its nine screens. Also runs the multi-plex in Finchley Rd, northwest London, and Shepherd's Bush, West London.

Shopping

London...a kind of emporium for the whole earth.

Joseph Addison

London has been a cosmopolitan place to shop since the Romans traded their pottery and olive oil for cloth, furs and gold back in the 1st century AD. Until comparatively recently the best shopping was for the rich, in prestigious department stores such as Harrods, or smaller establishments in St James's and South Kensington offering exceptional service and attention to detail. The Carnaby St spirit of the 1960s changed that, and now you can find cheap clothes and jewellery, unusual music and exotic food, all over town in fleamarkets and gaily coloured shops. Carnaby St itself, regrettably, has long since sold its soul to the cause of tourist kitsch, but you will find its successors in Covent Garden, down the King's Rd, around Notting Hill and at Camden Lock Market. Thanks to the 1990s design boom, some of the dingier old addresses have been spruced up and transformed, San Francisco-style, into dinky pastel-coloured boutiques selling the work of idiosyncratic small artisans. Here at least, the encroachment of chainstore blandness appears to have hit its limit.

The major department stores and prestige stores are famous enough to need no introduction. Have a good look by all means at Harrods or Liberty's or Fortnum & Mason, but think hard about price and quality before whipping out the old credit card. Often you will find the same thing for much less elsewhere. Neither of the two classic shopping districts is ideal – Knightsbridge is snooty and expensive, while the area around Oxford St and Regent St is very crowded and noisy. Both areas reach a fever pitch of activity before Christmas and during the winter and summer sales – that is, January and July. So don't be afraid to look further afield.

A note on VAT: if you leave Britain for a non-EU country within six months of arriving, you are entitled to a refund on the Value Added Tax, or VAT, that you have paid on any goods you have bought from shops displaying a 'tax free for tourists' sign. You must pick up a form in the shop where you make your purchase, and then hand it in at the airport when you leave the country. Since the rate of VAT is 17.5%, this is well worth the hassle.

Opening hours: Traditionally, shops stay open Mon–Sat from around 9am to 5.30 or 6pm. Late opening for shops is becoming more and more common, however, particularly on Wednesday and Thursday, and Sunday trading is much more flexible than in the past: areas like Queensway, the Edgware Rd, Hampstead, Greenwich, Tottenham Court Rd and most of the Oxford St department stores are open on Sunday.

Oxford Street

Oxford St is forever packed with shoppers and tourists, for whom its wide pavements and large department stores symbolize the very essence of the big city. This rather puzzling mystique is not at all borne out by the reality, which is impersonal, uniform and unremittingly grey. The most prestigious address is Selfridge's, which for sheer size and range of goods is the closest rival in London to Harrods. But for the most part, Oxford St can only offer outsize outlets of high-street regulars like Marks & Spencer, River Island and The Gap – evidence that Oxford St is really just Nowheresville plopped into the centre of London. Most shops are open on Sunday, except John Lewis.

Off and behind Oxford St are a few sidestreets with interesting small stores: at the Selfridge's/Bond St end, try walking down South Molton St, Davies St,

St Christopher's Place, James St, Duke St and Wigmore St; past Oxford Circus there's Great Portland St, Argyll St and pedestrianised Carnaby St.

Borders Q8
197 Oxford St; tube Oxford Circus.
Open till 11pm and on Sundays.
Huge branch of the US book and music shop, with readings, performances and a coffee shop.

Browns O9
23–7 South Molton St,
w www.brownsfashion.com;
tube Bond St.
Centre of an empire of fashion shops along this bijou pedestrian street off Oxford St.

Electrum Gallery O9
21 South Molton St; tube Bond St.
Classic jewellery from around the world – at a price.

Forbidden Planet T8
71 New Oxford St; tube Tottenham Court Rd.
The best sci-fi bookshop around.

Gray's Antique Markets O9
58 Davies St, w www.egrays.co.uk;
tube Bond St.
An enclosed antiques market with over 200 dealers in a large Victorian building. Mainly silverware, glassware, jewellery, toys, ancient artefacts and china. Some odder stalls, such as Wheels of Steel model train sets stall, or Pete McAskie's Dinky toys. The Thimble Society of London is a stall dedicated to antique and modern thimbles.

James Smith and Sons T8
53 New Oxford St; tube Holborn.
Fend off the British weather with a trip to this Victorian shop dedicated to umbrellas. Also stocks walking sticks, often with carved handles.

John Lewis P8
278–306 Oxford St; tube Oxford Circus. Open Mon–Sat.
With its slogan 'Never knowingly undersold', this cheerful and efficient department store promises to refund the difference if you find anything cheaper elsewhere. Well-stocked departments of

household goods and accessories, and for decades one of London's largest retailers of dressmaking and furnishing fabrics and haberdashery.

Lush Q9
*40 Carnaby St; **tube** Oxford Circus.*
You can smell this shop from yards away. Stocks handmade soaps and toiletries using only natural ingredients.

Marks & Spencer M9
*458 Oxford St; **tube** Marble Arch, **w** www.marksandspencer.com, and branches all over London.*
Suppliers of cheap, comfortable clothes and underwear to the nation – and the world. Don't overlook the food section, with excellent pre-prepared dishes and stunningly good ice cream. It's even got its own café.

Muji Q9
*26 Carnaby St and 187 Oxford St; **tube** both Oxford Circus.*
Minimalist Japanese paper, fabric, fashion and edible goods.

NikeTown P8
*236 Oxford St (overlooking Oxford Circus); **tube** Oxford Circus.*
Supermodern sports shop with loud music, encouraging slogans ('Life is a Verb') and odd sculptures.

Octopus Q9
*28 Carnaby St; **tube** Oxford Circus.*
All kinds of gifts and gimmicks: lamps made of brightly coloured rubber, bags with holograms on, glasses mounted on toy cars. Great fun.

Selfridge's N9
*400 Oxford St; **tube** Bond St.*
Classic department store. There are also perfume and make-up demonstrations and a travel agent's in the basement.

Storm Q9
*21 Carnaby St and 6 Gees Court; **tube** Oxford Circus.*
Unusual modern watches as well as fashion, sunglasses, lava lamps and so on.

TopShop Q8
*214 Oxford St (overlooking Oxford Circus), **w** www.topshop.co.uk; **tube** Oxford Circus.*
Haven of cheap trendy gear for style-obsessed but cash-poor teenage girls (and their trendy mums).

Vivienne Westwood O10
*6 Davies St; **tube** Bond St.*
The punk queen of British fashion has real clothes as well as eccentric pieces of tailoring art.

Regent Street

Regent St was once the finest street in London; now all it boasts are a few decent shops (particularly men's clothes stores) and some rather stuffy, impersonal buildings livened up once a year by the overhead display of electric Christmas decorations.

Aquascutum Q10
*100 Regent St; **tube** Oxford Circus.*
Raincoats, cashmere scarves and endless sober suits. Clothes to last, not look hip in.

Boosey and Hawkes P8
*295 Regent St, **w** www.boosey .com/musicshop; **tube** Oxford Circus.*
Sheet music – mainly classical but some pop and jazz. Sheet music can be downloaded inexpensively from the Web site, too.

Crabtree and Evelyn Q9
*239 Regent St; **tube** Oxford Circus.*
Herbs and fruit scents, all beautifully packaged. Ideal for gift-hunting.

Dickins and Jones Q9
*224–44 Regent St, **w** www.house offraser.com; **tube** Oxford Circus.*
Department store for counties matrons. Good cosmetics – and unbeatable sales.

The European Bookshop Q10
*5 Warwick St, off Regent St, **w** www.esb.co.uk; **tube** Piccadilly Circus.*
Makes up for Grant & Cutler's deficiencies, especially with

French literature, in which it excels.

Grant & Cutler Q8
*55–7 Great Marlborough St, off Regent St, **w** www.grant-c .demon.co.uk; **tube** Oxford Circus.*
Uneven, but nevertheless the best bookshop in London for obscure and not so obscure foreign-language books.

Hamley's Q9
*188–96 Regent St, **w** www.hamleys .com; **tube** Oxford Circus.*
London's biggest and most famous toy emporium.

Liberty Q9
*210–20 Regent St, **w** www.liberty-of-london.com; **tube** Oxford Circus.*
A labyrinth of a store. Famous for print scarves; also good for fashion, china, rugs and glass.

L'Occitane Q9
*237 Regent St; **tube** Oxford Circus.*
Provençal herbs and fruit scents, all beautifully packaged. Ideal for gift-hunting.

Zara Q10
*118 Regent St, **w** www.zara.com; **tube** Oxford Circus.*
Spanish fashion store chain.

Bond Street

Two kinds of shopkeeper dominate Bond St: jewellers and art dealers, whose gaudy if not always particularly attractive shop fronts make for a diverting stroll.

Bulgari Q10
*172 New Bond St; **tube** Bond St.*
Italian jewellery.

Calvin Klein P9
*55 New Bond St; **tube** Bond St.*
Famous for jeans, underwear and scents.

Chanel Q10
*173 New Bond St for jewellery; 26 Old Bond St for everything else; **tube** Bond St.*

Church's P10
*163 New Bond St, **w** www.churchs shoes.com; **tube** Bond St.*
Solid, sober shoes to last half a lifetime.

DKNY Q10
27 Old Bond St; ***tube*** *Bond St.*
Donna Karan's diffusion label:
streetwear for women. With a
trendy café.

Donna Karan P10
20 New Bond St; ***w*** *www.donna
karan.com;* ***tube*** *Bond St.*
Sleek, minimalist women's
fashion.

Fenwick P9
New Bond St; ***tube*** *Bond St.*
Traditional department store
for the lady who lunches:
strong on accessories and
women's clothes.

Hermès P10
155 New Bond St; ***tube*** *Bond St.*
Source of the famous scarves and
accessories.

Louis Vuitton P10
17 New Bond St; ***tube*** *Bond St.*
The famous monogrammed bags
are in again.

Miu Miu P9
123 New Bond St; ***tube*** *Bond St.*
The funkier offspring of Prada.

Mulberry P9
41 New Bond St; ***tube*** *Bond St.*
Traditional high-quality bags and
leather goods, stamped with the
recognisable mulberry tree
symbol.

Spymaster N8
3 Portman Square; ***tube*** *Bond St.*
Everything you ever needed for
surveillance ...

Yves Saint Laurent P10
137 New Bond St; ***tube*** *Bond St.*

Tottenham Court Road

As late as the 1870s, cows grazed
along this road, now all too
crowded with traffic. Its main
attractions are its furniture stores
– Heal's, Habitat and shop after
shop selling sofa-beds and futons
– and its discount computer and
hi-fi shops. Visit plenty of shops,
ask to see write-ups in trade
magazines to back up the
recommendations, and haggle.
North Americans will find prices

rather high, but Europeans will be
astounded at how cheap
everything is. Most shops open
on Sundays.

Computer Exhange R6
70 Tottenham Court Rd;
tube *Tottenham Court Rd.*
A wide variety of secondhand PCs,
monitors, etc. Staff know their
stuff and there are lots of good
bargains.

Habitat R6
196 Tottenham Court Rd,
w *www.habitat.net;* ***tube*** *Goodge
St.*
Everything for the house, from
glasses and corkscrews to fitted
cabinets. Moderately priced and
practical.

Heal's R6
196 Tottenham Court Rd,
w *www.heals.co.uk;* ***tube*** *Goodge
St.*
Upmarket sister to Habitat, with
innovative designs.

Charing Cross Road

Charing Cross Rd is the traditional centre of the London book
trade, although the pressure of
high rents is pushing many original establishments out into other
areas, like Notting Hill. The once-
gentlemanly publishing and book
trade has become something of a
cut-throat environment. Stores no
longer stock the eclectic range of
titles that they once did, preferring to focus on titles they know
will sell in large numbers. The
abolition of the Net Book
Agreement that fixed retail prices
has made mainstream titles
considerably cheaper, but it has
also intensified competition
between sellers, favouring the big
chains at the expense of the
smaller specialists.

On the plus side, many assistants still give expert advice on
titles and subjects. Browsing is not
only tolerated, it is welcomed;
letting yourself drift for hours
from shelf to shelf is one of the

great pleasures of the London
bookshop.

Borders Books and Music S8
*120 Charing Cross Rd and many
branches,* ***w*** *www.borders.com;*
tube *Tottenham Court Rd, Leicester
Square.*
The giant US chain has a strong
line-up of titles, including a lot of
American imports which don't
make it onto the shelves of other
stores.

Foyles S8
113–19 Charing Cross Rd,
w *www.foyles.co.uk;*
tube *Tottenham Court Rd.*
Love it or hate it (and there are
plenty in both camps), this chaotic
and maze-like bookshop is an
institution on this street.

Henry Pordes T9
58–60 Charing Cross Rd,
w *home.clara.net/henrypordes;*
tube *Charing Cross.*
One of many secondhand
and antiquarian booksellers
near here.

Murder One T9
71–3 Charing Cross Rd;
tube *Leicester Square.*
New and secondhand genre
fiction, mainly science fiction
and crime.

Waterstone's S8
*121–5 Charing Cross Rd, and many
branches;* ***tube*** *Tottenham Court
Rd, Leicester Square.*
Probably the best chain, with
outstanding selections at
every branch.

Zwemmer T9
80 Charing Cross Rd; ***tube*** *Leicester
Square.*
London's leading art bookshop –
and worth a visit.

Jermyn Street and Savile Row

Jermyn St, in St James's, boasts
some of the fanciest shopping in
town. Royal and aristocratic
patronage has showered down on
its old-fashioned emporia for
centuries. Don't miss the two

arcades just off Jermyn St: Princes Arcade and Piccadilly Arcade.

North of Piccadilly is the place for men's bespoke tailoring, Savile Row. Classic menswear can still be found here, although the styles on offer are beginning to look impossibly old-fashioned. The street has hit hard times recently, although you'll still find some atmospherically traditional establishments, and you can see tailors working away in the basements as you pass. Also north of Piccadilly is Burlington Arcade, which contains a host of little shops selling Irish linens, old pens, leather, pashmina shawls, costume jewellery, perfumes and accessories.

Bates R10
21A Jermyn St, w www.bates-hats.co.uk; tube Piccadilly Circus, Green Park.
Men's hatter, with straw Panamas and other traditional styles.

Davidoff Q11
65 Jermyn St; tube Piccadilly Circus, Green Park.
Fine cigars.

Floris R11
89 Jermyn St, w www.florislondon.com; tube Piccadilly Circus, Green Park.
Old-fashioned, long-established perfume shop.

Gieves and Hawkes Q10
1 Savile Row, w www.gievesand hawkes.com; tube Piccadilly Circus.
One of the last gentlemen's outfitters in Savile Row. Unwavering attention to detail, and atmospherically traditional.

Immaculate House Q11
Burlington Arcade; tube Piccadilly Circus, Green Park.
All manner of strange and wonderful objects for the home.

Paxton and Whitfield R11
93 Jermyn St; tube Piccadilly Circus, Green Park.
Impeccable, old-fashioned cheese shop with specials of the day and nibbles at the counter.

Taylor of Old Bond Street Q11
74 Jermyn St; tube Piccadilly Circus, Green Park.
Old-fashioned barber paraphernalia: shaving brushes and so on.

Turnbull and Asser Q11
69–72 Jermyn St; tube Piccadilly Circus, Green Park.
One of many old-fashioned clothing boutiques on Jermyn St, with lots of shirts and silk ties.

High Street Kensington

This is a really fun place to shop, and not that expensive either. It's basically a mini-Oxford St, more compact and less busy. It's got its very own department store, Barker's, which is especially good for cosmetics, furniture and Christmas goods. There are big branches of Marks & Spencer, BHS and Boots. At the western end of the High St are all the women's fashion chains (H&M, Kookai, Jigsaw, Zara, Warehouse, Hobbs, Monsoon, French Connection), a selection of shoe shops and a large branch of Waterstone's.

Turn right from the station to find trendier clothes shops, like Diesel and and Urban Outfitters. For antiques, look around the lower end of Kensington Church St and the cobbled passage, Church Walk, that snakes behind the Victorian-era St Mary Abbots church.

Children's Book Centre B13
237 Kensington Church St, w www.childrensbookcentre.co.uk; tube High St Kensington.
Books, CDs, story-telling and now jewellery and chocolate, too.

Claire's Accessories D14
171 Kensington High St and branches; tube High St Kensington.
Pink ribbons, plastic earrings and hairslides: a little girl's paradise.

Cologne & Cotton E13
39 Kensington Church St; tube High St Kensington.
Luxury linen for the stylish bedroom, mostly in tasteful white, cream and blues.

Crabtree and Evelyn E13
6 Kensington Church St and branches, w www.crabtree evelyn.com; tube High St Kensington.
Herbs and fruit scents, health and beauty products all beautifully packaged. Ideal for gifts.

Diesel F13
38A Kensington High St; tube High St Kensington.
Streetwear by the well-known, ultra-trendy Italian designers.

Ehrmann's E13
Lancer Square, off Kensington Church St, w www.ehrmann tapestry.com; tube High St Kensington.
Tapestry kits and equipment: make your own medieval cushion.

Habitat F13
26 Kensington High St; tube High St Kensington.
Brand-new branch of the interior-design emporium opening in mid-2002.

Miss Sixty F13
42 Kensington High St; tube High St Kensington.
Hip, offbeat and very sexy streetwear for young women.

Muji F13
157 Kensington High St and branches, w www.muji.co.jp; tube High St Kensington.
Minimalist Japanese store selling kitchen equipment, stationery and clothes.

Past Times D14
179 Kensington High St, w www.past-times.com; tube High St Kensington.
Gift shop trading on nostalgia for the British past. As tacky as it sounds.

Snow and Rock C14
188 Kensington High St; tube High St Kensington.
Everything for skiing and mountaineering.

Urban Outfitters F13
36 Kensington High St; tube High St Kensington.
Kitsch, young and fun, but you have to be fit to climb the stairs to the cool café.

Wolford E13
28A Kensington Church St;
tube *High St Kensington.*
Expensive underwear and
fashionable tights worn by
the most fashionable legs in
London.

King's Road

*For all the following shops, the
nearest **tube** is Sloane Square, then
take **bus** 11, 19, 22.*

Like Carnaby St, the King's Rd let
its hair down in the 1960s and
filled up with cafés and fashion
shops selling mini-skirts and
cheap jewellery. Old-fashioned
shops were superseded by the
likes of Terence Conran, who
opened his first household store
Habitat on the King's Rd as a
direct challenge to the fusty, old-
fashioned goods of Peter Jones on
Sloane Square. Nowadays, most of
the boutiques have either gone
upmarket or been replaced by
generic high-street chainstores.
Some of the 1960s spirit lives on,
however, in the delightfully
sprawling antiques markets (*see*
'Chelsea Antiques Market', below)
on the south side of the road.
Behind the King's Rd to the
north, Cale St and Elystan Place
have nice little shops and a
certain charm.

American Classics Off maps
400 King's Rd.
All you need for that authentic
'street' look.

L'Artisan Parfumeur K17
17 Cale St.
Beautifully gift-wrapped, elegant
scents and colognes.

Bluebird I19
*350 King's Rd, **w** www.conran.com.*
Part of the Conran empire, a
converted 1930s garage
containing a luxury food store,
cookware shop, flower stall,
restaurant and café.

Boy London/Ad Hoc K18
153 King's Rd.
OTT selection of fun,
kitsch clothing and clubbing
accessories.

Brora I19
*344 King's Rd, **w** www.brora.co.uk.*
Scottish cashmere, tweed and
wool with a modern twist.

Chelsea Antiques Market K18
245–53 King's Rd.
All sorts of antiques.

The Chelsea Courtyard J18
Sydney St.
Pleasant haven from the main
drag, with Bikepark, a bike shop
where you can buy, hire and park
bikes and get them repaired; an
antiques centre; and the only
authentic Vietnamese street
barrow in London.

Chelsea Town Hall K18
Corner of Manor St and King's Rd.
Venue for antique sales and
craft fairs.

Daisy and Tom's K18
181–3 King's Rd.
Children's emporium, set up by
Tim Waterstone of bookshop fame
and named after his children, with
hairdressing salon, carousel, toys,
clothes and shoes.

Designer's Guild J19
*269 King's Rd, **w** www.designers
guild.com.*
Bright and colourful textiles,
pottery and furniture.

Habitat K18
206 King's Rd.
Everything for the house, from
glasses and corkscrews to fitted
cabinets. Cheap and practical.
Good café.

Heal's K18
*234 King's Rd, **w** www.heals.co.uk.*
Upmarket sister to Habitat, with
innovative furniture, beds,
lighting, etc.

The Holding Company J19
241 King's Rd.
A wealth of storage solutions
for every room in the home or
office.

John Sandoe Books L17
*10–11 Blacklands Terrace, just off
the King's Rd, **w** www.john
sandoe.com.*
An old-fashioned, higgledy-
piggledy bookshop with
knowledgeable staff.

Mac Cosmetics K18
*109 King's Rd, **w** www.mac
cosmetics.com.*
Stylish New York make-up and
beauty products.

Monsoon L17
*33D King's Rd and branches,
w www.monsoon.co.uk.*
Strong-coloured cotton and silk
clothes with an oriental
influence. Accessories, too.
Mostly for women. Unusual
homewares department in
this branch.

Peter Jones M17
Sloane Square.
A West London institution.
A branch of John Lewis renowned
for wedding lists and Chelsea
'ladies who lunch'.

Rococo I19
*321 King's Rd, **w** www.rococo
chocolates.com.*
Zany chocolate shop – an
Aladdin's cave of edible
delights.

R. Soles K18
*109A King's Rd, **w** www.r-soles
.com.*
Cowboy boots.

Steinberg & Tolkein J18
193 King's Rd.
Vintage clothing and accessories
beloved by the 'in-crowd'.

V. V. Rouleaux M16
*54 Sloane Square, **w** www
.vv.rouleaux.com.*
An irresistible shop filled to the
ceiling with rolls of ribbon and
brocade, beads, feathers
and sequins.

Knightsbridge

The Great Exhibition turned
Knightsbridge into the birthplace
of the late Victorian department
store. Harvey Nichols is the most
stylish (and the absolute favourite
of Patsy and Edina in *Absolutely
Fabulous*). But the most famous is
Harrods. Brompton Rd and Sloane
St parade designer shops, some of
them too scary to enter. Farhi,
Dior, Lacroix, Chanel, Gucci, Kenzo
and a clutch of others stretch

down Sloane St, while past Harrods in the Brompton Rd lurk Emporio Armani and Issey Miyake. The streets behind Harrods have hidden treasures, and halfway down Brompton Rd to the left is Beauchamp Place, with tiny exclusive shops selling underwear, jewellery or designer cast-offs. Yet around the station are branches of Monsoon and Miss Selfridge, Jigsaw and Laura Ashley as well.

La Bottega del San Lorenzo K15
23 Beauchamp Place; ***tube*** *Knightsbridge.*
Divine Italian deli.

Descamps L14
197 Sloane St, ***w*** *www.descamps .com;* ***tube*** *Knightsbridge.*
French linen.

Emporio Armani K15
191 Brompton Rd; ***tube*** *Knightsbridge.*
The king of classic Italian tailoring. The café is a great place for a breather.

Gant USA L13
17 Brompton Rd, ***w*** *www.gant.com;* ***tube*** *Knightsbridge.*
US men's casual wear.

Harrods L14
Brompton Rd; ***tube*** *Knightsbridge.*
A shopping institution that demands to be seen. Exotic foods, kitchenware, silverware and toys are excellent, clothes less so. Look out for bargains on mundane things like CDs during the sales.

Harvey Nichols L13
109–25 Knightsbridge; ***tube*** *Knightsbridge.*
High-class fashion and an excellent food hall.

Isabell Kristensen L15
33 Beauchamp Place; ***tube*** *Knightsbridge.*
Ballgowns.

Joseph Menswear L14
26 Sloane St; ***tube*** *Knightsbridge.*
Sharply tailored men's fashion.

Marni L14
16 Sloane St, ***w*** *www.marni.com;* ***tube*** *Knightsbridge.*
Light, floaty Italian fashion.

Mulberry K15
185 Brompton Rd, ***w*** *www .mulberry-england.co.uk;* ***tube*** *Knightsbridge.*
Classic English leather bags and luggage.

Rigby and Peller K14
2 Hans Rd, ***w*** *www.rigbyandpeller;* ***tube*** *Knightsbridge.*
Sublime underwear, including made-to-measure corsets.

Space NK Apothecary J16
305 Brompton Rd, ***w*** *www.spacenk .co.uk;* ***tube*** *Knightsbridge.*
Make-up and beauty products not available elsewhere: Nars, Kiehl's, Stila.

Brompton Cross

Further along Brompton Rd is a small enclave of shops and restaurants at the start of Fulham Rd known as Brompton Cross. Its most striking building, at its centre, is Terence Conran's remarkable Art Nouveau Michelin Building (at No.81), containing the Conran Shop. Behind and parallel to the Brompton Rd, first left off Draycott Av, Walton St is a quiet enclave of unmissable classy little shops.

Agnès B J16
111 Fulham Rd, ***w*** *www.agnesb.fr;* ***tube*** *South Kensington.*
One branch of the women's design shop: elegant clothes and make-up.

Bentley's K16
190 Walton St; ***tube*** *South Kensington.*
Leather goods and luggage.

Conran Shop J16
Michelin House, 81 Fulham Rd, ***w*** *www.conran.com;* ***tube*** *South Kensington.*
Baskets, chairs, lighting, even notebooks, all beautifully designed, in this tremendous Art Deco building.

Cox and Power K16
95 Walton St, ***w*** *www.coxand power.com;* ***tube*** *South Kensington.*
Flamboyant modern jewellery.

Czech and Speake J17
125 Fulham Rd; ***tube*** *South Kensington.*
Incense burning by the door lures you into this haven of scents for the body and home.

Dinny Hall J16
54 Fulham Rd; ***tube*** *South Kensington.*
Trend-setting jewellery designer.

Divertimenti J17
139 Fulham Rd; ***tube*** *South Kensington.*
Pots and pans of the highest quality and inventiveness.

Farmacia di Santa Maria Novella K16
117 Walton St; ***tube*** *South Kensington.*
Hand-milled soaps and fragrances, friendly staff and a trademark Tuscan pot pourri.

Formes Off maps
313 Fulham Rd; ***tube*** *South Kensington.*
French fashion for pregnant women.

Jerry's Home Store J17
163–7 Fulham Rd; ***tube*** *South Kensington.*
American goods and food: shiny chrome blenders and authentic brownie mixes.

Jo Malone K16
154 Fulham Rd, ***w*** *www.jomalone .co.uk;* ***tube*** *South Kensington.*
Her own range of expensive toiletries from the queen of the facial.

Maman Deux K15
79 Walton St; ***tube*** *South Kensington.*
For the street-smart baby.

The Ringmaker J17
191–3 Fulham Rd; ***tube*** *South Kensington.*
Huge jeweller's with stylish designs.

Elizabeth Street

This short street in Belgravia is fantastic for shoppers with luxury tastes and a dislike of crowds.

Even if you can't quite affor d to splash out, it's the perfect street to windowshop, with wonderful delis and chocolate shops, as well as exclusive hat shops and chi chi designers all nudged up together with villagey cosiness.

Ben de Lisi O16
40 Elizabeth St; tube/train Victoria.
Cashmere, sequins and velvet transform simple creations into something really special. One of the most sought-after designers around.

The Chocolate Society O16
36 Elizabeth St, w www.chocolate .co.uk; tube/train Victoria.
Every chocaholic's dream – the homemade ice cream is out of this world.

Philip Treacy N16
69 Elizabeth St, w www. philip treacey.co.uk; tube/train Victoria.
Perhaps the best-known hat-maker in the world – Madonna wore one of his creations to the 2001 Grammy awards.

Poilane O16
46 Elizabeth St; tube/train Victoria.
New outpost of the chi chi French baker and delicatessen.

Covent Garden

Apart from the market, there are many shops that make this a rewarding area. Neal St, Seven Dials and the streets radiating from it, Thomas Neal's Arcade, Long Acre, New Row and the streets around the market are the places to head for.

The Africa Centre U9
38 King St; tube Covent Garden.
African crafts and a restaurant-café (see p.323).

The Astrology Shop T8
78 Neal St; tube Covent Garden.
Have your personal horoscope done; also books, CDs and astro-logical objects.

Camper U9
39 Floral St; tube Covent Garden.
Part of the Spanish chain. Trendy, quirky and affordable.

Crime in Store T8
4 Bedford St, w www.crimein store.com; tube Covent Garden.
Specialist crime and mystery bookshop, including many titles unavailable elsewhere in Britain.

Culpeper Herbalists U9
8 The Market; tube Covent Garden.
Herbs, spices, bath salts and pot pourri, mostly taken from home-grown sources.

Dr Martens Department Store U9
1–4 King St, w www.drmartens .com; tube Covent Garden.
Four floors of DMs for men, women and children; also sells clothing.

Dress Circle T9
57 Monmouth St, w www.dress circle.co.uk; tube Covent Garden.
'The greatest showbiz shop in the world,' they claim, with sheet music, scores, books, posters and CDs.

Duffer of St George T8
29 Shorts Gardens, w www.the dufferofstgeorge.com; tube Covent Garden.
Very trendy menswear store, selling street- and clubwear.

Face Stockholm T10
5 New Row, w www.facestockholm .com; tube Leicester Square.
Fantastic range of mid-priced pampering and beauty products from a Swedish mother and daughter team. Elegant, mini-malist packaging.

Gold Kiosk T10
St Martin's Lane Hotel, w www .goldkiosk.com; tube Leicester Square.
A Philip Starck-designed frosted-glass box, this gift shop has everything from sweets and mags (all very stylish, of course) to designer clothing and jewellery.

Jones T9
13 Floral St, w www.jones-clothing.co.uk; tube Covent Garden.
At the cutting edge of fashion for men; established and up-and-coming labels.

Koh Samui T9
65 Monmouth St; tube Covent Garden, Leicester Square.
This is a wonderful boutique which stocks colourful, feminine clothes from a range of labels.

Muji T9
39 Shelton St and branches, w www.muji.co.jp; tube Covent Garden.
Minimalist Japanese store selling kitchen equipment and stationery.

Neal Street East U9
5 Neal St; tube Covent Garden.
An oriental emporium of books, clothes and home-decorating ideas.

Neal's Yard Dairy T8
17 Shorts Gardens; tube Covent Garden.
More than 70 varieties of cheese, matured and served with love.

Neal's Yard Remedies T8
15 Neal's Yard; tube Covent Garden.
Lots of oils and homoeopathic remedies, all very natural.

Neal's Yard Wholefood Warehouse T8
Off Shorts Gardens; tube Covent Garden.
Organic everything.

Nicole Farhi U9
12 Long Acre and Unit 4, East Piazza; tube Covent Garden.
Stylish, elegant women's clothes.

Oasis U9
13 James St and branches, w www.oasis-stores.com; tube Covent Garden.
Fashionable womenswear at reasonable prices.

Ordning & Reda T10
21 New Row, w www.ordning reda.com; tube Covent Garden.
Stylish, colourful, Swedish-designed stationery and office accessories.

Paul Smith U9
40–44 Floral St, Covent Garden, w www.paulsmith.com; tube Covent Garden.
High-class gloss on the bovver-boy look. Mostly for men, but there is now a women's collection.

Penhaligon's U9
*41 Wellington St, w www
.penhaligons.co.uk; tube Covent
Garden.*
Own-brand *eau de toilette* and
other fragrances, some packaged
in beautiful stoppered glass jars.
Also delicious air freshener sprays.

Ray's Jazz Shop S9
*180 Shaftesbury Av; tube Leicester
Square.*
Old classic LPs and new CDs: jazz
and blues.

Sam Walker T8
*27 Shorts Gardens; tube Covent
Garden.*
Vintage clothing for men.

Segar & Snuff Parlour U9
The Market; tube Covent Garden.
A tiny shop selling pipes, lighters,
and hand-rolled cigars from Cuba.

Stanfords S9
*12–14 Long Acre, w www.stanfords
.co.uk; tube Covent Garden,
Leicester Square.*
Map specialist. Also travel guides,
travel literature and walking
guides.

The Tea House T9
15A Neal St; tube Covent Garden.
All kinds of teas from around the
world: herbal, green, organic
and fruit.

Uth U9
9–10 Floral St; tube Covent Garden.
Slick, quirky urban fashion for men
and women.

Markets

Street markets are where the
city comes alive, showing off the
vitality and variety of the neighbourhoods lucky enough to have
them. Some, such as Covent
Garden and Portobello, are
described in the main sections of
this book; what follows is a list of
what to expect and details of
opening hours.

**Bermondsey Antiques
Market** Off maps
*Bermondsey Square; tube Borough.
Held Fri 6–8am.*
Antiques, junk, knick knacks and a
seriously good silver collection.
Apparently, it's the only place in

London where you can legally flog
stolen goods for a couple of hours
before dawn. Makes an entertaining morning when combined
with a trip to Borough Market.

Berwick Street R8–9
*Soho; tube Oxford Circus,
Tottenham Court Rd. Held Mon–
Sat around 9am–4pm, with
lunchtime closing on Wed.*
Outstanding fruit and veg.
See p.134.

Borough Market BB11–12
*Stoney St, off Borough High St;
tube/train London Bridge. Farmer's
market Fri noon–6pm, Sat
9am–4pm; some stalls and fruit
and veg Thurs noon–6pm.*
A wide array of small, mainly
organic, food-producers gathered
together underneath a delicate
Victorian wrought-iron canopy.
Close by is the spectacular Neal's
Yard Dairy cheese shop, Konditor
and Cooke's fine pâtisserie, and
the Borough Café, probably the
best café in all of London.
Fantastic.

Brick Lane Off maps
*Whitechapel; tube Aldgate East,
Shoreditch. Held Sun dawn–noon.*
Brick Lane is now so hip that this
market isn't the place it was. In
the centre, it's almost impossible
to rummage and come up with a
bargain. But, if you stick to the
outskirts of the market, you'll
come across a few East End
barrows trying to offload their
junk, especially furniture and old
books. Keep a hard nose and you
might haggle a bargain.

Brixton Off maps
*Electric Av; tube Brixton.
Held Mon–Sat, with lunchtime
closing on Wed.*
London's biggest Caribbean
market, with music, exotic
vegetables, goat's meat and
wafting spices.

Camden Lock Off maps
*Between Camden High St and
Chalk Farm Rd; tube Camden Town,
Chalk Farm. Some stalls and shops
open Mon–Fri 9.30am–5.30pm, but
the best time to visit is Sat and Sun
10am–6pm.*

A weekend institution, with an
array of books, clothes, records
and assorted antiques by the
canal. Huge crowds guarantee a
festive atmosphere, and there are
lots of excellent refreshments on
hand. *See p.235.*

Camden Passage Off maps
*Islington; tube Angel. Antiques
shops and stalls best visited Wed
10am–2pm or Sat 10am–5pm.
Farmers' market held Sun am.*
High-class antiques market in a
quiet street next to the bustle of
Upper St. *See p.236.*

Chapel Market Off maps
*Islington; tube Angel. Held Tues–
Sun, with lunchtime closing Thurs
and Sun.*
An exuberant North London food
market, with excellent fish and, as
a sideline, lots of household goods
and cheap clothes.

**Columbia Road
Flower Market** Off maps
*Off Hackney Rd about three-
quarters of a mile north of
Liverpool St Station; tube Liverpool
St. Held Sun 8am–1pm.*
A wide range of cut flowers and
pot plants. The shops on the street
offer homemade bread and farm-
house cheeses. *See p.271.*

Earlham St T9
*Earlham St, between Shaftesbury
Av and Seven Dials; tube Covent
Garden. Held Mon–Sat 10am–4pm.*
Extraordinary flowers, and
secondhand clothes.

Greenwich Off maps
*College Approach; train Greenwich;
DLR Cutty Sark. Held Sat and Sun
9am–5pm.*
Lots of crafts, books, furniture
and coins and medals. Worth
a detour.

Petticoat Lane Off maps
*Middlesex St, Whitechapel;
tube/train Liverpool St. Held Sun
9am–2pm.*
Leather, cheap fashion and household goods at London's most
famous Sunday market. Look out
for the jellied eel and whelk sellers
on the fringes. *See p.269.*

Portobello Road B8–C10
*Notting Hill; **tube** Ladbroke Grove. **Antiques market held** Sat 7am–5.30pm; **fruit and vegetable market held** Mon–Wed, Fri and Sat 9am–5pm, Thurs 9am–1pm.*
Perhaps the most atmospheric market in London. The southern end is stuffed with antique dealers, while the northern end is a mixed bag of design shops, cafés, food stalls, jewellery stands, record stores and more. *See p.244.*

St James's R11
*St James's Churchyard, Piccadilly; **tube** Piccadilly Circus. **Held** Tues–Sun 10am–6pm.*
Lots of books, old prints, coins and medals on a Tuesday, and ethnic crafts the rest of the time.

South Bank W11
*Riverside Walk, in front of the NFT; **tube/train** Waterloo. **Held** Sat and Sun.*
Secondhand books and prints along the riverside, open rain or shine.

Sports and
Green Spaces

The English have a peculiar knack for inventing games and then failing dismally at them in international competition. Football (soccer, not the US variety), tennis and cricket all originated on the fields and meadows of merry England; nowadays, though, all the country seems to produce is an endless string of plucky, or not so plucky, losers. The only sports in which the British really dominate internationally are darts and snooker – both about as far away from real exercise as you can get.

London is nevertheless rich in sports facilities and venues thanks to its extensive parkland and plentiful supply of reservoirs and lakes. It boasts several first-rate venues, including Twickenham for rugby, Crystal Palace for athletics, Lord's and the Oval for cricket, and Wimbledon for tennis. The famous football ground at Wembley has been demolished and plans for the stadium's replacement are unclear as controversy continues to dog the project. London has 11 professional soccer teams, roughly six of them in the top division. It has two major cricket teams, Middlesex and Surrey, and any number of rugby sides.

The number of last resort you should call with any sporting query, whether for participation or spectating, is **Sportsline** on **t** (020) 7222 8000.

Spectator Sports

Athletics

Crystal Palace Stadium Off maps
Near Sydenham, **t** *(020) 8778 0131,* **w** *www.runtrackdir.com/uk/ london(cp).htm;* **train** *Crystal Palace (from Victoria).*
Major meetings take place here in southeast London.

Boxing

There's plenty of boxing through the year at the **Royal Albert Hall** (**t** *(020) 7589 8212,*
w *www.royalalberthall.com*) and the **London Arena** (**t** *(020) 7538 1212,* **w** *www.londonarena.co.uk*); otherwise you could try the East End Club at **York Hall** (*Old Ford Road, Bethnal Green,* **t** *(020) 8980 2243*).

Cricket

A game surely invented to be incomprehensible to the uninitiated, cricket incites great passions in its most ardent fans and sheer tedium in everyone else. Games last at least a day, and at international level can go on for five days, with no guarantee of an outcome. The rules defy description, at least on paper. Atmosphere's the thing, and a visit usually provides plenty of good drink and conversation as well as an introduction to the world of silly mid-offs, googlies and short legs.

During international matches (called Test matches) you will hear people in parks and bars listening avidly to the ball-by-ball commentary on BBC radio. Cricket unseen is even more abstracted than the real thing, but at least the commentators show a certain potty enthusiasm and good humour. Most of the time they pore over old statistics and thank kindly listeners who have sent them fruitcakes.

Lord's Off maps
St John's Wood Rd, **t** *(020) 7289 1611,* **w** *www.cricket.org;* **tube** *St John's Wood. To book a* **tour**, *call the MCC at* **t** *(020) 7432 1033,* **f** *(020) 7266 3825,* **e** *tours@mcc .org.uk, or write to Lord's Tour Office, Lord's Ground, London NW8 8QN.*
The most famous cricket venue in the world, and home to the original governing body of the sport, the Marylebone Cricket Club, as well as the local side, Middlesex. The MCC Museum is located here; *see* p.234.

The Oval Off maps
Kennington, **t** *(020) 7582 6660;* **tube** *Oval.*
Home to Surrey. Usually hosts the last Test match of the summer.

Greyhound Racing

The ultimate working-class pastime was once to go to the dog races at the weekend – but the sport's now very popular with everyone. The dogs chase a dummy rabbit round the track while the betting punters look on between rounds of beer. One of the most famous venues is at Walthamstow in northeast London (**t** *(020) 8531 4255,* **w** *www.wsgreyhound.co.uk*). You won't catch the Ascot crowd there.

Horse-racing

All the following racecourses (apart from Ascot) can be contacted on the United Racecourses Hotline number: **t** *(01372) 470047.*

The closest race courses are at **Sandown Park** in Esher, Surrey; **Kempton Park** near Hampton Court (**w** *www.kempton.co.uk*); **Epsom**, also in Surrey and venue for the Derby in early June (**w** *www.epsomderby.co.uk*); and **Ascot** in Berkshire (**t** *(01344) 622211,* **w** *www.ascot.co.uk*), where the Queen turns up along with cohorts of aristocratic horse-lovers for the Royal meeting in June.

Rugby

Rougher and more complex than soccer, rugby football involves hand as well as foot contact and is played with an ovoid ball.

International fixtures are held at Twickenham in southwest London (*see* below). Not far away are the home grounds of two of the best London sides, **Harlequins** (*Stoop Memorial Ground, Craneford Way, Twickenham,* **t** *(020) 8410 6000*) and **London Wasps** (*Loftus Rd Stadium, South Africa Rd, Shepherd's Bush, W12 7PA,* **t** *(020) 8743 0262*).

The Rugby Football
Museum Off maps
Rugby Rd Stadium, Twickenham,
***t** (020) 8892 2000;* **train** *Twicken-
ham (from Waterloo or Victoria);
wheelchair accessible.* **Open** *Tues–
Sat 10am–5pm, Sun 2–5pm, on
match days 11am until kick-off and
for one hour after the game;*
***adm** £4, concessions £3, joint price
for museum and stadium tour,
adults £6, concessions £4, families
£19.* **Guided tours** *four times daily;
book in advance on **t** (020) 8892
8877.*
Offers guided tours of the
changing rooms and field, a
history of the game and an array
of trophies.

Soccer

Soccer is the English national
obsession, with a season lasting
from mid-August through to May.
The best place for a foreigner to
start watching is probably on television, where you get a feel for not
only the game but also the peculiar mixture of national pride,
mixed metaphor and self-
derision displayed by the
commentators.

Traditionally the two strongest
London sides are **Arsenal** (*Avenell
Rd, Highbury, **t** (020) 7704 4000*)
and **Spurs**, or Tottenham Hotspur
(*White Hart Lane, Tottenham,
t (020) 8365 5050*). London is still
waiting for an international
football stadium to replace
Wembley.

Tours
Chelsea FC Off maps
*Stamford Bridge, Fulham Rd, SW6
1HS, **t** (020) 7385 0710; **tube** Fulham
Broadway.*
Tours take place at the week-
ends except during school
holidays.

West Ham United FC Off maps
*Green St, Upton Park, E13 9AZ,
t (020) 8548 2707; **tube** Upton
Park.*
The home of the Hammers. Tours
held on the first Thursday of each
month.

Stock-car Racing

Wimbledon Stadium Off maps
*Plough Lane, Wimbledon, SW17,
t (020) 8946 8000, **e** info@
spedeworth.co.uk; **w** www
.spedeworth.co.uk; **tube**
Wimbledon.*
Stock-car racing – including
Bangers, Hot Rods, Superstox and
Stock Cars. Firework shows and
demolition derbys.

Tennis

**Stella Artois
Tournament** Off maps
*Queen's Club, Palliser Rd, London
W14, **t** (020)7 3853421; **tube** Barons
Court.*
Easier to get tickets for than
Wimbledon, and many of the top
names turn up.

**Wimbledon
Championships** Off maps
*All England Lawn Tennis Club,
Church Rd, SW19, **t** (020) 8944
1066, **w** www.wimbledon.org;
tube Southfields; wheelchair
accessible.*
The Wimbledon lawn tennis
championships take place in the
last week of June and the first
week of July. You'll need to apply
nine months in advance for a seat
on the Centre Court or Number
One Court – they are allocated by
ballot. However, if you turn up
early in the competition you'll see
plenty of action on the outside
courts, and can enjoy strawberries
and cream under the pale
English sun.

**Wimbledon Lawn Tennis
Museum** Off maps
*Address as above, **t** (020) 8946
6131, **w** www.wimbledon.org/
museum. **Open** Tues–Sat 10.30am–
5pm, Sun 2–5pm; closed 1 Jan, Good
Fri, 25 Dec and during championships exc. to ticketholders;
adm adults £5.50, concessions
£4.50, 5–16s £3.50.*
Tells the history of the famous
tennis tournament, including the
quantity of strawberries
consumed by spectators and the
ever-changing fashion in

hemlines; also has a video gallery
replaying great moments of the
past. A visit can include an individual tour of the grounds (*adults
£12.75, concessions £11.75, 5–16s
£10.75*). Otherwise, group tours are
held daily between 29 March and
15 Sept (*closed between 5 June and
15 July for the tournament*); phone
to book.

Activities

Boating

**Regent's Park
Boating Lake** L3–N5
***t** (020) 7486 4759.*
Rent a boat during the summer
and idle away a few hours on
either the large adult or the tiny
children's lake between the
Inner and the Outer Circle of
Regent's Park. Cheap and
wonderful.

Dance and
Performance Arts

For full listings of dance classes
– you'll find everything from salsa
and tango to street dance and
ballet – check *Time Out*, available
from all newsagents.

The Circus Space Off maps
*Coronet St, Hoxton, N1, **t** (020) 7613
4141, **w** www.thecircusspace.co.uk;
tube Old St.*
Mainly for adults. Learn to walk on
stilts, fly on a trapeze, clowning
and acrobalance.

Danceworks N9
*16 Balderton St, **t** (020) 7629 6183;
tube Bond St.*
High teaching standards, with
entrance fees for any time from an
hour to a year.

Pineapple T9
*7 Langley St, **t** (020) 7836 4004;
tube Covent Garden.*
Another first-class dance studio
for all categories.

Go-karting

For a comprehensive list of
tracks around London, visit
w *www.karting.co.uk.*

Dayton Indoor Karts Off maps
*Union Gate, Atlas Rd, Park Royal,
NW10 6DN,* **t** *0500 145 155,* **t** *(020)
8961 3617,* **e** *sales@daytona.co.uk,*
w *www.daytona.co.uk;*
tube *Willesden Junction.*
Popular indoor karting track.

F1 City Off maps
*Gate 119, Connaught Bridge, Royal
Victoria Dock, E16 2BS,* **t** *(020) 7476
5678,* **t** *(020) 7476 3456,* **e** *sales@
f1city.co.uk,* **w** *www.f1city.co.uk;*
DLR *Silvertown.*
Three outdoor tracks; 500m, 550m
and 1000m circuits; and 45mph
and 75mph high-performance
karts.

Golf

There are courses at Richmond
and all around the outskirts of
town. For more information, visit
w *www.thelondongolfer.com,*
which has a comprehensive list of
greens around London. Call first to
check that they accept non-
members or people without proof
of handicap.

Gyms

Many London clubs charge an
annual membership, so are
impractical for visitors. All London
boroughs have (much cheaper)
public sports centres – ask
Sportsline (*see* p.375) for your
nearest one, or try:

**Britannia Leisure
Centre** Off maps
40 Hyde Rd, Hackney, N1, **t** *(020)
7729 4485;* **tube** *Old St.*
Rock-climbing wall, sports courts,
circuit classes, pool with wave
machine.

Cally Pool Off maps
239 Caledonian Rd, **t** *(020) 7278
1890,* **w** *www.aquaterra.org;* **tube**
Caledonian Rd, King's Cross.
Large pool plus training and baby
pools. There's also a gym with
sauna and sunbeds.

Chelsea Sports Centre K18
Chelsea Manor St, **t** *(020) 7352
6985;* **tube** *Sloane Square, South
Kensington.*

Offers everything from
badminton to yoga, via canoeing,
netball and sub-aqua.

The Oasis T8
32 Endell St, **t** *(020) 7831 1804;*
tube *Covent Garden.*
With an open-air swimming pool
which is even popular in winter
among stalwarts.

**Queen Mother
Sports Centre** Q16
223 Vauxhall Bridge Rd, **t** *(020)
7630 5522;* **tube** *Victoria.*

Horse-riding

**Battersea Park Equestrian
Centre** Off maps
14A Winders Rd, SW11 **t** *(020) 7350
0419;* **train** *Clapham Junction.*
Riding in Battersea Park.

Hyde Park Livery Stables H15
11 Elvaston Mews, SW7, **t** *(020) 7823
7300;* **tube** *Gloucester Rd.*
Riding in Hyde Park.

Hyde Park Stables I9
63 Bathurst Mews, W2, **t** *(020) 7723
2813;* **tube** *Lancaster Gate.*
Riding in Hyde Park.

**Wimbledon Village
Stables** Off maps
24A High St, Wimbledon, SW19,
t *(020) 8946 8579;* **tube/train**
Wimbledon.
Good for beginners, with the
whole of Wimbledon Common
and Richmond Park in which to
roam free.

Ice Skating

Broadgate Ice Rink DD7
Broadgate Circle, **t** *(020) 7505
7608,* **w** *www.broadgateestates
.co.uk/ice/introduction.htm;*
tube *Liverpool St.* **Open** *Oct–April.*
Tiny outdoor ice rink, with
Christmas trees and fairy lights.

Queens Ice Skating Club F10
17 Queensway, W2, **t** *(020) 7229
0172;* **tube** *Queensway.*
Lessons, ice discos and more at
London's most famous club.

**Somerset House Open-air
Ice Rink** V9–10
Somerset House, The Strand,
t *(020) 7845 4600,* **w** *www*

*.somerset-house.org.uk/attractions/
icerink/index.html.* **Book** *well in
advance for tickets.*
Beautiful outdoor ice rink in the
courtyard of Somerset House.

Jogging

Hyde Park, St James's Park,
Regent's Park, Primrose Hill,
Battersea Park and Hampstead
Heath (*see* below for all parks) are
all great for jogging. Otherwise,
jog beside the river along the
Thames Path, or along the canal
between Little Venice and
King's Cross.

Sailing and
Watersports

**Docklands Watersports
Club** Off maps
*Tereza Joanne (name of the boat),
Gate 14, King George V Dock,
Woolwich Manor Way, E16,* **t** *(020)
7511 7000,* **w** *www.tereza-
joanne.com;* **DLR** *to Galleon's
Reach, or* **tube** *to Canning town,
then bus 474.*
Wet-biking and jet-skiing. Boat for
hire for functions.

**Shadwell Basin Outdoor
Activity Centre** Off maps
3–4 Shadwell Rd, Wapping, E1,
t *(020) 7481 4210,* **w** *www
.shadwell-basin.org;* **tube** *Wapping.*
Canoeing, dragon-boating, sub-
aqua and fishing, plus sailing
courses.

Shoal Divers Q16
*Queen Mother Sports Centre, 223
Vauxhall Bridge Rd,* **t** *(020) 7630
5522;* **tube** *Victoria.*
Scuba-diving courses in the river.

**Surrey Docks Watersports
Centre** Off maps
t *(020) 7237 5555;* **tube** *Canada
Water, then 5-minute walk.*
Sailing, windsurfing, canoeing
and sub-aqua in Docklands. A
surprisingly attractive venue.

Skiing

For complete listings of dry
slopes in the London area, visit
w *www.dryslope.co.uk.*

Alexandra Palace Ski Centre Off maps
Alexandra Park, N22, t (020) 8888 2284; tube Wood Green; train Alexandra Palace (from Moorgate).
Call for details.

Beckton Alps Off maps
Alpine Way, E6, t (020) 7511 0351, w www.becktonalps.co.uk; DLR Beckton.
Don't laugh: the former chemical waste dump in Beckton in Docklands has been sealed and converted into a 200m dry ski slope called the Beckton Alps.

Snooker

Centre Point Snooker Club S8
Centre Point, New Oxford St, t (020) 7240 6886; tube Tottenham Court Rd.
Open all day and most of the night.

Squash

Almost impossible to play without joining a private club. If you know a member or are staying long enough to make it worth joining, try **Cannon Sports Club** next to Cannon St Station in the City (**t** (020) 7283 0101), **Lambs Squash Club** by the Barbican (**t** (020) 7638 3811), or the **South Bank Squash Club** (124 Wandsworth Rd, **t** (020) 7622 6866), which has 11 courts. Or try:

Dolphin Square Apart-hotel Complex R18
Chichester St, Pimlico, t (020) 7798 8686. Sessions cost £8 for 30mins and £15 for one hour.
There are 5 courts here and membership is not necessary

Swimming

The foolhardy can break the ice on the Serpentine on New Year's Day; the rest of us choose from public pools run by each borough (ask Sportsline for your nearest one) or clubs like The Oasis (*see* 'Gyms', above).

But there are some superb outdoor venues for summer, notably the Bathing Ponds on

Hampstead Heath (*see* p.242). Council-run lidos worth trying are at Bankside, Tooting, Brixton and Parliament Hill (lidos are large unheated open-air pools, usually built in the 1930s).

Tennis

There are courts in virtually every London park – check with Sportsline for details and booking procedure. Battersea Park has some of the cheapest courts, while Holland Park has the smartest. Most charge a membership fee, but this may entitle you to play at other London venues. Often you have to book in person. Give up all thoughts of playing at Wimbledon, unless you have lots of money, impeccable connections and plenty of time for your membership to be considered.

Ten-pin Bowling

Rowans Off maps
10 Stroud Green Rd, t (020) 8800 1950; tube Finsbury Park.
For a little late-night exercise.

Yoga and Pilates

Breathe Off maps
13 Cranhurst Rd, t (020) 8452 8322, t 07977 451 574, e info@breathe online.com, w www.breatheon line.com; tube Willesden Green.
Astanga vinyasa yoga, dynamic or gentle hatha yoga, yoga for kids and pre- and post-natal yoga taught for all levels in classes or privately to individuals or small groups.

Iyengar Yoga Institute Off maps
223A Randolph Av, W9, t (020) 7624 3080, w www.iyi.org.uk; tube Maida Vale.
More than 50 classes a week to all levels.

TriYoga Off maps
6 Erskine Rd, Primrose Hill, t (020) 7483 33 44, w www.triyoga.co.uk; tube Chalk Farm.
Offers massage and holistic treatments as well as yoga and pilates.

The Yoga Place Off maps
Ist floor, 449–553 Bethnal Green Rd, E2, t (020) 7739 5195, w www .yogaplace.co.uk; tube Bethnal Green.
Yoga classes, courses and workshops; all levels.

Green Spaces

Parks

Alexandra Park Off maps
Tube Wood Green; train Alexandra Palace (from Moorgate).
The park at the northeastern end of Muswell Hill contains Alexandra Palace, the reconstructed hall from the ill-fated second Great Exhibition of 1862, but much rebuilt since because of fire. It is used as a cultural and sports centre, and has fine views over the North London townscape.

Battersea Park Off maps
t (020) 8871 0530; train Battersea Park (from Victoria).
Battersea park sits right next to the river and is a favourite with kids. There's a small zoo (*see* p.384), an adventure playground, and a boating lake. Grown-ups will like the art exhibitions at the Pump House (**t** (020) 7350 0523), elegant gardens and roseries, overlooked by the graceful Peace Pagoda, donated by Japanese monks in 1985. Sports facilities include tennis courts, a running track, and an all-weather pitch.

Chelsea Physic Garden L19–20
Tube Sloane Square.
See p.248.

Clapham Common Off maps
Tube Clapham Common.
Clapham Common is a flat green expanse surrounded by huge mansions, dotted with three small ponds and not much else. It may be fairly modest by the standards of some London parks, but it's a big favourite with locals. There are always plenty of families out for a picnic, one or two games of football or rounders being played, and lots of walkers out with their dogs. There are a couple of netball

courts and a bandstand, but little in the way of sports facilities.

Green Park O12–Q13
Tube Green Park.
See p.118.

Greenwich Park Off maps
***DLR/train** Greenwich.*
See p.264.

Hampstead Heath Map p.284
***Train** Hampstead Heath, Gospel Oak; **tube** Hampstead.*
Hampstead is London's wildest park; it's occasionally possible to forget you are even in a city as you scramble between huge oak trees and down brambly tracks. Parts – especially the West Heath – are notorious gay cruising areas, but the cruisers are pretty much invisible by day. Hill Garden is a lovely, forested walk, and knobbly Parliament Hill is great for kite-flying. There are three swimming ponds (one for each gender and one mixed), where you can swim in the murk with the ducks, and lots of sports facilities including a running track, tennis courts, a lido and a bowling green near the Gospel Oak end of the park. On a slope overlooking the Heath is the elegant Kenwood House, with a placid lake and huge, grassy gardens. Concerts are held here in the summer (*see p.241*).

Highbury Fields Off maps
***Tube/train** Highbury and Islington.*
Highbury Fields are surprisingly small. Surrounded by trees and grand Islington houses, they make a useful and attractive spot to walk the dog. There are a couple of tennis courts and a swimming pool.

Highgate Wood and Queen's Wood Off maps
***Tube** Highgate.*
At the north end of Highgate, up the hill from the Tube station, these two enchanting woods are relics of the forests that once covered the whole of North London. There is an excellent café in Highgate Wood, and a good children's playground.

Holland Park B12–C14
Tube Holland Park.
Holland Park turns reality on its head: it seems much bigger, much wilder, much more remote than it really is. Covering only about 40 acres (a fraction of the size of Kensington Gardens, for example), it feels like something out of a magical children's story, a maze of winding paths, wooded hide-aways, rolling fields and formal gardens, with wild flowers, birds and even the odd peacock. The park is what remains of the estate of Holland House, a grand Jacobean mansion devastated beyond recognition during the Second World War, which survives only in truncated form, about two-thirds of the way down towards Kensington High St. It was taken over after the war by the municipal authorities, who preserved what they could of the house and opened the park to the public. You can see some of the ground-floor stonework of the original building, but little else. The east wing has been entirely rebuilt as a youth hostel (a wonderful place to stay if you are a student), while part of the ruined main house has been converted into an open-air theatre with an eclectic summer season of plays, concerts and opera (*see p.357*). Around the house to the north is a series of formal gardens, including the peaceful Kyoto Garden with its still lake and lawns lined with gentle blooms. On the south side is a terrace café overlooking a cricket pitch and tennis courts – this is where David Hemmings played metaphysical tennis with mime artists in Antonioni's *Blow Up*.

Hyde Park J10–N12
Tube Hyde Park Corner, Marble Arch, Lancaster Gate, Knightbridge.
See p.196.

Kensington Gardens E10–I13
Tube Queensway, Lancaster Gate.
See p.195.

Kenwood Map p.284
Tube Highgate, then bus 210.
See p.241.

Kew Gardens Off maps
Train Kew Gardens.
See p.251.

Little Venice Off maps
Tube Warwick Av.
See p.246.

Marble Hill Off maps
Train Richmond, then walk.
See p.254.

Parliament Hill Map p.284
Train Hampstead Heath.
See p.242.

Primrose Hill Off maps
Tube Chalk Farm, then 5-minute walk.
Primrose Hill is a favourite with Londoners. It's a smallish park, criss-crossed with walkways, and divided from Regent's Park by a canal and a road. It's set on a hill, from the top of which you can get some of the best views of the city's skyline in London. There are a couple of flat stretches which are good for a game of rounders in the summer, and behind the hill is a pretty enclave of ice-cream-colloured houses, pubs, teashops and restaurants.

Queen Mary's Rose Garden N4
Tube Regent's Park, Baker St.
See p.182.

Regent's Canal K3–M1
The Regent's Canal goes through the lower end of St John's Wood and the north side of Regent's Park, running from Paddington and Little Venice and heading off, via some underground sections, towards Camden and Islington. The whole expanse winds through some attractive residential districts, and you will see brightly decorated barges, tugs, houseboats and pleasure boats. To take a boat trip yourself, contact one of the private boating companies such as the London Waterbus Company (*t (020) 7482 2660*), which runs services April–Oct on the hour from 10am–5pm between Little Venice (*tube Warwick Av*) and Camden Lock (*tube Camden Town*). During Nov–March the service is restricted to Sat and Sun 10am–3pm.

Follow the canal on foot through Regent's Park, ducking under bridges and passing the tennis courts and jogging tracks used by the residents of the imposing 19th- and early 20th-century mansions on Prince Albert Rd.

Regent's Park K1–O5
Tube Regent's Park, Baker St.
See p.180.

St James's Park Q13
Tube St James's Park.
See p.118.

Syon Park Off maps
Tube Gunnersbury, then bus 237 or 267; *train* Kew Bridge, then bus 237 or 267.
See p.250.

Victoria Embankment Gardens U11–V10
Tube Temple.
See p.146.

Waterlow Park Map p.284
Tube Highgate.
See p.238.

Squares

Berkeley Square O–P10
Tube Piccadilly Circus.
This is perhaps Mayfair's most famous square, but it's been a long time since nightingales sang here – they have all been scared away by the traffic which blasts around the edge of the grassy plot at the centre.

Grosvenor Square N9–10
Tube Bond St.
Perhaps the grandest square in Mayfair, this large grassy square is surrounded by palatial white mansions and the US embassy. Roosevelt surveys the picnickers with disdain from his plinth in the centre of the park.

Hanover Square P9
Tube Oxford Circus.
This is a perfect retreat from the crowds on Oxford St; tall shady trees (watch out for the one infested by pigeons – easy to spot, as it's the only one with no one sitting beneath it), benches, lovely rose gardens and a great view of Vogue House, where fashionistas can catch up on the latest trends by watching the Vogue girls leave for lunch at 1pm.

St James's Square R11
Tube Piccadilly Circus.
This quiet, elegant 18th-century square in the heart of Clubland is home to several of London's most exlusive clubs, as well as its most eccentric library (members only). The patch of grass in the middle has a sprinkling of benches shaded by trees, and it's fun to watch the aristocracy tottering off to their clubs for the first sherry of the day.

Soho Square S8
Tube Leicester Square, Tottenham Court Rd.
This little square is a pocket of green in the heart of Soho, with a gabled hut in the centre and a few rose bushes. It comes into its own in summer, when it gets crammed with office workers and runners from the nearby film studios enjoying picnic lunches and a spot of sunshine.

Children's London

Children have traditionally come somewhere beneath dogs and horses on the scale of human affection in England. The Edwardian short-story writer Saki frequently depicted them as malicious pests, while George Bernard Shaw – who admittedly had none of his own – compared them unfavourably to farmyard animals; chickens, he said, were at least cheaper to keep. A rather more progressive way of thinking has held sway in recent times, but still the prevailing view is that children should be neither seen nor heard in public. If some pubs, bars and restaurants now admit children, and even provide high chairs and nappy-changing facilities, it is often more out of a sense of obligation than any real enthusiasm. Nevertheless, there is plenty to keep children occupied and amused in London.

Look out for child reductions; anyone under 14 should qualify most of the time, and under-16s a fair lot. The transport network insists that 14- and 15-year-olds have a photo pass to qualify for child fares, so have passport photos and proof of age at the ready. Note that under-16s are not allowed to buy cigarettes, and that under-18s can't buy alcohol or consume it in public.

For much more on taking children around London, read Cadogan's *Take the Kids: London*.

Attractions and Museums

Children are a diverse bunch, and there is no reason why they shouldn't enjoy nearly all the adult sights recommended in the rest of this book. But among the most popular and absorbing sights for children are: the **Science Museum** (where they can even spend the night; see p.193), the **Natural History Museum** (see p.192), **Pollock's Toy Museum** (see p.174), the **Bethnal Green Museum of Childhood** (see p.270) and the **Theatre Museum** in Covent Garden (see p.141).

The **Tate Modern** (see p.205), **V&A** (see p.186), **Courtauld** (see p.150) and **National Gallery** (see p.103) all offer special workshops and tours for arty kids. Look out too for events at the **Museum of London** (see p.223), the **British Museum** (see p.166) and the **Horniman Museum** (see p.266), which all offer an impressive list of activities, workshops and courses for kids and young people.

Avoid such crowd-pullers as the **London Dungeon** (see p.259) and **Madame Tussaud's** (see p.179). The former is horribly inauthentic and overblown; queuing at the latter will try the patience of all the family to breaking point. For gore and ghoulishness, try instead **The Clink** in Southwark (see p.208) or the **Tower of London** (see p.229).

Note that children under 14 are not allowed into the Old Bailey, and that infants are barred from the Houses of Parliament.

Entertainment

Options are many: funfairs in the parks during the summer (see *Time Out* or ask in a tourist office for details); Punch and Judy shows at Covent Garden; children's films and theatre performances; and a daily schedule of sometimes first-rate children's television in the late afternoons on both BBC and ITV. At Christmas time there are pantomimes galore all over London, and you are sure to find a performance of *The Nutcracker* ballet.

Cinema Clubs

Barbican Centre AA–BB6
Silk St, t (020) 7382 7000, booking t (020) 7638 8891, w www .barbican.org.uk; tube Barbican.
Ages 5–12. Children's films; they also organize art workshops, story-telling and puppet shows.

BFI IMAX Cinema W12
Belvedere Rd, t (020) 7902 1234; tube Waterloo.

Clapham Picture House Off maps
76 Venn St, SW4, t (020) 7498 3323, w www.picturehouse-cinemas .co.uk; tube Clapham Common.
Saturday-morning screenings for families.

Everyman Hampstead Map p.284
5 Holly Bush Vale, NW3, t (020) 7435 1600, t 7431 1777, w www .everymancinema.com; tube Hampstead.
Saturday-morning screenings and workshops. For ages 8–12; under-8s with accompanying parents.

Junior NFT W11
National Film Theatre 2, BFI, South Bank Centre, t (020) 7928 3232, w www.bfi.org.uk; tube Waterloo.
Ages 5–11. Matinées for children are held on Saturdays at 3pm with accompanying workshops at 2pm.

Science Museum IMAX I15
Exhibition Rd, t 0870 870 4771, w www.sciencemuseum.org.uk; tube South Kensington; wheelchair accessible.

Tricycle Off maps
269 Kilburn High Rd, NW6, t (020) 7328 1000, w www.tricycle.co.uk; tube Kilburn.
Family cinema every Saturday at 1pm.

Theatre

Little Angel Theatre Off maps
14 Dagmar Passage, Islington, t (020) 7226 1787; tube Angel.
A delightful puppet theatre. Weekend performances at 11am and 3pm, plus holiday features. Over-4s only.

London Bubble
t (020) 7237 4434, w www.london bubble.org.uk.
A roving theatre company that performs in London's parks during summer. Plays for under-12s. Workshops for 3–6s.

Polka Adventure Theatre Off maps
240 The Broadway, Wimbledon, t (020) 8543 4888, w www.polkatheatre.com; tube/train Wimbledon.

A complex for under-13s including the main theatre (4 shows a day in holidays, 2 in term time), a playground, two shops with cheap toys, and an adventure room for under-5s.

Puppet Theatre Barge Off maps
Blomfield Rd, W9, **t** *(020) 7249 6876,* **w** *www.movingstage.co.uk;* **tube** *Warwick Av.*
An old working barge moored at Henley, Marlow and Richmond from June to October, and Little Venice in the winter, putting on high-quality shows.

Tricycle Off maps
269 Kilburn High Rd, NW6, **t** *(020) 7328 1000,* **w** *www.tricycle.co.uk;* **tube** *Kilburn.*
Around 300 workshops a year for all ages, in acting, puppetry, circus skills and more.

Theatre and TV Backstage Tours

Budding thesps or TV presenters might want to take a backstage tour of London's best-known theatres and TV centres.

BBC: Backstage tours of Television Centre Off maps
Wood Lane, W12 7RJ, advance booking **t** *0870 603 03 04;* **tube** *White City.*
For 14 years and over. For free audience tickets, call **t** (020) 8576 1227, **e** tv.ticket.unit@bbc.co.uk.

Royal Opera House U9
Covent Garden Piazza, **t** *(020) 7304 4000,* **w** *www.royalopera.org;* **tube** *Covent Garden.*
See p.143 for tour details.

Shakespeare's Globe AA11
21 New Globe Walk, **t** *(020) 7902 1500,* **w** *www.shakespeares-globe.org;* **tube** *Southwark.*
Runs guided tours between 9am and midday May–Sept, and daily 10am–5pm the rest of the year.

Sports and Activities

When museums and sight-seeing pall, take your kids out for a spin around a Go Kart track or an adventure park.

See also the 'Sports and Green Spaces' chapter, p.374.

Parks

The parks are of course great for children. They can swim and row on the Serpentine in **Hyde Park** (see p.196) and play in playgrounds in **Regent's Park** (see p.182) and **Kensington Gardens** (see p.195). They can fly kites and go on nature trails on **Hampstead Heath** (see p.242), and they can play mini-golf at **Alexandra Park** (see p.378). A number of parks, including **Battersea Park** (see p.378), **Holland Park** (see p.379) and Alexandra Park, have special play areas for the under-fives called One O'Clock Clubs, where your littl'uns will find sandpits, paddling pools, climbing frames and toys galore.

Sports Centres and Adventure Playgrounds

Most sports centres offer child-friendly activities. Good bets for kids include:

Burgess Community Playground Off maps
Albany Rd, Camberwell, SE5, **t** *(020) 7277 1371;* **tube** *Elephant and Castle;* **adm** *free.*
Indoor and outdoor adventure playground for kids aged 5–15. Swings, slides, sandpits, a football pitch and a small tennis court, table tennis, arts and crafts, cooking and basketball. Let your kids loose on the Kart Track (8–16-year-olds only); lessons for beginners.

Fantasy Island Playcentre Off maps
Vale Farm, Watford Rd, Wembley, Middx HA0 3HG, **t** *(020) 8904 9044;* **tube** *Wembley Central.*
A purpose-built adventureland with slides, rope bridge, climbing nets, ball pond, witch doctor's den and a monster serpent slide.

Kimber BMX/Adventure Playground Off maps
Kimber Rd, Southfields, SW18, **t** *(020) 8870 2168;* **tube** *Southfields.* **Adm** *free.*
Indoor and outdoor playground with a BMX track (bikes for hire), rope swings, monkey bars, a basketball court, table tennis, arts and crafts, and even a kitchen.

Theme Parks

Most of the theme parks in the following list are outside London (and off our maps), but they are all easily accessible by public transport.

Alton Towers Off maps
Alton, Staffordshire, ST10 4DB, **t** *(01538) 702 200,* **w** *www.alton-towers.co.uk;* **train** *Stoke-on-Trent then bus service.*
Possibly the UK's best-known theme park, with dozens of white-knuckle rides, but a 3hr journey.

Chessington World of Adventures Off maps
Leatherhead Rd, Chessington, Surrey, KT9 2NE, **t** *0870 444 7777,* **w** *www.chessington.com;* **train** *Chessington South then 10min walk.*
Nine theme lands and 15 rides, including the Vampire roller coaster, Dragon River Log Flume and Terrortomb Dark Ride.

Dreamland White Knuckle Theme Park Off maps
Belgrave House, Belgrave Rd, Margate, Kent, CT9 1XG, **t** *(01843) 227 011;* **train** *Margate.*
More than two dozen thrilling rides. Height restrictions apply.

Legoland Windsor Off maps
Windsor, Berkshire, SL4 4GP, booking **t** *08705 626 364, info* **t** *08705 626 375,* **w** *www.legoland.co.uk;* **train** *Windsor/Windsor and Eton Riverside, then shuttlebus.*
Huge, popular theme park; the new advance-booking system means that the park will never get too crowded.

Snakes and Ladders Off maps
Syon Park, Brentford, Middlesex, TW8 8JQ, **t** *(020) 8847 0946;*

tube Gunnersbury; **train** Syon Lane, Gunnersbury, Kew Bridge.
Slides, ropes, ball pond, climbing frame, roller skating (£1 extra), electric cars (50p extra).

Thorpe Park Off maps
Staines Rd, Chertsey, Surrey, KT16 8PN, **t** 0870 444 4466, **w** www .thorpepark.co.uk; **train** Staines, then shuttlebus.
Geared towards younger kids, this hasn't got much for over-12s.

City Farms and Zoos

Battersea Park Children's Zoo Off maps
Battersea Park, SW11, **t** (020) 8871 7540; **train** Battersea Park.
Home to Yum Yum the pot-bellied pig; there's also a reptile house, monkeys, flamingoes, ponies, deer and wallabies.

Crystal Palace Park Farm Off maps
Crystal Palace Park, SE20 8DT, **t** (020) 8778 9496; **train** Crystal Palace (from Victoria).
Free-roaming pigs, cows, goats, rabbits, chickens, donkeys, otters and sheep. Shire-horse cart rides around the park. The summer fair is best for under-7s.

Freightliners Farm Off maps
Sheringham Rd, N7 8PF, **t** (020) 7609 0467; **tube/train** Highbury and Islington.
Feed the sheep, cows, pigs, goats, ducks, geese and chickens, and explore the Sensory Garden.

London Butterfly House Off maps
Syon Park, Brentford, Middlesex, TW8 8JQ, **t** (020) 8560 0378; **tube** Gunnersbury; **train** Syon Lane, Gunnersbury, Kew Bridge.
Hundreds of free-flying butterflies in tropical greenhouse gardens and ponds, and an insect house full of creepie-crawlies.

London Zoo M–N1
Regent's Park, **t** (020) 7722 3333; **tube** Camden Town.
See p.181. Collect a daily events guide on your way in, to make sure you see the animals being fed.

Mudchute Farm Off maps
Pier St (off Manchester Rd), Isle of Dogs, E14 3HP, **t** (020) 7515 5901; **DLR** Mudchute.
Britain's largest city farm, with a working farm, wildlife area, horses, woodland and parkland.

Wetland Centre London Off maps
Queen Elizabeth's Walk, Barnes, SW13 **t** (020) 8409 4400, **e** info@ wetlandcentre.org.uk, **w** www.wet landcentre.org.uk; wheelchair accessible. **Open** summer daily 9.30am–6pm, winter daily 9.30am–5pm, last adm one hour before closing; **adm** adults £6.75, concessions £5.50, children £4, families £17.50; **tube** Hammersmith, then bus 283 or special Duck Bus; **train** Barnes, then 10min walk. **Café** and **shop**.
Built around some long-disused water reservoirs, the centre was the first created wetland habitat in any capital city. It's won a handful of awards for its thoughtful presentations, from the interactive computer exhibits in the Discovery Centre, to an observatory with great views out across the reservoirs. There are outdoor exhibition areas giving an insight into the creatures which inhabit wetlands, from the floodplains of Africa to the ponds of suburban England. Trails meander through the marshes, and budding twitchers might spot a bittern or a kingfisher – there are lists posted on the Web site each week of the birds spotted.

Tours

See also 'Guided Tours', p.71.

Jason's Canal Boat Trip
Opposite 60 Blomfield Rd, Little Venice, W9, **t** (020) 7286 3428; **tube** Warwick Av.
A 45min narrow boat cruise from Little Venice, past London Zoo, Primrose Hill and up to Camden Lock Market.

Star Safari
t (01932) 854 721.
A special walk past the homes of London's rich and famous.

Shopping

There's no lack of outlets in which to shop for kids: for most toy or clothing needs you should be satisfied by the many branches of the Early Learning Centre, Toys R Us or Next. As for shopping with kids, here are a few hardy perennials:

Benjamin Pollock's Toy Shop U9
44 Covent Garden Market, **w** www.pollocks-coventgarden .co.uk; **tube** Covent Garden.
Shop selling the famous toy theatres (see p.174).

Children's Book Centre D14
237 Kensington High St, **w** www.childrensbookcentre.co.uk; **tube** Kensington High St.
Just for kids. CD-Roms too.

Daisy & Tom's K18
181–3 King's Rd; **tube** Sloane Square.
A complete department store for kids: toys, books, even a hairdressers. Founded by Tim Waterstone, of bookshop fame.

The Disney Store R10
104 Regent St; **tube** Oxford Circus, Piccadilly Circus.

Hamley's Q9
188 Regent St, **w** www.hamleys .com; **tube** Oxford Circus, Piccadilly Circus.
One of the world's great toyshops: loads of puzzles, computer games, teddy bears and gadgets. The escalators alone can keep kids happy for hours. Lots of demos by staff.

Harrods L14
Old Brompton Rd, **w** www.harrods .com; **tube** Knightsbridge.
The Christmas window displays and the toy department on the fourth floor are both big draws.

Lego Kids Wear Q10
137 Regent St, W1, **w** www.lego .com; **tube** Oxford Circus.
Kids can play with the Lego while you rummage among the colourful clothes.

Warner Brothers Studio Store Q9
178–82 Regent St; **tube** *Oxford Circus, Piccadilly Circus.*

Eating

The following places cater for kids particularly well:

Belgo Centraal T9
50 Earlham St, **t** *(020) 7813 2233,* **w** *www.belgo-restaurants.com;* **tube** *Covent Garden.*
Laid-back Belgian chain with branches throughout London. Special colour-in 'Mini Belgo' menu for under-12s; children eat free (max two kids per adult) at any time.

Chicago Rib Shack L14
1 Raphael St, **t** *(020) 7581 5595;* **tube** *Knightsbridge.*
Balloons, activity menus, colouring books, and competitions for kids on Sunday lunchtimes.

Luna Nuova T8
22 Shorts Gardens, **t** *(020) 7836 4110;* **tube** *Covent Garden.*
Friendly pizzeria where one Sunday a month Spotty Dotty will entertain the kids between 1pm and 3pm.

Maxwell's U9
8–9 James St, **t** *(020) 7836 0303,* **w** *www.maxwells.co.uk;* **tube** *Covent Garden.*
Staff dress up in silly costmes for Halloween and Christmas, and there are special menus, colouring books and games.

New World S9
1 Gerrard Place, **t** *(020) 7734 0396;* **tube** *Leicester Square, Piccadilly Circus.*
One of the best places to introduce your children to Chinese food. Dim sum a speciality, with child-size varieties available. Very child-friendly.

Rainforest Café R10
20 Shaftesbury Av, **t** *(020) 7434 3111,* **w** *www.therainforest cafe.co.uk;* **tube** *Piccadilly Circus.*
Exciting rainforest-themed place which will delight kids. Face-painters, animal sounds, and waterfalls.

Smollensky's U10
105 The Strand, **t** *(020) 7497 2101,* **w** *www.smollenskys.co.uk;* **tube** *Charing Cross, Covent Garden.*
A very popular family restaurant. At weekend lunchtimes there are Punch and Judy shows, magic, balloons and colouring books.

TGI Fridays S10
25–9 Coventry St, **t** *(020) 7839 6262,* **w** *www.tgifridays.co.uk;* **tube** *Piccadilly Circus.*
The formulaic chain is always a big hit with kids, with special menus, games and face-painters.

Veeraswamy Q10
101 Regent St, **t** *(020) 7734 1401;* **tube** *Oxford Circus.*
A great child-friendly Indian restaurant. Sunday is family day, with a special children's menu, crayons, colouring books and goodie bags.

Yo Sushi! R8
52 Poland St, **t** *(020) 7287 0443,* **w** *www.yosushi.co.uk;* **tube** *Oxford Circus.*
Kids love the novelty of sushi from a conveyor belt, and drinks from a robotic trolley. There are fun packs, special kids' menus, easy-to-use chopsticks, and clip-on baby seats. Under-12s eat free from Monday to Friday.

Babysitting

Childminders N6
6 Nottingham St, W1, **t** *(020) 7935 3000,* **w** *www.babysitter.co.uk;* **tube** *Baker St.*
An agency for babysitters.

Pippa Pop-Ins Off maps
430 Fulham Rd, **t** *(020) 7385 2458;* **tube** *Fulham Broadway.*
Nursery school and kindergarten run by highly trained nursery teachers. Parties, holiday and weekend activities and a crêche for working parents.

Simply Childcare Off maps
16 Bushey Hill Rd, SE5, **t** *(020) 7701 6111,* **w** *www.simplychildcare.com;* **train** *Denmark Hill.*
Nannies and nanny-shares.

Universal Aunts
t *(020) 7738 8937 (daytime child-minding),* **t** *(020) 7386 5900 (babysitting in the evenings).*
Provides babysitters, entertainers, people to meet children off trains, and guides to take children around London.

Gay and Lesbian London

London has one of the most vibrant gay scenes in Europe. For years Earl's Court was the focal point for gay clubs and bars, but the focus has shifted to Soho, Hampstead and Clapham. Old Compton St in Soho is something of a gay high street, with specialist bars, shops, a travel agency, hairdressers and taxi company.

Some of London's best nightclubs, such as Heaven, The Fridge and Turnmills, either have a strong gay element or else are completely gay. There are also plenty of gay bars and cafés. You'll find zillions of suggestions and write-ups in one of London's gay magazines, such as *Boyz*, *QX*, or the *Pink Paper*, which are all available free from gay venues. You can pick up the more glossy magazines, such as *Attitude*, *Diva*, *Gay Times*, *Axiom* and *Fable*, from most newsagents.

Male homosexuality was legalized in 1967, although the age of consent was fixed for years at the high age of 21 (heterosexuals are legal at 16); it is now down to 18 and, under pressure from the European Court of Justice, the battle for 16 continues in Parliament. Female homosexuality, meanwhile, has never been criminalized, because Queen Victoria did not believe it existed.

Organizations

Gay London Policing Group (GALOP)
2J Leroy House, 436 Essex Rd, N1, **t** *(020) 7704 6767,* helpline **t** *(020) 7704 2040.* **Open** *Mon 5–8pm, Tues 1–3pm, Wed 3–6pm, Fri noon–2pm.* Help for gay men and lesbians who have been victims of homophobic violence or need support with dealing with police.

Gay Men Fighting Aids
Unit 43, The Eurolink Centre, 49 Elfra Rd, SW2, **t** *(020) 7738 6872,* **w** *www.gmfa.org.uk.* Geared towards supporting people with HIV and Aids but involved in all aspects of educating people about sexual

health – and advising on the nearest clinic for sorting out any little problems.

Metropolitan Community Churches
Find them at community centres in Brixton, **t** *(020) 8678 0200, Mile End,* **t** *(020) 8304 2374, and Camden,* **t** *(020) 8802 0962,* **w** *www.ufmcc.com.* Proud of its 'inclusiveness', this church was set up for 'gay, lesbian, bisexual and transgendered communities' to worship together – and offers blessings if you feel like tying the knot.

OutRage!
PO Box 17816, SW14 8WT, **t** *(020) 8240 0222,* **w** *www.outrage.org.uk.* Headed by notorious activist Peter Tatchell, this is a campaigning group known for jumping on archbishops and generally taking direct action in its fight for equal rights for gay men and lesbians and to stamp out homophobia.

Regard
2J Leroy House, 436 Essex Rd, N1, **t** *(020) 7738 6191,* **t** *7688 4111.* Organization for disabled lesbians, gay men and bisexuals.

Stonewall
46–8 Grosvenor Gardens, SW1, **t** *(020) 7881 9440,* **w** *www.stonewall.org.uk.* Campaigning group that also offers advice on legal issues and discrimination. Named after the gay bar in New York where riots against police in 1969 marked the beginning of a campaign against discrimination and homophobia.

Helplines

Lesbian and Gay Helpline
t *(020) 7837 3337.* **Open** *daily 7.30-10pm.* Lesbian Helpline, **t** *(020) 7837 2782.* **Open** *Sun–Thurs 7.30pm–10pm.* Lesbian Line, **t** *(020) 7251 6911.* **Open** *Mon and Fri 2–10pm, Tues–Thurs 7–10pm.* Bisexual Helpline, **t** *(020) 8569 7500.* **Open** *Tues–Fri (Thurs* **t** *(0131) 557 3620).*

Lesbian and Gay Switchboard
t *(020) 7837 7324,* **w** *www.llgs.org.uk.* A 24-hour service offering all kinds of information, from bars and clubs in London to where to get medical advice.

Accommodation Agencies

Much of the gay-run hotels and B&B accommodation is still in Earl's Court, once the centre of London's gay world in the good old days. Tourist Information Centres (*see* p.81) will provide you with lists of gay-friendly places to stay, but there are also specialist agencies such as:

Central London Bed and Breakfast
t *(020) 7251 3535,* **w** *www.gayaccom.co.uk.* For accommodation in Soho, the West End, Islington, Barbican and East End.

International Gay Travel Association
4331 North Federal Highway, Suite 304, Fort Lauderdale, FL 33308, **t** *1800 448 8550,* **w** *www.igita.org.* Lists of gay-friendly travel agents and accommodation.

Outlet S9
60–62 Old Compton St, Soho, W1, **t** *(020) 7287 4244,* **w** *www.outlet4homes.com;* **tube** *Piccadilly Circus, Leicester Square.* If you're planning a short or a longer stay, there's this excellent specialist accommodation service in the heart of Soho (now being run by sexy Josh from Britain's *Big Brother* TV show). You can arrange short-term or long-term accommodation, with gay-friendly roommates or landlords, by phone, Internet or dropping by in person.

www.pinkhotels.com
An online reservations service for gay-friendly hotels across London.

www.sbr22.dircon.co.uk
Details of gay-friendly accommodation, with useful links.

Hotels

Buosi Private Hotel Off maps
50 Nevern Square, SW5, **t** *(020) 7370 3325,* **w** *www.hotelbuosi.com;* **tube** *Earl's Court. Single £30; double £55; family £80.*
Privately run informal B&B over-looking a leafy square, with a small courtyard garden.

Noel Coward Hotel O16
111 Ebury St, Belgravia, SW1, **t** *(020) 7730 2094,* **w** *www.noelcoward hotel.com;* **tube/train** *Victoria. Single £55–60; double £70–75; triple £90–97.50; quadruple £120.*
An opportunity to stay in the Victorian house where gay play-wright Sir Noel Coward lived from 1917 to 1930. Friendly, accommo-dating bed and breakfast with high standards of service.

Number Seven Off maps
7 Josephine Av, Brixton, SW2, **t** *(020) 8674 1880,* **w** *www.no7 .com;* **tube/train** *Brixton. Single £39–69; double £59–109; triple £99–129; quadruple £109–139.*
This friendly B&B is in a Victorian townhouse in a quiet street in Brixton, but close to clubs such as the Fridge.

Philbeach Hotel Off maps
30–31 Philbeach Gardens, Earl's Court, **t** *(020) 7373 1244,* **w** *www .philbeachhotel.freeserve.co.uk;* **tube** *Earl's Court. Single £35–60; double £65–90.*
One of the best-known and well-established hotels for gay travellers, with Appleby's bar and the Wilde About Oscar Garden Restaurant. 40 bedrooms, 24-hour reception, TV and Internet lounge.

Prince William Hotel H9
42–4 Gloucester Terrace, W2, **t** *(020) 7724 7414;* **tube** *Lancaster Gate. Single £45; double £60; triple £80.*
Friendly small B&B.

Restaurants

Balans
w *www.balans.co.uk; 239 Old Brompton Rd (off maps),* **t** *(020) 7244 883;* **tube** *Earl's Court; 60 Old Compton St (S9),* **t** *(020) 7437 5212;* **tube** *Piccadilly Circus, Leicester Square; 187 Kensington High St (D14),* **t** *(020) 7376 0115;* **tube** *High St Kensington; 239 Brompton Rd (off maps),* **t** *(020) 7584 0070;* **tube** *Knightsbridge.*
The most well-known chain of gay-run, gay-friendly restaurants, now with four branches across London. The first was in Earl's Court but the biggest and most popular is in the heart of the 'gay village' in Old Compton St. They attract a mixed clientèle and serve modern international cuisine and great brunches in relaxed café-style surroundings.

Old Compton Café S9
34 Old Compton St, **t** *(020) 7439 3309;* **tube** *Piccadilly Circus, Leicester Square. Open 24 hours.*
Popular meeting place with seating outside offering a good view of the gay strip of Old Compton St. Fresh snacks, sand-wiches, coffee and cakes for an international clientèle.

Wilde About Oscar Off maps
30 Philbeach Gardens, Earl's Court, **t** *(020) 7835 1858,* **w** *www .philbeachhotel.freeserve.co.uk;* **tube** *Earl's Court. Open Mon and Wed–Sat 6–11pm.*
Smart gay restaurant with a garden, part of the Philbeach Hotel.

Pubs and Bars

London's gay life centres on Old Compton St in Soho, where media suits mingle freely with fashion queens. Past squabbles between restaurateurs and Westminster Council over tables thrust onto wobbly narrow footpaths have been resolved in an untidy but lively compromise. The tidal pink pound has seen the rise and de-mise of many places to be seen in; what follows is a snapshot of the current scene in Soho and beyond.

Admiral Duncan S9
54 Old Compton St, **t** *(020) 7437 5300;* **tube** *Piccadilly Circus, Leicester Square. Open Mon–Sat noon–11pm, Sun noon–10.30pm.*
Small laid-back traditional pub. Bombed by a bigot in 1999 (when three people died), it has acquired a certain iconic status as a symbol of resistance to prejudice.

Bar Aquda U10
13–14 Maiden Lane, **t** *(020) 7557 9891;* **tube** *Covent Garden, Leicester Square. Open Mon–Sat noon–11pm, Sun noon–10.30pm.*
Stylish café-bar.

BarCode R10
3 Archer St, **t** *(020) 7734 3342;* **tube** *Piccadilly Circus, Leicester Square. Open Mon–Sat noon–11pm, Sun noon–10.30pm.*
Clubby bar for muscle boys and cropped hair. The comedy club in the basement offers some gay-themed nights.

Bar Fusion Off maps
45 Essex Rd, **t** *(020) 7688 2882;* **tube** *Angel. Open daily 1pm–midnight.*
Small modern bar with sofas and laid-back atmosphere.

Black Cap Off maps
171 Camden High St, **t** *(020) 7428 2721;* **tube** *Camden Town. Open Mon–Thurs noon–2am, Fri and Sat noon–3am, Sun noon–3pm.*
Friendly local pub upstairs and late-night bar and club down-stairs with regular cabaret.

The Box T9
32 Monmouth St, **t** *(020) 7240 5828;* **tube** *Leicester Square. Open Mon–Sat 11am–11pm, Sun noon–10.30pm.*
Stylish café-bar with brasserie-style food.

Brompton's Off maps
Old Brompton Rd/Warwick Rd, **t** *(020) 7370 1344,* **w** *www .bromptons-club.com;* **tube** *Earl's Court. Open Mon–Sat 4pm–2am, Sun 1pm–midnight.*
Local bar and club on two floors playing disco and pop.

Candy Bar S9
23 Bateman St, **t** *(020) 7437 1977,* **w** *www.candybar.easynet.co.uk;* **tube** *Tottenham Court Rd. Open Mon–Tues 5pm–1am, Wed–Fri 5pm–3am, Sat 4pm–3am, Sun 5pm–midnight.*

Modern friendly bar – London's best-known and longest-running venue for lesbians and their male guests.

Compton's S9
53 Old Compton St, **t** (020) 7479 7961, **w** www.comptons-of-soho.co.uk; **tube** Piccadilly Circus, Leicester Square. **Open** Mon–Sat noon–11pm, Sun noon–10.30pm.
Notorious long-established dimly lit bar on two levels.

The Edge S8
11 Soho Square, **t** (020) 7439 1313, **w** www.edgesoho.com; **tube** Tottenham Court Rd. **Open** Mon–Sat noon–1am, Sun 1–10.30pm.
Stylish funky bar on four floors for a fashionable crowd.

Escape R9
8 Brewer St, **t** (020) 7734 2626, **w** www.kudosgroup.com; **tube** Leicester Square. **Open** Mon–Sat 4pm–3am, Sun 4–10.30pm.
Small modern bar with a lively late-night young and stylish crowd.

First Out Café Bar S8
52 St Giles High St, **t** (020) 7240 8042; **tube** Tottenham Court Rd. **Open** Mon–Sat 10am–11pm, Sun 11am–10.30pm.
Great veggie food served at this café-bar, the first of its type in the West End. Women only on Friday evenings.

Freedom S9
60–66 Wardour St, **t** (020) 7734 0071; **tube** Piccadilly Circus, Leicester Square. **Open** daily 11am–3am.
Large café-bar serving good food and cocktails to a trendy mixed crowd posing in designer gear. Downstairs club open until 3am.

Friendly Society R9
79 Wardour St, **t** (020) 7434 3805; **tube** Piccadilly Circus, Leicester Square. **Open** daily noon–11.30pm.
Basement bar with chilled music and cocktails, given an alternative look with Barbie dolls on the wall.

Gloucester Off maps
1 King William Walk, SE10, **t** (020) 8293 6131; **DLR** Greenwich; **train** Greenwich. **Open** Mon–Sat noon–11pm, Sun noon–10.30pm.
Long-established friendly gay pub, next to Greenwich Park and with good views.

Kazbar Off maps
50 Clapham High St, SW4, **t** (020) 7622 0070, **w** www.kudosgroup.com; **tube** Clapham North. **Open** Mon–Sat 5pm–midnight, Sun 5pm–11pm.
Modern stylish bar with DJs and video screens.

King William IV Off maps
77 Hampstead High St, NW3, **t** (020) 7435 5747; **tube** Hampstead. **Open** Mon–Sat noon–11pm, Sun noon–10.30pm.
Traditional friendly pub with garden, serving hearty pub food.

Ku Bar S9
75 Charing Cross Rd, **t** (020) 7437 4303 **w** www.ku-bar.co.uk; **tube** Leicester Square. **Open** Mon–Sat 4–11pm, Sun 4–10.30pm.
Friendly bar on two levels for a young fashion-conscious crowd.

Kudos T10
10 Adelaide St, **t** (020) 7379 4573, **w** www.kudosgroup.com; **tube** Charing Cross. **Open** Mon–Sat 10am–11pm, Sun noon–10.30pm.
Modern café-bar with a darker cruisey basement bar.

Manto S9
30 Old Compton St, **t** (020) 7494 2756, **w** www.mantogroup.com; **tube** Piccadilly Circus, Leicester Square. **Open** Mon–Sat 11am–midnight, Sun 11am–11pm.
Modern bar on three floors, with dancefloor and stylish restaurant; popular with the fashion crowd.

Quebec M9
12 Old Quebec St, **t** (020) 7629 6159; **tube** Marble Arch. **Open** Mon–Sat noon–11pm, Sun noon–10.30pm.
If you're tired of all the bright young things, this is the best place for the more mature gentlemen and their admirers.

Retro Bar U10
2 George St, **t** (020) 7321 2811; **tube** Charing Cross. **Open** Mon–Sat noon–11pm, Sun noon–10.30pm.
Attitude-free two-storey pub for lovers of indie and retro sounds.

Ye Rose and Crown Off maps
1 Crooms Hill, Greenwich, **t** (020) 8293 1898; **DLR** Cutty Sark, Greenwich; **train** Greenwich
Traditional, friendly but rather small local pub, with large plate-glass windows looking out onto bustling maritime Greenwich.

Rupert St R9
50 Rupert St, **t** (020) 7734 5614; **tube** Piccadilly Circus, Leicester Square. **Open** Mon–Sat 11am–11pm, Sun noon–10.30pm.
Modern café-bar segueing into a busy venue in the evenings for men in suits and designer labels.

79 CXR S9
79 Charing Cross Rd, **t** (020) 7734 0769; **tube** Leicester Square. **Open** Mon–Thurs 1pm–2am, Fri and Sat 1pm–3am, Sun 1–10.30pm.
Unpretentious 'attitude-free' bar on two floors, popular with a late-night cruisey crowd.

The Shadow Lounge R9
5 Brewer St, **t** (020) 7287 7988; **tube** Piccadilly Circus, Leicester Square. **Open** Mon–Sat 7pm–3am.
Upmarket style bar with cocktails and DJs, attracting a fashion-conscious crowd and a few celebrities.

Two Brewers Off maps
114 Clapham High St, SW4, **t** (020) 7498 4971; **tube** Clapham Common. **Open** Mon–Thurs noon–2am, Fri and Sat noon–3am, Sun noon–midnight.
Friendly modern bar, with late-night club and nightly cabaret.

Vespa Lounge S8
Beneath Centre Point, St Giles Circus, **t** (020) 7836 8956; **tube** Tottenham Court Rd. **Open** daily 6–11pm.
Laid-back bar for lesbians and their male guests.

Village R9
81 Wardour St, **t** (020) 7434 2124; **tube** Piccadilly Circus, Leicester Square. **Open** Mon–Thurs 11am–11pm, Fri and Sat 11am–midnight, Sun 11am–10.30pm.
Modern stylish bar on two floors for a young lively crowd.

West Central S9

29 Lisle St, t (020) 7479 7981;
***tube** Leicester Square.* **Open** *Mon–Sat noon–11pm, Sun noon–10.30pm.*
Modern venue on three storeys, including a friendly pub for theatre fans on the first floor. Basement club open from 10.30pm nightly to as late as 3am.

West Five Off maps

Popes Lane, W5, t (020) 8579 3266;
***tube** Ealing Common.* **Open** *Mon–Sat noon–11pm, Sun noon–10.30pm.*
Large, friendly traditional pub with a garden and pub food, offering DJs, dancing and cabaret in the late evening.

The Yard R9

57 Rupert St, t (020) 7437 2652;
***tube** Piccadilly Circus, Leicester Square.* **Open** *Mon–Sat noon–11pm, Sun noon–10.30pm.*
Good food and an outdoor courtyard attract a mixed stylish crowd.

Clubs

Many of London's gay bars have late licences, so around 11pm the lights start to dim and the disco beat is turned up. Expect to stay out late at venues like the Shadow Lounge, Freedom, Escape, the Black Cap or the Two Brewers (*see* above). But there is also an ever-changing calendar of excellent club nights – check *Boyz* for the most comprehensive listings. There are a few club nights exclusively for women, such as the Royal Vauxhall Tavern, but it seems to be mainly a male thing.

Atelier T8

The End, 18 West Central St, t (020) 7419 9199, w www.cocolatte.net;
***tube** Tottenham Court Rd.* **Open** *Thurs 10pm–4am.*
Clubby late-night bar for designer labels and muscle boys, created by the team behind established club night Coco Latte.

Backstreet Off maps

Wentworth Mews, Burdett Rd, Mile End, E3, t (020) 8980 8557;
***tube** Mile End.* **Open** *Thurs–Sun.*
Out-of-the-way black leather and rubber nightclub for men, rather wilder than most of the other clubs.

Club Kali Off maps

*The Dome, Dartmouth Park Hill, Tufnell Park, N19; **tube** Tufnell Park.* **Open** *1st and 3rd Friday of the month 10pm–3am.*
London's biggest night for Asian gay men and lesbians featuring bhangra mixed with pop and house.

Crash Off maps

*66 Goding St, Vauxhall, SE11, t (020) 7820 1500; **tube/train** Vauxhall.* **Open** *Sat 10.30pm–6am.*
Two dancefloors playing techno for an almost exclusively muscle-boy crowd.

DTPM Y7

*Fabric, 77A Charterhouse St, EC1, t (020) 7439 9009, w www.dtpm .net; **tube/train** Farringdon.* **Open** *Sun 10pm–late.*
Disco, R&B, house and Latino music on three dancefloors for a fashionable clubby crowd.

G.A.Y. S8

*London Astoria, 157 Charing Cross Rd (Thurs–Sat); The Mean Fiddler, 165 Charing Cross Rd, (Mon), t (020) 7734 6963; w www.g-a-y.co.uk; **tube** Tottenham Court Rd.* **Open** *Mon (Pink Pounder) 10.30pm–4am, Thurs 10.30pm–4am, Fri 11pm–4am, Sat 10.30pm–5am.*
Ever-popular superclub for mainly younger lovers of pop and trash, with chart-toppers on stage most Saturdays.

Heaven U11

*The Arches, Villiers St, t (020) 7930 2020, w www.heaven-london.com; **tube** Embankment, Charing Cross.* **Open** *Mon 10pm–3am, Wed 10.30pm–3am, Sat 10pm–5am.*
Long-established gay club with three dancefloors playing a mix of music from house and R&B to disco and garage.

Love Muscle Off maps

*The Fridge, Town Hall Parade, Brixton Hill, t (020) 7326 5100; w www.fridge.co.uk; **tube/train** Brixton.* **Open** *Sat 10pm–6am.*
Funky music and a packed dance-floor, next to the gay-friendly Fridge Bar for pre-dancing drinks.

Popstarz U2

*The Scala, 278 Pentonville Rd, King's Cross, N1, t (020) 7738 2336, w www.popstarz.co.uk; **tube/train** King's Cross.* **Open** *Fri 10pm–5am.*
Three floors of indie, trash and house for a mainly younger set.

Royal Vauxhall Tavern Off maps

*373 Kennington Lane, Vauxhall, SW8, t (020) 7582 0833; **tube/train** Vauxhall.* **Open** *Fri–Sun.*
Shabby but fun late-night bar and club playing retro sounds, renowned for alternative cabaret night Duckie on Saturdays. There is a women-only night the second Friday of every month.

Sound on Sunday S10

*Sound, Leicester Square, The Swiss Centre, t (020) 7287 1010, w www .sound-on-sunday.com; **tube** Leicester Square, Piccadilly Circus.* **Open** *Sunday 7pm–2am.*
Sunday is no longer the day of rest, so this friendly night packs out with a mix of mainstream dance tunes.

Substation South Off maps

*9 Brighton Terrace, Brixton, SW9; **tube/train** Brixton.* **Open** *Mon 10pm–2.30am, Tues 10.30pm–2am, Wed 10.30pm–3am, Thurs 10.30pm–2.30am, Fri 10.30pm–5pm, Sat 10.30pm–6am, Sun 10.30pm–late.*
Dingy but popular hard-core basement club playing house, with specialist midweek nights for leather or sportswear.

Trade Off maps

*Turnmills, 63B Clerkenwell Rd, EC2, t (020) 7250 3409, w www.turn mills.co.uk; **tube/train** Farringdon.* **Open** *Sat 4am–1pm.*
Long-running night (or rather Sunday morning) of hard house for muscle and leather boys.

West Central S10

*29 Lisle St, t (020) 7479 7981; **tube** Leicester Square.* **Open** *10.30pm–3am.*
Small friendly basement club beneath West Central bar spinning out disco and retro sounds.

White Swan Off maps
*556 Commercial Rd, Limehouse,
E14, t (020) 7780 9870;
tube Aldgate East; DLR Limehouse.
Open Mon 9pm–1am, Tues–Thurs
9pm–2am, Fri and Sat 9pm–3am,
Sun 5.30pm–midnight.*
Friendly no-nonsense local bar
and club playing disco music, with
regular cabaret.

Wig Out S8
*The Tube, Falconberg Court, off
Charing Cross Rd, t (020) 7738 2336;
tube Tottenham Court Rd.
Open Sat 10pm–4am.*
Retro, trash and chart pop at a fun
attitude-free night for men and
women. More mainstream but
less fun gay night on Fridays.

XXL BB12
*53 Southwark St, t 07967 304335,
w www.fatsandsmalls.com;
tube/train London Bridge.
Open Sat 10pm–4am.*
Dubbed a club for 'men who are
proud, hairy, hunky and beery' as
well as their leaner friends, but
this is just a fun attitude-free
night of pop and house.

Entertainment

Many gay bars keep the tradition of cabaret alive in London. It's
still mostly transvestites camping
it up to pop and show tunes, but a
number of top comedy and music
acts have started their careers on
the gay circuit. Bars and clubs
worth checking out are the Two
Brewers, Black Cap and the Royal
Vauxhall Tavern (*see above*).

While there are enough musicals in London to delight the most
dedicated of show queens, a
number of theatres and venues
have a reputation for including
excellent gay drama and cabaret
in their programmes.

The Arts Theatre T9
*Great Newport St, t (020) 7836
3334, w www.artstheatre.com;
tube Leicester Square.*
With a history of shocking the
censors with avant-garde productions, this historic theatre, in its
current sleek and modern guise,

continues to include drama and
cabaret with a gay theme within
its wider programme.

Bush Theatre Off maps
*2 Goldhawk Rd, Shepherd's Bush,
W12, t (020) 7610 4224;
tube Shepherd's Bush.*
With a broad programme of
drama, this theatre above a pub is
one of the best fringe venues,
often presenting plays tackling
gay themes.

Drill Hall S6
*16 Chenies St, t (020) 7637
8270, w www.drillhall.co.uk;
tube Goodge St.*
London's biggest gay and lesbian
theatre presents its own work and
brings in shows from around the
world. Mondays are women only
from 6pm.

**The Institute of
Contemporary Arts** S11
*The Mall, t (020) 7930 3647,
w www.ica.org.uk; tube Charing
Cross.*
With a reputation for the most
challenging avant-garde, the ICA
often presents gay and lesbian
performances and movies.

Madame Jo Jo's R9
*8–10 Brewer St, t (020) 7734 2473;
tube Piccadilly Circus.*
With a whiff of old Soho, outrageous transvestite cabaret and
other gay-oriented shows.

Oval House Off maps
*52–4 Kennington Oval, Oval, SE11,
t (020) 7582 7680, w www.oval
house.com; tube Oval.*
A leading venue for gay and
lesbian productions, with two
theatres, often attracting
respected, subsidised companies.

Shops

Clone Zone S9
*64 Old Compton St, t (020) 7287
3530, w www.clonezonedirect
.co.uk; tube Piccadilly Circus,
Leicester Square; 266 Old
Brompton Rd, t (020) 7373 0598;
tube Earl's Court.*
Gay books, videos, clubby tops and
gifts, with a section full of bewildering sex toys and porn mags.

Gay's The Word T5
*66 Marchmont St, t (020) 7278
7654, w www.gaystheword.co.uk;
tube Russell Square.*
London's leading gay bookshop.

Prowler R9
*3–7 Brewer St, t (020) 7734 4031;
w www.prowlerstores.co.uk;
tube Piccadilly Circus, Leicester
Square; 283 Camden High St, NW1,
t (020) 7284 0537; tube Camden
Town.*
Gay books, streetwear and club
fashion, videos and gifts, with a
section of leather, sex toys and
porn magazines.

Rob London Q7
*24 Wells St, t (020) 7735 7893,
w www.rob.nl; tube Oxford Circus.*
Established in 1992, this is a
straightforward store for all
your leather, rubber and
'twisted' needs.

Miscellaneous

Taxis

For a safe ride back to your
home or hotel, there are a couple
of well-known taxi firms:

Cruisers Off maps
*Abbey Business Centre, Ingate
Place, SW8, t (020) 8333 6747.*
A friendly gay-run taxi firm mainly
serving South London.

Freedom Cars R9
*2nd floor, 52 Wardour St, t (020)
7734 1313; tube Piccadilly Circus.*
A well-established firm for getting
into and out of the West End.

Health
and Beauty

Compton's Hair S9
*7 Old Compton St, t (020) 7434
0969; tube Piccadilly Circus,
Leicester Square.*
Hairdressers in the heart of the
'gay village'.

Covent Garden Health Spa T8
*29 Endell St, t (020) 7836 2236;
tube Covent Garden.*
Strictly non-sleazy health club for
men. Includes beauty therapy,
Jacuzzi and solarium.

It's Marvellous R9
5 Greens Court, t (020) 7287 8748;
tube Piccadilly Circus.
Gay-friendly hair salon.

M.O.T. R9
7 Silver Place, off Lexington St,
t (020) 7287 3334; tube Piccadilly
Circus.
Men-only salon for a wide range
of treatments to make you more
beautiful.

Paris Gym Off maps
Arch 73, Goding St, Vauxhall, SE11,
t (020) 7735 8989, w www.paris
gym.com; tube/train Vauxhall.
London's only exclusively gay gym,
geared towards bodybuilders. If
you're staying for only a few
weeks, you can pick up a carnet

that allows you a number of visits
at a reasonable price without
becoming a full member.

Soho Gyms
12 Macklin St (U8), t (020) 7242
1290; tube Covent Garden,
Holborn; 254 Earl's Court Rd, SW5,
t (020) 7370 1402; tube Earl's Court;
193 Camden High St, NW1, t (020)
7482 4524; tube Camden Town;
95–7 Clapham High St, SW4,
t (020) 7405 3214; tube Clapham
North; w www.sohogyms.com.
A high-quality chain of gyms
throughout London. It's not just
for gay bodypumpers, but it's gay-
run and gay-friendly. You don't
have to be a member to use the
facilities, although the day rates
are steep.

Saunas

Chariots Roman
Baths Off maps
201–207 Shoreditch High St, EC1,
t (020) 7247 5333; tube/train
Liverpool St.

Chariots III Y6
57 Cowcross St, Farringdon, t (020)
7251 5553; tube/train Farringdon.

Pleasuredrome Central X12
125 Alaska St, Waterloo, t (020)
7633 9194; tube/train Waterloo.

Sailors Off maps
572–74 Commercial Rd, E14, t (020)
7791 2808; DLR/train Limehouse.

Festivals and Events

London has a packed programme of festivals and special events. The 'season', that whirligig of balls, parties and sporting events for upper-crust Londoners and aspiring toffs from the country, can be seen in action at the Royal Ascot races, the Wimbledon Tennis Championships and the Henley Royal Regatta. Dates for many of the events below change every year. Phone numbers are given where possible.

January

London Parade
1 Jan
Display of 6,000 real American majorettes starting from Parliament Square at noon and finishing in Berkeley Square at 3pm.

Harrods After-Christmas Sale
Early Jan

London International Mime Festival
Mid-Jan
Held in various venues across London, **t** (020) 7637 5661, **w** www.mimefest.co.uk.

Chinese New Year
Mid-Jan–early Feb
Celebrations around Gerrard St in Soho. Lots of food and colourful floats.

February

Fine Art and Antiques Fair
End Feb
Olympia.

Great Spitalfields Pancake Day Races
Shrove Tuesday
Sprints down Spitalfields, with participants tossing pancakes in a pan, **t** (020) 7375 0441.

March

Ideal Home Exhibition
Second week March
At Earl's Court Exhibition Centre: kitchens and bathrooms galore, **t** (01895) 677 677.

Oranges and Lemons Service
One Sun in March
At St Clement Danes in the Strand, at which local school-

The Queen's Golden Jubilee

2002 marks the 50th anniversary of the Queen's accession to the throne and, despite a lot of media hullabaloo about public apathy, a string of events have been organized to celebrate the Golden Jubilee with plenty of pomp and circumstance. For a full list of events and institutions that are part of the festival, log on to **w** www.stringofpearls.org.uk.

There will be extended public access to the Houses of Parliament, special exhibitions in many museums, parades and other events. There will be a whole weekend of festivities in early June, and some institutions that are rarely open to the public will throw open their doors to the hoi polloi. There will be a series of open days at the Foreign and Commonwealth Office; special

---

tours of Lincoln's Inn, as well as a series of free lunchtime concerts in the Inn's Chapel (*see* p.156); Eton College's (*see* p.289) five gardens, normally closed to the public, will, exceptionally, be open to visitors; Charterhouse (*see* p.222) will be open for tours every Wednesday at 2.15pm and Saturday at 11am from April to August (pre-booking is essential on **t** (020) 7251 5002); Horse Guards (*see* p.95), the Headquarters of London District Military who organize all the royal regimental duty such as the Changing of the Guard, will be open to the public; the Royal Hospital Chelsea (*see* p.247) is hosting the first public concert ever to be held in its State Apartments on 18 June, and on 22 June the only London performance of *The Triumphs of Oriana* will take place in the Chapel.

---

children are given an orange and a lemon each as per the nursery rhyme (*see* p.152).

Head of the River Race
End March
Regatta in Hammersmith, **t** (01932) 220 401.

April

April Fool's Day
1 April
Check newspapers for April Fool's Day hoaxes.

Oxford and Cambridge Boat Race
Sat before Easter
Teams from the universities row from Putney to Mortlake, **t** (020) 7611 3500, **w** www.theboatrace.org.

Easter Day Parade
Easter Sun
In Battersea Park, complete with funfair and sideshows.

Easter-egg Hunts
Easter Sun
Easter-egg hunts at Kew Gardens, **t** (020) 8940 1171.

London Marathon
Mid-April
From Blackheath to the Mall; vist **w** www.london-marathon.co.uk

---

for details of the route and how to enter.

May

Spring Bank Holiday
First Mon in May
Funfairs on Hampstead Heath, on Blackheath and in Alexandra Park.

London Tattoo
Military parades, bands and performers from around the world, **t** (01189) 303 239.

Beating the Bounds
Ascension Day (40 days after Easter)
Boys of St Dunstan's beat on the City's boundary markers with willow sticks in an ancient ritual. Starts at 3pm at All Hallows by the Tower.

Chelsea Flower Show
Late May
At the Royal Hospital Gardens, **t** 0870 906 3781.

June

The Derby
First Sat in June
Derby horse race at Epsom racecourse, Surrey (*see* p.375).

Greenwich Festival
Early June
Concerts, theatre and children's events, plus fireworks on the opening night, **t** (020) 8305 1818.

Hampton Court Festival
Opera, music and dance, **t** (020) 8781 9500.

Beating the Retreat
Floodlit evening display by the Queen's Household Division outside Buckingham Palace.

Trooping the Colour
Second Sat in June
The Queen's Guards in a birthday parade for Ma'am, **t** (020) 7414 2497.

Spitalfields Festival
Throughout June
Classical music in Christ Church, plus guided walks of the area, **t** (020) 7375 0441.

Royal Ascot
Mid-June
Society horse-races at Ascot in Berkshire (*see* p.375).

Wimbledon Tennis Championships
Late June–early July
The world-famous championships, **t** (020) 8944 1066.

Henley Royal Regatta
Late June–early July
Rowers row on the Thames while very posh spectators get sozzled in their champagne tents.

Summer Exhibition at the Royal Academy
June–Aug
More than 1,000 works by living artists, **t** (020) 7300 8000.

Coin Street Festival
Buskers and free street performances at Gabriel's Wharf. Includes Gran Gran Fiesta, an outdoor Latin dance event, Celtic and Caribbean events and more, **t** (020) 7401 2255.

Kenwood Lakeside Concerts
June–Sept
Open-air concerts at the top of Hampstead Heath. Magical if the weather's good, **t** (020) 7973 3427.

July

City of London Festival
Classical concerts, **t** (020) 7377 0540.

Hampton Court Flower Show
t (020) 7821 3042.

Gay Pride Day
First week in July
w www.pridelondon.org.uk.

Doggett's Coat and Badge Race
Late July
A rowing contest from London Bridge to Cadogan Pier.

Respect Festival
End July
Celebration of London's diversity with live acts and bands at Victoria Park, Hackney, **t** (020) 7983 6554, **e** info@respect festival.org.uk, **w** www.respect festival.com.

The Proms
July–Sept
Famous concerts at the Albert Hall (*see* p.359), **t** (020) 7589 8212.

August

Buckingham Palace Open to the Public
Aug–Sept

Notting Hill Carnival
Last weekend in Aug
Steel bands, dancing and general Caribbean fun around Portobello Rd and Ladbroke Grove.

September

Chelsea Antiques Fair
Mid-Sept
t (01444) 482514, **f** 483412.

Open House Weekend
Third week in Sept
Houses and buildings that are normally closed to the public open up for free; also walking tours, **t** 09001 600061 (60p per minute), **e** send@londonopenhouse.org, **w** www.londonopenhouse.org.

Clog and Apron Race
Late Sept
A sprint through Kew by gardening students in strange attire, **t** (020) 8940 1171.

October

Pearly Harvest Festival
First Sun in Oct
At St Martin-in-the-Fields: folklore Cockneys in button-splashed coats, **t** (020) 7766 1100.

November

London Film Festival
Based at the NFT on the South Bank but with showings all over town, **t** (020) 7928 3232.

Bonfire Night
5 Nov
Fireworks and bonfires, plus plenty of booze, in parks all over London to commemorate Guy Fawkes' attempt to blow up Parliament in 1605. Highbury Fields, Alexandra Palace and Battersea Park are good venues, but telephone the London Tourist Board, **t** 09068 66 33 44 (calls cost 60p per minute) or check *Time Out* for details.

State Opening of Parliament
First week in Nov
The Queen sets out from Buckingham Palace for Westminster, where she reads out the government's programme for the forthcoming year. Crowds follow her around.

London to Brighton Veteran Car Run
First Sun in Nov
Starts in Hyde Park; **t** (01753) 765 100 for details.

Lord Mayor's Show
Early Nov
The new Lord Mayor goes on a grand procession through the City in his 18th-century gilded coach, **t** (020) 7332 1906, **t** (01992) 505396.

Remembrance Day
Sun nearest 11 Nov
Service to commemorate the war dead at the Cenotaph in Whitehall.

Christmas Lights Go On
Along Oxford St, Regent St, Bond St and in Trafalgar Square.

December

New Year's Celebrations
31 Dec
Crowds count down to midnight beneath the Christmas tree in Trafalgar Square.

Language

Language in London is all about class. Despite the levelling effects of television and social mobility, the elite remains suspicious of the way that ordinary Londoners talk, and the feeling is mutual. Pernickety middle-class folk despise the double negatives, dropped l's and h's and swallowed consonants of the Cockney dialect, which they think of as unforgivably bad English; in return, ordinary people poke fun at the preciousness of society ladies in their Kensington drawing rooms who talk about 'snare', when what they mean is the white stuff that falls out of the sky on an exceptionally cold day. London is a city divided by a common language.

The very term Cockney, traditionally used to denote anybody from the East End, the heart of working-class London, is in its origin disparaging. Derived from the Old English for 'cock's egg', it was used by Chaucer to mean a spoilt child and by Shakespeare to denote a fool. Pierce Egan, in his classic 1821 study *Life in London*, defined the Cockney as 'an uneducated native... pert and conceited, yet truly ignorant' – an attitude that neatly sums up Professor Higgins's opinion of his young charge Eliza Doolittle in George Bernard Shaw's *Pygmalion* (later turned into the hit musical *My Fair Lady*). 'A woman who utters such depressing and disgusting sounds has no right to be anywhere – no right to live,' he says as he embarks on his wager to teach her the sounds and sophistications of 'proper' English.

But in fact, from a historical point of view, it is Eliza who speaks the more proper English. The London dialect known as Cockney has been around since before the Norman invasion of 1066. As the philologist M. MacBride wrote in 1910, three years after *Pygmalion* was first performed, 'The London dialect is really, especially on the south side of the Thames, a perfectly

legitimate and responsible child of the old Kentish tongue... The dialect of London north of the Thames has been shown to be one of the many varieties of the Midland or Mercian dialect, flavoured by the East Anglian variety of the same speech, owing to the great influx of Essex people into London.'

The ruling classes have always sought to distinguish themselves from the rabble with a more rarefied form of speech, but Received Standard English as we now understand it – that is to say, talking posh – dates back only to the late 18th century. It was the 'public' schools, the private establishments where the elite pay to send their children, which set the agenda in speech and writing. In standardizing the English language's notoriously irrational spelling habits, the schools set the rules to suit themselves, paying scant attention to considerations of either etymology or current usage. Thus it was that 'often' gained its t, 'assault' and 'vault' gained their l's, and 'advantage' and 'advance' their d's. Etymologically there is no justification for these additions, and yet when Cockney-speakers drop any of them they suffer the indignity of being told they do not speak properly. The Cockney use of 'remember' to mean remind, or 'learn' to mean teach, is generally frowned upon by the chattering classes; and yet it was perfectly acceptable in Elizabethan times and crops up in Shakespeare.

The class war over language reached its height with the arrival of broadcasting in the 1920s. The BBC became the unofficial arbiter of correct speech, and since most of its producers and announcers had been to public school, the soft, drooling vowels of the English upper classes became the linguistic benchmark for the nation. If you've ever seen Pathé wartime newsreels or films like *Brief Encounter*, you'll know how hilariously fake this 'correct'

speech sounded, as though everyone had half a dozen marbles stuffed into their cheeks. Cockney, on the other hand, was deemed common and generally kept off the airwaves except as an illustration of the quaintness of working-class life. When television first came into its own in the 1950s, Cockney speech was often subtitled as though it were a foreign language. It wasn't until the 1980s that regional or working-class accents became acceptable in broadcasting.

At the same time as Cockney was being derided in the corridors of power, a whole folklore about it was building up among those who supposedly despised it the most. Even today, you'll often hear public-school-educated voices mimicking the 'innits' and 'yerwots' of Cockney dialect, or holding lengthy disquisitions about the peculiarities of rhyming slang (on which more below). There is even a theory that the affectations of upper-class English speech derive from the imperfect imitation of working-class accents. What really set off the fad for Cockney folklore was the rise of the music hall at the end of the 19th century. Working-class performers like Albert Chevalier, who wrote the classic Cockney song 'My Old Dutch', created a folksy version of the East End with which to entertain middle-class audiences. This was a world of pearly kings and queens wearing jackets sewn with a thousand buttons (originally the traditional costume of the costermonger, or barrow seller) and toothy old men plucking at ukeleles. Needless to say, this world did not have much to do with reality, but soon well-to-do Londoners were coming out with phrases like 'put a sock in it' or 'keep yer 'air on' and finding it endlessly amusing. The folklore Cockney – crafty, cheeky and all right for a laugh – started popping up all over the place, in plays like *Pygmalion*, in films like *Alfie* (starring that ultimate Cockney performer Michael Caine), and in musicals like *My Fair Lady*, *Underneath the Arches* and Lupino Lane's *Me and My Girl*, which is still doing the rounds in the West End and on Broadway today. In fact, *Me and My Girl* might be said to be the definitive Cockney musical. The plot revolves around a group of Cockneys who baffle a group of aristocrats with their peculiar expressions. The aristocrats quickly catch on, however, and soon they are joining in the fun and coming out with the best rhyming slang. All mutual suspicion melts away and in the end everybody joins in for a rousing grand finale of reconciliation.

In fact rhyming slang, more than any other aspect of Cockney, highlights the disparity between the language of the stage and the speech of ordinary people. It seems to have originated in the first half of the 19th century. Henry Mayhew, in his *London Life and the London Poor* of 1851, remarked on 'the new style of cadgers' cant... all done on the rhyming principle'. The idea was that criminals could talk without fear of being betrayed by police narks, and that stallholders in Smithfield and Billingsgate markets could converse about prices without their customers understanding them. In other words, the whole point of rhyming slang was that it should be exclusive and comprehensible only to a chosen few. As soon as *Me and My Girl* popularized expressions like 'apples and pears' (stairs) or 'Dicky Dirt' (shirt), there was no point in using them any more on the street. Other exclusive languages emerged, including Billingsgate backslang in which the letters of a word were simply reversed (for example, 'reeb' to mean beer or 'delo woc' for old cow). But these, too, were soon worn down by overuse. The English language is now littered with relics from Cockney sub-dialects. You'll commonly hear Londoners of all classes talking about taking a

'butcher's' (butcher's hook, look) or accusing each other of telling 'porkies' (pork pies, lies). The word 'yob', meaning hooligan, was originally Billingsgate backslang for boy.

No kind of language or dialect remains fixed, but changes and grows with usage. Cockney has been modified with every new influx of immigrants, be they Huguenots, Jews, Pakistanis, Bengalis or West Indians. Expressions like 'wicked', meaning either super-cool or excitingly dangerous ('man, that shirt is wicked', 'whatever you put in those drinks is wicked'), or 'serious' as a synonym for 'lots of' ('serious money', 'serious trouble'), are Caribbean in origin. More recently, London speech has been vastly influenced by American English as used in films and on television ('no way', 'beat it', 'movie', etc).

Geographically, Cockney has spread from the East End all over London and beyond into the Kent and Essex suburbs. Most significantly, the erosion of the working class since the 1970s has created profound shifts in the usage of Cockney dialect. The emergence of a new category of upwardly mobile entrepreneurs in the Thatcher era changed the whole definition of Standard English. Public-school accents have catapulted out of fashion in favour of a more populist middle register, largely dictated by television. At the same time, many people from working-class backgrounds have worked hard to smooth off the rough edges of their accent to make themselves more socially acceptable. The two old registers are beginning to meet somewhere in the middle. The result has been studied by linguists and christened New London Dialect or, more vulgarly, Estuary English, after the Thames Estuary that divides Essex and suburban Kent. Tory cabinet ministers and even Princess Diana have been caught referring to 'foo'bauw' and

'St Pauw's Caffedraw'. It is now trendy for middle-class Londoners to say 'cheers' instead of the usual 'thank you', and 'motor' or even 'mo'er' instead of 'car'.

It is hard to say what the significance of this linguistic shift is. Certainly, it suggests that the relaxing of class strictures has led to a corresponding shift in speaking habits. But it does not signal the end of the class war over language, or at least not yet. For all the new Estuary speakers on television and in the House of Commons, deep prejudices about language still remain. It is easy enough to tell, just from turn of phrase or use of grammar, whether an Estuary speaker is a middle-class person going down-market or a working-class person striving to go up. The social codes have become more complicated to read, but they are still very much there. They depend primarily, now as in the past, on education. Public schools are still very much in the business of grooming rich children to take their place in the elite, while the state system continues to be eroded by inadequate resources and an ingrained inferiority complex. The difference in accent between the two systems may be diminishing, but the gap in linguistic culture remains as broad as ever. As long as Britain's education system is divided along class lines into a private and a public sector, the linguistic battle is unlikely to go away.

Cockney

The main characteristics of Cockney speech have not changed all that much, although a good deal of the vocabulary has modified or disappeared in recent years. Broadly speaking, its salient features are:

- **dropped h's**: as in 'orrible, 'Ackney, 'oppit! for horrible, Hackney, hop it (clear off)
- **swallowed consonants**: as in bu'er, bo'le, dau'er for butter, bottle, daughter

dropped l's: as in baw, St Pauw for ball, St Paul

f for soft th: as in fink, nuffink for think, nothing

v for hard th: as in bruvver, muvver for brother, mother

multiple negatives: as in 'you ain't never done nuffink for nobody'

Glossary

bat n. price in a market, as in 'to pay the full bat'

beef n. disagreement or argument, as in 'to 'ave a beef'

bird n. woman, as in 'yer bird's a bit of all right'

bloke n. man, as in 'me bruvver's a smashin' bloke'

blotto adj. drunk (now in general use)

blow yer top phr. to get very angry

bonce n. head, synonym for *nut* or *noddle*

boozer n. pub. 'Down the boozer' means at the pub

boss-eyed adj. cross-eyed

bread-basket n. stomach

brickie n. bricklayer

clippie n. ticket collector, bus conductor

clod'opper n. twit, fool

cock n. term of endearment, as in 'wotcher, cock!' A bit old-fashioned. Alternatives include *mate*, *mush* and *tosh*

coffin nails n. pl. cigarettes. Also *Irish jigs* (rhyming slang for cigs)

conk n. nose. Also *schnozzle*, *hooter*

coppah n. policeman, from the verb 'to cop' meaning 'to snatch'. Less polite variants include *fuzz*, *pig*, *filth*, etc

cor blimey! interj. expression of surprise. Synonyms include *strewth* (from God's truth), *strike a light*, *love a duck*, *stone the crows*, etc, etc

cuppa n. cup of tea

ear'ole n. ear, or side of face generally, as in 'to slug someone round the ear'ole'. Also *lug'ole*

flag n. shirt, as in 'I've ironed me flag'

flap n. pocket

flappers n. ears

gob n. mouth. 'I'm gonna smash yer gob' means 'I'm going to beat you up'

goner n. dead person. 'To be a goner' means to be a marked man, or to die. Other phrases for dying include *conk out*, *peg out*, *push up the daisies*, *turn yer toes up*, *kick the bucket*

gumption n. intelligence, as in 'use yer gumption'. See also *loaf*

guv or **guv'nor** n. polite way of addressing important people or customers

innit adv. multi-purpose word stuck on the end of sentences for effect, a bit like *n'est-ce pas* in French, but not so classy. As in 'it's bleedin' freezin', innit?' Similar words include *innee* and *dinn'l*

keep yer 'air on phr. don't get over-excited

kisser n. mouth

learn vb. teach, as in 'I'm gonna learn yer good'n'proper'

loaf n. head, as in 'use yer loaf'

lolly n. money. Also *dosh*

London dressing phr. old-fashioned way of describing soot

London flit phr. 'to do the London flit' means to move house surreptitiously (usually overnight) without paying the outstanding rent

mate n. most common term of endearment (see also *cock*)

moggy n. cat

mo'er n. car

the moon's wet phr. it's going to rain

nosh n. food

nut n. head. 'It did me nut' means it annoyed or frustrated me

oi! interj. used to get attention, as in 'oi, you!'

'oky-poky man n. old word for an ice-cream seller who came round on a bicycle

'oppit! vbl phrase. clear off, scram

'oppin' the wag vbl phr. playing truant

peepers n.pl. eyes

preggers adj. pregnant. Also *up the pole*, *in the puddin' club*

put a sock in it! phr. keep the noise down, shut up

put wood in the 'ole, to vbl. phr. to shut the door

punter n. customer, client of any kind

scarper vb. run, scram, clear out. Rhyming slang (from *Scapa Flow*, go)

scrump vb. old-fashioned word for steal

spark n. electrician. Also, clever person as in 'a bright spark'

spiv n. dishonest person, usually a well-turned-out hustler rather than a petty thief. Also *wide boy*

spud n. potato. Also *tayter*

swede-basher n. person from the country

to talk peas over sticks or **to talk right cut glass** phr. to talk posh

tallyman n. debt-collector

tizz n. fuss, bother, as in 'to get into a tizz'

turf accountant n. bookmaker

up the dancers adv. upstairs

wallop n. to hit, esp. parents hitting children

wotcher n. hello

yer wot? phr. I beg your pardon?

Rhyming Slang

As explained above, rhyming slang is more folklore than reality. Nevertheless, some phrases have entered the language and others, although never said with a straight face, are still well-known enough to merit entries in dictionaries. There are two types of rhyming slang: straight rhymes with the original word, such as 'mince pies' for eyes or 'pig's ear' for beer; and abbreviations or contractions of the original phrase, which take longer to work out. For example, 'on 'is Jack' meaning 'on his own' (Jack, Jack Jones, own) or 'nanny' for 'coat' (nanny, nanny goat, coat). Here are some of the better-known and more colourful phrases:

Adam and Eve believe

apples and pears stairs

Artful Dodger lodger

Barnaby Rudge judge

battle cruiser boozer (pub)

bell ringers fingers

board'n'plank Yank

borassic out of cash (borassic lint, skint)

Brahms and Liszt a little the worse for drink (incidentally, also the name of a wine bar in Covent Garden)

bricks'n'mortar daughter

Cape of Good 'Ope soap

Charlie twit, fool, as in "'e made me feel like a right Charlie' (derivation probably Charlie, Charlie Ronce, ponce)

Crimea beer (also *pig's ear* or *far'n'near*)

daisy roots boots

dicky bird or **Richard III** word, as in 'don't believe a dicky that man tells yer'

Dicky Dirt shirt (Dicky Dirt's was the name given to a chain of cheap clothing stores in the 1970s, though the phrase came first)

Dunlop tyre liar

elephant's trunk drunk

fairy snuff fair enough

fisherman's daughter water

flounder'n'dab cab

Fourth of July tie

frog'n'toad road

Gawd forbids kids (also, *saucepan lids*)

glass case face, as in 'shut yer glass case'

Khyber Pass arse (or *North Pole* for arsehole)

Mae West chest

mince pies eyes

Mrs Thatcher equalizer in soccer (Thatcher, matcher)

nanny coat (nanny goat, coat)

needle'n'thread bread

pot'n'pan old man (husband)

Rosy or **Rosy Lea** tea (Rosy Lea was a gypsy who told fortunes by reading tea-leaves)

swear'n'cuss bus

titfer hat (tit for tat, hat)

trouble'n'strife wife (also, *fork'n'knife*)

turtles gloves (turtle doves, gloves)

Vera Lynn gin (also *needle'n'pin*)

West Ham reserves nerves, as in 'you get on my ...'

whistle and flute suit

Pronunciation

Modern English spelling was standardized at the end of the 18th century by a small group of educationalists who evidently thought it would be hilarious to make pronunciation as difficult as possible for the uninitiated. Foreign tourists are forever

inviting ridicule by asking for 'Glaw-sister Road' or 'South-walk'; it is hardly their fault if they're merely following the written word. Here is a survival guide to some of London's more common spelling anomalies:

Written/Spoken

Balham Bal'm

Berkeley Square Barkly Square

Berwick St Berrick St

Cadogan Ca-DUG-gan (Square or Guides!)

Charing Cross Charring ('a' as in Harry)

Cheyne Walk Chainy Walk

Chiswick Chizzick

Cholmondeley Walk Chumly Walk

Clapham Clap'm

Dulwich Dullitch

Gloucester Rd Gloster Rd

Greenwich Grennitch

Grosvenor Place Grove-ner Place

Holborn Hoeburn

Leicester Square Lester Square

London Lund'n

Marylebone Marleyb'n or Marilebon

Southwark Suthuk

Thames Tems

Wapping Wopping

Woolwich Woolitch

Index

Numbers in **bold** indicate main references. Numbers in *italic* indicate maps.

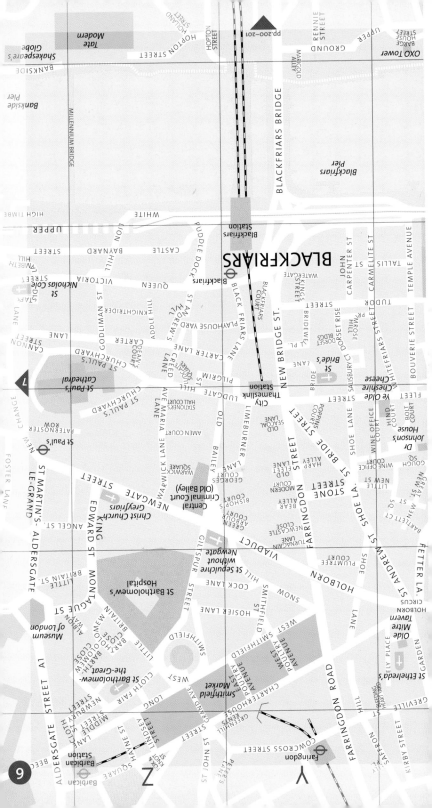

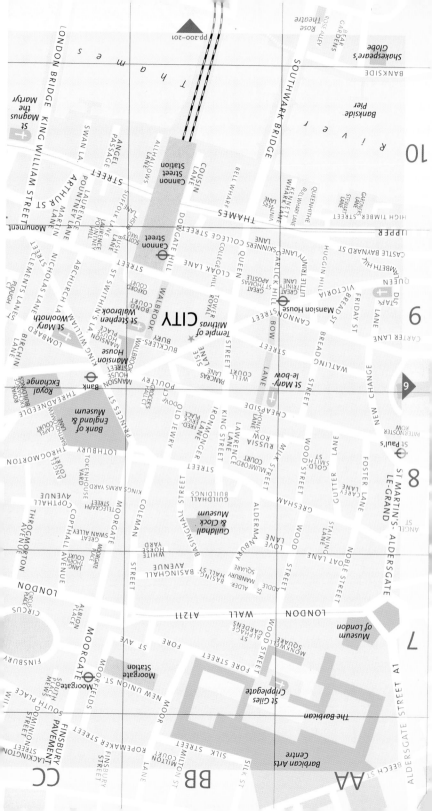

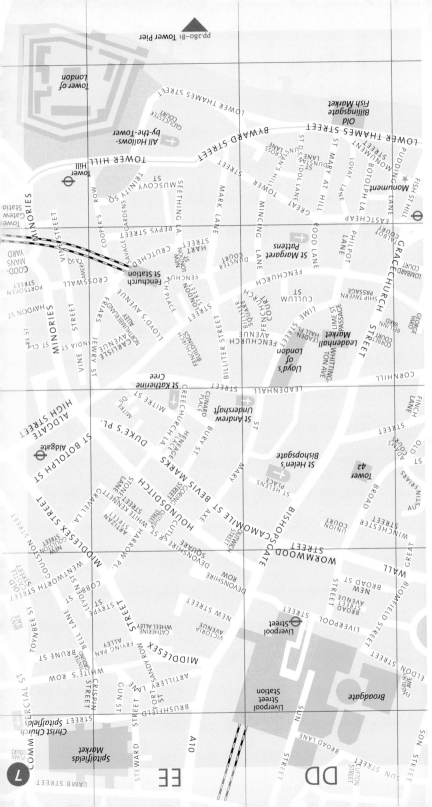

Spitalfields Market

COMMERCIAL ST

Christ Church Spitalfields

STEWARD STREET

A10

Liverpool Street Station

Broadgate

LAMB STREET

PLUMB COURT

7

EE

DD

Spitalfields / Bishopsgate area

STEWARD STREET
BRUSHFIELD STREET
GUN STREET
ARTILLERY LANE
FORT STREET-SANDYS ROW
ARTILLERY ROW
WHITE'S ROW
BELL LANE
CRISPIN STREET
FRYING PAN ALLEY
CATHERINE WHEEL ALLEY
BRUNE ST
TENTER GROUND
CROWN ST
FORT STREET
TOYNBEE ST
WENTWORTH ST
CROYDON ST
NEW GOULSTON STREET
OLD CASTLE STREET
COBB STREET
STRYPE ST
NEW STREET
VICTORIA AVENUE
DEVONSHIRE ROW
DEVONSHIRE SQUARE

MIDDLESEX STREET

MIDDLESEX STREET

COMMERCIAL STREET

TOYNBEE ST

WENTWORTH ST

BELL LANE

ST BOTOLPH ST

ALDGATE HIGH STREET

ST BOTOLPH ST

ALDGATE ⊖

DUKE'S PL.

DUKE'S PLACE

MITRE ST

MITRE ST

CREECHURCH LANE

HENEAGE LANE

BURY ST.

CUNARD PLACE

St Katherine Cree

St Andrew Undershaft

HEN-EAGE PLACE

ARTIZAN STREET
WHITE KENNETT STREET
STONEY LANE
GRAVEL LANE
CUTLER STREET
HARROW PL.
GORING STREET

HOUNDSDITCH

BEVIS MARKS

ST MARY AXE

CAMOMILE ST

WORMWOOD STREET

BISHOPSGATE

St Helen's Bishopsgate

ST HELENS PLACE

Tower 42

BROAD STREET

NEW BROAD ST

WALL

BLOMFIELD STREET

LIVERPOOL STREET

Liverpool Street ⊖

BROAD ST AVENUE
NEW ST
OLD BROAD STREET

WINCHESTER STREET
WINCHESTER COURT
UNION COURT
GREAT WINCHESTER STREET

FINSBURY AVE

ELDON STREET

BROAD LANE
SUN STREET
CLIFTON STREET
SON STREET

City of London area (Tower / Monument)

MINORIES

GOOD-MANS YARD

PORTSOKEN STREET

HAYDON ST

ST CL ARE ST

VINE STREET

MINORIES

VINEGAR STREET

AMERICA SQ.

CRESCENT

INDIA ST

JEWRY ST

CARLISLE AVENUE

NORTHUMBERLAND ALLEY

FRIARS

LLOYD'S AVENUE

FENCHURCH BUILDINGS

FENCHURCH STREET

BILLITER STREET

LEADENHALL STREET

CREECHURCH PLACE

Lloyd's of London

Leadenhall Market

FENCHURCH AVENUE

LIME STREET

LIME STREET PASSAGE

WHITTING-TON AVE

HALL PL.

LEADENHALL STREET

LEADENHALL STREET

CORNHILL

CORNHILL

FINCH LANE

CLEMENT'S LANE

GRACECHURCH STREET

LOMBARD COURT

TALBOT COURT

GEORGE YARD

CORBET COURT

BELL INN YARD

SHIP TAVERN PASSAGE

CULLUM ST

FENCHURCH ST

FENCHURCH STREET

Tower Gateway ⊖ Statio

Tower Gateway Statio

Fenchurch St Station

COOPER'S ROW

SAVAGE GARDENS

PEPYS STREET

CRUTCHED FRIARS

CRUTCHED FRIARS

HART STREET

NEW LONDON ST

LONDON STREET

NORTHUMBERLAND ALLEY

FRENCH PLACE

FENCHURCH PLACE

TRINITY SQ.

COOPER'S ROW

MUSCOVY ST

SEETHING LANE

SEETHING LA.

MARK LANE

MARK LANE

MINCING LANE

MINCING LANE

DUNSTER COURT

St Margaret Patterns

ROOD LANE

PHILPOT LANE

LOVAT LANE

BOTOLPH LANE

PUDDING LANE

ST MARY AT HILL

GREAT TOWER ST

GREAT TOWER HILL

TOWER STREET

BYWARD STREET

ST DUNSTAN'S HILL

IDOL LANE

ST MARY AT HILL

FISH ST HILL

Monument

Monument ⊖

EASTCHEAP

EASTCHEAP

LOWER THAMES STREET

MONUMENT STREET

Old Billingsgate Fish Market

LOWER THAMES STREET

BYWARD STREET

GLOUCESTER COURT

Tower Hill ⊖

TOWER HILL

Tower of London

All Hallows-by-the-Tower

Tower Pier

pp.280–81

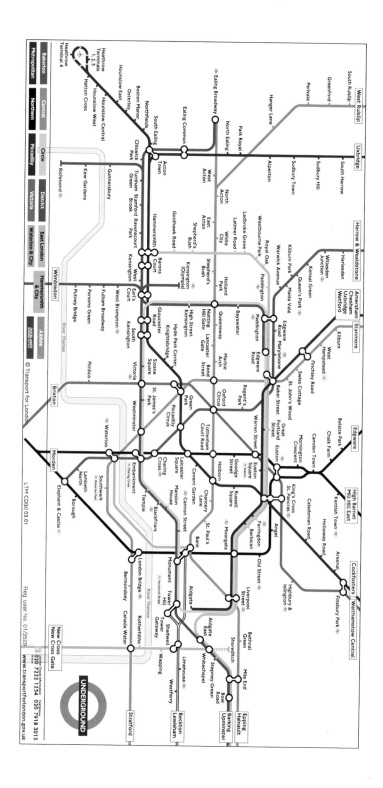

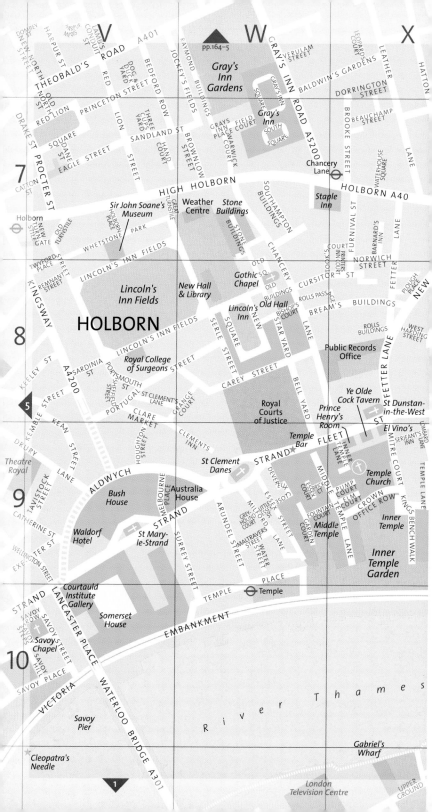

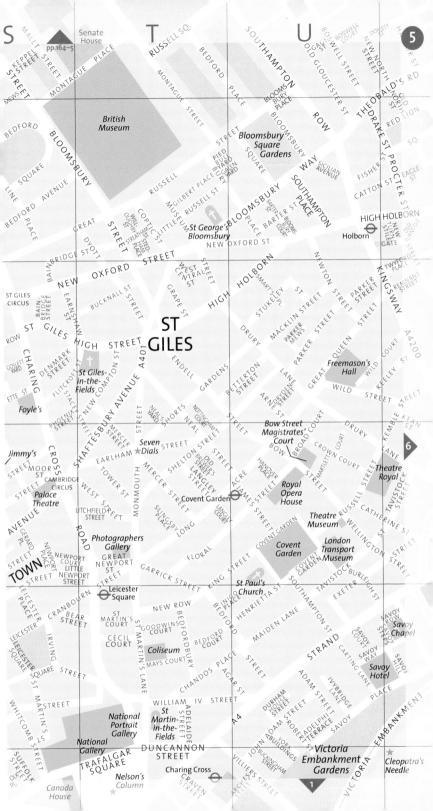

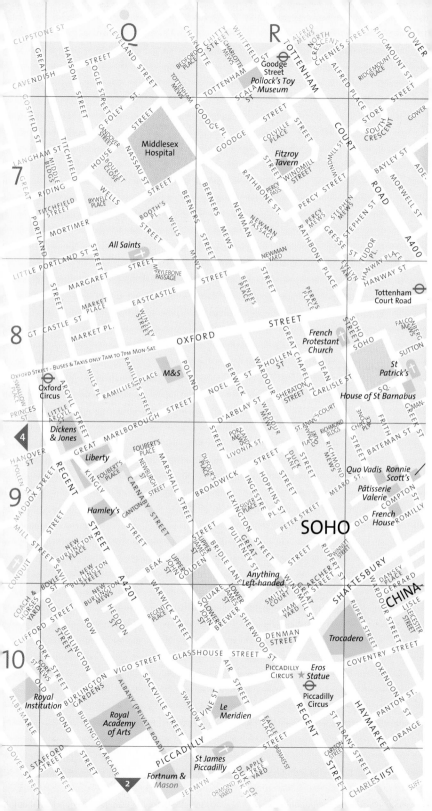

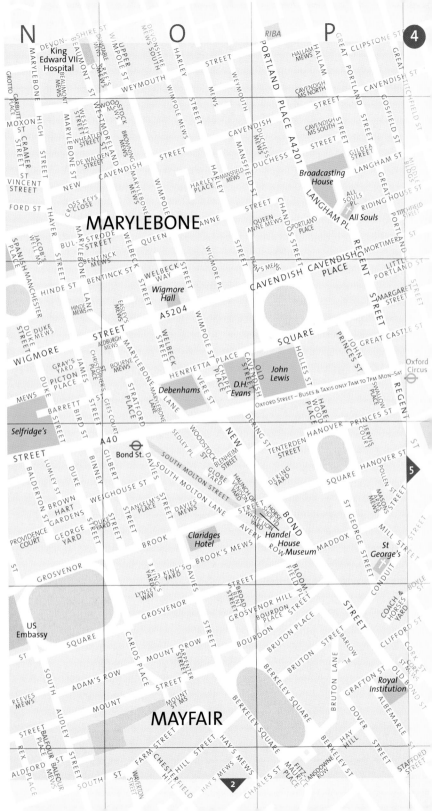

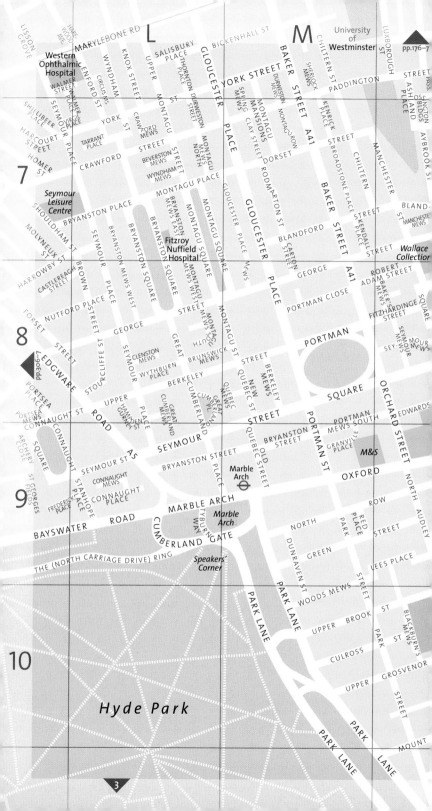

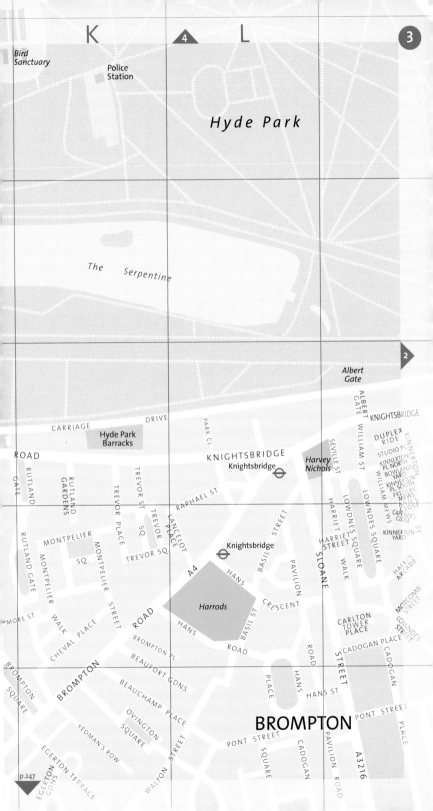

Bird
Sanctuary

Police
Station

Hyde Park

The   Serpentine

Albert
Gate

ALBERT
GATE

KNIGHTSBRIDGE

CARRIAGE   DRIVE

PARK CL.

Hyde Park
Barracks

SEVILLE ST

WILLIAM ST

DUPLEX
RIDE

STUDIO PL.

KINNERTON

ROAD

RUTLAND
GATE

KNIGHTSBRIDGE

Knightsbridge

Harvey
Nichols

KINNERTON
PL NORTH
BOWLAND
YARD
KINNERTON
SOUTH
FREDERIC
MEWS

CAPENER'S
CLOSE

KINNERTON
YARD

RUTLAND
GARDENS

TREVOR ST

RAPHAEL ST

HARRIET
STREET

LOWNDES SQUARE

WILLIAM MEWS

HALKIN
ARCADE

RUTLAND
GATE

MONTPELIER

SQ.

TREVOR PLACE

TREVOR
SQ.

TREVOR

LANCELOT
PLACE

Knightsbridge

BASIL   STREET

HARRIET
WALK

SLOANE

KINNERTON

MONTPELIER

MONTPELIER   STREET

TREVOR SQ.

A4

HANS

PAVILION

MOTCOMB
STREET

LOWNDES
STREET

MORE ST

CHEVAL PLACE

Harrods

HANS

CRESCENT

BASIL ST.

CARLTON
TOWER
PLACE

CADOGAN PLACE

CADOGAN

ROAD

BROMPTON PL.

ROAD

HANS

ROAD

PLACE

HANS

HANS ST

STREET

BROMPTON
SQUARE

BROMPTON

BEAUFORT GDNS.

BEAUCHAMP PLACE

OVINGTON
SQUARE

WALTON   STREET

PONT   STREET

BROMPTON

PONT   STREET

SQUARE

CADOGAN

PAVILION   ROAD

PONT   STREET

PLACE

A3216

YEOMAN'S ROW

EGERTON TERRACE

EGERTON
GDNS.

p.247

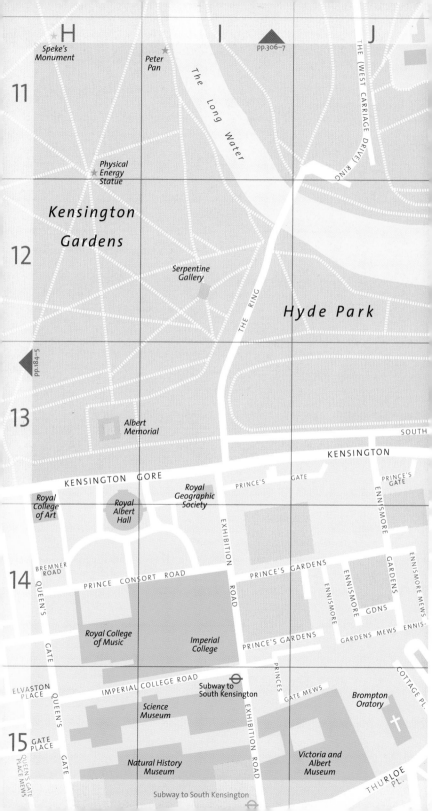

H I J

Speke's
Monument

Peter
Pan

The Long Water

pp.306-7

THE (WEST CARRIAGE DRIVE) RING

11

Physical
Energy
Statue

Kensington

Gardens

12

Serpentine
Gallery

Hyde Park

THE RING

pp.18-5

13

Albert
Memorial

SOUTH

KENSINGTON

PRINCE'S GATE

PRINCE'S
GATE

KENSINGTON GORE

Royal
Geographic
Society

ENNISMORE

Royal
College
of Art

Royal
Albert
Hall

EXHIBITION ROAD

BREMNER
ROAD

PRINCE CONSORT ROAD

PRINCE'S GARDENS

ENNISMORE GARDENS

ENNISMORE MEWS

14

QUEEN'S

ENNISMORE

ENNISMORE GDNS

Royal College
of Music

Imperial
College

PRINCE'S GARDENS

GARDENS MEWS

ENNIS-

GATE

ELVASTON
PLACE

QUEEN'S

IMPERIAL COLLEGE ROAD

Subway to
South Kensington

PRINCES GATE MEWS

COTTAGE PL.

Brompton
Oratory

Science
Museum

EXHIBITION ROAD

GATE
PLACE

15

QUEEN'S GATE
PLACE MEWS

GATE

Natural History
Museum

Victoria and
Albert
Museum

THURLOE
PL.

Subway to South Kensington

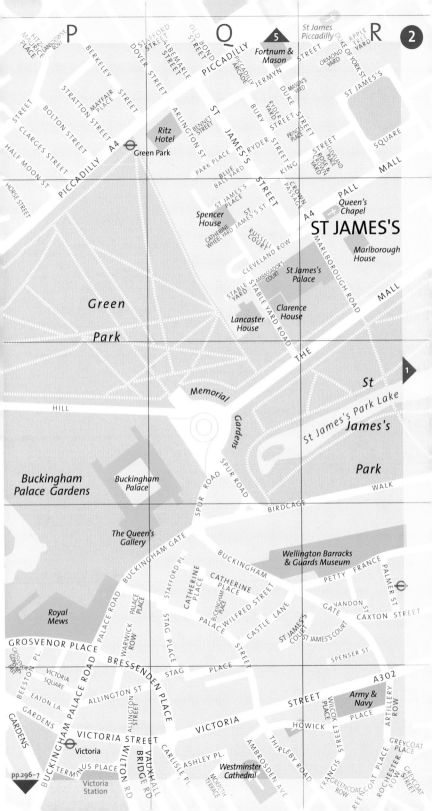

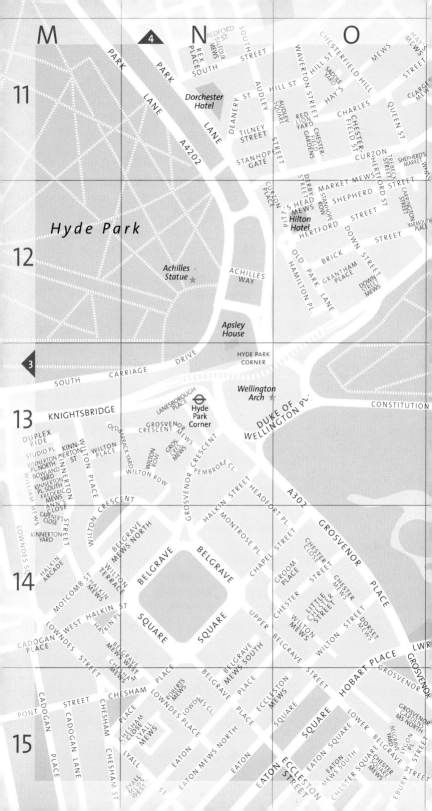

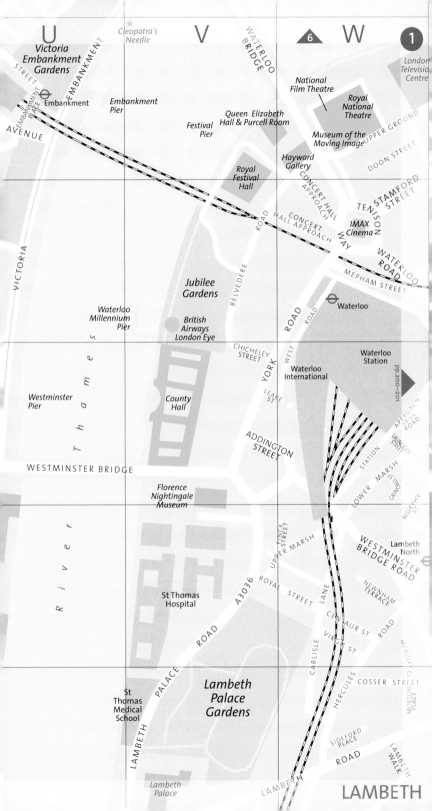

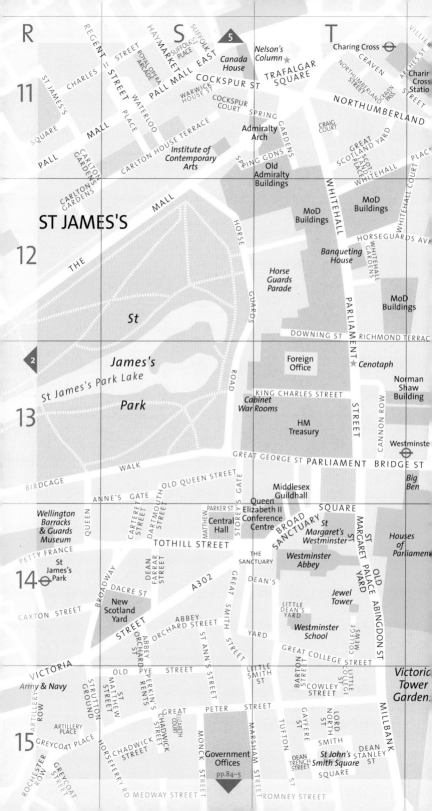

London Street Maps

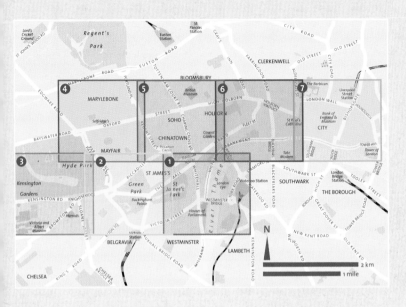

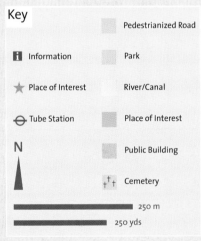

Key

i	Information		Pedestrianized Road
⭐	Place of Interest		Park
⊖	Tube Station		River/Canal
N ▲			Place of Interest
			Public Building
		† † †	Cemetery

250 m
250 yds